The
Illusion
of
Peace

Also by Tad Szulc

Twilight of the Tyrants
The Cuban Invasion (with Karl E. Meyer)
The Winds of Revolution
Dominican Diary
Latin America
The Bombs of Palomares
Czechoslovakia Since World War II
Portrait of Spain
The Invasion of Czechoslovakia
Compulsive Spy
Innocents at Home

TAD SZULC

The Illusion of Peace

Foreign Policy in the Nixon Years

THE VIKING PRESS • NEW YORK

This book is for J. O. Szereszewski

Copyright © Tad Szulc, 1978
All rights reserved

First published in 1978 by The Viking Press
625 Madison Avenue, New York, N.Y. 10022

Published simultaneously in Canada by
Penguin Books Canada Limited

LIBRARY OF CONGRESS CATALOGING IN PUBLICATION DATA
Szulc, Tad.
The illusion of peace.
Includes index.
1. United States—Foreign relations—1969–1974.
2. Nixon, Richard Milhous, 1913–   3. Kissinger,
Henry Alfred. I. Title.
E855.S98   327.73   77–25978
ISBN 0–670–39255–3

Printed in the United States of America

Set in Videocomp Baskerville

Prologue

Richard Nixon—and with him much of America and the world—firmly believed that foreign policy was the most constructive and positive aspect of his presidency. This, he claimed, would be the most enduring contribution of the years he spent at the White House. And until the very end, Nixon used his foreign policy as his principal defense in the Watergate crisis.

For many years, indeed, America and the world saw him as an immensely innovative policy-maker and—together with Henry Kissinger—as the statesman of peace. He ended the Vietnam war for the United States, established détente with the Soviet Union, opened the dialogue with China, and brought a semblance of peace to the Middle East.

But this Nixonian image obscures much of the truth, hiding the real story of these astonishing and complex years. As the perspective lengthens, it becomes clearer and clearer that what Nixon gave America and the world was only the illusion of peace.

This book is a factual account of Nixon's foreign-policy stewardship. I have been especially concerned with the public as well as the secret aspects, and with the contradictions between these two in the execution of American policy.

Some of the information and impressions contained herein derive from my own experience as a newspaper correspondent in Washington covering, on a day-to-day basis, the *visible* conduct of American foreign policy during Nixon's first term in the White House. I have read all I could of the published accounts in books, congressional reports, periodicals, and newspapers pertaining to Nixon's and Kissinger's performances; obviously all this material was helpful in broadening my own personal observations.

Public documents of the entire Nixon era were used in this reconstruction along with material, some of it still kept secret by the United States government, gained from a wide variety of sources in Washington and abroad. This material helps to establish, I believe, the important contrast between the public and private attitudes during the Nixon administration.

Vastly more important to me, however, was the opportunity I had to study confidential materials (from some of which I quote directly) and to discuss the history of the Nixon years with American and foreign officials —civilian and military—who in varying degrees were involved in the making of American foreign policy between 1969 and 1974. Among them were former cabinet officers, United States ambassadors, subcabinet officers, top White House advisers, executive staff aides, diplomats, and soldiers. It was in talking to them that I began to acquire a sense of perspective on many of these events; it was also when I realized, with a touch of professional shock, how little we—we the American people and we the reporters whose job it was to keep the public informed—knew and understood about Nixon's and Kissinger's management of policy. It is an understatement to say that we were as often as not fed mistruths and led astray.

The preparation of this book included dozens upon dozens upon dozens of interviews—some of them extended over many days—with high-ranking officials as well as with lesser figures who also had access to parts of the truth. Inevitably, perceptions and interpretations on different themes varied considerably. I have endeavored, however, to convey these differences while taking upon myself the elaboration of the conclusions and judgments that, for better or worse, I reached in the end.

The Americans who through their cooperation in my research contributed to my reconstruction of events are dedicated and honest public officials—some still active in the government, others already retired— whose principal concern, I believe, was to assist me in the quest for the truth. In an overwhelming majority of cases, they did not try to impose their views on me, although our assessment of events did not always coincide. I am deeply grateful for their trust in me and for their time and effort in providing me with the accounts of their experiences.

Foreign statesmen and diplomats provided me not only with precious nuggets of knowledge, some of it never revealed before, but even more important, with their special appreciation of situations hitherto considered only from the American vantage point.

Specialists in congressional and military affairs, some of them participants in the events of the day, guided me through the areas where they were acknowledged experts, and this helped me greatly to understand the background of many policies.

I thank them all. And finally, my thanks go to my publishers, The Viking Press; my editor, Elisabeth Sifton; my literary agent, Carl D. Brandt; my friend Daniel I. Davidson, whose advice I found highly valuable; Richard Holbrooke, who as managing editor of *Foreign Policy* magazine encouraged me in the reconstruction of the history of the Vietnam peace negotiations; and, last but not least, my wife, for their patience and help during the four long years this book was in preparation.

                                                                    T. S.

Washington, D.C.
October 1977

Contents

BOOK ONE

1969
The Year of Promise

Chapter 1

Let us take as our goal: Where peace is unknown, make it welcome; where peace is fragile, make it strong; where peace is temporary, make it permanent. . . .

After a period of confrontation, we are entering an era of negotiation. . . .

We seek an open world—open to ideas, open to the exchange of goods and people—a world in which no people, great or small, will live in angry isolation. . . .

We cannot expect to make everyone our friend, but we can try to make no one our enemy. . . .

With those who are willing to join, let us cooperate to reduce the burden of arms, to strengthen the structure of peace, to lift up the poor and the hungry. . . .

But to all those who would be tempted by weakness, let us leave no doubt that we will be as strong as we need to be for as long as we need to be. . . .

Let this message be heard by strong and weak alike: The peace we seek—the peace we seek to win—is not victory over any other people, but the peace that comes "with healing in its wings"; with compassion for those who have suffered; with understanding for those who have opposed us; with the opportunity for all the peoples of this earth to choose their own destiny.

With these words—carrying a touch of Wilson and the rhythm of John F. Kennedy—Richard Milhous Nixon, the thirty-seventh president of the United States, set forth in his inaugural address on January 20, 1969, the immensely ambitious foreign-policy objectives of his incoming administration. In the ensuing 2026 days, until his culpability in Watergate forced his resignation on August 9, 1974, Nixon presented the United States and the world with a spectacular, innovative, and controversial foreign-policy performance. This dazzling display of sound and light diverted attention away from the many flaws in Nixon's policies. Nevertheless the Nixon years—and the building of what he grandiloquently called the "structure of peace"—were extraordinarily rich in milestones, breakthroughs, imaginative if devious diplomacy, stunning shocks, inhumane application of sheer destructive power, brinkmanship and risk taking, contrived and real crises, cynicism, hard-eyed *Realpolitik,* a penchant for deception, and obsessive secrecy. Much of this new American policy was deeply thought out and meticulously planned, but a lot was improvised and sloppily executed.

The great lines of policy under Nixon—the détente with the Soviet Union, the opening to China, and the Vietnam peace settlement—evolved gradually. They made conceptual sense, but had to be fitted into a congruous body of international politics, properly timed, and related to other world trends. They had to be molded by dexterous negotiation and, sometimes, by the use or threat of extreme military force. The latter, indeed, was a constant element in the complex equation of Nixonian war-and-peace strategies. Friend and foe also had to be manipulated, misled, or bought off. Occasionally, what was made to appear as a triumph turned out to be a compromise at best, an illusion at worst.

Richard Nixon, the restless traveler, played out his strategies publicly as a consummate actor with a flair for the dramatic on practically every world stage. He planned them in the secrecy of his Oval Office and such hideaways as the upstairs Lincoln Sitting Room in the White House, a special office in the ornate gray Executive Office Building next door, the lodge at Camp David in the Maryland mountains, his San Clemente estate, and his Key Biscayne compound. Some of his policies and initiatives emerged from long nocturnal deliberations and meditation in the Lincoln Room. His personality thrived on extraordinary foreign exposure as it did on self-imposed seclusion. A passionate believer in personal diplomacy, Nixon was the most traveled American president, even more so than Franklin D. Roosevelt, whose wartime trips took him to Casablanca, Cairo, Tehran, and Yalta. Nixon visited thirty-one countries and territories while in office, from South Vietnam to the Soviet Union, China, Saudi Arabia, and Spain—some of them several times.

Travel and personal contact were an essential part of Nixon's diplomacy, but inevitably the brutal deadline pressures of the summit meetings forced him into quick decisions to be regretted later. This is where the compromises and improvisations came: the last-minute agreement on strategic arms with the Russians in 1972, the way the dollar devaluation was agreed to in the Azores in 1971, and the commitments made to the Arabs during a breathless Middle East tour in 1974. On the one hand, Nixon held out for careful preparations of his meetings with foreign leaders, but on the other hand, he was carried away by the dynamics of summitry: a Nixon summit could not be permitted to *look* as if it had failed.

Strands of foreign policy are by definition so intertwined that it is often impossible to separate long-range creativeness from breathless crisis management. This was especially evident under Nixon's steward-ship.

His first major foreign trip—to Western Europe—began a month and three days after his inauguration. For the next five and a half years, Nixon's jet, *Air Force One,* which he named *The Spirit of '76,* crisscrossed oceans and continents, making him the first American president to visit Peking and Moscow as well as Bucharest and Warsaw plus the Middle East. Visits to Western Europe became almost routine, and he went literally around the world logging 147,686 miles in international travel between 1969 and 1974. In 1969, the record year, Nixon flew 46,173 miles overseas.

Most key national leaders—from the Soviet Union's Leonid Brezhnev to successive British and Japanese prime ministers, the shah of Iran, Israel's Prime Minister Golda Meir, Yugoslavia's Marshal Tito, Romania's President Nicolae Ceauşescu, and West Germany's Chancellor Willy Brandt—came to see Nixon one or more times. (The great exception was the Chinese.) The sight of Nixon gravely welcoming these foreign digni-taries on the south lawn of the White House and entertaining them at state dinners became a feature of Washington life, and he went to the extreme of dressing the White House police in operetta-like uniforms to add to the spectacle.

Foreign policy was unquestionably the environment in which Nixon was at his statesmanlike best. It was his favorite subject in reading and conversation. Until the bitter end, foreign policy was his stronghold. That is where he was the safest. He felt passionately that history would judge him primarily for his conduct of foreign policy; it probably never oc-curred to him that one day his marks might be much less than perfect *even* in foreign policy.

In the broad sweep of Nixonian thinking, the first priorities were, of course, to extricate the United States from the Vietnam war and to im-prove relations with the Communist world. But because the Nixon ad-ministration developed from the outset the concept of secret "linkage" of various situations, particularly in the American relationship with the Soviet Union, it was hard to tell what the state of policy play was at different stages of its evolution. In Nixon's mind, from before the first inaugural, Vietnam and détente were clearly linked, and the Middle East crisis could be defused only in the context of Soviet-American cooperation. In the case of Vietnam, Nixon understood in time that détente with the Russians and an understanding with China had to precede the end of the war on terms ultimately acceptable to him. Détente was a long-range proposition; Vietnam, excruciating as it was, was a short-term one; but Nixon also understood that the success of détente was conditioned on a Vietnamese settlement.

These were the fundamental assumptions upon which Nixon constructed his foreign policy. He could not spell them out in so many words —though he offered strong hints in his inaugural address—and he could never be sure that the other sides had similar perceptions. In any event, Vietnam, the Middle East, the military posture of the United States, and East-West relations—in that order—were among the first ten subjects of systematic study ordered by the White House during Nixon's first week in office. All four were interconnected in his mind.

Aside from the basic parameters of policy, uncertainties continuously arose to suggest or create crises. Not surprisingly, Moscow periodically tested Nixon's mettle (often he just *thought* it did), as it had done with every other postwar American president, while feeling out détente possibilities. Interestingly, the Chinese refrained from playing this game. Global linkages, or imagined linkages, tended to confuse broad policies with crisis management, producing a distorted image of the moves on the world chessboard. Thus nervous reactions to sudden crises and improvisation were easily accepted, even by sophisticated independent analysts, as thoughtful responses or initiatives in the context of broad and well-planned strategies. And needless to say, Nixon too knew how to play the crisis card. Artificial military alerts and crises were produced to achieve diplomatic advantage and leverage. Dealing with the Russians, Nixon methodically worked to keep Moscow involved in linkage. The Cuban "minicrisis" of 1970 over Soviet nuclear-submarine facilities was a case in point. Washington brought this issue into play just as major crises were developing in the Middle East: the Soviet-abetted Egyptian violations of the precarious Suez Canal cease-fire with Israel, and the Syrian invasion of Jordan by Soviet-supplied armor. Simultaneously, Vietnam peace talks were frustratingly stalemated, and a Marxist was elected president in Chile.

Nixon's instinct was to hit militarily when he was provoked or perceived a provocation. Sometimes, "preventive" or "protective" military measures were secretly ordered. The history of the Vietnam peace talks shows that air strikes of varying magnitudes were carefully coordinated with diplomatic moves in Paris and elsewhere. As the curtains of secrecy are gradually drawn aside, it becomes clear that Nixon's "structure of peace" was studded with bombings and plans and threats to bomb—from Indochina to North Korea. Nixon's conduct of foreign policy was not so serene as portrayed by the White House or suggested in the idealism of his first inaugural address. Above all, Nixon could not tolerate the notion that the United States—or its president—could be regarded as a helpless giant.

Another paradox was that Nixon frequently did what he professed he would never do: for example, not insisting on a North Vietnamese military withdrawal from South Vietnam, or agreeing to devalue the dollar. Whether altering his public policy commitments or suddenly turning to the use of military power, Nixon used his unpredictability as a diplomatic weapon. Yet in time he found himself the political and intellectual prisoner of some of his own concepts—such as détente. In the end, he used foreign affairs to shield himself from his domestic disgrace: his frantic tour of the Middle East and his trip to Moscow in mid-1974 were as much anti-Watergate ploys as exercises in foreign relations. Yet only in the last year or so of his administration did a certain amount of "revisionism" begin to appear in serious analyses of Nixon's foreign policy.

Taken together, Nixonian policies set the United States, for better or for worse, on a wholly new course in its foreign relations. These policies, irreversible in many areas, marked a most momentous shift in America's posture toward allies and adversaries alike. Basic relationships were realigned, and progressively, new truths were recognized: that in Indochina and elsewhere there were real limits to American political, military, and economic power; that the countries of the third world were a major factor in world politics; that the United States must learn to live in nuclear parity and nonconfrontation with the Soviet Union; that mainland China must be brought into the international polity; and that it was time to diminish America's role as world gendarme. This last concept, widely advertised as the Nixon Doctrine, seemed the logical conclusion to be drawn from all the other policy notions, but it was one goal Nixon never really achieved—perhaps it was truly beyond reach—and it is now for the Carter administration to determine America's proper place in a rapidly changing world. The question remains whether the United States can altogether afford to relinquish the responsibilities of world gendarme.

Thus during the Nixon years the United States went a long distance to adjust its position to the global realities of the 1970s, even if many of these adjustments were incomplete and ill conceived—perhaps none of them more so than those that destabilized American relations with Western Europe and Japan. For much too long Nixon and his advisers dealt offhandedly with monetary, inflationary, and trade issues—to say nothing of the great energy crisis and matters concerning food supply—issues that were intimately linked with the viability of these alliances. And in terms of assuring the United States of an adequate and uninterrupted supply of oil, clearly a foreign-policy requirement for a nation depending at the time on imports for a quarter of its petroleum requirements, Nixon was, to say the least, irresponsible. In 1970, when it was obvious to most independent experts that the energy demands of industrial nations were coming into conflict with the producing nations, Nixon, responding to pressures from the domestic oil industry, vetoed the recommendation of the majority of his cabinet that petroleum import quotas be lifted. The National Security Council's first systematic study of the world oil situation was not undertaken until January 15, 1971—two years after Nixon took office—and it was done on a crash basis to cope with the rebellion of Persian Gulf and North African producers. It is a tenable argument that the skyrocketing oil prices of 1973 and 1974, contributing to worldwide inflation and the nearest thing to a depression in more than forty years, could have been largely averted if the Nixon administration had developed a coherent oil policy in time.

When it came to violations of human rights abroad (in the Soviet Union, under rightist dictatorships from Chile to South Korea or in Pakistani-ruled Bangladesh) the Nixon administration remained conveniently and studiously silent. It quietly helped racist white regimes in Africa. This Washington "pragmatism" had no place for the human rights of others; besides, Richard Nixon had a special respect for dictators.

Nixon's overwhelming and almost exclusive concentration on big-power or superpower relationships—everything from Vietnam to the Middle East and the Indian subcontinent was viewed through this prism —distorted much of his foreign policy. Even Vietnam was a "cruel side-show" to Russian-American détente, and so was the 1973 Arab-Israeli war. The smaller nations were in the anteroom of power—unless their actions threatened direct superpower confrontations. Subversion of a Marxist regime in Chile and joy at its ouster by Chilean military forces were the highlights of United States Latin American policy. The broad desire to negotiate with "adversaries" on basic themes was, of course, not new. It began with John F. Kennedy's initiatives for a partial nuclear-test–

ban and nonproliferation treaties and Lyndon B. Johnson's efforts to
"build bridges" to the East. But it was Richard Nixon who was given, and
knew how to grasp, the unique opportunity to forge ahead with a "structure of peace." The conjuncture was right. Thus Nixon was able to pull
the United States out of direct participation in the decade-long nightmare
of the Vietnam war. But he achieved it, after further tearing his own
country asunder, through unparalleled military brutality throughout Indochina coordinated with skillful diplomacy in a half-dozen world capitals
—in the end leaving Vietnam and Cambodia as far away as ever from the
peace he sought. Bloodshed and death were still a massive reality when
Nixon stepped down from office eighteen months after the signing of the
Paris peace agreement. The rapprochement with China after twenty-five
years of mutual hostility, and the détente with the Soviet Union, including
the signing, at the height of the Vietnam conflict, of the first nuclear-
arms–limitation treaty, were Nixon's greatest diplomatic triumphs: he
rode the crest of the wave with his 1972 visits to Peking and Moscow.
These spectaculars, televised in color via satellite, and the apparent imminence of the termination of the Vietnam war unquestionably helped his
landslide reelection for a second term. By the time of his downfall in the
dust of Watergate, however, détente with the Russians was beginning to
erode, as Nixon discovered during his second Moscow visit in 1974.

Again, paradoxically, the Nixon administration succeeded in stopping
Egyptian-Israeli warfare in 1970, but it bore heavy responsibility for the
October 1973 Arab-Israeli war. Illusory as are the works of diplomacy,
the farewell triumph of the Nixon administration (or so it was portrayed)
was the military disengagement between Israeli and Egyptian and Syrian
forces—but it came after a war that could have been prevented. And
Nixon went down in defeat in the midst of the Cyprus war for which his
administration was likewise partially responsible.

Nixon's foreign policy, representing his greatest claim to glory, also
carried the seeds of his own destruction. His obsession with secrecy and
his inclination toward deception led him to exclude most of the government from participating in policy formulation. This exclusion was accompanied by a paranoid fear of news "leaks" and a miasmatic conspiratorial
climate at the White House. When "leaks" did occur, as they always have
in Washington, Nixon and his men responded with secret wiretaps on
National Security Council members, key aides to the secretaries of state
and defense, and newsmen. And when the president launched secret
domestic intelligence operations through his White House "Plumbers,"
allegedly to protect his foreign policy, it was just a short step to the

horrors of Watergate, the bizarre by-product of Nixon's building the "structure of peace." The wiretaps became part of the article of impeachment against him for his abuse of presidential power.

In its very first year, Nixon's administration was deeply involved in domestic political espionage. Aimed principally at antiwar militants and other "radicals," it was conducted by the Central Intelligence Agency under the code name of Chaos—in violation of the CIA's own charter forbidding domestic activities. To be sure, Nixon inherited Chaos from Lyndon Johnson, but this was not enough for him. In 1969, he added the NSC wiretaps and, a year later, the broad internal intelligence program, the jumping-off point for Watergate.

The United States' secret bombings of Cambodia in 1969 and 1970, concealed from the American people and most members of Congress through a deceptive system of double reporting, were also included in the list of activities examined during the impeachment process. Impeachment—induced resignation—then, was how the circle closed.

Pledges to struggle for world peace are customary in inaugural speeches by American presidents. Nixon's address, drafted by him with the assistance of two White House speech-writers, gave his audience no reason to think that this conservative Republican with the reputation of being a cold war warrior and professional anti-Communist would produce dramatic changes in the traditional foreign policy of the United States pursued by four presidents since the end of World War II.

America's postwar history was containment, confrontation, and negotiation from a position of strength. It was the Truman Doctrine for Greece and Turkey; the Marshall Plan for Western Europe; the breaking of the Berlin blockade; the creation of the North Atlantic Treaty Organization; the Korean war; the Lebanon landings; the U-2 incident that killed the earlier Eisenhower-Khrushchev "spirit of Camp David" and wrecked the "summit" meeting they had planned; the Bay of Pigs, designed to overthrow Fidel Castro in Cuba; a deepening involvement in Indochina; the Cuban missile crisis, which nearly brought a nuclear war with the Soviets; intervention in the Dominican Republic; the arming of the Middle East rivals by the two superpowers; and, finally, the full entry of the United States into the Vietnam war, including heavy bombing of North Vietnam.

It certainly had been a period of confrontation, due as much to Communists as to Americans, and those listening to Richard Nixon's inaugural address gave short shrift to his rhetoric about an "era of negotiation."

The international situation was still unpromising as the president stood in the cold January wind on the steps of the Capitol talking of his "structure of peace," and there seemed to be little reason to expect profound changes. But the Nixon administration was barely an hour old when its aggressive and ambitious foreign policy was being launched from a suite of basement offices in the West Wing of the White House.

Several hours before the president was sworn in, Henry Alfred Kissinger, a rotund, bespectacled German-born Harvard professor of political science, who had been named by Nixon during the transition period to be his assistant for national security affairs, had moved with his new staff into the offices of the National Security Council, divided between the West Basement and the Executive Office Building across the West Executive Alley from the White House.

An energetic, compulsive man, then forty-five years old, Kissinger would not wait a few hours, let alone a day, to set in motion what was to become the most carefully designed operation in the history of American foreign policy and that in time would propel him to world fame and the post of secretary of state. In that capacity, he would receive Nixon's resignation from the presidency in 1974—the law requires that a president submit his resignation in writing to the secretary of state, the senior member of the cabinet—after acting during the height of the Watergate crisis as the nearest thing to a prime minister of the republic.

On inauguration day 1969, however, Kissinger was virtually unknown to most Americans. In addition to holding a Harvard chair, he had been a White House consultant and an adviser to New York's Governor Nelson Rockefeller, but his reputation was largely confined to academic circles and foreign-policy experts. The public neither knew nor cared what Kissinger was doing while Nixon stood in the limelight on a grandstand in front of the White House, beaming as he reviewed the inaugural parade.

While the troops marched past Nixon along Pennsylvania Avenue, Kissinger was drafting the first of the uncounted thousands of classified telegrams he would be sending over the years to American ambassadors abroad, foreign ministers, and chiefs of government. This first telegram was addressed to an American ambassador in a foreign capital. But it suddenly occurred to Kissinger that in order to be able to send it, he needed clearance from William P. Rogers, the new secretary of state. All telegrams to embassies abroad must carry the formal signature of the secretary. Kissinger would soon establish his personal channels to ambassadors and leaders of foreign governments but the immediate problem

was to get the secretary's clearance. Kissinger strolled over to the grandstand and found Rogers standing near the president. Rogers, one of
Nixon's old and close personal friends, and attorney general in the Eisenhower administration, smilingly gave Kissinger the required signature.

Secretary Rogers, an amiable and decent man with fairly limited experience in foreign policy, thus symbolically signed his own political death
warrant. Even before the inauguration was over, Kissinger had woven an
institutional web around the White House—acting with Nixon's assent—
that effectively excluded Rogers and the State Department from substantive policy-making. Redesigning the mechanism of the National Security
Council, ostensibly the government's highest-ranking policy-making
group in the area of foreign policy, Kissinger created seven NSC committees to develop and study new policies, and he assigned himself to chair
six of them. As the president's assistant for national security affairs,
Kissinger not only controlled the council itself, sitting at Nixon's elbow,
but from the first day took charge of every move within the NSC mechanism. This is how power affecting foreign, defense, and intelligence policies became centralized in the White House or, in other words, in Kissinger's hands. Kissinger, who, of course, understood the basic principle
of centralized power, later developed a private system for bypassing the
council, too.

The reorganization of the machinery of the National Security Council
—by statute composed of the president, who chairs it, the vice president,
the secretaries of state and defense, the chairman of the Joint Chiefs of
Staff, the director of central intelligence, and then the director of the
Office of Emergency Preparedness—and its supporting committees was
contained in three decisions Nixon made a few days before he took office.
Kissinger had prepared the documents during the preinauguration transition period at the Pierre Hotel in New York and his temporary office in the
Executive Office Building in Washington. They were called National
Security Decision Memoranda—NSDMs for short—and Kissinger arranged for copies of NSDM–1, NSDM–2, and NSDM–3 to be placed on the
desks of all the statutory members of the National Security Council during
the afternoon of January 20. NSDM–3, the most important of the three,
was entitled "The Direction, Coordination and Supervision of Interdepartmental Activities Overseas." This paper became Kissinger's operational charter. Inasmuch as Rogers had already lost the bureaucratic fight
for a strong voice in the NSC operation—he fought it badly in the weeks
before inauguration when Nixon was resting at his vacation home in
Florida—the three NSDMs sealed the State Department's fate. Over the

years, most major decisions were incorporated in NSDMs, which remain highly classified documents.

On January 20, while Secretary Rogers performed ceremonial acts, Kissinger was busy writing his first telegrams and opening direct channels between the White House and foreign governments. Prior to the inauguration, Nixon and he had drafted personal presidential letters to at least fifteen heads of government, including the Soviet Union's Brezhnev, France's de Gaulle, Yugoslavia's Tito, and Romania's Ceauşescu. Now, unbeknown to Secretary Rogers, the letters, over Nixon's signature, were delivered by NSC aides to the Washington embassies of these countries for transmission home. They were the first Nixon-Kissinger secret. Although these letters simply expressed Nixon's desire to improve relations between the United States and the recipient country, an NSC official described them as "the beginning of the effort to establish channels directly from the White House. . . . It was one of the early incidents of bypassing the State Department."

As it developed, it was also the first step in establishing total White House tyranny and secrecy over the conduct of foreign policy. Indeed, Nixon's and Kissinger's penchant for secretiveness may have been among the reasons, along with foreign-policy concepts, that these two men, who met only once before the 1969 Republican convention, so quickly achieved their extraordinary personal rapport. Besides, both the president and his assistant had contempt for the Washington bureaucracy— most notably in the State and Defense departments and the CIA. In a 1968 speech at a California college, Kissinger had said:

> Foreign policy is . . . complicated by the fact that the actual decision-making process leads to a fragmentation of the decisions. Also, research and intelligence organizations, either foreign or national, attempt to give a rationality and consistency to foreign policy which it simply does not have. . . . Once the American decision-making process has disgorged an answer, it becomes technically very difficult to change the policy because even those who have serious doubts about it become reluctant to hazard those doubts in an international forum.

This, basically, was Kissinger's rationale for keeping the bureaucracy out of the decision-making process. At State and Defense, he argued, policy could be influenced only at the level of an assistant secretary, and not above that, because "that is the highest level in which people can still think. . . . Above that, the day-to-day operation of the machine absorbs most of the energy, and the decisions that are made depend very much on internal pressures of the bureaucracy."

Kissinger made the case for the kind of preponderant role he would carve out for himself at the White House: "Most of the people who advise the president are plausible, so he constantly sees individuals who sound very convincing. His time is so budgeted and the pressures on him are so great that it is almost impossible for him to know whether he should listen to one convincing individual or the other." The inevitable conclusion had to be that the president should be advised by one man alone in whom he had trust. When the time came, Kissinger made himself into this indispensable man.

Kissinger's recipe for policy-making went as follows:

Because management of the bureaucracy takes so much energy and precisely because *changing course* is so difficult, many of the most important decisions are taken by extra-bureaucratic means. Some of the key decisions are kept to a very small circle while the bureaucracy happily continues working away in ignorance of the fact that decisions are being made, or the fact that a decision is being made in a particular area. One reason for keeping decisions to small groups is that when bureaucracies are so unwieldy and when their internal morale becomes a serious problem, an unpopular decision may be fought by brutal means, such as *leaks to the press or to congressional committees.* Thus the only way secrecy can be kept is to exclude from the making of the decision all those who are theoretically charged with carrying it out. . . . Another result is that the relevant part of the bureaucracy, because it is being excluded from the making of a particular decision, continues with great intensity sending out cables, thereby distorting the effort with the best intentions in the world. You cannot stop them from doing this because you do not tell them what is going on. . . . On the whole, if we could get rid of the bottom half of the Foreign Service, we might be better off [italics added].

Kissinger, showing a remarkable scorn for politicians, suggested that "only in the rarest cases is there a relationship between high position and great substantive knowledge. . . . Most of our elective officials had to spend so much of their energy getting elected that they can give relatively little attention to the substance of what they are going to do when they are elected. . . . *It is literally the case that you are starting with a* tabula rasa, *and that the position the political leader takes is much influenced by the type of intellectual that almost quite accidentally winds up in his entourage"*[italics added].

Kissinger had been an anti-Nixon Republican for a long time—his patron was Nelson Rockefeller, who lost the 1968 nomination to Nixon —and he had made no bones about bad-mouthing Richard Nixon. He had told his liberal academic associates that Nixon was not fit to be president of the United States. What, then, so radically changed this skeptical Harvard professor's view and made him the new president's intimate adviser?

The short answer, of course, is power. Kissinger was amazed when Nixon offered him the key foreign-policy post at the White House. In effect, Nixon was handing him power in its purest form, and with it an extraordinary opportunity to put into practice his ideas and philosophies on themes ranging from the control of nuclear weapons (one of his favorite topics, on which he had written extensively) and the modalities for settling the Vietnam conflict to the establishment of new international relationships.

Even as early as 1966, Kissinger was keenly aware of the trappings of power from the sublime to the trivial. When his wallet was lifted by a Saigon pickpocket—Kissinger, then a White House consultant, was on his way to a champagne breakfast at the apartment of an American diplomat on Vietnam's National Day—his instant reaction was that "what bothers me is not the money I lost, but my White House pass."

From Nixon's viewpoint, the selection of Kissinger was more logical than perhaps even he realized at the time. Nixon was deeply interested in international problems and was a dedicated student of foreign policy. He had visited more than sixty countries and had met many national and political leaders the world over. After his defeat by Kennedy, he had spent eight years studying foreign affairs and evolving positions that would become the basis of new policies once he became president—a goal he had always believed he would achieve. Moreover, Nixon was convinced that through foreign policy he could make his greatest mark on history. He had the illusion that domestic problems, one way or another, would take care of themselves.

Marshall Green, a State Department specialist on Asian affairs, described in an interview with me the impression Nixon made on him when he came to Djakarta in April 1967. Green was then ambassador to Indonesia and Nixon was traveling as a private citizen. As a former vice president, Nixon rated the courtesy of VIP treatment, and Green was among those abroad who granted it to him. "I introduced Nixon to the leaders of Indonesia, President Suharto, Foreign Minister Malik, and so on," Green recalled. "The thing that struck me was that Nixon was all ears. He had a little yellow pad with him, and while he was talking with

Suharto, he was taking down his own personal notes. He was a very good listener. We came back to the embassy that evening and sort of compared notes until two o'clock in the morning about Indonesia, the conversations we had had, and all the rest of it. We particularly discussed this question of the American presence, the question of profile, the question of our responsibility of trying to find the right degree of involvement in the affairs of other countries. . . . The Indonesian experience had been one of particular interest to [Nixon] because things had gone well in Indonesia. I think he was very interested in that whole experience as pointing to the way we should handle our relationships on a wider basis in Southeast Asia generally, and maybe in the world."

A number of other American diplomats had similar experiences with the perambulating and ever-curious Richard Nixon. He had all his detailed notes neatly transcribed after each foreign trip and filed away, cross-indexed, at his New York law office. By the time he entered the White House, he had his own personal archive on international affairs.

(Incidentally, he had a talent for remembering those who had helped him as a private citizen—American ambassadors as well as heads of state. Because of the cordial treatment accorded him during his lean years by Romania's President Ceauşescu and Pakistan's president, General Agha Mohammad Yahya Khan, they later became his favorite statesmen, and subsequently he used them as his prime secret diplomatic channels for the opening to China.)

Nixon had in mind a broad sweep of international strategies, but he needed a tactician and an implementer to transmute these ideas into action. Inasmuch as he had decided long before that he himself would devise the great strokes of foreign policy, Nixon did not want the kind of strongheaded secretary of state that, for instance, Eisenhower had had in John Foster Dulles. As vice president, Nixon had observed at close quarters the Eisenhower-Dulles relationship; he was determined to avoid such a situation.

William Rogers, as a former senior White House official wrote later, "was selected not primarily because of his experience in foreign affairs (which was negligible), but because he was thought to have the intellect, negotiating skill, and judgment to meet the Russian, Chinese and North Vietnamese, or any other potential antagonist on an equal ground. . . . In addition, he was an expert on handling the Congress and the press —problems which have stumped most Secretaries of State in years past." Still, as Nixon saw it, Rogers would be confined to the role of an "up front" negotiator while real policy formulation would be done at the

White House. What Nixon needed was a man of ideas who would assemble the building blocks for the "structure of peace" and who shared his taste for White House decision-making. And, indeed, in foreign affairs—unlike domestic affairs, where he had a knack for picking all the wrong people—Nixon usually showed a fine instinct for selecting the best men available, and Kissinger certainly was one of them.

All the evidence suggests that at least at the outset of his administration Nixon himself was the grand strategist while Kissinger stayed in the background as the chief tactician. In this sense, then, the two men complemented each other.

Aware that there were no really competent conservative foreign-policy thinkers around, Nixon had no qualms about reaching into liberal ranks to find his man in Kissinger, as he did in naming Rogers to the cabinet and Elliot Richardson to be under secretary of state. All three were members in good standing of the liberal Republican Eastern establishment, a group heartily disliked by Nixon's "California clique." But Nixon was not planning on conducting a conservative cold war foreign policy. It was going to be the "new Nixon."

Despite their special brand of compatibility, the relationship between Nixon and Kissinger was strangely ambivalent. Nixon had no personal attachment to Kissinger, and he never felt quite at ease with the professor except when they worked together. "Nixon and Kissinger spent hours and hours together, just the two of them," a former White House official recalled, "but it was always sort of impersonal, and that's the way both of them wanted it. They were not on buddy-buddy terms."

As for Kissinger, he was impatient and suspicious in his dealings with politicians—and Nixon was first and foremost a politician. A brilliant and somewhat authoritarian man, he displayed a sense of superiority that seemed rooted in an essential feeling of insecurity. As a historian of nineteenth-century politics and diplomacy, he evidently never forgot that Bismarck, one of his heroes, had been fired by Kaiser Wilhelm after years of outstanding and dedicated service. His insecurity seemed to stem from fear that his nascent influence might wane if any of his ideas was questioned by Nixon (as they may well have been on occasions, especially at the beginning); he intended to be invulnerable and indispensable at the White House.

Yet Kissinger knew that his power derived entirely from Nixon, and he resented the president accordingly. (Kissinger's associates believe that he had no true admiration for *any* contemporary figure with the possible exception of Premier Chou En-lai and President de Gaulle. For Secretary

Rogers, he had absolute contempt, and he saw a dangerous adversary—
a man who was "out to get him"—in Defense Secretary Melvin R. Laird.
Richardson was one of the few Washingtonians for whose intellect Kissinger had respect.) A former aide recalled Kissinger's reactions to Nixon
in these first months: "A couple of times I heard him talk about the
president with great disdain, great disdain for the president's intelligence. I was shocked. This was early in the game. . . . It was about
[Nixon's] ability to understand some of the complicated matters that, he,
Henry, was trying to deal with on his behalf. . . . I suspect the president
is much more intelligent than Henry made him out to be. . . . Henry would
say, 'How do you make this man understand?' and so forth and so on, a
kind of impatience, the way I would talk to my wife about difficulties in
getting my son to understand the importance of emptying the trash
regularly."

Yet Nixon and Kissinger had shared their enthusiasm for a centralized
staff system, and Kissinger had a finely honed instinct for understanding
the president's views on foreign policy. "If you wanted a diplomacy of
surprise and secret maneuver," another Kissinger aide observed, "it was
a perfect system; you couldn't have done better. . . . If you had a president
with Kennedy's pragmatism or Johnson's kind of consensus building,
wanting to hear things and smell out where to go, Kissinger would be a
disaster and that system would be a disaster. But this president was not
about to be persuaded by opposing points of view; obviously he didn't
want to hear them.

"When American ambassadors would go in to see Nixon, it almost
became a joke. You know, ambassadors going abroad would always raise
two or three sorts of issues, parochial concerns in those foreign countries,
and Nixon would start getting very friendly and smile and appear to be
agreeing—and obviously he had no intention of doing anything about it,
but he wouldn't argue it through or confront it. He would let them say
their piece, go away, and then write them off as fools for having misused
their time with the president to try and get something out of him."

One such ambassador recalls his visit to Nixon in 1969, made before
he returned to his not unimportant diplomatic post: "As I was walking
into the Oval Office, I produced a pad and a pencil to write down what
I thought would be the president's instructions. But I think it was Kissinger who stopped me at the door and whispered, 'Put them away,
because we would rather you didn't make any notes. . . . The last time
you saw the president you wrote a memorandum to the secretary of state,
and this just isn't necessary.' "

.   .   .

On the afternoon of inauguration day, Henry Kissinger held his first meeting with the new NSC staff, each man handpicked by him, including two holdovers from Johnson's White House whom he wanted to keep. It began in a typical Kissinger way with a mixture of defensively self-deprecating humor, explanations of internal White House politics, a pep talk on high policy, and trivia. This is how one of the participants recalls that first meeting in a large room in the Executive Office Building:

"Kissinger came in, sat down, and started off with a joke by saying, 'Look, I've been in office now whatever it is—several hours—and I haven't had a thought yet.' Everybody laughed. Then he said, 'I took this job to think, but ever since I came on, all I've been doing is reading cables, putting out fires, and trying to keep the State Department from selling us down the river.' Looking at his notes, Kissinger said: 'I have to inform you all that there will be no mess privileges in the White House mess for you. I talked to Bob [H. R.] Haldeman, the president's chief of staff, and it's been decided that only the domestic staff will have mess privileges.' There ensued a lengthy discussion with those among us who felt their prerogatives were being slighted, and Kissinger said: 'I'll see what I can do, but I can't do very much. We're in a delicate position here. The most important thing is that all of you instantly are to sever your relations with the press. I observed from reading *The New York Times* and *The Washington Post* that the Johnson administration was the leakiest ship afloat. That will not happen here: the penalty is being fired. If anybody leaks in this administration, I will be the one to leak. You are not to talk to the press at all. In certain instances I may ask you to establish contact with the press. To your friends in the press you are simply not in, from here on.' "

It is useful to cite this admonition to his staff about the press—and even about something as trivial as White House mess privileges—because it emphasizes how vulnerable Kissinger felt vis-à-vis Nixon's "palace guard." One of his aides put it this way: "I don't think he anticipated at all the fierce partisanship of Haldeman, [John] Ehrlichman, and [Charles] Colson. I don't think he had any real portent at all of what kind of a shark tank the White House would become or how isolated and how partisan the Nixon administration would be. Originally he saw even his own appointment and Nixon's 'Bring Us Together' speech after the election as a kind of honeymoon, as a genuine effort to reestablish the consensus in foreign policy. It may have been a forlorn hope, but I think it was genuine for a while."

Another assistant to Kissinger remembered these first days as "an incredibly hopeful and fresh start," after the virtual standstill in foreign policy in the closing months of the Johnson administration, "when everything was [Vietnam] peace negotiations and the election." He said:

"Kissinger was doing all the right things and he was saying all the right things. At that first staff meeting he told us, 'We are going to review every policy from scratch: . . . I'm well aware of all the mythology that is fastened on Vietnam. . . . I'm well aware of how the bureaucracy makes policy and is locked into positions, and the sense of inertia and the departmental rivalries, and all the rest. We are going to overcome that. We are going to have an open system in which all the options are reopened and reconsidered, and the president will then decide, as the president should, between a number of choices well argued and fairly presented. All the unfinished questions will be resolved in some way, and I want you, my NSC staff, to submit suggestions for policy reviews, policies in your areas which need to be looked at afresh.' "

But Kissinger's political problem within the White House was the fact that his NSC staff was formed principally of relatively young liberals, many of whom had worked in the preceding Democratic administrations. The White House palace guard, always suspicious of "outsiders," never quite trusted Kissinger's team. That Kissinger leaned so much on liberals was his chief vulnerability, and his permanent concern was to protect himself and his staff from the White House "gestapo."

The gestapo were principally Haldeman and Ehrlichman, the tough California political pros and political ultraconservatives whom Nixon had brought into the White House from the campaign trail. Parochial and authoritarian, they had no use for the likes of Kissinger, whom they regarded as a dangerous "liberal"—the word itself was derogatory in the new White House. Haldeman as chief of staff and Ehrlichman as head of the Domestic Council (the newly invented domestic counterpart of the NSC) were determined to run Nixon's administration with an even greater sense of ideological discipline—a rightist one—than the president himself.

In a way, it was a tribute to Kissinger that he insisted on a free hand to hire the best staff he could regardless of his assistants' political or ideological beliefs. But it was a virtue born from necessity. One of Kissinger's associates described the situation as follows:

"The people who were around Nixon on foreign policy were abominable intellectually and Henry had no respect for them at all. He sort of kept two of them as a sop to Nixon. . . . I think Kissinger behaved like a typical establishment appointee in recruiting his staff. He went around, he talked to the moguls, he talked to Mac Bundy, he talked to Dean Rusk, he talked to Walt Rostow. . . . So, in the end, it was the kind of staff that you would expect a typical member of the Council on Foreign Relations to put together. It was a staff of people composed on hearsay and reputation inside the establishment—and the establishment was basically liberal Democratic at that point. People with experience in foreign policy over the last five or six years were all Democrats."

Another Kissinger aide thought that "Kissinger was uneasy about the ideological bent of the whole thing" and tried to make up for it by emphasizing to his prospective assistants that the NSC staff was to work for "the presidency" and not for a Republican politician named Richard Nixon. In any event, key people on Kissinger's staff included Morton Halperin, who was brought in from his post in the Pentagon's International Security Affairs unit; Roger Morris, who had worked for Walt Rostow under President Johnson; Laurence Lynn, a Pentagon expert on nuclear matters under Robert McNamara; and Richard Moose, a defense expert. Even Alexander M. Haig, then an unknown colonel, had worked at the Pentagon for a Democratic political appointee. The greatest irony was that Kissinger brought from the RAND Corporation to the group that met at the Pierre Hotel before the inauguration a young man named Daniel Ellsberg to act for a while as a consultant on Vietnam. Kissinger had first met Ellsberg in Vietnam in 1965 and was highly impressed with him. Though he never dreamed of the problems Ellsberg would pose for him and the Nixon administration in the future, he was always self-conscious in those early days about all the NSC staff. "We were outsiders. . . . I think that Henry felt he was an outsider," one young aide recalled. "Any time there was a feeling that Henry was edging into some controversy or issue over which there were strongly held political views on the domestic side, Henry would defer to Haldeman and Ehrlichman. He would pull back, he didn't want us to get into any fights with any of those people. He would pull in his horns rather than get into a scrap with any of them."

Thus the new foreign policy was born in the shadow of an internal conflict on the highest White House level, setting the stage for the political battles ahead.

Chapter 2

One of the first decisions taken by Nixon and Kissinger when they were still working at the Pierre was that there would be a methodical and meticulous review of all U.S. foreign policies and all international situations, area by area and subject by subject, before any new moves would be made. Each study, controlled and coordinated by Kissinger's NSC staff and personally approved by him, would contain a series of policy options, usually four or five, and Nixon could then select the one he wanted—theoretically with the advice and concurrence of the full National Security Council. Embassies and other Washington agencies would be asked to contribute to the studies, but the key to the whole operation was Kissinger's NSC *apparat,* a mini State Department.

Vietnam, relations with the Soviet Union and China, and problems in the Middle East were naturally at the top of the list. But Nixon and Kissinger were not ignoring other subjects. The first request for a policy study—dealing with the Nigerian civil war—was made by Kissinger early in January with instructions to Roger Morris to have it ready for Nixon on inauguration day. Still at the Pierre, Kissinger himself tried to undertake a private mediation effort between the Nigerian government and the Biafra secessionists, but he never had the time to start it.

The policy studies by the NSC staff were known as National Security Study Memoranda—NSSMs for short. They were numbered serially. On January 21, Kissinger issued requests for the first six NSSMs: on Vietnam, the Middle East, military posture, foreign aid, NATO, and international monetary policy. The preinauguration study on Nigeria was not a NSSM, but one was ordered on that subject on January 28. In the first two months, thirty-four NSSMs were requested from the increasingly frantic and overworked NSC staff. (The total for 1969 stood at eighty-five NSSMs.)

Early in February, Nixon and Kissinger asked for a NSSM on China: it marked the start of the Nixon administration's immense effort to prepare itself for the opening to Peking. As far back as October 1967, Nixon, then still a private citizen, first publicly broached the notion that it was inevitable and necessary for the United States and mainland China to establish a serious and permanent relationship. His thoughts were contained in an article in the Council on Foreign Relations quarterly, *Foreign Affairs;* it attracted only limited attention at the time. Now, the State Department and other agencies were asked to contribute voluminous material to the NSC study, though, following Kissinger's style, they were not told why the White House was suddenly interested in China. Most of the contributors remained essentially ignorant of the purpose of their work until Nixon announced more than two years later that he would be going to Peking. The NSSMs and their contents were all classified Secret. One of the reasons for the urgent White House concentration on China was that between election day and the inauguration the Chinese had sent word to the Johnson administration that they wanted diplomatic contacts with the United States via the American and Chinese embassies in Warsaw; these contacts, limited as they were, had been interrupted for a year. In any event, NSSM–14, partly a response to the Chinese feelers, became the cornerstone of the developing new policy.

At his first news conference, on January 27, Nixon said he looked forward to a new Warsaw meeting to see whether any change in the Chinese attitude "on major, substantive issues may have occurred." But emphasizing that it would be "a mistake" for the United States to support Peking's entry into the United Nations, he told newsmen, "I see no immediate prospect of any change in our policy." It was, of course, much too soon for Nixon to show his hand. But on March 28, he and Kissinger requested NSSM–35, dealing with "Trade with Communist China," and on July 3 they asked for a study on "Sino-Soviet Relations," which became NSSM–63.

The Vietnam war was, both in private and in public, Nixon's first and most immediate concern. The important fact to grasp here is that, his claims notwithstanding, Nixon before he took office had no clear plan for ending the war. At best, he and Kissinger had outlines of possible strategies.

Still at the Pierre, a special task force had prepared an "options" paper on Vietnam. Kissinger, with Morton Halperin, and with Ellsberg, Henry S. Rowen, and Fred C. Ikle of the RAND Corporation, were among those who worked on it. The secret "A to Z" options offered to Nixon ranged from an open-ended and gradual beginning of withdrawal of American forces from Vietnam to their indefinite presence there. At

Nixon's direction, the option for an immediate commitment to a complete U.S. withdrawal within a year or two was deleted from the paper. The document also presented a series of specific options on bombing North Vietnam: from maintaining the agreement not to bomb negotiated by W. Averell Harriman in October 1968, to bombing Hanoi and mining the port of Haiphong—a step that had been advocated by the Pentagon for several years but resisted by President Johnson. There was no mention of tactical nuclear weapons. On the diplomatic front, the options ranged from Johnson's basic position that the United States would promise to withdraw militarily from South Vietnam six months after the North Vietnamese troops' departure, to some sharing of political power in Saigon between President Nguyen Van Thieu and the Communists. As one of the authors of the paper put it, "The options were choices in a combination of the ground strategy, bombing strategy, and negotiating strategy."

Simultaneously Daniel Ellsberg prepared a list of twenty-eight questions to be asked of various government departments on different aspects of the Vietnam picture. The tenth question was actually suggested by Kissinger, concerning the impact of Cambodia as a supply route for the Communists in South Vietnam. As subsequent events showed, there was a good reason for this query. The questions were submitted to the bureaucracy on January 21; the replies and comments became the basis for NSSM–1. The principal innovation in this process was that the government agencies—the State and Defense departments; the CIA; the Military Assistance Command, Vietnam (MAC/V); and the American embassy in Saigon—were being asked to submit separate replies to each question rather than to present jointly agreed-upon assessments. Kissinger believed that after receiving all the available information and opinion, it was the White House's privilege to mold this material to its own policies.

The full National Security Council, presided over by Nixon, held its first formal meeting on January 25, a session devoted almost entirely to Vietnam and based on the options paper prepared by the Kissinger-Ellsberg team. Two days later, Nixon sought to give the public impression that he knew exactly where he was going on Vietnam. To the first question at his first presidential news conference—"Now that you are president, what is your peace plan for Vietnam?"—Nixon replied smoothly, "We have been quite specific with regard to some steps that can be taken now on Vietnam. Rather than submitting a laundry list of various proposals, we have laid down those things which we believe the other side should agree to: the restoration of the demilitarized zone as set forth in the Geneva conference of 1954; mutual withdrawal, guaranteed withdrawal of forces by both sides; the exchange of prisoners. All these are matters that we think can be precisely considered and on which progress can be made. Now, where we go from here depends upon what the other side offers in turn."

To be sure, there was nothing new in this, and not surprisingly, Nixon made no reference to the options he had under consideration. But it is relevant to note that he used the news conference to commit the United States to two concepts which in time he would be forced to abandon: one was his insistence on "mutual withdrawal," and the other his opposition to a cease-fire in place. In response to a question, he said that he did not believe in a cease-fire because "when you have a guerrilla war, in which one side may not even be able to control many of those who are responsible for the violence in the area, the cease-fire may be meaningless." He seemed to believe, along with Kissinger, that a military victory in Vietnam, achieved through the destruction of the North Vietnamese potential for aiding the Viet Cong, was still possible. And his response also suggested that his administration had misread Hanoi's intention to engage in a large-scale protracted conventional war in South Vietnam; it was still thinking of the war as a guerrilla situation.

When the answers to the twenty-eight questions were received by Kissinger on February 21, the resulting document—NSSM–1—made it evident that the kind of military pressure applied in Vietnam by the Johnson administration, particularly the bombings, simply had not worked. This is what the CIA reported in its secret paper:

> There were some indications in late 1967 and 1968 that morale was wavering, but not to a degree that influenced the regime's policies on the war. The regime was quite successful, however, in using the bombing threat as an instrument to mobilize people behind the Communist war effort. There is substantial evidence, for instance, that the general populace found the hardships of war more tolerable when it faced daily dangers from the bombing than when this threat was removed and many of the same hardships persisted. . . .
> Communist military and economic aid to North Vietnam to a large extent offset the physical destruction and the disruptive effects of the U.S. bombing. . . . Communist countries provided all of the weapons; enough food, consumer goods, and materials to compensate for lost domestic output; and most of the equipment and materials to maintain the transport system. Without Communist aid, most of it from the Soviet Union and China—particularly given the pressures generated by the bombing—the Vietnamese Communists would have been una-

ble to sustain the war in both South and North Vietnam on anything like the levels actually engaged in during the past three years. . . .

North Vietnam's air defenses significantly reduced the effectiveness of the U.S. bombing, resulted directly or indirectly in the loss of almost 1,100 U.S. aircraft, and provided a psychological boost to morale. . . . Since early 1965, the U.S.S.R. has provided North Vietnam with most of its air defense systems including surface-to-air missiles, jet fighters, a radar network, and antiaircraft artillery.

Almost four years of air war in North Vietnam have shown—as did the Korean War—that, although air strikes will destroy transport facilities, equipment, and supplies, they cannot successfully interdict the flow of supplies because much of the damage can frequently be repaired within hours. . . . The air war did not seriously affect the flow of men and supplies to Communist forces in Laos and South Vietnam. Nor did it significantly erode North Vietnam's military defense capability or Hanoi's determination to persist in the war.

The office of the secretary of defense took a similarly negative view:

The external supply requirements of VC/NVA forces in South Vietnam are so small relative to enemy logistic capacity that it is unlikely any air interdiction campaign can reduce it below the required levels. . . . The enemy can continue to push sufficient supplies through Laos to South Vietnam in spite of relatively heavy losses inflicted by air attacks. . . . It is generally agreed that the bombing did not significantly raise the cost of the war to North Vietnam. . . . North Vietnam is better off today than it was in 1965.

The State Department made this judgment:

Our interdiction efforts in Laos do not appear to have weakened in any major way Communist capabilities to wage an aggressive and protracted campaign in South Vietnam as well as to support military operations against Royal Laotian Government forces in Laos itself. . . . There is little reason to believe new bombing will accomplish what previous bombings failed to do, unless it is conducted with much greater intensity and readiness to defy criticism and risk of escalation.

Nixon's and Kissinger's reaction to NSSM–1 was that the way to win the war would be precisely "to defy criticism and risk of escalation" through bombing of unprecedented intensity throughout Indochina. The point, as the White House interpreted the new study, was not that bombing should be ruled out because it had proved ineffective, but that it should be increased to maximal levels in order to *become* effective. From the outset the White House held the view that the key to a diplomatic solution lay in decisive military action.

Kissinger was telling friends and associates in those first weeks of the new administration that the war would end suddenly in a final spasm of violent fighting. History, of course, proved him right, but only many years later. Now, in January 1969, he was pleading for six months of patience by Americans to achieve Vietnamese peace. We now know in retrospect that Nixon and Kissinger were convinced that Communist exhaustion on the battlefield would create diplomatic conditions for a settlement. This philosophy of letting wars run their course characterized the administration's approach to Vietnam as well as to all future military situations.

NSSM–1 theorized that inasmuch as Hanoi had made concessions late in 1968 to bring about the bombing halt, it would do likewise in the new military-diplomatic round:

> Once Hanoi is convinced the new Administration is not going to "quit" in Viet-Nam or give the game away for free in Paris, and after a period of propaganda exchanges, we would expect renewal of "serious" talks. The primary aim of these for Hanoi will be U.S. withdrawal coupled with the best attainable political settlement. Hanoi will dangle issues such as prisoners before us to achieve these ends and in pursuit of their tactical objectives. . . . Hanoi will try to obtain their ends at minimum cost to themselves in terms of their own withdrawal, effective supervision of a settlement, and the like. Yet we think the prospects on the ground are bleak enough for them so that they will, in the end, make significant concessions (in terms of their own withdrawal) to get us out. They may even relinquish their effort to obtain a favorable political settlement in the negotiations, provided they feel the play of forces in South Viet-Nam in the wake of the agreements reached holds out good promise for their military or political takeover of South Viet-Nam in the next few years.

On another level, Nixon was determined that the United States would not be "humbled" by Vietnamese Communists because, in his opinion, American credibility in Moscow and Peking would be undermined—thus weakening Washington's hand in all future dealings with its "adversaries." Nixon always saw Vietnam in terms of worldwide relationships with the big Communist powers and of the whole future of Asia. In a sense, then, Vietnam was truly an ancillary issue—no matter how the war overshadowed other issues within the United States and affected overall foreign policy.

Moral considerations which weighed heavily with American domestic opposition to the war—such as whether the United States had the right to intervene with awesome military power in an Asian civil war—never seemed to have entered White House deliberations. Kissinger's view was amply demonstrated when he told the newsman Gerald Astor, "I can understand the anguish of younger generations. . . . They lack models, they have no heroes, they see no great purpose in the world. But conscientious objection is destructive of a society. The imperatives of the individual are . . . in conflict with the organization of society. Conscientious objection must be reserved for only the greatest moral issues, and Vietnam is not of this magnitude."

As for Nixon, he understood that the United States could not remain in Vietnam forever; as a corollary, he believed that a way must be found to build up the South Vietnamese regime so that it could survive without the support of American combat forces. In a preelection speech in 1968, he said, "It is a cruel irony that the American effort to safeguard the independence of South Vietnam has produced an ever-increasing dependency in our ally. . . . If South Vietnam's future is to be secure, this process must now be reversed." This was the kernel of the "Vietnamization" policy Nixon launched along with new tactics in "pacification," a bloody program for stamping out Viet Cong insurgency. From the first days of his rule, Nixon realized that Vietnamization, which implied a *gradual* withdrawal of American troops, was essential in domestic political terms. The military draft, the flag-covered caskets steadily streaming back from Vietnam, and the return of wounded veterans by the thousands were intolerable to Americans in the long run—and, therefore, politically unacceptable to Nixon.

Morton Halperin, who as senior adviser to Kissinger was intimately connected with the initial Vietnam policy planning, summarized the attitude toward Vietnam in these words:

"For Nixon what was going on in Vietnam was irrelevant. What was important about Vietnam was that it was seen as a struggle between the United States and the Soviet Union, and it was a question of American ability to meet its commitments, to use force effectively, and so on. He was being tested, and the fact that the situation in Vietnam was not very good and the pacification program wasn't really working—well, none of these things really fundamentally mattered to him.

"Nixon's and Kissinger's view was that the problem with the bombing in the Johnson administration was that the escalation was gradual and accompanied by assurances of limited political gains. In their view, escalation, to be successful, had to threaten first what the president used to call decisive escalation—that is, sudden, very large increases in escalation. Second, it had to threaten the existence of the North Vietnamese regime, and the point of the escalation was to raise sufficient concern in Hanoi, Moscow, and Peking as to what American intentions were and how far the United States would go toward actually destroying North Vietnam. They believed that this kind of escalation would be effective, indeed was necessary, because as they always say in negotiations, 'You'd better be threatening something as well as promising something.'

"The issue was to effect an American disengagement—which was necessary for domestic political reasons—in a way that would preserve the current Saigon government in power. This meant you had to buy time during which you could strengthen the South Vietnamese army and put more destruction on the North Vietnamese so that when you actually withdrew, there was more of a chance that the South Vietnamese government would survive.

"In the beginning, Kissinger was telling everybody that we would be out in six months. You buy time and use that time, first of all, for the Vietnamization program; second, to convey credible threats to the North Vietnamese that you will destroy [them] if they engage in offensive operations after you withdraw; and, third, to build up political relations with China and Russia so that they have an incentive to try to deter the North Vietnamese from renewed escalations of war once the United States withdraws. That, I think, was the basic strategy: to buy time at home and carry out these policies overseas."

When Kissinger took over responsibility for planning Vietnam policies with Nixon, he had already had direct exposure to Vietnamese problems, although his special fields of expertise were nuclear strategy and European affairs. In broad terms, nineteenth-century concepts of the balance of power as applied to the nuclear world were Kissinger's favorite theme as a historian, political scientist, and policy thinker. He had written extensively on these subjects—his books included *Nuclear Weapons and Foreign Policy, A World Restored: Metternich, Castlereagh and the Problems of Peace, 1812–22,* and *The Troubled Partnership: A Re-appraisal of the Atlantic Alliance*—but, inevitably, Vietnam invaded his area of interest, and just as inevitably, he began considering the Vietnamese problem as an extension of his balance-of-power theories.

Kissinger first visited South Vietnam in 1965 and again in 1966 as a consultant to the Johnson administration, preparing a series of reports on the state of pacification in the areas held by the Saigon forces and on the intricacies of Vietnamese politics. By all accounts, he was properly skeptical about what he encountered. He also engaged in secret studies concerning a possible cease-fire, something that occupied him throughout Nixon's first term in the White House. It was during his 1965 trip to Saigon that Kissinger first met President Thieu, the man destined to become one of his most difficult diplomatic interlocutors.

Acting on behalf of the Johnson administration, Kissinger engaged in 1967 in fruitless secret negotiations with the North Vietnamese through two French intermediaries who agreed to carry American messages between Paris and Hanoi. This diplomatic effort, code-named "Pennsylvania," was Kissinger's introduction to the tortures of secret negotiations with North Vietnam, preparing him for his subsequent direct diplomacy with Hanoi's men.

Between this first experience and his work as a policy planner and then negotiator, Kissinger put down his thoughts on Vietnam in a lengthy article written while he was still teaching at Harvard and published in the January 1969 issue of *Foreign Affairs.* Because Kissinger had already been named as Nixon's foreign-policy adviser when his article on "The Vietnam Negotiations" reached the public, it was construed as something of a policy document. In it Kissinger interestingly showed greater perception and sensitivity about the problems of negotiating an end to the Vietnam war than when he handled it months later as a presidential adviser. Power, evidently, alters the perspective. His critique of how the Johnson administration had conducted the war and its negotiations between 1965 and 1968 could later be applied to the Nixon-Kissinger policies. But in the article there was no hint of the options for destroying North Vietnam that emerged as soon as Nixon took office:

> We fought a military war; our opponents fought a political one. We sought physical attrition; our opponents aimed for our psychological exhaustion. . . . The North Vietnamese used their main forces the way a bullfighter uses his cape—to keep us lunging into areas of marginal political importance. . . . All this caused our military operations to have little relationship to our declared political objectives. Short of a complete collapse of the opponent, our military deployment was not well designed to support a negotiation.

Kissinger made two other important points in his analysis, points that became structurally crucial in his own negotiating approach to the North Vietnamese. One was that "American 'victories' were empty unless they laid the basis for an eventual withdrawal." The other was that "our diplomacy and our strategy were conducted in isolation from each other." In the first instance, Nixon and Kissinger decided on a policy of gradual withdrawal of American troops—but with the clear determination to strike with utmost brutality at North Vietnam if Hanoi did not reciprocate. But inasmuch as both men knew that the North Vietnamese were in no mood to give up their objective of controlling the South—Kissinger himself wrote that this was immutable Hanoi policy—American aerial escalation of the war was predetermined. There was considerable subtlety—and cynicism—in this approach. In the second instance, Nixon and Kissinger immediately and intimately related American actions on the battlefield and in the air to the diplomatic negotiations in Paris. Yet it took an extraordinary combination of unacknowledged American political concessions and overwhelming military power before the United States—with its war prisoners—was extricated from the Vietnam quagmire.

The first hundred days of the Nixon administration—from inauguration to the beginning of May 1969—were a frantic period in American foreign policy. A part of this activity was in full public view, but much of it was covert and secret, certainly more so than many of the president's closest associates realized at the time. Publicly, Nixon embarked on traditional American presidential diplomacy in Western Europe. Semipublicly, he dealt with a sudden Korean crisis that, out of rashness, he nearly transformed into a new Asian war. Secretly and covertly, within weeks of moving into the White House, he escalated the aerial war in Indochina, wasting no time in ordering many of the bombing options outlined in the basic document Kissinger gave him just before the inauguration and later discussed in NSSM–1. Subsequently, Kissinger sought to convey the impression that NSSM–1 was no more than an effort to acquaint the new administration with the war's problems, but a close study of this paper strongly suggests it actually provided the rationale for the air escalation.

At the same time, Nixon was quietly moving toward negotiations with the Soviet Union over the control of nuclear weapons, a Middle East settlement, and a whole range of other issues. Kissinger quickly established a private "back channel" to Anatoly Dobrynin, the enormously knowledgeable Soviet ambassador to the United States, who had been in Washington since early 1962, arriving six months before the Cuban missile crisis. Nixon's was the third successive administration to which Dobrynin had been accredited, and he knew his way around Washington better than most diplomats. His first secret meeting with Kissinger at the White House in February marked the beginning of an extraordinary diplomatic partnership that spanned the next eight years.

Just as secretly, Nixon and Kissinger probed China's attitudes toward a rapprochement, using other back channels. And the NSC staff worked virtually around the clock, preparing new studies and recommendations on every conceivable policy problem. Some NSC officials kept two shifts of secretaries and typists working regularly—a day shift and a night shift after dinner to ready papers for presentation to Kissinger and Nixon the first thing the next morning.

Consciously or not, Nixon had a penchant for imitating John Kennedy. He had a grudging admiration for Kennedy's easy personal style, and he, too, was eager to develop a distinctive style for dealing with foreign nations and their leaders. It may not have been altogether accidental that Nixon's first presidential overseas voyage was to Western Europe, in February 1969, which had also been Kennedy's first trip, in June 1961.

A visit to America's NATO allies was, of course, a natural move—relations with the Europeans and particularly the French were again at a low ebb—but there was no special urgency surrounding Nixon's trip. For Kennedy the principal purpose had been to meet in Vienna with Soviet Premier Nikita S. Khrushchev, as well as to seek a personal relationship with France's President de Gaulle. But Nixon was far from even contemplating a conference with the Soviet leadership. His European grand tour was more in the nature of a diplomatic gesture.

Nixon's approach to his personal diplomacy was extremely meticulous. Ronald L. Ziegler, the White House press secretary, who seldom left the president's side, recalled that "The president would have briefings from government specialists or meet with a task force to refresh himself about bilateral situations. Then, aboard the plane, he would further update himself from briefing books he took along. He would keep conferring with Kissinger. . . .

"He had an unbelievable grasp of issues and a great awareness of subtleties in foreign affairs. . . . In meeting foreign leaders, especially adversaries, Nixon looked first at the human strength of the man he faced and then at his intellect. He watched the man's strength of position and recognized his ability to discuss positions."

Nixon had every conceivable product of technology at his command when he traveled abroad. *The Spirit of '76* was linked by radio to the Tactical Air Command headquarters at Langley Air Force Base in Virginia and, through it, to the White House telephone switchboard. Just by picking up a white phone in the plane (or a red one for a scrambler-equipped line), he could reach any of his civilian advisers or military commanders around the world. Should an emergency or conflict develop while he was aloft, Nixon could use his air communications system to act as commander in chief. The National Military Command Center at the Pentagon, the North American Defense Command in Colorado Springs, and the Strategic Air Command headquarters at Omaha, Nebraska, controlling the Minuteman missiles and B-52 bombers, could respond instantly if he issued orders in a sudden crisis, no matter where he was.

Nixon announced his European visit within two weeks of his inauguration, saying in a formal statement that "the future of the countries of the West can no longer be an exclusively American design. It requires the best thought of Europeans and Americans alike." And now, in the chilly, rainy semidarkness of early morning on Sunday, February 23, Nixon was saying good-bye to dignitaries and diplomats seeing him off at Andrews Air Force Base, outside Washington:

> It is a trip, I wish to emphasize, which is not intended [to] and will not settle all of the problems we have in the world. The problems we face are too complex and too difficult to be settled by what I would call "showboat" diplomacy. . . . Before we can make progress . . . it is necessary to consult with our friends. And we are going to have real consultation because we seek not only their support but their advice and their counsel on the grave problems that we face in the world— the problem of Vietnam, of the Mideast, monetary problems, all the others that may cause difficulties between nations.

The rhetoric continued at Nixon's first stop, which was Brussels, where he was met by King Baudouin in midevening. At a NATO Council meeting he reassured the nervous Europeans that he would do nothing behind their backs:

> I know there have been rumblings of discontent in Europe—a feeling that too often the United States talked at its partners instead of talking with them, or merely informed them of decisions after they were made instead of consulting with them before deciding. The United States is determined to listen with a new attentiveness to its NATO partners —not only because they have a right to be heard, but because we want their ideas. I believe we have a right to expect that consultation shall be a two-way street.

In London, Nixon followed American presidential ritual in reassuring the British about the "special relationship" between the two countries—

and then it was on to Bonn for a speech before the West German Bundestag and to West Berlin for a day's stay. After Berlin, it was a one-night stop in Rome and then the short hop over to Paris for the most important part of the European tour, talks with de Gaulle. During four days in Paris, Nixon succeeded in temporarily improving relations with the touchy French president, as Kennedy had done eight years earlier. But more important, Nixon and de Gaulle conferred at length about the Vietnam war and the possibility of an American rapprochement with China. De Gaulle volunteered France's diplomatic resources to help in the tangled peace negotiations—Kissinger's secret diplomacy on Vietnam was really born during these Elysée Palace conversations—and in establishing channels to Peking.

Nixon also used his Paris stay to take a close personal look at how the negotiations were proceeding between the Americans and the North Vietnamese. This diplomatic confrontation had just entered a new phase —with both the South Vietnamese and the Viet Cong joining the Americans and the North Vietnamese—and quiet Russian pressure on the Communists had helped to resolve a long argument about the shape of the negotiating table and the places where the negotiators would sit. Diplomacy is full of such apparent trivialities—at the 1815 Congress of Vienna the issue was through which door different kings and emperors would enter the negotiating room—and Nixon was encouraged that Soviet Ambassador Valerian Zorin had been willing to conciliate. He took it as a sign that the Russians would be helpful in settling the Vietnam war.

On his last day in Paris, Nixon paid an unpublicized visit to the American delegation to the peace talks, in their separate wing of the embassy building on the Place de la Concorde. Nixon had ostensibly gone to the embassy to address the entire assembled staff, but after his speech he was taken to the delegation's "secure" room (protected from electronic eavesdropping) to meet with the American negotiators.

It was a brand-new delegation, one that he himself had named to replace the team headed by Averell Harriman, which the previous October had worked out the secret "understanding" with the North Vietnamese concerning a cessation in the bombing of North Vietnam. The new chief delegate was Henry Cabot Lodge, the former Republican senator and Nixon's 1960 running mate, who served as Kennedy's and Johnson's ambassador in Saigon in the early and mid-1960s. A man of considerable international prestige, Lodge was well versed in South Vietnamese politics; it was during his ambassadorial tenure that the United States forced the military coup against President Ngo Dinh Diem ending in

Diem's death. Nixon appointed Lodge to the Paris post publicly to emphasize the importance he gave the peace talks. But in reality, it was an empty diplomatic gesture because Nixon and Kissinger insisted on conducting secret and substantive diplomacy themselves. It became a pattern for Nixon to name outstanding personalities to crucial diplomatic posts —to provide the "theater," as a White House official explained later— and then to bypass them altogether when it came to serious business. When Kissinger, who had been Lodge's consultant in South Vietnam, took over the secret talks with the North Vietnamese in Paris soon afterward, he left Lodge in the dark about what he was doing.

Nixon was accompanied by Secretary of State Rogers and Kissinger when he arrived at the delegation's "secure" room. Lodge; his deputy, Lawrence Walsh, a New York lawyer; and Marshall Green, who after finishing his tour as ambassador to Indonesia was temporarily attached to the Paris negotiating team, were there. The discussion went on for four hours as Nixon busily scribbled notes on his yellow pad. An American official asked Kissinger after the meeting what Nixon did with his notes. "Well, he calls me in the evening and we go over whatever he has collected in his pad, and then he requires action," Kissinger replied.

The embassy meeting was largely in the form of questions and answers, but, as one participant recalled, "Nixon was certainly bound and determined to complete a peace settlement and the withdrawal of American forces during his first term in office." So the session revolved around "how we were going to get out of Vietnam the right way," as another participant explained it later. Nixon's emerging policy was still known as "de-Americanization" (the term "Vietnamization" was coined subsequently), and "we thought it was probably a somewhat easier job than it turned out to be. We probably had many illusions as to what the North Vietnamese were willing to do." While Nixon emphasized battlefield escalation, he was also willing to make certain parallel concessions to Hanoi on the diplomatic track. The United States would consider withdrawing its forces from South Vietnam on a "systematic basis," he told the delegation, and it was ready to discuss South Vietnam's political future and an exchange of war prisoners. (The latter had not yet become a problem in the negotiations: in fact, neither side had made an issue of it.) But he also wanted Hanoi to respect the demilitarized zone that had divided the two Vietnams since the end of the French war in 1954.

But Nixon and Kissinger evidently did not realize that gradual American withdrawals were not sufficient to bring about the kind of peace Hanoi had in mind and that, regardless of the scope of American bombing, it was determined to keep on fighting until most of the United States troops had been repatriated.

Nixon left Paris on March 2 to fly to Rome for a private meeting with Pope Paul VI—spending just a few late-afternoon hours in the Eternal City. Nixon had been keen on crowning his European tour with a Vatican visit, and he told Paul VI in a speech in the Papal Salon that "the fact that we have your prayers will sustain us in the years ahead."

With this, the president recrossed the Atlantic and, landing late in the evening at Andrews Air Force Base, informed the large welcoming committee (the White House had arranged for Vice President Agnew, cabinet members, a number of senators and congressmen, and a group of foreign ambassadors to be on hand) that his overall impression of the European trip could be summed up by the word "trust." "I sensed, as I traveled to the capitals of Europe, that there is a new trust on the part of the Europeans in themselves. . . . Also, I think I sensed a new trust in the United States growing out of the fact that they feel that there are open channels of communication with the United States, and a new sense of consultation with the United States," Nixon said. Again, the Nixon rhetoric was not quite in tune with the realities. "Trust" has rarely been a notable characteristic of American-European relations.

Back in Washington, Nixon's first priority was still Indochina. The president had concluded on the basis of recommendations from the Joint Chiefs of Staff; the Military Assistance Command, Vietnam (MAC/V); and the American embassy in Saigon contained in the "answers" section of NSSM–1 that an escalation of air action in Vietnam and Laos—as well as bombing in Cambodia—was essential to satisfactory progress. Military people were certain that a significant volume of Communist supplies was moving down the Ho Chi Minh Trail in Laos and up along the Cambodian border from the port of Sihanoukville in the south. Soviet, Chinese, and Soviet-bloc freighters as well as North Vietnamese coastal vessels and sampans were sailing around the Indochina peninsula to unload in Sihanoukville.

The decision to strike, like so many other decisions taken on Indochina, was the result of a White House predilection for accepting "worst case" interpretations made by the armed forces and justifying harsh action over much less sanguine estimates and more cautious recommendations from the CIA and the State Department. The United States government was sharply split over what was the *reality* in Indochina and, therefore, over what should be done about the war. NSSM–1 made it clear how little resemblance each government agency's perceptions about the "truth" in Indochina bore to the others. The document said that the responses to the twenty-eight questions forming it "show agreement on some matters as well as very substantial differences of opinion . . . on many aspects of the Vietnam situation. . . . While there are some divergencies on the facts, the sharpest differences arise in the interpretation of those facts, the relative weight to be given them, and the implications to be drawn." Interestingly, disagreements usually occurred between two groups "with generally consistent membership." NSSM–1 said that "Group A," including MAC/V; Commander in Chief, Pacific (CINC-PAC); the Joint Chiefs of Staff (JCS); and Embassy Saigon, "takes a hopeful view of current and future prospects in Vietnam." But "Group B," made up of the Office of the Secretary of Defense (OSD), the CIA, and to a lesser extent the State Department, "is decidedly more skeptical about the present and pessimistic about the future."

As to the specific matter of escalating the aerial war, NSSM–1 observed that "Group A assigns much greater effectiveness to bombing in Vietnam and Laos than Group B." The document reported that MAC/V attributed greater military power to the Communists than did the CIA and the State Department—and that "MAC/V-JCS and Saigon consider Cambodia (and especially Sihanoukville) an important enemy supply channel while CIA disagrees strongly." The disagreements went further:

> MAC/V-JCS assign very much greater effectiveness to our past and current Laos and North Vietnam bombing campaign than do OSD and CIA. . . . MAC/V-JCS believes that a vigorous bombing campaign could choke off enough supplies to Hanoi to make her stop fighting, while OSD and CIA see North Vietnam continuing the struggle even against unlimited bombing. . . . The MAC/V-JCS and State/CIA/OSD fundamentally disagree over whether our bombing campaign either prior to or after November [1968] has reduced the enemy's throughput of supplies so that the enemy in South Vietnam receives less than he needs here. The MAC/V-JCS feel the bombing has succeeded; State/CIA/OSD think it has failed. . . .
>
> If all imports by sea were denied and land routes through Laos and Cambodia attacked vigorously, the MAC/V-JCS find that North Vietnam could not obtain enough war supplies to continue. In total disagreement, OSD and CIA believe that the overland routes from China alone could provide North Vietnam enough material to carry on, even with an unlimited bombing campaign.

The White House was thus faced with two bureaucratic alliances representing and pushing divergent views. The uniformed officers in Washington, Honolulu (CINCPAC headquarters), and Saigon, together with the embassy in Saigon headed by Ambassador Ellsworth Bunker, were the gung-ho group, believing that the war was winnable and that all that was needed for victory in the battlefield were decisive actions through overwhelming American power. The civilian Office of the Secretary of Defense (which meant Secretary Laird and his immediate advisers) chose to align itself with CIA and the State Department to present what turned out to be a vastly more realistic assessment. The CIA, in particular, understood the limitations of American power in the Vietnam situation better than most of the other agencies.

In the end, it was up to Nixon and Kissinger to mediate these differences and formulate what they thought to be adequate American policy. And the record shows clearly that Nixon and Kissinger chose the route of violence, convinced that North Vietnam and the Viet Cong could not withstand the savage blows of American military power. This notion flew in the face of some of the best analyses available in Washington, and it produced four more years of destructive warfare.

Even before Nixon gave the green light for B-52 air strikes in Cambodia, American involvement in Indochina as a whole was formidable. In South Vietnam there were more than half a million United States troops, an inheritance from the Johnson reign. Much of Asia, in fact, was enmeshed in United States military, paramilitary, and intelligence operations aimed chiefly at Vietnam, but fitting into a broader Asian strategy. This strategy was concerned with the situation throughout Southeast Asia, from Vietnam in the east to Thailand in the west. It included scenarios and contingencies for dealing with China, if the need arose, as well as special operations around North Korea (this for reasons that were unclear at best and downright perilous at worst). Years were to elapse before the American public and members of Congress, indeed before even many senior government officials, became fully aware of the scope and diversity of these United States activities in Asia.

In addition to the presence of American ground troops in South Vietnam, the navy permanently maintained aircraft carriers and other warships on "Yankee Station" in the general area of the Gulf of Tonkin for tactical air strikes and naval bombardment of the Vietnam coast. The coast guard devoted itself to the interdiction of Communist supply movements in Vietnamese inland waters. B-52s of the Strategic Air Command (SAC) were stationed on Okinawa (before the island reverted to Japan) and Guam. Nuclear weapons were stored on both Okinawa and Guam, as they were on Taiwan and in the Philippines. Under secret agreements negotiated in the Johnson era, B-52s and fighter-bombers plus an array of specialized aircraft were based in Thailand. *That* country was the center of so-called electronic battlefield operations in Vietnam, Laos, and Cambodia: sophisticated electronic control for combat and intelligence missions. There was even a special squadron whose mission was weather-modification over Indochina, meaning rain-making attempts (generally unsuccessful) over Communist infiltration trails.

From Okinawa, Guam, and Thailand, SAC's B-52s flew constant bombing missions against North Vietnamese and Viet Cong concentrations in South Vietnam—the huge planes often struck within earshot of Saigon—as well as against the trails in eastern Laos. Sometimes the huge bombers went out against the North Vietnamese and Pathet Lao rebels in the contested Plaine des Jarres area in central-northern Laos.

In Laos, since the early 1960s the CIA had been operating its "Clandestine Army," largely made up of tough Meo tribesmen headed by General Vang Pao, in support of the totally ineffective Royal Lao Army. Whether General Vang Pao and his hill people were patriots or mercenaries is a moot point; the principal reality was that the 40,000-man Clandestine Army was supplied and directed by the CIA, whose officers kept Vang Pao on a short leash. CIA aircraft disguised as planes of Air America, a CIA-owned airline, flew the Meos and provided them with supplies and tactical support. Later, Thai "volunteers," secretly paid by the United States, were added to the Laotian operation.

The concept behind the CIA's secret army, which had been organized during the Kennedy and Johnson administrations and which was expanded by Nixon, was to prevent the Communist take-over of Laos without actually introducing American combat troops, which would have been an open violation of the 1962 Geneva accords on Laos. That the North Vietnamese had been violating the accords all along by keeping troops in Laos was not sufficient reason for a direct United States presence. Deception, then, was deemed the answer, and all things considered, it was working reasonably well. The United States government hid behind the CIA, not to show its hand openly, and the agency, in turn, used other covers. One of them was the Agency for International Development (AID), whose official mission in Laos was to provide humanitarian assistance—food deliveries and care of the refugees—except that a lot of AID's rice went to Vang Pao's soldiers rather than to war victims. It was all very convenient.

Laos was an essential component of the Southeast Asian military equation. The old domino theory, which went back to John Foster Dulles in the 1950s, was easily accepted by Nixon and Kissinger, just as it had been by previous Democratic administrations: the fall of Laos to the North Vietnamese and their local Pathet Lao allies would not only lead to the fall of Cambodia and South Vietnam but, even worse, open up Thailand's northeastern border to the Communists. China was in the north and Communist-supported insurrection was developing within Thailand itself. With the collapse of Laos, the Washington reasoning went, Thailand would quickly be ripe for a take-over. The main concern, therefore, was to keep the Communists from installing themselves on the northern bank of the Mekong, the river that divides Laos from Thailand.

The key to central Laos was the Plaine des Jarres, where for years the Communists moved forward during the rainy season and pulled back in the dry season. It was never entirely clear that the North Vietnamese really planned to "go for broke" and capture the administrative capital at Vientiane and the royal capital at Luang Prabang, but this remained a major American fear. Thus the Vang Pao/CIA army operated almost exclusively in the Plaine des Jarres with air support from the United States, a fact that Washington would never confirm officially even though American fighter-bombers and pilots were being lost there, and B-52s were secretly added to the strike force in 1970.

It was no great secret, on the other hand, that the B-52s had been raiding in the Laotian panhandle in the south, day in and day out, to interdict the flow of men and matériel from North to South Vietnam along the Ho Chi Minh complex of trails. It was, indeed, a separate Laotian war, wholly disconnected from the fighting in the Plaine des Jarres. The B-52 strikes in South Vietnam and over the trails were code-named "Arc Light." Bombing decisions for the panhandle were made far away from Laos, just as future invasions of the area were planned in Saigon and Washington.

When it came to the Clandestine Army, however, all the activities, including supportive U.S. air strikes, were coordinated jointly by the American ambassador in Vientiane and the resident CIA station chief. For all practical purposes, the American embassy in Vientiane was a military command. The embassy and the CIA jointly set targets for air strikes in the Plaine des Jarres in coordination with MAC/V and the Seventh Air Force headquarters in Saigon. In a sense, they were directly responsible for the massive bombardment of Laos, its villages, and its people for nearly a decade. Between the Plaine and the panhandle, 2 million tons of bombs were dropped on Laos between 1960 and 1970. Many years later, CIA Director William Colby made the important and often overlooked point that the Laotian operations were authorized by the president of the United States, that the agency was not acting on its own. This is crucial in understanding *all* covert United States operations worldwide. The CIA never undertakes *major* projects without clearance from the White House. The ultimate responsibility always was—and is—the president's, although the official inclination was to dissociate him from unpalatable acts under the tattered doctrine of "plausible denial." Laos was no exception.

When Colby, answering questions at his confirmation hearings before the Senate Armed Services Committee on July 2, 1973, said: "The agency's activities in Laos were undertaken in direct response to presidential and National Security Council direction in order to carry out U.S. policy and at the same time *to avoid the necessity for uniformed involvement in Laos,*" he was perpetrating yet another Indochina war fiction. American military and CIA men in civilian garb ran the secret army just as efficiently as if they were in uniform. It was an immensely cruel war-by-proxy on the ground, supported from the air by U.S. Air Force planes.

A senior State Department official who served in Laos during the first year of the Nixon administration described to me the American objectives in running the Clandestine Army:

"Basically, what we were envisaging was that the war in Laos would be contained within certain rather well-defined parameters with the recognition that the solution in Laos could only come with the solution in Vietnam. . . . If one wanted to avoid the presence of the North Vietnamese on the northern bank of the Mekong, which they otherwise would be capable of doing with all the implications that meant for relations with Thailand, I think the decision of using the Meo mountain tribes as, if you like, paid mercenaries, I think that was successful, I think it was in our interest to have done so." He made no bones about the fact that Vang Pao's army could not have existed without the CIA's logistic support, because "they were supplied firearms and they were supplied rice, the basic staple of their diet."

Having frequently dealt with General Vang Pao, the official had vivid memories of the elusive commander: "He was a very unusual human being. He wore several hats or had several responsibilities. He was a very good military leader. It was almost to the point of rashness that he himself got down to the front lines with his own troops. There were always efforts to restrain him. He was [also] a tribal leader, and, as such, he had to hold court a couple of times a week when he adjudicated some of the tribal or community problems with the Meo people, and he was looked up to and respected as a very judicious man."

But Vang Pao was wholly subject to United States control. To maintain the fiction of American "neutrality," his channel to the embassy was through Premier Souvanna Phouma; it was to the premier that Vang Pao presented his military proposals and these, in turn, were submitted to the American ambassador, G. McMurtrie Godley (whose tenure in Laos spanned most of the Nixon years), and to CIA representatives.

Godley, a rough, tough Yale man and career Foreign Service officer, presided over the most intensive period of the Clandestine Army's activities. He had replaced William H. Sullivan, a Laos expert who had helped to oversee the organization of the Vang Pao army and whose CIA partner was Theodore Schackley, later station chief in Saigon and a man his own associates described as "cold" and "arrogant." When Godley took over in Laos in 1968, he arranged to have as CIA station chief his former colleague from the Congo, Lawrence Devlin (Godley and Devlin had been deeply involved in the CIA's Congo activities in the mid-1960s, when Godley had been ambassador in Kinshasa). Devlin lasted until late in 1970, when he was replaced as CIA boss in Laos by another top operative, Hugh Tovar. Godley, Devlin, and Tovar were the principal paramilitary American chiefs in Laos during the first Nixon administration.

Vang Pao's proposals were reviewed by the ambassador, his deputy, the CIA station chief, and the military attaché. A former senior embassy official reported, for example, one occasion when Souvanna Phouma "came to me, saying that Vang Pao thought it would be militarily advantageous and wise to attempt to take the Plaine des Jarres, and in order to do so he needed certain specific U.S. military support. . . . I refused to give it to him because I didn't believe this was a wise move."

Thus Laos was in effect a military protectorate of the United States and the ambassador was the proconsul. This is how it worked in practice, according to a ranking member of the embassy in Vientiane:

"The embassy country team met six mornings a week at nine o'clock from Monday through Saturday. On the walls in the embassy room where staff meetings were held, there were maps showing the current position of the Pathet Lao and the North Vietnamese. The defense attachés were there, the CIA people were there, AID people, and others, and each morning the tactical situation was looked at very carefully. Decisions were made by the ambassador or, in his absence, his deputy. On occasion, the CIA station chief would make certain recommendations; sometimes they were accepted, sometimes not, but the final decision was the ambassador's."

As for the air operations, American tactical and later B-52 support was given the Laotian regulars and Vang Pao's hill people fighting in the ebb and flow of battles for the Plaine des Jarres by aircraft flying from Thai and South Vietnamese bases. Laotian T-28s simply could not do the job. But the American embassy often had to compete with its counterpart in Saigon when it came to Seventh Air Force raids. As a former attaché in Vientiane recalls, "There was a constant conflict of demand on the Seventh Air Force in Saigon between the need for strikes in Vietnam and in Laos. Often we felt we got the short end of the stick."

State Department officials have insisted that the embassy, not the CIA, had the final say in Laotian deployments. Colby made the point that the agency, in Laos as elsewhere, primarily carried out presidential directives. But there are many indications that the CIA often bypassed embassy and State Department channels, particularly on military affairs, dealing directly with the White House via its Langley, Virginia, headquarters. Because of Nixon's and Kissinger's penchant for working through their own back channels, American ambassadors were often in the dark about military operations.

Laos was an exception, but the CIA's active role was extensive. Fred Branfman, an Indochina expert, wrote that "the CIA on a typical day in 1971 had direct control of over 2000 Americans and 45,000 Asians fighting the war within Laos; could call upon another 65,000 Americans and Asians in Laos indirectly involved in the war; and was supported by another 50,000 Americans outside Laos, mostly involved in the air war, who were directly and fully involved in waging war against Laos."

If Vietnam and Laos were the major and largely visible American operations in Indochina, there was a plethora of ancillary efforts, largely in the area of combat intelligence, that spread all over Asia. The Nixon administration's inclination, as it assumed responsibility, was to expand rather than reduce the scope of these activities.

When Nixon took office, there were 28,000 Americans working for the Pentagon in intelligence and psychological-warfare operations in East Asia. This figure appears in a still secret study prepared for the White House late in 1969 by Elliot Richardson, then under secretary of state, on proposed reductions in the number of American officials serving abroad apart from organized military forces. Nixon had ordered a 10 percent cut in American personnel abroad under Operation Reduction, but Richardson reported that the White House had granted an exemption for those employed by the Defense Department in Asia in intelligence and related activities. (The exemption, incidentally, was the result of a directive from Kissinger, who wanted intelligence and psychological-warfare operations to proceed at an undiminished rhythm throughout Asia. Kissinger already seemed to trust the military more than the CIA.) The document warned Nixon that under the exemptions for the Pentagon, "the military psychological-warfare units" would assume "a disproportionate role in comparison to civilians. . . . In Southeast Asia and Korea, civilian agencies are reducing the level of operations, but the Department of Defense does not plan to reduce the level of psychological warfare operations." (This was written months after U.S. intelligence operations around Korea nearly led to a war.)

And indeed, the Pentagon was stepping up its most secret operations in Southeast Asia. These were ground penetrations into Laos and Cambodia by United States military-intelligence teams, usually with South Vietnamese participation, in clear violation of the neutrality of the two adjacent countries. Laos, of course, was a war theater, but ground incursions into Cambodia were launched in 1967 under the Johnson administration, two years before Nixon started bombing Cambodian targets. The incursions were the responsibility of a secret military-intelligence unit attached to the U.S. Command in Saigon: the Military Assistance Command Studies and Operations Group or MAC/SOG. MAC/SOG teams were made up of the army's Special Forces (Green Berets) operatives and electronic technicians from a National Security Agency group also stationed in Saigon. The very fact that an NSA group operated in Vietnam was a military secret. Its operations were financed as a separate classified line item in the navy's budget, and even a trained budget reader would never have guessed that "NOP 345" represented ground-intelligence activities in Laos and Cambodia.

The secret ground missions, designed to obtain intelligence on Communist movements in the staging areas in the Laotian panhandle and in Cambodian sanctuaries contiguous to South Vietnam, were supported by tactical air strikes, when needed, and by helicopter gunships. The usual practice was for an electronic NSA aircraft, typically an EC-47 (a C-47 plane packed with electronic gear), to fly overhead when the penetration teams moved into Laos or Cambodia. If any intelligence was obtained, the SOG men radioed the EC-47, which, in turn, relayed the information to the Saigon command. An air strike in Laos or Cambodia could thus be ordered literally within minutes.

This practice, incidentally, gave the lie to subsequent assertions that the first secret U.S. intervention in Cambodia came only with the B-52 bombings in March 1969. In fact, starting in March, one of the SOG teams' principal missions was to comb the Cambodian sanctuaries for "lucrative" targets for the B-52s.

SOG teams also placed sensors, which are tiny radio transmitters, along Communist infiltration routes, and they tried to capture prisoners. In the latter endeavor, however, they were rather unsuccessful; between 1965 and 1972 only twenty-six were taken in Laos, and between 1967 and mid-1972 only twenty-four were captured in Cambodia.

A report issued late in 1973 by the Department of Defense provided the first comprehensive account of these secret activities. It showed that there were 1798 SOG missions in Laos, code-named "Prairie Fire," and 1885 cross-border operations in Cambodia, code-named "Salem House," by the time they were ended in April 1972. The department's study also emphasized how the rate of these incursions—some in platoon or multiplatoon strength—increased after Nixon took office. Whereas there were 327 such missions in Laos in 1968, the number went up to 452 in 1969. Supportive sorties by helicopter gunships went up from 287 in 1968 to 689 in 1969 and 1116 in 1970. In Cambodia, the number of Salem House missions grew from 287 in 1968 to 454 in 1969 and 558 in 1970. Helicopter gunship sorties over Cambodia rose from 359 in 1968 to 398 in 1969 and 1548 in 1970.

Assertions that secret cross-border operations of this type were purely a military affair and did not involve top policy-makers in Washington are contradicted by the Pentagon report, for it indicates that "targets, dates, penetration points, and landing zones" were submitted for approval to the Saigon command and the Pacific command in Honolulu, with copies to the Joint Chiefs of Staff, the secretary of defense, and the secretary of state. The report said that "approval of the schedule was assumed if no objections were raised."

As in many other U.S. operations in Asia, deep deception covered Prairie Fire and Salem House. For security reasons, the data bank of the Joint Chiefs of Staff was deliberately fed false information as to the location of casualties incurred in Prairie Fire and Salem House, and next of kin were advised that men had been killed in "Southeast Asia," "along the border," or in a "classified" area. Only in May 1973 were Congress and the families of those men told the truth: 76 American servicemen had been killed in Prairie Fire operations and 27 in Salem House. The report acknowledged that for years these casualties "were grouped with the South Vietnamese data" in Pentagon computers.

In Laos, Prairie Fire's objectives included the search for the ever-elusive Viet Cong headquarters known to American intelligence as

COSVN (Central Office for South Vietnam). Until the end of the war, however, the Americans could not discover just where COSVN was located, and for that matter, whether it really existed. They looked for it in both Laos and Cambodia, never quite sure whether it was a fixed-site command that occasionally moved from one place to another, or whether it was a mobile headquarters, changing locations all the time. Actually, American intelligence became aware of COSVN only because captured Communist documents occasionally included so-called COSVN Directives—political-military guidance papers. It may well be that COSVN Directives were written by Hanoi, and even that they were intended as "disinformation" to confuse the United States. However, American intelligence considered the capture of a COSVN document a major triumph. Much planning in the Indochina war was based on what had been gleaned from COSVN Directives; this may have been exactly what the Communists had in mind. In any event, the United States, its intelligence and technological resources notwithstanding, never broke the North Vietnamese–Viet Cong communications and command system. But the efforts to do so—on the ground and from the air—certainly cost quite a few American lives.

In South Vietnam, the principal intelligence effort, aside from battlefield intelligence, was Operation Phoenix, staffed by the CIA and the Defense Department and aimed at eradicating Viet Cong cadres (known in official parlance as VCI, or Viet Cong Infrastructure). Phoenix was part of the broader pacification program, called Civil Operations and Rural Development Support (CORDS), which, with the advent of the Nixon administration, was designed to parallel in the civilian realm the Vietnamization policy in the South Vietnamese armed forces.

Pacification was run by William Colby, who reported to the chief of the U.S. Military Command in Saigon rather than to Ellsworth Bunker, the American ambassador. Colby had served earlier as CIA station chief in Saigon, but his performance as the head of the 10,000-man pacification operation gained him recognition in Nixon's Washington and, in time, ascent to the post of director of Central Intelligence.

Operation Phoenix was primarily a murderous enterprise. American Phoenix teams working with the South Vietnamese National Police had the task of flushing out Viet Cong or suspected Viet Cong wherever they hid. Those caught were imprisoned, often tortured, and quite frequently executed. During the years 1969–72, as many as 20,000 Viet Cong or suspected Viet Cong are believed to have been murdered under the aegis of Operation Phoenix. Colby confirmed this figure in congressional hearings, although he took exception to senators who referred to Phoenix teams as "assassination squads."

Along with the My Lai massacre of Vietnamese civilians by American troops, Operation Phoenix unquestionably looms as one of the most degrading enterprises carried out by Americans in Vietnam. Yet the Nixon administration saw it as a perfectly acceptable intelligence operation. Under Nixon, both pacification and Phoenix grew in scope and importance.

In escalating the air war, the first major step taken by the new administration was to increase American reconnaissance flights over North Vietnam. This may have seemed a relatively small thing at the time, but in the later judgment of many experts, including that of Kissinger's assistant Morton Halperin, these reconnaissance flights may have contributed to delays in ending the war.

The decision to maintain the flights was made under the outgoing administration, whose policy-makers assumed that Hanoi understood that flights by *unarmed* reconnaissance planes would go on despite the October 1968 bombing halt. American negotiators had made it clear to the North Vietnamese in Paris that the United States intended to continue these flights. When Hanoi's diplomats failed to insist that reconnaissance missions be discontinued as a condition for the expanded peace talks, to open in the new year, Washington took it for granted that this was no longer an issue. But what the North Vietnamese had refrained from doing was to indicate affirmatively that they would *not* shoot at these reconnaissance planes. This nuance was lost on both the Johnson negotiators and the incoming Nixon team, causing problems that were not fully resolved until after the 1973 peace agreement.

Nixon had no problem in authorizing continuance of the observation flights, inasmuch as they were being done anyway up to the eve of his inauguration. The Pentagon condition for halting bombings had been that "recon" would be kept up, and when it said the flights should be stepped up, the White House agreed; Nixon, too, must have assumed that Hanoi would not shoot at the surveillance aircraft.

But misunderstandings can serve useful purposes. When Hanoi's gunners, including surface-to-air–missile (SAM) batteries, started firing at the unarmed recon planes, the Pentagon, with Nixon's approval, authorized "protective reaction strikes" to neutralize antiaircraft fire. This meant either arming reconnaissance aircraft or assigning them armed escort. Apparently, Nixon felt that he was being "tested" by the Communists, one of his obsessions, and presently the "protective strikes" led to "preventive strikes" and to the gradual resumption of bombing in North Vietnam.

There has been so much false reporting by the air force on its North Vietnamese operations—usually quietly condoned by the Joint Chiefs of Staff, Defense Secretary Laird, and the White House—that it will probably never be known which strikes were truly "protective" and which were "preventive." In air force parlance, "preventive" can mean anything a commander wishes. There were instances of reconnaissance pilots calling for "protective strikes" when North Vietnamese SAM radars locked in on them, and instances when they only thought this had happened. Air force pilots I interviewed made clear that, as one of them said, "nobody would get mad" back at headquarters if he falsely radioed back that his radar had picked up the SAMs.

In time, the "preventive strike" became an accepted operational concept. Sorties would be flown against areas where SAMs were *believed* to be located. On the way home, fighter-bombers occasionally got rid of their ordnance if they spotted an inviting target—a truck or a convoy or a concentration of troops. "Protective strikes" were occasionally announced, but only in 1973 did the American people and Congress become aware of the magnitude of these theoretically unauthorized bombings, including the covert air activities of Lieutenant General John D. Lavelle, then Seventh Air Force commander.

The nomenclature of the air war became increasingly complex and byzantine. Early in 1971, Defense Secretary Laird would invent the "reinforced protective reaction strike" to justify the then steadily mounting air offensive against North Vietnam—a contribution made during a visit to MR-I, or Military Region I, the northernmost area of South Vietnam. One of his aides described it thus:

"Laird had discovered that U.S. planes were continuously violating the North Vietnamese air space, crossing the demilitarized zone for strikes at the enemy. We couldn't call it plausibly 'hot pursuit,' so Laird coined this new term, 'reinforced protective strike.' This was being done on an increasing scale, and later it was strongly pushed by the White House, especially Kissinger. Operational orders read as follows: 'Suppressive strikes at SAM sites, equipment and supporting elements. . . .' The latter meant everything. Sometimes we sent out a hundred or two hundred planes, and we took advantage of the missions to hit truck concentrations, where the North Vietnamese were building up, and everything in sight. . . . The bombing of the trails in Laos was essentially futile: we rarely hit anything worthwhile. Still, the White House wanted missions flown perilously close to China. They never understood how difficult precision bombing was in North Vietnam, trying to avoid taboo targets. Then, there was [also] the unsolved problem of command and control."

This last problem was that the southern part of South Vietnam was controlled by the Saigon headquarters and the northern part, adjoining the demilitarized zone, by CINCPAC, the Pacific command in Hawaii. Militarily, this was a nonsensical situation, but politically it had an advantage. In theory, bombing orders went from the White House to Secretary Laird, who, in turn, transmitted them to the Joint Chiefs of Staff, who passed the directives on to Saigon for operations in the southern area and to CINCPAC for strikes in the northern sector. The political advantage for the White House was that when Nixon and Kissinger wanted surreptitious raids in the North, the Saigon command could conveniently be kept in the dark.

On certain occasions, even Laird was bypassed, and Kissinger went directly to the Joint Chiefs of Staff. Kissinger had his own back channel to the Office of the JCS, whose director at the time was air force Lieutenant General John Vogt, once Kissinger's student at Harvard. When General Lavelle increased the scope of his unauthorized raids against the North, General Vogt was dispatched to Saigon to replace him as Seventh Air Force commander. A senior air force staff officer told me that despite the command and control division in Vietnam, it could not be excluded that General Lavelle's Seventh Air Force was directly responsible to the Joint Chiefs and CINCPAC, without clearance by General Creighton Abrams, the supreme U.S. commander in Saigon. "In the Pentagon, we often suspected that Lavelle wouldn't have undertaken 'unauthorized' raids if he didn't have reasons to think that the White House quietly approved of his actions," this officer told me.

Another senior air force staff officer explained that, particularly during key negotiation periods, the White House was ordering so many strikes everywhere that the air force had trouble finding targets. Inasmuch as the White House and the Pentagon issued bombing "quotas" every month for the next thirty-day period, the air force devised the system of "banking" them, that is using up later the sorties that could not be flown during the designated time. The White House, was, in effect, forcing deception on its air commanders.

"When a pilot spotted a shirt on a tree, he would bomb it on the theory that there might be Viet Cong or North Vietnamese under it," one officer told me. "This was over South Vietnam. So we invented the sorties banking system. We always assumed at the Pentagon that the high quotas were ordered by Nixon and Kissinger as part of political pressure on the Communists. . . . But we didn't need so many tactical sorties because there were no real targets. This applied to the B-52s over the demilitarized zone, South Vietnam, and Laotian trails as well. The White House theory seemed to be that if we showed the enemy we were flying fewer sorties, Hanoi might think we were weakening in our resolve. Some of our officers even proposed falsifying public reports on the number of sorties —to show *more* than were actually flown. In the case of the B-52s, the monthly quota in 1971 and 1972 was between fourteen hundred and eighteen hundred sorties over South Vietnam. This was programmed a year ahead, which was absurd, because how can you know a year in advance what the target situation would be? General [George] Brown, who was then air deputy commander in Saigon [he subsequently became chairman of the JCS], knew he was getting more sorties than he needed; he couldn't find enough targets. So the operations cost us more men and planes than necessary. Our intelligence was lousy. Sensors on the ground were no help. The North Vietnamese would capture our sensors and play tapes of truck movements, you know, truck rumbles, to confuse our surveillance. . . . Sometimes hours of bombing in the South would produce no more than two dead bodies."

It may be argued that Hanoi forced Nixon's hand in the resumption of bombing in the North, but the White House probably welcomed its firing at American recon aircraft, for this fitted perfectly into the escalation concept and provided an official rationale for it. Curiously, one question never raised at the time was whether the reconnaissance missions were really necessary from a strictly intelligence viewpoint or simply represented the payoff to the Pentagon for its assent to the bombing halt. In a paper on "Implications of Decision-Making for Covert Operations," Morton Halperin wrote in 1974 that the decision to maintain these missions

> was made without any careful evaluation of the likely impact on the North Vietnamese, or the need for the kind of reconnaissance which involved an intrusion into North Vietnamese air space. . . . Intelligence analysts in the intelligence branches of the CIA, the Department of State, and even the Department of Defense, as well as those involved in Vietnam policy-making on the civilian side of the Pentagon and in the Department of State, were excluded from the decision-making process, both because it involved a tightly held political decision and because it involved operational, covert programs.

If such decisions were held tightly in the Johnson administration, they were held even more tightly when Nixon and Kissinger took over. More and more specialists were excluded from the process of analysis; decisions and events took on their own life. It was a classic case of self-perpetuating decisions taken on the highest level because the men at the top seemed to fear analytical examination of their work.

As Halperin wrote,

There does not appear to have been any serious study, either before or after the decisions to continue reconnaissance while curtailing the bombing, on the utility of the manned reconnaissance operations [and on whether] . . . that same information, or virtually all the same information, could have been obtained by alternate intelligence means.

Instead, the reconnaissance went on, the North Vietnamese began shooting at the airplanes, the United States responded first by firing back and then by a program described as "protective reaction. . . . All this proceeded without any real assessment of the need for the reconnaissance program itself, and it illustrates how the decision-making procedures for covert operations—including technical operations—can have wider repercussions in a major policy area."

Chapter 3

One step leads to another when there is a basic policy decision to raise the ante in a frustrating war such as Nixon faced in Vietnam. Stepped-up reconnaissance flights over North Vietnam led to resumed bombings. Clandestine ground crossings into Cambodia by SOG teams and simultaneous air photo missions strengthened the hand of the armed forces in demanding secret B-52 strikes against suspected Communist bases in Cambodia. Once that move was authorized by the White House, it was logical that a full-fledged invasion of Cambodian territory had to follow sooner or later.

The bombing of Cambodia was Nixon's first *major* decision as president. It was, to be sure, a military decision, but it carried immense political implications. In addition to a strong Pentagon recommendation for the strikes, submitted on February 11—the Saigon command and the Joint Chiefs of Staff naïvely argued that such action would cripple the Communists operating in South Vietnam from across-the-border bases in Cambodian jungles—Nixon had before him political options prepared by Kissinger's NSC staff. These options were contained in three secret National Security Study Memoranda—NSSM–21, NSSM–22, and NSSM–29—that outlined the political risks involved in bombing Cambodia. The suggestion that on balance the advantages outweighed the risks was expressed in the strongest terms in NSSM–29, presented to Nixon on March 12. This argument carried Kissinger's personal support, although as usual he refrained from making a formal recommendation. Besides, this would not have been really necessary because during his first week in office Nixon had already privately opted for the Cambodian move.

In reconstructing the decision-making process, it appears that Nixon used the limited North Vietnamese offensive in February (known as the mini-Tet offensive, including the shelling of some cities in violation of the "understanding" that had led to the bombing halt) to rationalize the need for bombing Cambodia. Nixon was quite concerned over the developing battlefield situation—to the point that he conceded at his March 4 news conference that he had "given thought" to the possibility of bombing North Vietnam in retaliation. In his usual style, he said he would not "threaten" it publicly: "I will only indicate," he said, "that we will not tolerate a continuation of this kind of attack without some response that will be appropriate."

On March 12, he received the NSC recommendation to begin bombing Cambodia—a full-fledged air offensive against North Vietnam was not seriously considered at the time—and he decided to authorize it. The reasoning was that a long-range air operation against North Vietnam was neither politically feasible nor militarily sustainable, whereas the bombing of Cambodia, in secret from the rest of the world, would show Hanoi how determined Nixon was to curb the Communists. Besides, Nixon had been persuaded by his advisers that action in Cambodia would be sensible.

Nevertheless, Nixon had briefly entertained the notion of bombing North Vietnam, after the Communists began to shell South Vietnamese cities in violation of the 1968 "understanding." In the last days of February—just before Nixon's departure for Europe—Kissinger summoned his NSC Vietnam specialists to order an urgent study on retaliatory bombing in the North. The staff was given twenty-four hours to prepare the paper and draft a presidential speech announcing a decision to resume bombing. But by the time Nixon and Kissinger returned from Europe, the White House mood had shifted again, and the president made the final determination to proceed, instead, with the Cambodian operation. Nixon was evidently alluding to the emergency NSC study when he acknowledged he had "given thought" to the bombing of North Vietnam.

At a news conference on March 14, while the North Vietnamese offensive was still in progress, Nixon did not show his hand. Instead, he told newsmen at the White House that he had already warned the North Vietnamese once, and that "it will be my policy as president to issue a warning only once. . . . Anything in the future that is done will be done . . . there will be no additional warnings." What he failed to say was that his "appropriate response" would be secret bombings of Cambodian sanctuaries. The following day, March 15, the full National Security Council was apprised of the decision to start bombing. There is nothing to suggest any opposition to it. On March 18, the B-52s began raiding the Khmer kingdom.

Just as he was discussing armed retaliation, Nixon also made a point of predicting that secret peace talks would resume in Paris. "That is where this war will be settled—in private rather than in public," he said, in one of his more prescient statements.

The manner in which the bombing of Cambodia was decided set the pattern for future White House decision-making. Once Nixon and his top adviser resolved to go ahead with it, and the staff put together the required studies, the full National Security Council was informed of it in a general way—rather than consulted about it. The emphasis on secrecy was so great that not only did the military men set up their own top-secret system—the false reporting mechanism—but every effort was made to confine knowledge of the raids to the fewest possible administration officials. In the Pentagon, Secretary Laird along with the Joint Chiefs obviously had to know about the operation. Secretary of State Rogers and Under Secretary Richardson knew generally about the bombing decision, but only in 1973, when the whole story came out, did Rogers learn their real extent. Both Laird and Rogers went along with Nixon's view that the administration should neither announce the bombings publicly nor inform Congress—even on a confidential basis, through the military-affairs committees. It did not occur to anyone that, strictly speaking, it was illegal to use funds appropriated for the war in Vietnam to bomb Cambodia, a country with which the United States was at peace. This cavalier approach to war-making in Southeast Asia soon became the rule rather than the exception.

Richardson held the view that appropriate members of Congress should be told about the move in Cambodia. He was in favor of informing them immediately that the bombings were an incidental but necessary consequence of the situation in Vietnam. His opinion did not prevail. Yet quite a few senators and representatives did learn about the bombings from published news leaks and other sources—and chose to remain silent about them, thereby sharing culpability with Nixon.

The first raid against Cambodia was carried out by B-52s flying from Guam on the night of March 18, 1969. This first phase of the top-secret bombings was known as Operation Menu; it lasted until May 26, 1970. During that period, the Strategic Air Command's B-52s flew 3875 sorties against the Cambodian sanctuaries, dropping a total of 108,823 tons of bombs. After that, air strikes in Cambodia ceased to be a secret—for one thing, American forces invaded that country on April 30, 1970—but they went on until August 1973, when Congress finally and specifically forbade all aerial activities there. The overall bomb tonnage dropped on Cambodia in a little more than four years was 540,000.

The official explanation offered later for the extraordinary secrecy surrounding Menu bombings was that Prince Norodom Sihanouk, then Cambodia's chief of state, acquiesced in them on the condition that there would be no publicity given to the raids. Otherwise, American officials explained, he would be forced to make diplomatic protests, thus creating an untenable political situation for the United States.

This version was entirely accurate, and it is confirmed in a heretofore unpublished memorandum of conversation between Prince Sihanouk and Senate Majority Leader Mike Mansfield of Montana, an old friend of his. Sihanouk received Mansfield at the royal palace in Phnom Penh on August 22, 1969, five months after the bombings began. (If the prince had not known about the bombings from the outset, he certainly learned it from a page-one article by William Beecher published in *The New York Times* on May 9, which reported that "American B-52 bombers in recent weeks have raided several Vietcong and North Vietnamese supply dumps and base camps in Cambodia for the first time . . . but Cambodia has not made any protest.")

The relevant portion of the memorandum on their conversation clarifying the prince's position on protests reads as follows:

The Prince had protested to the [United States] Ambassador against American bombing, but not against bombing [Viet Cong] sanctuaries in areas of Cambodia not inhabited by Cambodians. American intelligence people know where these sanctuaries are. They have been bombed many times. "I never protest such bombings," the Prince said. He added that he learned of such bombing when he read *Time* or *Newsweek,* but he never protested. It is in one's own interest, sometimes, to be bombed—in this case, the United States kills foreigners who occupy Cambodian territory and does not kill Cambodians.

But, the Prince continued, he did protest the bombings of Cambodian villages and the killing of Cambodian peasants. Sometimes the United States has false information and bombs places where there are no Viet Cong. The Prince then gave an example. It is difficult for Cambodia to cooperate with the United States. Cambodia is neutral and wants the U.S., the Viet Cong and the Viet Minh to respect her. But Cambodia cannot cooperate with the U.S. in the military field— in information, for example. The Prince then said he requested that incidents which might possibly involve Cambodian lives be avoided. But how? War is war. The Prince suggested that the U.S. withdraw from Vietnam.

Sihanouk, worried about the presence of Communist troops within his borders and the flow of Communist arms to his domestic foes, was willing to string along with the American bombings so long as Cambodians were not killed. Senator Mansfield had an opportunity to discuss this situation in detail with Sihanouk, but he failed to turn it into a major issue with the Nixon administration. Every member of Congress who read the *Times* story was also informed about the bombings, but this knowledge produced no major outcry.

A significant element in the decision to strike in Cambodia was Nixon's clear wish to signal Hanoi that while Americans negotiated peace in Paris, they were also prepared to engage in a battlefield escalation that even Lyndon Johnson had avoided. Administration officials admitted this at the time to Beecher, the *Times* reporter who first publicly revealed the raids on May 9. Sending military "signals" to adversaries soon became a staple in the White House stick-and-carrot approach to diplomacy.

The most blatantly cavalier attitude toward the whole matter was taken by Nixon himself, when he addressed the nation on television on April 30, 1970, to announce the "incursion" into Cambodia thirteen months after B-52s had begun hitting Cambodian territory. Where others simply chose to remain silent, Nixon offered an outright lie. "For five years, neither the United States nor South Vietnam has moved against these enemy sanctuaries because we did not wish to violate the territory of a neutral nation," he said. Not a word about the SOG teams covertly crossing into Cambodia since May 1967, or about the B-52 bombings.

What is probably the most complete account extant on Menu raids— including the explanation of how secrecy was maintained over them— appears in the Pentagon's report on "Selected Air and Ground Operations in Cambodia and Laos," issued September 10, 1973, in response to a request from Missouri's Senator Stuart Symington, chairman of the Senate subcommittee investigating United States commitments abroad. This virtually unnoticed report provides a rare insight into the military mind as well as into the Pentagon's secret procedures.

First, the strategic concept of the raids: "The purpose of MENU was to protect American lives during the preparation for and actual withdrawal of U.S. military personnel from Southeast Asia by preempting imminent enemy offensive actions from the Cambodian sanctuaries into South Vietnam and against U.S. servicemen and women." Here, even so many years after the event, the Pentagon overstated its case and provided a misleading rationale. When the B-52s were dispatched over Cambodia, Nixon had not yet made a final decision to withdraw American forces from Indochina (although the subject was reviewed in depth in secret NSSMs on Vietnam in January, February, and March). Likewise, there was no imminence of a major Communist offensive; the North Vietnamese and the Viet Cong had been engaged in a series of "high points" against the Americans and the South Vietnamese, but this mini-Tet offensive was nothing like the savage onslaught of the original Tet offensive at the time of the lunar New Year the year before.

What did trouble the American commanders was that the Communists were able to concentrate a considerable volume of war matériel and supplies in underground depots on the Cambodian side of the Cambodia-Vietnam frontier, in support of their forces operating northwest of Saigon and farther down in the Mekong Delta. This traffic from North Vietnam was subject to B-52 strikes on the Ho Chi Minh Trail in Laos, but it was immune from attack when it reached Cambodia. Four Communist divisions—the First and Seventh North Vietnamese divisions, and the Fifth and Ninth Viet Cong divisions—were operating freely in southwestern Vietnam from the Cambodian bases. The real purpose of bombing Cambodia, therefore, was to take out these bases rather than to protect still hypothetical U.S. withdrawals.

The Menu B-52s concentrated on six Communist base areas on the Cambodian side of the border. Each area was identified by a number for operational purposes—they were the 350, 351, 352, 353, 609, and 704 areas—but Pentagon planners could not resist the temptation of also giving each base area a special code name in a curious display of semantic taste. Thus the jungle bases were called Dessert, Snack, Dinner, Breakfast, Lunch, and Supper. For reasons understood only by air force intelligence specialists, Lunch, Snack, and Dinner received the heaviest punishment; Breakfast was on the light side.

The Pentagon's system of double reporting worked so that all existing official records would suggest that the missions flown in Cambodia were nothing more than routinely reported strikes in South Vietnam. (Actually, each Menu mission was assigned an alternate target in Vietnam.) Except for pilots and navigators, who had to know where they were flying, the B-52 crews were never told that their planes were actually striking Cambodia.

> Knowledge of the operation was limited to those personnel essential to its successful administration and execution. The special security or "back" channel communication system for insuring optimum security in highly sensitive matters was used for TOP SECRET sensitive aspects of MENU. . . .
> A B-52 strike on a target in South Vietnam would be requested through normal communication and command channels. Through the special security communication and command channel, a strike on

the MENU [Cambodia] target nearest a requested target in South Vietnam would be requested. Upon approval, the mission would be flown in such a way that the MENU aircraft on its final run would pass over or near the target in South Vietnam and release its bombs on the enemy in the MENU sanctuary target area. On return of the aircraft to its base, routine reports on the mission would be filed in normal communication channels which did not reveal the MENU aspect of the mission. Separate reports were provided by "back" channel on the MENU aspect.

The B-52s flying from Guam, always at night, were guided to Cambodian targets by ground control radar sites, known as Combat Skyspot. According to the Pentagon report, "In MENU operations, the radar site crews received instructions that resulted in the aircraft releasing their bombs on the MENU targets rather than on the targets in South Vietnam."

Before takeoff from Guam, B-52 pilots and navigators received "special guidance" about their real targets. This was necessary

since the entire crew was briefed routinely, as they normally had been throughout the war, to make every effort not to bomb in Cambodia. . . . MENU . . . sorties were included in overall Southeast Asia statistical totals but not identified with Cambodia in any but the special security channels. . . . When the routine data base was subsequently utilized in providing Congress a country-by-country breakout of sorties—first in classified and then in unclassified form—the MENU sorties were reflected in South Vietnam as they were routinely carried in that data base rather than in Cambodia as they were carried in the closely held MENU records.

As for the range of knowledge about Menu, the Pentagon report explained that "there was a careful selection of individuals who, in addition to TOP SECRET clearance, had a need-to-know about MENU. . . . Everyone in the reporting chain received and reported that information for which he had a need-to-know. Those who had no need-to-know about MENU could not perceive any difference between MENU and any other sorties." Although Congress was not being informed, "all appropriate civilian and military decision makers had accurate and complete command and control data throughout MENU." Nixon and Kissinger received daily top-secret reports on Menu strikes, and in addition, these were seen by a handful of senior NSC staffers. Secretary of State Rogers was *not* shown these reports.

Top-secret requests for Cambodian air strikes were forwarded from the U.S. Saigon command to the Joint Chiefs of Staff. Each request "included current intelligence confirming that no Cambodians were known to be located in the enemy target area." This, of course, was a chancy procedure, because there was no way to ascertain whether some Cambodians might walk into the target area between the time the request was made and the B-52 strike. As it happened, Cambodians were killed; NSC records indicate that the United States quietly paid compensation seven times for the killing of Cambodians.

Once the Joint Chiefs approved a Menu strike, they sent a brief memorandum to Secretary of Defense Laird asking for White House clearance. "Only after additional appropriate civilian authority was obtained," the report said, "did the Secretary of Defense authorize the OJCS [Office of the Joint Chiefs of Staff] to dispatch an execute message" through special security channels.

In Vietnam, extraordinary security precautions also applied. Before each Menu strike, a Strategic Air Command officer went to a ground radar site to provide its operators with coordinates and other data for a Cambodian target. Subsequently,

> computations, worksheets and the plotting board trace sheet showing the aircraft's final track to the target were destroyed in order to preserve the security of the operation. . . .
>   On days when there were MENU missions, the number of MENU sorties may have constituted as much as 60 per cent of the B-52 missions. This was a sufficiently large portion of the total that failure to indicate a level of operation consistent with the total missions would have almost certainly led to speculation that unreported operations were being conducted. For this reason, the procedures supporting MENU operations included the selection of cover targets in South Vietnam which would indicate a level of activity consistent with the clearly observable number of B-52 missions launched. This selection of cover targets provided the same type of security cover historically characteristic of military operations of particular sensitivity.

Kissinger's NSC staff also had a hand in the deception to "minimize," as the Pentagon put it, "the likelihood of public speculation or disclosure." Thus the NSC instructions issued for the first Menu mission directed that the U.S. Command spokesman in Saigon publicly announce missions on "enemy activity, base camps and bunkers and tunnel complexes 45 kilometers northeast of Tay Ninh city." (Actually, *other* B-52s hit that area on the day of the first Cambodian strike, on March 18, so, in the literal sense, the spokesman was not lying.)

The report added that "in every instance the generalized press guidance would deal with an approved and executed South Vietnam strike taken from the MAC/V request or would reflect a general geographic locale without specifying that the target—listed as so many kilometers from a reference point in South Vietnam—was, in fact, in Cambodia." Ironically, however, the Pentagon noted that "there were no persistent inquiries so it was not necessary to implement any further guidance."

The Pentagon report made no reference to the knowledge possessed by Senator Mansfield concerning Menu, but it claimed that six senators and congressmen had been informed about it, including Gerald Ford, who then served as House minority leader.

Although Menu appeared to be a success, Secretary Laird, in time, developed some second thoughts about it. In a top-secret memorandum to General Earle G. Wheeler, chairman of the Joint Chiefs of Staff, Laird asked for answers to a series of questions concerning "risk versus value" in the Cambodian strikes. General Wheeler, replying a week later in a top-secret memorandum of his own, assured Laird that "the value of MENU strikes against Cambodian Base Areas should be classed as one of the most significant contributions of the war by B-52's." Wheeler noted that "heavy jungle canopy limits the analysis of some MENU results; however, practically all have revealed extensive destruction of bunkers, supply caches, structures, and trenchworks. Increasing evidence of cave-ins indicates damage far more extensive than bomb damage assessments could support."

Were not these superoptimistic reports on Menu just as exaggerated as the "kill ratio" figures trumpeted by the army earlier in the war? If, indeed, Menu was so "significant," one may wonder why General Wheeler and his associates pushed for a ground invasion of Cambodia several months later to achieve precisely what he said the B-52s were doing so well.

Still in the upbeat manner, Wheeler advised Laird that "there are indications that the enemy has taken steps to compensate for MENU strikes." The level of activity in at least two base areas had decreased and "supplies have been moved into densely covered, unstruck areas on the periphery of base areas." A bit contradictorily, Wheeler observed that "even with his increased dispersal of personnel and supplies, the enemy continues to use portions of his old areas." Earlier in November "an increased number of enemy troops have been located in the target area by SOG reports. . . . Last week four SOG ground teams received heavy opposition from enemy combat troops and were unable to enter the area."

Not surprisingly, then, General Wheeler asked Secretary Laird for authorization for two additional Menu strikes during the week of November 23. "The concept of operation," he wrote, "is to employ 41 B-52s against MENU targets on each of two nights during the week of 23 November. The remaining available aircraft will be employed to strike cover targets as well as targets elsewhere in-country and in Laos. Strikes on these latter targets will provide a resemblance to normal operations there by providing a credible story for replies to press inquiries."

Wheeler also undertook to quiet Laird's fears that too many Cambodian civilians might be killed by Menu strikes. (This is what the secretary had meant by the problem of "risk versus value.") The general informed Laird:

Steps are being taken on a continuing basis to minimize the risks of striking Cambodian people and structures . . . by extensive visual and photographic aerial reconnaissance, use of SOG ground teams. . . . Suspected areas of habitation identified from these sources are objects of additional reconnaissance with special emphasis given to SOG low level aerial photography and visual observation. . . . Doubtful areas are considered as containing Cambodian personnel and structures and are carefully avoided in targeting. This criteria [sic] is applied even when the area in question is surrounded by identified VC/NVA military facilities. Application of this criteria [sic] has precluded the targeting of many otherwise lucrative areas.

Still, Wheeler conceded that on two nights in October at least eleven Cambodian villagers were killed by Menu strikes after "visual and photo reconnaissance of the areas . . . failed to reveal the presence of any Cambodians." As Prince Sihanouk told Senator Mansfield, "War is war," and this was the view the Joint Chiefs were taking of Menu risks. Wheeler's overall conclusion was that "in view of the favorable results from previous Menu operations, the high military value of the available targets, and the minimal risk to Cambodians, strikes against these base areas should be continued as long as the threat persists."

While warfare increased in intensity in Cambodia and Vietnam, the conduct of that warfare insofar as it was known and understood by the American people was increasingly unpopular. Nixon, already hoping to be reelected in 1972 for a second term, obviously did not want to be victimized by the Vietnam war as Lyndon Johnson had been. Besides, Indochina stood in the way of the "structure of peace" he had promised in his inaugural, and blocked his plans for global policies whose success would elevate him to great statesmanship.

But Nixon was trapped from the very outset. His first alternative was a total unilateral withdrawal from Vietnam. But this would have meant capitulation, a "bug out," something Nixon could not tolerate viscerally or intellectually. The second alternative, so long as the Communists kept fighting, was military escalation. To be sure, the president had already decided on this route. But time was against him. American casualties were still averaging three hundred to four hundred a week. The military draft was still in full swing. Mounting sentiment against the war was rapidly narrowing choices. Nixon knew that soon he would have to start reducing American troop levels in Vietnam, no matter what the other side did, in order to satisfy public opinion and strengthen his negotiating position in Paris.

To cope with the complexities of this situation, a new policy—seeking, in effect, to bridge the unbridgeable—began to be formulated during March in a series of secret studies. The options and assessments produced in NSSM–1 in January were no longer satisfactory. The National Security Council, presided over by Nixon, met on March 15 (mainly to hear about the Cambodian bombing decision) and again on March 28 to look ahead. On April 1, Kissinger issued a so-called Study Directive to the NSC staff, in which he again asked the staff, and the relevant government departments and agencies, to consider a whole spectrum of options ranging from unilateral and relatively rapid American pullout (this option was immediately rejected, as it had been in January, and the White House reacted angrily to published reports that it was even under consideration) to a series of gradual withdrawals, initially small, tied to the battlefield situation and to what the White House earnestly hoped would be an improved quality of Saigon's armed forces. Kissinger had persuaded Nixon that making such force reductions might give the Americans some leverage in the Paris negotiations. He was still looking for the elusive mutual-withdrawal formula. The NSC staff was also requested to prepare the outlines of a formal peace proposal that Nixon could announce publicly before too long. It was urgent for the United States to launch a diplomatic offensive.

On April 10, Kissinger transmitted to Nixon two top-secret NSC studies—NSSM–36 and NSSM–37—setting forth, with appropriate rationalizations, a number of political and military options from which the president could select the ones that would form his new public and secret policies. It must be remembered, as we consider this next phase of Vietnam policy, that from their first day in office, Nixon and Kissinger dealt with Vietnam on parallel public and secret tracks, which had the effect of keeping both the enemy and American public opinion completely in the dark regarding the administration's real plans. This approach initiated the Kissinger practice of committing the United States to a variety of secret enterprises throughout the world. In the case of Vietnam, the double-track system was maintained until the very end.

The April line simply restated the ideas of the preceding months. It provided for the *quid pro quo* of North Vietnamese withdrawals from the South as a condition for peace (even though Hanoi had never acknowledged publicly that its forces were in the South in the first place) or for more war if the enemy refused to go along. A cease-fire in place was still ruled out as unacceptable before a general agreement was reached. The only new ingredient was a secret plan to begin soon to cut down, by small increments, the American forces in Vietnam. This crucial new factor committed Nixon to continue reducing troop levels over the ensuing years, and thus created the public impression that, notwithstanding North Vietnamese obduracy, the United States was getting out of the war. It was, of course, making a virtue out of necessity: Nixon had to keep paying on the installment plan for congressional willingness to let him pursue his "peace plan." Congress, already remiss enough in its responsibilities in the conduct of the Vietnam war, was unaware that the air war was Nixon's *real* secret weapon.

At the same time, the White House turned to its secret Soviet channel to convey messages to Hanoi. The secret back channel was through Soviet Ambassador Dobrynin, with whom Kissinger had already dealt on a number of issues. In the first week of May, Kissinger informed Dobrynin that the war would be escalated—and violently so—if Hanoi failed to respond to the American overtures. One of his aides remembers that their conversation took place on the day a team of navy frogmen succeeded in penetrating Haiphong harbor undetected to survey the possibility of mining that North Vietnamese port. Dobrynin, of course, had no inkling of this; Kissinger tended to speak in ominous generalities. This was when Kissinger first put into practice his ploy—over the years it became the most noticeable feature of his diplomatic style—of arguing that if he could not produce results through negotiations, Nixon would not be restrained from sinister and unpredictable acts. The president, who liked this image of unpredictability and toughness, went along willingly with this "good guy–bad guy" charade.

The game with the Russians was a complicated one. With their "linkage" concept in dealing with Moscow, Nixon and Kissinger felt that

Vietnam should be part of a package for improving Soviet-American relationships. Yet Dobrynin insisted that despite their massive military and economic aid to North Vietnam, the Russians had no real leverage in Hanoi. Still, they were willing to be a channel for information back and forth; Moscow, of course, did not wish to jeopardize détente possibilities. This implied to Kissinger, and rightly so, that the Russians would look the other way while the United States escalated the Vietnam war. In Kissinger's view, this was a useful arrangement, though it fell short of his best hopes, and the back channel went on functioning. Secretary of State Rogers was, meanwhile, completely cut out of it. A Kissinger aide re-marked later, "We were always afraid that through a slip of tongue Dob-rynin might tell Rogers about his secret meetings with Henry." But Dob-rynin, a cautious diplomat, knew who wielded real power in Washington —and there were no slips of the tongue.

While constructing his new diplomacy, Nixon remained publicly silent about Vietnam between March and May, except for a news conference comment in mid-April that the Communist "spring offensive at this time either has run its course or is in a substantial lull." But despite the end of this offensive, the B-52s kept up the raids on Cambodia; it was too good a thing to call off.

On May 14, the president summoned the National Security Council to display his Vietnam package; Lodge and his Paris deputies were also on hand. (By then, the full council was meeting less and less frequently; Nixon had no time for it, and he and Kissinger were making decisions by themselves, bypassing its advice. The real infighting over national secu-rity issues was conducted on a one-to-one basis in the Oval Office.) That evening Nixon went on nationwide television to announce publicly his eight-point peace plan for Vietnam.

The outstanding feature of this plan was its utter unreality. It called for an agreement in principle to halt the war, to be followed over a twelve-month period by the withdrawal of most U.S. and North Viet-namese forces from South Vietnam (the North Vietnamese would also leave Laos and Cambodia). An international supervisory body would be created afterward to arrange—then and only then—for "supervised cease-fires." The next step would be for this international body to super-vise elections in South Vietnam. Nixon also proposed an exchange of war prisoners "at the earliest possible time." (In 1969, the fate of American POWs had not yet become a major issue: there were only 328 of them.)

It is difficult to perceive what made Nixon think that this plan had the slightest chance of becoming a basis for serious negotiations—let alone of being accepted by the Viet Cong and North Vietnamese in the form in which it was presented. Whatever might be said for Nixon's desire to settle the war on his own terms, it was immediately clear that he was either naïve or duplicitous. As seen from Hanoi, his proposal was equivalent to an invitation for a Communist capitulation—and it took no genius to realize that the North Vietnamese were not about to oblige Nixon. To withdraw from South Vietnam would be tantamount to recognizing President Thieu's indefinite sway over that country—the Viet Cong cadres alone were no lethal threat to Saigon—and to abandoning any hope of reuniting Vietnam. This may have suited the United States and the Thieu regime, but realistically, it was a bit much to to expect Hanoi to give up the struggle after years of war.

Since it is difficult to believe that Nixon or Kissinger could have been that naïve, the thought occurs that the White House was engaging in duplicity. World public opinion was being presented with a pious-sounding peace plan, although Nixon must have known that it could lead only to continued fighting. Moreover, the president was misleading public opinion in asserting that "we have ruled out attempting to impose a purely military solution on the battlefield" and that "reports from Hanoi indicate that the enemy has given up hope for a military victory in South Vietnam." Neither side was ruling out anything of the sort.

Concerned as Nixon always seemed to be with the public credibility of the United States, it is astonishing that he went on to say, "We have also ruled out either a one-sided withdrawal from Vietnam, or the acceptance in Paris of terms that would amount to a disguised American defeat." Quite aside from the fact that Nixon would have to swallow his words a few years later, this pronouncement only underscored the plan's essential emptiness. Thus:

> Abandoning the South Vietnamese people . . . would jeopardize more than lives in South Vietnam. It would threaten our long-term hopes for peace in the world. A great nation must be worthy of trust.
>
> When it comes to maintaining peace, "prestige" is not an empty word. I am not speaking of false pride or bravado—they should have no place in our policies. I speak rather of the respect that one nation has for another's integrity in defending its principles and meeting its obligations.
>
> If we simply abandoned our effort in Vietnam, the cause of peace might not survive the damage that would be done to other nations' confidence in our reliability.

He also underlined his conceptual misunderstanding of big-power Communist politics. His explanation sounded contrived:

Another reason for not withdrawing unilaterally stems from debates within the Communist world between those who argue for a policy of confrontation with the United States, and those who argue against it.

If Hanoi were to succeed in taking over South Vietnam by force—even after the power of the United States had been engaged—it would greatly strengthen those leaders who scorn negotiation, who advocate aggression, who minimize the risks of confrontation with the United States. It would bring peace now but it would enormously increase the danger of a bigger war later.

If we are to move successfully from an era of confrontation to an era of negotiation, then we have to demonstrate—at the point at which confrontation is being tested—that confrontation with the United States is costly and unrewarding.

What Nixon appeared to misperceive was that in accepting his notion of a new American "era of negotiation," China and Russia were acting for reasons of long-term national interests of their own wholly unrelated to any concept of American "prestige." Both the Russians and the Chinese knew that it was only a question of time before the fighting involving the United States would end.

Three weeks after unveiling this so-called peace plan, President Nixon flew to Midway Island in the Pacific for a one-day meeting with South Vietnam's President Thieu. The purpose of this conference was much more political and "cosmetic" than substantive: Nixon wanted a fitting forum to announce his decision to withdraw 25,000 United States combat forces from Vietnam, the first troop reduction in Indochina since the American buildup had begun in 1961. The decision had no real military meaning—it was less than 5 percent of the total—but it would be a useful political gesture at home as well as a convincing demonstration of the sincerity of his peace offer. The time had come to set the Vietnamization policy in motion.

Actually, Nixon had decided on the withdrawal even before May 14. It had been recommended in the April NSC studies, but the White House hoped to save it for the June 8 Midway meeting so as to give it added significance and enhance Thieu's prestige. After his conference with the South Vietnamese leader, Nixon said:

President Thieu informed me that the progress of the training program and the equipping program for South Vietnamese forces had been so successful that he could now recommend that the United States begin to replace U.S. combat forces with Vietnamese forces. This same assessment was made by General [Creighton] Abrams when he reported to me last night and this morning.

As a consequence of the recommendation by the president and the assessment of our own commander in the fields [*sic*], I have decided to order the immediate redeployment from Vietnam of a division equivalent of approximately 25,000 men.

Thieu, beaming broadly, replied to a questioner that yes, indeed, he had made such a recommendation to Nixon earlier in the day, at the residence of the commanding officer of the U.S. Naval Station on Midway. But this was a diplomatic charade: Thieu had agreed to the withdrawal sometime during May, and both *The New York Times* and the *Washington Evening Star* had reported a week earlier that Nixon and Thieu would announce it at the Midway session. Thieu had also been told—and Nixon reiterated it on Midway—that after the first withdrawal was completed, in August 1969, the levels of American troops in Vietnam would be reviewed at regular intervals.

Although the new American military doctrine in Vietnam called for increased reliance on air power, Nixon was determined to synchronize gradual American ground-force withdrawals with the progress of Vietnamization, progress in the Paris peace talks, and the scope of Communist military activity. This was Nixon's parting warning at Midway: "No actions will be taken which threaten the safety of our troops and the troops of our allies. . . . No action will be taken which endangers the attainment of our objective, the right of self-determination for the people of South Vietnam." Returning to Washington, Nixon waved the olive branch: "By the May 14 speech that I made setting forth an eight-point program for peace, and by our action in withdrawing 25,000 American combat forces from Vietnam, we have opened wide the door to peace. . . . And now we invite the leaders of North Vietnam to walk with us through that door, either by withdrawing . . . their forces from South Vietnam as we have withdrawn ours, or by negotiating in Paris, or through both avenues."

Meanwhile, Henry Kissinger, speaking as an anonymous "administration official," began telling selected newsmen that the time had come for "substantive negotiations" to begin in Paris. It was his way of beginning to send "signals" to Hanoi.

Chapter 4

During the first six months of 1969, Nixon's activist foreign policy ranged over an impressively broad front. His administration was engaged, aside from Vietnam, in preparations for strategic-arms negotiations with the Soviet Union, peace mediation in the Middle East, and the thorny question of relations with Japan. Simultaneously, an increasing effort was being made to define and set in motion a new policy toward China.

The central concern in Nixon's mind, however, was relations with the Soviet Union. In his and Kissinger's judgment, both the United States and the Soviet Union had reached the point in their nuclear-weapons capabilities where a lethal confrontation could occur unless an agreement were made on limiting the further development of strategic weapons. The theory was that the danger of nuclear war rose as new arms were deployed. A related notion was that in order to create a climate in which negotiation was possible, both nations should make every effort to "defuse" situations throughout the world that might lead to superpower confrontations. This was the origin of "linkage." In his March 4 press conference Nixon explained:

> I think it is that overwhelming fact—the fact that if the situation in the Mideast and Vietnam is allowed to escalate, it is the fact that it might lead to a confrontation—that is giving the Soviet Union second thoughts, and leads me to, what would I say, the cautious conclusion at this point: that the Soviet Union will play, possibly, a peacemaking role in the Mideast and even possibly in Vietnam. . . . Let's face it, without the Soviet Union's cooperation, the Mideast is going to continue to be a terribly dangerous area—if you continue to pour fuel on those fires of hatred that exist on the borders of Israel. And without the Soviet Union's cooperation, it may be difficult to move as fast as we would like in settling the war in Vietnam.

Earlier comments from the White House had suggested that the Soviet Union, given her inferiority in nuclear weaponry, would be more eager than the United States was to move into the Strategic Arms Limitation Talks (SALT), and Nixon was certainly trying to keep alive the impression that the United States was holding out on SALT, pending Soviet demonstrations of goodwill in other areas. He went on in this vein:

> I think their interests and ours would not be served by simply going down the road on strategic-arms talks without, at the same time, making progress on resolving these political differences that could explode. Even assuming our strategic-arms talks were successful, freezing arms at their present level, we could have a very devastating war. . . . Most wars have come not from arms races, although sometimes arms races can produce a war, but they have come from political explosions. . . . Our attitude is very conciliatory, and I must say that in our talks with the Soviet ambassador, I think that they are thinking along this line now, too.

But Nixon's and Kissinger's assumption that the Soviet Union was prepared to sacrifice her interests in Asia or the Middle East for the sake of strategic-arms negotiations was proved by events to be wrong. Thus Moscow was able to engage the United States in the SALT talks *without* making concessions. In the end, it was the United States that made most of the concessions, and Nixon and Kissinger were outmaneuvered by the Kremlin.

Yet the Soviet Union, for profound reasons of its own national policies, had a definite interest in negotiating with the United States over a whole spectrum of issues. Tensions with China were dangerously high, and the Soviet leaders needed a relaxation of pressures on their Western flank. On another level, the Russians must have felt that their influence in Southeast Asia and the Middle East would be further enhanced if they were to participate in international negotiations affecting those regions. Prior to the 1967 Arab-Israeli war, the Soviet Union was regarded as essentially an interloper in the Middle East. Now, busily rearming Egypt and Syria, she was aspiring to equal diplomatic status in discussions over the future of the area, and Nixon was, in effect, granting her this status. In Vietnam, the Soviet Union was, of course, in a much more delicate diplomatic posture. And it must have occurred to Kremlin policy planners that SALT was a convenient means by which to remain involved in the entire sequence of international negotiations. It was the Soviet idea of linkage in reverse.

From the American point of view, the diplomatic situation seemed inviting. The White House analysis was that Russia needed an accommodation with the United States, given her Chinese problem, her less developed nuclear arsenal, and growing domestic pressures for higher living standards that required an infusion of Western and, most especially American, technology. The word from Moscow was that the Soviet leaders wanted badly to expand trade with the United States as part of General Secretary Leonid Brezhnev's economic-development programs. Whether these Soviet policies were designed for a long or short term, Nixon and Kissinger concluded that an opportunity was presenting itself and the United States should take advantage of it.

In any event, Nixon had resolved from the first days of his administration to embark on a gradual policy of improving relations with Moscow. He approached this policy in a cold, nonideological fashion, reasoning that only a viable relationship between the United States and the Soviet Union could guarantee world peace in the long run. That Nixon had launched his political career in the late 1940s on the basis of visceral and outspoken anti-Communism (to wit, his role in the Alger Hiss case) and that he remained an unforgiving foe of Communism had absolutely nothing to do with this. The president thought in power terms in erecting his "structure of peace," and the stark reality was that the Russians were a superpower and had to be treated accordingly. Otherwise, Nixon believed, Moscow would move from mischief to mischief politically, endangering international peace. The lesson of the 1962 Cuban missile crisis had not been lost on Nixon and Kissinger. And Nixon knew that his personal record as an anti-Communist placed him in a virtually invulnerable domestic political position: he could never be accused of being "soft" on Communism. This was a crucial dimension of the détente policy; a Democratic president could not have pursued it with equal vigor. The diplomatic community—and the Communist diplomats—were keenly aware of this. A senior East European diplomat remarked years later, "Any United States government would have taken advantage of détente possibilities after 1969," but "Nixon was better equipped for it than a Democratic president in terms of handling the political right wing at home." And Ambassador Dobrynin further encouraged the administration to explore possibilities of cooperation with the Russians by skillfully advancing the idea in formal conversations with Secretary Rogers (after a few weeks they were addressing each other intimately as "Beel" and "Toly") or in dealings with "Henry."

Immediately after Nixon's inauguration, Romania's president Nicolae Ceauşescu instructed Corneliu Bogdan, his ambassador in Washington, to invite the new president to visit Bucharest.

The Romanians had their own special reasons for making this overture. Ceauşescu had for years been steering an independent foreign policy line between the Soviet Union and China. In practice, this meant that the Romanians had found a way of maintaining a warm relationship with Peking without antagonizing the Russians to the point where their regime's survival might have been in question. Romania remained a member of the Warsaw Pact, the Communist military alliance, but Romanian territory was closed to the pact's forces and Romanian troops refused to participate in joint exercises elsewhere in the area. Premier Chou En-lai was received in Bucharest as an honored and beloved guest despite Moscow's annoyance. Ceauşescu's own hour of great peril had come in August 1968, when Soviet-led Warsaw Pact forces invaded Czechoslovakia to smash the Czech liberal Communists, and the Romanians thought they might be next. Ceauşescu had ordered the mobilization of his army and territorial guard to defend his frontiers. His contacts with the United States had preceded even the 1968 crisis, however, since during Johnson's presidency, Romanian officials had undertaken to act as a secret channel between the Americans and the North Vietnamese, though with limited success. Now they no longer wanted to be peace brokers in Vietnam: Ceauşescu's judgment was that Romania could be more helpful in a broader context, including the development of American-Chinese relations. Ambassador Bogdan first approached the White House in February but had no immediate response to his soundings about an invitation to Nixon. But after Nixon returned from Western Europe, Kissinger suddenly became interested in the idea. Nixon was already planning a trip to Asia for the summer of 1969, and Kissinger thought it would be useful if the president added Bucharest as a stop at the end of his itinerary. He and Nixon believed this could be a useful prelude to a future meeting with Brezhnev, and besides, it would intriguingly test Soviet reactions. The decision to go to Bucharest was also specifically intended as a gesture toward China, certain not to be lost on Peking.

Despite an adverse reaction from the American ambassador in Moscow, Llewellyn Thompson, who feared a damaging show of Soviet displeasure, the White House proceeded by mid-June with secret preparations for the Romanian visit.

But the most important element in relations with Russia concerned nuclear weapons and the arms race. The idea of having talks with the Russians on limiting strategic arms—the SALT talks—had been under active consideration during the Johnson administration, when the 1968 Soviet invasion of Czechoslovakia forced the last-minute cancellation of a planned Johnson meeting in Leningrad with Soviet leaders. But as soon as Nixon took office, Moscow communicated to Washington that it wished to resume the discussions aimed at setting SALT in motion.

Nixon was attracted by this prospect but at first wary of it. He indicated in his news conferences that SALT must be a part of a wider "linkage" concept in dealing with the Soviet Union. Also, his administration was divided over the whole issue of strategic-arms controls. The so-called arms controllers—the State Department, the Arms Control and Disarmament Agency (ACDA), and the CIA—supported a SALT agreement and believed that Soviet compliance with any specific terms in a treaty could be satisfactorily verified with overhead satellite observation and other intelligence means. The Joint Chiefs of Staff opposed SALT, and Defense Secretary Laird was of two minds; for one thing, the specialists in the Office of the Secretary of Defense were themselves split over it. Kissinger, as his aides recalled later, was cautiously neutral.

Still, Kissinger, a long-time student of nuclear strategy, took the view that the United States government knew too little about the subject, including the precise extent of Soviet capabilities, to be able to make instant SALT decisions. Consequently, he directed the NSC staff on January 21, the day after the inauguration, to undertake what he later described as "an overall study . . . regarding the United States strategic force posture for the internal use of the government and for use in the SALT negotiations." The fundamental requirement of this study on "Military Posture," which was NSSM–3, was, in Kissinger's words, "to determine what programs should be adopted to insure credibility of our country's strategic deterrent." David Packard, deputy secretary of defense, was in charge of the study, and he drew on the resources of the Pentagon, State Department, ACDA, CIA, Treasury Department, and Budget Bureau. NSSM–3, which also concerned itself with the cost of various options it proposed, was described at the time by a senior administration official as "the most comprehensive review of national security policy since the end of World War II."

The NSC study, completed early in March, offered Nixon five basic options. One was maintenance of the existing strategic posture inherited from the Johnson administration. This involved improving the strategic force (made up of the triad of the new land-based Minuteman III intercontinental missiles, missile-equipped nuclear submarines, and nuclear-armed B-52 bombers) through the deployment of MIRV warheads (multiple independent reentry vehicles, weapons that have clusters of independently targeted missiles contained in each warhead) on Minuteman and submarine weapons. Now, the development of MIRV was the most important technological breakthrough in American nuclear weaponry since the perfecting of the hydrogen bomb in the 1950s; it gave the United States a major qualitative advantage over the Soviet Union.

The first option made the assumption that the Soviets would not develop their own MIRV in the foreseeable future—although nobody could quite define foreseeable future. In general, the belief was that the United States possessed a second-strike capability—that is, the power to annihilate the enemy even after being hit by its initial nuclear strike—and having it was regarded as the principal deterrent against attack by the Russians. For defensive purposes, the United States had for a year been developing the Sentinel system of antiballistic missiles (ABMs), a "thin line" essentially designed to protect the country from Chinese intercontinental missiles (which the Pentagon thought would be deployed by the late 1970s) and from accidental missile launches. It remains a mystery to this day why anyone expected a Chinese nuclear attack. The cost of maintaining this existing nuclear posture was estimated in the study at $10 billion annually.

The second option, costing $16 billion annually, provided for a massive buildup of American strategic offensive forces to create an overwhelming United States first-strike capability. Achieving this, the study noted, would have made it possible for an American attack to disarm the enemy, but the counterargument was that a major arms race would immediately get under way. This option ruled out SALT.

The third option, estimated at $60 billion, called for an expanded defensive ABM system, to include Alaska and Hawaii, and a limited increase in MIRV deployment.

The fourth option contemplated a unilateral freeze by the United States of its offensive forces without a MIRV deployment, and the limitation of the ABM system to two Minuteman sites. The NSC staff never expected Nixon to accept this option.

Finally, the fifth option called for no expansion of any kind in the offensive forces, which meant no new MIRVs, but for a "thick" ABM system covering between twenty-five and fifty-two American cities as well as the Minuteman sites.

But as the first "Military Posture" study was being completed, Nixon and Kissinger moved ahead to eliminate some of the opposition to SALT in the Pentagon, as well as opposition to MIRV in Congress, by deciding to arm the United States with an expanded ABM system. This complicated maneuver was designed to buy time to prepare the SALT negotiating position and to cope with the fact that, stripped down to its essentials, the basic argument in Washington was between ABM and MIRV. Nixon did not want at that point to be locked into a hard policy, however, and he had Kissinger order additional studies from the NSC staff: "U.S. Military Forces" (NSSM–8, requested on February 8), "East-West Relations" (NSSM–10, of January 28), "Disarmament" (NSSM–20, of February 12), "Defense Budget" (NSSM–23, of February 20), and another "Military Posture" study (NSSM–24) commissioned on February 20.

Simultaneously, the United States Intelligence Board—a group of top officers from all the intelligence agencies, which was chaired by Richard M. Helms, who was both director of Central Intelligence and CIA director—was engaged in a supersecret study of the Soviets' missile testing and especially of their degree of advancement in MIRV. Inasmuch as the Soviets' MIRV capability, and the time in which it was expected to be reached, was a measurement of their first-strike capability, Nixon obviously had to defer his decisions on how to proceed with SALT until he received this report.

On March 5 the National Security Council reviewed the president's ABM plan (which, of course, was still subject to congressional approval). Nixon's idea was to have a "phased" ABM system, starting with deployments around two Minuteman sites in North Dakota, and calling for an annual review with a view to expansion if warranted by Soviet actions. The new system, to be called Safeguard, would replace President Johnson's plans for the thin Sentinel system that was meant to protect the United States from a Chinese nuclear attack.

Nixon announced his ABM proposal at a news conference on March 14, saying that Safeguard would defend the United States from the Soviets as well as from China. This, of course, was a new dimension in the defense concept: it was a signal to Moscow that the United States wanted to start the SALT talks from a position of greater strength; it was a payoff to the Pentagon for agreeing to the principle of SALT in the first place. And there were other subtleties: Nixon proposed to remove existing Nike Hercules and Nike Zeus ABM defenses (they were rather unsophisticated systems) around Washington and other American cities in favor of constructing modern ABM systems at the Minuteman sites. Nixon explained this new concept in strategic-arms control in these words: "Moving to a massive city defense system, even starting with a thin system and then going to a heavy system, tends to be more provocative in terms of making credible a first-strike capability against the Soviet Union. I want no provocation that might deter arms talks."

The idea was that when a superpower builds heavy defenses around its cities—the Russians already had sixty-seven ABM sites of the Galosh system around Moscow, as well as the Tallin system around their intercontinental missile launchers—the other side might conclude that an attack was being planned against it. Why otherwise would massive city defenses be constructed? Nixon's theory, subsequently embraced by most American arms experts, was that it is safer in the long run to leave the cities undefended and concentrate on the protection of the second-strike capability as a deterrent against war. This was the new psychology of the nuclear age. Nixon added another explanation:

> Where you are looking toward a city defense, it needs to be a perfect or near perfect system to be credible because, as I examined the possibility of even a thick defense of cities, I found that even the most optimistic projections, considering the highest development of the art, would mean that we would still lose thirty to forty million lives. . . . When you are talking about protecting your deterrent, it need not be perfect. It is necessary only to protect enough of the deterrent that the retaliatory second strike will be of such magnitude that the enemy would think twice before launching a first strike.

The Russians evidently understood this psychology. Having first insisted that their ABM deployments around Moscow were defensive and thus could not be regarded as an escalation in the arms race, they had proposed the SALT talks four days after the United States announced the Sentinel ABM system in 1968. Nixon duly noted this as he explained the reasons for Safeguard.

Now deeply interested in SALT, Nixon tried to reassure the Russians still further. He said: "We could increase our offensive capability, our submarine force, or even our Minuteman force or our bomber force. That I would consider to be, however, the wrong road because it would be provocative to the Soviet Union and might escalate an arms race." Nixon and Kissinger had developed a new doctrine of "sufficiency"—a flexible notion doing away with such obsolete notions as "superiority" or even "parity"—based on MIRV deployments. In fact, his public justification of ABM was in reality a justification for a continuing MIRV program. And he pointed out in a separate statement: "The Soviet Union is continuing the deployment of very large missiles with warheads capable of destroying our hardened Minuteman forces. The Soviet Union has also been substantially increasing the size of their submarine-launched ballistic-missile force. The Soviets appear to be developing a semi-orbital nuclear weapon system."

While public debate raged over ABM, Nixon and Kissinger were quietly preparing the United States negotiating stance for SALT. One of the basic documents in this endeavor was a study on "SALT Criteria" (NSSM–28), drafted by the Quantitative Analysis Staff of the NSC and completed on March 13, supplementing the previous studies on military posture and its implications for SALT. NSSM–28 expanded to nine the original five options contained in NSSM–3, refining some of the possible courses of action.

A study of Nixon's public pronouncements during this period suggests that he decided to proceed with SALT even in the absence of Soviet concessions on Vietnam and the Middle East because of his growing concern over a rapid Russian nuclear buildup. He noted that American intelligence had reported that the Soviet Union had developed the huge new SS–9 missile, expected to be operative in 1972 or 1973, and that "if we allow those plans to go forward without taking any action on our part, either offensively or defensively, to counteract them, they will be substantially ahead of the United States in overall nuclear capability. . . . We cannot allow that to happen." On April 18, he put it in the classic Nixon way: "I do not want to see an American president in the future, in the event of any crisis, have his diplomatic credibility be so impaired because the United States was in a second-class or inferior position. We saw what it meant to the Soviets when they were second. I don't want that position to be the United States' in the event of a future diplomatic crisis."

But to bring off the SALT talks, Nixon had to negotiate simultaneously with the Soviets and with the Washington establishment. For both, the question was what the real nature of the strategic negotiations was. In other words, it was necessary to define what precisely would be negotiated in SALT. Kissinger, now an ardent convert to SALT, did most of this preliminary negotiating, which involved some of the most bitter bureaucratic infighting Washington had witnessed in a long time, although the public was wholly unaware of it.

Working with Dobrynin, Kissinger tried to outline the basic areas that might be covered in talks. The American position, as set forth at National Security Council meetings on June 13 and 25, was to go for limiting both offensive and defensive weapons; Dobrynin repeatedly made it clear to Kissinger that the Russians preferred to concentrate first on an agreement on defensive weapons (the ABM systems) and to leave offensive weapons for a future SALT round. The obvious reason was that they wanted time to perfect their MIRV before accepting any limitations on it. On the other hand, Kissinger was wary of the Soviet insistence on "comprehensive" agreements, preferring his own "building blocks" approach, in which each element could be symmetrically set off against the other, a step-by-step negotiation leading to a well-constructed agreement —rather than an overall declaration of principles, which the Russians were proposing.

Kissinger kept requesting masses of technical information from the Pentagon as he negotiated with Dobrynin. For example, one of his aides said, "He would ask the Defense Department how long it would take the United States and the Soviet Union respectively to move MIRV missiles from storage to actual deployment." But several Pentagon experts who dealt with Kissinger at the time have agreed that despite his conceptual mastery of nuclear strategy, he seemed to lack even "minimal technical expertise." He tended, a Pentagon specialist observed, "to be sloppy . . . and we never knew whether he fully understood the technical aspects of the situation." But his main problem was to convince the military that the SALT negotiations would be in the American interest. Nixon's announcement on ABM had served to mollify the Joint Chiefs of Staff, but they remained opposed to American-Soviet agreements on offensive weapons, on the grounds that the United States must keep on developing new systems in order to stay ahead of Soviet advances—unless Moscow accepted a ban on MIRV development.

Another raging argument was over how to ensure that a strategic–arms–limitation agreement would be observed—or, in the jargon, "verified." Kissinger had set up a Verification Panel at the White House to study how the United States could best assure itself that the Russians would not cheat by deploying unauthorized weapons systems. But the battle spilled over from the White House to Congress, where the Senate Foreign Relations Committee was receiving widely differing assessments from the Pentagon and the CIA on Soviet nuclear capabilities and verification possibilities. Defense Secretary Laird, influenced by the Joint Chiefs of Staff and the Defense Intelligence Agency, gave the committee the "worst case" projection of Soviet power—he insisted that the Soviets had already "MIRVed"—while CIA Director Helms tended to be less alarmist, and concluded that the Soviets could not have an operational MIRV until around 1972 (actually it did not happen until late in 1973).

This controversy went to the heart of the American negotiating stance on SALT. If the Russians had indeed developed the MIRV, as Laird claimed, then it was imperative to make an agreement on MIRV limitations part of any SALT accord. If they had not, as Helms testified, then one could proceed comfortably with a defensive-weapons treaty in the first stage of negotiations, and leave an offensive-arms pact for SALT II.

The view of the arms controllers was that Moscow would never agree to a treaty banning MIRV development before it had completed its testing and acquired an operational capability, but if it agreed to a numerical limitation on MIRVs, the United States would acquire a five-year certainty (Washington was thinking along the lines of a five-year SALT pact) concerning Soviet MIRV potential.

In any event, the logic of the disarmament case was dependent on the "diplomatic cushion," the time elapsing before the Kremlin achieved the MIRV breakthrough. It was vital for the United States to know when this would happen, and this is why the Laird-Helms controversy was important militarily as well as politically.

As for Helms, his presentation was based on a secret National Intelligence Estimate (NIE) in which the military intelligence agencies had grudgingly concurred. The NIE said that the Russians had already developed a MRV, a multiple reentry vehicle, but lacked a sophisticated full-fledged MIRV, with independently targeted warheads, which it would take them at least three years to produce. The CIA's judgment was that the testing of a full-fledged MIRV in the atmosphere could be detected by telemetry—with a very small margin of error. Testing, Helms testified, had not yet occurred.

Laird and Helms testified before the Senate committee in executive session; their testimony was never made public. But Senator J. William Fulbright, then chairman of the committee, protested publicly that different administration spokesmen could not get together on their estimates of various situations affecting SALT. At that point, the secret battle within the administration became vicious. Kissinger, in what a senior intelligence officer described as "the last bit of skulduggery," sided with Laird against Helms in the MIRV controversy—for two reasons. One was that in espousing Laird's view, Kissinger was strengthening his hand vis-à-vis the Russians: by assuming that the Russians already had MIRV, he thought he would force them into making an agreement on offensive arms. The other was that he had decided to seize this opportunity to discredit Helms and the way Helms conducted business in what Washington calls "the intelligence community." Kissinger had long been contemptuous of Helms and had been trying to undermine him. Thus Kissinger "bought" the Pentagon's estimate that the "footprint" of Soviet intercontinental missiles suggested that the MRV (their vehicle) was so designed as to be able to send three warheads against American Minuteman silos by advance guidance—as distinguished from the independent targeting of warheads in a full MIRV system. To many experts, this was not convincing, but Kissinger translated it into politics by emphasizing to Nixon that the CIA was being "complacent."

Then it was back to the verification problem. Helms took the view that electronic surveillance and telemetry would keep the United States informed of Soviet MIRV testing. He and the rest of the intelligence experts also believed that after signing a SALT agreement, the United States could monitor Soviet compliance through overhead satellites, the so-called national verification means. But both Laird and Kissinger were doubtful. Kissinger told his aides that Helms had a "vested interest" in a SALT treaty requiring extensive verification procedures because it would increase the "power" of the CIA and its allied agencies. Whereupon the CIA began to complain that Kissinger was deliberately passing out the word that American intelligence was deficient. And its officials charged that the Pentagon was introducing "weasel" words in interagency papers and was even suppressing data it considered unfavorable to its cause.

As to Kissinger, his behavior may have appeared erratic, inasmuch as he, like Helms, advocated a SALT treaty with ironclad verification procedures. But one must bear in mind his byzantine personality. He knew that Nixon had to obtain a disarmament agreement with the Russians, but to reinforce the White House position in Washington as well as in the forthcoming negotiations, he was playing the Pentagon against the CIA. He wanted to avoid the impression that he was "soft" in preparing the United States position for SALT: this was a crucial matter in his relations with Nixon, a man obsessed with the need for toughness, and with the Pentagon. Also, Kissinger's relationship with Laird was not good—the two men were deeply suspicious of each other—and Kissinger was not about to provide him with ammunition. But in those days few people understood Kissinger's talent for disguising what he really thought, and for maintaining his credibility while telling different people what he thought they wanted to hear. And no one realized that the SALT fight marked the beginning of Helms's fall from grace at the White House.

The confusion over Soviet nuclear planning became even worse in June when the United States Intelligence Board concluded its top-secret report to Nixon on the Soviet Union's plans for a first-strike capability within the next two or three years. The board, presided over by Helms but including the military-intelligence agencies, speaking the arcane language of intelligence, suggested that the Soviets might be seeking more than parity with the United States, that although there might be a "desire" on the part of some Soviet leaders to achieve a first-strike capability, there was nothing to indicate that the Kremlin had taken such a policy decision, and that in any case the Russians could not reach that goal in the "foreseeable future."

This was obviously annoying to Kissinger, but what annoyed him most about the board's report was that *The New York Times* was able to publish a summary of its conclusions on June 18. In 1974, explaining his concern over news leaks—and justifying the wiretapping of NSC officials and newsmen—he put it this way:

> Each of these disclosures was of the most extreme gravity. As presentations of the Government's thinking on these key issues, they provided the Soviet Union with extensive insight as to our approach to the SALT negotiations and severely compromised our assessments of the Soviet Union's missile testing and our *apparent inability to accurately assess* their exact capabilities. . . . The disclosure of the assessment of the Soviet's first strike capability . . . would provide a useful signal to the Soviet Union as to the . . . efficacy of our intelligence system. It would also prematurely reveal the intelligence basis on which we were developing our position for the impending strategic arms talks [italics added].

Problems with the Washington bureaucracy and with the Russians inevitably delayed the start of SALT. Although Nixon told a news conference on June 19, "We have set July 31 as a target date for the beginning of [SALT] talks, and Secretary Rogers has so informed the Soviet ambassador," five more months elapsed before the negotiations actually began. And during July, Kissinger asked the NSC staff for additional studies on SALT and "Military Capabilities." (They became NSSM–62 and NSSM–64.) In mid-September, Nixon complained in a speech before the United Nations that the Russians still had not replied to Secretary Rogers.

Nixon and Kissinger bought Laird's and the Joint Chiefs' reluctant assent to the SALT negotiations with a commitment for new funds to develop the Trident nuclear submarine to replace the Polaris and Poseidon, already becoming obsolescent, and to go ahead with the development of the B-1 bomber that the air force wanted as a replacement by the end of the 1970s for the B-52 jet bomber. This was the final tradeoff. Still, Laird and the chiefs remained skeptical. Laird, for one, had the uncomfortable feeling that the Russians would be getting "something for nothing," as he told one of his aides.

.   .   .

Richard Nixon's new diplomacy was evolving slowly and painstakingly, but the administration also had to face sudden emergencies that threatened to upset its long-range plans.

Thus Nixon faced his first major international crisis in the presidency at dawn on Tuesday, April 15, when Henry Kissinger woke him with an urgent telephone call. Rousing the president from sleep was a privilege reserved only for key people during the greatest emergencies, a privilege that Kissinger had been granted from the outset and one that neither the secretary of state nor the secretary of defense would normally exercise. Kissinger was the one and only link between Nixon and the rest of the United States government when it came to international affairs.

What Kissinger had to tell Nixon on that spring morning was that North Korean MiG jet fighters had just shot down an unarmed United States Navy electronic plane, an EC-121, with a crew of thirty-one men, somewhere over the Sea of Japan, presumably near the North Korean coast. The slow propeller-driven navy aircraft had gone down at 1:50 p.m., Korean time, on April 15, or ten minutes before midnight of the fourteenth, Washington time. A few hours later, an English-language broadcast from Pyongyang announced the incident, adding that the EC-121, a "reconnaissance plane of the insolent U.S. imperialist aggressor army," had been spotted by the MiGs while "reconnoitering, after intruding deep into the territorial air of the northern half of the republic." Two MiGs, the radio said, "scored the brilliant battle success of shooting it down with a single shot at a high altitude."

The Pyongyang broadcast was monitored by U.S. intelligence facilities in the Far East and immediately relayed to the White House basement Situation Room. The navy plane evidently had had no time to radio back to its base in Atsugi, near Tokyo, that it was under attack.

The American public was not informed about what happened next in Washington. The administration was able to conceal the fact that Nixon nearly plunged the United States into a serious confrontation, if not outright war, at a time when the other Asian war, in Vietnam, was being escalated. Instead, the country and the world were fed a reasonably plausible diplomatic story, while Nixon fought for three days with his top advisers over what course of action the United States should take.

As soon as he could study the Pyongyang broadcast, the president ordered a heavy punitive air strike against North Korea. Nixon, of course, had bitterly criticized the Johnson administration for its inaction the previous year when North Koreans had captured the navy's intelligence ship *Pueblo* not far from the spot where the EC-121 had just gone down.

Nixon had said that a "fourth-rate military power" like North Korea should be taught to "respect" the United States. Now, after conferring with Nixon in the White House living quarters an hour or so after his phone call, Kissinger summoned the NSC action officer and instructed him to pass the word on to the Pentagon that a "surgical strike" against the North Koreans was to be carried out in the next twenty-four to forty-eight hours. What Nixon and Kissinger had in mind was a one-time attack on a selected North Korean airfield by some 150 American war-planes. But the White House instantly ran into fierce opposition from most of the top military and civilian officials involved in preparing such an action.

The first problem was that the United States did not have sufficient air or naval deployments in the area to carry out the reactive strike that Nixon wanted. The attack was simply impossible. It would take a number of days to put a carrier task force in place in the Sea of Japan—the only practical way of staging the raid—and the Pentagon and State Depart-ment agreed that a strike a week later would look absurd in both military and political terms. A big power strikes at once or not at all.

The other options were equally impossible. The air force kept 128 jets permanently stationed at South Korean bases, but it was quickly realized that a strike flown from South Korea could easily reopen a Korean war. It was assumed that Pyongyang would retaliate immediately against the South Koreans, and the North Koreans had, at the time, 444 MiG jets and 80 Il-28 bombers. The last thing the South Koreans would want was to be involved in a shooting match between Americans and North Koreans. Flying combat missions from Japan was also out of the question. Under the provisions of the 1960 U.S.–Japan Treaty of Mutual Cooperation and Security, Japanese permission was needed to send up American planes from the insular bases for war missions—and the Japanese were unlikely to grant it. Finally, the air force had grave doubts about the wisdom of engaging Okinawa-based B-52s over North Korea. The big planes would be an easy target for North Korean SAM batteries and MiGs.

"Henry doesn't understand that you can't just send five planes for a mission like that," a senior official said later. "You need a protective cover and suppression against antiaircraft fire. And we didn't have avaiiable the 150 planes Henry was talking about." Speaking more generally about Kissinger's approach to crises, another official remarked, "Henry always wanted to use Defense Department hardware, not realizing the problems of the budget, wear and tear, and the difficulty of keeping aircraft carriers too long on station."

The Joint Chiefs of Staff took the view that once the United States decided to hit North Korea, it had to be in a position to follow up. A single strike was senseless. The chiefs reasoned that the North Koreans would certainly respond with strikes against American bases or other targets in South Korea, and then the United States would have to be prepared to take additional measures. Formally, they advised the White House that the navy could mount one limited carrier-based strike fairly quickly, but to do more would require shifting additional carriers and assigning more planes to Japan—if the Japanese agreed. Privately they made it clear that the United States was already overextended militarily in Southeast Asia, and that a new involvement in Northeast Asia, unpredictable in its consequences, was more than could be handled without weakening the overall American posture.

Politically the opposition to the strike was as strong at Defense as it was at State. Secretary Laird argued strenuously with Nixon that such a move made no political sense at a time when domestic antiwar sentiment over Vietnam was on the rise. A North Korean adventure would damage Nixon's incipient "generation of peace" policy and become his equivalent of John Kennedy's Bay of Pigs. At the State Department, U. Alexis Johnson, then the influential deputy under secretary of state for political affairs, took the view that the United States would risk unpredictable Soviet and Chinese reactions. He privately told associates that he could not understand how Kissinger could have gone along with Nixon's idea of bombing North Korea. Secretary Rogers was quickly converted to this position.

Now Rogers, Laird, and the Joint Chiefs of Staff were solidly aligned against Nixon. Rogers, who recalled later that there was "immense pressure" from the White House to retaliate for the loss of the EC-121, tried to convince Nixon that if the punitive strike was carried out, "the sons of bitches would come back at us, then we would hit again, and we'd have a second war in Asia parallel with Vietnam." He too was concerned that a conflict in Korea would affect the détente policies Nixon was preparing, and along with Laird, he found the Bay of Pigs analogy fitting.

The battle within the administration raged for three days. The public, however, was happily unaware of it; the administration let it be known that American armed forces were placed on alert in the general area of Korea, but *only* against the contingency of a further deterioration of the situation.

This was not entirely true. Laird and the chiefs, playing a delaying-action game, had convinced Nixon on the first day, Tuesday, that a strike could not be mounted instantly for logistic reasons. But obeying presidential orders, they began moving three aircraft carriers and a battleship toward the Sea of Japan. The carrier *Kitty Hawk,* on a visit in Hong Kong, was ordered to steam back immediately to waters off Vietnam; the carrier *Bon Homme Richard* raced to Vietnam from her base at Subic Bay in the Philippines. This deployment made it possible for the carriers *Enterprise, Ticonderoga,* and *Ranger* to leave their station off Vietnam and move toward the Sea of Japan. The battleship *New Jersey,* en route home to Long Beach, California, after six months of operations off Vietnam, was turned around in mid-Pacific with orders to meet the three carriers in the Sea of Japan. At the same time, orders went out for navy and air force fighters to fly escort on future EC-121 intelligence missions in the Korean region. Aerial tankers were assigned to refuel the fighters in flight.

During Tuesday, Nixon met several times with Kissinger, Laird, Rogers, and General Wheeler. The result was a compromise of sorts: no immediate action was ordered against North Korea—the early morning attack order was rescinded in the face of military realities—but naval and air movements got under way. Nixon still wanted to strike as soon as possible.

Publicly there were various efforts to make the administration appear reasonable while keeping its options open. Some of these efforts were in fact intended to commit President Nixon to a peaceful course. Thus Rogers, addressing a convention of editors, said on the subject of the EC-121 incident that "the weak can be rash; the powerful must be more restrained. . . . Complexity in world affairs should teach us the need to act responsibly, to substitute cooperation for coercion, and to move from confrontation to negotiation on the issues that divide nations." Rogers seemed to be reminding Nixon of his own inaugural speech.

Kissinger's role was murky. Privately he sided with Nixon, but he subtly created the impression that he really opposed military retaliation. This pattern Kissinger would follow throughout his years as America's top foreign-policy official. When the National Security Council met to consider the situation, Rogers and Laird expressed their opposition to taking military action; Nixon, extremely well briefed on the situation, argued for it. Kissinger, as was his custom at NSC meetings, said nothing, but it was Kissinger who had briefed the president.

(Nixon's own version of these events surfaced in 1977 when he said in a television interview with David Frost that it was Kissinger who had urged him to hit North Korea; it was a version that officials involved in the EC-121 affair consider to be inaccurate. "Frankly, I tilted toward it,"

Nixon told Frost, adding that he later changed his mind because of advice from others. "Kissinger came down hard . . . [but] I figured having one war on our hands was enough.")

Nixon was vigorously supported by Vice President Spiro Agnew and Attorney General John Mitchell. (The attorney general was not a statutory NSC member, but Nixon asked him to attend this particular meeting, presumably to bolster his case.) And although the session produced no agreement, a major internal political development occurred, one that was not fully understood in Washington for a long time. When Kissinger saw that Nixon had brought Mitchell into the NSC meeting for "hard-line" support, he made a tactical decision: *he* would become the administration's "secret hawk," as one of his close associates put it. Knowing that Mitchell would be likely to be in regular attendance at NSC sessions, Kissinger opted for hawkishness to retain the president's confidence and support. In those early months he had not yet achieved real personal power, and he was aware of the hostility from the "domestic" side of the White House. "Henry chose to be a hawk over the EC-121 incident as the price of his admission to power and the inner circle," an NSC official told me. "It was the Mitchell thing that did it. Henry had to side with Nixon to guard his White House flanks."

The final confrontation in the Korean affair occurred on Thursday, April 17 (the eighth anniversary of the Bay of Pigs), in Nixon's Oval Office. There, Kissinger came out openly in support of the president and together with Mitchell advocated a strike against North Korea. But Rogers, Laird, and General Wheeler argued so convincingly in opposition that Nixon ultimately accepted their views. Besides, the political momentum had been lost: nearly four days had elapsed since the navy plane had been shot down.

From then on, the lines were clearly drawn in the formulation of foreign policy: on highly controversial issues, it was generally Nixon and Kissinger on one side, pushing for tough solutions, and Rogers and Laird on the other side, counseling moderation. This pattern prevailed during the entire four years of Nixon's first term.

The EC-121 incident was historically significant because it also defined even more clearly than did the secret Cambodia bombings Nixon's approach to the use of power in the conduct of foreign policy, even though in this case he drew back from the brink. And the Korean infighting defined once and for all Henry Kissinger's role in the administration. From the tactical shift to hawkishness over Korea, it was only a step to acquiescence in the illegal wiretapping of his NSC aides and his friends in the Washington press corps.

As for Korea, the epilogue was anticlimactic. On April 17, after the Oval Office meeting, the United States confined itself to a diplomatic protest, and the Defense Department temporarily suspended reconnaissance flights. On April 18, Nixon announced at a news conference that flights were being resumed under armed escort and that a powerful naval task force was being assembled in the Sea of Japan to support the whole operation. It was clearly a face-saving maneuver, as the president said that further action would depend "upon what is done as far as North Korea is concerned, its reaction to the protest and also any other development that occurs as we continue these flights." On April 23, North Korea replied that she would go after American planes violating her air space, and warned that "we will not sit with folded arms, but will take resolute measures for safeguarding our sovereignty as ever." This was the end of the affray.

One of the arguments between Washington and Pyongyang had been whether the EC-121 was shot down over the high seas forty miles off the Korean coast, as the United States claimed, or within North Korea's twelve-mile territorial airspace, as it insisted. But a much more relevant question is whether the United States, then and subsequently, had not been running unnecessary risks in its far-flung intelligence operations. Both the United States and Soviet Union have over the years tacitly accepted the existence of mutual military-intelligence activities—by ships, planes, and "spy-in-the-sky" satellites. Each insists on the freedom to observe the other's moves so that alerts can be called in the event of suspicious, war-threatening actions. Satellites have been used, for example, as "national verification means" in the implementation of the strategic-arms–limitation agreements by both sides since 1972. The Russians would not think nowadays of shooting down a U-2, as they did in 1960, and aircraft track each other's fleet movements in the Mediterranean and elsewhere.

But the problem is that the United States government has an unquenchable thirst for intelligence. It has the technology and trained manpower to go after it. The National Security Agency, in conjunction with the CIA and the armed services, maintains a formidable and immensely sophisticated worldwide observation and eavesdropping intelligence system. NSA facilities—such as secret bases in Turkey (until the Turks closed them down in 1975 in a Cyprus-related dispute), Morocco, Japan, Vietnam, Thailand, India, Alaska, and the Aleutians—around the clock track radio, telephone, microwave, and Telex communications in all the Communist countries and many non-Communist ones. The agency takes pride in being able to monitor pilot-to-pilot radio exchanges over the Soviet Union, China, Poland, or Cuba.

But for the satisfaction of this intelligence greed, land facilities must be supplemented with ships and planes packed with electronic gear. *Liberty,* the ship sunk by the Israelis during the 1967 Middle East war, was an electronic intelligence craft intercepting Israeli and Arab communications. The *Pueblo* was eavesdropping off North Korea when it was captured in 1968, as was the EC-121. Scores of intelligence ships ply the oceans in quest of secret knowledge, and countless electronic spy planes are involved in similar operations. These intelligence ships and planes as a rule perform specific missions requested by the NSA, the CIA, or the Joint Chiefs of Staff. The operations are not haphazard, and missions are approved individually or, in the case of aircraft, in "batches," for precisely defined periods. When particularly risky operations are requested, authorization may have to be sought from the White House.

In the case of the EC-121, its special mission, in addition to routine monitoring of North Korean military communications, was electronic eavesdropping on Soviet and Chinese forces facing each other across the border. Tensions between the Soviets and the Chinese were rising at the time, and Kissinger along with Richard Helms was convinced that the Russians were on the verge of making a preemptive strike against China's nascent nuclear arsenal. Kissinger ordered a special NSC study (NSSM-63) on "Sino-Soviet Relations"; the nature of these relations, Kissinger correctly believed, had a direct bearing on détente with Moscow and Peking, which he and Nixon were beginning to develop.

For this reason, then, the ill-fated EC-121 found itself cruising off the northern part of North Korea, close enough to the Soviet-Chinese frontier for its powerful electronic equipment to pick up communications from both armies. But even if we accept the need to know what the Russians and the Chinese were up to, was the intelligence obtained by the EC-121 sufficiently important to warrant the risk not only of losing a plane and its crew, but of the kind of conflict that nearly developed? The odds are certainly against a spy plane's casual interception of a nuclear-strike order from Moscow.

As Elliot Richardson's secret report pointed out, there was an excess of American intelligence operations in East Asia anyway. Subsequent hearings before the Senate Subcommittee on U.S. Security Agreements and Commitments Abroad brought out the fact that American intelli-

gence and military psychological-operations teams were engaged in astonishing activities throughout Asia. For example, North Korea was
among the principal targets of the Okinawa-based Seventh Psychological
Operations Group of the U.S. Army, known as the 7th Psyops Group. The
group, working with a $10-million budget for 1969, was responsible for
unbridled propaganda work in North Korea, Laos, Thailand, Vietnam,
and China. One of its operations was the Voice of the U.N. Command
radio station in Seoul, which, according to Richardson's report, the
American embassy had unsuccessfully tried to abolish as useless: whereas
official American policy was to reduce tensions between North and South
Korea, the Voice, according to a subcommittee investigator, insisted that
there could be no relaxation, "that the North is continually on the offensive militarily and that there can be no cooling of tensions until there is
a change of government in North Korea."

The 7th Psyops also published a monthly propaganda magazine, *The
Friends of Freedom,* with a circulation of a half-million copies, and produced
literally billions of leaflets that were dropped by planes over North Korea,
sent in balloons floated across the demilitarized zone in Korea, and
bundled in floating packages out to the sea so that they would wash up
on North Korean beaches. This was a program known as Focus Truth.
Other leaflets were dropped over Vietnam, Thailand, and northern Laos.
The subcommittee discovered that the 7th Psyops produced a total of
11.8 billion leaflets in 1969 and 16.2 billion in 1970. More than 200
million were dropped every month over Laos.

In Thailand in 1969, the Psyops distributed some 10,000 bars of
"propaganda soap" manufactured in Taiwan as part of its counterinsurgency efforts. According to the description by a subcommittee investigator, "As you wash yourself with it, at each level there is a new message.
. . . As the soap washes down there is a new message with each layer of
soap. . . . It is probably a secret message."

On Taiwan, the 7th Psyops worked with the U.S. Army's Special
Forces and the U.S. Air Force as late as 1969 to prepare the Chinese
Nationalists to assault the mainland. As it happened, they were engaging
in these operations just as Nixon and Kissinger were secretly preparing
their breakthrough to Peking. The army obviously was not informed of
this, but the question is whether the White House knew what the military
were up to in Taiwan.

The Taiwan operation, known as Forward Thrust, included urgings
by the 7th Psyops that "the Chinese [Nationalist] Government has to
maintain a strong armed force for return to the mainland" and joint

paratroop exercises with Chinese Special Forces units. This is how Forward Thrust, using U.S. Air Force C-130 transport planes, was described to the subcommittee:

> The exercise included parachute drops on Taiwan simulating a drop behind enemy lines. American and Republic of China's Special Forces people dropped together to open the exercise, and they were simulating high-altitude drops into a territory controlled by an enemy. . . . American pilots who carried the paratroopers, who then dropped, described the exercise as understood by the Chinese as practicing return to the mainland.

Propaganda and psychological warfare are not always intelligence activities, but this was certainly the case with the 7th Psyops. An army document setting forth the Psyops mission thus provided that the group "maintains contact with U.S. intelligence agencies . . . to insure a maximum regular flow of appropriate intelligence to Headquarters, 7th PSYOP Group." A special Psyop detachment "conducts PSYOP research on 16 PACOM [Pacific Command] countries . . . in the form of assessments, research notes, propaganda trends, topical reports, psychological opportunities, and propaganda analyses." On Taiwan, the group "obtains PSYOP intelligence through liaison with U.S. military and civilian intelligence agencies."

From the very beginning, Nixon and Kissinger were convinced—and probably rightly so—that the greatest danger to world peace lay in the Middle East. Given the overriding political and security interests in that region of the two superpowers, a new escalation of the Arab-Israeli conflict, they reasoned, might lead to a Soviet-American confrontation, possibly a nuclear one. A war of attrition was raging across the Suez Canal between Israel and Egypt, as massed Egyptian artillery fired at Israeli positions behind the Bar-Lev Line on the Sinai side of the waterway, and Israeli jets hit back at the Egyptian emplacements on the western bank. Not two years had passed since the Six-Day War of 1967, and the two opponents seemed to be squaring off for another round. The Soviets were rearming the battered Egyptians while the United States, more cautious, was limiting its military support to Israel to a slow trickle of F-4 Phantom jets despite the Israelis' increasingly strong requests for more planes and arms.

To cope with this disturbing situation, President Nixon embarked on a series of policies that could not but fail. Briefly, he concluded that the way to bring peace to the Middle East was to negotiate a settlement plan directly with the Soviet Union. Both parties in the area—Israel and Egypt —would be kept virtually in the dark during this diplomatic process. This bizarre approach to trying to settle the quarter-of-a-century-old conflict behind the backs of the principal protagonists was carried out by Secretary of State Rogers—with Henry Kissinger's noncommittal backing at the White House. It was, not surprisingly, welcome to the Soviet Union, which, in this manner, was brought for the first time into the heart of Middle East diplomacy. If this attempt to impose a superpower solution on the warring parties in the Middle East has a viable explanation, it lies in the Nixon-Kissinger obsession with involving the Russians in global "linkage" situations. But Moscow outmaneuvered Washington, politically and militarily, in the Middle East in 1969, and it is worthwhile to reconstruct the history of this period in order to throw additional light on Nixon's and Kissinger's philosophy.

This reconstruction is based on interviews with U.S. officials and foreign diplomats involved in the 1969 negotiations, as well as on U.S. government documents and studies that served as the foundation for Middle East policies.

The story actually begins before Nixon took office. Early in January, during the transition period, Kissinger ordered his nascent NSC staff to prepare a National Security Study Memorandum on the subject to be ready the moment the new administration assumed power. NSSM–2 was put together by Harold H. Saunders, an old Middle East hand who had served on the NSC staff under Presidents Kennedy and Johnson (following a stint with the CIA), and it was presented to Kissinger on January 21. (Retaining Saunders had been one of Kissinger's first decisions when he began to work for Nixon after the election.) Saunders had to work under extraordinary pressure, for rumors kept sweeping Washington that a new conflagration was imminent, and a secret intelligence alert was called on inauguration day so that the United States could respond instantly to any new crisis in the Middle East.

NSSM–2, a blend of views provided by the State Department's Bureau of Near Eastern and South Asian Affairs, the Defense Department, the CIA, and the NSC staff, offered two basic policy options in response to a series of questions posed by Kissinger. In fact, the study was the government's first full review of the Middle East situation since the 1967 war. The first option was for an essentially passive policy, that is, with the United States continuing to provide Israel with just enough military equipment so that it could remain in strategic balance with its neighbors,

and leaving diplomacy to the care of Gunnar Jarring, the Swedish diplomat who had been acting as United Nations mediator in the Middle East
under the 1967 U.N. Security Council Resolution 242. But the problem
with Jarring was that he was wholly ineffective—although it was not entirely his fault—and the war of attrition was picking up momentum as he
made his diplomatic rounds.

The second option proposed that the United States act as a principal
in the Middle Eastern crisis, injecting itself more intensively in diplomatic
efforts toward a settlement. Both Nixon and Kissinger preferred the
second option, fearing that American passivity would lead to drift and a
new war. The National Security Council was informed at its meeting on
February 1 that the president had chosen option 2.

Having made this fundamental decision, however, Nixon had to
define precisely how the United States would get involved. The White
House viewed the problem in a very complex way, striving to link the
Middle East question with other aspects of diplomacy. Late in 1968,
President de Gaulle had proposed that the Big Four members of the U.N.
Security Council initiate talks among themselves to look for a Middle East
solution. (De Gaulle, of course, was pushing for a major role for France
in the Middle East even if that meant the British were brought in as well.)
Johnson had left this decision to the incoming administration, and the
new president was exposed to it when he met with de Gaulle in Paris. But
by that time he and Kissinger had already made up their minds to seek
a Middle East settlement through direct negotiations with Russia. Leaving Paris, Nixon assured de Gaulle that the United States would go along
with the Big Four formula. But almost simultaneously, Kissinger was
working with Dobrynin to engage the Russians in a secret direct dialogue.
Concentrating on the talks with Moscow was among the options presented in another NSC study on the Middle East (NSSM–17) that was
completed on February 6. Secretary Rogers was familiar with White
House policy in its main outlines, but for the time being he was excluded
from active participation in the preliminary talks with Dobrynin. As a
senior administration official described the situation in March: "Nixon
[accepted] de Gaulle's proposal . . . in order to have better relations with
France. It served to butter up de Gaulle. In other words, Nixon's inclination to accept the French ideas was for *European,* not Middle Eastern
reasons. But we knew that the really relevant talks would be between the
two major powers, the United States and the Soviet Union. So we had to
explore, at the same time, a way to have parallel talks with the Soviets—
this time for *Soviet,* not Middle Eastern reasons. You must remember that

the détente concept was already in the wings."

If European and Soviet reasons were two ingredients for the emerging United States policy in the Middle East, the third ingredient was Kissinger's personal view (which he discussed with some of his aides at the time) that Israel must not be allowed to become too strong militarily while the secret negotiations were under way. Kissinger's idea, from which he never deviated, was that the United States must use its flow of arms to the Israelis as leverage in efforts to persuade them to give up, sooner or later, territories they had conquered in 1967. This issue dominated American-Israeli relations during Nixon's entire presidency—and Kissinger played on it, with varying degrees of success (as well as deception), in all the negotiations with Jerusalem.

The Big Four talks on the Middle East began at the United Nations in New York during March, just as Kissinger and Dobrynin agreed to conduct parallel Soviet-American negotiations in Washington. The overall situation was further explored in two more NSC studies on the Middle East—NSSM–30 of March 19 and NSSM–33 of March 21–and Secretary Rogers was formally given the responsibility for the entire Middle East diplomatic operation. Kissinger allowed this for his own reasons (some of his aides say that being Jewish he wanted to keep a low profile on the Middle East), although he and Nixon remained very active in the background. One reason could have been his concern that the effort might fail, in which case he did not wish to have the White House identified with a fiasco. If it succeeded, it would never be too late for Nixon and Kissinger to claim credit—Rogers could be nudged aside at the right time. Obversely, if it aborted, the secretary of state would be further weakened; considering Rogers his arch rival, Kissinger had no qualms about exposing him to the perils of Middle East diplomacy. It is curious to note how Henry Kissinger's personal insecurities provide a steady counterpoint to American diplomatic history of this era.

The publicly announced Big Four meetings in New York served principally as an "umbrella" for the secret Soviet-American talks in Washington, and this is how it was explained to the increasingly alarmed Israelis. Both Prime Minister Golda Meir in Jerusalem and her ambassador in Washington, Yitzhak Rabin, regarded the Big Four conversations as a political triumph for Egypt's President Gamal Abdel Nasser and, therefore, as a setback for Israel, reasoning quite accurately that one reason Nasser was waging his war of attrition was precisely to force the big powers to intervene diplomatically and bring their influence to bear on Israel to agree to far-reaching concessions so that a new full-fledged war could be averted. To be sure, both Egypt and Israel rejected the basic notion of an imposed settlement—it was the only thing they had in common—but the message Nasser's guns were booming over the Suez Canal was that unless the Big Four forced Israel to make territorial concessions, the war could escalate beyond control.

But Kissinger and Rogers kept emphasizing privately that the quadripartite talks in New York were merely a feint to please the French and the British, and that the real business would be transacted with the Russians in Washington. This, of course, did not wholly allay Israeli concern. Mrs. Meir and her cabinet, including Defense Minister Moshe Dayan, took a dim view of Israel's fate being decided by Richard Nixon and Leonid Brezhnev. Invariably they were assured that the United States was committed to the survival and security of Israel, and that the secret negotiations with the Russians were principally aimed at convincing them to cut back on their military deliveries to Egypt. Kissinger saw no reason the Israelis should be told that a broader détente with the Soviet Union loomed, and Egyptian diplomats have since acknowledged that Moscow also kept its thoughts on détente to itself.

In this sense, virtual collusion developed between the United States and the Soviet Union. Each of them supposedly spoke for its respective client, Israel or Egypt, and both concealed that they were actually endeavoring to write their own peace plan for the Middle East. The theory behind this performance was that substantive consultations with Israel and Egypt during the negotiating process would lead to instant paralysis. So the tacit agreement between the Russians and Americans was that there would be no consultation with the "clients," and only after they had ironed out a peace plan would they seek to "sell" it to the Egyptians and the Israelis.

But there was another element: Nixon and Kissinger, caught up as they must have been in their diplomatic linkage acrobatics, were acting basically in good faith. The Russians, on the other hand, appear to have been playing a tactical delaying game, in the full knowledge that Nasser would never accept a compromise worked out in Washington. They knew that the United States was keeping the Israelis on a short leash, in terms of deliveries of aircraft and weapons, while the secret talks went on. Egypt was simultaneously being rearmed.

The secret talks began late in March following a series of preliminary meetings between Dobrynin and Rogers. Rogers now tended to leave the actual negotiations to a team headed by Joseph J. Sisco, assistant secretary of state for Near Eastern and South Asian affairs, and including his deputy, Alfred L. Atherton, Jr., and Walter B. Smith III, the Near East expert in the State Department's Bureau of Intelligence and Research. On the Soviet side, Dobrynin was the principal negotiator, though he always brought along his minister counselor, Yuli Vorontsov, and at least one Middle East specialist from Moscow. The first meeting was held at the Soviet embassy on Sixteenth Street, but all the subsequent sessions took place in the conference room of the Near Eastern Affairs Bureau, on the sixth floor of the State Department building.

The Americans made no secret of the fact that they were engaged in private talks with the Russians over the Middle East; what was kept secret was the *content* of the discussions. Both Sisco and Dobrynin were skilled negotiators: Dobrynin could be both firm and suave while Sisco, one of the department's toughest operators (resembling Kissinger in approach and personality traits), blended ribald humor with streaks of stubbornness and deviousness. Dobrynin was, of course, at a certain disadvantage: though he was Moscow's most famous diplomat and a full member of the Communist Party's Central Committee, he had virtually no plenipotentiary powers and was forced to refer every important point for decision back home. This inevitably slowed down the negotiating process, something the Russians did not seem to mind. Sisco, on the other hand, had more personal latitude; besides, he could consult with Rogers (and through him with Kissinger) just by leaving the conference room and picking up the phone in his office.

To begin with, the United States wanted to obtain an agreed-upon interpretation of the Security Council's Resolution 242, covering Israeli withdrawals from occupied territories as well as Arab obligations to assure Israel of secure borders; and to proceed from there to hammer out a peace plan. The Soviets, however, insisted on a prior commitment that Israel would make withdrawals, arguing that once such an agreement was reached, the other elements would "fall into place." In other words, Sisco wanted to build from specifics toward the general while Dobrynin's instructions were to win a general agreement and then fill in the specifics. But the situation was even more complex than that. As an American diplomat observed later, "What we had to do was to look for tradeoffs to be able to reach some form of understanding."

To understand the existing situation clearly, it is necessary to quote from Resolution 242, which since 1967 had been the diplomatic centerpiece of the Middle East situation. The operative part of the resolution, which was approved by the U.N. Security Council on November 22, 1967, said:

the fulfillment of [U.N.] Charter principles requires the establishment of just and lasting peace in the Middle East which should include the application of both the following principles:

(i) Withdrawal of Israeli armed forces from territories of recent conflict;

(ii) Termination of all claims or states of belligerency and respect for and acknowledgement of the sovereignty, territorial integrity and political independence of every state in the area and their right to live in peace within secure and recognized boundaries free from threats or acts of force;

The second part of Resolution 242 affirmed

the necessity:

(a) For guaranteeing freedom of navigation through international waterways in the area;

(b) For achieving a just settlement of the refugee problem;

(c) For guaranteeing the territorial inviolability and political independence of every state in the area, through measures including the establishment of demilitarized zones.

Finally, the resolution provided for the designation of a "special representative" of the U.N. secretary general—Gunnar Jarring became this "special representative"—"to proceed to the Middle East . . . to promote agreement and assist efforts to achieve a peaceful and accepted settlement."

This text was a masterpiece of compromise. And the most important compromise was locked in clause (i) providing for "withdrawal of Israeli armed forces from territories of recent conflict." It took a furious battle by the United States, Britain, and their allies (Israel was not a member of the Security Council) to prevent the insertion by the Soviet Union of the word "the" before "territories." It was not just semantics in the official English-language version: had "the" been included, it would have had the effect of ordering Israel to withdraw from *all* the territories taken in 1967—the Sinai, the Golan Heights, the West Bank, and East Jerusalem. Without this tiny word, however, Israel was given the flexibility of negotiating pullbacks from certain, but not necessarily *all,* territories. The precise interpretation of clause (i) became the central point in the Dobrynin-Sisco talks.

The first negotiating clash was over the meaning of "withdrawal" by Israel. Because agreement on this point was not possible, the American team came up with the ploy of producing a "prototype" of an Israeli-

Egyptian peace accord. The central American notion was to develop language that would link the obligations of the Arab states and Israel to each other under the provisions of Resolution 242. Using the resolution's call for a "special representative," Sisco kept emphasizing the role that Jarring could and should play. The corollary was that, sooner or later, Israel and the Arabs would have to negotiate with each other in some manner—something the Arab side steadfastly opposed on the grounds that it would imply the recognition of the existence of the state of Israel. Dobrynin argued, however, that such arrangements should *follow* an Israeli withdrawal commitment. Likewise, he hedged on the U.S. proposal for a formal end of Arab belligerency toward Israel and renunciation of war. The U.S. draft was based on clause (ii) of Resolution 242, but Dobrynin took the position that Egypt would never agree to a written pledge.

U.S. negotiators patiently explained to Dobrynin that, in the end, the whole concept of a settlement had to repose on the premise of Arabs "living at peace with Israel." Therefore, Sisco argued, there was a need for specific understandings, such as the establishment of controls over commando operations by both sides. In outlining the "prototype" agreement, the Americans began working around such central issues as withdrawal and instead tried filling in other provisions of a less controversial nature. Thus Dobrynin was able to agree to a section on "freedom of navigation" and other minor points. Occasionally, he came back with counterproposals. (When he proposed critical new language, Sisco would consult Rogers. Often, Rogers would have to go to Kissinger and even Nixon for White House authority to accept or reject specific Soviet ideas. It soon became clear that he had no final say in the matter.)

Among various American formulations, Sisco put forward a draft that did not exclude—the word was carefully chosen—Israeli pullbacks to the 1967 lines. In return, however, the Americans wanted a Soviet commitment to the demilitarization of the Sinai in a final peace agreement (this, too, was inspired by Resolution 242) and "security" for Israel at the Sharm al-Sheikh outpost on the Strait of Tiran. (A special formula would be devised for the Gaza Strip, possibly to give Jordan an outlet to the Mediterranean.) By the end of June, a tentative draft was agreed on by Sisco and Dobrynin—although a precise definition of Israeli "withdrawal" was left vague for further discussions. However, neither Egypt nor Israel had been fully consulted by the superpowers on the preliminary text, and nobody knew how the two capitals would respond to it. American officials claimed later that Israel was kept fully informed throughout the talks with the Soviets, but there is no evidence that this was so. The Israelis have always insisted that the whole negotiation was conducted behind their backs. We do not know, of course, what, if anything, the Russians were telling Nasser.

In any event, Sisco, Atherton, and Smith flew to Moscow in July for quiet negotiations with Soviet Foreign Minister Andrei Gromyko and his advisers. The Americans spent a week there without any further progress being made. Gromyko was holding out for an Israeli commitment to withdraw to the 1967 lines. Back in Washington, Sisco and Dobrynin resumed their painstaking talks. But the Americans were encouraged again: now the Russians accepted the United States draft on "secure and recognized boundaries" for Israel—this, of course, was tied to still undefined Israeli pullbacks—and by late August it appeared possible that a deal might finally be struck.

In September, the scene switched to New York. Nixon, delivering an address before the U.N. General Assembly on September 18, argued forcefully for a settlement in the Middle East. He spoke in general terms of "extensive consultations" with the Soviet Union, but he was clearly preparing world opinion for the possibility that a settlement, "which both sides have a vested interest in maintaining," might be beyond reach. He also let it be known that the Soviet Union was less than cooperative over such issues as a mutual limitation of arms deliveries to the Middle East.

> Peace cannot be achieved on the basis of anything less than a binding, irrevocable commitment by the parties to live together in peace. Failing a settlement, an agreement on the limitation of the shipment of arms to the Middle East might help to stabilize the situation. We have indicated to the Soviet Union, without result, our willingness to enter such discussions.

It is unclear whether Nixon's pronouncements had anything to do with it, but within days of his speech the negotiations picked up again in a more optimistic mood. Dobrynin and Sisco had several meetings in a thirty-fifth-floor suite at the Waldorf Towers where the impression was that the Russians may have been dragging their feet, but they did not wish to break off the talks entirely.

The intriguing aspect of this diplomatic exercise is that the White House never gave the State Department its full support on what was becoming known as the "Rogers Plan." This was so even though on October 19 the National Security Council chaired by Nixon "signed off on" (i.e., approved) the final draft of the peace plan to be presented to the Russians and, ultimately, to Israel and Egypt. In Washington, there is a large difference between formally approving a policy, often just for the record, and politically supporting it. In the absence of such support from the White House, a policy simply dies.

An essential element in Nixon's and Kissinger's diplomacy was theater. And theater is what Israel got when its prime minister, Golda Meir, visited Nixon on September 25 and 26. Mrs. Meir had arrived in Washington just after the president's speech at the United Nations—it was her first direct contact with the Nixon administration—to urge the United States to accelerate deliveries of arms, especially jet aircraft, to Israel and to learn what she could about the Soviet-American negotiations. What she found was that the United States government itself appeared to be rather divided in its attitudes toward the Israeli cause. A certain coldness at the State Department contrasted with the warmth displayed at the White House. What Mrs. Meir may not have realized at the time was that this was part of a complicated scenario, a classic Kissinger-inspired charade devised for the occasion. The State Department was hinting that arms deliveries would be forthcoming only if Israel were willing to be more flexible diplomatically in the context of the Rogers Plan (although, in reality, Rogers and Sisco favored increased military assistance). The real opposition was to be found in the Pentagon, notably from Warren Nutter, then assistant secretary of defense for international security affairs (ISA), representing what might be called the "Arabist view" in the government. The White House line, however, was that the United States believed in a strong Israel: Nixon told Mrs. Meir that he had to fight his own bureaucracy over this issue in order to meet Israel's requests for arms. This was the favorite Kissinger ploy, espoused by Nixon, of suggesting to "difficult" clients that their real friends were in the White House. Nixon and Kissinger thought it gave them greater diplomatic leverage.

Mrs. Meir and her advisers noticed with some surprise that Nixon was not pushing the Rogers Plan (about which they still knew very little); instead he kept pointing to Kissinger, who was mostly mute, and telling her that Kissinger was most anxious to be helpful in the efforts for a Middle Eastern peace. (This was a neat way of undercutting Rogers.)

At that point, Kissinger's assessment of the problem, as he outlined it privately to his aides during Mrs. Meir's visit, was that military support for Israel would serve a twin purpose: it would make the Israelis more dependent on the United States and, therefore, more responsive to its diplomatic pressures; and it would demonstrate to the Arabs that reliance on the Soviet Union was not sufficient to help them with their objectives and that they would be better served by accepting American diplomatic guidance. To Kissinger, the Middle East was essentially a United States–Russia problem, and he felt that the Soviet penetration in the region was traceable to the Arab-Israeli conflict. The corollary was that the Russians were benefiting from tensions between the United States and Israel as well as from Arab frustrations.

Not surprisingly Mrs. Meir's visit produced no major diplomatic decisions. The prime minister discovered precious little about American diplomacy—the Americans were not ready to take her into their confidence about their talks with the Russians—and she went away somewhat perplexed about the White House diplomatic theater. She did learn, however, a few things about baseball—thanks to Nixon's proclivity for discussing sports on the most improbable occasions with the most unlikely people. Bidding her farewell in the Roosevelt Room at the White House, Nixon noted that before returning to Israel, Mrs. Meir would visit Milwaukee, where she had taught school for many years as a young woman. "Milwaukee," the president said, "lost the Braves, but they got you back. . . . As a matter of fact, the Braves could use you as a pinch hitter right now in order to win." Nixon then informed Mrs. Meir that the Braves had moved to Atlanta—"you know that."

After Mrs. Meir's departure, the administration shifted to a mix of two strategies: somewhat increasing military aid to Israel and maintaining the diplomatic process with the Russians, although the White House was careful to remain dissociated from the Rogers Plan. Basing its decision on NSSM–40, a study on "Israeli Arms" produced on April 11, and NSSMs–81 and –82 written on November 6 on the general subject of Israel (plus supplementary State Department papers), the White House authorized a secret resumption of Phantom jet deliveries to Israel. It was on a limited scale: during November, two Phantoms were flown to Israel by U.S. Air Force pilots under instructions to behave as discreetly as possible during refueling stops and while around Lod Airport near Tel Aviv, and four more F-4s were similarly delivered in December. The pilots wore civilian clothes in public and they were forbidden to discuss their mission. Nixon's condition was that Israel would give no publicity to these deliveries to avoid hostile Arab reactions. The Israelis were delighted to oblige, although they were sharply disappointed over the small number of planes. They continued to press the United States for larger deliveries, but this was not in the cards for quite a while.

To be sure, the Phantoms went to Israel while the Soviet-American negotiations were at a critical stage. After the National Security Council reviewed the Rogers Plan on October 19, Rogers and Soviet Foreign Minister Gromyko had a long working dinner at the secretary's Waldorf Towers suite; it produced what the Americans thought was an agreement in principle on wording of an agreement that the two governments would present to Israel and Egypt. (At that point, Israel still had not received a precise formulation of the peace plan from the United States. The Americans assumed that the Russians were likewise refraining from telling Cairo too much.) The principal feature was that Israel would return to Egypt the territories conquered in 1967, except for "insubstantial alterations" (this phrase, personally contributed by Rogers, related to an area formerly held by Jordan crossed by the new Jerusalem–Tel Aviv highway built after the war, the so-called Latrun salient), in exchange for Egyptian political concessions assuring the security of Israeli borders. The plan was deliberately vague as to how this security would be defined. The idea was that once the principle of withdrawal-for-guarantees was accepted, the Israelis and the Egyptians could negotiate the specific points through Jarring in indirect "proximity" talks: the two delegations would be in the same city—Nicosia on Cyprus and New York were suggested—and even in the same building, with Jarring shuttling between them. (This expedient, based on the "Rhodes formula" used in the 1949 armistice talks, was intended to finesse the Egyptian objection to face-to-face discussions.)

The plan's vagueness was both its strength and its fatal flaw. It achieved a Soviet-American compromise on the controversial question whether the Israelis should pull back *before* the Egyptians agreed to a formula on secure borders. The idea was that the two parties would simultaneously accept both concepts, then try to implement them through Jarring. That the Soviets agreed to it was regarded by the Americans as something of a breakthrough. Moreover, it did not run the risk of failure that might occur if the specific concepts of implementation were spelled out; the demilitarization of the Sinai, the future of the Gaza Strip, and Israel's control of Sharm al-Sheikh, for example, were subject instead to subsequent negotiation.

But the plan's vagueness carried an immense potential for misunderstanding and suspicion, so great, in fact, that it could not survive even its first political test. Because the United States was not "clearing every step of the way" with Israel, as an American negotiator explained it later, a diplomatic accident was inevitable. That accident came when Israeli newspapers, improperly briefed by their inadequately informed government, published articles late in October announcing that the Soviet-American peace plan called for "direct negotiations" between Jerusalem and Cairo. The immediate result was a protest from the Egyptian foreign minister, Mahmoud Riad, to Secretary Rogers; Cairo, Riad said, had agreed only to "indirect talks," which already represented a major concession. It is possible, of course, that the Israelis deliberately torpedoed the plan, sensing, as they were to say later, that they were being "sold out." But in any event, this was the beginning of the end of the Rogers Plan.

Still, many American diplomats believe that the plan could have been saved if Rogers had enjoyed full White House support. There were indications that the Soviets seriously pushed Nasser to get the talks back on the track, but this effort could have been successful only if the Russians were convinced that Nixon really wanted the Rogers Plan to work. It is conceivable, on the contrary, that Dobrynin, via Kissinger, gained the impression that the White House had lost interest in the plan. "We gambled on this deal and we lost," an American diplomat recounted some years later. "But it might have still worked if the White House had been fully aboard. As it was, there existed a serious question about a political decision in the White House to proceed with it. There was no desire to back Rogers. He was left on his own, out on a limb, with no commitment from the White House."

Why did Nixon let the Rogers Plan abort without any attempt to save it? There are several explanations, none of them documentable. One of them, adduced by some American officials, is that the White House had come to the belated conclusion that American public opinion would have opposed a vague plan that was based on secret arrangements with Russia and that Israel would denounce as a "sellout." Another is that Nixon and his principal adviser were disenchanted with the Russians over their lack of cooperation in Vietnam and their continuing to hold back on the SALT talks. Finally, there is the view that Kissinger persuaded Nixon to dissociate himself from the Rogers Plan to avoid embarrassment in the event of failure. At that point, the White House was interested only in foreign-policy triumphs—and Nixon and Kissinger were able to draw distinctions between the White House and the State Department when it came to foreign-policy performance.

Curiously, there was a hiatus of quite a few weeks between the Egyptian protest to Rogers in October and the formal communication to the State Department that the Russians could no longer go along with the Rogers Plan. When Dobrynin delivered the word to Rogers in the first week of December, the official argument was that the Egyptians could not accept the American proposals. But the State Department also contrived to create a major political upheaval over the way in which it handled the matter. Inexplicably, it failed to inform Israel of the Soviet rejection, as well as of the full details of the peace plan, until Rogers told the whole story publicly in a speech at a dinner at a Washington hotel on December 19. The Israelis were furious, all the more so because, although Rogers had met with Foreign Minister Abba Eban the day before, he had failed to tell him about the forthcoming speech. Prime Minister Meir personally advised Nixon that Israel rejected the imposition "from the outside" without any "element of negotiation" of a peace settlement that called on Israel to withdraw to the 1967 lines without an acceptable guarantee of secure borders, as specified in Resolution 242, and she insisted that the Rogers Plan could not have worked in any case because Egypt was not ready for peace.

The 1969 Middle East peace effort was thus a complete fiasco, and Washington's erratic diplomacy resulted in the loss of a serious chance for a modicum of peace in the Middle East. If nothing else, this experience proved the fallaciousness of policies aimed at settlements imposed by the big powers.

Chapter 5

An understanding between the United States and the Soviet Union on major world issues was a basic condition for international security, but Richard Nixon became quickly convinced (and eventually convinced a somewhat skeptical Kissinger) that Russia's interest in improved relations with Washington would be enhanced by the simultaneous development of a Sino-American relationship. "The road to Moscow leads through Peking," as a senior administration adviser remarked. Nixon concluded correctly that the Russians could not afford to be isolated by both the Chinese and the Americans; conversely, China's fear of Russia would induce it in time to accept American friendship as a form of added international insurance. Nixon perceived that this convergence of political forces and interests offered the United States a unique opportunity to seek a functioning détente with the two major Communist powers. He also expected that the Russians and the Chinese would be helpful in settling the Vietnamese war.

This "triangular" strategy likewise looked forward to a certain balance of power in the Pacific that would operate even before the Indochina war ended. Nixon's vision was an Asia where Soviet and Chinese interests would cancel each other out, thereby requiring a permanent American presence, in one form or another, throughout the Pacific. He believed that both Moscow and Peking, each for its own reasons, would welcome such an American presence to provide strategic balance, and he was not disturbed by the anti-American verbiage emanating from the two Communist capitals. What counted, he thought, were the real pragmatic interests of each side—not official propaganda.

The exception to his big-power calculations in the Pacific was Japan. Its strategic location and economic might required that it be included in the new Pacific security equation. Under the 1960 Treaty of Mutual Cooperation and Security, the United States retained military bases and facilities on Japanese territory (although their number was reduced from an astonishing 3800 in 1952 to 148 at the start of 1969); Japan was the cornerstone of America's security arrangements in East Asia. But Nixon faced complicated problems in Tokyo. Japanese public opinion was pressing for the return of Okinawa, and this would mean, among other things, that the United States would have to remove its nuclear weapons from the island. This was a very touchy point with the Joint Chiefs of Staff, and Nixon first had to win the Pentagon's concurrence to proceed with Okinawa's reversion before being able to enter into actual negotiations with the Japanese. He realized that failure to return Okinawa might compromise the planned extension in 1970 of the ten-year security treaty and, in general, poison relations with Tokyo. Washington was already at odds with Japan over a textile agreement, a secondary economic issue but one with far-reaching political implications, and over such nagging questions as the regulation of American private investments in Japan. It was thus necessary to move carefully and delicately.

Obviously, attention had to be paid to other strategic parts of Asia: South Korea, Taiwan, the Philippines, and Thailand—countries that were vital to the smooth functioning of the American military machine in Asia. Yet when Nixon entered the White House there was no coherent, long-range United States policy in Asia other than the determination to pursue the Indochina war. Also, Washington had only a murky view of Asian attitudes, because there had been no systematic effort in previous years to ascertain what Asians thought and wanted. What Asian policy there was, was determined in Washington on the basis of a variety of misconceptions, aggravated by the propensity of most Asian governments to tell U.S. ambassadors what they thought these envoys wanted to hear.

The Nixon administration's first comprehensive attempt to understand Asian attitudes better came in March and April 1969, when the new assistant secretary of state for East Asian and Pacific affairs, Marshall Green, visited eleven Asian capitals, plus Hong Kong and the American bases in Thailand. On his return, Green wrote a lengthy report to Nixon, dated April 21 and classified Secret-Limdis (limited distribution). Nixon scrawled, "This is Great," on the top page of Green's report, and a month later Kissinger sent copies of it to the secretaries of state and defense, the administrator of the Agency for International Development, and the director of the U.S. Information Agency with a covering memorandum on White House stationery (also marked Secret-Limdis) saying, "The President has read the attached East Asian trip report prepared by Assistant Secretary of State Marshall Green and believes it is excellent. He has asked that you circulate it to key officials in your agencies."

The Green report is one of the most interesting foreign policy documents of the early Nixon years.

Here are some excerpts from it:

Most Asian leaders I met feel that Peking has never been so extreme, unreasonable, intransigent, and hostile as it is at present. They foresee no change until Mao passes from the scene. Some of them agree that Peking, despite its belligerent rhetoric, is cautious in foreign affairs, pushing its expansionist designs primarily by manipulating Communist parties and other proxy entities, and through subversion and psychological warfare. There was less of a consensus on whether Peking's growing nuclear capability would lead to adventurism. Some thought it would and all agreed that Peking would certainly exploit its nuclear capability to the full in terms of psychological warfare and blackmail.

Washington's own evaluation of Peking's posture was completely at variance with this, of course; both Nixon and Kissinger—and, for that matter, Green—saw China moving ever so cautiously to new forms of accommodation, especially with the West: it was emerging from the maelstrom of the Cultural Revolution, and it had been shocked by the Soviet invasion of Czechoslovakia. Despite Lyndon Johnson's notion of building an ABM shield in the United States against Chinese missiles, no serious American analyst thought that the Chinese were considering nuclear blackmail against anybody. Subversion, of course, was an on-going Chinese effort around her borders, but this was done in order to expand her political influence rather than to fulfill "expansionist" designs. But to go on with Green's report:

It is interesting to note in talks with Asian leaders the different ways in which Communist China's threat presented itself to their respective countries. President Suharto said that Peking is infiltrating trained cadres into Indonesia to rally Communist forces, and he cited evidence of Chicom economic manipulation to upset Indonesia's fragile economy. Prime Minister Lee [Singapore] and Deputy Prime Minister Razak [Malaysia] saw the Chinese Communist threat in terms of a conjunction of Peking-supported insurgency movements with communal strife. The Burmese Foreign Minister portrayed a complex Chinese design involving intimidation of Rangoon, actual PLA [People's Liberation Army] control of the Sheveli district, stirring up tribal groups in North Burma and exfiltrating Naga insurgents trained in China to Eastern India. The Prime Minister of Laos and the Lao Delegate for Foreign Affairs depicted Peking as exerting new efforts to control northern areas of Laos and to influence the Pathet Lao. President Marcos [Philippines] emphasized his concern over nuclear blackmail at some future date for which reason he expressed appreciation for President Nixon's views given him in Washington on the ABM decision.

Green, acting on instructions (he had met with Nixon and Kissinger, but not Secretary Rogers, before embarking on his trip), had informed many of the Asians he met that the United States "would make moves from time to time designed to prove that it is Peking, not Washington, that is isolating China." Though he was not yet privy to Nixon's plans for major approaches to China, he was used to suggesting to Asians that the United States might be shifting its policies. "Reaction to this line," Green wrote, "ranged from equanimity to strong approval."

Then Green came up with this striking line: "No one seemed to share the Soviets' concern that the U.S. was contemplating normalization of relations with Peking." But then, as Green stressed, the Asians had as little notion of Soviet policy as they had of Chinese plans. He quoted Indonesia's President Suharto and Foreign Minister Malik as "theorizing that Moscow may be holding back on military deliveries to Hanoi in order to pressure Hanoi toward a peaceful settlement and that Hanoi is countering by insisting on military guarantees before agreeing to do so." Green's own conclusion was more accurate: "Moscow may not have any clear idea as to how to proceed in Asia. Moscow must have been left in a deep dilemma by the widening Sino-Soviet rift, the upheaval in Indonesia, and the costs and risks of supporting Hanoi and Pyongyang in the years ahead."

Green's talks in Saigon produced this wholly befuddled view of the war:

President Thieu believed that the Communists are sufficiently realistic to go for a negotiated settlement while they have enough strength with which to bargain. They know that, if they persist too long, there will be little left of their cadre force with which to seek a take-over after the peace. He concluded that, after one more offensive, of some three months' duration, the DRV/NLF [Democratic Republic of Vietnam/- National Liberation Front] would enter into serious negotiations which would be concluded six months from now.

However, Green wrote, he was inclined to go along with the forecast of a "top-level American official" in Saigon that "serious talks would start sooner that that, but would continue for many months marked by Hanoi's fight and talk tactics." There Green was closer to the truth than Thiêu, and he also discovered something which the Nixon administration never told the American people:

> I was appalled to hear from General Abrams that the three worst ARVN [Army of the Republic of Vietnam] divisions are located in the most critical area, between Saigon and the Cambodian frontier, where enemy strength is being massed. It seemed absolutely incomprehensible to General Abrams that President Thieu, whatever his political reasons, had permitted this situation to persist. General Abrams commented that if the third-rate Generals now commanding these three divisions were replaced by good officers, the effect would be to upgrade significantly each of the divisions concerned. I believe this is an issue of such critical concern to our forces that we must press hard for its correction immediately.

Green's comment is illuminating because it was made at a time when Nixon was publicly boasting of the progress of Vietnamization—and constructing his broad war policies on that basis, never revealing what actually went on with the Vietnamese armed forces and how Thieu played politics with them. But it is also "absolutely incomprehensible" that the late General Abrams, then the top United States commander in Vietnam, had allowed this situation to develop. After all, the entire war effort was built upon a system of American advisers to the South Vietnamese together with half a million American troops. Where, then, was the American leverage, and why was Washington so reluctant to challenge Thieu's politics? What Green reported, appalled, in 1969 was a portent of things to come.

As it turned out, Green was also prescient about another aspect of the United States role in Asia—the perils of the overwhelming American presence:

> As long as the war in Vietnam continues, it will be difficult to decrease the official American presence in such countries as Japan, the Philippines and Thailand. We must nevertheless bear in mind that an excessive U.S. presence in East Asia presents a serious political liability not only in terms of our relations with the countries concerned but also prospectively in terms of weakening governments we seek to strengthen.

Green was probably the first senior American official to realize that the obsession with being everywhere and doing everything for everybody all the time was bound to backfire sooner or later, undercutting the pro-American regimes so painstakingly constructed as anchors of Asian "regional mutual security." He noted that the Philippines provided "the best example of too large an American presence and too close contact over too long a period," observing that there were 30,000 "official Americans" and 18,000 tax-free U.S.-owned vehicles in the country, that the U.S. government was "the second largest employer" in the country, operating "the largest printing press and the largest radio station. . . . Our rest camp at Camp Hay is perhaps the biggest resort area in East Asia." He added: "I leave it to others to decide whether all our bases in the Philippines are essential, but I am certain that we must reduce our presence and visibility as part of a long over-due intensive look at U.S.– Philippine relationships."

Among Green's other discoveries was that 1000 U.S. Army engineers were busy building a road in northeast Thailand, between Nakhon Phanon and Sakon Nakhon, in the general direction of the Chinese border. This fact was generally unknown to Americans at home (as were so many other American activities around the world), and Green wondered why the job could not have been done by the Thais. In Vietnam, Green cited the complaints of an American assistant province chief that "his office was being continuously inspected by U.S. officials from Saigon and was required to prepare an avalanche of reports, most of them unnecessary," and he learned about the arrival of a science adviser with twenty-nine assistants "who were to advise the South Vietnam Government's Research and Development staff"—but it turned out that the GVN had no such staff.

"There are perhaps tens of thousands of unnecessary American officials in East Asia who should be removed as quickly as possible for political as well as budgetary reasons," Green wrote. "I believe that explicit White House instructions must be issued to the Secretary of Defense to investigate this problem with a view to eliminating all unnecessary American personnel throughout the area." This included fourteen separate intelligence groups on Taiwan and 6,000 excess intelligence personnel in Japan.

In his conclusion, Green touched on a basic problem that was to haunt the Republican administration for years—the obsessive need to prove its *machismo:*

We must avoid over-reacting in certain situations as though our manhood was at stake. We must preserve selectivity in our handling of issues. Some of the ailments of this world require a major surgical operation, but there are others that respond better to therapy or even, like acne, to no handling at all. Perhaps this is why, when a blizzard closed the State Department for three days in the late 1950's, a variety of problems in the latter category were automatically resolved. . . . We often fret about other countries' lack of responsibility without realizing that we may have contributed to that state of affairs by our having taken on too many responsibilities for others. Others may best learn by their own mistakes.

The idea that the United States entertain some form of relationship with the government of China in Peking was not a bolt out of the blue produced by Nixon. Every administration since Harry Truman's played with the notion (for it seemed unreal for the United States not to have any kind of direct communication with the world's most populous nation). But Washington and Peking had always been out of phase: when one side showed some desire to open a "meaningful dialogue," the other refused. Besides, American domestic politics almost invariably rendered a relationship impossible.

In 1949, General George Marshall, then secretary of state, had favored the establishment of relations with the new regime in Peking. Dean Acheson advocated it quietly in 1950, just before the Korean war. But Acheson realized that the powerful China Lobby, supporting the exiled Chiang Kai-shek regime on Taiwan, and the Republican Party, would never stand for it. This was a shame, because Chairman Mao Tse-tung was personally interested in relations with Washington.

The Korean war and virulent McCarthyite anti-Communism at home ruled out any possibility of an *approchement* with Peking for the balance of Truman's term in office and during the first Eisenhower years. Premier Chou En-lai remembered his sense of humiliation at the Indochina Conference in Geneva in 1954, when John Foster Dulles, Eisenhower's secretary of state, refused his proffered handshake. Dulles, as a former aide remarked, was too much a prisoner of his "ethical Presbyterianism" to allow himself to "flirt with the devil." This, again, was a missed opportunity because China, after an initial period of self-imposed isolation, wanted to deal with the West. Likewise, there was no response from Washington after Chou En-lai enunciated his "Five Principles of Coexistence" at the Bandung Conference in April 1955.

But even Dulles, suspicious as he was of the Chinese, felt the need for a diplomatic contact with Peking. Documents in State Department archives record that during Eisenhower's summit meeting with Soviet leaders in Geneva later in 1955, Dulles convinced the president that the United States must seek a channel of communications with China. The gravity of the 1954 and 1955 crises over Quemoy and Matsu, the islands off the mainland coast that were Chinese Nationalist outposts, had convinced Dulles that it was necessary and "imperative" to talk with "the enemy." He warned Eisenhower that Senator William Knowland, then the Senate majority leader, would be "horrified" and mobilize public opinion against a permanent contact with Peking, but he told the president that "it had to be done." With Soviet assistance, contacts were set up, first in Geneva, then in Warsaw.

Under the Kennedy and Johnson administrations, the State Department began quiet studies of how diplomatic relations with China might possibly be established. To be sure, these studies were generated by lower-ranking officials—not on White House instructions—and they led to no practical results. Nevertheless they formed the basis for subsequent policies toward China. In 1962, for example, the department's Policy Planning Staff produced a huge two-volume study on China. Under Secretary of State George Ball and Walt Rostow, then the Planning Staff's director, immediately raised the question of the study's practical implications. A secret memorandum prepared by the department's East Asian Affairs Bureau in response fell short of recommending that the United States negotiate with Peking to establish diplomatic relations. It proposed, however, a phased series of modest unilateral actions—economic, political, and military—in order to initiate some movement in the frozen diplomatic wasteland. The idea was to send "signals" to China that the United States would welcome a change in the status quo. Washington should not expect immediate reciprocity from Peking to its "signals," the memorandum said; the experts knew that the Chinese position had hardened, for the record of the on-and-off Warsaw talks showed that they were offering absolutely no encouragement to veiled American hints about improved relations. Peking was interested neither in trade nor in cultural exchanges. (Some years earlier, it had rejected Dulles's proposal for exchanges of journalists.) Stiffly Chinese diplomats would tell the Americans that there was nothing to discuss so long as the Taiwan question remained unresolved, i.e., so long as Washington recognized Chiang Kai-shek's regime on Taiwan. At the infrequent Warsaw meetings, discussion was generally confined to restatements of political positions and arguments about such practical matters as the conditions of a handful of Americans imprisoned in China.

For a variety of reasons—including concern about political repercussions at home—the Kennedy administration failed to implement the proposals coming from the State Department. The only gesture made toward China was Kennedy's offer of American food during a 1962 famine, but the Chinese turned it down. Still, the thought of improved relations continued to intrigue State Department experts. In 1963, for example, Marshall Green, completing a long stint as consul general in Hong Kong (in this post, he was America's principal "China watcher"), wrote a lengthy dispatch discussing the ways to lessen tensions with the Chinese. But no action was taken on it.

In late 1968, a group of senior State Department officials suggested that, to begin with, the United States might review the controls on Chinese assets in this country, as a new "signal" to China, but Secretary of State Dean Rusk vetoed it. The idea was to remove the provisions of the Foreign Assets Control Regulations from overseas subsidiaries of American corporations wishing to do business with China. Since 1950, when China entered the Korean war, all forms of trade with the mainland had been forbidden, and Johnson and Rusk took the view that any relaxation of controls over Chinese trade would affect overall American policy in Asia and "it should be done by someone else."

It was Peking that took the first step in the new phase in Chinese-American relations. On November 26, 1968—less than three weeks after Richard Nixon's election—China's chargé d'affaires in Warsaw, Lei Yang, delivered a note to Walter J. Stoessel, Jr., the American ambassador, proposing that the two sides hold a formal meeting the following February 20. The note came as a complete surprise to the Johnson administration. There had been no meetings with the Chinese in Warsaw since January 8—that was the one-hundred-thirty-third session in the series that began in Geneva in 1955—and since 1965, when the Cultural Revolution erupted in China, there had been only one or two a year.

The Chinese offered no direct hint as to why they suddenly wished to resume diplomatic contacts with the United States. But on the same day that Lei Yang presented his note, the Peking radio carried a short item reporting this event and, even more interestingly, referring to the "Five Principles of Coexistence." As far as China experts in Washington could recall, this was the first time since the start of the Cultural Revolution that the Chinese had publicly invoked the "Principles." The tentative Washington conclusion was that Peking was sending out a signal that it was ready to return to the international scene. Interpretations of the Chinese gesture varied: Was Peking, concerned over the rising tensions with the

Russians and shocked by the invasion of Czechoslovakia, building a countervailing policy in the West? Or had the Chinese noted Nixon's article in *Foreign Affairs* advocating normalization of relations with China and chosen to respond to it as soon as he was elected to office? The latter speculation was correct: Chinese diplomats later confirmed that Nixon's article was read at the highest levels in Peking with deep interest.

In any event, the Chinese move was an opening gambit in an exquisitely complex and refined diplomatic chess game. Secretary of State Rusk's reaction was first that the United States should certainly accept the Chinese proposal, but that the decision now lay in the hands of the incoming Nixon people. Word was passed to Robert Murphy, the retired diplomat who was acting as Nixon's representative on foreign affairs during the transition period. Murphy immediately told Nixon at his Pierre Hotel headquarters. The president-elect forthwith instructed him to request the State Department to advise the Chinese that the new administration would welcome a Warsaw session in February, and that it would act on it as soon as Nixon was inaugurated. This was Nixon's personal decision; Kissinger was not yet aboard. He had as yet no idea what the Chinese had in mind for the Warsaw meeting.

Established at the White House, Nixon, now with Kissinger's assistance, set in motion the enormous and mostly secret effort of developing a new policy toward China. On February 5, two weeks after assuming office and acting through Kissinger, he ordered the NSC staff to prepare the administration's first major study on China, NSSM–14. This reviewed possible options for the United States, including the crucial question of whether *any* changed relationship was possible with China as long as Washington maintained support for the Nationalist regime on Taiwan. The key option offered Nixon was, in effect, to move toward a two-Chinas policy, preserving ties with Taiwan while gradually establishing a better understanding with Peking. Nixon's own assessment was that the Chinese Communists would in time accept this—provided that an acceptable formula could be devised. Naturally, he had no illusions about the difficulties —in terms both of Peking's responses and of domestic political reactions —or about the time and the patience required to achieve a breakthrough. But Kissinger, as his aides recalled later, was less sanguine.

In fact, less than two weeks after Nixon ordered the drafting of NSSM–14, the United States and China found themselves in a crisis. The crisis resulted from the defection of a Chinese diplomat in the Netherlands— a minor incident, but one that on February 16 Peking seized upon as a reason to cancel the Warsaw meeting slated for February 20. The Chinese

appeared to suspect that at worst the United States might have engineered the defection and at least was exploiting it politically. There was
no evidence of any direct American involvement, but in any case the
resumption of Chinese-American contacts was delayed by nearly a year.

Peking's rebuff did not discourage Nixon from the formulation of
policies aimed at an opening to China. White House planners ignored the
cancellation of the Warsaw session and proceeded with their work—they
were concentrating on long-range policies—as if nothing had happened.
Although the impetus for an active China policy had come from the State
Department's Asian experts during the last months of the Johnson administration, it now developed that Nixon was prepared to move faster
and more decisively than they. But he was operating in total secrecy at
the White House, and kept the State Department wholly in the dark about
what he was doing. Secretary Rogers had a general idea of Nixon's China
policies, but Marshall Green and the men at the Chinese Communist
affairs desk were told nothing substantive; they were requested only, with
growing urgency, to assemble studies on every aspect of mainland China.
Green and the others soon began to suspect that something important
was afoot, but it was a long time before they learned how advanced
Nixon's plans actually were.

China was among the topics Nixon discussed in Paris with President
de Gaulle less than two weeks after the cancellation of the Warsaw meeting. He returned more convinced than ever that the United States must
work toward a relationship with the Chinese regardless of the Warsaw
setback. For his part, de Gaulle instructed his ambassador in Peking,
Etienne M. Manac'h, quietly to convey to the Chinese the "sincere"
American interest in a new relationship. Thus the Paris conference between the two presidents marked the beginning of top-secret, high-level
diplomacy on China.

On March 28, Kissinger asked the NSC staff to produce a study on
"Trade with Communist China," a voluminous paper designated NSSM–
35. This request may well have been triggered by a memorandum Under
Secretary of State Elliot Richardson had sent Nixon earlier in March. This
was a period when Richardson, representing State, worked very closely
with Kissinger; usually the two lunched at least once a week and talked
about a wide variety of issues. Kissinger, whose own insecurities during
a good part of Nixon's first term included a fear of being upstaged by
Secretary Rogers, preferred to deal with Richardson, for whom he had
considerable respect but who was not a rival. Under this informal arrangement, Richardson proposed in a four-point memorandum (marked

Secret) the lifting of certain restrictions on trade with and the freeing of travel to China. (Rogers had authorized his deputy to send the memo to the president; his style was affable passivity.) A few days later, Nixon returned the Richardson memorandum with "affirmative comments" in his own hand. For all practical purposes, the new China policy—with specific American initiatives running parallel to Nixon's secret diplomacy —was launched in this manner.

Although NSSM–35 was being prepared by a NSC staff group (headed by John Holdridge, a West Pointer turned diplomat who was Kissinger's top expert on China), the State Department's cooperation was needed. And Richardson handled this State–White House liaison even though he, too, was unaware of Nixon's broad plans. He requested Robert W. Barnett, then acting assistant secretary of state for East Asian and Pacific affairs (Green had not yet taken office), to prepare answers to a series of questions to be discussed at the White House's Interdepartmental Group (IG) on China, which he chaired, and which included representatives from the NSC, the Pentagon, the CIA, and the Joint Chiefs of Staff. What the IG wanted from the State Department was a plan for dismantling the controls on trade with China. Were there legislative obstacles? (None, except for a ban on exports of strategic materials to countries, such as China, that were actively assisting North Vietnam.) When and how best could commerce with Peking be authorized? A special working group was set up in the State Department under Barnett's chairmanship, with representatives from the Treasury and Commerce departments, to study the political implications and international ramifications, as well as the method and timing of an announcement. Treasury and Commerce had traditionally opposed trade with Communist China, but once the White House ordered the study, they went along without a murmur.

The State Department's experts were never told what, if anything, the White House proposed to do beyond liberalizing trade regulations concerning China. But as a senior official remarked subsequently, "We sensed it was a big operation. The questions the NSC was asking carried a colossal impact. It was the first time in twenty years that we could analyze Chinese problems without bogging down in a bureaucratic miasma." Yet a basic difference of opinion immediately developed in the working group. Barnett and other Asian specialists favored the "fell swoop" approach—simply junking the whole machinery of trade controls. The other view called for an "artichoke" policy of gradually peeling off layers of trade restrictions.

The opponents of the "fell swoop" line were supported by Bryce

Harlow, Nixon's liaison man with Congress, and William Macomber, who was in charge of the State Department's liaison with the Capitol; they were both apparently backed by H. R. Haldeman, who took the view that in doing away with all the trade controls against China the global system of export controls would collapse. Haldeman and Harlow were pushing for congressional renewal of the control legislation, and they reached the curious conclusion that if Congress failed to act on it, the vote would affect the passage of the ABM bill that Nixon wanted approved. Their theory was that if trade with China were no longer restricted, Congress might raise the question why it was necessary to erect an antiballistic system against a possible Chinese attack. But apart from the substantive issue, this was a good illustration of top-level bureaucratic infighting in the White House, often pitting Haldeman and John Ehrlichman against Kissinger.

In the end, the "artichoke" approach prevailed, and the State Department presented its recommendations to the IG in mid-April, and they were incorporated into NSSM–35, which proposed to the president that the first step be permission for American travelers to spend up to one hundred dollars on goods of Chinese origin, say, in Hong Kong. Up to then, it was unlawful for Americans to buy and bring into the United States *any* goods of Chinese origin. This very minor move was the first specific positive step taken in China policy since before the Korean war, and the State Department's experts felt it had vast symbolic significance. What was not resolved in April, however, was its timing.

The next move was made by Secretary Rogers. He knew, of course, about the work of Richardson's IG experts and he shared the president's notions about global détente (a word that was not, in fact, used initially). This subject was covered in many discussions he had with Nixon—and with Nixon and Kissinger—on policies toward the Soviet Union and China. "The basic idea," Rogers said later, "was that the Communist world was no longer monolithic. And the most compelling fact was the Soviet-Chinese split and that it could not be healed. Intelligence reports on it continued to flow—and massive troop concentrations on the two sides of the border were the proof. Our view was that United States policy should recognize this fact in order to improve relations with both the Russians and the Chinese, but not . . . deviously. We had to take steps, not just toward the Soviets or the Chinese, but toward both. . . . There was no real road map. The important [question] was, what would be the responses to United States signals? And this we didn't know. . . . We had a policy, but we had to improvise the implementation."

The occasion for the first diplomatic signal to Peking was Rogers's visit in May to Pakistan, a country that had good relations with both the United States and China and thus was was the ideal go-between. This was so in the former case even though Pakistan had refused to support American policy in Vietnam, though Lyndon Johnson had suspended U.S. participation in an international consortium providing economic aid to Pakistan, and though (after the Pakistanis had set up regular airline service to China) Johnson had withdrawn a loan for the improvement of the Dacca airport. France and Romania could be helpful, but only to a degree: the French had active diplomatic relations with China, and de Gaulle was highly regarded by the Chinese, but they were a NATO ally; the Romanians, on the other hand, with excellent ties to the Chinese (they were continuously at odds with the Russians), could go only so far as a broker for Washington. But Pakistan was an Asian country with whom China had ever stronger common interests—as well as a common border. The Chinese were not disturbed by Pakistan's military arrangements with the United States through SEATO and CENTO (Southeast Asia Treaty Organization and Central Treaty Organization), both relics of Dulles's days, and they were willing to listen to the Pakistanis.

The United States was fully aware of this situation—and Rogers moved to take advantage of it. On May 24 in Lahore, Secretary Rogers discussed China at great length with President Agha Mohammad Yahya Khan and in effect inquired whether Pakistan could help the United States establish a secret diplomatic contact with the Chinese. Specifically, he asked Yahya Khan to pass on the message to Peking that the United States was serious and "forthright" in its approaches. Yahya Khan was quite receptive to Rogers's suggestions, and the secret American diplomatic offensive was launched.

China was very much on Nixon's mind as he prepared for the grand tour which in July and August was to take him across the Pacific, across the length of Southeast and South Asia, and finally to Romania on his way home. He had been listening to arguments, mostly from the State Department, that he simply could not travel through Asia without making some kind of overt gesture toward China. And State's China experts also argued that his planned visit to Romania had to be accompanied by a pro-Chinese gesture. The matter came up aboard *Air Force One* when Nixon, flying home on June 8 from his meeting with President Thieu on Midway, invited Marshall Green to join him in the plane's forward cabin (where his airborne office was located) for an hour-long discussion. Rogers and Kissinger left the cabin after a few minutes, and Green was alone with Nixon. As usual, the president was busily taking down notes on a yellow pad. Among other things, Green advanced the notion that the United States would have more leverage in Moscow if it developed better relations with Peking, and Nixon, who had been thinking for some time along these lines, indicated his concurrence.

Coincidentally or not, two days after Nixon's return from Midway, the State Department received a memorandum from Kissinger requesting still another study on American-Chinese relations. The department came up with a position paper proposing once again a relaxation of trade restrictions, and this time the administration was prepared to act. Nixon personally cleared the proposals, and then the White House busied itself with the orchestration of public gestures toward Peking.

Although the president denied it when replying to a news-conference query, the decision was to relate those gestures to Nixon's approaching Asian trip and the Romanian visit. On July 21, three days before he left for the Pacific (where his first job was to greet the American astronauts just back from the first moon mission), the State Department quietly issued its historic press release:

> The Department of State announced on July 21 that new regulations will permit American tourists and residents abroad to purchase limited quantities of goods originating in Communist China. This modification, made by the Treasury Department in its Foreign Assets Control Regulations, will reduce the inconvenience caused to American travelers desiring to purchase Chinese goods for noncommercial purposes.
>
> In this same spirit of reducing restrictions on U.S. citizens' activities abroad, the Department of State has decided to authorize automatic validations of passports for travel to Communist China for the following categories of persons: (1) Members of Congress; (2) journalists; (3) members of the teaching profession; (4) scholars with postgraduate degrees and students currently enrolled in colleges and universities; (5) scientists and medical doctors; (6) representatives of the American Red Cross.
>
> These new measures become effective on July 23. Consistent with this decision, persons in these categories receiving new passports can have the restriction on travel to Communist China automatically removed from their passports. To facilitate the processing of requests for removal of this restriction in passports which already have been issued to persons in these categories, the Department is authorizing all Foreign Service posts to validate their passports for travel to Communist China, without reference to the Department.

The next day, Nixon went out of his way to speak publicly about China. To some three thousand foreign exchange students on the White

House South Lawn, Nixon contrived to bring the Chinese, along with the Russians, into a discussion about the moon landing:

> I thought one of the, shall we say, rather sad things about that great day on Monday when man first stepped on the moon was that while most of the peoples of the world saw it on television or participated in it on television or radio, that there was approximately one-half the world that did not see it, the whole of Communist China, and the world of the Soviet Union. . . . I know the Russian people. I have visited them. They are a great people. . . . And I know the Chinese people. I have never seen them on the mainland of China, but I have seen them on Taiwan and I have seen them in Manila and I have seen them in Indonesia and I have seen them in Thailand and I have seen them in New York and I have seen them in San Francisco, and I want the time to come when the Chinese people and the Russian people and all the peoples of this world can walk together and talk together.

And during his July–August grand tour, there is no doubt that Nixon worked hard on the China front. In Lahore on August 1, a good part of his discussions with President Yahya Khan concerned American relations with China, taking up where Rogers had left off two months earlier. Yahya Khan was able to tell him that Pakistani soundings taken in Peking had brought neither discouragement nor affirmative responses, and the two men agreed that the circumstances warranted keeping open the Pakistani channel to China. Needless to say, not a word of the private Nixon–Yahya Khan discussions reached the public, and even senior State Department officials assumed that the only new China policy was the announced relaxation of trade controls and travel.

On August 2 and 3 in Bucharest, with Romania's President Ceauşescu, Nixon again made the point that the United States had a serious interest in an improved relationship with Peking, and Ceauşescu volunteered to make his views known to the Chinese. But the only public hint that the subject had come up was this phrase in Nixon's toast to Ceauşescu at the formal dinner at the Council of State palace: "Your country pursues a policy of communication and contact with all nations—you have actively sought the reduction of international tensions. My country shares those objectives." This comment was of course meant as another subtle signal to China—particularly in juxtaposition with the next sentence: "We are seeking ways of ensuring the security, progress, and independence of the nations of Asia, for, as recent history has shown, if there is no peace in Asia, there is no peace in the world." The point was not lost on the Chinese.

A week later, on August 8, Secretary Rogers was addressing himself to the Chinese problem in public in a speech before the National Press Club in Canberra, Australia. Curiously, however, this speech was not part of Nixon's overall plan, since Rogers was not informed about the president's talks with Yahya Khan and Ceauşescu, and his speech was not cleared with the White House. But after a stop in Hong Kong and a meeting with "China watchers" at the American consulate general there, Rogers decided that his long-scheduled Canberra speech would offer an excellent opportunity to send an *open* signal to the Chinese. Green was urging him to devote the entire speech to China, but the secretary concluded that this would be premature. Still, Rogers said more in Canberra than had yet been said by any senior member of the Nixon administration, and although it went unnoticed in the press, the Chinese listened to it carefully:

> We recognize, of course, that the Republic of China on Taiwan and Communist China on the mainland are facts of life. We know, too, that mainland China will eventually play an important role in Asian and Pacific affairs—but certainly not as long as its leaders continue to have such an introspective view of the world. . . . Public expressions of attitude toward the United States from Communist China since the inauguration of our administration in Washington certainly have been strident. They pretend to feel they are encircled by hostile forces. . . . Communist China obviously has long been too isolated from world affairs. This is one reason why we have been seeking to open up channels of communication. Just a few days ago, we liberalized our policies toward purchase of their goods by American travelers and toward validating passports for travel to China. Our purpose was to remove irritants in our relations and to help remind people on mainland China of our historic friendship for them. Previously, we had suggested other steps such as an exchange of persons and selected trade in such goods as food and pharmaceuticals. . . . We were prepared to offer specific suggestions on an agreement for more normal relations when the Chinese canceled the scheduled resumption of the ambassadorial talks in Warsaw last February. None of our initiatives has met with a positive response. Apparently the present leaders in Peking believe that it serves their purposes to maintain a posture of hostility toward the United States. They seem unprepared for any accommodation. Their central position is that they will discuss nothing with us unless we first abandon support of our ally, the Republic of China. This we do not propose to do. We nonetheless look forward to a time when we can enter into a useful dialogue and to a reduction of tensions. We would welcome a renewal of the talks with Communist China. We shall soon be making another approach to see if a dialogue

with Peking can be resumed . . . in Warsaw or at any other mutually acceptable site. . . .

In Washington, the administration was trying to sell the new China policy to another constituency: the American armed forces. The spokesman was Under Secretary of State Richardson and his audience was the National War College. Richardson undertook to convince his military listeners that the United States should steer a "middle course" in Asia between the Soviet Union and China rather than become associated with either. The policy, he said, would be "one of making clear to each, the Soviet Union and China, that we intend to pursue—and in the case of China over time progressively to develop—normal relations of the kind that ordinarily exist between countries. . . . This in turn helps to make clear why it was important to make known the fact that we were not about to embark upon a process of carving up the world between ourselves and the Soviet Union either as a condition to or as a by-product of entering into strategic arms limitation arrangements."

Addressing a specialized private audience has the advantage of enabling the speaker to be quite candid in a way that would be impossible in a public forum (the text of his speech was marked Confidential and declassified only many years later), and Richardson made full use of that advantage:

> For the long run in Southeast Asia one can visualize a triangular relationship between the Soviet Union, Communist China, and the United States in which there is in effect a standoff between us. Each is concerned that neither of the others acquires the capability of dominating the area. . . . We face, in the case of China and the Soviet Union, countries both exceedingly touchy, if not paranoid, with respect to any approach by the United States toward the other. Each at the very moment is accusing us of collusion or contemplated collusion with the other. Although the Soviet Union has been relatively quiet about it, there is no question that they were very sensitive toward the President's visit to Bucharest, not alone because of Bucharest's place among the Warsaw Pact countries but perhaps even more because of Rumania's refusal to participate in any joint Communist Party condemnation of China. . . . We have to avoid the impression on the part of the Soviet Union that we are seeking to exploit their tension with China to our own direct short-range advantage. Similarly, if we are ever to achieve more normal relations with China, we must succeed in conveying to China that the steps we take toward the resolution of conflict between us—that is, the USSR and us—are not a part of an attempt to encircle and to contain China. . . . We are about to embark

on a careful balancing process—a process which seems to me an inescapable course for the indefinite future.

Nixon was in fact impatient to move ahead. On September 9, he and Kissinger conferred at the White House with Ambassador Stoessel, who was about to return to his post in Poland. Nixon quickly brushed aside Polish-American problems and asked the ambassador to try to reestablish contacts with the Chinese. It would, of course, have to be done most secretly, since he insisted that the United States could not let it be known that it sought *direct* contacts with the Chinese. Nixon thought that the feelers put out through the Pakistanis, the Romanians, and the French were not working as rapidly as he wished. In short, Stoessel was to catch the Chinese in Warsaw—in the most literal sense.

Stoessel's Warsaw assignment turned into a frantic chase. He could not approach the Chinese overtly; he had to contrive an "accidental" social encounter with the elusive Chinese chargé d'affaires, Lei Yang, that could lead to a seemingly innocent party chat and then, one would hope, a secret business meeting. Stoessel, a dignified white-haired man, overnight became Warsaw's leading social butterfly, accepting every diplomatic invitation that came his way. But for nearly two months, Stoessel could not conveniently approach the Chinese at any of the receptions he attended. (In November, he almost grabbed Lei at the Swedish embassy, but the party was such a mob scene that he had to give up.) Nixon, immensely anxious about Stoessel's activities, had Kissinger send him three cables (again ignoring the State Department) urging that the ambassador come up with results. Kissinger claimed later that Stoessel was paying no attention to these White House communications, since he did not reply to them, but the truth was that he still had nothing to report.

Finally, Stoessel's break came in early December. At a fashion show sponsored by the Yugoslav embassy and given at the nightclub in Warsaw's huge Palace of Culture—an event that the American ambassador would probably ordinarily have ignored—Stoessel and his wife were sitting at a table near the dance floor in the company of several Polish officials. Suddenly one of the ambassador's aides spotted Lei Yang and his interpreter at a nearby table. At that moment, the orchestra began to play, and a Polish model dressed as a bride in a see-through dress walked onto the dance floor. Whether for puritanical or other reasons, the Chinese rose to leave. Stoessel jumped up from his table and followed them to the door, where they stopped to bid good-bye to the Yugoslav ambassador. As Stoessel exited, the Yugoslav inquired whether he, too, were leaving; no, no, Stoessel reassured him, he'd be right back.

The Chinese marched toward the cloakroom and up a flight of stairs toward the street exit with Stoessel in hot pursuit. On the front steps, Stoessel grabbed the Chinese interpreter by the coat, introduced himself, and said he would like to speak with the chargé. But the Chinese diplomat was already in his limousine, and the interpreter told Stoessel that a meeting was impossible at that point. Speaking urgently in Polish, Stoessel told him that he had recently returned from Washington with instructions to establish a contact with the Chinese embassy. Politely, the interpreter promised Stoessel to relay the message to Lei Yang. The Chinese limousine departed, and Stoessel dispiritedly returned to his nightclub table.

Two days later, the American embassy received a telephone call from a Chinese official who had previously acted as the liaison man in arranging Chinese-American meetings. He understood, he said, that the American ambassador wished to see the Chinese chargé d'affaires, who would be pleased to receive him. Lei Yang had evidently reported to Peking on the nightclub scene and had received instructions in an amazingly short time. Stoessel called Washington for *his* instructions and was authorized by the State Department to accept the invitation to visit the Chinese embassy. (The invitation in itself was something of a breakthrough. All past Chinese-American meetings were held at a Polish government office with the full knowledge of the Poles—and, therefore, the Russians. But this time the Chinese seemed to want the secrecy and security their own premises could offer. Besides, Stoessel theorized, they might have felt it more correct to have the American ambassador come to them.)

On December 12, Stoessel arrived at the Chinese embassy; the American flag, usually flown by his diplomatic limousine, was not in evidence. Lei Yang received him at his residence, in the back of the walled-in embassy compound. Everything was very polite—tea, cookies, and cigarettes were offered—but the conversation was extremely difficult. For one thing, Stoessel spoke in English; his aide, Thomas W. Simons, Jr., translated into Polish; and the Chinese interpreter then translated into Chinese for Lei Yang. The reverse occurred when Lei responded in Chinese. Essentially, Stoessel simply proposed that formal talks be resumed between the two countries and called his host's attention to recent "positive" American statements on relations with China. Lei seemed attentive and interested, but he was not very responsive. After an hour, he told Stoessel that he would report to Peking and await new instructions.

A week later, the Chinese liaison officer telephoned to say that Lei

Yang would like to call on Stoessel. Stoessel and Simons received him in a small room on the second floor of the chancery, rather than at the ambassador's private office, in order to avoid calling attention to the meeting. (The embassy had Polish employees.) There had been some discussion among the Americans whether tea or coffee would be served, but the final decision was for coffee. This time Lei was prepared for a substantive conversation. Stoessel outlined to him the American proposal for a long-range resumption of contacts, with meetings to be held alternately at the Chinese and American embassies. Lei said he was authorized in principle to accept the proposal, and a date was set for the first formal session: January 20, 1970, at the Chinese embassy. The arrangements were confirmed by liaison officers several days later, but they were kept secret until the meeting actually took place.

Chapter 6

By the middle of 1969, halfway through his first year as president, Nixon had engaged the United States in a series of major foreign-policy initiatives around the world. American policy was more active, searching, intellectually aggressive, and diversified than at any time since the end of World War II. Truman (with Dean Acheson's conceptual guidance) had concentrated on "containment" of what was perceived as a Soviet expansionist threat: he presided over the reconstruction of Western Europe, devised the Truman Doctrine to protect Greece and Turkey from Communism, created the North Atlantic Treaty Organization, and involved the United States in Korea as part of "containment." Eisenhower, influenced by Dulles's hard-nosed and sternly moralistic view of the world, negotiated the end of the Korean war, but his eight-year term saw essentially unrevised cold war politics, despite two summit meetings with the Russians. Kennedy (who made his own foreign policy) began to break out of the cold war mentality—he negotiated, for example, the nuclear-test–ban treaty—but, at the same time, he kept alive the idea of "containment" and engaged the United States in new (and unnecessary) foreign commitments. Johnson had been obsessed and wholly preoccupied with Vietnam although he, too, sought accommodation with the Russians. But Nixon had new policies going everywhere. Détente with the Soviet Union and the opening to China were in the works. Troops were being withdrawn from Vietnam, albeit slowly (a year earlier Johnson had been asked by his commanders to *add* 200,000 men to the 500,000 already there), and secret negotiations with North Vietnam were being considered. The United States and the Soviet Union were busily (if not successfully) searching for a solution to the Middle East conflict. A negotiating position was being prepared for the SALT talks with the Russians. Now Nixon began groping for something resembling a philosophical definition of his overall policies—and almost by accident, the "Nixon Doctrine" was born in the middle of the Pacific on a quiet summer evening.

Unlike the other important foreign-policy documents of the Nixon era, the doctrine was neither researched by the NSC staff nor even put down on paper in a coherent way. Instead, it gradually emerged at a background briefing for newsmen accompanying the president on his trip to Asia. Close presidential aides such as Press Secretary Ziegler said later that Nixon had not intended beforehand to announce so casually anything as formidable as a new foreign-policy doctrine. The White House had promised a "backgrounder" with Nixon at the outset of the trip, and only after it was arranged did Nixon, Kissinger, and other White House people decide to call it the "Nixon Doctrine" and to make it into the rhetorical basis of Nixonian foreign policy. But only some time afterward did the White House make public the text of the Guam briefing. (At the time it was held, newsmen were allowed to attribute the comments to Nixon, but without direct quotation.)

Nixon had gone to Agana, Guam, on July 25 after spending a day aboard the aircraft carrier *Hornet* near the astronauts' splashdown site in the Pacific. He had wanted personally to congratulate Neil A. Armstrong, the mission commander, and Colonel Edwin E. Aldrin, Jr., on their return to earth. Indeed, his Asian trip had been geared from the beginning to coincide with the moon mission, for, as William Safire, then a Nixon speech-writer, recounts in his book *Before the Fall,* an enormous effort had been undertaken to extract maximum public-relations mileage from the planned Armstrong-Aldrin moon walk.

That evening, Nixon met with newsmen at the Top o' the Mar Officers' Club. This is what, in his rambling fashion, he said to them:

The United States is going to be facing, we hope before too long— no one can say how long, but before too long—a major decision: what will be its role in Asia and in the Pacific after the end of the war in Vietnam? We will be facing that decision, but also the Asian nations will be wondering about what that decision is. . . . This is a decision that will have to be made, of course, as the war comes to an end. But the time to develop the thinking which will go into that decision is now. I think that one of the weaknesses in American foreign policy is that too often we react rather precipitately to events as they occur. We fail to have the perspective and the long-range view which is essential for a policy that will be viable.

As I see it, even though the war in Vietnam has been, as we all know, a terribly frustrating one, and, as a result of that frustration, even though there would be a tendency for many Americans to say, "After we are through with that, let's not become involved in Asia," I am convinced that the way to avoid becoming involved in another war in

Asia is for the United States to continue to play a significant role.

I think the way that we could become involved would be to attempt withdrawal, because, whether we like it or not, geography makes us a Pacific power. . . . We, I think, realize that if we are thinking down the road, down the long road—not just four years, five years, but ten, fifteen, or twenty—that if we are going to have peace in the world, that potentially the greatest threat to that peace will be in the Pacific. . . .

So, what I am trying to suggest is this: as we look at Asia, it poses, in my view, over the long haul, looking down to the end of the century, the greatest threat to the peace of the world, and, for that reason the United States should continue to play a significant role. It also poses, it seems to me, the greatest hope for progress in the world—progress in the world because of the ability, the resources, the ability of the people, the resources physically that are available in this part of the world. And for these reasons, I think we need policies that will see that we play a part and a part that is appropriate to the conditions that we will find.

Now, one other point I would make very briefly is that in terms of this situation as far as the role we should play, we must recognize that there are two great, new factors. . . . A very great growth of nationalism, nationalism even in the Philippines vis-à-vis the United States, as well as other countries in the world. And, also, at the same time that national pride is becoming a major factor, regional pride is becoming a major factor.

The second factor is one that is going to, I believe, have a major impact on the future of Asia, and it is something that we must take into account. Asians will say in every country that we visit that they do not want to be dictated to from the outside, Asia for the Asians. And that is what we want, and that is the role we should play. We should assist, but we should not dictate.

At this time, the political and economic plans that they are gradually developing are very hopeful. We will give assistance to those plans. We, of course, will keep the treaty commitments that we have. But as far as our role is concerned, we must avoid that kind of policy that will make countries in Asia so dependent upon us that we are dragged into conflicts such as the one that we have in Vietnam.

In response to questions, Nixon expanded on his philosophy:

I believe that the time has come when the United States, in our relations with all of our Asian friends, be quite emphatic on two points: one, that we will keep our treaty commitments, our treaty commitments, for example, with Thailand under SEATO; but, two, that as far as the problems of internal security are concerned, as far as the problems of military defense, except for the threat of a major power involving nuclear weapons, that the United States is going to encourage and has a right to expect that this problem will be increasingly handled by, and the responsibility for it taken by, the Asian nations themselves. . . . If the United States just continues down the road of responding to requests for assistance, of assuming the primary responsibility for defending these countries when they have internal problems or external problems, they are never going to take care of themselves.

I should add to that, too, that when we talk about collective security for Asia, I realize that at this time that looks like a weak reed. It actually is. But looking down the road—I am speaking now of five years from now, ten years from now—I think collective security, insofar as it deals with internal threats to any one of the countries, or insofar as it deals with a threat other than that posed by a nuclear power, I believe that this is an objective which free Asian nations, independent Asian nations can seek and which the United States should support. . . .

One of the reasons for this trip is to leave no doubt in the minds of non-Communist Asia that the United States is committed to a policy in the Pacific—a policy not of intervention but one which certainly rules out withdrawal—and regardless of what happens in Vietnam that we intend to continue to play a role in Asia to the extent that Asian nations, bilaterally and collectively, desire us to play a role. . . .

Each of these countries . . . poses an entirely different question. I would simply say we are going to handle each country on a case-by-case basis, but attempting to avoid that creeping involvement which eventually simply submerges you. . . . The military involvement, the military assistance, military aid programs and the rest, and particularly the commitment of military personnel—that type of program would recede. However, as far as economic programs are concerned, and particularly those of a multilateral character . . . I would say that the level of U.S. activity would be adequate to meet the challenges as it develops, because it is very much in our interest in terms of economic assistance, economic assistance through loans and other programs, to help build the economies of free Asia. . . .

Certainly the objective of any American administration would be to avoid another war like Vietnam any place in the world. . . . I realize it is very easy to say that. I will be quite candid when I admit that to develop the policies to avoid that is taking an enormous amount of my time and those of my associates. But what we can do is to learn from the mistakes of the past. I believe that we have, if we examine what happened in Vietnam—how we became so deeply involved—that we have a good chance of avoiding that kind of involvement in the future.

Taken at face value, the Nixon Doctrine as enunciated on Guam appeared to mean that the United States would maintain its nuclear umbrella over all friendly Asian countries, including Japan, in the event of a Soviet or Chinese nuclear attack (or threat of one), but that in the cases of conventional wars waged by Communist states or of internal insurgency, each nation would have to defend itself—albeit with equipment provided by the United States. But the crucial point was that this new policy of noninvolvement would become effective *only when the Vietnam war ended.* The implication was that, in the meantime, the United States would continue to do what it had been doing all along: remain deeply involved in the affairs of at least a half-dozen Asian countries and, in effect, dictate their policies—all in the name of what Nixon called "collective security."

Besides, as the president pointed out, the United States proposed to honor all its standing treaty commitments: to go to the active defense of Thailand under the SEATO pact; the defense of Japan, South Korea, the Philippines, and Taiwan under bilateral mutual-security treaties; and the defense of Australia and New Zealand under their ANZUS treaty with the United States. Moreover, in Nixon's words, the United States was a Pacific power and was determined to go on playing a major role in Asia. We were to help Asians help themselves. Even as Nixon talked of the new forces of nationalism and the Asians' desire to run their own lives, he seemed to be singularly insensitive to them, for the immediate reality was that so long as the Indochina conflict dragged on, the United States would remain in command.

A high State Department official, appalled at what the United States had been doing in Indochina, put it this way several years later: "We have for a long time let the tail wag the dog. The military guys go out there, get their vested interests, and then start defending them. We justify it, then [we] build the military machine further and further—and so on. Really, the relationship with these countries should be a matter of just a political and diplomatic relationship—and not getting the hell in there and doing it all for them. But we can't bring outselves to do it this way." Yet, the same diplomat thought, the Nixon Doctrine had merit so long as it was a "recognition that other nations are both more capable and desirous of running their own affairs in their own manner, seeking out their own destiny," and that the Americans want "to play less of a role and carry less of the burden. . . . The basic force going in Asia is the force of nationalism, and the object of a successful policy is to touch the quick of that nationalism, but doing it through indirection. . . . You do yourself a disservice, really, if you go there and try to take over."

On Nixon's grand tour, his message to his hosts was essentially unvarying, but there was room for nuances appropriate to each country.

In Manila, Nixon told President Ferdinand Marcos that "now we reach a new period—a period in which there will continue to be assistance and cooperation, particularly from the United States of America as a Pacific power . . . and in which there will continue to be . . . a military presence as far as the United States is concerned." The Philippines, of course, was the country where the United States maintained its principal naval and air bases in Southeast Asia, and it was also a country facing pro-Communist insurgency as well as a dangerous religious split. Much Filipino nationalist sentiment was pure anti-Americanism, but Marcos, soon to become a full-fledged dictator, was a friend of the United States—and a friend of Nixon's.

In Djakarta, Nixon, remarking that President Suharto had overthrown the leftist Sukarno regime some years earlier, thought that "what happens here, the future of the 115 million people of Indonesia, will have an enormous effect on the future of peace in the Pacific and, therefore, on peace in the world." Suharto's Indonesia was a model for Southeast Asia, and Nixon commended him for "that hard, daily drudgery of building again after the revolution has necessarily destroyed some of the institutions of the past." (He did not have to repeat that among the reasons he often cited for the continued American involvement in Indochina was the fear that a Communist victory there would lead to a new leftist take-over in Indonesia.)

In Bangkok, the president told King Bhumibol Adulyadej, a figurehead monarch, and Prime Minister Thanom Kittikachorn that "Thailand has a special interest in the strategy for achieving a durable peace—that is, one which guarantees to the people of South Vietnam the right to determine their own future without outside coercion." Thailand, of course, had sent troops to Vietnam, as it had to Korea almost two decades earlier, and now it served as a principal base area for the U.S. Air Force in Indochina. Thus, as Nixon told his hosts, "The Thai contribution to the struggle . . . has been of great significance." But Thailand also faced direct dangers from across the Chinese border, and it was fighting insurgency along its northern and southern frontiers. Hence Nixon was reassuring: "We are bound by the [SEATO] treaty. . . . As far as Thailand and the United States are concerned, a treaty means far more, because we share common ideals; because what we want for Asia and the world is the right of freedom which Thailand enjoys for all peoples here."

Even in Thailand, Nixon felt compelled to demonstrate that he was a "regular guy," a president who shared the interests of the average American. Sports, inevitably and bizarrely, was the theme. In a standard Foreign Service pep talk to American embassy employees in Bangkok, Nixon remarked, "I particularly feel at home [at the embassy] when I find here that somebody read that I had received in the White House the other day an insignia from the commissioner of baseball indicating that I was the Number 1 baseball fan. So here is the cap for it. . . . [He produced the cap.] It is certain our Americans can leave the United States, but you can never take baseball out of an American boy. I see a great number of them over there. I only wish that I had the time to see one of your games."

Nixon took a quick side trip to Saigon—he was back in the Thai capital in time for a dinner given by Prime Minister Kittikachorn—in order to spend several hours conferring with President Thieu, and then visit (in a helicopter ride to Di An, a town thirteen miles north of Saigon) the officers and men of the Second Brigade of the First Infantry Division. His remarks to the troops were not the kind of thing the president usually said in Washington or at a formal diplomatic forum:

> Certainly this is the most difficult war any army of the United States of America has fought. Because this is the first time in our history when we have had a lack of understanding of why we are here, what the war is all about, *where we have had real division at home.* . . . I just visited three countries in Asia, and in each of those countries I can tell you they are watching Vietnam. What happens in Vietnam, how this war is ended, may well determine what happens to peace and freedom in all of Asia. . . . *If* we can bring this war to an end, and an early end, and that is our goal, and *if* that war is ended in a way that the people of South Vietnam have a right to choose their own way, and that is all we are asking—*if* we do that, then the chance for all of the people of Asia to have a chance to have a peace in Asia, the possibility that we can discourage aggression and reduce the chances of more wars in the future—that is what we want to accomplish [italics added].

In Saigon, however, the president was back to the official diplomatic line. Nixon said the administration had reviewed the situation since he and Thieu had conferred on Midway seven weeks earlier: "The steady progress in pacification, involving the people in greater political participation and in decisions about their future; the elections of village and hamlet officials . . . ; the improving performance of the Vietnamese armed forces . . . and their determination to take over an increasing share of the burden of the conflict; the plans for a revolutionary land-reform program; and most importantly the moves we together have made toward peace." But did Nixon and his advisers really believe that there had been progress in pacification, that the village elections were more than a self-serving political farce staged by Thieu to please Washington, that the South Vietnamese armed forces were truly capable of improved performance, and that the land reform, likewise engineered by Americans, would cause Viet Cong militancy to melt away? And were American officials in Saigon, including Ambassador Bunker and General Abrams, misleading Washington as to the true state of affairs in South Vietnam, or were they, in turn, led astray by Thieu and his ministers and generals, who needed to impress Nixon?

In the Saigon statement, Nixon also recapitulated the most recent peace moves, including his eight-point proposal of May 14 and Thieu's recent offer on July 20 to negotiate directly with North Vietnam on the subject of having the two nations reunified on the basis of free and internationally supervised elections. The problem, of course, was that Hanoi had no intention of negotiating with Thieu on any subject. Still, Nixon was totally committed to Thieu, and United States policy in Vietnam presumed that he was the only viable leader. Besides, Nixon believed that sooner or later Hanoi would do business with Washington.

The concluding paragraph of Nixon's statement contained a hint, little understood at the time, that negotiations with Hanoi would soon enter a new phase: "It is now time for the other side to sit down with us and talk seriously about ways to stop the killing, to put an end to this tragic war, which has brought so great destruction to friend and foe alike. We have put forward constructive proposals to bring an end to the conflict. We are ready to talk with the other side about their proposals." What Nixon did not say was that arrangements had already been made by Henry Kissinger, who was traveling with him, to meet secretly with the North Vietnamese in Paris at the end of the presidential grand tour. It is not clear whether Nixon told Thieu about this during their Saigon conference. The pattern of Nixonian diplomacy was to hide the cards from everybody: allies and adversaries alike—to say nothing of the public.

Following his day in Vietnam and the dinner in Thailand, Nixon flew to India on July 31. There he faced a different problem. Despite ringing declamations by every American president about India's being the biggest democracy in the world, United States–India relations were never satisfactory—and more often than not were irksome. Washington resented India's neutralism, or "nonalignment," along with her leaders' penchant for moralizing about other countries' foreign policies, notably America's. The Indians, on the other hand, uncomfortable because they were recipients of massive—sorely needed—aid from the United States, and having fought inconclusive wars with China in 1962 and Pakistan in 1965—two nations that they regarded as their natural enemies—were touchy and sensitive about their own policies. They distrusted the United States (although they received American arms during the China war) and, increasingly, shifted their friendship toward the Soviet Union. (The American arms embargo against India and Pakistan was a factor here.)

Nixon's fence mending was carried out in private talks with Prime Minister Indira Gandhi (with whose father, Prime Minister Jawaharlal Nehru, he had dealt as vice president sixteen years earlier) and Acting President Mohammed Hidayatullah, as well as in a series of public statements. He noted that he was keenly aware that "the people of this great nation desire to choose their own way to progress" and "I respect that. . . . We want to work with you to the extent that you feel we can and should, for the goals that you believe are best for India, and not for the goals that we may think are best for India." But these sentiments were not wholly successful: in a dinner toast, Acting President Hidayatullah remarked that "there are tensions, both national and international, which arise from basic factors—economic, social, and political." The problems, he told Nixon, "are not amenable to simple explanations of power politics and power vacuum. . . . A military solution cannot remove the main causes of weakness and tension." He was not, it was clear, letting Nixon off the Vietnam hook.

By the time Nixon reached Lahore, in contrast, Pakistani-American relations were improving after the tensions during the Johnson administration. Since Secretary Rogers's visit in May, the opinion was emerging that Pakistan might be a more reliable partner in South Asia than India. (This was never said publicly, but it was consistent with Nixon's appreciation of the Asian situation.) Nixon had to tell Yahya Khan that for considerations of South Asian stability, the United States was not ready to lift the arms embargo imposed against India and Pakistan during their 1965 war, but the Pakistani president, who had a keen sense of priorities, did not make it a major issue. Instead, to demonstrate his interest in close relations with the United States, he awarded Nixon the Nishan-e-Pakistan, the country's highest civilian medal, and at their private session was highly receptive to Nixon's suggestions that Pakistan serve as a secret diplomatic intermediary between China and the United States. The two presidents went into no details, but from then on, the State Department, including Secretary Rogers, was excluded from the private exchanges set up via Pakistan with Peking; the White House dealt directly with Yahya Khan, who, in turn, communicated with the Chinese through his embassy in Peking.

Lahore was Nixon's last Asian stop, and there remained only Romania, on the way home. In Bucharest, hundreds of thousands of Romanians lined the highway leading from the new airport (inaugurated with Nixon's arrival direct from Pakistan aboard *Air Force One*) and the city's broad avenues in the early afternoon of August 2, a Saturday, to see and cheer the visitor—easily the most enthusiastic reception Nixon ever enjoyed as president (and reminiscent of his vice-presidential visit to Warsaw in 1956). But in its simplest terms, it was a demonstration of pro-American and anti-Soviet sentiment—and everybody knew it.

And indeed, as far as Ceauşescu was concerned, the invitation to Nixon was another act demonstrating his independence from Moscow in foreign affairs even though at home he maintained a model Communist dictatorship. The Romanians never experienced the political relaxation that characterized Yugoslavia under Tito and certainly nothing resembling the freedom-under-Communism practiced in Czechoslovakia during 1968. This may have been one reason the Russians had tolerated Ceauşescu for so long. Still, inviting an American president was a gamble, and the evening before Nixon's arrival, Foreign Minister Corneliu Manescu confided to friends over glasses of chilled white wine that he was keeping his fingers crossed that "all goes well tomorrow."

It did. Nixon and Ceauşescu, after stating publicly the obvious about their politics, spent the afternoon conferring, Vietnam and China being the principal topics, along with various bilateral questions mainly concerning trade. (Romania was eager to be granted most-favored-nation tariff treatment by the United States so that her exports could be competitive on the American market. Among Communist nations, only Poland and Yugoslavia enjoyed this treatment; it was routinely given to most other countries.) While the president inquired how best the United States could move toward a relationship with Peking, he did not specifically invite Romania to mediate. Still, Ceauşescu told Nixon that he would be pleased to relay the general American sentiment to Peking.

In the evening, President and Mrs. Nixon attended a glittering reception and dinner at the Council of State palace. For nearly an hour, the Nixons, the Ceauşescus, and their interpreters moved slowly through the huge crowded reception room, greeting cabinet ministers, high Communist Party functionaries, generals and admirals, Eastern Orthodox priests, and foreign diplomats. (The Soviet ambassador was among these last.) In an after-dinner toast, Ceauşescu told Nixon that the American landing on the moon "was a source of joy for us" (Romania and Yugoslavia were the only Communist countries to afford their citizens live television coverage of the moon mission, through a hookup with the Eurovision network) and then proceeded to outline his foreign policy: "Being a Socialist country, Romania places in the center of her foreign policy the many-sided cooperation with the Socialist countries, to which she is bound by a common social system. At the same time, she steadily develops fruitful relations in all the fields with the other countries in the world. . . . In our view, at the present the condition *sine qua non* of peace is to establish in the relations between all states the principles of independence and national sovereignty, to liquidate once and for all the policy of domination and interference in the internal affairs of others." Ceauşescu's words could be read as being addressed both to the United States and to the Soviet Union; he was content to let his audience draw its own conclusions.

In his reply, Nixon likewise accentuated the need for contacts among *all* nations regardless of systems and philosophies. This was the central message he brought to Bucharest, and he wanted it to be heard throughout Eastern Europe as well as in Peking. Increasingly, he was using the occasion of after-dinner toasts to reveal significant bits of new policy. Such toasts are replete with platitudes, but nonetheless diplomats and newsmen began paying attention to Nixon's. In Bucharest, of course, he said all the right things about international peace, but then, he went on: "Your country pursues a policy of communication and contact with all nations—you have actively sought the reduction of international tensions. My country shares those objectives. . . . As I told you today in our meetings, we seek normal relations with all countries, regardless of their domestic systems. We stand ready to reciprocate the efforts of any country that seeks normal relations with us. We are flexible about the methods by which peace is to be sought and built. We see value neither in the exchange of polemics nor in false euphoria. We seek the substance of détente, not its mere atmosphere."

(The president also had a special message for the Russians, who were still holding back on starting the SALT negotiations: "We are prepared to negotiate seriously on the crucial and complex problem of strategic arms, and will consider any arrangement that equitably protects the security of all concerned while bringing the qualitative and quantitative growth of arsenals under control.")

The Nixons' second day in Bucharest was largely devoted to the lighter side of diplomacy, and the president went along with Ceauşescu's eagerness to give his American guest the maximum of public exposure. In the morning, the Nixons visited a housing project and a modern suburban supermarket, where they were met by smiling and applauding Sunday crowds. Local authorities had obviously spread the word, even though the tour was not listed on the official schedule. At the huge supermarket, the Nixons darted from fish counters to vegetable stands, with the Ceauşescus barely keeping up. At one stand, Nixon picked up a lemon, looked at it admiringly, and commented that he was reminded of his boyhood, when he had got up at dawn to help out at his father's grocery in Whittier, California. This seemed to please the crowd as Nixon's words were translated into Romanian and repeated over and over by supermarket employees and shoppers. He was carrying on in the best campaign tradition.

Nixon kept it up at the luncheon he gave for the Ceauşescus at the lakeside government guest house where he was staying. Having arranged to have on hand a U.S. Air Force dance combo from the headquarters in Wiesbaden, West Germany, to play at the lunch, Nixon informed his guests that *everything,* in fact, was American: the place cards, the menus, and the matches; the beef from Kansas City, the peas from California, the tomatoes from Florida, and the hearts of palm from Hawaii. The Romanians seemed delighted: Mrs. Ceauşescu requested the combo to play a selection from *My Fair Lady,* and Nixon made a point of mentioning it in his toast.

Landing that evening at Andrews Air Force Base, outside of Washington, Nixon still had Romania on his mind. The reception in Bucharest, he said, "was the most moving experience that I have had in traveling to over sixty countries in the world. . . . In this country in which we have an entirely different political philosophy from our own, people were out by the hundreds of thousands, not ordered by their government, but cheering and shouting—not against anybody—but showing their affection and friendship for the people of the United States. . . . This means to me one simple thing: that deep differences in political philosophy cannot permanently divide the peoples of the world. . . . It means that we can live in peace in the world, live in peace with other nations who may have different political philosophies."

The grand tour, it appeared, had been an even greater success than the president had anticipated. But now he was back to the harsh realities of policy-making—and most specifically to the reality of Vietnam.

Actually, Vietnam was very much on Nixon's mind as he streaked across Asia and Europe. Eight days before his departure, the president had taken the first step to set secret negotiations with North Vietnam in motion, a diplomatic exercise in frustration that was to be conducted, on and off, for nearly two and a half years. On July 15, he signed a conciliatory three-paragraph secret letter to President Ho Chi Minh (addressing him as president of the Democratic Republic of Vietnam, a form not habitually used in those days by the American government in relation to the Hanoi regime) urging new efforts toward ending the war.

The idea of a direct appeal to Ho Chi Minh had originated with Kissinger, who also thought that it would be useful to establish a private and unpublicized contact with the North Vietnamese in Paris (as Averell Harriman had done in 1968 to negotiate the bombing pause), parallel with the weekly semipublic sessions involving the United States, North Vietnam, South Vietnam, and the National Liberation Front, which had resumed on January 25.

Actually, Ambassador Lodge held eleven private and unpublicized meetings, beginning in March, with Xuan Thuy, his North Vietnamese counterpart. But these sessions, with Lodge and Xuan Thuy operating on strict instructions, were basically unproductive, and offered no room for what Kissinger envisaged as creative diplomacy; besides, Kissinger had a rather low regard for Lodge's diplomatic acumen. He had privately decided by late spring that to be profitable negotiations had to be conducted on the highest possible level and in the greatest possible secrecy. He convinced Nixon that he, Kissinger, should take over the secret negotiations. Given Kissinger's preoccupation with secrecy and his fear of State Department leaks, it is not surprising that he also found it necessary to bypass Lodge in making the approach to the North Vietnamese. Lodge, therefore, was not asked to arrange for Kissinger's personal entrée into Vietnam diplomacy, nor was he informed of Nixon's letter to Ho. (He learned of the presidential correspondence only in November, when Nixon made it public.)

The chosen channel for the secret communication with Hanoi was Jean Sainteny, a retired French diplomat and banker with close personal ties to President Ho. Kissinger and Sainteny had known each other "for a long time," as the Frenchman later remarked, and when he visited Washington in February, Kissinger took him over to the White House for a long secret meeting with Nixon. The three men discussed in depth the possibility of new diplomatic initiatives to break the Vietnam deadlock, but nothing was decided at that time. When Sainteny returned to Washington in the early part of July, he met several times more with Kissinger. Now that Nixon had proposed his eight-point peace plan and announced the first withdrawal of American troops from Vietnam, Kissinger and Sainteny agreed, the time was ripe for an approach to Ho. Sainteny had informally sounded out Xuan Thuy in Paris, and he felt encouraged by the response he elicited, so Kissinger took Sainteny to see Nixon again.

This time it was decided that Sainteny would deliver to Xuan Thuy, for transmittal to Hanoi, an oral message and a letter from Nixon to Ho:

Dear Mr. President:

I realize that it is difficult to communicate meaningfully across the gulf of four years of war. But precisely because of this gulf, I wanted to take this opportunity to reaffirm in all solemnity my desire to work for a just peace. I deeply believe that the war in Vietnam has gone on too long and delay in bringing it to an end can benefit no one—least of all the people of Vietnam. My speech on May 14 laid out a proposal which I believe is fair to all parties. Other proposals have been made which attempt to give the people of South Vietnam an opportunity to choose their own future. These proposals take into account the reasonable conditions of all sides. But we stand ready to discuss other programs as well, specifically the 10-point program of the NLF.

As I have said repeatedly, there is nothing to be gained by waiting. Delay can only increase the dangers and multiply the suffering.

The time has come to move forward at the conference table toward an early resolution of this tragic war. You will find us forthcoming and open-minded in a common effort to bring the blessings of peace to the brave people of Vietnam. Let history record that at this critical juncture, both sides turned their face toward peace rather than toward conflict and war.

Sincerely,
Richard Nixon

President Ho took over a month to reply formally to Nixon's letter of July 15, but Hanoi responded almost instantly to the proposal for secret negotiations. A North Vietnamese message accepting it and suggesting an early August date reached Nixon, via classified communications through Paris and Washington on July 26, as *Air Force One* flew over Asia. Without informing Secretary Rogers, the president decided that Kissinger should be his emissary in meeting Xuan Thuy. The only American in Paris to know about the Xuan Thuy contact was Lieutenant General Vernon A. Walters, the defense attaché at the embassy, who had his own communications link with Washington. Nixon had known Walters for many years—Walters, who is a phenomenal linguist, had served as Nixon's interpreter during his stormy vice-presidential tour of South America in 1958—and Nixon trusted him completely. It became Walters's responsibility to arrange the Kissinger–Xuan Thuy session. Numerous top-secret messages were exchanged between *Air Force One* and Walters, and August 4 was set as the date. Sainteny was to introduce Kissinger and Xuan Thuy.

On August 3, Nixon had stopped off at Mildenhall Air Force Base to meet with Prime Minister Wilson on his way home from Bucharest to Washington. Nobody seemed to notice that Kissinger and two of his NSC assistants, Anthony Lake and Helmut Sonnenfeldt, left the presidential party to board a United States military aircraft that immediately flew them to Paris. There they were met by Walters and spent the night at his apartment on the rue Commandant Charcot, in suburban Neuilly. The next morning, Kissinger became publicly visible. The embassy announced that he was in Paris to brief President de Gaulle on Nixon's Asian and Romanian trip and to confer with Lodge; the next day, the embassy said, Kissinger would go to Brussels to brief NATO officials. The theory was that it was better to have this cover story than to run the risk of Kissinger's unexplained presence in Paris being discovered by newsmen or others. Consequently, Kissinger chatted amiably with newsmen at the embassy after conferring with Lodge (who was told nothing of the secret mission), and at the Elysée Palace he told de Gaulle of his forthcoming meeting with Xuan Thuy and asked for discreet French help in maintaining secrecy in future sessions with the North Vietnamese. De Gaulle promptly agreed.

In the early afternoon, Kissinger, Walters, and Lake (Sonnenfeldt was left behind, although he was privy to the secret) got into an embassy car for the short drive to Sainteny's apartment at 204 rue de Rivoli. Sainteny met the Americans at the door, introduced them to Xuan Thuy and his aide, and left after telling his guests where they could find refreshments. The Kissinger–Xuan Thuy conference, though it lasted well over two hours, accomplished nothing substantive: the only agreement was to hold further meetings—and to keep them secret—but no new date was set. Kissinger was somewhat disappointed that this first encounter was so unproductive, but he was not discouraged. He left Paris that same evening for Brussels after confirming to an American reporter that he had seen Sainteny during the day. The reporter, who happened to know of Kissinger's friendship with Sainteny, had asked the question as a shot in the dark. Kissinger decided to be truthful—up to a point. Stories were published the next day about Kissinger's seeing Sainteny, but more than two years elapsed before the full truth of what he was doing in Paris on that August 4 became known. Back in Washington, Kissinger went to Nixon's living quarters at the White House to describe his conversation with Xuan Thuy.

One of the last acts of Ho Chi Minh's life was to dictate his reply to Nixon's July 15 communication. He signed it on August 25, and the letter was delivered to the White House via the Paris channel on September 1, the day before Ho died suddenly. It was not the kind of answer Nixon had expected.

> Mr. President:
> I have the honor to acknowledge receipt of your letter.
> The war of aggression of the United States against our people, violating our fundamental national rights, still continues in South Vietnam. The United States continues to intensify military operations, the B-52 bombings and the use of toxic chemical products multiply the crimes against the Vietnamese people. The longer the war goes on, the more it accumulates the mourning and burdens of the American people. I am extremely indignant at the losses and destructions caused by the American troops to our people and our country. I am also deeply touched at the rising toll of death of young Americans who have fallen in Vietnam by reason of the policy of American governing circles.
> Our Vietnamese people are deeply devoted to peace, a real peace with independence and real freedom. They are determined to fight to the end, without fearing the sacrifices and difficulties in order to defend their country and their sacred national rights. The overall solution in 10 points of the National Liberation Front of South Vietnam and of the Provisional Revolutionary Government of the Republic of South Vietnam is a logical and reasonable basis for the settlement of the Vietnamese problem. It has earned the sympathy and support of the peoples of the world.
> In your letter you have expressed the desire to act for a just peace. For this the United States must cease the war of aggression and withdraw their troops from South Vietnam, respect the right of the population of the South and of the Vietnamese nation to dispose of themselves, without foreign influence. This is the correct manner of solving the Vietnamese problem in conformity with the national rights of the Vietnamese people, the interests of the United States and the hopes for peace of the peoples of the world. This is the path that will allow the United States to get out of the war with honor.
> With good will on both sides we might arrive at common efforts in view of finding a correct solution of the Vietnamese problem.
> Sincerely,
> Ho Chi Minh

Ho's letter, like Nixon's, was not meant as propaganda. (Its text was not made public by Hanoi; it was Nixon who released both letters to the press two months later for his own domestic political reasons.) Yet the extraordinary thing was that neither Nixon nor Kissinger—irritated as they were with the tone of Ho's missive—took it seriously. In the first place, they refused to believe that the North Vietnamese were so obstinate as to persist indefinitely in demanding the withdrawal of American forces as a condition *sine qua non* for a peace settlement. The White House view was that Ho was presenting a hard negotiating position, from which, in time, he would bargain down. In the second place, the White House —most especially Kissinger—found it inconceivable that the North Vietnamese could much longer withstand the brunt of American military power.

The Nixon-Ho exchange demonstrated dramatically the vast gulf in understanding separating Washington and Hanoi. It was not just "the gulf of four years of war," as Nixon put it, but a total intellectual, cultural, and political misunderstanding of the Vietnamese situation on the part of the American government. Whereas Nixon took the view that the United States was rightfully in South Vietnam, fighting on behalf of its Saigon ally, Ho Chi Minh believed that his country was the victim of direct American aggression.

Thus the inconclusive Kissinger–Xuan Thuy meeting in Paris on August 4 and Ho Chi Minh's letter of August 25 led the administration to decide that continued military toughness, combined with appropriate political gestures, was the proper policy—until the North Vietnamese saw the error of their ways and came to terms.

When the White House received word of Ho's death, it was considered good news. With the passing away of this great figure, the North Vietnamese leadership might be not only weakened, but actually brought to its knees.

But in fact American intelligence and political analysts knew very little (and understood even less) about North Vietnamese politics—a remarkable condition when one considers the enormous degree and length of the American involvement in Vietnam. Only a handful of North Vietnamese experts could be found in Washington or in the Saigon embassy, and with one or two honorable exceptions even these experts were next to useless. Their basic sources were the Hanoi press and radio, South Vietnamese intelligence (usually self-serving and often misleading), captured North Vietnamese and Viet Cong documents (offering few real clues to Hanoi's intentions and subsequently responsible for several major American errors), and whatever could be picked up on the diplomatic circuit. At best, the information was meager.

(As late as August 1970, Kissinger asked Daniel Ellsberg during a private conversation in San Clemente if he could give him names of "anyone who knows anything" about North Vietnam. As Ellsberg recalls it, Kissinger remarked that "as you know, no one in this government understands North Vietnam." Ellsberg told Kissinger that just twenty miles away at the RAND Corporation, there was at least one outstanding expert on North Vietnam. There is no record, however, that Kissinger ever contacted Ellsberg's colleague.)

This intelligence vacuum was compounded by Nixon's and Kissinger's own prejudices and ignorance of Asian situations. Kissinger, for one thing, seemed to believe in the theory that one strong man was a precondition for the functioning of a Communist society: Brezhnev in Moscow, Mao in Peking, Kim Il Sung in Pyongyang, Castro in Havana, Ceauşescu in Bucharest, Tito in Belgrade, and so on. And there had been Ho Chi Minh in Hanoi. But with Ho's death, he could no longer say how North Vietnam was run. Ho was replaced as president by a senile figurehead, and power appeared to have been transferred to the Politburo of the Workers' (Communist) Party. A number of names were known in Washington: Le Duan, the new first secretary of the party; Truong Chinh, the chairman of the Standing Committee of the National Assembly; Premier Pham Van Dong; and Defense Minister Vo Nguyen Giap. But nobody in Washington had the slightest idea which, if any, of these men had become Ho's real successor. Information about Le Duan and Truong Chinh, the two men believed to hold most power in the Politburo, was inconclusive, and experts argued in position papers over their relative importance. A great deal of time was spent discussing whether Le Duan was "Moscow's man" and Truong Chinh "Peking's man," or vice versa. Theories were evolved about possible power struggles within the Politburo and the way these might affect Moscow's and Peking's gain or loss of influence. Public North Vietnamese pronouncements, needless to say, were no help in clarifying this situation. Hanoi's stated policy was to fulfill Ho's "testament," which meant expelling the Americans and reunifying the two Vietnams. Presently the conclusion was reached that North Vietnam was run by a collective leadership, busy papering over its deep differences, and that this offered an opportunity to end the war on terms that would not have been possible under Ho. Ignorance and wishful thinking were the hallmarks of this policy—with the inevitably catastrophic results. In the circumstances, Nixon's policy turned into a strange blend of secret diplomacy, highly advertised public gestures, and unabating military action.

A curious footnote to Kissinger's secret Paris diplomacy involved an ancillary intermediary role between Kissinger and Xuan Thuy played by the late Joseph R. Starobin, who had once been foreign editor of the New York *Daily Worker,* the organ of the American Communist Party. Starobin, who had left the party in 1954 and subsequently became a professor at York University in Toronto, met Xuan Thuy in Paris on July 26, renewing an old acquaintanceship dating back to 1953, during the first Indochina war. On the basis of some intriguing comments Xuan Thuy made, Starobin decided that he should convey what he thought were fresh North Vietnamese views to Nixon, and he did so in a conversation with Kissinger in San Clemente on August 12. Kissinger, who in those days was willing to receive almost anybody with Hanoi contacts, naturally failed to inform Starobin that he had secretly seen Xuan Thuy eight days earlier, but he encouraged the professor to report back to him if he had further information. Starobin returned to Paris for a long session with Xuan Thuy on September 1, receiving what he considered to be a set of proposals for transmission to Kissinger. It is unclear whether Xuan Thuy (who had also not told Starobin of the secret talk with Kissinger) had developed a new position since his August 4 encounter with Kissinger or was simply restating what he had told the Americans earlier.

In any event, Starobin took the proposals to Kissinger at the White House on September 10. Briefly, as Starobin recounted it, Xuan Thuy was indicating Hanoi's willingness to enter into private talks with the United States on the basis of Washington's acceptance of the "principle" of complete American withdrawal from Vietnam. Hanoi, Starobin reported, no longer demanded total American departure as a precondition for private talks, would be satisfied with the withdrawal of 100,000 troops as soon as possible (the 25,000-man pullout announced by Nixon in June was not considered sufficient), and would agree to a negotiated coalition regime in Saigon, including "some members of the present administration," rather than insisting on a Viet Cong government. To be sure—and unknown to Starobin when he reported to Kissinger—Hanoi had already entered into secret talks with the United States. What remains obscure is whether Kissinger had, as a precondition for them, given North Vietnam assurances of a complete American withdrawal. It is unlikely that Kissinger would have given Xuan Thuy an overall withdrawal timetable. Starobin took the view that Hanoi was showing "flexibility" in agreeing to a coalition regime in Saigon, including members of President Thieu's government, but—even if this did represent a concession—the Nixon administration was so totally committed to Thieu's survival that the proposal was rejected out of hand. The intriguing thing is why Xuan Thuy, already in private contact with Kissinger, chose to use Starobin as a parallel intermediary and why Kissinger played the game.

.   .   .

At about this same time, in late August, President Nixon turned his attention to South Korea, one of the "forward" countries in America's global system of defenses. When Nixon took office, there were in excess of 60,000 American troops there. Two National Security Council studies —NSSM–27 ordered on February 22 and NSSM–34 on March 21— reaffirmed the need for preserving the United States military presence there and providing the Seoul regime with substantial military and economic assistance. The administration's view, as expressed in subsequent Senate testimony, was that the 1954 Mutual Defense Treaty with South Korea was based on the "so-called Monroe Doctrine formula"—a rather startling extension to the western Pacific of the early nineteenth-century concept that declared any threat to the Americas to be a direct danger to the United States. The repercussions of the shooting down of the EC-121 by the North Koreans on April 15 fell short of an open conflict between the two countries, but the incident served to focus Nixon's attention on American arrangements in South Korea. On April 26, the NSC staff produced NSSM-53, still another study of the Korean situation and its implications. The White House had the distinct suspicion that the North Koreans were preparing to take advantage of the American preoccupation with Vietnam to launch a new adventure in South Korea.

These considerations led Nixon to decide to meet with South Korea's President Park Chung Hee less than three weeks after he had returned from his Asian grand tour (which had not included Seoul). The problem, however, was that Park was one of the most repressive dictators on the American payroll. Given the mounting antiwar sentiment in the country and the rising revulsion against America's dictatorial clients (we had them in Vietnam, Greece, and Brazil as well), Nixon realized that it would be bad politics to bring Park to Washington for a formal visit, complete with White House honors and ceremonies. The decision was to receive him in San Francisco.

Park arrived at Crissy Field (an air force base near San Francisco), not at the International Airport, on August 21, where Nixon greeted him in a relatively low-key manner. In his brief welcoming address, Nixon noted that South Korea maintained armed forces "that are strong enough to assume the major share of the responsibility for defending Korea against the threat from the North" and that, at the same time, the South Koreans furnished "more fighting men fighting in South Vietnam than any other nation" except for the United States and South Vietnam itself. This was a reference to the 50,000-man South Korean contingent in South Vietnam, whose Tiger Division, for example, was a far better fighting force than the ARVN. (Thailand, Australia, and New Zealand were the other nations with troops in Vietnam; the Philippines had sent an unarmed engineers' battalion.) The South Korean presence in Vietnam was welcome, because it served to show that Americans were not the only foreigners fighting in Vietnam.

What Nixon—and his administration—did not explain at the time, however, was that the South Korean assignment of troops to Vietnam was a colossal economic bonanza financed by the United States. Subsequent Senate hearings produced the information that it cost the United States $927 million to transport, equip, and maintain the South Koreans in Vietnam in fiscal years 1965–70. This was apart from ongoing military assistance to South Korea. Additionally, South Korea earned $546 million from the United States between 1965 (when Korean forces first went to Vietnam) and 1969, in direct purchases for Vietnam under military-commodity procurement, construction contracts, military- and civilian-personnel remittances, and commercial exports. As a State Department witness told a Senate committee in 1970, "The war in Vietnam, as is the case with all wars, created a substantial demand for goods and services. The Koreans made it clear that they wanted to be assured an opportunity, provided they were competitive, to provide as much as they could of these goods and services. . . . The Koreans felt it only reasonable that if they were sending men in large numbers to fight in Vietnam, they should be allowed to share in markets created by the war. In other words, they wanted to participate in the opportunities as well as the risks."

United States direct financial aid to South Korean forces in Vietnam included funds for overseas allowances for the soldiers as well as the noncombatant units—as was the case with the Philippines. Employment was "extensively" created in Vietnam for South Korean workers, such as stevedores. Finally, the United States committed itself to provide Seoul with $15 million annually in economic loans "for the support of exports to Vietnam."

For reasons the administration never adequately explained, United States financing of South Korea's participation in the Vietnam war was for years kept secret—even from Congress. But when Senator Stuart Symington asked a senior State Department official at the 1970 hearings whether "the Koreans would have made the Vietnam deal without the money they received," the answer was, "No, sir; because they could not support the expenses involved." The direct cost to the United States of maintaining South Korean troops in Vietnam was $250 million in 1969, roughly $5000 per soldier (the annual cost of maintaining an American soldier in Vietnam was $13,500).

At a state dinner at the St. Francis Hotel, Nixon told Park that Koreans had proved their courage in the 1950 war "for their own freedom" and "they are proving it by fighting alongside the persons of the United States and those of South Vietnam and other countries in the war in Vietnam with 50,000 Koreans there. And they prove it by maintaining one of the largest armed forces in the world in order to meet the threat which is posed against them in the North."

Park used the occasion to digress at length on this northern threat, his constant justification for his repressive policies:

> Frankly speaking, I realize through my own experience that, as far as Communists are concerned, there can be no peace as we understand it. Theirs in reality is no more than a peace in disguise during which they prepare for a larger-scale aggression. Through my own long experience in dealing with Communists in Asia, I am firmly convinced that the only, and the best, way to restore peace in the region is to convince the Communists of our superior strength, which they cannot defeat, so that they may abandon their futile theme of aggression. It is because of this belief that at every opportunity I have emphasized the importance of the principle of responsive actions in our dealings with the Communists.

This was the kind of tough language Nixon appreciated. In a joint statement issued the next day, August 22, Nixon and Park agreed that South Korean forces and American forces stationed in Korea "must remain strong and alert." They also "reaffirmed the determination of their Governments to meet armed attack against the Republic of Korea in accordance with the Mutual Defense Treaty. . . ."

In September, Nixon launched a series of new moves in his Vietnam policy. Whereas to Kissinger the war was essentially a foreign-policy problem, a quasi abstraction to be worked out through complex formulas forming a comprehensive power equation, Nixon increasingly had to look at Vietnam as a domestic issue. The president, of course, psychologically or morally, was not any more averse than Kissinger to the extreme use of force in imposing his own solution to the war or showing the world that American prestige could not be challenged with impunity.

But Nixon was keenly aware that the nation was turning against the war—was confused and fatigued by it. He could not forget Lyndon Johnson's political defeat at the hands of the antiwar movement. He heard the rumblings in Congress and watched the ominous mobilization in the streets by antiwar militants. There was mounting resistance to the draft (now draft evaders and deserters numbered in the high thousands). The nation was shocked every week when American casualty figures in Vietnam were published; the KIA (killed in action) figure for September 1969 was 510—though down from 949 the previous year. Nixon had campaigned for election on the platform of a quick peace with adequate honor. When he entered the White House, Nixon asked the country to be patient and trust him that he wanted a settlement as soon as possible. Kissinger was privately pleading with the liberals for "six months" to end the war.

But now it was September, the eighth month of the administration, and no progress was visible. If anything, the United States was even more deeply embroiled in Indochina—what with the secret Cambodia bombings launched in March and the stepped-up air war over Vietnam. To be sure, Nixon had presented his peace proposals in May, ordered the first withdrawals of American troops from Vietnam in June, and set in motion the secret negotiations with Hanoi in August. But the deadlock seemed unbreakable.

In Paris, the day before Ho died, Xuan Thuy suggested to newsmen that there might be diplomatic progress if Nixon announced a timetable for larger United States withdrawals. Some observers chose to interpret Thuy's remarks as a sign of flexibility, but the White House did not. Nixon reasoned that to announce a firm withdrawal timetable without a meaningful *quid pro quo* by Hanoi would be tantamount to a unilateral concession, an open-ended commitment to get out of the war without fulfilling the objectives that had led to the original American involvement. This he was not prepared to do.

Nevertheless he had to do something—if not to inspire Hanoi toward more rewarding diplomacy, at least to placate American public opinion. This took the form of an announcement on nationwide television and radio on September 16 that another 35,000 United States troops would be withdrawn from Vietnam by December 15. (This would mean a total of 60,000 men withdrawn for the year, more than 10 percent of the total strength.) This decision was taken by the president following a meticulous secret review of the overall Vietnam situation by him, Kissinger, and other top advisers, culminating in a National Security Council meeting on September 14. The results of the review were not, in Nixon's words, "overly optimistic," although he drew some encouragement from the fact that Hanoi had not launched an anticipated summer offensive and that the troop infiltration rate from North to South "was down by two-thirds," suggesting that a fall offensive was also less likely. This remark was in tune with the standard intelligence judgments furnished to the White House by civilian and military experts, judgments that almost always proved to be wrong. The United States continually misread North Vietnamese capabilities and intentions, expecting offensives when Hanoi planned none and missing the real indications when a major assault was being prepared.

On the subject of a successor to Ho Chi Minh, Nixon indicated that the administration was wholly uninformed. "The major problem in a Communist system of government is the problem of succession, and the North Vietnamese are going through that," he said grandly. "There is a tendency for uncertainty and rigidity as the contest for power goes on. We think that is going on within North Vietnam at the present time."

Nixon's brief announcement did not go into the military implications of the new withdrawal. Nor did he touch on the domestic political aspects. Instead, he presented it as a "significant step" toward "meaningful negotiations" with Hanoi. Curiously the last sentence of his announcement was taken verbatim (except for a single word) from the last paragraph of his still unpublished July letter to Ho Chi Minh: "Let history record that at this critical moment [he used the word "juncture" in the letter], both sides turned their faces toward peace rather than toward conflict and war." Then he went over the list of Washington's and Saigon's peace proposals earlier in the year, and disclosed for the first time an intriguing negotiating point: that the United States and South Vietnam would settle "for the *de facto* removal of North Vietnamese forces so long as there are guarantees against their return." This was intended as a face-saving device for Hanoi, which had never publicly acknowledged that its regular troops were fighting in the South. But the *de facto* withdrawal formula threatened to do away with his concept of *mutual* withdrawals. And if it were *de facto*, it obviously could not be written into a peace agreement, which suggested that the United States was beginning to think of possible secret deals—presumably the only way that guarantees against the return of the North Vietnamese could be given. Nixon could not say that this concession had been offered to Xuan Thuy by Kissinger in August and that the North Vietnamese had shown no interest in it.

In purely military terms, the decision to withdraw another 35,000 troops from Vietnam during 1969 was much less meaningful than Nixon would have had the American public believe. The military establishment in Vietnam was bloated to begin with; Nixon was actually only trimming the fat. U.S. strategy in Vietnam was also changing: the Pentagon had finally abandoned General William Westmoreland's "search-and-destroy" concept as unworkable, shifting instead to a more defensive doctrine in support of the South Vietnamese forces and placing greater emphasis on Vietnamization and pacification. On another level, the United States relied increasingly on air power. In brief, the new withdrawals made little military difference, did not impress Hanoi, and had no real effect on domestic opinion.

Two days later, Nixon went to New York to address the United Nations General Assembly. In a broad policy speech, touching on most aspects of foreign relations, Nixon called attention to his announcement about the withdrawals from Vietnam; quite clearly it had been timed to enhance the importance of his speech. Nixon's principal theme was that the United States had done its share in seeking peace, that now it was up to Hanoi to respond, and that all the member governments should assist in the search for a solution.

> I urge all of you here—representing 126 nations—to use your best diplomatic efforts to persuade Hanoi to move seriously into the negotiations which could end this war. The steps we have taken have been responsive to views expressed in this room. And we hope that views from this organization may also be influential in Hanoi. If these efforts are successful, this war can end. . . .
>
> When the war ends, the United States will stand ready to help the people of Vietnam—all of them—in their tasks of renewal and reconstruction. And when peace comes at last to Vietnam, it can truly come with healing in its wings.

The implied offer of postwar economic aid to North Vietnam was another carrot. It soon would become part of the secret negotiations. As for the appeal for "best diplomatic efforts to persuade Hanoi . . . seriously" to negotiate, it was obviously directed at the Soviet Union, inasmuch as nobody else in the United Nations could influence Hanoi.

Back at the White House, Nixon became much more forceful about his Vietnam policies—in relation both to Hanoi and to domestic dissent. The administration's attitude on Vietnam was hardening in response to the North Vietnamese stonewalling, and Nixon was becoming more and more annoyed by attitudes in Congress and the activities of the antiwar movement. It was around this time that he began equating in his mind congressional and other criticism of the war with virtual subversion of United States interests. This was becoming obsessive with him, as it had been with Lyndon Johnson, and imitating his predecessor, Nixon secretly ordered the FBI, the CIA, and other intelligence agencies to look for relationships between the antiwar movement and hostile foreign governments. Surreptitious spying on the antiwar movement spread into other forms of domestic espionage and harassment. On September 26, at a noontime news conference halfway through the Washington visit of Mrs. Meir, Nixon hammered away at his differences with his congressional foes:

> It is my conclusion that if the administration were to impose an arbitrary cutoff time, say the end of 1970, or the middle of 1971, for the complete withdrawal of American forces in Vietnam, that inevitably leads to perpetuating and continuing the war until that time and destroys any chance to reach the objective that I am trying to achieve, of ending the war before the end of 1970 or before the middle of 1971.
>
> I think this is a defeatist attitude, defeatist in terms of what it would accomplish. I do not think it is in the interest of the United States. I also believe that even though these proposals, I know, are made with the best of intentions, they inevitably undercut and destroy the negotiating position that we have in Paris. We have not made significant progress in those negotiations. But any incentive for the enemy to negotiate is destroyed if he is told in advance that if he just waits for eighteen months, we will be out anyway. Therefore, I oppose that kind of arbitrary action.

From a diplomatic standpoint, Nixon may have been right but politically he was applying a dangerously divisive charge of "defeatism," and it was not so far from talking treason if the president of the United States claimed that his critics were undercutting American diplomacy. Nixon delivered the message that Americans who did not follow his leadership were, in effect, prolonging the war:

> I think we are on the right course in Vietnam. We are on a course that is going to end this war. It will end much sooner if we can have to an extent, to the extent possible in this free country, a united front behind very reasonable proposals. If we have that united front, the enemy then will begin to talk, because the only missing ingredient to escalating the time when we will end the war is the refusal of the enemy in Paris to even discuss our proposals. . . . I understand that there has been and continues to be opposition to the war in Vietnam on the campuses, and also in the nation. . . . We expect it. However, under no circumstances will I be affected whatever by it.

Nixon's stern attitude soon set in motion a critical chain of events. The White House was turning its attention again to military solutions in Vietnam while the domestic unrest grew. Then, early in October, the president decided that the absence of North Vietnamese responses to his overtures required a new toughness; at the same time, he was counseled to go before the nation to explain his policy once more. During October, Nixon faced contradictory pressures from his top advisers, as the antiwar protest spilled into the streets with a huge October 15 moratorium (which is what the militants called their demonstration) in Washington and attendant rioting.

Kissinger instructed a special task force on the NSC staff to undertake a top-secret study of new military options that might include the use of a tactical nuclear weapon in a single, carefully controlled situation.* About October 1, Kissinger assembled a hand-picked group of ten or so trusted aides to discuss with them what he called a "very, very sensitive matter." Those present included Colonel Alexander Haig; Helmut Sonnenfeldt, the Soviet expert; Rear Admiral Rembrandt C. Robinson, the head of the Joint Chiefs of Staff liaison office at the NSC; Colonel William Lemnitzer, an army officer attached to the NSC staff; and specialists in other fields: Winston Lord, Laurence Lynn, Anthony Lake, Roger Morris, William Watts, and Peter Rodman. Each man had been separately told by Kissinger beforehand that he would be asked to work on a very secret project. Kissinger opened the meeting by saying that this would be a "special group on Vietnam," remarking that he was setting it up because "the war is not going very well in the South." Then he took the group in his confidence, telling them of his secret meeting with Xuan Thuy in Paris (only Sonnenfeldt and Lake had known about it before) and other diplomatic efforts. "We've been very forthcoming," he said; "we've attempted to make concessions which have been unrequited."

Then Kissinger made his central point: "I refuse to believe that a little fourth-rate power like North Vietnam doesn't have a breaking point. The Johnson administration could never come to grips with this problem. We intend to come to grips." He paused for effect, and went on: "It shall be the assignment of this group to examine the option of a savage, decisive blow against North Vietnam, militarily. You are to start without any preconceptions at all. You are to sit down and map out what would be a savage, decisive blow. You are to examine the option from every angle, you are to examine every detail of how it should be executed militarily, what the political scenario would be."

---

*The story of this Kissinger study is reconstructed here from confidential interviews with members of the special study group and senior Pentagon officers who were acquainted with the project on a "need-to-know" basis. Quotations attributed to Kissinger are based on the best recollections of those interviewed; in some cases they are composite.

Kissinger said he wanted everything put together in a large loose-leaf notebook. The last thing in the book, he said, would be a presidential speech in which Nixon announced his decision to apply the "decisive blow," leveling with the American people and telling them, in effect, that the United States had tried to negotiate but to no avail, and that therefore "tonight, pursuant to my orders, American planes are, etc., etc." One of the participants recalled later, "I guess we were all in a sort of a mild state of shock." But Kissinger continued, explaining that "my view is that the bureaucracy is constitutionally unable to come up with a fresh initiative on the war. If there is to be a negotiated settlement, if the war is to end, I am convinced that I have to do it. I must take the president along with me, and we must, in turn, carry the Congress and the American people." He offered the comment that "we don't want a long nightmare of recrimination afterward," and "the war has to be ended in a way in which it doesn't disturb the basic structure of peace that we are going to be trying to build in the next few years."

Kissinger told his group that what he wanted was a "fresh perspective." Thus far only Haig and Lake had worked on Vietnam, but each of the others would have a special assignment in the context of the study. Sonnenfeldt, for example, would consider possible Soviet reactions. Haig, Lemnitzer, and Robinson would look into purely military aspects of the operation in conjunction with the Joint Chiefs of Staff. Watts was to study possible domestic political repercussions. Lynn would be in charge of a general critique of the project. As usual, Kissinger wanted the study compartmentalized, each man working in his own area until the options were all "staffed out" and ready. One of the aides was given the task of keeping track of the entire project.

The study, Kissinger said, had to be completed as soon as possible although he did not tell his group when Nixon proposed to deliver his planned Vietnam speech. (Actually, the date had not yet been set, and Kissinger was aiming at the end of October—*after* the moratorium.) There was some general conversation in the room after Kissinger requested the "savage blow" study, an expression he repeated several times. Then, as one of the men remembered it, "someone raised the question of nuclear weapons."

Kissinger said, "It is the policy of this administration not to use nuclear *weapons,* and we shall not, so this option excludes that one thing." But "you are not to exclude the possibility of a nuclear *device* being used for purposes of a blockage in the pass to China, if that seems to be the only way to close the pass."

Several participants assumed Kissinger meant using a tactical nuclear weapon to close the mountain pass over which the railroad line runs from China to North Vietnam. This railway was one of the most important routes for deliveries of Chinese war matériel, fuel, and food to Hanoi, and railroad bridges and tracks in Vietnamese territory were often hit by American aircraft throughout the war. But the special group never considered in its study the possibility of using a nuclear device as part of the proposed blockade of North Vietnam, and Kissinger is not known to have alluded to it again.

(In March 1976, Kissinger admitted publicly for the first time that he would not exclude the use of nuclear weapons in certain limited situations. In an interview with *U.S. News & World Report,* he remarked that "the peace of the world will be threatened, when it is threatened, not primarily by strategic forces but by geopolitical changes, and to resist those geopolitical changes we must be able to resist regionally." The interviewer asked him whether this meant American response by nuclear or non-nuclear means. Kissinger said: "By non-nuclear means, or perhaps even by nuclear means geared to the local situation. Non-nuclear means would always be preferable, but I don't want to exclude nuclear means in certain situations." Later, he repeated this before a Senate committee, adding that there was a need to compensate for Soviet superiority in conventional forces.)

As drafted by the officials in charge of the military aspects of the operation, the plan called for mining Haiphong harbor and sinking ships towed there for that purpose, mining rivers and coastal waters, carpet-bombing Hanoi, and bombing Red River dikes. The Joint Chiefs of Staff provided details on how these objectives could be achieved—along with private comments that "we should have done this three or four years ago. . . . It would have saved a lot of lives and a lot of torture and torment." And indeed Pentagon contingency papers for this kind of action had been in existence for some time. Late in August, a copy of a 150-page Pentagon document was shown at the command post at Nixon's Key Biscayne compound to several NSC staffers, including Haig and Watts. The military referred to it as the "November Option." When Kissinger convoked the special group in October, its task was to review this Pentagon blueprint and fit it into a broader policy context.

Kissinger's name for the overall project was "Duck Hoop" because, as he explained it, all the "ducks" of American power would be "circling in" for the kill; a drawing of a flight of ducks appeared on the cover of all documents pertaining to Duck Hoop.

The Pentagon refined its earlier plans down to the smallest detail when its updated contingency documents were presented to Kissinger in mid-October during another Key Biscayne retreat. For example, the military men projected that there would be no more than five civilian casualties if a given target were struck, say, between 5:00 a.m. and 5:08 a.m. But in staff discussions they conceded they could not be really sure of their estimates.

According to one member of the group, "The scenario was for savage air blows and mining, to be repeated at intervals." The idea was to hit North Vietnam, then suspend the attacks to give Hanoi time to respond diplomatically in some way. The speech the special group drafted for Nixon said that if no response were forthcoming, the attacks would be repeated "again, again, and again." A participant explained, "You were talking about one very savage punch to be followed by others at regular intervals as long as they could take it. You'd give them breathing space in which to respond, then you'd come back and hit them again."

The whole study was conducted on a purely pragmatic level, considering only whether the operation was feasible and whether it would achieve the desired results. No moral considerations entered the picture. In the words of an NSC aide, "The whole exercise struck me as being very cool and amoral, not judging it in terms of the loss of life or in terms of the escalation of the war, but simply in terms of effectiveness." Politically Sonnenfeldt offered the judgment that the "savage blow" would have the tacit acquiescence of both the Soviet Union and China, although he expressed concern about the risk of hitting Soviet ships in Haiphong and about the Chinese reaction if the frontier passes were attacked even with conventional weapons.

But in the end, the group—mainly influenced by civilian analysts— recommended against the "savage blow" on the grounds that no matter how intensive, it would never achieve a complete blockade or destruction of North Vietnam. As one of the civilian analysts put it, "We made a very, very persuasive case on technical and military grounds that it just wouldn't work." The conclusion was that "in effect, you can get by a blockade." To maintain it, he said, "would require stationing the fleet off the coast, and the chances for a direct confrontation with the Soviets were very high." Besides, he added, "when it came to bombing, they could rebuild most of the damage inside North Vietnam fairly quickly.

"It boiled down to the fundamental reality of Vietnam. You were trying to fight a war with North Vietnam as if they were an industrial society when, in fact, they were not. They were only a quasi-industrial society that would survive militarily and politically in a state to which one could reduce them by bombing, but beyond which you really couldn't reduce them by conventional bombing."

The special group also had in hand elaborate CIA studies, complete with charts and statistics, offering the conclusion that the "savage blow" would not significantly decrease the capability of North Vietnam to wage a major offensive in the South. This was the same assessment the CIA had produced in January as its contribution to NSSM–1, and it kept repeating it over and over again, but by and large, it was ignored by Nixon and Kissinger, who tended to go along with the Pentagon's opinion that if the bombings were adequate—and the military concept of "adequate" was an all-out effort engaging the maximal American air capability—they would produce the desired results. The White House and the Pentagon were, for all practical purposes, espousing the doctrine enunciated some years earlier by General Curtis LeMay, a former air force chief of staff, that North Vietnam should be bombed back to "the stone age." But on this occasion the CIA's assessment was accepted by Kissinger's special study group.

The overall critique of the "savage blow" plan was written by Laurence Lynn, with the assistance of at least two NSC colleagues. Taking into account the CIA's estimates as well as other material, the critique made these points: strategic bombing in general had limited advantages; carpet-bombing of Hanoi would cause immense civilian casualties and, in fact, reinforce the political will of the North Vietnamese society to go on fighting; Soviet-supplied SAM missiles would take a heavy toll of the B-52s; seeding and reseeding mines in Haiphong harbor, coastal waters, and rivers would be a very difficult and costly operation offering uncertain results; the long-run capability of North Vietnam to absorb this kind of punishment would not basically affect its war-making potential in the South because the Soviets and the Chinese would find ways—an airlift or other means—to keep Hanoi supplied.

Politically the group also opposed the Kissinger plan. There was the feeling that the Nixon administration could not afford a repeated number of "savage blows" in terms of domestic opinion. "If you predicated the whole strategy on a savage, decisive blow to bring North Vietnam down to its knees, it was not reasonable to expect the support of public opinion unless you prefaced it by much more elaborate and probing negotiations than we had done in the past," one analyst said. "You could perhaps get away with it if the negotiations were at a stage where it was really a matter of not surrendering a major point that stood between us and peace. But in fact, there had been no serious negotiations, only a series of ambiguous meetings on general principles, including Henry's secret talks with Xuan Thuy."

The analysts also argued that the timing was wrong. The mood of the country was such that to engage in an operation of this magnitude, with some 450,000 American troops still in Vietnam, would be to invite domestic wrath against the administration. Besides, the argument ran, a "savage blow" would look to the world as if the United States was still intent on *winning* the war militarily despite Nixon's official disclaimers. The cost to American troops in Vietnam might be very heavy if in retaliation against the air offensive and the blockade, the Communists raised the level of violence in the South. After the end of the winter mini Tet offensive, the North Vietnamese and Viet Cong had significantly scaled down their military activities. One NSC official summed it up: "We just argued in general that it was the wrong time, the wrong place, that it was an erroneous strategy to pursue." And a top-secret memorandum written by Watts on October 13 warned that Duck Hoop might provoke serious civil unrest and the probability that the National Guard would have to be mobilized to quell disorders.

The "savage blow" study was completed late in October. The plan, the critique, the political comments, and the draft of a presidential speech were pulled together, placed in a loose-leaf book marked Top Secret, and delivered to Kissinger. What happened next remains unclear.

Defense Secretary Laird was informed of Duck Hoop before it went to Nixon, and in the words of an NSC official, "was actually appalled, stunned by the whole thing on political grounds." Laird's basic view was that the war had to be "Vietnamized" as soon as possible and American troops brought home, that the administration could not survive politically unless it did this, and the idea of the "savage blow" was political insanity. He seized on Lynn's critique and on the uncertainties concerning the military success of the operation—the navy and the air force admitted they could not guarantee results—as a basis for his opposition. He also made the point that the administration would be unable to enlist Soviet and Chinese assistance in convincing Hanoi to accept the settlement proposed by Nixon if the United States appeared to be starting the war anew.

It is not known whether Secretary of State Rogers was consulted about Duck Hoop. He indicated many years later that he had no recollection of any major military option in 1969. And it is virtually certain that the full National Security Council never discussed it. However, Kissinger did

submit the study to Nixon—and the president rejected it. Only the two
of them know why: Kissinger never explained it to his staff nor did he say
whether he recommended for or against it. This was Kissinger's cardinal
rule in his relations with Nixon. Other cabinet officers, notably Laird and
Rogers, often let it be known in a quasi-public way whether they agreed
or not with a presidential decision. Kissinger, on the other hand, encouraged the impression that all he did was to present Nixon with a series of
options—and no recommendations. But this does not appear to be true.
He seemed to have a way of divining what options would appeal to Nixon
and what options would not. Seeing Nixon alone every morning for an
hour—and frequently spending long nocturnal hours with him in the
Lincoln Sitting Room or in the hideaway in the Executive Office Building
—he had developed a sense of how the president's mind worked. This
gave him a flexibility in formulating policies for Nixon's approval that was
not enjoyed by others in the government. His total identification with the
president also made him virtually invulnerable in Washington power
terms. The deep secrecy always surrounding his deliberations with Nixon
served to isolate the two men from the rest of the government, the
despicable "bureaucracy," which was the way they wanted it.

In the case of the "savage blow" decision, it is possible that Kissinger
became convinced by the NSC staff critique that the plan was not workable. Perhaps, although he may have favored the "savage blow," he
concluded that it would be a losing battle with Nixon if he pushed for it.
And Kissinger never believed in waging lost battles. Some members of
the NSC study group think that the initial idea may have come down to
Kissinger from Nixon and that he was simply carrying out the president's
instructions in ordering the study. Others suspect that Kissinger was
playing the devil's advocate, knowing that the staff would recommend
against it and that the study could be used to dissuade Nixon. Still other
NSC staffers are convinced that Kissinger, at least at the outset, truly
favored the "savage blow." "Why else would Henry be so insistent in
giving us our marching orders, in repeating over and over that 'I just can't
believe that there is an organized society on earth that doesn't have a
breaking point'? Maybe he was applying the European concept of organized societies to North Vietnam."

Perhaps the commanding reason that Nixon vetoed the "savage blow"
was that he had resolved to defuse the antiwar movement politically in
a forthcoming speech, that this had become his first political priority—
and he would not let anything interfere with it. Certainly he viewed the
speech, which he was to deliver on November 3 (he chose this date as

falling roughly between the October 15 antiwar moratorium, when he arrogantly let it be known that he was watching a football game on television the Saturday afternoon of the demonstration, and the planned November 15 moratorium) as his first major political test since assuming the presidency. William Safire recounts that the president treated the speech "with the seriousness of an Inaugural or an acceptance address, doing it all himself." He also quotes Kissinger as saying that "there is nothing the President has thought more deeply about or reflected on with greater anguish than what he is about to say. . . . Night after night he has worked until two or three in the morning, producing draft after draft."

The speech, the longest Nixon had thus far made as president, offered no new diplomatic initiatives, no fresh thoughts, not even a promise that the war would wind up in the foreseeable future. Instead, it was a restatement of his policies in Vietnam, an incomplete account of his efforts at secret negotiations with Hanoi—he released the texts of the letters in the exchange with Ho Chi Minh, but made no mention of Kissinger's secret meeting with Xuan Thuy in August—and a ringing appeal to the nation to stand behind the position taken by the United States government: "If a vocal minority, however fervent its cause, prevails over reason and the will of the majority, this nation has no future as a free society. . . . And so tonight—to you, the great silent majority of my fellow Americans—I ask for your support."

Nixon invoked for his audience the specter of a Communist-directed bloodbath in South Vietnam if the United States agreed to a "precipitate withdrawal" of its forces. This, he said, "would inevitably allow the Communists to repeat the massacres which followed their takeover in the North fifteen years before. . . . They then murdered more than fifty thousand people, and hundreds of thousands more died in slave-labor camps." Actually, this was a fairly credible point at that stage. The North Vietnamese, who should have known better, did kill a large number of civilians when they briefly held the northern city of Hue during the 1968 Tet offensive (Nixon said three thousand South Vietnamese were thus murdered), and this was fresh in the minds of Americans who had seen on television and in newspapers the pictures of piles of bodies. Many people, therefore, took Nixon seriously when he said that "with the sudden collapse of our support, these atrocities of Hue would become the nightmare of the entire nation—and particularly for the million and a half Catholic refugees who fled to South Vietnam when the Communists took over in the North." Nixon's mention of Vietnamese Catholics was, of course, a deft appeal to the sensibilities of American Catholics, millions of whom the president thought fitted in the "silent majority" category.

Another thing Nixon did, as he would do in subsequent speeches, was to challenge the American sense of honor and patriotism as well as of American greatness in the world. Speaking of proposals for a "precipitate withdrawal" from Vietnam, he said: "For the United States, this first defeat in our nation's history would result in a collapse of confidence in American leadership, not only in Asia but throughout the world." And he added: "Three American presidents have recognized the great stakes involved in Vietnam and understood what had to be done." This was calculated to give his position a politically nonpartisan flavor as he cited actions taken in Vietnam by Eisenhower, Kennedy, and Johnson. The crux of Nixon's performance was to deflect what he perceived as partisan political pressures on him to change his policy. Early on, he made the central point: "Let us all understand that the question before us is not whether some Americans are for peace and some Americans are against peace. The question at issue is not whether Johnson's war becomes Nixon's war. The great question is: How can we win America's peace?" In fact, by November, the president had become very seriously concerned that, indeed, the Vietnam war would become known as "Nixon's war." He often raised this point in private conversations with his advisers—and with increasing irritation. "But," he said in the speech, "I had a greater obligation than to think only of the years of my administration and of the next election. I had to think of the effect of my decision on the next generation and on the future of peace and freedom in America and the world."

The November speech in fact set the stage for three more years of hard conflict. But Nixon did succeed in deflecting for a while the domestic antiwar pressures—the November 15 moratorium failed to create serious political problems for him—and this is what the whole exercise was all about. As recounted by Jeb Stuart Magruder in his book, *An American Life,* Nixon was so enchanted with the results that on November 5 he told his aides that he had "floored those liberal sons of bitches with the TV speech" and "we've got those liberal bastards on the run now; we've got them on the run and we're going to keep them on the run." Safire, another White House insider, says that Nixon told him, the day after the speech, "My object was to go over the heads of the columnists. . . . We have been getting the reaction from across the country, and it's been pretty good. We've got to hold American public opinion with us for three or four months and then we can work this Vietnam thing out."

Having firmed up the political base for the pursuit of his policies,

Nixon warned the North Vietnamese that he would not tolerate their increased military activity. He threatened, among other things, that the rate of Communist military activity in Vietnam would be a factor in determining additional American troop withdrawals (which was not true, because he understood the political necessity of taking out U.S. units at regular intervals no matter what) and that he would retaliate massively. The specific option of the "savage blow" had been rejected, but its spirit was very much alive.

Very little of importance concerning Vietnam, except for a new announcement on troop pullouts, occurred between Nixon's November 3 speech and the end of the year. It was essentially low-level diplomacy and a steady flow of rhetoric from the White House. In a television interview on November 5, for example, the president remarked, without elaboration, that "we have a plan now that will end the war, and end it in a way that we think will contribute to the cause of a just and lasting peace." Two days before the moratorium events, addressing the House of Representatives, he expressed "appreciation" to members of both parties "for their support of a just peace in Vietnam." He noted with evident pleasure that three hundred members of the House had joined in sponsoring a resolution "for a just peace in Vietnam along the lines of the proposals that I made in a speech on November 3." Nixon repeated this performance one hour later before the Senate (the source of many of his difficulties over Vietnam), thanking the more than sixty Senators who had written a letter to Ambassador Lodge in Paris in support of "some" of Nixon's peace proposals. And while grateful for the backing "of more than half the membership of this body, I also have respect for those who may have disagreed with the program for peace that I outlined." And then there was this pure hyperbolic Nixonism: "I know that this war is the most difficult and most controversial of any war in this nation's history. But I know that while we have our differences about what is the best way to peace, there are no differences with respect to our goal. I think Americans want a just peace; they want a lasting peace."

On November 20, Nixon accepted "with great regret" the resignation of Henry Cabot Lodge as chief United States delegate to the Paris peace talks. However, he made a point of not naming a successor immediately —a way of showing his displeasure to the North Vietnamese. The weekly public Paris sessions were to be conducted for some time by Ambassador Philip Habib, a very competent career diplomat.

At a news conference on December 8, new contradictions arose. On the one hand, Nixon said that the chances of a negotiated settlement were

"not good" because "the enemy's line continues to be hard, their proposals quite frivolous, as the one by the VC today [the Provisional Revolutionary Government (PRG) delegation in Paris had just presented another multipoint proposal, basically restating its position], and I do not
anticipate any progress on the negotiating front at this time." On the
other hand, he disclosed that another American troop withdrawal, the
third in 1969, would be announced in a few weeks, presumably coinciding
with Christmas. Although he had said in the past that diplomatic progress
in Paris would be one prerequisite for the partial withdrawals, this reduction was now explained on the grounds of "more progress . . . than we
had anticipated" in training South Vietnamese troops, an improved situation in American casualties, and a lower Communist infiltration rate.

At the same news conference, Nixon had to cope publicly with the
story of the My Lai massacre, an incident involving a U.S. Army infantry
company and the killing of more than a hundred South Vietnamese
villagers that had occurred in March 1968. The story had not become
known until mid-November 1969, and now, amid public furor, the president chose to face it squarely. He said: "We cannot ever condone or use
atrocities against civilians in order to accomplish [our] goal. . . . I believe
that it is an isolated incident. . . . Certainly within this administration we
are doing everything possible to find out whether it was isolated and so
far our investigation indicates that it was. . . . If it is isolated, it is against
our policy and we shall see to it that what these men did, if they did it,
does not smear the decent men that have gone to Vietnam in a very, in
my opinion, important cause."

(Though Nixon spoke so forcefully against condoning "atrocities
against civilians," he made no reference then or ever to the brutalities
committed by South Vietnamese authorities against Communist war prisoners or the thousands of political detainees in the South. By 1969, there
were more than sixty thousand of them. This information was available
to the government because American advisers were attached to the South
Vietnamese prison system and because Washington received periodic
detailed reports from the International Committee of the Red Cross
[ICRC]. It is unknown whether this material ever reached Nixon's desk
or was kept back by zealous State Department officials who did not wish
to upset him. But in any case, the reports spoke vividly of the treatment
of prisoners in the South. For example, ICRC inspectors wrote after a
visit in November to Saigon's Chihoa prison that they were told by prisoners that many of them had been beaten and put into irons for refusing
to salute the South Vietnamese flag and refusing to chant "Down with Ho

Chi Minh!" The same report related that Chihoa held a group of inmates whose lower limbs had atrophied to the point where they could hardly walk. At the Quinhon prison, the ICRC found in October inmates who had been beaten and women prisoners who regularly underwent hysterical attacks. Also in Quinhon, unruly inmates were confined in barbed-wire cages, 4 feet by 4 feet.)

On December 15, a week after the news conference, Nixon asked for early-evening television time to deliver an address to the nation on "Progress toward Peace in Vietnam." The principal purpose of this pre-Christmas address was to announce that by next April 15 another fifty thousand American troops would be withdrawn from Vietnam. It was the largest single withdrawal since Vietnamization had been set in motion.

But Nixon's reasoning for ordering this new reduction contradicted his own criteria for withdrawals. First, he told his audience, "with regret," that "there has been no progress whatever on the negotiating front since November 3." And for the first time, he injected the issue of American war prisoners in North Vietnam, charging that "typical" of Hanoi's attitude was its "absolute refusal to talk about the fate of the American prisoners they hold and their refusal even to supply their names. . . . This cruel, indefensible action is a shocking demonstration of the inflexible attitude they have taken on all issues."

That the North Vietnamese were indeed cruel on the subject (and certainly in violation of the Geneva Convention on war prisoners) was beyond question. But what Nixon may not have fully understood was that they had concluded that the POWs were one of their most important assets in negotiating with Washington. The prisoners were literally hostages, and Hanoi made it clear that the men—mostly pilots and air crews shot down over the North—would be released only when Nixon accepted its principal settlement points. This decision forced Nixon to place the POW issue at the top of the list of his diplomatic priorities. There was immense irony in this: Nixon, politically, had to keep emphasizing the prisoners in terms of the peace settlement, probably realizing in time that this was undercutting his stance in other areas of the negotiation. But as the tempo of the air war increased, there were more and more American POWs in North Vietnamese hands. Hanoi thus succeeded in setting a trap.

Another criterion for troop withdrawals that Nixon chose to overlook was the rate of North Vietnamese infiltration to the South. In fact, he was contradicting himself—or American intelligence was deficient. Just one week earlier he had said that "enemy infiltration" was down. "The infiltration rate is not as great as we thought [two weeks ago]. . . . It is higher than it was a few months ago . . . it is still lower than it was a year ago. . . . We do not consider the infiltration significant enough to change our troop withdrawal plans." Now, however, he argued that "enemy infiltration has increased substantially. . . . It has not yet reached the point where our military leaders believe the enemy has developed the capability to mount a major offensive, but we are watching the situation closely to see whether it could develop to that extent." Now anyone familiar with North Vietnamese infiltration patterns knew that with the advent of the dry season in November and December movement along the trails did not fluctuate wildly from week to week. Once men and matériel started out in the North, they kept moving down systematically until they reached their planned destination. Despite the use of the most sophisticated ground and air monitoring systems, American intelligence was either wholly inadequate in tracking this North Vietnamese traffic or the data were not properly evaluated. This was a recurring problem in the Vietnam war: the capability of a "fourth-rate" Asian power, day in and day out, to outsmart the electronic resources of a superpower.

Misunderstanding Vietnam was a problem Americans shared for a long time with Sir Robert Thompson, a British counterinsurgency expert who caught first John Kennedy's eye, then Nixon's. Thompson had served as chief of the British police mission in Malaya during the rebellion there in the 1950s and was one of the few Western specialists on insurgency. His credentials seemed impeccable, because the British succeeded, to a large extent, in annihilating the Malayan guerrillas. Kennedy heard about Thompson, a highly articulate Englishman, and invited him to be a private confidential adviser on Vietnam; Thompson had recommended that a system of "strategic hamlets"—fortress-like villages—be established in South Vietnam. (The strategic hamlets were one of the principal defensive-war features in President Diem's strategy; later the idea was dropped as unworkable.)

Now Nixon brought Thompson back into the picture. After having read Thompson's book *No Exit from Vietnam,* he said, he had invited him to the White House on October 7 to discuss the situation. Thompson's book "was very pessimistic about the conduct of the war in Vietnam" largely because of the South Vietnamese failure "to take over the responsibilities for their own defense." This was understood by Nixon as a confirmation of the validity of the administration's Vietnamization program. Presently, the president asked Thompson to go secretly to Vietnam in order to prepare for him "a firsthand, candid, and completely independent report on the situation there."

> After five weeks of intensive investigation, he gave me his report on December 3. His full report, which makes several very constructive recommendations, must remain confidential since it bears on the security of our men. But let me read to you from his summary of his findings: "I was very impressed by the improvement in the military and political situation in Vietnam as compared with all previous visits and especially in the security situation, both in Saigon and the rural areas. A winning position in the sense of obtaining a just peace (whether negotiated or not) and of maintaining an independent, non-Communist South Vietnam has been achieved but we are not yet through. We are in a psychological period where the greatest need is confidence. A steady application of the 'do it yourself' concept with continuing United States support in the background will increase the confidence already shown by many South Vietnam leaders." Mr. Thompson's report, which I would describe as cautiously optimistic, is in line with my own attitude and with reports I have received from our civilian and military leaders in Vietnam.

Actually, Thompson was much more pessimistic about the security situation in Vietnam when he attended a secret high-level conference at the Pentagon on December 4. There, under questioning by intelligence experts, he acknowledged that pacification in the countryside was not going well at all although Vietnamization seemed more promising. This reporter received shortly thereafter a summary of the Pentagon meeting from one of the participants and reported it in an article in *The New York Times*. White House Press Secretary Ziegler responded with a somewhat murky denial of the story; Thompson, back in England, did likewise. As far as the public record was concerned, the Vietnam situation, as set forth by Thompson to Nixon, was a "winning" one. This was the impression the president wished the nation to have.

Nixon might have been better advised if, instead of listening to Thompson, he had been paying attention to General Vo Nguyen Giap, the North Vietnamese defense minister and the architect of the 1954 victory against the French at Dienbienphu. In a series of seven articles published between December 14 and 20 in the party newspaper, *Nhan Dan,* and reprinted in the army newspaper, *Quan Doi Nhan Dan,* the North Vietnamese general outlined his strategy for the next year or two. The central theme of Giap's articles was that Hanoi would now be concentrating on the development of "high quality" in its armed forces, accentuating mobile strike units in place of the massed forces that had been used in recent years. Evidently Giap had learned that the deployment of large units in battle was prohibitively expensive so long as the United States maintained a strong combat presence and lethal air capability in Vietnam. His new strategy was to practice an economy of forces by avoiding large-scale confrontations with the Americans, and to keep both the Americans and the South Vietnamese off balance with mobile-unit strikes. This was Giap's updated version of the "protracted warfare" of the 1950s and, more important, a signal to Washington, if it cared to listen, that he was preparing himself for years of conflict. As it turned out, his strategy worked remarkably well, encouraging Nixon to keep withdrawing United States forces.

Some Americans who read the Giap articles concluded erroneously that Hanoi was, in effect, returning to a form of guerrilla warfare and, due to confessed manpower shortages, making a virtue out of necessity. What they failed to understand was that Giap was evolving a sophisticated doctrine to meet the requirements of a new situation. As Giap explained it:

> Army-building and combat realities have clearly shown that a high-quality army is one that possesses a high combat morale; an intense determination to attack the enemy; satisfactory technical and tactical levels; skillful fighting methods; neat, light, and scattered organizational patterns; good equipment; and a cadre corps and command units possessing firm organizational capabilities; discipline; a stanch perseverance and high mobility in all terrains and under all weather conditions; and one whose material and technical requirements are adequately and satisfactorily met.
> . . . If all our units possess a high quality and are capable of fighting the enemy with high combat efficiency, we can greatly increase the combat strength of our limited armed forces and, at the same time, reduce organizational and leadership problems, replenish our forces, meet our armed forces' material requirements, and use our forces economically.
> We must pay attention to the development of forms of war so that they can respond to the requirements of each period. When it is necessary, we must change in time outdated forms of warfare, taking up new ones which are more appropriate. . . . We must know how to apply already obtained experiences and always consider the practical aspects on the battlefield in order to improve constantly our strategic, operative, and tactical guidance. We should not apply old experiences mechanically, or reapply outmoded forms of warfare.
> In general, in every battle we must use our forces rationally and

have superior fighting methods so that we can destroy many enemy troops and suffer as little as possible. However, sometimes in war there are important battles which, whatever the difficulty may be, we must be determined to overcome at all costs to destroy the enemy.

Nobody in Washington was paying Giap heed. It was on this note—of ignoring a major North Vietnamese hint—that Nixon ended his first year of the war in Vietnam.

Chapter 7

Vietnam, the Middle East, and the general détente approach to the Soviet Union and China dominated Richard Nixon's foreign policy during his first year in office. But there were other complex problems requiring the president's attention. With Japan, there loomed the unresolved question of returning Okinawa—where the United States had important military bases and stored nuclear weapons—to Japanese sovereignty after twenty-five years of American control. There was the need to take a fresh look at the endemically difficult relations with Latin America and to formulate a more coherent policy in Africa. And finally, there was oil.

In 1969, oil price and supply were of no particular concern to Americans. Oil was cheap—imported crude oil cost around $2.30 a barrel delivered at East Coast ports, while the more expensive domestic crude ran around $4.00—and it was plentiful. Under the mandatory oil-import program, instituted in 1959, imports were regulated by a quota system. It was devised under the pressure of major oil companies, which feared that an unrestricted flow of cheap foreign crude would undermine domestic prices. Inasmuch as the majors owned or controlled most oil in the United States as well as in the Middle East, Venezuela, and Canada—our chief suppliers—the quota system was in effect an artificial market-distribution arrangement with strong monopolistic overtones. To make it palatable, the companies invoked national-security reasons (the argument was that excessive foreign competition from abroad would remove domestic production incentives and thus endanger national security in terms of petroleum availability in an emergency), and the Eisenhower administration (Richard Nixon, vice president) went along with it.

By 1969, the situation had changed. For one thing, domestic production was just barely increasing, despite the quota protection: the big companies neatly balanced their cheap imports with the costlier domestic output to arrive at the most favorable profit formula. And while domestic consumption was growing at an astounding rate, a recalculation of United

States resources showed that America's proved reserves were a billion barrels less than had been estimated. This was roughly one-third of total annual domestic production—or one-thirtieth of all proved reserves. Not only was the United States a net *importer* of energy (in the 1950s it had been a net *exporter*), but the gap between domestic supply and consumption was enlarging. Another fairly ominous factor in the equation was that since 1960, most of the producing nations had come together in the Organization of Petroleum Exporting Countries (OPEC), and now this unit was beginning to flex its muscles.

The United States was not taking OPEC seriously, but Nixon had seen enough statistics on production and consumption to realize that something might be wrong with the existing system. On March 25, 1969, he appointed a Cabinet Task Force on Oil Import Control, headed by Labor Secretary George Shultz, to review the entire policy on imports. The basic question was whether the quota system should be abolished and replaced with free imports operating under higher tariffs. The task force took almost a year to complete its study and make recommendations.

Meanwhile the president had a visit from Mohammed Riza Shah Pahlevi, the shahanshah of Iran. The shah, who was journeying to the United States for the ninth time in twenty years, arrived on October 21, to be greeted with full military honors and a brief speech in which Nixon congratulated him on Iranian land reform, "a revolution in terms of social and economic and political progress." (He referred again to the Iranian "revolution" in his toast to the shah at a state dinner, declaiming that "today Iran stands as one of the strongest, the proudest among all the nations of the world.") It was a ceremonial, goodwill visit on the part of the shah, whom succeeding American administrations regarded as a close friend (it was the CIA that had restored him to the throne in 1953 after his ouster by the populist premier Mohammed Mossadegh, the first Iranian politician to demand that his country control its oil) and a useful ally in the volatile Middle East. Nixon and the shah did, nevertheless, discuss the emerging security problems in the Persian Gulf as Britain was giving up her historic responsibilities "East of Suez."

Earlier in the year, the NSC staff had begun a study of the Persian Gulf situation—NSSM–66, which Kissinger ordered on July 12—and the policy conclusion was that Iran, militarily and economically supported by the United States, would fill the vacuum left by the British. Nixon told the shah that the United States hoped Iran would become the dominant power in the strategic Persian Gulf. Not only was it vital in terms of its extraordinarily rich oil basin, but Iran controlled the narrow Strait of

Hormuz, the tanker route in and out of the Persian Gulf. At that point, the United States thought of Iran principally as a strategic junior partner, even possibly a surrogate power, in a region close to Soviet borders. The policy decision in 1969 was, indeed, to make Iran "one of the strongest . . . nations of the world." Sophisticated American arms and training teams were beginning to flow to Iran.

Curiously, however, Nixon and the shah had nothing to say publicly —and very little privately—about oil. Iran was a founding OPEC member, and taking a leaf from Mossadegh's book, it was starting to think about nationalizing foreign oil companies and subjecting consumer countries to price and supply *Diktats*. But none of this came up in the amiable White House encounters. Evidently, it had not occurred to Nixon that before long the Iranians would be grabbing the United States by the jugular.

As a lawyer for a number of American-owned multinational corporations (Pepsi-Cola was one and Precision Valve, owned by his friend Robert Abplanalp, was another), Nixon had often visited Japan on behalf of his clients during his "private" years. Not only did the president regard Japan as the security bulwark of Asia, but he was personally a Japanophile (unlike Kissinger, who, as an aide put it, found it hard to relate to the Japanese) with wide acquaintance in Tokyo's conservative political and business circles. When he entered the White House, he made Japan his top noncrisis priority. One of the first NSC studies—NSSM–5, ordered the day after inauguration—was on Japan, and at an early NSC meeting, Nixon talked at length about Japanese-American relations. His principal point was that the administration should address itself as soon as possible to the reversion of Okinawa. Remembering the wave of anti-American sentiment that forced the cancellation of Eisenhower's visit to Tokyo in the 1950s, Nixon considered Okinawa a potential irritant, and though the Japanese government was not actually pressing Washington on Okinawa, it had privately made it clear that reversion would be welcome. "Nixon really listened to the Japanese case on Okinawa," a former NSC staffer recalled. "The Japanese were too cautious to stick their heads out on it officially, but Nixon understood that it was up to the Americans to make the case for Japan."

Here, the president's main problem was that the Joint Chiefs of Staff opposed the removal of American nuclear weapons from Okinawa (Japan would not agree to have them on its territory), and he also had to contend with a certain amount of foot dragging by Kissinger. It was the State

Department that became his principal supporter on this issue. The department took the view, as Nixon did, that it was inconsistent with Japanese-American relations to hang on indefinitely to Okinawa. It also felt that to wait too long would mean the loss of leverage in negotiations with the Japanese for the maintenance of American nonnuclear bases, particularly those for the B-52s needed over Indochina or for other contingencies. Secretary Rogers proposed that reversion take place in 1970, on the tenth anniversary of the Treaty of Mutual Cooperation and Security with Japan. An agreement, Rogers suggested, could be negotiated during 1969. Kissinger disagreed with Rogers, but this was one of the few times he was actually overruled by Nixon.

According to one State Department official, "Henry's basic problem is that he never gets to a problem until there is a crisis. He would let pressure reach the boiling point. He's a great tactician, but a lousy strategist." And in the case of Japan, he was also hampered by his personal attitude toward the Japanese: "Henry always felt that the Japanese are not conceptual, that they have no long-term vision, that they go for decisions by consensus," one associate said. "Besides, his staff never put Japan into a context for him so that he could understand it."

During May, Nixon won over the Joint Chiefs of Staff to the notion that American security would not be seriously damaged if nuclear weapons were removed from Okinawa. Laird needed no convincing. The chiefs also went along in the end with the State Department's argument that, as in the case of metropolitan Japan under the 1960 treaty, the United States would have to consult with the Japanese government before using Okinawa as a base for combat operations. The State Department's point was that inasmuch as the acquiescence of the Okinawa population was required to maintain American bases there after reversion, it was worthwhile to sacrifice the freedom of action in order to keep the facilities. So long as the United States administered Okinawa, the question of consultation did not arise in launching B-52s against Indochina targets.

Nixon's decision to remove nuclear weapons from Okinawa came late in May, before the United States and Japan opened actual negotiations. But before this decision could be communicated to the Japanese, *The New York Times* reported it, on June 3, which enormously annoyed the White House. "The consequences of this disclosure," Kissinger commented many years later, probably with more anger than accuracy, "in terms of compromising negotiating tactics, prejudicing the government's interest, and complicating our relations with Japan were obvious, and clearly preempted any opportunity we might have had for obtaining a more favorable outcome during our negotiations with the Japanese." Actually, anyone who had followed the Okinawa problem for the previous two or three years, including the Japanese, knew that the United States would sooner or later have to remove its nuclear weapons from the island. It is difficult to see what better terms could have been negotiated, and Kissinger was clearly defending diplomatic secrecy for its own sake.

The Okinawa reversion agreement was hammered out by Nixon in three days of White House negotiations—November 19 to 21—with Japan's Prime Minister Eisaku Sato. This artful piece of diplomacy, which took into account the military requirements of the United States and the political requirements of Japan, hinged on the idea, oft repeated in the communiqué, that Okinawa's reversion would be accomplished "without detriment to the security of the Far East including Japan." Nixon and Sato agreed that "the United States would retain under the terms of the Treaty of Mutual Cooperation and Security such military facilities and areas in Okinawa as required in the mutual security of both countries," and that the treaty would "apply to Okinawa," meaning that the United States and Japan would consult on the use of bases for combat missions. (Sato had said that in the event of a new Korean war, for example, Japan would respond instantly to let the United States use *all* Japanese bases for the defense of Korea.)

The tricky point was the continued use of Okinawa by the American B-52s in the Indochina war. This was handled in the following passage of the joint statement: "The President and the Prime Minister expressed the strong hope that the war in Vietnam would be concluded before return of the administrative rights over Okinawa to Japan. . . . [If not,] they agreed that . . . the two governments would fully consult with each other in the light of the situation at that time so that reversion would be accomplished without affecting the United States efforts to assure the South Vietnamese people the opportunity to determine their own political future without outside interference." Privately Sato told Nixon that the Americans could go on using Okinawa in their Vietnamese efforts even after the reversion.

Nixon and Sato dealt with the problem of nuclear weapons in a similarly deft fashion. The United States, according to the communiqué, accepted "the particular sentiment of the Japanese people against nuclear weapons and the policy of the Japanese government reflecting such sentiment," but with the caveat that it was doing so "without prejudice to the position of the United States government with respect to the prior consultation system under the Treaty. . . ." In the negotiations, Nixon told Sato that the United States would respect the Japanese position "so long as it existed." This, in effect, became a nuclear loophole, allowing the United States to bring nuclear weapons back to Okinawa if the basic Japanese policy changed or if permission to do so could be obtained through consultation—if ever necessary. (And the actual Okinawa reversion treaty, to be signed in 1970, made no reference whatsoever to nuclear weapons; it only mentioned the consultation system in general.) The communiqué said that actual reversion would take place in 1972; complex negotiations, as well as treaty ratification by both countries' legislative bodies were still needed.

Where Nixon and Sato made no progress at all was in the dispute over textiles. The crux of the problem was that Washington, under pressure from the depressed American textile industry, wanted to limit Japanese exports of synthetic textiles to the American market. The Japanese, who had shifted much of their production to synthetics after accepting some years earlier the export limitations imposed by the Long-Term Textile Agreement on Cotton, felt they had been betrayed. The dispute was a curious one, for it was a textbook case of bad economic politics on both sides. The political forces involved were much larger than the industries they represented, and the argument for a time poisoned overall relations between the two countries.

On the American side, a major error had been committed by Maurice Stans, then commerce secretary, who had gone to Tokyo in April to negotiate a textile agreement but, in the words of a State Department expert, "blew" it right away. Stans had personal instructions from Nixon to act low-key in the Tokyo conversations, but as soon as he arrived in Japan, he began making public statements. According to State Department officials, he wanted "to put pressure on the Japanese by going public, against all advice, and it blew up in his face." Not only did his negotiating effort fail, but a political storm ensued. After Stans's return to Washington, Peter Flanigan, a White House adviser, tried to carry on the negotiations with the Japanese ambassador, Nobuhiko Ushiba, but to no avail. When Sato came to Washington, Nixon was under strong pressure to relate the textiles issue to the Okinawa reversion. But he resisted, and raised the subject only privately with Sato, who gave him a private commitment that Japan itself would seek to limit exports ("It was a bit Delphic," an aide recalled). The problem went unresolved for two more years. It was a good example of sloppiness in the conduct of foreign-economic policy, and it also showed that Kissinger could not care less about Japanese textiles.

One curious sentence in the Nixon-Sato communiqué was a portent of things to come: "The President stressed his determination to bring inflation in the United States under·control." Inflation was not yet a major issue in the United States in 1969, but the Japanese economy, heavily dependent on American imports, was beginning to suffer from what economists would later call "the export of inflation by the United States"—and Sato tried hard to call Nixon's attention to it.

By midautumn, the United States and the Soviet Union were able to come to terms on when their negotiations on the limitation of strategic nuclear arms would start. The Senate's passage on August 6 (by one vote) of the law authorizing the construction of the ABM shield was the final element in the elaboration of the American position; as far as Kissinger was concerned, it was simply a bargaining chip in the game with the Russians, who had already developed antiballistic defenses. The Russians, who had been dragging their feet for months, also seemed to have resolved their doubts, and on October 20, Soviet Ambassador Dobrynin secretly called at the White House to inform Nixon and Kissinger that Moscow was ready to proceed.

On October 25, the two governments announced jointly that SALT negotiations, intended to cover offensive as well as defensive weapons, would begin in Helsinki on November 17. The Finnish capital was chosen as a convenient neutral site, although provisions were made for the rotation of SALT sessions between Helsinki and Vienna, another neutral ground. It was agreed that the negotiations would be conducted in absolute secrecy—with no information given the news media, except for dates of sessions—and that all substantive announcements would be made jointly. Both governments appeared to be taking SALT with utmost seriousness, and neither seemed interested in turning it into a propaganda forum.

On November 17, Nixon sent a message to Ambassador Gerard C. Smith, director of the Arms Control and Disarmament Agency, who had been named the previous July to lead the American delegation. "Today," he wrote solemnly, "you will begin what all of your fellow citizens in the United States and, I believe, all people throughout the world, profoundly hope will be a sustained effort not only to limit the build-up of strategic forces but to reverse it. . . . I do not underestimate the difficulty of your task; the nature of modern weapons makes their control an exceedingly complex endeavor. . . . Nor do I underestimate the suspicion and distrust that must be dispelled if you are to succeed in your assignment." He went on to explain in general terms the United States negotiating position worked out by Henry Kissinger over the past months, and reflected in specific secret instructions. Addressing himself as much to the Russians as to Smith, he took a conciliatory tone:

> I have stated that for our part we will be guided by the concept of maintaining "sufficiency" in the forces required to protect ourselves and our allies. I recognize that the leaders of the Soviet Union bear similar defense responsibilities. I believe it is possible, however, that we can carry out our respective responsibilities under a mutually acceptable limitation and eventual reduction of our strategic arsenals.
> We are prepared to discuss limitations on all offensive and defensive systems, and to reach agreements in which both sides can have confidence. . . . We are prepared to deal with the issues seriously, carefully and purposefully. We seek no unilateral advantage. Nor do we seek arrangements which could be prejudicial to the interests of third parties. We are prepared to engage in bona fide negotiations on concrete issues, avoiding polemics and extraneous matters.

Nixon was saying, in effect, that the United States had abandoned the earlier concepts of "superiority" and even "parity" in nuclear forces. But "sufficiency," of course, was an elusive and subjective concept.

The talks opened in Helsinki with Ambassador Smith, Soviet Deputy Foreign Minister Vladimir S. Semyonov, and their delegations toasting each other in champagne. Formal speeches were exchanged, and then a curtain dropped over the proceedings. For the next three weeks, the two teams—each included diplomats specialized in disarmament questions, military officers, and scientists—exchanged general views on how the negotiations should be conducted. The American delegation started out by presenting to the Russians four "illustrative" rather than specific proposals on how problems of defensive and offensive weapons could best be handled. Kissinger had wanted first to establish the limits, then settle down to the specific aspects.

On December 8, the United States asked for a brief recess. At a news conference, Nixon explained that it was done for "the purpose of developing positions in a proper way." Actually, he and Kissinger wanted to give some thought to the presentation made by Semyonov, a much more narrow proposal emphasizing negotiations on defensive arms only, before having Smith return to the table in Helsinki. But, Nixon said, progress thus far was "encouraging" because "both sides are presenting positions in a very serious way and are not trying to make propaganda out of their positions. . . . Here you have the basic security of the United States of America and the Soviet Union involved. Therefore, both must bargain hard. . . . The prospects are better than I anticipated they would be when the talks began."

Presently, the delegations resumed their meetings. They adjourned on December 22, with plans to open a new round of talks in Vienna the following April. Such was the complexity of the issues that both governments needed at least three months to study the situation. Smith and the American delegation, home for Christmas, gave Kissinger a detailed briefing, and Kissinger reduced it to a top-secret position paper to be considered by the White House Verification Panel, the special NSC body set up to deal with SALT.

During the autumn, Nixon was also busy in other areas of control of modern weapons. On November 25, he signed the instrument of ratification of the Treaty on the Nonproliferation of Nuclear Weapons that the Senate had ratified in March. The idea behind the treaty, originally negotiated by President Kennedy for the United States, and signed by 108 governments, was to restrict the possession of nuclear weapons to the members of the "atomic club"—the United States, the Soviet Union, Britain, France, and China—and to bind the other signatories not to develop or acquire them. France and China, however, did not sign. A number of "threshold countries," those such as India and Israel with a theoretical or quasi-practical nuclear capability, likewise refused to sign it. As Nixon was signing the American ratification instrument, the danger remained that the "club" would grow in coming years.

The same day, Nixon announced that the United States was renouncing chemical warfare through a commitment not to make first use of lethal chemical weapons and incapacitating chemicals. The renunciation would take the form of United States adherence to the 1925 Geneva Protocol, and Nixon said he was submitting it for ratification by the Senate. He also announced America's renunciation of the use of lethal biological agents and weapons, "and all other methods of biological warfare." Nixon said the United States "will confine its biological research to defensive measures such as immunization and safety measures" and that the Pentagon "has been asked to make recommendations as to the disposal of existing stocks of bacteriological weapons." This action was taken in response to a proposed U.N. convention banning biological warfare.

Nixon's moves on chemical and biological warfare were major breakthroughs. Forty-four years had elapsed since the Geneva Protocol, and Nixon recalled that "during the eight years that I sat on the National Security Council in the Eisenhower administration . . . these subjects, insofar as an appraisal of what the United States had, what our capability was, what other nations had, were really considered taboo." But, he said, he had ordered a comprehensive study of chemical and biological warfare "because it has always been my conviction that what we don't know usually causes more fear than what we do know." This study, ordered on May 28, the National Security Council's NSSM–59 on "Chemical-Biological Agents," took almost six months to complete. There was the inevitable opposition from the Pentagon, but Nixon went ahead with the renunciation. This decision, he said, was "an initiative toward peace."

However, as Senate investigators would discover in 1975, the CIA simply ignored Nixon's suggestions to explore means of destroying the stocks of toxins that came under the rubric of biological weapons. The agency admitted that it secretly kept in storage for six years 10.9 grams of Saxitonit, one of the deadliest known toxins, derived from shellfish. Six-tenths of a milligram of Saxitonit is sufficient to cause instant death, so what the CIA had on hand was enough to murder 6540 persons with Saxitonit pellets fired from special dart guns. Though the agency claimed that Saxitonit was mainly intended as a suicide toxin for CIA agents who might be captured, it did not deny that it could be used against "the enemy" as well. The Pentagon, which controlled bacteriological and biological weapons, apparently offered its stocks for "research" to other government agencies when Nixon ordered their disposal—and the CIA immediately volunteered to take its quota. The army kept Saxitonit for the CIA at its Fort Detrick facility in Maryland. Other poisons, such as cobra venom, were also retained in contravention of presidential orders.

As is clear from the patterns emerging in the White House, Nixon's global policies took the so-called third world only marginally into account. The president never set foot in Latin America (except for Mexico) during his tenure, and he never visited Africa as president. (His only African visitor in the first year was Ethiopia's Emperor Haile Selassie, not exactly an emissary of the new Africa.) Though he dispatched Governor Nelson Rockefeller on a "fact-finding" mission to South America, virtually none of Rockefeller's recommendations was ever implemented.

Kissinger seemed totally uninterested in Latin America—except for Cuba, where he kept urging CIA Director Helms to build up again the program of infiltrating secret agents. Helms resisted this on the ground that the risks were greater than the potential benefits.

Yet during 1969 the NSC staff produced six special studies on Latin America: two general ones, the others addressed to trouble spots—Cuba, Haiti (where the dictatorial rule of President François Duvalier threatened Caribbean stability), Brazil (a major investment target for United States private capital and the scene of leftist-guerrilla activities), and Peru (where the new military regime had nationalized an American oil company).

Nixon's fundamental approach to Latin America was to keep an eye on problems while making the goodwill gestures that were expected of an American president. Having suffered physical attacks during his 1958 vice-presidential tour of South America, he harbored a certain resentment toward Latin Americans in general, and he advocated a "low profile" for U.S. policies in the Hemisphere. He addressed the foreign ministers of the Organization of American States in April; received Colombia's President Carlos Lleras Restrepo in June; went to the inauguration of the Amistad Dam on the Rio Grande on September 8; and on October 31, delivered a speech before the annual meeting of the Inter American Press Association, making a promise that the United States would be unable to fulfill. In this latter effort, he proclaimed that the United States would lead "a vigorous effort" to reduce nontariff barriers erected by industrialized nations against Latin American products and "press for a liberal system of generalized trade preferences for all developing countries, including Latin America." The Latin Americans were delighted, but actually, the State Department had advised Nixon against promising "the generalized trade preferences" on the grounds that Congress, in its protectionist mood, would never grant them.

The same approach prevailed when it came to Africa. There was only one really major crisis in the area, and that was the Nigerian secession war, where Nixon and Kissinger saw no need for new policies. For a time, Nixon considered recognizing Biafra—possibly because American public opinion, aroused by the tales and pictures of starving Biafran children, was strongly in favor of the rebels—and Kissinger tried halfheartedly and vainly to arrange secret mediation between the Nigerians and the Biafrans. But in the end, Kissinger concluded that nothing would be served by recognizing Biafra—he had an instinctive dislike of seeing nations break up—and he so advised Nixon. The president dropped the idea after six options contained in NSSM–11, on Nigeria, were discussed by the National Security Council on February 11.

For both strategic and domestic reasons, the White House took a special interest in South Africa, since the preservation of the status quo there was deemed important: oil-tanker routes from the Persian Gulf to Western Europe and the United States ran around the Cape. Still, Nixon was aware of American sentiment against white-rule regimes in South

Africa and Rhodesia. In April, Kissinger ordered a NSC study on southern Africa to determine whether any change in U.S. policies was warranted. NSSM–39 was submitted to the National Security Council on December 19, a meeting at which Vice President Agnew continually confused South Africa with Rhodesia, and Nixon kept gently correcting him. NSSM–39 offered five policy options, ranging from support for black liberation movements in southern Africa, including Mozambique, to a policy of "communication" with the South African government. ("Communication" would mean a *de facto* relaxation of restrictions on the sale to South Africa of equipment that could be used militarily against black insurgents.) The intermediary option recommended that existing policies be maintained. The National Security Council reviewed the NSSM–39 options, but Nixon deferred the decision for a number of weeks.

Early in May an internal fight had developed in the White House over Rhodesia. After receiving a visit from several executives of Union Carbide, Patrick Buchanan, a special assistant to the president, sent a private memorandum to Nixon recommending that the corporation be permitted to retrieve 150,000 tons of chromium ore from Rhodesia. Obeying the U.N. decision to impose economic sanctions on the regime of Prime Minister Ian Smith for declaring "unilateral independence" (and ruling out the participation of black-majority representatives in the new government), the United States had suspended all trade with Rhodesia. Union Carbide's argument was that the embargo caused it serious hardship, and the corporation wanted a one-time exception to import the bottled-up ore. On the margin of Buchanan's memo, Nixon scrawled the notation, "Yes, let them have it." The memo then went to Kissinger for execution.

Roger Morris, Kissinger's NSC specialist on Africa, was of a different opinion. "You can't just go around abrogating international law any time you feel like it," he argued; the United States was bound by the U.N. resolution and President Johnson's executive order implementing it. There might be a legal way of satisfying Union Carbide, but "this needs careful deliberation. . . . It should be decided in the context of the overall United States policy in Africa." He reminded Kissinger that the NSC staff was preparing a general review of southern African policies and this could be resolved as part of it.

Kissinger, according to Morris, agreed and asked for one memorandum for Nixon explaining why the exception should not be granted to Union Carbide, and another for Buchanan, setting forth the NSC reasoning, which Buchanan could submit to Nixon. The president went along with Kissinger's opinion; but a few days later, Buchanan complained,

"This is not what I expected from you, Henry." He knew, he remarked, that the person who had handled the chromium matter for Kissinger was Roger Morris, "a well-known Democrat." As a result of the Rhodesian incident, the political backgrounds of NSC staff members were carefully checked on instructions from Nixon's domestic advisers. This was part of the beginning of secret police operations inside the White House. (Union Carbide was granted its exception the following year, apparently with no further opposition from Kissinger.)

The roots of Richard Nixon's ultimate personal disaster are to be found in the practices developed during 1969 around his conduct of foreign policy. Very quickly, Nixon's planning and execution of that policy became caught in a web of obsessive secrecy, in ever-increasing suspicions of the "bureaucracy" and the news media.

On one level, Nixon shared with his national security adviser as well as the domestic palace guard—Ehrlichman, Haldeman, Colson, Buchanan, and others—the increasingly paranoid belief that bureaucrats, liberals, Democrats, journalists, and the permanent Washington establishment were "out to get us." They convinced themselves that secret information was being leaked to the news media by an envious and embittered bureaucracy in order to torpedo their initiatives, and even went so far as to suspect selected bureaucrats and newsmen of possible ties with foreign (i.e., Soviet) intelligence services. But curiously and perhaps inevitably, the greater the secrecy in which the president and Kissinger conducted foreign policy, the greater the leakage. It was almost a geometric progression. Nixon and Kissinger took the view that public opinion—and Congress—should know only what the White House was prepared to reveal, that the diplomacy in which they were involved demanded utmost secrecy. It seems never to have occurred to them that a reasonably honest explanation of foreign policy could be offered the public without exposing state secrets. And, as we have gradually come to learn, their secrecy was also used to conceal policies and actions that almost certainly public opinion would have opposed.

On another level, there were unabating personal tensions in the highest echelons of Nixon's administration, and again, these tensions would be reflected in Nixon's and Kissinger's suspicions that hostile people were leaking information to embarrass them. As for their own personal relationship, it remains unclear, apart from Kissinger's carefully masked intellectual contempt for the man he served. (Kissinger, as one of his former associates related, "never spoke well of *anyone* in private—unless the person was present.")

According to NSC aides, Kissinger tried to protect himself in the Nixon White House by having his secretary monitor, through a "dead key," all his telephone conversations with the president and then type up summaries of the conversations for his private files—a practice about which Nixon, the aides assumed, was never informed. Kissinger himself acknowledged in a court affidavit that it was standard procedure that all his telephone calls were monitored by his secretary and summarized for the files. This is not uncommon in the offices of senior government officials, but it *was* unusual to eavesdrop on the president of the United States—who, himself, of course was also having his talks recorded.

The ripples of mutual distrust spread out from the White House into the cabinet. Nixon distrusted Defense Secretary Laird, and so did Kissinger, but all three men joined in a certain contempt for CIA Director Helms. Kissinger also disliked Secretary of State Rogers—yet never ceased to consider him a rival for Nixon's favors. Laird distrusted Kissinger as a general proposition, and the palace guard—especially Ehrlichman, Haldeman, and Colson—had reservations about him because he had loaded his NSC staff with what one aide called "a very liberal crowd." They also resented the fact that his foreign-policy–NSC structure gave him control of the process at every sensitive point.

Kissinger set up a system through which he thought he could control the press by making himself accessible to key newsmen and commentators. This was how he did his own leaking. An aide recalled ruefully, "It was awfully hard for us to see Henry because his schedule was so crowded with newsmen in addition to his official duties." When an NSC staffer got to see Kissinger, he would be "squeezed between Rolly Evans [a columnist] and Joe Kraft [another columnist], between Max Frankel [then *The New York Times*'s Washington bureau chief] and Murray Marder [*The Washington Post*'s diplomatic correspondent], or between a variety of people Henry was seeing from the media. . . . It was Herb Kaplow [of NBC] at eleven o'clock and somebody else at noon, and one had the impression that Henry was conducting quite vigorous press relations." Nixon's domestic advisers, always uncomfortable with newsmen, never established such an operation.

One NSC staffer, obeying Kissinger's instructions, severed his relations with his friends among newspapermen. Soon he received an angry letter from one, a *New York Times* correspondent, protesting that "I'm being confronted with a sort of East European, totalitarian treatment of the First Amendment." So he took the letter to Kissinger, and told him that "I thought we were inviting much more difficulty [with secrecy] than it seems to be worth. Someone sooner or later is going to do a story about how the NSC staff has been muzzled. I told Henry I could assure him that people in the State Department are talking to newsmen quite normally. Isn't it better to trust us? If an indiscretion occurs, you can check on it. And isn't it better for us to have cordial relations with these people and not create this kind of animosity? No response from Henry."

One way the NSC staff learned a lot about personal relations in the White House was from memos taken down in the president's office by Alexander Butterfield, one of Nixon's aides. An official recalled: "Alex would sit in a corner of the Oval Office taking down everything Nixon said —this was ages before the tape recorders were put in—and we used to call his memos 'Butterfieldgrams.' Sometimes they were simply instructions from Nixon. They were headed: 'Memorandum for Dr. Kissinger from Alexander Butterfield,' and would say, for example, 'The President says: Henry, I have decided that we should have a policy review on Korea. . . . I want an options paper up here in four days.' " But the Butterfieldgrams also told quite a bit about Nixon's private attitudes, as another official recounted: "I remember one Butterfield memo that sent us all into hysterics. Al Haig called us over to read the damn thing—it was Butterfield's notes on Nixon's comments while reading the newspapers, thinking out loud. Nixon would read the *Times* or the *Post* and he would identify leaks—all as being Laird's. The memos were on separate pieces of paper that came down to us through Henry, who was usually present when Nixon did his reading. So Nixon would say: 'I see this goddamn c . . . s . . . . . story about troop levels, this is Laird again. The son of a bitch is up to his old games. What's he trying to do? Next page: Henry, what is this goddamn c . . . s . . . . . . story by Beecher? Is this Laird? It must be Laird. It's Laird, isn't it? Next page: What's this editorial in the *Post?* I've seen this before, it's the same line of reasoning. You know who this is? It's Laird.' This particular batch was about five or six sheets, and all of them were Laird, and Nixon treating his secretary of defense as a sort of foreign government out to get him. The level of suspicion, the quality of human relationships between these two men was a source of constant amazement to us."

Kissinger, too, fed his staff morsels of gossip about his enemies. One aide recalled occasions when Kissinger would return from National Security Council meetings and tell them: " 'Oh, Laird stomped up and down, bashed on the table, took his shoe off . . . and Rogers did his usual nonsensical presentation.' Henry would make curious, humorous, sort of deriding remarks about Laird. He didn't care for Laird, distrusted him, thought he was ambitious, thought he wanted to be president, thought

he was basically in cahoots with the military against Henry, although he
was never quite sure how that worked. He thought Laird had friends in
the White House who were conspiring against him."

But Kissinger was equally suspicious of his own staff. One of the NSC
aides was told one day in the spring of 1969 by Lawrence S. Eagleburger,
a key assistant, "You're in trouble. . . . Henry doesn't know what you're
doing. . . . He said the other day, 'I don't know what that son of a bitch
is doing. . . . Is he doing something against me?' " Eagleburger's advice
was: "What you've got to do is to send him every week a little piece of
paper which tells him what you're doing—specifically, what you're doing
in the bureaucracy, about what you did, what meetings you went to, what
you said, what you're trying to do, and whom you're trying to monitor.
. . . Give him some insights into the State Department and some intelligence about the people there and their weaknesses, and the bureaucratic
infighting that's going on—and so on. Give him the details."

What came next were secret wiretaps on American officials involved
in foreign-policy planning and execution, and on a group of Washington
news correspondents who specialized in the coverage of diplomatic and
defense news. The official justification for this eavesdropping exercise, as
it was presented many years later, was that President Nixon and Special
Assistant Kissinger were so disturbed over the dissemination of secret
information that they had to turn to wiretapping to track down the
sources of the leakage. But considerable evidence suggests that both men
also wanted to know what was being said by people about them and their
policies. In any event, before his fourth month in office was over, President Nixon had launched a spying operation against his own aides; Kissinger's role was to supply the names of his own (hand-picked) personal
assistants and other functionaries whom the FBI should wiretap.

To turn to the FBI to spy on key government officials was, of course,
an extremely serious political decision on Nixon's part, a decision that,
one would think, would be ordered only under the most critical conditions affecting national security in its most serious sense. But the chronology of events, pieced together from FBI documents and testimony before
the Senate Foreign Relations Committee, does not suggest that such
critical conditions ever existed. What *did* exist was a police-state mentality
in the White House.

To begin with, only five major news stories were published that could
be considered as containing serious leaks (and even this characterization
is debatable concerning three of the five) before the president ordered

the wiretapping. The first story in this batch (all of them, incidentally, appeared in *The New York Times*), published on April 6, dealt with the fact that the new administration was considering unilateral withdrawal among various Vietnam options.

Presumably on the strength of this particular article Nixon set the spying process in motion. According to Kissinger's deposition in a lawsuit in January 1976, he "authorized an electronic surveillance to be conducted" on suspected "leakers" during an Oval Office meeting on April 25 with FBI Director J. Edgar Hoover, Attorney General Mitchell, and Kissinger. That same evening, at Camp David, Nixon, Hoover, and Mitchell discussed leaks during dinner. Kissinger was not present.

At this point contradictions emerge concerning the responsibility for selecting the wiretap targets. Kissinger's deposition emphasized that "while his [Nixon's] authorization was general in terms and not limited to specific individuals, my understanding was that he then directed surveillance" against specific individuals. And he also claimed that Hoover specifically proposed at the Oval Office meeting the name of at least one NSC official to be wiretapped. But in an earlier deposition, Mitchell had said he could not recall that Nixon had ordered specific wiretaps, and he thought Kissinger had been responsible for preparing a list of names. Nixon himself, in an oral deposition taken in San Clemente on January 15, 1976, insisted that although he had been in full accord with the wiretaps, he never personally selected the targets. This, he said, was left up to Kissinger, who was asked to provide the names of officials suspected of leaking information. Nixon added that Kissinger could have stopped the wiretaps if they were unproductive. On January 29, in response to this assertion, which so flatly contradicted his own, Kissinger said he "cannot believe" Nixon had denied his role in picking the names to be wiretapped.

In any case on May 2, 1969, *The New York Times* published an article disclosing five strategic options the administration was studying while evolving the American negotiating position on SALT; as we have seen, these options were discussed in the newspaper even before they were presented to the National Security Council. By White House standards, this was a fairly serious leak; that very evening, the president called Hoover at home—the FBI logs say the "subject of conversation [is] unknown." It is significant that this Nixon-Hoover conversation took place one week *after* the president had approved the wiretaps.

On May 4, the *Times* came up with a story discussing possible military responses the United States might make if North Korea were to shoot down other American aircraft—as it had done a month earlier. This was a "soft" story, as this kind of reporting goes, but it alarmed the White House. The next afternoon, May 5, Kissinger secretly visited Hoover at FBI headquarters, and while there is no known record of their conversation, this was the first such visit Kissinger is known to have made. On May 6, the *Times* was back with a story reporting that Nixon would order retaliation if the North Koreans again shot down a plane.

At dawn on May 8, Nixon, Kissinger, and Mitchell arrived at Nixon's home at Key Biscayne. The following morning, May 9, the *Times* ran a page-one story under the byline of its Pentagon correspondent, William Beecher, reporting that American B-52s had been secretly bombing Cambodia since March. This was when Nixon and Kissinger really hit the roof, as a presidential assistant later recalled. Beecher's article was considered immensely embarrassing to the administration, and Kissinger feared that its disclosures would place the United States as well as Prince Sihanouk in an untenable position (this was not, as it turned out, the case). Curiously there was very little public or congressional outcry over this news story, although the White House was enraged.

President Nixon decided at once that the FBI should be brought into the picture, and Kissinger, in effect, took command of the operation for him. FBI logs show that Kissinger telephoned Hoover from Key Biscayne at 10:35 a.m. on May 9 concerning Beecher's article. Hoover's own memorandum of the conversation quotes Kissinger as requesting "a major effort to find out where that came from." Thirty minutes later, Kissinger called again to ask that two earlier news articles written by Beecher—the one about SALT and the latest North Korea one—be included in the "inquiry." "Hoover promised to call him the next morning if not sooner." At 1:05 p.m., Kissinger was once more on the phone to suggest that the inquiry concerning Beecher be handled discreetly, "so no stories will get out." Hoover, according to FBI file memos, replied that he had decided not to contact Beecher himself, and instead the bureau's agents were checking with other reporters "to see if they can find out where it came from." This comment in itself emphasizes the unreality of their whole undertaking: did Hoover and Kissinger really imagine that other Washington reporters knew Beecher's sources and that if they did they would tell the FBI about them?

At 5:05 p.m., Hoover telephoned Kissinger in Key Biscayne (this was now the fourth conversation that day) to make a report. This is how the chronology assembled by the staff of the Senate Foreign Relations Committee described the conversation: "[Hoover] stated that their 'contacts' believed that the Beecher leak came from a staff member of the National Security Council and Hoover said the speculation was that [deleted] may have been responsible, citing what he considered to be unfavorable material in his record. He also named as possibilities [deleted] of the NSC staff and [deleted] of the Defense Department. Hoover said Kissinger said he 'hoped I would follow it up as far as we can take it and they will destroy whoever did this if we can find him, no matter where he is.' There was no direct suggestion that wiretapping was either asked for or would be used."

At this point the story becomes even more complicated. Although the FBI log thus disclaimed any "direct suggestion" of wiretapping, it listed at 6:20 p.m. *of that same day* "the first entry from the tap on [deleted]'s home phone." The wiretap was thus installed on May 9, *before* Attorney General Mitchell formally authorized it. The "deleted" target of this first wiretap was Morton Halperin, who had been a deputy assistant secretary of defense under Lyndon Johnson and was one of Kissinger's most intimate associates. And it was Halperin whom Hoover had in mind when he referred to "unfavorable material in his record."

As far as is known, this "material" included the fact that Halperin was a Democratic holdover with liberal views. Besides, Halperin did work on Indochina on the NSC staff, and Hoover and Kissinger perhaps concluded he might have told Beecher the Cambodia information. According to Kissinger's 1976 deposition, Nixon had singled out Halperin on April 25 as one of those to be wiretapped. One way or the other, the tap on Halperin's home phone was maintained until October 2, 1971, more than two years after he had left the government.

The two other "deleted" NSC names mentioned by Hoover to Kissinger were Helmut Sonnenfeldt, the Soviet expert on the staff, and Daniel I. Davidson, also a Democratic holdover, who had served on the American delegation to the Paris peace talks under Averell Harriman. The "deleted" name at the Defense Department was that of air force Lieutenant General Robert E. Pursley, senior military assistant to Defense Secretary Laird.

On May 10, Colonel Alexander Haig, a principal assistant to Kissinger, called on William Sullivan, a top Hoover aide, at the FBI offices. A memorandum later written by Hoover to Attorney General Mitchell said that Haig "came to the Bureau to advise that a request was being made on the highest authority which involves a matter of most grave and serious consequences to our national security." Sullivan's own memo to Hoover was even more specific. It said that Haig requested FBI wiretaps on Halperin, Sonnenfeldt, Davidson, and General Pursley, adding that the taps "will only be necessary for a few days to resolve the issue," and that Haig would come to the FBI "to review any information developed."

Mitchell signed Hoover's memorandum authorizing the wiretaps late in the afternoon of May 12. Halperin's tap, of course, had already been on for three days; the taps on Sonnenfeldt, Davidson, and General Pursley were installed during the evening of May 12. In a legal deposition in 1975, General Haig (he had risen from colonel to four-star general during the Nixon years) said that while his initial task was to read the FBI wiretap logs and pass on their information to Kissinger, the White House soon changed this procedure. Instead of Haig's giving the FBI information orally to Kissinger, the bureau submitted written reports to both Nixon and Kissinger. Haig explained that this was because some White House officials might not have been "totally comfortable with Dr. Kissinger's own reporting of information" to Nixon. "He was suspect, to some individuals—I cannot say who—to some he may have been perceived to be part of the problem." "Loyalist and partisan" White House staffers may have been suspicious of him because he had worked for Kennedy and Johnson and "there were many people at that time that were accusing him of being very left of center."

(In relation to Halperin, Kissinger too applied something of a double standard. FBI logs showed that on August 9, 1969—three months after the tap was put in place—Kissinger telephoned Halperin to plead with him to remain on the NSC staff. Halperin had been planning to resign for his own reasons—and of course he was unaware at the time of the wiretap—but Kissinger praised "Halperin's work as being extraordinary for him [Kissinger]." The FBI summary added: "It was strongly stated by Kissinger that Halperin had a 'damned frustrating position there and some of my operators have behaved very poorly.' Kissinger wants Halperin to know that his work was 'certainly the most creative of anyone on the staff,' and he doesn't want to give up on that without a struggle." Presumably, Nixon read this summary.)

One naturally wonders what sort of mind would have conceived or concurred in the idea of spying on one's closest associates. Perhaps it is explicable in terms of Kissinger's own insecurity in the White House and his fear that he might be damaged if the leaks came from his staff. Questions of morality, trust, and loyalty toward his colleagues probably did not even arise. Kissinger knew that Halperin and Davidson had many friends in the Washington press corps and even Sonnenfeldt, a dour man known around the NSC as "Kissinger's Kissinger" (he, too, was a Jewish refugee from Germany), had a friend or two among newsmen.

But General Pursley's case was quite different. He had no known friends among reporters, and he was the most unlikely leak prospect in town. Here, then, another dimension to the White House spying comes in. No knowledgeable official believes that Pursley was wiretapped because of news leaks; instead, many of them are convinced that this was a form of spying, indirectly, on Defense Secretary Laird. The presumption is that by monitoring conversations between Laird and Pursley—they were friends, and often had occasion to call each other at home (Pursley's tap was on his home phone in suburban Maryland)—the president and Kissinger could learn about Laird's private views on any number of policy issues.

General Pursley's wiretap was removed after two weeks, on May 27 (officially on Colonel Haig's request), but he was wiretapped again, presumably for the same reasons, during most of 1970 and 1971—a period when relations between Kissinger and Laird were at their worst. Neither Nixon nor Kissinger ever told Laird that Pursley's phone was being tapped; and of course had Pursley really been suspected of leaks, any rational president would have informed the general's boss of it. With enormous indignation, Laird said years later that he did not learn of the Pursley tap until 1974.

Meanwhile, the FBI and Kissinger kept playing sleuth. On May 13, Hoover informed Kissinger, "I have alerted our most sensitive sources." On May 15, a memo from Sullivan declared that "no information has been developed that would identify sources of leaks." On May 20, Kissinger and Haig drove over to the FBI to read the wiretap logs as if Kissinger had no weightier matters on his mind. According to Sullivan, Kissinger told him then that "it is clear that I don't have anybody in my office that I can trust except Colonel Haig here." Haig was the only member of the NSC staff who knew of the wiretaps put on his colleagues. Sullivan also noted Kissinger asked that the four initial wiretaps continue a "little while longer" and that two more names be added. Later that day, Mitchell signed authorizations to place taps on the home phones of two more NSC aides: Richard L. Sneider, who was a specialist on Japan and Korea, and Richard Moose, another Democratic holdover. Sneider and Moose were tapped for a full month. They were also tailed by FBI agents. Davidson's tap was removed after four months. Sonnenfeldt was under coverage until June 20, and again in 1970.

On May 28, Hoover sent Kissinger a long letter reporting on intercepted conversations involving three NSC staffers. Two of them, Hoover reported, made references to Kissinger. The next day, another letter arrived telling Kissinger about contacts between an NSC staffer and "deleted," who was placed under phone surveillance six days later. This latest "deleted" turned out to be Henry Brandon, the Czech-born Washington correspondent of the London *Sunday Times.* Brandon was a newsman with excellent Washington connections; Kissinger himself was one of his friends. Thus, merely because of a telephone conversation with a suspected NSC staff aide, Brandon became on May 29 the first journalist to be wiretapped. The request for this tap was sent to the FBI by Colonel Haig, but, Sullivan noted in an internal memo, "Dr. Kissinger is aware of this request."

On June 4, *The New York Times* published an article by Hedrick Smith to the effect that Presidents Nixon and Thieu would announce at their coming Midway meeting the first reduction in American troops in Vietnam. Kissinger and Hoover met during the morning of that day, and according to a Sullivan memo, Kissinger used the occasion to request a wiretap on Smith, "who has been in contact with the individuals on whom we have had telephone coverage in this case." The FBI obliged at once. On June 20, however, Sullivan reported to Hoover that "there has been nothing of late . . . relevant to the leaks. In view of this fact, I have suggested to Colonel Haig that he might want to consider discontinuing some of them. He agreed." The bureau removed Sneider's and Moose's taps the same evening.

The FBI was evidently becoming impatient with the White House's wiretapping program. On July 8, Sullivan wrote to Hoover again that "nothing has come to light that is of significance from the standpoint of the leak in question. I am suggesting that some of this coverage be removed." For the balance of July, the FBI kept on sending logs of intercepted conversations to Kissinger, but it was unable to come up with any more information.

At this point, the attention of the White House mysteriously turned in another direction. On July 23, Attorney General Mitchell authorized, "on behalf of the president," the wiretapping and physical surveillance of John P. Sears, a deputy counsel to the president in charge of Republican Party patronage. On August 4, he approved a wiretap on William Safire, one of Nixon's favorite speech-writers. There was no clear explanation as to why Sears and Safire, who had virtually nothing to do with foreign policy, would be so treated. In requesting the tap on Safire, Haig informed Mitchell that it was being made on "the highest authority." But the fact that *Haig* was making the request suggests that the recommendation came from Kissinger's office. Safire's greatest offense may have been that he was a sociable man with extensive friendships in the press and that he was overheard on Henry Brandon's wiretap, discussing a forthcoming presidential speech. Safire was tapped until September 15 and Sears until October 2.

Throughout the summer a stream of letters and reports on the wiretap logs continued unabated, including a fourteen-page memorandum from Hoover to Kissinger on August 1 summarizing the information picked up to date. The reports were replete with such nuggets of major information as the fact that one tap had revealed that the target and another person "are friends." On September 10, Mitchell told the FBI that Nixon wanted an "immediate" wiretap put on CBS diplomatic correspondent Marvin Kalb, whose FBI file the president had just read. Nixon thought that Kalb "might be receiving information." Kalb, who may have aroused suspicions because of an earlier stint as CBS correspondent in Moscow, was wiretapped for nearly two months, and evidently the FBI really did have the wild notion that Kalb had "contacts" with Soviet and Hungarian intelligence.

Meanwhile, the absurdity of the wiretap program was highlighted by the fact that William Beecher, the reporter who had caused the White House such grief, was never placed under surveillance during 1969. He was not wiretapped until 1970.

On September 15, Kissinger himself evidently concluded that the telephone eavesdropping was producing no results. Colonel Haig advised the FBI that wiretaps on all White House personnel—except Halperin—could be discontinued. It remains unclear why the tap on Halperin was to be maintained—particularly considering that he had been effectively cut off from access to highly sensitive material even before May. Davidson likewise no longer saw the most sensitive material. Sonnenfeldt, on the other hand, had constant access to almost everything Kissinger handled. Some friends of both men believe that the wiretap on Sonnenfeldt was the price Kissinger had to pay within the White House, where Sonnenfeldt was disliked and suspected, in order to keep him on; others believe that it was entirely Kissinger's doing. In any case, Sonnenfeldt was tapped again in 1970—on Haldeman's request.

Early in November (after wiretaps were removed from Smith's and Kalb's phones), the White House instructed the FBI to place Joseph Kraft, the syndicated columnist, under physical surveillance by agents. Kraft, a very well-informed journalist, was a friend of Kissinger's, but this was no bar to the treatment he received from the White House. All in all, the Nixon "leak-plugging" program produced in 1969 eleven wiretaps and four cases of physical surveillance of White House aides, journalists, and a senior Pentagon official.

The questions this 1969 wiretap program raised are many—and disturbing. It is known that the decision to initiate the operation was taken by Nixon after the meeting with Kissinger, Mitchell, and Hoover in the Oval Office on April 25. Nixon took the view that he had the right to order wiretapping without a court warrant when national security was involved and when the attorney general approved it. Given the personal relations between Nixon and Mitchell, there could never be any doubt that the attorney general would authorize whatever taps Nixon wished to have placed. Subsequent court opinions reopened the question of the legality of warrantless taps—even in national-security situations. But the broader issue was, as it had been from the beginning, one of political motivations and the president's own concept of morality.

As to Henry Kissinger, the man who supervised the program for Nixon, the question was never satisfactorily answered whether he had personally initiated the wiretaps under a broad presidential authority or whether he had simply suggested the names of targets for the FBI to monitor. But either way, it is impossible to dissociate him altogether from Nixon. They were inseparable in the sordid infighting of the White House as they were in their foreign-policy creativeness.

To the outside observer, 1969 had been a year of promise in American foreign policy. What America saw was a president who asserted he had a plan to end the Vietnam war and was already withdrawing troops from Asia; a president who was working for a "generation of peace" through new approaches to the Soviet Union and China; a wise leader acclaimed from Manila to Bucharest and from Paris to Washington; a man who was breaking away from the mold of the past to guide the United States—and the world—toward a new era of negotiations while wisely preserving the power of America. That was Nixon's image, and his first year did shine like a true year of promise.

BOOK TWO

1970

The Year of Wars

Chapter 8

To listen to President Nixon, his foreign policy was progressing by giant strides—and in the right direction. The administration, still enjoying relative credibility, succeeded for a while in projecting a positive image of this "foreign policy of the seventies," emphasizing initiatives while concealing weaknesses. Public opinion at home was still prepared to believe him—and let him have his way in Vietnam. Congress, equally uninformed, was reluctant to challenge his decisions, and there were only feeble congressional efforts to place restrictions on his conduct of the war. Only Senator J. William Fulbright, chairman of the Senate Foreign Relations Committee, and a few other stalwarts kept up a barrage of criticism. The administration also chose to ignore publicly a number of signs—including classified reports—indicating that Hanoi was not greatly impressed by Vietnamization and that pacification efforts in the South were not really working. There was a built-in resistance to unfavorable news from Vietnam.

The accent was on selling the administration's foreign policy—to the world and to Americans. The president himself assumed the role of the principal salesman. The year began with a veritable public-relations offensive.

The opening shot in this offensive was fired by President Nixon when he went before a joint session of Congress on January 22 to deliver his first State of the Union message. Because Nixon was planning to follow up the message with a special report to Congress on foreign affairs, he confined himself to generalities, but all the Nixonian hallmarks were there: the hyperbole, the promise of peace, and the stress on the administration's break with the sterile past.

> The major immediate goal of our foreign policy is to bring an end to the war in Vietnam in a way that our generation will be remembered —not so much as the generation that suffered in war, but more for the

fact we had the courage and character to win the kind of a just peace
that the new generation was able to keep. We are making progress
toward that goal. The prospects for peace are far greater today than
they were a year ago.

Yet throughout January it was clear that the prospects were *worse:*
fresh North Vietnamese units were steadily infiltrating into the South,
according to State and Defense Department briefings, and Henry Kissinger's secret contacts with the North Vietnamese had been discouraging. But having announced that peace was closer than it had been in 1969,
when the Democratic administration was leaving office, Nixon played
another political card:

> A major part of the credit for this development goes to the Members
> of this Congress who, despite their differences on the conduct of the
> war, have overwhelmingly indicated their support of a just peace. By
> this action, you have completely demolished the enemy's hopes that
> they can gain in Washington the victory our fighting men have denied
> them in Vietnam.

This gratuitous *non sequitur* was part of Nixon's battle with the "liberals." He was saying, in effect, that any congressman opposing his Vietnam
policies was helping Hanoi to win the war over the bodies of "our fighting
men." But the president resumed a statesman-like tone:

> We have based our policies on an evaluation of the world as it is, not
> as it was twenty-five years ago at the conclusion of World War II.
> . . . Then . . . America had to assume the major burden for the defense
> of freedom in the world. In two wars, first in Korea and now in
> Vietnam, we furnished most of the money, most of the arms, most of
> the men to help other nations defend their freedom. Today the great
> industrial nations of Europe, as well as Japan, have regained their
> economic strength; and the nations of Latin America—and many of
> the nations who acquired their freedom from colonialism after World
> War II in Asia and Africa—have a new sense of pride and dignity and
> a determination to assume the responsibility for their own defense.
> That is the basis of the doctrine I announced at Guam. Neither the
> defense nor the development of other nations can be exclusively or
> primarily an American undertaking. . . . We shall be faithful to our
> treaty commitments, but we shall reduce our involvement and our
> presence in other nations' affairs. To insist that other nations play a
> role is not a retreat from responsibility; it is a sharing of responsibility.

Nixon did present Congress with fresh thoughts about America's
relationships with the Communist powers. He had spoken of this often

enough during the past year in the White House but now he was summing up his policies for Congress in a philosophical mold:

> I would not underestimate our differences [with the Soviet Union], but we are moving with precision and purpose from an era of confrontation to an era of negotiation. Our negotiations on strategic arms limitations and in other areas will have far greater chance for success if both sides enter them motivated by mutual self-interest rather than naïve sentimentality. It is with this same spirit that we have resumed discussions with Communist China in our talks at Warsaw. . . . I believe our new policies have contributed to the prospect that America may have the best chance since World War II to enjoy a generation of uninterrupted peace.

Eight days after the State of the Union message, Nixon called his first news conference of the year. In this more flexible forum, newsmen could raise direct questions and occasionally force him to answer questions he would just as soon ignore. During 1969, something of a honeymoon year, the president had held only eight conferences, an all-time low in the modern presidency, and it was clear that he much preferred television, where alone before the cameras he was the master of the audience, never challenged or contradicted. Still, news conferences, as the White House saw it, were a necessary evil.

In the case of the January conference, Nixon decided that there had been so many developments in foreign policy since he had last met with the press, on December 8, that it would be to his advantage to hold another question-and-answer session. For one thing, a news conference enabled him to make foreign-policy statements in a less formal way than in a speech, even to float trial balloons, which was quite convenient. It was a good way to address foreign governments, friends or foes, without official commitments. For another thing, it was thought that a news conference would help to maintain momentum between the State of the Union message and the special foreign-policy report the president planned to issue in late February. Nixon, a methodical man, prepared himself carefully for news conferences: the White House press office put together a fat briefing book covering all the topics that newsmen were likely to raise; Kissinger and his NSC staff (sometimes with State Department assistance) contributed material; and Nixon usually held a special meeting with Kissinger (in addition to their daily one-hour morning conference) just before facing the microphones.

Vietnam and the Middle East were at the center of attention when Nixon took his place at the podium in the East Room of the White House in the early evening of January 30. (To the despair of the newsmen, Nixon insisted on making all his speeches and holding his press conferences in the evening, to command prime television time, which created immense problems for regular evening network news shows and for morning newspapers.) On Vietnam, the questions reflected concern with the possibility of a new Communist offensive. And Nixon's answers were more sober than his assurances before Congress a week earlier had been:

> The infiltration in Vietnam . . . has gone up in January. However, the number of infiltrators is still not of a size to provide what we believe is the capability the enemy would need to mount and sustain a prolonged offensive beyond that which we are able to contain. . . . If, at a time that we are attempting to deescalate the fighting in Vietnam, we find that they take advantage of our troop withdrawals to jeopardize the remainder of our forces by escalating the fighting, then we have the means—and I will be prepared to use those means—strongly to deal with that situation, more strongly than we have dealt with it in the past.

His listeners naturally assumed that the president had in mind heavy air bombardment of North Vietnam when he spoke of dealing with the situation "more strongly than . . . in the past." What was unknown was that, in greatest secrecy, top administration figures were beginning to think in terms of a ground intervention in Cambodia to capture the Communist command for South Vietnam—the mythical and elusive COSVN (Central Office for South Vietnam), which was thought to be operating somewhere in the jungles on the Cambodian side of the border —and to interdict North Vietnamese infiltration routes through Cambodia. Nixon and Kissinger had been discussing such an operation on and off for months, partly under pressure from the Pentagon, but no decision had yet been taken. The public and the press were, of course, also unaware that the United States had been bombing Cambodia for *ten-and-a-half months.*

Nixon, who used the news conference to say that there would be fresh announcements at an unspecified time on further American troop withdrawals from Vietnam, came close to revealing his secret diplomatic contacts with Hanoi. This was in the context of a question whether the arrival in Paris earlier that week of Le Duc Tho, a member of the North Vietnamese Politburo, would provide an opportunity for the United States to make new peace proposals. Le Duc Tho, a man who had been very close to Ho Chi Minh, was officially listed as "Special Adviser to the

Chief of the Delegation," Xuan Thuy, but it was no secret that Tho was the one who really counted; he had been in and out of Paris ever since the start of the peace talks.

Sometime in mid-January, Washington and Hanoi had arranged for a new round of secret sessions. The contacts were handled, as they had been before, by General Walters, the defense attaché in Paris, and Mai Van Bo, the permanent delegate of North Vietnam in France. This time, it was agreed that a meeting would be held early in February, when Le Duc Tho was to confer with Kissinger. In Washington this was taken as an encouraging sign: the North Vietnamese were raising the diplomatic level. But Le Duc Tho was in Paris ostensibly to attend the congress of the French Communist Party, and Nixon was not about to blow his cover altogether:

> As you know, Le Duc Tho, at least according to press reports, has arrived in Paris to attend a Communist Party meeting that is being held there. Now, whether he will now participate in the negotiations again or whether we could have an opportunity to have discussions with him remains to be seen. I can only say that we have a very competent ambassador there in Mr. [Philip] Habib. He has instructions to explore every possible avenue for a breakthrough in the negotiations, and if an opportunity is presented, he will do so.

The president's other comment on Indochina—a reply to a question concerning the extent of American involvement in Laos—was to say only that "the North Vietnamese have 50,000 troops in Laos and thereby threaten the survival of Laos" and that "our activities there are solely for the purpose of seeing that the Laotian government . . . [is] not overwhelmed by the North Vietnamese and other Communist forces." He avoided mentioning that B-52s were bombing the Ho Chi Minh Trail on the Laotian side of the Vietnamese frontier, that other American planes were providing combat support to the Laotian Army in the Plaine des Jarres, and that the CIA was fully supporting a clandestine army of Laotian irregulars in the Plaine des Jarres. Nixon liked to keep America's secret wars as secret as possible.

The other major issue raised at the January news conference was the situation in the Middle East, where the "attrition war" between Egypt and Israel was increasing in intensity. With the collapse of the Rogers Plan, a new full-blown war seemed in the offing. The Soviet Union was shipping more and more modern arms to Egypt, and the Israelis, who regarded air superiority as an absolute requirement in offsetting the Arabs' numerical strength on the ground, were pressing hard to get additional Phantom F-4 and Skyhawk jets. Early in the month it had become known that France was selling Libya a number of Mirage jets; the Israelis did not hide their fears that the Mirages would wind up in Egyptian hands, to supplement the advanced MiG jet fighters and Sukhoi bombers supplied by the U.S.S.R. Mrs. Meir had exacted a promise in 1969 that the United States would sell Israel fifty Phantoms and one hundred Skyhawks. Only twenty-five Phantoms had been delivered by mid-January, and to make matters worse, the Americans had made it clear that they had reservations about selling Israel the other Phantoms or any Skyhawks. The State Department's advice was to hold back on deliveries of new planes. To the worried Israelis, this meant that the Nixon administration was turning against them. They had nervously read that Nixon had met on December 9 with a group of leading American bankers, oil-company executives, and industrialists who warned him that continued U.S. support for Israel and further arms supplies would result in the loss of political and economic influence in the Arab countries. There could be nothing worse for Israel than an "evenhanded" United States policy in the Middle East (a Rogers phrase)—and they thought this was what they were seeing emerge in Washington.

Actually, Middle East policy at that point was indecisive, not to say murky. On January 9, a State Department spokesman blamed the Soviet Union for preventing Gunnar Jarring, the United Nations mediator, from resuming his peacemaking efforts after the collapse of the Rogers Plan. And on January 26, Nixon sent a message to a conference of Jewish leaders in Washington declaring: "The United States is prepared to supply military equipment necessary to support the efforts of friendly governments, like Israel's, to defend the safety of their people. We would prefer restraint in the shipment of arms to this area. But we are maintaining a careful watch on the relative strength of the forces there, and we will not hesitate to provide arms to friendly states as the need arises."

This last remark was thrown back at Nixon at the January 30 news conference in the form of a question as to whether France's planned sale of Mirages to Libya justified the sale of additional jets to Israel. Nixon demurred. Then he disclosed that it would take the administration thirty days to decide whether Israel needed additional arms "in order to meet that threat. . . . We are neither pro-Arab nor pro-Israeli. We are pro peace. We are for security for all the nations in that area." But the truth was that Nixon's Middle East policy was being improvised from day to day, and both the Israelis and the Arabs were left up in the air pending the promised review of the military situation—the thirty days Nixon had mentioned. What Nixon failed to clarify was that he wanted to make his decision on Israeli arms in the light of resumed private talks with the Russians. He was hoping to persuade Moscow to join the United States in what would amount to an embargo on all arms shipments to the Middle East. This was what he had meant on January 26 by "restraint" on Middle East arms.

The occasion for the detailed, in-depth, and philosophical presentation of the new American foreign policy was Richard Nixon's "First Annual Report to the Congress of the United States: Foreign Policy for the 1970's," submitted on February 18. This third foreign-policy pronouncement of the winter season was a formidable effort. Indeed, nothing on this scale had ever been attempted before. In the past, a president confined foreign-policy declarations to the State of the Union message and special statements. But what Nixon now sent Congress was an encyclopedic study of American foreign policy divided into six parts: a lengthy introduction; chapters on "The National Security Council System," "Partnership and the Nixon Doctrine," "America's Strength," and "An Era of Negotiation"; and a ringing conclusion entitled, "A New Definition of Peace." When it was printed for publication, it became a 160-page *book*, with the title gold-embossed on white.

The report was Henry Kissinger's pride and joy. It was precisely the kind of exposition that excited his methodical professorial mind—and his taste for broad philosophical formulations. His concern was to codify the foreign-policy doctrines and achievements of the Nixon administration for the year in the form of a spectacular library volume, a monument to the ideas of the Nixon-Kissinger team. The notion was to issue such a volume for every year of the administration so that when Nixon bowed out of office after what it was assumed would be two presidential terms, there would exist a body of Nixonian history, instant history, to be sure, written by the historian himself.

But the first report—Nixon and Kissinger called it "A New Strategy for Peace"—was not serious historical material. It was bombastic, hortatory, overblown—enshrining the Nixon Doctrine as a centennial milestone of American foreign policy. One must wonder whether Kissinger really believed that this "doctrine," the casual product of a news conference on Guam, would enter serious history books, as the Truman Doctrine or the Marshall Plan had, or whether he was simply being obsequious.

It had taken almost four months to prepare the foreign-policy report.

Work had begun on October 27, 1969, when Kissinger instructed the NSC staff to draft a study to serve as the basis for the report; this was called "President's Annual Review," designated NSSM–80. This project consumed most of the time of Kissinger's staff, and except for an occasional emergency—there were not too many—the staff worked on little else. Actually, Kissinger's requirement for NSSMs in general was decreasing. Of the eighty-five written in 1969, sixty had been ordered in the first six months of the year, as he set out to define the problems and options facing the new administration; these NSSMs became his principal background resource for every international situation. But only sixteen NSSMs were prepared during all of 1970.

Besides, more and more sensitive policy planning was being done outside regular NSC channels (the October study on the "savage blow" against North Vietnam was not a formal NSSM), and the frequency of full-fledged National Security Council meetings also diminished. Nobody really seemed to have the time for lengthy NSC meetings, and they became limited to occasions when long-range policy decisions had to be reviewed. To cope with sudden crises, Kissinger had invented the Washington Special Action Group—WASAG—which acted as the White House crisis-management center though it had no statutory powers. Its small and select membership consisted of senior State and Pentagon officials plus the director of the CIA and the attorney general (added during the Korean crisis in April to look after Nixon's political interests). Kissinger directed WASAG, reporting directly to the president. WASAG helped Kissinger to deal with occasional opposition from Secretary of State Rogers and Defense Secretary Laird, who were left with the only recourse of taking their battles to the Oval Office, obviously in disadvantageous conditions. John Kennedy had "managed" his crises through a small informal group known as EXCOM (Executive Committee). But Kissinger reconstituted and expanded the NSC system that had existed under Eisenhower (it had largely withered away in the Democratic administrations) *and* revived Kennedy's EXCOM operation in the form of WASAG.

The bulky foreign-policy report went through more drafts and revisions than any NSC staff member could remember having done before. Kissinger read personally every word of every section, ordered changes and new drafts up to the last moment. The final touches were applied at frantic meetings at Key Biscayne, where Kissinger and his writers joined Nixon for a long February weekend in the sun. Then Nixon's own White House speech-writers went over the final text under Kissinger's watchful eye. The president, proud of his own style, made personal contributions, mostly to the introduction and the conclusion, writing the first drafts in longhand on a yellow legal pad and last-minute changes in ink on the final version, scribbling in the margins.

Increasingly, the president was isolated from outside thinking and influences during long periods, including the time when the report was being hammered together. As a rule, Nixon was not interested in the informal opinions of outsiders, and American experts and foreign-policy "elder statesmen" were invited only very rarely to the Oval Office. Nixon preferred the one-to-one relationship with Kissinger. Rogers saw the president once or twice a week (usually in Kissinger's presence) and, as he recalls it, talked with Nixon on the telephone at least once a day, mostly to answer his questions on specific situations. But he was rarely asked for his opinion and of course was often kept in the dark.

The full text of the foreign-policy report, quickly dubbed the "State of the World Message," belongs to the bibliography of the Nixon years, but certain passages provide a vivid expression of the mood and flavor of the time. Also, Nixon's actual achievements—and failures—during his five-and-a-half years in the White House can be fairly measured against the goals he set for himself and the United States at the opening of the decade:

> When I took office, the most immediate problem facing our nation was the war in Vietnam. . . . Yet the fundamental task confronting us was more profound. We could see that the whole pattern of international politics was changing. Our challenge was to understand that change, to define America's goals for the next period, and to set in motion policies to achieve them. . . .
>
> The postwar period in international relations has ended. . . . Then we were confronted by a monolithic Communist world. Today, the nature of that world has changed—the power of individual Communist nations has grown, but international Communist unity has been shattered. . . . The Soviet Union and Communist China, once bound by an alliance of friendship, had become bitter adversaries by the mid-1960's. . . . The Marxist dream of international Communist unity has disintegrated.
>
> Then, the United States had a monopoly or overwhelming superiority of nuclear weapons. Today, a revolution in the technology of war has altered the nature of the military balance of power. . . . Communist China has acquired thermonuclear weapons. Both the Soviet Union and the United States have acquired the ability to inflict unacceptable damage on the other, no matter which strikes first. . . . Thus, both sides have recognized a vital mutual interest in halting the dangerous

momentum of the nuclear arms race.

Then, the slogans formed in the past century were the ideological accessories of the intellectual debate. Today, the "isms" have lost their vitality—indeed the restlessness of youth on both sides of the dividing line testifies to the need for a new idealism and deeper purposes.

Nixon based his "New Strategy for Peace" on these principles: *partnership* ("its obligations, like its benefits, must be shared"), *strength* ("American weakness could tempt would-be aggressors to make dangerous miscalculations"), and *willingness to negotiate* ("In partnership with our allies, secure in our own strength, we will seek those areas in which we can agree among ourselves and with others to accommodate conflicts and overcome rivalries").

Discussing America's strength, Nixon said that "this Administration has established procedures for the intensive scrutiny of defense issues in the light of overall national priorities. . . . We have re-examined our strategic forces; we have reassessed our general purpose forces; and we have engaged in the most painstaking preparation ever undertaken by the United States Government for arms control negotiations." And this was his own approach to negotiations:

> Our commitment to peace is most convincingly demonstrated in our willingness to negotiate our points of difference in a fair and business-like manner with the Communist countries. We are under no illusions. We know that there are enduring ideological differences. We are aware of the difficulty in moderating tensions that arise from the clash of national interests. These differences will not be dissipated by changes of atmosphere or dissolved in cordial personal relations between statesmen. They involve strong convictions and contrary philosophies, necessities of national security, and the deep-seated differences of perspectives formed by geography and history. . . . No nation need be our permanent enemy.
>
> Skeptical and estranged, many of our young people today look out on a world they never made. They survey its conflicts with apprehension. Graduated into the impersonal routine of a bureaucratic, technological society, many of them see life as lonely conformity lacking the lift of a driving dream. Yet there is no greater idealism, no higher adventure than taking a realistic road for peace. It is an adventure realized not in the exhilaration of a single moment, but in the last rewards of patient, detailed and specific efforts—a step at a time.

The response to Nixon's State of the World Message was all that he and Kissinger hoped. In Congress, approval came from both sides of the aisle. Pleasure was expressed in most capitals—and quietly but strongly in Moscow and Peking. *The New York Times* printed the full text of the report as a special insert, and editorial comment everywhere was favorable. People were starved for new ideas. Americans were fatigued by the unending Indochina war. And Nixon seemed to be pointing the way to that "generation of peace" the world so ardently desired.

But reality was less kind and promising. On February 1, Le Duan, the first secretary of the Vietnamese Workers' (Communist) Party, had warned that his nation was prepared to fight the United States for "many years more" to obtain the full withdrawal of American forces from Vietnam. And Nixon's warnings that he would apply stern measures to protect U.S. forces remaining in Vietnam were dismissed as an "insolent threat, an argument of pirates" by the Hanoi newspaper *Nhan Dan* on the same day that Le Duan was proclaiming that "our people are sure to win total victory."

Lines were being drawn tighter for more war. In the Middle East, the Arab-Israeli crisis was worsening almost daily. Late in January, Nasser had secretly gone to Moscow to ask for additional Soviet military assistance, and early in February, Nixon became engaged in a frustrating exchange of secret correspondence with Premier Aleksei Kosygin over the supply of arms to the Middle East.

The only satisfaction Nixon could derive in foreign affairs was his moderate but encouraging progress vis-à-vis China. In the slow diplomatic minuet with Peking, the administration was perfectly willing to measure progress in inches. So everyone was quietly pleased when Peking freed two Americans who had been held captive for ten months (even though six other Americans remained in prison).

The two governments were closely watching each other, sometimes reciprocating one another's goodwill gestures, and there was a sense in Washington that all these "small steps" portended the development of a major new policy. For instance, Romanian Deputy Foreign Minister Gheorghe Macovescu had visited Nixon early in December 1969, and it was known that the two men discussed China, though the White House would not talk about it publicly. Later in the month, Secretary Rogers said at a news conference, somewhat mysteriously, that it would "depend on events" whether the United States would reconsider its standing opposition to Peking's membership in the United Nations.

The next step came on January 20, 1970, when Ambassador Stoessel and his aides drove to the Chinese embassy in Warsaw for the first formal meeting with Lei Yang, the chargé d'affaires. This was the result of

Stoessel's preliminary activities during December. By common agreement, the two governments confined themselves to the simple public announcement that a meeting was held, but the two-hour conversation touched on a number of substantive matters—the Vietnam war and the fate of Taiwan, for example. The mood was "polite, but not effusive." Lei conducted himself with a certain stiffness, the American diplomats thought, but he refrained from tirades, polemics, and propaganda—quite a change from past sessions with the Chinese—and this enabled Stoessel to make an important proposal. On instructions carefully drafted by Marshall Green and cleared with Rogers and Kissinger, Stoessel told Lei that under favorable conditions the United States might consider dispatching a "high-level emissary" to Peking to pursue the new discussions on a more elevated level. No names or dates were suggested, but Stoessel left no doubt that the Americans were extremely interested in the idea. No American official had set foot in Peking since the Communists assumed power in 1949. Lei appeared to be "receptive" but told Stoessel he had to consult his government before submitting a formal reply.

When the State Department drafted Stoessel's instructions, the thought was that Marshall Green would be the "high-level emissary"—if Peking agreed to accept one. This, associates said later, was Green's notion, too. The subject came up again when Stoessel and Lei met next, on February 20, at the American embassy on Warsaw's tree-lined Aleje Ujazdowskie. Lei again sounded "receptive," but evidently, Peking had not yet made up its mind, and he could not give Stoessel a firm answer. He did, however, give Stoessel some general replies to questions raised the month before about Vietnam and Taiwan. Stoessel felt that the concept of a "permanent contact" between Washington and Peking—in Warsaw or elsewhere—had moved forward significantly. At the end of the meeting, they agreed to resume the conversations a month hence.

In the words of a senior administration official engaged in the China policy, "Warsaw was important because it was there that the Chinese in reality conveyed their message of readiness for contacts with the United States, which led to the future relationship and laid the groundwork for all that came later." Stoessel himself felt that "these contacts showed that the Chinese were ready for some form of relations with the United States and that they were more reasonable." This, an official recounted, "was clear in the way in which they stated their positions." Among other things, Lei indicated the extent of the Chinese concern about the threat of Russia, something Peking had never before discussed with the Americans. The first months of 1970 were the "right psychological moment" to enter into talks with the Chinese, the Americans thought, and "the Chinese gave the first sign of moderation, the foretaste of the style of diplomacy they would follow in the months and years to come."

In his "State of the World Message," Nixon had set forth the new policy toward China:

> The principles underlying our relations with Communist China are similar to those governing our policies toward the USSR. United States policy is not likely soon to have much impact on China's behavior, let alone its ideological outlook. But it is certainly in our interest, and in the interest of peace and stability in Asia and the world, that we take steps we can toward improved practical relations with Peking.
>
> The key to our relations will be the actions each side takes regarding the other and its allies. We will not ignore hostile acts. We intend to maintain our treaty commitment to the defense of the Republic of China. But we will seek to promote understandings which can establish a new pattern of mutually beneficial actions. . . . We have avoided dramatic gestures which might invite dramatic rebuffs. We have taken specific steps that did not require Chinese agreement but which underlined our willingness to have a more normal and constructive relationship. . . . The resumption of talks with the Chinese in Warsaw may indicate that our approach will prove useful. . . .
>
> Our desire for improved relations is not a tactical means of exploiting the clash between China and the Soviet Union. We see no benefit to us in the intensification of that conflict, and we have no intention of taking sides. Nor is the United States interested in joining any condominium or hostile coalition of great powers against either of the large Communist countries.

Though Nixon insisted that "we have avoided dramatic gestures" in the approaches to China, the fact is that even then he and Kissinger were playing with the notion that Kissinger himself should go to Peking—as soon as possible. Kissinger never mentioned this specifically to State Department planners, but when Stoessel reported that the Chinese had shown interest in receiving an emissary, Kissinger sent word that events could move a "little harder and faster." Though the Warsaw meetings scheduled for March and April were delayed on China's request—Peking was obviously thinking hard about the whole situation before committing itself to a new course—the White House had high hopes that the May meeting might produce the kind of Chinese answer that would open the door to Kissinger.

There is no question that the mounting tension between the Soviet Union and China was a factor in the "triangular" American policy. While the United States indeed had no desire to "exploit" the split, as Nixon had stressed, the administration saw this rivalry as a geopolitical reality that forced both sides to have better relations with the Americans. At the same time, however, Kissinger was concerned that the incidents along the Soviet-Chinese border might lead to full-scale warfare.

It is hard to judge how justified Kissinger was on this latter point. He could measure warlike signs, but he could not judge the intentions of the two parties. For more than half a year, Soviet forces had been massing on the Chinese border, and Peking was continuously accusing the Russians of aggressive plans. United States intelligence also reported considerable Soviet political penetration into the Chinese government, weakened as it was by the Cultural Revolution. There was steady talk of the possibility of a Soviet preemptive strike against China's nuclear arsenal, although the CIA and military intelligence agencies could not point to actual Soviet contingency planning for it. (In fact, the intelligence people were divided on the matter of a Soviet nuclear attack on China. Soviet specialists thought it was plausible, and Helms tended to side with them. China experts, on the other hand, were more skeptical, and took the view that Peking was deliberately exaggerating the danger for political reasons.)

In any event, in mid-February Kissinger set up a secret Special Projects Staff to develop contingency planning for the United States in the event of a Sino-Soviet war. Several of his NSC staffers worked on this project in an out-of-the-way suite in the Executive Office Building. As one of them recalled, Kissinger said: "I'm very worried that war is going to break out and that we'll be caught unawares." He had asked the "bureaucracy" to provide some studies on the subject, "but it is very unsatisfactory, and I want you to take a fresh look at it." He ordered a complete scenario: what American reactions should be toward the Soviet Union and China, what the United States could do in the United Nations, how it would affect the Vietnam war and American troops in Indochina, and so on. Actually, the task force could draw on an NSC study on "Sino-Soviet Relations" that had been ordered the previous July 3 as NSSM–63, but the material urgently needed updating.

In the meantime, the ever-volatile situation in the Middle East was putting American policy-makers to a severe test. In the months gone by, Israeli and Syrian tanks and artillery had been engaged in heavy duels on the Golan Heights, the most severe fighting since the 1967 war. Both sides, of course, depended on outside military supplies—Israel on the United States, and the Arabs on the Soviet Union—and each superpower felt an obligation to support *its* ally. At the same time, each feared that if the situation went out of control, they would confront each other in a fashion that neither desired. Washington and Moscow were hostages to the Middle Eastern dynamics that they kept feeding.

Nasser, still smarting from the 1967 humiliation, had conceived the notion that a sustained war of attrition would place an intolerable burden on Israel, possibly forcing her into a desperate offensive response such as she had effectively used in the 1967 war but that the Egyptians would now be prepared to rebuff. Nasser seemed almost eager to goad the Israelis into a new war, on the theory that by fighting on his own territory west of the Suez Canal—he expected that Israel would launch a blitzkrieg across the waterway—he could inflict awesome losses on the enemy; and that this, in turn, would lead to a diplomatic settlement under which Egypt would regain most if not all of the territories lost in 1967. The Soviets had already effectively reequipped Nasser's army, especially in artillery and armor, and, he reasoned, they would have to continue supplying him in time of war. Nasser also believed that if his war of attrition provoked Israel to ever-greater responses, the West would intervene politically to allay the danger of a major war, indeed, would force Israel to make significant territorial concessions. Nasser's "big ploy," as an Israeli diplomat put it at the time, was to "sow the fear of war" in Washington.

This master plan, like so many of Nasser's other initiatives, was flawed in many respects. (For one thing the Arabs had not divined, in 1969, the "oil weapon.") But the truth was that the war of attrition *was* hurting the Israelis badly. The Bar-Lev Line—the complex of Israeli fortifications on the eastern bank of the Suez Canal—was being eroded. Israeli personnel losses were numerically small, perhaps two or three soldiers killed every day, but dramatically poignant in a nation of two and a half million inhabitants. Besides, the Israelis had to contend with constant armed penetrations from Jordan, Syria, and Lebanon—and this, too, cost lives and damage to the outlying *kibbutzim.*

Initially, the Israeli response had been to use air power to hit Egyptian artillery positions. But pinpoint bombing raids against artillery emplacements were extremely difficult, and they took their toll in lost planes and crews.

In December, the Israelis had reached a basic decision to make the war of attrition painful to the Egyptians. The strategy was to hit at Egypt's military machinery not only at the canal but in depth. Israel simply had to escalate its military responses, Mrs. Meir told her cabinet colleagues.

Various contingency plans were evolved during the closing weeks of December and the first weeks of January, and eventually deep-penetration air strikes against targets in Egypt were approved by the Ministerial Committee for Defense. Weighing all the pros and cons in the situation, they accepted the likelihood that Nasser would ask the Russians for sophisticated air-defense systems and that he might be driven to an all-out war against Israel. Still, Israel had no way of knowing how deeply the Soviet Union would wish to become involved, and, Mrs. Meir reasoned, it had to take the risk of hitting Egypt's neuralgic points. Israeli contingency plans also, as Nasser suspected, called for a full-scale crossing of the Suez Canal if the deep-penetration raids failed to produce the necessary results—or as a reaction against an Egyptian preemptive attack.

Although Nasser had correctly predicted that Israel would escalate the war of attrition, he was taken by surprise by the deep-penetration raids. And by late January, the Israeli Air Force was fully in control of Egyptian skies, hitting targets from Alexandria to Aswan. Israeli air commandos raided the coast; they briefly captured Shadwan Island in the Gulf of Suez, making off with a complete radar station. Nasser was further humiliated when the Israelis repeatedly raided the Cairo-West air base, right under his nose. The Egyptian Air Force was powerless despite its Soviet instructors. As many as five MiG jets flown by Soviet instructor-pilots were shot down over a period of a few weeks (a fact the Russians never acknowledged), and reliable reports said that a senior Soviet general had been killed in an Israeli air raid.

This was the background when on January 31 Ambassador Dobrynin delivered a secret two-page missive from Premier Aleksei Kosygin to President Nixon, hinting that the Russians might move to equip Egypt with sophisticated air-defense systems if the United States continued sending military supplies to Israel and failed to dissuade the Israelis from their activities. However, the letter—the first direct message from Kosygin to Nixon—was low key. (The texts of this and subsequent letters between Kosygin and Nixon remain secret. At that stage, Kosygin still acted as Moscow's principal spokesman on foreign affairs; Communist Party General Secretary Leonid Brezhnev had not yet fully assumed that responsibility. Similar Kosygin letters were handed to the British and French governments.)

Nixon's position in this new crisis tended to be ambiguous. Senior American and Israeli officials concur that his administration had reacted rather "mildly" to the Israeli deep-penetration raids, and there is no record of any American demarche with Israel suggesting opposition to the raids. The feeling seemed to have been that Israel's in-depth strikes against Egypt might serve their purpose, i.e., to persuade Nasser to slow down the war of attrition. The basic policy was to let Israel have free rein over Egypt, but to control it to some extent through indefinite delays in deliveries of new aircraft so urgently demanded by Jerusalem. But by February there were some demonstrations of concern over civilian losses in Egypt inflicted by Israeli raids.

The White House reading of the Kosygin letter was that it should not be construed as an actual threat—although Moscow was likely to provide Nasser with *some* equipment—but, rather, as a high-level gesture of solidarity with Egypt. Kissinger's assessment was that the Russians probably would shy away from giving massive military support to Nasser lest the nascent détente with America be jeopardized; he evidently believed that Moscow took the "linkage" concept as seriously as he did.

On February 4, Nixon's reply to Kosygin was handed to Dobrynin. The letter urged the Russians to join the United States in discussing limitations on arms shipments to the Middle East. Nixon rejected Kosygin's charge that Washington was to blame for the new Middle East dangers, and reminded him that the United States had been pushing all along for observance of the U.N. cease-fire lines established after the 1967 war. He invited Kosygin to resume, in a more constructive manner, the Soviet-American negotiations for a Middle East peace formula that had broken off in December when the Rogers Plan aborted.

The Nixon-Kosygin exchange had no tangible results. But it soon became evident that the Russians were delivering advanced MiG-23 jet fighter-bombers and SAMs to the Egyptians as part of a new integrated air-defense system. More and more Soviet military specialists were turning up in Egypt, according to intelligence reports. Israel was pressing for the still-undelivered twenty-five Phantoms and one hundred Skyhawk jets from the batch promised in 1969—its losses were increasing as a result of the deep-penetration raids—but Nixon, strongly supported by Kissinger, was delaying the decision. In fact, Kissinger as well as Rogers was advising him to *turn down* the Israeli request for the time being, on the ostensible grounds that Soviet deliveries to Egypt had not *yet* upset the strategic balance (they chose to regard the deployments of equipment provided by the Soviets as a "defensive" rather than an offensive move), but actually because they still hoped to engage Moscow in new negotiations; they argued that restraint on the part of the United States might persuade the Soviets to apply similar caution.

On February 24 and 25, when Nixon met in Washington with French

President Georges Pompidou, he apparently extracted a promise that France would delay its sale of Mirage jets to Libya—in any case, it would have taken the French at least a year to begin the deliveries—but they could not agree on the main lines of a policy approach to the Middle East. Pompidou remained faithful to the Gaullist line that Israel must make major concessions to the Arabs in terms of military withdrawals—virtually without a *quid pro quo*. He told a joint session of Congress that "there is no assured future for Israel outside a lasting entente with the world which surrounds it—an entente which implies renunciation of military conquest and the solution of the Palestinian problem."

As March rolled along, the Israelis were beginning to feel the effect of Egypt's new air-defense system. SAM-3 missile batteries were being installed in clusters around key Egyptian targets. Soviet personnel were known to be manning the SAM-3 radars, and Soviet pilots were flying MiG-23s against invading Israeli jets. To avoid severe losses—and having no assurance that Washington would make up for them—Israel had to curtail the deep-penetration raids although Egypt continued waging the artillery attrition war across the Suez Canal.

At a news conference on March 21, Nixon announced that the American decision on Israeli requests for jet aircraft would be disclosed within forty-eight hours by Secretary of State Rogers, but he made it clear that it would be a negative "interim" one. The administration review was supposed to have taken thirty days, according to Nixon's promise in January, but it had taken fifty-two days—and still it was not final. Nixon took note of Soviet activities in Egypt, however:

> In recent days, there have been disturbing reports that the Soviet Union, by deliveries of new SAM-3s to the U.A.R. and through the insertion of military personnel, may be taking actions which could change that balance [of power]. It is too early to say whether that is the case. We are watching the situation closely. If the U.S.S.R., by its military assistance programs to Israel's neighbors, does essentially change the balance, then the United States would take action to deal with that situation.

Yet his hopes of a deal with Moscow were still high, and he added, "There have been some developments in the Middle East in our bilateral discussions with the Soviet Union that have been, I would say, modestly encouraging, and we trust that that trend, rather than this latest trend, will be the one that will prevail."

Nixon and Kissinger had developed a system of leaving the announcement of politically unpopular decisions to Secretary Rogers—particularly when they could produce adverse domestic reactions—and this was the case with the arms for Israel: the White House was aware of the strong sentiments of American Jews and many other Americans on the subject of Israel. So on March 23 it was Rogers who had to get up and say that the Israeli requests for the Phantoms and the Skyhawks would be held "in abeyance for now" inasmuch as the administration believed that Israel's air capacity was "sufficient to meet its needs for the time being."

This was a major blow to the Israelis, but Rogers added that "we have no intention of jeopardizing the security of Israel"—a statement that officials in Jerusalem found incomprehensible in light of the continuing war and the scope of Soviet military deliveries to Egypt. Their judgment was that the Middle Eastern crisis would now deepen rather than recede.

Despite publicly expressed hopes, Nixon and Kissinger were puzzled when Moscow now suddenly moved to reopen the negotiations on a Middle East peace formula, and State Department specialists were surprised that when Dobrynin called on Rogers on March 11, he indicated an interest in pursuing the ideas that seemed to have died the previous December. Dobrynin's visit, not announced publicly at the time, was obviously what Nixon had had in mind when he spoke of "modestly encouraging" developments, and on March 25, the Rogers-Dobrynin talks were formally resumed. Contrary to expectations, the Russians showed no interest in negotiating a limitation on weapon supplies in the Middle East.

The administration now developed the opinion that the crisis in the Middle East could be resolved only through an Egyptian-Israeli cease-fire agreement. As the State Department saw it, the situation was getting out of hand and urgent diplomatic action was required. Policy planners thought with horror of a situation in which Israel would fight Soviet units —there already were some fifteen thousand Soviet military personnel in Egypt—and the United States found itself under growing pressure to do "something." Talking to the Russians alone was not enough. Egypt had to be brought directly into the picture.

The United States and Egypt had had no diplomatic relations since 1967, but Nasser now agreed to receive a senior American official to discuss the situation. Joseph Sisco, assistant secretary of state for Near Eastern affairs, stopped in Cairo on April 9—he was en route to Tehran for a conference of American ambassadors in the region. His first question to Nasser was how "all this killing can be stopped." He was not at liberty to apprise Nasser of the substance of the secret Soviet-American talks back in Washington, but he could discuss the outlines of a possible "Rogers Plan II" leading to a cease-fire. A week or so later, Nasser said in a television interview that he would agree to a limited-duration cease-fire. This was immediately picked up by the State Department officials, who thought they were on the verge of a breakthrough. Working through diplomatic channels in Cairo (an active "American Interests" section was attached to the Spanish embassy), they discreetly inquired what Nasser had meant by his remark. The reply was: "Make us a proposition." By the end of April, the department began to put together elements of a stand-still cease-fire along with a broad negotiations formula.

The question of oil, meanwhile, was wholly alien to the American diplomatic effort in the Middle East. To be sure, Arabists in the State Department, some of the oil companies, and businessmen with invest-ments in the Middle East occasionally warned the administration that a pro-Israeli policy might result in Arab antagonism expressed in anti-American economic measures. But nobody had suggested that the United States might be in danger of not getting petroleum. The conventional wisdom in those days of low crude-oil prices was that the producers could not "eat their oil" and had to sell it to the West no matter what. Con-versely, the Arab governments were not thinking, either, of oil as a weapon in the Middle East crisis. They were interested in the prices paid them by the multinational companies, and the extent of control they exercised over their own oil resources.

Nevertheless, the supply of oil was an increasing source of concern within the United States. Consumption was growing while domestic pro-duction had decreased since the early 1960s. However, in 1959, to pro-tect domestic producers—and prices—the Eisenhower administration had imposed the mandatory oil-import–quota system, in which quotas were regulated by levels of domestic demand.

By 1969, given the enormous increase in the demand for oil, it had become clear that the quota system was obsolete. On March 25, Nixon had appointed a cabinet task force, headed by George Shultz, then labor secretary, to determine whether it should be replaced with tariffs. The task force's monumental study, entitled "The Oil Import Question: A Report on the Relationship of Oil Imports to the National Security," was submitted to Nixon on February 9, 1970. The recommendation by the majority—Shultz, Rogers, Laird, Secretary of the Treasury David M. Kennedy, and Director of the Office of Emergency Preparedness General George A. Lincoln—was to abolish the quotas and return by stages to the tariff system. Only Interior Secretary Walter J. Hickel and Commerce Secretary Maurice H. Stans dissented, arguing for the maintenance of the existing system.

Now the oil companies had fought tooth-and-nail against dismantling the quota system, and they had mounted one of the most intensive lobbying campaigns seen in Washington in years. The majority's argument— that under the quota system Americans were forced to use the more expensive domestic oil rather than the cheaper foreign oil although there was no convincing "national security" reason for this—was not what the big oil companies wanted to hear. They opposed the importation of cheap foreign oil (having, earlier, driven its prices down through their overseas subsidiaries to be more competitive in European, Latin American, and Asian markets) because they wanted to protect their domestic earnings. The lowering of the prices for foreign-produced oil in 1969–70 also served to increase artificially the differential between foreign and domestic costs. With these figures in hand, the companies argued that it would be absolutely uneconomical for the industry to develop a greater domestic-production potential, thereby threatening national security in a crisis situation. (They overlooked the fact that, aside from Alaska, little effort had been made to discover new oil sources in the United States during the noncompetitive period from 1959 when import controls protected producers at home.)

The majority's conclusion was that

the present import control program is not adequately responsive to present and future security considerations. . . . The fixed quota limitations . . . bear no reasonable relation to current requirements for protection either of the national economy or of essential oil consumption. The level of restriction is arbitrary and the treatment of secure foreign sources internally inconsistent. The present system has spawned a host of special arrangements and exceptions for purposes essentially unrelated to the national security, has imposed high costs and inefficiencies on consumers and the economy, and has led to undue government intervention in the market and consequent competitive distortions. . . . The present import control system, as it has developed in practice, is no longer acceptable.

Under the majority's plan, the quota system would be replaced by a flexible import-control system based on gradually liberalized tariff levels. Special preferences would be granted oil imports from the Western Hemisphere: Canada, Venezuela, and other Latin American countries. The freeing of imports would force domestic producers to become more competitive both in price and volume. If domestic producers wanted to sell more, even at lower prices, they would have to produce more.

A wise statesman, equipped with the knowledge provided by the cabinet task force, should have understood the overall oil situation as it affected the United States. Given the fundamental supply and consumption problems, he should have acted providently. Thanks to Nixon, however, the United States had no contingency plans in the vital area of energy. The president found it more expedient to bow to the pressures of the big oil companies than to serve the national interest.

On February 20, Nixon announced his decision. It was an extraordinary one because in effect he rejected the recommendations of the 5-to-2 majority. He did not so say flatly in his formal statement: he simply failed to act on their recommendation and, instead, established a permanent Oil Policy Committee, headed by General Lincoln, to study further the question of oil imports. The quota system was retained.

In terms of relations with the Soviet Union, the SALT negotiations loomed importantly in Nixon's global policies. In 1970, however, no visible progress was achieved in these talks, disappointing the president. In January, Nixon announced that, after consulting with the National Security Council, he had decided to proceed with both the first and the second phases of the ABM system.

It was a curious decision. The first phase was the deployment of the antiballistic system around the launch sites of Minuteman missiles. This related directly to the American position in SALT negotiations; Nixon had explained at length the year before that the United States had chosen to concentrate its ABM defenses on the Minuteman sites rather than around Washington and other cities. The American doctrine was that the protection of retaliatory capability against a first strike was paramount for national defense while "area defense" of cities against the Soviet Union was impractical and, besides, might lead the Russians to suspect that the United States was preparing for a first strike. For this reason, Nixon said, the United States decided to forgo a comprehensive ABM system.

The second phase, however, was something else altogether. It called for the construction of a "thin" ABM system as an area defense along the Pacific coast. This was essentially what Lyndon Johnson and Robert McNamara had in mind in 1968 as a political-strategic compromise before the United States and the Soviet Union agreed to proceed with the SALT exercise. At his January 30 news conference, this is how Nixon explained his decision to develop the second ABM phase as an area defense of cities:

> Our decision involves area defense. The Minuteman defense is only effective insofar as an attack by a major power, taking out our retaliatory capacity. The area defense, on the other hand, is absolutely essential, as against any minor power, a power, for example, like Communist China. I don't anticipate an attack by Communist China, but if such a power had some capability with ICBMs to reach the United States, an area defense, according to the information we have received, is virtually infallible against that kind of potential attack, and, therefore, gives the United States a credible foreign policy in the Pacific area which it otherwise would not have. . . .
>
> Ten years from now the Communist Chinese, for example, among others, may have a significant nuclear capability. They will not be a major nuclear power, but they will have a significant nuclear capability. . . . With a significant nuclear capability, assuming that we have not made a breakthrough—and we are going to try to make the breakthrough in some normalization of our relationships with Communist China—then it will be very important for the United States to have some kind of defense so that nuclear blackmail could not be used against the United States or against those nations like the Philippines with which the United States is allied in the Pacific, not to mention Japan.

This was extremely bizarre reasoning. The idea of China using nuclear blackmail against the United States in 1980 or thereafter was quite unconvincing given the obvious American nuclear superiority. The chances of Peking closing this gap appeared remote in 1970. Curiously, while Kissinger was worrying about a Sino-Soviet nuclear war, Nixon was expostulating about a Chinese nuclear attack on the United States. As to Chinese nuclear blackmail against the Philippines or Japan, Nixon's remarks were plainly irrelevant. His own Guam "doctrine" promised the protection of the United States nuclear umbrella to friendly Asian nations. The United States maintained means of nuclear delivery in the immediate vicinity of the Chinese mainland. Thus it was difficult to make a logical connection between the second ABM phase in the United States and a "credible foreign policy" in the Pacific. The only explanation was that the "second phase" related to domestic politics and Nixon's tradeoffs with the Pentagon.

At his March 21 news conference, Nixon seemed somewhat annoyed that the Senate Foreign Relations Committee had reported out a "sense of the Senate" resolution urging a Soviet-American freeze on offensive and defensive missiles. "Of course, that is what SALT is all about, so I think the resolution really is irrelevant to what we are going to do," he said. "That is our goal. It takes two, however, to make a deal." Nixon then suggested that the negotiations were more intricate than the senators seemed to think and that it was far from certain that the United States would succeed in persuading Moscow to agree on limiting both offensive and defensive weapons. This was Nixon's first public hint that the United States might, in the end, settle for no more than a defensive agreement —which was what the Soviets seemed to want. Pending the development of their MIRV, the Soviets had no immediate interest in an accord on offensive arms. Nixon said:

> We found in our preliminary discussions that the Soviet Union did not come in with generalized language, which had been previously their tactic in arms negotiations, but they came in with very precise weapon-systems-by-weapon-systems analysis. Now whether we eventually have a comprehensive agreement or a system-by-system agreement remains to be seen. We are prepared for either.

The SALT negotiations resumed as scheduled in Vienna on April 16, and Nixon dispatched a message to the chief American delegate, Gerard Smith, expressing hopes that an agreement would be reached "on the limitation and eventual reduction of strategic arsenals with proper recognition of the legitimate security interests of the United States and the Soviet Union and of third countries."

Nixon told Smith that his new instructions "will enable you to move from general explorations to a discussion of more specific proposals." These instructions were the product of three months of studies by Kissinger's Verification Panel at the White House of the status of the negotiations during the opening phase in Helsinki in 1969. Nixon also told Smith that "you have authority to approach the issues in the most comprehensive manner," but this was a purely hortatory phrase. Neither Nixon nor Kissinger really trusted the State Department–led delegation. As Smith would find out in time, the negotiations he was conducting were a mere backdrop to the top-secret back-channel talks that Kissinger preferred to pursue directly with the Russians on the highest level. However, nothing would develop in the SALT area during 1970—neither in the formal negotiations nor in the Kissinger back channel. The Soviets maintained the talks deadlocked for the whole year with their refusal to consider a comprehensive accord on both offensive and defensive weapons.

In SALT, linkage was as deceptive as it was in other areas of Soviet-American relations.

Dealing with America's adversaries presented—by definition—a host of fundamental problems for the administration. But when it came to the allies in Western Europe, Nixon found diplomacy just as difficult. For one thing, the imperial White House was impatient with democratic governments that had to take public opinion into account. It was easier to do business with totalitarian leaders in the Communist world whose personal decisions were the final word in the formulation of policies. For another thing, the United States had to deal not only with the Atlantic alliance as an entity—via NATO, for example—but with major policy problems in relationships with each individual ally. Finally, the European allies did not always see eye to eye even on NATO-type situations (France, for instance, had withdrawn from NATO's military structure in de Gaulle's time) affecting East-West relations in general. Nixon, visiting Western Europe in 1969, claimed that "trust" was the underlying characteristic of the Atlantic alliance. But this had never been true, and now, in 1970, the administration had to face serious problems with America's allies.

Thus much of the winter and spring of 1970 was spent on European questions while simultaneously concentrating on détente, China, the Middle East, oil, the Vietnam war, and Africa. Most of these problems were also part of the diplomatic relationship with the West Europeans—and Nixon sought to tackle this skein of criss-crossing interests in separate Washington meetings with Britain's Prime Minister Harold Wilson, France's President Georges Pompidou, and West Germany's Chancellor Willy Brandt during the early part of the year. These visitors, not surprisingly, used the occasion to sell American public opinion on their views and policies.

President Nixon's meeting with Wilson, who came to Washington on January 27, fitted the pattern of the Anglo-American "special relationship" of the past, but both men had to go to some effort to make it appear that this relationship still existed notwithstanding the waning of British power. Wilson confirmed the Labour government's plans to remove British forces from the Persian Gulf; he and Nixon discussed at length how this power vacuum could best be filled, at least politically, by the United States; and Wilson also told the president that Britain felt strongly that the American consulate general in Rhodesia should be closed to avoid giving an impression of support to Ian Smith's breakaway regime.

Pompidou came on February 24 for an eight-day visit that took him all over the United States. The two presidents handled each other with kid gloves in their public pronouncements, accentuating their agreement on basic long-range policies for the West, but acknowledging their differences on immediate issues such as the Middle East and Vietnam. In his congressional address, Pompidou openly called on the United States to find a quick solution for the Vietnam war. Concerning the Vietnam peace talks in Paris, he told Congress that France had at times "regretted [their] length and wondered whether the paths followed had always been the speediest and the surest."

What Pompidou did not reveal publicly, however, was that his government had been playing a significant role in helping to arrange the secret talks conducted by Kissinger with the North Vietnamese since the previous August. France was the only Western government aware of these talks. Consequently Nixon went out of his way to please the French. He attended the dinner given by Pompidou at the French embassy, the first time he had gone to a foreign embassy since he became president.

Brandt visited Nixon on April 10. This was a most difficult meeting because Kissinger, if not Nixon, held a suspicious view of the West German policy of seeking closer relations with the Soviet Union and Eastern Europe. None of this was ever mentioned publicly by the Americans, but German officials reported in private conversations that Kissinger had expressed to Brandt his doubts about the validity of *Ostpolitik*. On the surface, it seemed like a contradiction inasmuch as the Nixon administration's own policy was to seek a détente with the Russians. The catch, however, was that Kissinger's game plan was for the United States to lead Western détente efforts; he did not want Brandt to run interference or move too far ahead on his own before Washington was ready to proclaim détente.

Brandt, who had been getting this kind of message from Washington even before his visit to Nixon, was annoyed by the American pressures. Responding to Nixon's toast at the White House dinner, Brandt addressed himself to this problem with unusual frankness:

In our efforts we must start out from the existing situation, that is to say, from realities, in order to arrive at a more normal relationship with our Eastern neighbors. We pursue this task free from illusion but with perseverance. . . .

There have been voices that accused the Germans of being willing to plunge into a course of *Realpolitik* in a questionable sense. They implied that we tried to follow a policy of self-interest in disregard of the moral values which, of course, must also guide international policy. I am certainly not speaking in terms of that kind of *Realpolitik* when I speak of the necessity to accept realities.

Western Europe's—and West Germany's—constant nightmare had been the possibility that the United States would reduce its forces on the Continent. There had been heavy congressional pressure for such a cut. Brandt's conference with Nixon largely revolved around his hopes for an open commitment that there would be no reductions in American forces in Europe in the foreseeable future. Playing on the Nixon administration's policies aimed at a détente with the Russians, Brandt quickly made the point on his arrival that the success of any negotiations with Moscow depended on European strength that could only be achieved through the continued presence of United States troops in the NATO context.

The next day, the White House announced that the United States had no plans to reduce its forces in Europe even after the existing formal commitment expired in June 1971. Actually the administration needed no persuasion on this point—it had all along opposed efforts by Senate Majority Leader Mike Mansfield to obtain a Senate resolution urging a force cut in Europe—but the White House announcement gave Brandt the assurances he came to seek. The question of *Ostpolitik* remained unresolved. The Germans went on pursuing it, Kissinger's doubts notwithstanding, until their policy finally converged with that of the United States.

During 1969, the Nixon administration had been able, by and large, to ignore African problems even though the Nigerian secession battles had raged all year, and Portugal's colonial war against nationalist guerrillas in Angola, Mozambique, and Guinea-Bissau continued unabated. By 1970, however, the United States could no longer go on pretending that African situations could wait forever for American attention. But even with this new awareness rising in Washington, the administration contrived to do almost everything wrong in developing its African policies.

The Nigerian secession collapsed on January 10, 1970. Word of this reached Kissinger from Paris, where Ambassador Sargent Shriver had received a predawn call from the Elysée Palace with the news. The immediate American concern was to avoid bloody Nigerian reprisals against the Biafrans and to forestall starvation. On January 12, Nixon authorized $10 million in emergency foodstuffs and medicine to be sent to the defeated Biafrans—offering eight C-130 air force transport planes and four helicopters to help distribute the relief shipments—and discussed the situation with Prime Minister Wilson by transatlantic telephone. (He also sent cablegrams to the victorious Nigerian leader, Major General Yakubu Gowon.) Actually, the administration had been engaged in a limited relief operation for almost a year, but now, as the president put it at an NSC meeting, it wanted a "high profile" on humanitarian aid.

On February 7, Secretary of State Rogers left on a fifteen-day tour of ten African countries: Morocco, Tunisia, Ethiopia (in Addis Ababa, he addressed the Organization of African Unity), Kenya, Zambia, the Congo Democratic Republic (now known as Zaire), Cameroon, Nigeria, Ghana, and Liberia. All these countries were more or less friendly to the United States; Rogers stayed away from the more radical African states (such as Algeria and Tanzania) and, obviously, from South Africa. This was the first time, as he noted on his departure, that an American secretary of state would visit the sub-Sahara. "We have not announced a new policy toward Africa," he said, but when he came back, he shifted gears and promised that Nixon would have a "policy position to announce."

This, however, was wholly inaccurate. In January, Nixon had finally approved a new policy toward southern Africa and the black liberation movements, selecting the option he and Kissinger liked best from NSSM–39, which had been presented to the National Security Council on December 19, 1969. The secret decision—it was never announced or alluded to in public—was to "communicate" with South Africa and other white racist regimes, on the ground that they were going to remain in place for the foreseeable future. The new policy—nicknamed, remarkably, "Tar Baby"—secretly relaxed the standing embargo on sales of military equipment to South Africa and Portugal. From Nixon's and Kissinger's viewpoint, Tar Baby provided the rationale for secret military contingency planning by the United States and NATO for the defense of southern Africa. The idea was to extend NATO's air and naval operational responsibilities to the vast strategic vacuum stretching from the South Atlantic to the Indian Ocean, covering the sea lanes around South Africa's Cape of Good Hope and the approaches to the oil-rich Persian Gulf. (Under its 1949 charter, NATO's responsibilities ended at the Tropic of Capricorn.)

Meanwhile, Tar Baby made it possible for the Nixon administration to disregard the United Nations resolutions urging an arms embargo against South Africa and the United States' own embargo against providing Portugal with military equipment for the African wars. In brief, what

Nixon and Kissinger set out to do was to help the white regimes preserve the status quo.

The new policy was spelled out in a January 1970 NSDM, based on option 2 in NSSM–39:

> The whites are here to stay and the only way that constructive change can come about is through them. There is no hope for the blacks to gain the political rights they seek through violence, which will lead only to chaos and increased opportunities for the Communists. We can, by selective relaxation of our stance toward the white regimes, encourage some modification of their current racial and colonial policies and through more substantial economic assistance to the black states help to draw the two groups together and exert some influence on both for peaceful change. Our tangible interests form a basis for our contacts in the region, and these can be maintained at an acceptable political cost.

Option 2 had been something of a compromise between the more extreme option 1 and option 5 in NSSM–39. The first, rejected by Kissinger as politically untenable, made the point that since "the whites are in control and insurgent violence will not seriously threaten that control," the United States' "economic, scientific and strategic interests in the region . . . are worth preserving and expanding. The political costs of closer relations with the white states will not be excessive." It offered these "operational examples":

> Relax arms embargo against South Africa with liberal treatment of equipment which could serve either military or civilian purposes or which could serve the common defense;
> Authorize routine naval visits and use of airfields;
> Relax the unilateral U.S. embargo on the Portuguese territories to permit export of dual purpose equipment [dual purpose means capable of being used in metropolitan Portugal in the NATO context as well as in Africa against guerrillas];
> Limit economic aid to the black states to regional and multi-donor programs; [and]
> Publicly discourage insurgent movements.

As it turned out, of course, Tar Baby achieved in practice many of the notions incorporated in option 1. The United States subsequently sold Portugal a number of Boeing 707 jet transports, allegedly for the Portuguese airline TAP but knowing perfectly well that Lisbon would use them, as it did, to ferry troops to African war theaters. South Africa was able to buy Bell helicopters and small executive jets, allegedly for service in game preserves but clearly usable for military reconnaissance and counterinsurgency combat. And it could also buy in the United States the same herbicides and defoliants that were being used in Vietnam against the Viet Cong.

It is hard to determine whether the new policy was racist, strategically oriented, simply naïve—or all of those things. As spelled out in the January NSDM, it seemed to reflect the extraordinary belief on Kissinger's part that, indeed, a "selective relaxation of our stance toward the white regimes" would lead them to treat the blacks more humanely. It was this peculiar notion that gave the new policy its sobriquet, a reference to the device in the "Uncle Remus" stories that, through it's stickiness, traps Br'er Rabbit.

Whatever Kissinger had in mind, it was clear from the start that, in the words of a senior State Department official, Tar Baby was "hypocritical and immoral" and "gave us the worst of both worlds." He wistfully recalled the words of the late Adlai Stevenson addressing the U.N. Security Council on August 2, 1963:

> All of us sitting here today know the melancholy truth about the racial policies of the Government of South Africa. Our task now is to consider what further steps we can take to induce that government to remove the evil business of apartheid, not only from our agenda, but from the continent of Africa. . . . In the absence of an indication of change, the United States [will] not cooperate in matters which would lend support to South Africa's present racial policies.

Seven years later, the whole moral and practical tone of American policy had been changed. This is how the secret option 2 in NSSM–39 stated the "General Posture":

> We would maintain public opposition to racial repression but relax political isolation and economic restrictions on the white states. We would begin by modest indications of this relaxation, broadening the scope of our relations and contacts gradually and to some degree in response to tangible—albeit small and gradual—moderation of white policies.
>
> Without openly taking a position undermining the United Kingdom and the U.N. on Rhodesia, we would be more flexible in our attitude toward the Smith regime. We would take present Portuguese policies as suggesting further changes in the Portuguese territories. At the same time we would take diplomatic steps to convince the black states

of the area that their current liberation and majority rule aspirations in the south are not attainable by violence and that their only hope for a peaceful and prosperous future lies in closer relations with white-dominated states. We would emphasize our belief that closer relations will help to bring change in the white states.

This option accepts, at least over a three-to-five-year period, the prospect of unrequited U.S. initiatives toward the whites and some opposition from the blacks in order to develop an atmosphere conducive to change in white attitudes through persuasion and erosion. To encourage this change in white attitudes, we would indicate our willingness to accept political arrangements short of guaranteed progress toward majority rule, provided that they assured broadened political participation in some form by the whole population.

The document then recommended these "operational examples":

Enforce arms embargo against South Africa but with liberal treatment of equipment which could serve either military or civilian purposes. [This wording is identical with that in option 1.]

Permit U.S. naval calls in South Africa with arrangements for non-discrimination toward U.S. personnel in organized activity ashore; authorize routine use of airfields.

Conduct selected exchange programs with South Africa in all categories, including military.

Without changing the U.S. legal position that South African occupancy of South West Africa is illegal, we would play down the issue and encourage accommodation between South Africa and the U.N. [This was a reference to a U.N. decision that South Africa's mandate over South West Africa, first granted by the League of Nations, has lapsed and the territory should be given independence.]

On Rhodesia, retain consulate: gradually relax sanctions (e.g., hardship exceptions for chrome) and consider eventual recognition.

Continue arms embargo on Portuguese territories, but give more liberal treatment to exports of dual purpose equipment.

Towards African insurgent movements take public position that U.S. opposes use of force in racial confrontations. Continue humanitarian assistance to refugees.

Under this option, advantages accruing to the United States would preserve its "economic, scientific and strategic interests in the white states and would expand opportunities for profitable trade and investment." The secret paper further observed that "U.S. diplomatic support and economic aid offer the black states an alternative to the recognized risks of mounting Communist influence." Blithely the paper went on to say that the proposed policy "would reduce a major irritant in our relations with Portugal, and afford the Caetano government opportunity for liberalization."

Interestingly, however, the NSC study warned that Tar Baby could have negative consequences:

> Relaxation of the U.S. stance towards white states could be taken by the whites as a vindication of their policies. Many black states, led by Zambia and Tanzania, probably would charge us with subordinating our professed ideals to material interests and tolerating white-regime policies.
>
> There is a serious question whether pro-Western leaders of the black states could continue to justify their stance to their populations if the U.S. officially declared its opposition to current liberation efforts. Radical and Communist states would be the beneficiaries.
>
> Unilateral U.S. relaxation of sanctions against Rhodesia would be a highly visible violation of our international obligations and would be damaging both to the U.S. and to the U.N.
>
> The current thrust of South African domestic policy does not involve any basic change in the racial segregation system, which is anathema to the black states. There is virtually no evidence that change might be forthcoming in these South African policies as a result of any approach on our part.
>
> Requires extensive diplomatic and economic involvement in a situation in which the solution is extremely long-range and the outcome doubtful at best.

Despite these caveats, Nixon accepted most of the NSC recommendations in option 2 and, in some cases, even went beyond them. Starting in 1970, for example, Portuguese officers were trained in counterinsurgency at the U.S. Army's jungle-warfare school at Fort Gulick in the Panama Canal Zone. Portuguese jet pilots received advanced training in West Germany, the headquarters of the U.S. Air Force in Europe.

One of the strongest proponents of a prowhite policy in Africa was CIA Director Helms. At the NSC meeting on December 19, he had insisted so strongly on the stability and general durability of the African white regimes everywhere that Kissinger passed a note to one of his aides asking, "Why is he doing that?" Part of the answer was that the CIA had extremely close contacts with South African intelligence services through one of the special Commonwealth intelligence agreements, known as "UKUSA," as well as with Rhodesian intelligence. Helms, evidently, was eager to maintain these ties. When Nixon requested his views on the closing down of the American consulate general in Salisbury, Helms replied: "Well, Mr. President, I don't want to get in the business of commenting on policy . . . [but] we do have useful and workable relationships in Salisbury with our counterparts there. I think it would be a shame to sacrifice those if we didn't have to, and if we got rid of the consulate in Salisbury, we would have to run our operations out of some other context. I think it could be done, but I would like to see us keep a hand in there."

The tentative decision in December was to keep the consulate open as a listening post and as a possible kind of "venue," as an NSC official put it, for mediation with the British. However, Prime Minister Wilson expressed his displeasure with this decision when he visited Nixon in Washington late in January 1970. Early in March, Wilson sent Nixon a secret note—a "tough" one, according to NSC officials—stating that Rhodesia was British territory, despite its action on March 2 declaring itself a republic, and that because of the situation there the Crown was withdrawing the exequatur from the consulate general. Wilson's note was a virtual ultimatum for the United States to close down the consulate (he took the view that American presence in Salisbury would imply tacit recognition of the Smith regime), and this issue briefly became a secret storm in Anglo-American relations.

In the end, Kissinger decided to accept the British demands and the consulate was finally closed down on March 17. Kissinger's view was that the consulate was an expendable issue and that he would not fight with Wilson over it. Subsequently Secretary Rogers claimed that he had prevailed personally on the administration to do away with the consulate as a result of the views he heard during his African tour. But an NSC official denied it was so. "It was not Rogers, it was not African pressure, it was not domestic pressure from the congressional black caucus, or anybody else. It was, pure and simple, Henry's calculation that it wasn't worth making it an issue with the British at that point."

Rogers's African tour produced few tangible results from a policy viewpoint. As far as southern Africa was concerned, policy had already been set in motion. In public, however, Rogers was giving a different impression. At a news conference in Nairobi, Kenya, on February 15, he was asked about the American attitude toward African liberation movements. He replied: "We encourage independence movements in all countries. We very much believe in the policy of self-determination. We . . . do not think that those matters should be worked out by armed conflict; but we certainly support the independence movements in Africa, as we have always done." This was something less than a truthful statement of United States policy.

Chapter 9

The resumption of secret negotiations with the North Vietnamese came late in February, when Kissinger flew to Paris to hold his first meeting with Le Duc Tho, the Hanoi Politburo member. Kissinger had spent a great deal of time preparing himself; he seemed to expect a breakthrough and he wanted to be ready for it. He assigned three of his aides—Richard Smyser, who had just joined the NSC staff to work on Vietnam, Roger Morris, and Anthony Lake—to draft the "talking points" for his meetings with Tho. One of his aides recalled:

"We were engaged in refining these talking points. . . . Some of us would go to Henry's office, and he would pace back and forth, and talk through his negotiating stance. He'd start talking about how he was going to open the conversation with Le Duc Tho: 'We're both scholars, men with a sense of history. . . . I want you to know that we begin, that I begin these negotiations with an acute sense of the great sacrifice the people of North Vietnam have made in this struggle. I don't intend to negotiate any settlement which dishonors that sacrifice in any way. I look forward to the time when we can meet under different circumstances, when you can come to the U.S., and I can come to Hanoi, and we can both lecture. . . .' And so forth. . . . But it struck me at the time as almost grotesque —how much joking and light jocular talk went into this thing at the beginning to establish the ambience and the climate. Then Henry would sort of get down to business again. He planned to tell Tho, 'Now, it's our view that there ought to be a certain priority once these issues are to be settled. We believe that the military disengagement problem is terribly important. It's linked to the political settlement, and the political settlement is obviously something that ultimately has to be settled among the Vietnamese, North and South, but we think we can establish here some kind of schedule to deal with it.' "

The preparations for his sessions with Le Duc Tho, taken together with the accounts of the actual meetings (NSC files contain copies of some of his secret cables to Nixon as well as memoranda of conversations with

Tho, taken down by his aides), offer a fascinating study in Kissinger's negotiating technique. It was an astounding exercise in flexible diplomacy—never quite showing his hand and always keeping his *interlocuteur* slightly off balance. For one thing, Kissinger kept Le Duc Tho guessing as to what the *real* American negotiating position might be as distinct from publicly stated policies, and whether and how the United States might make concessions on a given point. Indeed, by the time Kissinger held his first session with Tho, the administration had developed a subtle pattern: Nixon would publicly state a posture, usually in a firm and specific manner; then Kissinger, closeted with Tho, would lead the latter to believe that under certain circumstances American policy had room for considerable nuance.

The best—and the most crucial—example concerned the question of mutual withdrawals from South Vietnam. It was official American policy, constantly reiterated by Nixon, that simultaneous American and North Vietnamese withdrawals from the South were the precondition for a settlement, but Hanoi had never publicly acknowledged that its troops were fighting in the South. It can be inferred from the secret accounts of the negotiations that Kissinger realized that if other conditions were met, the United States might in the end settle for a cease-fire in place and quietly drop the subject of mutual withdrawals. He did not say it to Tho in so many words, but he offered intriguing hints to that effect in his first encounters with him. A cease-fire in place, of course, could lead to a unilateral American withdrawal, and Kissinger must have known from the outset that, sooner or later, this would be the outcome. The only North Vietnamese condition Kissinger rejected was the removal of President Thieu, but even this rejection was communicated artfully. Kissinger seemed to be ahead of Nixon in his intellectual appreciation of what would be feasible in the end.

"The whole thing began with an insistence on mutual withdrawal," one of Kissinger's aides recalled. "Right away it ran into the question of North Vietnamese acknowledgment. But—and this was a portent of things to come—it never swayed Henry. I don't know whether he began these negotiations with the idea that he would ultimately abandon the mutual-withdrawal point, or that he would treat it as his trump card. Maybe, at the beginning, mutual withdrawals were a sticking point, and he tried to evade it, dance around it, or talk his way through it. But, whether he intended it or not, his handling of it was very skillful. He went right on talking about mutual withdrawal as if the other side had consented to discuss it. . . .

"In general, Henry had us draft his talking points as a very deliberately ambiguous, flexible presentation of possibilities on such things as a timetable for American withdrawals over a given period. For example, Henry would say to Tho that if we are to talk about military disengagement, this is the kind of thing that we ought to be talking about, these are the limits in which we should discuss them, or this is the kind of thing that we would be interested in putting forward. Henry phrased all of those things in a very tentative way. It wasn't just a matter of sitting down and saying, 'Here's our offer,' not a matter of saying, 'We believe in these or these principles.' The North Vietnamese did that, they were adamant. In comparative terms, they were the ones who were meticulous and precise. Henry was the one who was vague and elliptical and seemingly open to suggestion. But he was very persistent on coming back to the point of military disengagement. He was very vague, most vague of all, on the question of the South Vietnamese. He was always addressing the question in terms of what was politically possible for the U.S. It wasn't politically feasible for the U.S. to have a settlement in which we deposed the South Vietnamese government, Henry would tell Tho. He would say: 'Gentlemen, I understand perfectly your aversion to Thieu. I understand perfectly that from your point of view, there obviously has to be some kind of political settlement which guarantees the safety and security of your people in the South. But you must understand that from our point of view any settlement in which the U.S. deposed the regime in Saigon simply couldn't and wouldn't last. The president couldn't do it for domestic reasons. . . . Let's both be realistic: I'll be realistic about your imperatives, you must be realistic about mine.'

   "But there was a subtlety in Henry's approach. He never actually foreclosed the idea of replacing Thieu. It was always in terms of 'You must make it easy for us. . . . When the settlement comes, we may be able to do things about South Vietnam, we may be able to get them to accept certain things, but, please, bear in mind the political sensitivities of this thing.' It was always a tactical discussion—never a strategic presentation that the South Vietnamese are our allies, that they are to be protected, that 'I'm here to negotiate on their behalf.'

   "What I saw in those early negotiations was a portent of everything that was to follow: Henry was going to cave in on the military point—that was plain—we were going to have a kind of a leopard-spot settlement sooner or later, and we were going to hang in tough with the Saigon regime one way or another. And the critical ingredient in all this would be some kind of tangible concession over Thieu on the part of the North Vietnamese. The really moot point was the calculation in Henry's mind.

Was he thinking then about the circumstances in which Hanoi would come around to some kind of tacit acceptance of the Thieu regime? Was he, indeed, believing that only a final spasm of battle, initiated either by the U.S. or by them, would lead to a settlement? We were dealing with an extremely complex man whose appreciation of the subtleties of the whole thing was constantly evolving."

In any event, the first Kissinger-Tho meeting in February resulted in no tangible progress. Kissinger and Tho were sparring, looking for weak points. Tho was restating the official Hanoi line; Kissinger was trying out his flexible approaches. They parted in a deadlock. And when Kissinger went back to Paris in March for another session, it was more of the same, except that Kissinger decided to try some specific military proposals, largely to see the North Vietnamese reaction. Early in April, Kissinger ordered his staff (always working in utmost secrecy) to draft an American withdrawal timetable with specific numbers of troops to be taken out over several different periods of time—twelve months, eighteen months, twenty-four months, and so on. These alternate packages were designed to obtain Hanoi's responses rather than to be actual pullout plans that Nixon might set in motion independent of other considerations.

President Nixon remained silent about Vietnam proper—and about Kissinger's secret Paris negotiations—during all of February and most of March. However, developments in Laos were causing deep concern in the White House. There were reports of a heavy North Vietnamese buildup in the Lao kingdom and of increased involvement by Hanoi's troops in the seesaw battle for the strategic Plaine des Jarres.

The strategists were uncertain what all these movements meant: it could be a preparation for a final take-over of Laos, which could result in the flanking of the northern portion of South Vietnam; or it could be related to a redeployment of Communist forces in Laos and Cambodia, prior to a lethal blow at South Vietnam from the west and north. Generally speaking, Washington regarded all of Indochina as a single war theater. The North Vietnamese presence in Laos and Cambodia was perceived above all as a direct threat to South Vietnam. Communist forces were using Laos and Cambodia as sanctuaries; the Ho Chi Minh complex of trails in eastern Laos was the principal infiltration route from North to South Vietnam. Nixon resolved to launch a diplomatic offensive on the subject of Laos.

On March 6, the president requested the assistance of Britain's Prime Minister Wilson and Soviet Premier Kosygin in restoring the effectiveness of the Geneva accords on Laos. Britain and the Soviet Union had been cochairmen of the Geneva conference on Laos which in July 1962 produced an agreement providing for the withdrawal of all foreign troops from that country. The United States had complied with the accords by withdrawing the 5000 marines John Kennedy had sent there; the North Vietnamese removed some of their troops, but their cadres remained. Subsequently infiltration resumed, but this time, the United States countered by bolstering the Royal Lao Army with CIA elements who soon led the agency's Clandestine Army.

Along with his letters to Wilson and Kosygin, the president issued, from his vacation headquarters at Key Biscayne, a long public statement on the situation in Laos, explaining the reasons for his démarche. His letters, he declared, "note the persistent North Vietnamese violations of the accords and their current offensives." Britain and Russia "have particular responsibilities for seeing that [the agreements'] provisions are honored." Nixon went on:

> Hanoi's most recent build-up in Laos has been particularly escalatory. They have poured over 13,000 additional troops into Laos during the past few months, raising their total in Laos to over 67,000. Thirty North Vietnamese battalions from regular division units participated in the current campaign in the Plain of Jars with tanks, armored cars, and long-range artillery. The indigenous Laotian Communists, the Pathet Lao, are playing an insignificant role.

Much of Nixon's statement was devoted to the history of events in Laos since 1962. The president said he was releasing it "to set forth the record of what we found in January 1969 and the policy of this administration since that time." North Vietnam, he noted,

> appears to have two aims in Laos. The first is to insure its ability to use Laos as a supply route for North Vietnamese forces in South Vietnam. The second is to weaken and subvert the Royal Lao Government—originally established at its urging—to hinder it from interfering with North Vietnamese use of Laotian territory, and to pave the way for the eventual establishment of a government more amenable to Communist control.

Nixon acknowledged that, in response to the North Vietnamese escalation going back to 1963, the United States had all along been providing "military assistance to regular and irregular Laotian forces in the form of equipment, training and logistics," and that the levels of American assistance had "risen in response to the growth of North Vietnamese combat activities." He also admitted something that had been generally known for some time:

> We have continued to conduct air operations . . . to interdict the continued flow of troops and supplies across Laotian territory on the Ho Chi Minh Trail. As Commander in Chief of our Armed Forces, I consider it my responsibility to use our air power to interdict this flow of supplies and men into South Vietnam and thereby avoid a heavy toll of American and allied lives. In addition . . . we have continued to carry out reconnaissance flights in northern Laos and to fly combat supply missions for Laotian forces when requested to do so by the Royal Laotian Government. In every instance our combat air operations have taken place only over those parts of Laos occupied and contested by North Vietnamese and other Communist forces.

This had been the most complete statement to date by the United States government on its military involvement in Laos. Nixon had evidently resolved to be candid—up to a point—about military operations there because of a wave of journalists' reports that the United States had reintroduced combat forces in Laos or was contemplating doing so. He forcefully denied that this was the case, adding that there were only 1040 Americans in Laos employed by the U.S. government or by American contractors; only 320 military and civilian personnel engaged in military training or advisory capacities; and only 323 assigned to logistics. And, Nixon added, "No American stationed in Laos has ever been killed in ground combat operations."

But Nixon's candor was a relative thing. He spoke of "combat support missions" flown by American aircraft when requested by the Laotians, suggesting just occasional sorties, when in reality B-52s were steadily battering Laotian territory in the north. He confirmed American military aid to the Laotian Army and "irregulars," without making it clear that these "irregulars" were the ever-growing Clandestine Army. No Americans *stationed* in Laos had been killed, as far as anybody knew, but there were losses among men secretly infiltrating Laos under Operation Prairie Fire. Obviously, the North Vietnamese were violating the Geneva accords. Nixon's problem was that while he, too, was violating the accords (presumably for valid and symmetrical reasons, as he saw them), he wished to have this concealed.

.   .   .

Nixon's speech in November 1969 had gained him a respectable reprieve from criticism of his conduct of the war by the public, Congress, and even the antiwar movement. But in the new year, doubts were rising once more, and new questions were being asked as to what the United States was doing in Indochina. Challenging voices were heard again—in and out of Congress. On March 5, Senator Edmund S. Muskie of Maine urged a new national debate on Vietnam, arguing for a new approach to the Paris peace talks as well as to the Saigon regime—which, he said, "neither deserves nor receives much popular support." And Senator Eugene McCarthy went before the Senate Foreign Relations Committee on February 19 to charge that Nixon was "misleading" the nation about peace prospects in Indochina. The Minnesota senator, who had been in Paris in January to confer with North Vietnamese and Viet Cong diplomats, insisted that Vietnamization was neither desirable nor workable.

I believe that the nation is being misled over the issues at stake in Vietnam, as it was in 1966 and 1967, when this Committee took upon itself the responsibility of educating and informing the people and called the Johnson Administration to a public accounting. . . .
    Serious negotiations cannot proceed unless we are willing to support a coalition Government to control the process of transition. . . . The task of the interim Government would be to arrange a cease-fire and to assure the orderly withdrawal of foreign forces.

There were other Indochinese matters of concern to the Senate Foreign Relations Committee. At a hearing in February, Senator Fulbright charged that the United States was involved in "a program for the assassination of civilian leaders" in Vietnam through Operation Phoenix. His principal witness was William Colby, the career CIA official who, holding ambassadorial rank, served as head of the pacification program in Vietnam. Phoenix was of course a crucial element in the pacification program. Colby insisted that it was not a "counterterror" operation, but he told the committee that the year before a total of 19,534 suspected Viet Cong "political cadres" had been "neutralized": 8515 captured and imprisoned, 6187 killed, and 4832 had joined the Saigon side. In his cold voice, Colby then conceded that "there may have been some aberrations" and some "illegal killings" in Operation Phoenix.

The committee's hearings led to no specific action by Congress. Despite numerous attempts in the Senate to enact legislation controlling presidential war powers in Southeast Asia, Congress was not yet ready to block Nixon in any serious fashion. Late in 1969, it had approved legislation limiting to $2.5 billion the funds for military operations in Vietnam, Laos, and Thailand by local forces, but this made no noticeable difference. That was, in any case, all the money the administration needed for these activities; American combat activities were financed from Pentagon appropriations. An amendment proposed by Senator John Sherman Cooper, the Republican from Kentucky, forbade the introduction of American combat troops into Thailand and Laos, but this had no effect, either. The Senate had no inkling that the real danger area was in Cambodia.

By and large, congressional opposition to the war was expressed in rhetoric rather than in action. Three resolutions on the limitation of the president's war powers died in the House Foreign Affairs Committee during 1969 and 1970, and even some of the most outspoken senators and congressmen tended to back off when the administration invoked the need to allow the commander in chief to retain maximal freedom to protect American lives in Vietnam.

Despite the Senate Foreign Relations Committee's indignation about Operation Phoenix, no effort was made to take the United States out of the Viet Cong–chasing and assassination business in Vietnam. Yet classified directives issued by Colby's pacification-program office (its official name was Civil Operations and Rural Development Support, commonly known as CORDS) explained in detail the American involvement in Phoenix (whose name in Vietnamese was Phung Hoang). Assassinations were never mentioned; the emphasis was on what were called "An-Tri detentions," which were "administrative" rather than judicial detentions. Operations were conducted by South Vietnamese Province Security Committees (PSC) assisted by American CORDS advisers. Colby also established American Phoenix Coordinators to work in this vast counterintelligence operation. CORDS directives made it strikingly clear that Phoenix cases were handled in the manner of kangaroo courts whenever Viet Cong suspects were captured. A CORDS directive of January 22, 1970, for instance, concerned itself with "elements of proof" required to convict members of the Viet Cong Infrastructure (VIC). It declared that South Vietnamese laws on national security

> define mere membership or function in the Viet Cong Infrastructure as a threat to national security. . . . Membership or function may be inferred from acts or intelligence data. . . . There is no rigid rule regarding the amount or type of evidence necessary to support An-Tri detentions. Not being a criminal conviction, the burden of proof is

less than that required by a court. The theory of preventive detention is based upon the reasonable conclusion that the accused is a threat to the national security. The burden of proof is on the prosecution which must show that the accused is, in fact, a member of the communist party or exercises a position or function in the party or any associated front organization. Proof of position or function in the Viet Cong Infrastructure is sufficient to convict.

The directive then described "elements of proof":

> Membership, position or function in the VCI, as indicated by:
> a. Incriminating documents—to include, but not limited to, membership lists of communist organizations; enemy correspondence; diaries; notebooks. . . .
> b. Enemy weapons or material found in the possession of the accused upon apprehension.
> c. Witnesses—accomplices', accessories' or ralliers' [i.e., defectors'] statements regarding the position or function of the accused. . . .
> d. Interrogation statements or confessions—are admissible . . . in An-Tri hearings. . . .
> e. Intelligence reports—are admissible in that there is no prohibition against hearsay.
> f. If position or function within the Viet Cong Infrastructure is proven, sentencing is automatic. . . . Renewable An-Tri detention of up to two years may be given by the Province Security Committee.

American Phoenix Coordinators were to "stress the varied elements of proof sufficient to convict," and they were to "insure that members of the [provincial] center understand the importance of intelligence as evidence." The directive also noted that Province Security Committees "must hold meetings at least once every week, and in each meeting, the number of cases to be resolved should be reasonable so that the making of reports and dossiers proposing security detentions can be done rapidly." All reports "should be coordinated with the US advisor."

A separate CORDS document analyzed the procedures of the Province Security Committees, noting that "their purpose is political; their method is administrative detention of those persons reasonably believed to endanger national security, but against whom sufficient evidence for a trial is lacking." It remarked that suspect detainees "may appear before the Committee, but do not have the right to demand such appearance." And it explained that "due to the administrative nature and political mission of the PSC, procedures are far less exacting than those of the courts."

Inasmuch as under South Vietnamese regulations the provincial chief of internal security was responsible for recommending "the type and duration of detention," CORDS wanted to make sure that his performance was adequate. Therefore, the CORDS document said, "there is an urgent need to educate these . . . officers." American Phoenix advisers and their South Vietnamese counterparts were instructed to "determine what the chief of internal security considers to be necessary to have a dossier which is sufficient for him to recommend maximum 'An-Tri' detention." Clearly the Americans in Phoenix feared that the South Vietnamese might be too lenient with their own people. Phoenix procedures also covered trials in military courts that were held if "there was clear evidence of a violation of the national security laws, or if the suspect was apprehended in the act of committing an offense against the national security."

Having, in effect, established control over South Vietnamese military courts, Colby's CORDS needed assurance that suspects would not be prematurely released, in the absence of evidence, by the provincial committees. In what must have been the most blatant example of judicial lawlessness imposed by the American command on the South Vietnamese, the CORDS document set forth the following procedure:

> Where evidence for trial is lacking, but it is apparent that the suspect is a threat to the national security, the Committee may impose administrative ("An-Tri") detention. This is a type of preventative [sic] detention to protect the state from a known threat to its security. There is the additional provision of continual extension of two-year terms if the individual remains a threat to the national security. . . . A violation of the national security laws need not be proven; all that must be demonstrated is that a reasonable belief exists that the suspect threatens the national security. Once "An-Tri" detention is imposed there are no judicial remedies.

The CORDS document commented that the power of the provincial committees went "beyond that of the courts into the area of emergency political detention necessitated by the need of the State to survive." It added:

> There is no rigid rule regarding the amount of evidence necessary for detention, and the criteria may vary significantly from province to province. Each committee determines the existing threat to national security based on conditions within the particular province, and the function of the detainee within the VCI. This process, because it is

administrative, and political in nature, reflects the political "facts-of-life" in the province. It is encumbent [*sic*] upon each PHOENIX Coordinator to determine these local variances and tailor his advice accordingly.

A CORDS directive issued on May 18, 1970, proclaimed that the Viet Cong had an "unlawful status" as far as South Vietnamese law was concerned as well as "the laws of land warfare followed by the US Army." But, it said, American personnel participating in Phoenix "are specifically unauthorized to engage in assassinations or other violations of the rules of land warfare." Still, "they are entitled to use such reasonable military force as is necessary to obtain the goals of rallying, capturing, or eliminating the VCI in the Republic of Vietnam." There also was a word for the squeamish among Americans in Vietnam: "If an individual finds the police type activities of the PHOENIX program repugnant to him, on his application, he can be reassigned from the program without prejudice."

"Extraordinary efforts" were employed to combat the Viet Cong Infrastructure. The Pentagon's Advanced Research Projects Agency (ARPA), a very secret organization indeed, spent millions of dollars in Washington on a *VC Infrastructure Handbook*. As explained by ARPA's director at hearings before a Senate subcommittee in 1970, this handbook was developed for the agency by the RAND Corporation over a period of three years. It was based on interviews with "thousands of known Viet Cong who had been captured or turned themselves in . . . and who described how the basic Viet Cong organization worked right down to the lowest level and up to the top, the people who report to Hanoi." This research was analyzed scientifically so that ARPA could tell "how to dissassemble the Viet Cong." The handbook, published in both Vietnamese and English, was prepared so that "the Vietnamese police and the Government would be able to find the VC. . . . It has been one of the toughest problems of the war, how do you find out whether a Vietnamese is a VC or not?"

ARPA became interested in this fascinating issue as part of its wider, top-secret Project Agile, dealing with counterinsurgency in Southeast Asia and elsewhere. Most of ARPA's work is in advanced fields of nuclear studies, computer linkages, space and undersea research, laser weapons, and reconstruction of human speech. But such was the preoccupation of the United States government with the Vietnam war that even ARPA was harnessed to this effort. It was an intriguing example of how Americans deluded themselves into believing that their most esoteric technological resources could provide valid answers to the human questions of insurgency. Even ARPA's director raised the question of whether there is any way "of analyzing insurgent war . . . in the same way you can analyze nuclear war? . . . Can you somehow extract the moral considerations to see what the mechanics are?" In any event, the effort was made, and Phoenix became its recipient, if not its beneficiary.

Nobody will ever know how many real or suspected Viet Cong men and women were killed by the South Vietnamese or Americans as part of Phoenix. Given the enormous latitude enjoyed by Phoenix operators, it is likely that the use of "reasonable military force" must have led to executions on a number of occasions. Operating under vague rules of suspicion rather than evidence, the An-Tri–detention program helped to fill South Vietnamese prisons with tens of thousands of people who may, or may not, have been Viet Cong militants or sympathizers. Given the real "political 'facts-of-life' '' in the Vietnamese countryside, provincial officials obviously had no trouble engaging in vendettas and settling scores and grudges against rivals and personal enemies on the basis of undocumented charges of Viet Cong sympathies. All this was done with American encouragement and the application of the U.S. Army's "laws of land warfare." At the other end of this human conveyor belt, the United States provided the Saigon regime with "technical assistance" through AID's Public Safety mission in running the prisons where victims of An-Tri and other enemies of President Thieu were incarcerated. This included the "tiger cages" on offshore islands. According to U.S. Navy procurement documents, some of the prisons were prefabricated in California by navy contractors and shipped to Vietnam.

Most of these activities were unknown at the time to the American public, as the Nixon administration continued to justify the continuation of the war. In Paris, Kissinger argued with Le Duc Tho that the United States simply could not sacrifice President Thieu as part of a peace settlement, and in all its public comments the administration sounded a high moral note. Americans were fighting in Vietnam, Nixon kept reminding the country, to assure freedom and democracy for our allies in Asia—and especially for the South Vietnamese.

Cambodia had been part of the Indochina equation for at least fifteen years before 1970. Following the end of the French war in Indochina, Prince Norodom Sihanouk, the chief of state, proclaimed Cambodian neutrality and nonalignment and in 1955 signed an aid agreement with China. This cost him United States aid—Eisenhower did not take kindly to Asian flirtations with Peking—and subjected his country to an economic blockade imposed by South Vietnam and Thailand but apparently inspired by Washington.

In 1958 and 1959, just as the Viet Cong rebellion was getting under way in South Vietnam, a bizarre plot was hatched in Bangkok to remove Sihanouk. Thailand and South Vietnam (whose troops began to conduct raids into Cambodian border areas as early as 1958) appeared to be its prime movers, but there were strong indications that this operation had quiet United States blessing despite President Eisenhower's public disclaimers. The CIA, for one thing, helped to organize the Khmer Serei (Free Cambodia) movement, drawn from ethnic Cambodians in South Vietnam, as an anti-Sihanouk force. The traditional hostility between Cambodians and South Vietnamese was an element in this conspiracy, which laid the groundwork for future uses of the Khmer Serei. However, the plot failed and relations between Cambodia and its neighbors were temporarily repaired.

In 1960 Sihanouk was elected chief of state for life (he had earlier abdicated his throne in order to become a populist leader while retaining his princely rank) and moved to obtain international guarantees for his country. While the 1962 Geneva conference granted Laos neutral status and recognized its borders, it refused to do so for Cambodia, largely because of American and South Vietnamese opposition. With the United States increasingly engaged in Vietnam, Washington and Saigon favored Sihanouk's deposition: the prince, it was felt, could not be trusted. Cambodia's potential function as a sanctuary for Communist forces was obvious, and a pro-Western regime there was preferred to the uncertainty surrounding Sihanouk's tortuous policies. In 1963, the CIA reactivated the Khmer Serei for subversive activities in Cambodia, providing this rebel movement with radio transmitters in Thailand and South Vietnam.

In 1964, South Vietnamese forces resumed their penetrations into Cambodia; on at least one occasion (in March), a Saigon unit went in with an American adviser. Although Washington denied Sihanouk's charges that Americans were involved in these border incursions, it declined to support an international declaration of Cambodian neutrality until the kingdom settled its differences with Thailand and South Vietnam. This was probably one of the most important errors in American policy in Indochina; Sihanouk reacted by recalling his diplomatic mission from Washington. But when American intelligence discovered in the autumn of 1964 that the North Vietnamese had succeeded for the first time in infiltrating a large force of regular troops through Cambodia into the

Mekong Delta, southwest of Saigon, the United States suddenly showed an interest in negotiating with Sihanouk. Talks were quickly broken off when the Cambodians insisted on recognition of their boundaries, and the South Vietnamese resumed incursions into Cambodia in 1965; American aircraft bombed at least three Cambodian border villages. Late in 1965, Sihanouk severed diplomatic relations with the United States altogether. In 1966, however, Washington suddenly changed its mind and announced that it supported Cambodian neutrality. It coupled this announcement with charges that North Vietnam and the Viet Cong had been violating Cambodian neutrality. But once again the two governments could not find a common language.

In 1967, the CIA was instructed to turn to the Khmer Serei for covert actions in Cambodia. This time, Khmer Serei scouts were used in regular intelligence penetrations into Cambodia as part of Operation Salem House, whose teams included CIA, NSA, and the U.S. Army's Green Beret experts along with South Vietnamese and Khmer Serei combat units. Salem House was supported by helicopter gunships, and communicators attached to the teams were in radio contact with ELINT (electronic intelligence) aircraft circling overhead.

Sihanouk found himself pressed from all sides. He dispatched his own troops to fight the Communist-organized Khmer Rouge rebels in the provinces while other Cambodian units battled the rightist Khmer Serei. Because of leftist pressures in Phnom Penh, his capital, the prince fired General Lon Nol as his premier and refused to discuss with the United States the issue of how Cambodian territory was being used by the North Vietnamese. Increasingly—and desperately—he was playing both sides against the middle. He considered the Khmer Rouge his principal enemy, but in June he established diplomatic relations with Hanoi, presumably as a step to check the rebels he suspected the North Vietnamese of controlling. The American reaction was to step up the CIA-directed activities by the Khmer Serei, who were now permitted to go twelve miles into Cambodia.

In the course of 1968, the Cambodian situation became totally confused. Sihanouk simultaneously accused the Communists of fomenting a rebellion in northwestern Cambodia, near the Thai border, and the United States and South Vietnam of violating his borders in the south. Then he charged that the Communists were supporting the Khmer Rouge in the northeast, near the South Vietnamese borders. In the midst of this chaos, Washington charged, in September, that the North Vietnamese and the Viet Cong had tripled their use of bases in northeast

Cambodia, adjoining the Ho Chi Minh Trail, and in Svay Rieng Province in the salient west of Saigon. In December, Sihanouk complained that three hundred Cambodians in border villages were killed in United States air attacks, but he released four captured American airmen.

With the advent of the Nixon administration in 1969, Sihanouk's relationship with the United States came to reflect even more the contradictory pressures on Cambodia. On March 18, American B-52s had launched their secret raids against Cambodian territory with Sihanouk's tacit consent: the prince did not wish to have official knowledge of the daily strikes at Communist troop concentrations and depots in his country so that he would not be forced to protest. It was generally known that U.S. aircraft occasionally bombed Cambodian border areas, but this had gone on so long that nobody (except the border villagers) seemed to care. Hanoi, obviously, was in no position to protest the B-52 strikes against its forces in Cambodia because it never acknowledged their presence there. In April, Sihanouk offered to resume diplomatic relations with Washington in exchange for recognition of Cambodia's territorial integrity; it was his way of seeking an end to the warfare engulfing his nation. The United States replied, piously, that it "recognizes and respects the sovereignty, independence, neutrality and the territorial integrity" of Cambodia. A few weeks later, however, two American helicopters were shot down over Cambodia.

Sihanouk wanted to keep all his flanks covered. In May, he agreed to let the Viet Cong National Liberation Front mission in Phnom Penh be raised to embassy status, and by August, Cambodian relations with Washington had improved to the point where the American embassy was reopened with the arrival of Chargé d'Affaires Lloyd Rives. Lon Nol, the army chief of staff, was recalled as premier; his primary job appeared to be to coordinate actions against Khmer Rouge rebels while Sihanouk took upon himself negotiations with North Vietnam and the Viet Cong to persuade them to leave Cambodia. He raised this question with Hanoi's leaders in September when he attended Ho Chi Minh's funeral. From Washington's viewpoint, Cambodia now was on the "right track"; in time, it was hoped, it might become a valuable ally. The State Department began discussing economic aid. In October, Sihanouk issued a claim that forty thousand North Vietnamese and Viet Cong troops were in Cambodia, a figure in full accord with the Pentagon's own Enemy Order of Battle. But Sihanouk continued to protest the American bombings, and in January 1970, the United States paid Cambodia compensation for losses resulting from border clashes.

The tense situation in Cambodia notwithstanding, Prince Sihanouk left the country on January 6, 1970, for his annual water cure at Grasse, in the south of France. The timing could not have been worse. He was a mercurial and unpredictable chief of state, and his ill-timed vacation not only sealed his political doom, but served to alter radically the state of affairs in Phnom Penh. Leaving Premier Lon Nol and Deputy Premier Sirik Matak in charge during his absence, Sihanouk—whether he realized it or not—was opening the way for a coup designed to eliminate him. But the prince was loftily self-assured as he left for Europe. He told Lon Nol and Sirik Matak that after his French holiday he would go to Moscow and Peking and try to persuade leaders there to use their influence to prevent the use of Cambodian territory by Communist forces. This was a measure of Sihanouk's naïveté; he compounded it by lingering in France for two months before getting to Moscow on March 13. On March 12, in Paris, he refused to receive emissaries appointed by Lon Nol and Sirik Matak to seek his approval for an ultimatum to North Vietnam and the Viet Cong to leave Cambodia within seventy-two hours. The die was cast.

Actually, Sihanouk and Lon Nol had shared a deep concern about the Khmer Rouge. A report by Lon Nol in November described a "clear organization effort" on the part of the rebels, some of whose cadres had been trained in North Vietnam. He thought the Khmer Rouge headquarters were somewhere on the Cambodian–South Vietnamese border, probably northwest of the Vietnamese province of Tay Ninh. And Lon Nol predicted that the rebels "will seek to expand progressively their influence toward the west, the south and the north." The Cambodian government, assuming that the Khmer Rouge, with forces estimated at several thousand, were being supported by Hanoi and the Viet Cong, pressed the Vietnamese Communists to evacuate the country.

But it was not overly concerned about the North Vietnamese and Viet Cong presences. Sihanouk had worked out a quiet accommodation with the Communists, looking the other way while Hanoi's truck convoys moved from Sihanoukville, on the Gulf of Siam, toward staging areas on the South Vietnamese border and in the Mekong Delta. In the judgment of American commanders, the Sihanoukville supply route was becoming as dangerous as the old Ho Chi Minh Trail. Sihanouk's toleration of it (it was even alleged by American intelligence that the prince profited financially from the truck traffic) made him resented, and his parallel accommodation with the United States, including his tolerance of the secret B-52 bombings, seemed to count for less and less.

On March 12, despite Sihanouk's obduracy in Paris, Premier Lon Nol formally requested Hanoi and the National Liberation Front to remove their troops from Cambodia within seventy-two hours. It is not known whether he had been encouraged by the Americans to take this step, but clearly he could not have expected the Communists to oblige. As Sihanouk reached Moscow on March 13, Lon Nol and Cambodian Army commanders in Phnom Penh let loose crowds of young people to sack the North Vietnamese and NLF embassies in protest against Communist infiltration. The next day an inconclusive meeting was held between Cambodian and North Vietnamese and NLF representatives; the government set in motion further anti-Communist demonstrations in the capital. On March 15, South Vietnamese forces made one of their deepest incursions into Cambodia, apparently so as to put added pressure on the Communists. Lon Nol's deadline for the departure of Communist troops passed on March 16 with no visible reaction from Hanoi and the NLF.

On March 18, Lon Nol, supported by the army, staged a *coup d'état,* and Prince Sihanouk was removed from power. The premier reaffirmed Cambodia's neutrality, but pledged to expel the Communist troops from their eastern sanctuaries—a goal he could not possibly accomplish without outside assistance.

Sihanouk was apprised of the coup—and his political demise—by Soviet Premier Kosygin as he drove to the Moscow airport in a Kremlin limousine to board a plane for Peking. His talks with the Russians had been inconclusive; now that he had been overthrown *in absentia,* his influence in Moscow had vanished altogether. Kosygin—who had gotten the news in a message sent to the limousine by radio-telephone—was perceptibly cool as he told him of the events in Phnom Penh.

Sihanouk charged later that Lon Nol's coup was engineered by the CIA and the Khmer Serei. There is no hard evidence to support this claim, but there is no question that the Nixon administration welcomed the prince's fall. And there are indications that, if nothing else, Washington had reason to *anticipate* the anti-Sihanouk coup. Some intelligence sources allege that senior CIA officials met with Lon Nol in his room at the American Hospital in Paris, where he was convalescing from an illness in late 1969. And Forrest Lindley, a former U.S. Army Special Forces captain, told me that his unit was informed in mid-February 1970 that Sihanouk would be ousted. Lindley, who commanded the 8231st Special Forces Team at Tieu Atar in South Vietnam, some four miles from the Cambodian border, said that he received a radio message from Special Forces headquarters ordering him to dispatch two companies of his Viet-

namese *montagnard* irregulars (Green Beret teams in the Central Highlands were in charge of these guerrillas) to the nearby Bu Prang camp;
Sihanouk would be overthrown soon and the *montagnards* were needed to
replace Khmer Serei units that would be moving into Cambodia. (The
Khmer Serei were also under Special Forces control.) As Lindley understood the message, the Khmer Serei under Special Forces B-Team at Bu
Prang would be needed in Cambodia, where, according to radio messages, there would be a change in government favorable to the United
States.

Still when Kissinger received the first *press* reports of Sihanouk's
ouster—and subsequent telegrams from Chargé d'Affaires Rives—he appeared to be genuinely surprised, if not indeed at a loss as to what the
United States should do in the new situation. However, two immediate
actions were taken by the administration: the State Department advised
Cambodia that the change in government did not affect recognition by
the United States, and Defense Secretary Laird requested the Pentagon
and General Abrams to start urgent planning on "the various courses of
action that could be taken by our government." Abrams was specifically
asked to prepare plans for dealing with the Communist sanctuaries in
Cambodia. And one of Lon Nol's first moves was to close Sihanoukville
(quickly renamed Kompong Som) to Communist sea traffic.

Washington may have been eager to embrace Lon Nol and reject
Sihanouk, but military considerations enjoyed top priority. The departure of the mercurial and unreliable prince opened new perspectives in
Indochina. Yet politically the United States may have been less than
prudent. Unstable as Sihanouk was, he was now out of reach—and would
quickly align himself with Peking. (The Russians, incidentally, made a
similar miscalculation. They, too, chose to put all their eggs in the Lon
Nol basket, presumably on the theory that the prince was finished once
and for all.)

The Chinese received Sihanouk with open arms when he arrived from
Moscow. They treated him as an honored royal guest (the ideological
contradiction between the Chinese Communist system and Sihanouk's
royal lineage was no problem for Peking's pragmatists). It was an astute
Chinese move in the Indochinese chess game.

At a news conference on March 21, three days after the Phnom Penh
coup, Nixon told newsmen,

> These developments . . . are quite difficult to appraise. . . . The
> Cambodian political situation, to put it conservatively, is quite unpre-

dictable and quite fluid. . . . We have . . . established relations on a temporary basis with the government which has been selected by the Parliament and will continue to deal with that government as long as it appears to be the government of the nation. I think any speculation with regard to which way this government is going to turn, what will happen to Prince Sihanouk when he returns, would both be premature and not helpful. . . . We respect Cambodia's neutrality. We would hope that North Vietnam would take that same position in respecting its neutrality. And we hope that whatever government eventually prevails there, that it would recognize that the United States' interest is the protection of its neutrality.

Two days later, on March 23, Secretary of State Rogers said at a news conference that Cambodia's new regime "has not made any request for military assistance" and "we don't anticipate that any request will be made." He was either misreading the situation or misleading his audience: Lon Nol had already informally indicated to the American embassy at Phnom Penh that he was hoping for some form of military assistance. A little further on, Rogers conceded that Cambodia's neutrality and a possible request for American arms would not necessarily be incompatible, and if Lon Nol *were* to request military aid, "we will have to consider it on its merits."

The Cambodian coup came as the administration was preparing new diplomatic and military moves in Vietnam—Nixon had been planning for some time to announce new withdrawals from South Vietnam—and now he had to deal with a rapidly changing overall situation. National Security Council meetings on March 24 and 25 reviewed plans for withdrawing additional troops from Vietnam and the question was discussed of how best Cambodia could be assisted, and how best the United States could benefit from the new turn of events.

From the moment Sihanouk was overthrown, the administration's greatest concern was that Lon Nol would be unable to retain power and that the prince might return to Phnom Penh. Nixon himself had made this point when he cautioned against speculation on what would happen to Sihanouk "when he returns." Washington was so uncertain about Lon Nol's prospects that it virtually assumed either that he would be overthrown in another coup or that the North Vietnamese would mount an offensive to smash him. The fear was that if Sihanouk resumed his post, Cambodia would automatically become enemy territory, outflanking Vietnam from the west. Slowly it dawned on the Americans that Sihanouk's removal was a mixed blessing: the eastern provinces of Cambodia had been contested territory, but North Vietnam had made no attempt to take over the whole country; now it might do so.

The decision to send American troops into Cambodia evolved over a period of many weeks; it was finally taken only at the last moment. Laird's initial instructions to General Abrams in Saigon to prepare contingency plans for Cambodia suggested direct American involvement only as the last option. The notion of engaging American troops was not yet seriously entertained because the North Vietnamese were still concentrated in the border sanctuaries, and an attack on them would result in very high casualties.

Late in March, it was decided to persuade President Thieu to send South Vietnamese units on missions into Cambodia that would divert the Communists in the border area away from Lon Nol's army. These first thrusts, supported by U.S. helicopters, were about a mile or so deep, and they had the desired result of forcing counterattacks by the North Vietnamese. The Communists also hurriedly moved their units from the Memut area in Cambodia's Kompong Cham Province (an area known to Americans as the Fishhook) to the denser jungles of Tay Ninh Province in South Vietnam, where they felt better protected. The sanctuary area always straddled the official border line.

If anything, then, the American-orchestrated effort kept the Communists in the sanctuaries rather than chased them out. But the White House was dishonest about this even with the State Department. Thus, on April 2, Secretary Rogers found himself in the position of telling in good faith an executive session of the Senate Foreign Relations Committee that the United States was trying to discourage the South Vietnamese from the cross-border operations—although it was hard to understand how the South Vietnamese, so totally dependent on American military support, might have launched unwanted strikes into Cambodia strictly on their own. In any event, three days after Rogers's testimony, on April 5, two South Vietnamese Army battalions pushed their way ten miles inside Cambodia.

On April 8, Nixon presided over another National Security Council meeting to discuss both Vietnam and Cambodia. Laird presented Nixon and other NSC members with the Pentagon's contingency plans for action in Cambodia, plans drawn up by General Abrams, and modified by the Joint Chiefs of Staff and Laird himself. At that point, the plan was for a major South Vietnamese incursion into the Parrot's Beak salient in Cambodia, west of Saigon. (The Parrot's Beak comprised Cambodia's Svay Rieng Province, where a large part of the North Vietnamese forces were concentrated.) The idea was for the South Vietnamese to go in with American advisers and American air support.

The North Vietnamese, however, were changing their strategy. In the first place, they did not wish to be sitting targets along the border. In the second place, they were concerned because the Sihanoukville route was now closed to them. Communist units began moving west out of the sanctuaries around April 15, advancing into southern Cambodia. This shift resulted in greater rather than lesser pressure on Lon Nol's ill-organized and underequipped army, nullifying the American concept of keeping the Communists busy defending their sanctuary areas. On April 17, a Cambodian military spokesman announced that the North Vietnamese fully controlled three out of Cambodia's seventeen provinces and were occupying five more. As usual the Pentagon had underestimated Hanoi's tactical and strategic flexibility. The new Communist strategy, however, had additional results: now Laird and the U.S. commanders decided that a full-fledged thrust into Cambodia by South Vietnamese *and American* troops could successfully destroy Communist border bases without the risk of excessive United States casualties. This was a major turning point.

Kissinger's own thoughts on Cambodia at that stage were rather contradictory, or so they appeared in a private conversation with a Washington newsman with whom he had exceptionally close ties. The United States did not wish to have another client state in Southeast Asia, Kissinger remarked, and therefore, it did not want to get deeply involved with Lon Nol in Cambodia. On the other hand, it was a shame that the United States was in such a state (he was presumably referring to the domestic hostility toward the war) that the administration could not provide help to a little country of seven million inhabitants begging for it.

Actually, a decision to assist Cambodia surreptitiously had already been made. On April 17, American Chargé d'Affaires Rives informed the Cambodian government that shipments of captured Soviet- and Chinese-made AK-47 automatic assault rifles would start reaching Phnom Penh aboard South Vietnamese Air Force planes on April 30. No funds were authorized or appropriated to supply American equipment to Cambodia —and unauthorized military aid would violate the law—wherefore the State Department came up with the idea of turning over the AK-47s to the Cambodians. The AK-47s, which are among the best weapons of this type, were stored by U.S. authorities in South Vietnam along with other captured Communist equipment. This stratagem, so long as it could be kept secret, also protected the United States from charges that it was interfering in Cambodian affairs and violating the country's neutrality. That the administration envisaged this operation as a long-range enterprise was seen in the fact that, simultaneously, plans were made to manufacture ammunition for the AK-47s *in the United States.* The secrecy, however, lasted only a few days. On April 22, *The New York Times* broke the story, and paroxysms of fury shook the administration. One immediate result was to cut off senior State Department officials from all policy planning pertaining to Cambodia, since of course the White House suspected the State Department of the leakage.

In the April conversation with his newspaper friend, Kissinger fairly freely discussed the possibility of invading the Cambodian sanctuaries, although he did not make it entirely clear whether he was referring to the use of American combat forces along with the South Vietnamese. He noted that it would be militarily advantageous to do something about the sanctuaries, but, he added, military events in Cambodia are a plus in the short term and unknown in the long run.

Kissinger weighed the advantages of succumbing to the "temptation" of striking at the sanctuaries against the "unknown" factor of Hanoi's responses. He speculated that an attack might discourage the North Vietnamese from negotiating for peace in Vietnam, but he felt sure, even in the absence of clear evidence, that Hanoi had reached the point of considering the desirability of serious negotiations in Paris. (His certainty on this point was evidently based on his last secret session with Le Duc Tho, but he could not, of course, refer to it.) Although Le Duc Tho had left Paris on April 10, he was due to return in a month or so, and Kissinger also knew that Nixon was preparing a new announcement about withdrawing more American troops from Vietnam. Kissinger must have been worrying that an attack on the Cambodian sanctuaries could delay indefinitely the resumption of his secret negotiations. It was obviously quite a dilemma. He kept coming back, at length, to his "personal" view that before the end of 1970, there would be serious talks with Hanoi. Possibly to rationalize the situation to himself, he commented that the North Vietnamese might find it easier to negotiate in the larger context of Indochina and not just about Vietnam.

Kissinger must have been thinking that an extension of the war to Cambodia might require the convening of an Indochina-wide peace conference. Yakov Malik, the Soviet ambassador to the United Nations, had in fact suggested on April 16 that in Moscow's view "only a new Geneva conference could bring a new solution and relax tensions" in Southeast Asia. Kissinger believed that Malik had spoken on specific instructions from Moscow (where Le Duc Tho was visiting en route home from Paris). Two days later, however, Malik seemed to change his mind, declaring that he had been misunderstood and that a new Geneva conference would be "unrealistic." This did away with Kissinger's vision of a grandiose diplomatic exercise on Indochina.

Still, Kissinger was clearly tempted by the plan to move against the Cambodian sanctuaries. He remarked that if Cambodia and Laos were to fall to the Communists, the American effort in South Vietnam would come to appear illogical. The loss of Cambodia, he seemed to reason, would be a worse blow to the U.S. position in Indochina than a break in the negotiations with Hanoi. The latter could always be resumed, particularly if the Americans held a military advantage.

On April 18, Nixon flew to Honolulu to present the Medal of Freedom to the three Apollo 13 astronauts—James A. Lovell, Jr., Fred W. Haise, Jr., and John L. Swigert, Jr.—who had just returned from an aborted moon mission. The next morning, he breakfasted with Admiral John D. McCain, Jr., commander in chief, U.S. forces in the Pacific, and General Abrams to be briefed on the situation in Cambodia. Admiral McCain presented Nixon with the most up-to-date plan for Cambodian operations, including a strongly favored option for using American combat troops in the Fishhook. Nixon asked a number of questions, made notes, but gave no indication whether he would approve the Fishhook operation. The steady outflow of Communist troops from the sanctuaries threatened only limited American casualties in the Fishhook. And such an operation, McCain and Abrams argued, would achieve the twin objectives of destroying Communist arms and food caches in the sanctuaries and drawing North Vietnamese forces away from the actions farther inside Cambodia.

Nixon told McCain and Abrams that he had virtually decided to announce on his return to the United States the next day that the United States would withdraw an additional 150,000 men from Vietnam by the spring of 1971. This was essentially a political decision reached by Nixon and Laird on the basis of the domestic situation, but the effect on the peace negotiations in Paris was also taken into account. The new withdrawal had been strongly opposed by the Joint Chiefs of Staff, including Admiral Thomas Moorer, the acting chairman, and by Abrams. They had refused to support or recommend it, letting Nixon and Laird proceed on their own responsibility. In mid-March, when Abrams was first apprised of the plans to announce a single 150,000-man withdrawal schedule, he had bluntly told Laird that "unrealizable goals" were being set by the White House. Then he fought for a two-month delay in the announcement, counting from April 15, to avoid what he feared would be an adverse impact on the Vietnamization program at a particularly crucial moment.

Professionally, General Abrams was more honest in his assessments of the progress—or lack of it—in Vietnam than Nixon and Laird, who thought largely in political terms. He was particularly worried about the situation in the north, the I Corps and II Corps areas, where the South Vietnamese were facing the greatest organized threat: eight regiments of North Vietnamese regular troops and three more divisions just across the demilitarized zone. There was a deterioration, Abrams argued, and consequently, Vietnamization was not progressing satisfactorily. He was worried about new Communist infiltrations from the north coming during the wet season in August and September. Likewise, Abrams was conservative in his appraisal of the pacification program, which the White House kept insisting was progressing well. Abrams did not see it that way, and thought the whole enterprise was extremely "fragile" and subject to whims of the situation. There were new problems in II, III, and IV Corps areas, and Abrams pointed out that preliminary figures for April showed a slight reduction in the extent of the territory considered "safe" for the Saigon government.

Nixon left Hawaii slightly uncertain whether he would make his announcement as planned. He discussed the subject with Kissinger and others when he arrived at his house in San Clemente, California, and, according to Laird, he made the final decision only a few hours before he went on nationwide television on the evening of April 20 to deliver an address on "Progress toward Peace in Vietnam." It is difficult to understand how Nixon reconciled the withdrawal decision with the parallel plans to invade Cambodia. Perhaps he wanted to soften the political blow of the approaching Cambodian attack by showing the nation that, true to his word, he was reducing the American presence in Vietnam. But this is doubtful because Nixon had not yet decided to send U.S. forces into Cambodia. Another possibility is that the troop reduction was largely intended to impress Hanoi, which Kissinger optimistically hoped was moving toward "serious" negotiations. Like Kissinger, Nixon may have reasoned that the Cambodian operation would only delay, not kill altogether, such negotiations. Finally, it is possible that the attack on Cambodia and the withdrawals from Vietnam were wholly separate undertakings in Nixon's mind, one tactical and one strategic.

In any case, the situation in Cambodia was deteriorating as Nixon prepared to address the nation. That same day, he received a formal note from Lon Nol requesting military equipment and the services of American-controlled Khmer Serei mercenary troops in South Vietnam to bolster his position. Simultaneously, military reports showed that North Vietnamese forces had attacked the Cambodian towns of Snoul and Takeo in an apparent attempt to cut the convoy route from South Vietnam to Phnom Penh. The American military regarded these thrusts as "worrisome."

Nixon opened his speech with the reminder that he had always said the rate of American withdrawals from Vietnam would depend on the progress of Vietnamization, progress in the Paris negotiations, and the level of enemy activity. Then he proceeded to make a series of astonishing claims. Nixon declared that the first progress "has substantially exceeded our original expectations last June," and added, just as inaccurately, that "very significant advances have also been made in pacification." As for the Paris negotiations, he had to report

> with regret that no progress has taken place. . . . The enemy still demands that we unilaterally and unconditionally withdraw all American forces, that in the process we overthrow the elected Government of South Vietnam, and that the United States accept a political settlement that would have the practical consequences of the forcible imposition of a Communist government upon the people of South Vietnam. . . . That would mean humiliation and defeat for the United States. This we cannot and will not accept.

And on the matter of the level of enemy activity, Nixon sounded almost contradictory. First, he said, "that level has substantially increased" in several areas since December. Hanoi had "sent thousands more of their soldiers to launch new offensives in neutral Laos. . . . Almost 40,000 Communist troops are now conducting overt aggression against Cambodia, a small neutralist country that the Communists have used for years as a base for attack upon South Vietnam. . . . Men and supplies continue to pour down the Ho Chi Minh Trail; and in the past two weeks, the Communists have stepped up their attacks upon allied forces in South Vietnam." But Nixon found that "despite this new enemy activity, there has been an overall decline in enemy force levels in South Vietnam since December," and, consequently, "in the first three months of 1970, the number of Americans killed in action dropped to the lowest first-quarter level in five years." (This, of course, may have resulted largely from the fact, emphasized by Nixon himself, that as of April 15, a total of 115,500 men had returned from Vietnam.)

The point seemed to be that Nixon was determined to go ahead with the new withdrawal schedule even though none of the conditions he enunciated in 1969 had been met. His rationale (not shared by Abrams) was that by expanding the air war, if necessary, the United States could accomplish the same objectives in Vietnam with fewer troops. In any event, Nixon was seeking to justify a political decision without acknowledging publicly that this was what he was doing:

> We have now reached a point where we can confidently move from a period of "cut and try" to a longer-range program for the replacement of American by South Vietnamese troops. I am, therefore, tonight announcing plans for the withdrawal of an additional 150,000 American troops to be completed during the spring of next year. This will bring a total reduction of 265,500 men in our armed forces in Vietnam below the level that existed when we took office fifteen months ago.
>
> The timing and pace of these new withdrawals within the overall schedule will be determined by our best judgment of the current military and political situation. This far-reaching decision was made after consultation with our commanders in the field, and it has the approval of the Government of South Vietnam.

Nixon acknowledged that "this decision clearly involves risks" in view of the "enemy escalation" in Laos and Cambodia and the stepped-up attacks in South Vietnam:

> But I again remind the leaders of North Vietnam that while we are taking these risks for peace, they will be taking grave risks should they attempt to use the occasion to jeopardize the security of our remaining forces in Vietnam by increased military action in Vietnam, in Cambodia, or in Laos. . . . If I conclude that increased enemy action jeopardizes our remaining forces in Vietnam, I shall not hesitate to take strong and effective measures to deal with that situation.

Nixon referred to the Soviet hint about a possible new Geneva conference on Indochina (ignoring the fact that two days earlier Malik had backpedaled on his suggestion), and again proclaimed the American insistence on mutual withdrawals from Vietnam. He recapitulated the steps taken by the United States in the direction of peace, including the one whereby "the United States, over a year and a half ago, stopped all bombing of North Vietnam"—a somewhat inexact claim inasmuch as

American aircraft had been making "protective reaction strikes" for some time—and not always with justification. That new large-scale bombings of the North were already being planned was also not mentioned. What Nixon did say was that "it is Hanoi and Hanoi alone that stands today blocking the path to a just peace for all the peoples of Southeast Asia."

Next came this explanation:

> The decision I have announced tonight means that we finally have in sight the just peace we are seeking. We can now say with confidence that pacification is succeeding. We can now say with confidence that the South Vietnamese can develop the capability for their own defense. And we can say with confidence that all American combat forces can and will be withdrawn.
>
> The enemy has failed to win the war in Vietnam because of three basic errors in their strategy. They thought they could win a military victory. They have failed to do so. They thought they could win politically in South Vietnam. They have failed to do so. They thought they could win politically in the United States. This proved to be their most fatal miscalculation. In this great free country of ours, we debate —we disagree, sometimes violently, but the mistake the totalitarians make over and over again is to conclude that debate in a free country is proof of weakness. We are not a weak people. We are a strong people. America has never been defeated in the proud 190-year history of this country, and we shall not be defeated in Vietnam.

This strange, perhaps unnecessary, speech was delivered at a moment when the situation in Indochina was exceedingly fluid and dangerous, at a time when Nixon was contemplating a series of new and dramatic measures that would expand rather than limit the war. There was no visible purpose in making it—except to give Nixon the opportunity to announce the decision on troop withdrawals. Within ten days, he would be making an entirely different speech.

Why exactly Nixon resolved to commit United States troops to the Cambodian situation is a question that has never been satisfactorily answered. Since purely military rationale was certainly unconvincing, one may venture the guess that Nixon was motivated by domestic political reasons as much as by battlefield requirements in Indochina. This view is held by several former NSC officials who were intimately involved in the secret planning for the Cambodian assault. And given the special complexities of Nixon's character, it is not implausible that he may have created a foreign crisis to cope with politics at home.

The key event in this context may have been the Senate's rejection

April 8 of Nixon's nomination of G. Harrold Carswell, a Southern judge, to the Supreme Court, following an earlier rejection of another Southerner, Clement F. Haynsworth. On April 9, Nixon reacted angrily: "Judge Carswell, and before him, Judge Haynsworth, have been submitted to vicious assaults on their intelligence, on their honesty, and on their character. They have been falsely charged with being racists. But when you strip away all the hypocrisy, the real reason for their rejection was their legal philosophy, a philosophy that I share, of strict construction of the Constitution, and also the accident of their birth, the fact that they were born in the South." Privately, Nixon was even more abusive. He would show the Senate, he said, "who's really tough."

There is no evidence directly connecting the Carswell episode with the Cambodian invasion, but in the opinion of those who worked closely with Nixon, this interpretation cannot be ruled out. His administration was already facing its first major economic troubles—inflation was on the upswing—and there was more and more talk around Washington about Nixon being a "one-term president." Then came the anti-Carswell vote in the Senate. If he was to "show" the Senate his real mettle, Cambodia seemed to offer an extraordinary opportunity to do so.

In any event, it appears that Nixon began seriously considering the use of American troops in Cambodia around April 21, the day after his speech in San Clemente announcing new withdrawals from Vietnam. No more than a dozen senior officials were aware of the overall plan. In Washington, besides Nixon, only Kissinger, Laird, Rogers, the acting chairman of the Joint Chiefs of Staff, Admiral Moorer, CIA Director Helms, and Attorney General Mitchell were fully informed of the situation. Colonel Haig and a few key members of the NSC staff had access to a certain amount of the information. Even General William Westmoreland, army chief of staff, was cut out of the consultative process. J-3, the planning staff of the Joint Chiefs, was brought into the picture only in the final few days; J-5, the long-range planning staff, was kept in the dark until the end. At the State Department, Rogers was under instructions to keep Cambodian plans entirely to himself. Under Secretary of State Richardson was traveling in the Middle East and was caught by surprise. Marshall Green, the man in charge of Far Eastern Affairs in the State Department, was deliberately eliminated from the meetings of WASAG (Washington Special Action Group) after April 20. In the Pacific, only General Abrams and Admiral McCain plus a few of their closest aides had the full picture.

Nixon and Thieu were already in agreement that South Vietnamese troops would go into the Parrot's Beak. Then, included in the CIA's daily intelligence summary for Nixon on April 21 was a CIA radio intercept of a message from the North Vietnamese command to its units to the effect that "we don't have to worry about the Americans" in terms of being attacked in the sanctuaries. In preceding days, the intelligence reports from the CIA had been gloomy about Cambodia's internal situation, and the general impression was that the Communists were moving out of the sanctuaries in the general direction of Phnom Penh, cutting the Cambodian road network, and standing an excellent chance of taking over the whole country. As an intelligence officer recalled it, the CIA's view added up to the conclusion that "if the president doesn't act, a domino is going to fall."

Evidently, this was what Nixon wanted to hear. A move into Cambodia would accomplish the twin objectives of saving Lon Nol and destroying Communist caches in the sanctuary with very limited casualties for American forces. This was immensely tempting to Nixon, who appeared to feel, among other pressures, that the Communists were challenging him. Besides, Nixon and Kissinger convinced themselves that COSVN, the Communist headquarters for South Vietnam, had moved to the Fishhook. This, then, was an opportunity to destroy the Communist command structure. If this were to be done, American troops had to be used because that section of the border was the responsibility of the First Air Cavalry Division and the 25th Infantry Division. It made no sense to divert South Vietnamese units from the north or the Mekong Delta; other South Vietnamese troops, including some of the best elements, were already committed to the Parrot's Beak strike.

The fact that no serious military planning had been done for the Fishhook did not seem to disturb the White House. The plans prepared by General Abrams on Laird's request in late March and then in early May principally concerned a South Vietnamese incursion into the Parrot's Beak; the option for the use of American troops in the Fishhook was at the end of Abrams's list. The modifications introduced by McCain's staff in Honolulu and Moorer in Washington made little difference. Westmoreland thought the actual planning for the Fishhook operation was "very hastily thrown together, with very little warning." Even these plans were not really meant for action but, rather, to give the White House an appreciation of what was militarily possible.

Also on April 21, Le Duan, first secretary of the North Vietnamese Communist Party, said in a speech in Moscow that Hanoi was considering a "united front" against the United States in Indochina. This, he said, was essential because the Americans were preparing to widen the war in

Vietnam, Cambodia, and Laos. Le Duan's speech was duly noted in Washington, and it added to the sense of crisis. Acting on earlier instructions, Cambodian mercenary units from South Vietnam under the control of the U.S. Army's Special Forces moved on the same day into Cambodia's Svay Rieng Province—in the Parrot's Beak area—to relieve the pressures on Lon Nol. The first shipments of captured AK-47 rifles were about to be flown in great secrecy to Phnom Penh. The machinery for intervening in Cambodia was in motion.

On April 22, Nixon presided over a lengthy National Security Council meeting. He made the point that the North Vietnamese, instead of taking a conciliatory posture after his announcement of new American withdrawals, were stepping up their attacks in Cambodia (as if in only two days the North Vietnamese could have shown any tangible sign on the battlefield). Nixon was also disturbed by Le Duan's speech the previous day; he considered it a reply to his April 20 address on Vietnam. The NSC discussed the possibility of American involvement in Cambodia, but Nixon did not press for a decision. Laird and Moorer made their strategic presentation. As Kissinger told the story later, the real purpose of the meeting was to assign WASAG the responsibility for formulating hard plans for possible United States action in Cambodia. This was a very convenient way of managing the final preparations.

WASAG held two intensive sessions on Thursday, April 23, one in the morning and one in the evening. At the second meeting, it made the final decision to engage American forces in Cambodia. (Nixon almost never participated in WASAG meetings, but Kissinger kept him posted, and the assumption is that WASAG made its "recommendation" to the president with Kissinger's full assent.) Immediately—it was already April 24 in Saigon—the White House sent orders to General Abrams through a secret back channel (bypassing the Joint Chiefs of Staff) to prepare operational plans for an attack in the Fishhook. Abrams instructed Major General Elvy B. Roberts, commander of the First Air Cavalry Division, to start planning the operation. Within seventy-two hours, Roberts submitted his plan to the operational command of III Corps in Long Binh. It went up to Abrams and on to Moorer and the White House. In a real sense, then, the actual planning for the invasion was completed in less than three days.

In Washington, meanwhile, a complex charade was being played by other civilian and military figures for the benefit of public opinion. On April 23, as WASAG was reaching its decision to strike in Cambodia, Secretary Rogers testified in executive session before the House Appropriations Subcommittee that the administration had "no incentive to escalate" the Indochina war. "We recognize that if we escalate and get involved in Cambodia with our ground troops that our whole program is defeated," he said. It is quite likely, of course, that Rogers did not know at that point that the decision to escalate had already virtually been taken but he knew of the plans. In any event, he assured the congressmen that the administration would consult with Congress if it ever planned a "sizeable use" of American troops in Cambodia.

Almost simultaneously, General Westmoreland, the army chief of staff, was having lunch with a group of Washington news correspondents, arguing the merits of some U.S. military action to prevent the Communists from reopening the Sihanoukville supply route. Their ears perking up, several reporters concluded that Westmoreland was hinting at an invasion of Cambodia. At least one telephoned Kissinger to relate Westmoreland's remarks and to ask him point-blank if an invasion was being planned. Kissinger flatly denied it. Another senior NSC staff official told a reporter that Westmoreland should not be taken too seriously because of his inclination to "push the panic button"—as he had done in Vietnam in 1968 during the Tet offensive. Some time later, Westmoreland confessed to friends that he had not had the slightest inkling of the Cambodian decision on April 23: "Sometimes things moved so rapidly that we [the chiefs] were debriefed *after* things happened."

Still on the same day, the Chinese sponsored an Indochina "unity" meeting at an undisclosed site in southern China, probably Kunming. Premier Chou En-lai was present along with North Vietnamese Premier Pham Van Dong, Prince Sihanouk, NLF President Nguyen Huu Tho, and the Pathet Lao's leader, Prince Souphanouvong. They agreed that the Indochinese states should conduct an "unremitting" war against the United States. News of this meeting strengthened the resolve in Washington to act decisively in Cambodia.

On Friday, April 24, WASAG met again. This time, in a rare departure from his custom, Nixon was present, and others, too, made its composition unusual. Under Secretary of State U. Alexis Johnson and the Pentagon's David Packard were not invited, but Helms was told to bring his deputy, Lieutenant General Robert Cushman. Admiral Moorer was present in his capacity of military adviser to the president, rather than as acting chairman of the Joint Chiefs. The meeting had been convened on Nixon's telephoned request to Kissinger. Shortly after midnight, the president had called to explain that he wanted to go over military plans with Kissinger, Moorer, and the two CIA men; the session had to be at 7:15 a.m. Kissinger found William Watts, one of his aides, at the Jockey

Club, an elegant Washington restaurant, and instructed him to assemble all the relevant documents in time for the early-morning meeting. "Our peerless leader," Kissinger told Watts, "has flipped out."

In the course of the morning meeting, Nixon recalled that he had been the White House coordinator for the preparation of the Bay of Pigs invasion of Cuba, which Eisenhower left for Kennedy to carry out. "Ike lost Cuba," the president remarked, "but I won't lose Cambodia." Still, he shied away from a final decision, and held a separate conference with Kissinger later in the day, instructing him to inform Laird that American forces *might* be used in Cambodia.

At this point, the White House resolved that it was time to prepare American public opinion for what was coming. Press Secretary Ronald Ziegler told White House correspondents that the North Vietnamese and Viet Cong offensive in Cambodia was "a foreign invasion of a neutral country which cannot be considered in any way a pretense of a civil war."

The orchestration had begun. Nixon had originally planned to hold a full-fledged NSC meeting that afternoon, but he canceled it and went to Camp David for the weekend, scheduling an NSC meeting for Sunday. Kissinger, staying behind, summoned a small group of aides to his office to inform them that plans had been made to invade Cambodia. A rather heated discussion ensued. When one of the staffers raised the question whether a strike into the sanctuaries would not encourage the Communists to move on Phnom Penh, Kissinger dismissed this as "a sophomoric argument." He insisted that one of the crucial objectives of the operation was the capture of COSVN. A staffer took it upon himself to call the CIA and ask if the precise location of COSVN could be triangulated. The CIA replied in the negative. When this was reported, Kissinger seemed highly annoyed and changed the subject. Colonel Haig, who had already received the resignations of Anthony Lake and Roger Morris (but had refused to tell Kissinger about them), remarked that the opposition to the invasion seemed to reflect the views of the "Eastern establishment." (He and Kissinger had earlier dismissed Laurence Lynn's criticism that the invasion plans were inadequate.) Kissinger now asked William Watts to the NSC meeting planned for Sunday, but Watts refused on the grounds that he opposed the whole enterprise. (Watts soon left the staff, along with Lake and Morris.)

On Saturday, Nixon asked Kissinger to come by helicopter to Camp David. Later he cabled General Abrams requesting "the unvarnished truth" about the situation, adding that he would be "importantly guided" by the general's comments. A separate cable gave Abrams tentative approval for a South Vietnamese attack in the Parrot's Beak with American air support. Kissinger said later, however, that no permission was given at that point for American advisers to go in with the South Vietnamese. Nixon was still hedging his bets.

That same Saturday evening, Nixon, Kissinger, and Charles ("Bebe") Rebozo, the president's closest friend, left Camp David and flew by helicopter to the Washington Navy Yard, where they boarded the presidential yacht, *Sequoia,* for a long cruise on the Potomac. They dined aboard. Then Nixon had Kissinger and Rebozo join him in watching the movie *Patton.* This was Nixon's favorite film—he had already seen it four or five times at the White House—and he seemed to draw inspiration for drastic decisions from its portrayal of the "blood-and-guts" tank general. Patton as a legend and the actor John Wayne in real life were Nixon's great heroes. They symbolized the courage that he so admired.

At 4:30 p.m. Sunday, April 26, Nixon chaired a three-hour meeting of the National Security Council at his office in the Executive Office Building. He told the council that the United States had no choice but to go ahead with the Parrot's Beak and the Fishhook. Rogers registered mild dissent on domestic political as well as diplomatic grounds. Laird also raised the political issue, but he still believed the risk was worth taking because the North Vietnamese had moved out of the sanctuaries and posed only a limited risk to American forces.

Later Nixon went back to his hideout in the Executive Office Building to collect his thoughts. On a yellow pad, he made these jottings: "Time running out . . . Military aid—only symbolic." Failure to act might tempt the Communists to attack Phnom Penh; no action might lead to an "ambiguous situation," with the Cambodian government coming under Communist control or influence. Nixon jotted down the "pluses" and "minuses" of the operation. The pluses of the Fishhook were that the United States could withdraw more rapidly from Vietnam, divert the Communists from attacks on Phnom Penh, and possibly lead Hanoi to negotiate more seriously in Paris. The minuses were that the Communists might respond with an attack on Phnom Penh, there might be "deep divisions" in the United States, the Communists might break off the peace talks, and they might attack across the demilitarized zone. As to action by South Vietnamese troops only, Nixon wrote on his pad that this would be a minus in the sense of slowing down Vietnamization. The pluses would be that much less division would occur in the United States, and that all the minuses of an American operation in the Fishhook would be eliminated.

The White House deliberately made Nixon's jottings available to selected friends in the news media to show how the president considered all the options and wrestled with his conscience. The White House official who produced the Nixon doodlings said that when the president was warned by an aide that the academic community would be up in arms over an American involvement, he had replied, "Believe me, I've considered that danger," pointing to the phrase "deep divisions" on his yellow pad.

On Monday, Nixon met with Kissinger, Rogers, and Laird. Ziegler told the White House press corps that "we have an overriding interest" in Cambodia in the sense of "how a possible Communist take-over of Cambodia would affect the security of our forces in Vietnam and the Vietnamization program." In Vietnam, the First Air Cavalry command submitted its operational plans to III Corps and Abrams. In the afternoon, Rogers testified before the Senate Foreign Relations Committee on Lon Nol's request, received a few days earlier, for $200 million in military aid. On the one hand, he told the senators, "as of the moment," North Vietnamese/Viet Cong operations in Cambodia had not changed much from what they were before Sihanouk's fall (which, of course, contradicted Ziegler's statements at the White House). But, Rogers argued, Communist control of Cambodia would interfere with the success of the Vietnamization program and the withdrawal of American troops from Vietnam. Then he threw out a hint: "The president has the problem. Do you continue fighting the war in a way that doesn't make sense, or do you change it?"

In the evening of April 27, Nixon returned to the Executive Office Building with his yellow pad. He telephoned his wife at the White House, telling her not to wait dinner. Around 9:00 p.m., he called Kissinger, Ehrlichman, and Haldeman to inform them of two "final decisions." The first decision was that South Vietnamese troops would be allowed to move into the Parrot's Beak area with American advisers and air support. This operation—code-named "Rock Crusher"—was to take place one day before U.S. forces went into the Fishhook. Instructions were sent to Abrams to proceed with the Parrot's Beak operation on April 29. But Nixon chose to wait an extra day before issuing formal orders for the Fishhook. Kissinger, as aides related, spent the evening of April 27 "bobbing in and out" of the White House, talking to specialists on East Asian affairs, then returning to see Nixon. Appearing buoyant and self-confident, he told an NSC aide that "we intend to make our own mistakes in our own new ways."

The next morning, the president called Rogers and Laird to the Oval

Office to advise them that he had taken the Parrot's Beak and Fishhook decisions. This came as no surprise. At noon, the president dispatched final orders to General Abrams to launch Operation Prometheus, the code name for the Cambodian incursion. The First Air Cavalry—the Aircav—and the 25th Infantry Division were ready to move on April 29, but Nixon wanted the South Vietnamese to attack first in the Parrot's Beak; the Americans were to strike on April 30. WASAG held one more meeting late on April 28 to tie up loose ends.

On the morning of Wednesday, April 29, the world learned from an announcement in Saigon that South Vietnamese units, supported by the United States, had invaded Cambodia in the Parrot's Beak. This was Rock Crusher. But neither Saigon nor Washington offered the slightest hint that morning that a parallel American attack was to start within forty-eight hours in the Fishhook. While the news of the Parrot's Beak operation was being absorbed everywhere, the administration busied itself portraying it as a necessary move to save Lon Nol and destroy the Communist sanctuaries in Cambodia. The decision to support the South Vietnamese in their foray was, according to Kissinger and other high officials, the most difficult and agonizing ever made by Nixon as president— although they failed to say that it was over the Fishhook that he had *really* been agonizing. (Nixon was developing the habit of saying that every major decision he made was the "most agonizing" ever.) The administration also insisted that Lon Nol's fall and Communist rule in Cambodia would be an intolerable threat to American troops in South Vietnam and to the continued successful conduct of the war there.

At the White House, most of Wednesday and Thursday were spent drafting Nixon's speech announcing the Fishhook incursion. (Nixon stayed up until 5:00 a.m. on Thursday working in longhand on his text.) After lunch on Thursday, he invited Kissinger and Haldeman to the Oval Office to read them his speech. Later, Kissinger met once more with WASAG and, separately, with his own NSC staff. This was the first time staff members as a group were told about Fishhook in detail; several of them had known about it in general outline for nearly a week. Then Kissinger met with George Meany, the president of the AFL-CIO, to inform him that Nixon was about to announce the Fishhook attack. In the early evening, he briefed White House correspondents about the contents of the president's speech. There was no effort, however, to advise the congressional leadership that Cambodia was about to be invaded. At 9:00 p.m. on Thursday, April 30, Nixon went before the television cameras in the Oval Office.

The speech opened with a deception. The president recalled that despite his warning ten days earlier that if "increased enemy activity . . . endangered the lives of Americans remaining in Vietnam, [he] would not hesitate to take strong and effective measures . . . North Vietnam has increased its military aggression in all those areas [of Indochina] and particularly in Cambodia."

Nixon knew that all the Communists had done was to keep moving out of the border sanctuaries, a pattern initiated long before, but the public, with no access to actual battlefield information, had no way of knowing this. Nixon's ploy was to create the impression that after he had magnanimously ordered the new American troop withdrawal, the North Vietnamese responded with "aggression," endangering United States forces in South Vietnam. Although the reality was that the Communist movements had, if anything *decreased,* the pressures on Americans in Vietnam, Nixon explained the situation in this fashion:

> After full consultation with the National Security Council, Ambassador Bunker, General Abrams, and my other advisers, I have concluded that the actions of the enemy in the last 10 days clearly endanger the lives of Americans who are in Vietnam now and would constitute an unacceptable risk to those who will be there after withdrawal of another 150,000. To protect our men who are in Vietnam and to guarantee the continued success of our withdrawal and Vietnamization programs, I have concluded that the time has come for action.

(Nixon's claim was soon demolished by, among others, Senate Foreign Relations Committee investigators who visited Vietnam and Cambodia between April 29 and May 15. In a special report titled "Cambodia: May 1970," James Lowenstein and Richard Moose, both highly respected Senate investigators, wrote that

> neither in our briefings in Washington before we left on our trip, nor in the briefings and discussions we had in Vietnam on May 2 and 3, was there mention of an increased enemy threat to U.S. forces in Vietnam from the sanctuaries or of an increase in the size of enemy forces in Cambodia. Indeed, in both Washington and Saigon we were told that the size of the North Vietnamese and Vietcong forces in Cambodia had remained constant over the past six months, although it should be added that the estimate of that constant was higher in Saigon than in Washington—where it was estimated in late April to

be 40,000—and still higher in Phnom Penh—where, in early May,
enemy strength was said to be about 55,000.

Lowenstein and Moose also had a different explanation for the Cambodian operation:

> From our conversations in Saigon, it appeared to us that the United
> States and South Vietnam military regarded Sihanouk's fall as an
> "opportunity" to strike at enemy sanctuaries along the border. . . .
> Many U.S. military officers in Vietnam used this exact word and said
> that had it not been for the sanctuaries the war would have been over
> long ago. One sentence came up time and again in MACV briefings
> and in conversations with U.S. officers, the refrain that "No guerrilla
> war in history has succeeded without sanctuaries."

The investigators added a perspicacious observation of their own:
"No mention was made of the sanctuary still intact north of the DMZ
[demilitarized zone]." Nixon may have been ready to strike in Cambodia, but for obvious reasons, he certainly never considered invading
North Vietnam.)

To bolster his public case, Nixon next plunged into an outright lie.
He told his national audience that since Cambodia had become a neutral
state following the 1954 Geneva conference on Indochina, "American
policy . . . has been to scrupulously respect the neutrality of the Cambodian people. . . . For the past five years, we have provided no military
assistance whatever and no economic assistance to Cambodia." North
Vietnam, on the other hand, Nixon said, "has not respected that neutrality," establishing "military sanctuaries" that "are used for hit-and-run
attacks on American and South Vietnamese forces in South Vietnam."
These sanctuaries astride the Vietnamese-Cambodian border contained
"major base camps, training sites, logistics facilities, weapons and ammunition factories, airstrips, and prisoner-of-war compounds." The Communists, to be sure, had built up ammunition and food caches in the
sanctuaries and, obviously, maintained regional command posts there.
But Nixon grossly exaggerated the sanctuaries' importance: if, indeed,
the Communists had "factories," airstrips, and POW camps in the sanctuaries, *they were never found there by anybody.*

The president engaged in further untruths: "For five years, neither
the United States nor South Vietnam has moved against these enemy
sanctuaries because we did not wish to violate the territory of a neutral nation. Even after the Vietnamese Communists began to expand

these sanctuaries four weeks ago, we counseled patience to our South Vietnamese allies and imposed restraints on our own commanders."

Nixon, who kept pointing to a map of Indochina as he spoke, embarked on yet another major contradiction. First, he said, "the enemy in the past two weeks has stepped up his guerrilla actions and he is concentrating his main forces in these sanctuaries . . . where they are building up to launch massive attacks on our forces and those of South Vietnam." Then, in the same breath, he said that "thousands" of North Vietnamese soldiers were "invading" Cambodia from the sanctuaries, "encircling the capital of Phnom Penh. . . . They have moved into Cambodia and are encircling the capital." The picture that the president was presenting to the nation was that the Communists were launching a two-pronged offensive from the sanctuaries: one into South Vietnam and one into Cambodia. This, however, was inexact—as well as improbable. Although the Communists were moving west out of the sanctuaries, they certainly were not "encircling" Phnom Penh. A map attached to the daily CIA briefing bulletin that day showed that the Communists had blocked Route 7 between Kompong Cham and the capital, the main highway from South Vietnam, but that Cambodian forces controlled a wide area on both sides of the Mekong River. The Communists had succeeded in making only one thrust near the capital by occupying the town of Saang, twenty miles south of Phnom Penh.

This Communist westward movement in April had been the immediate result of Sihanouk's fall, an event that had forced Hanoi to devise a new strategy. Captured Communist documents, in which the Saigon command normally put considerable credence, had called for "no major engagements in 1970." Instead, instructions had provided for the rebuilding of Communist strength for large-scale actions in 1971; during 1970, the emphasis was to be on main-force reorganization in the Cambodian sanctuaries, the creation of new sapper squads, and, in Vietnam, nothing more than harassing actions in the IV Corps area, which covered the Mekong Delta. But the ouster of Sihanouk deprived the North Vietnamese of the south-north corridor above Sihanoukville, so the new strategy was to try to retake Sihanoukville—or take another harbor—and reopen the corridor to the sea.

Nixon chose to describe this in wholly different terms. He and Kissinger evidently planned to move ahead by permanently denying the sea link to the Communists and smashing their sanctuaries. It was essentially an offensive operation from which the White House hoped to extract maximal military profit. Nevertheless, the politics of the war required

Nixon to insist that the United States was engaging in a purely *defensive* operation—to "save" Phnom Penh and protect American forces in South Vietnam.

Having made the claim that Phnom Penh was being encircled by the Communists, the president continued in the same vein:

> Cambodia, as a result of this, has sent out a call to the United States, to a number of other nations, for assistance. Because if this enemy effort succeeds, Cambodia would become a vast enemy staging area and a springboard for attacks on South Vietnam along 600 miles of frontier—a refuge where enemy troops could return from combat without fear of retaliation. North Vietnamese men and supplies could then be poured into that country, jeopardizing not only the lives of our own men but the people of South Vietnam as well.

Nixon thus sought to make it appear that, to an important extent, the United States was responding to Lon Nol's appeals for help. But what Lon Nol had been requesting were arms and money, not an American–South Vietnamese invasion. The record shows that at no time did Washington consult with Lon Nol about a possible invasion either in the Parrot's Beak or in the Fishhook. (This was subsequently explained by administration officials in terms of the need to keep the planning secret —even from the presumed beneficiary of the imminent attacks. President Thieu would later claim in Saigon that he and Lon Nol had reached an "agreement in principle" concerning South Vietnamese entry into Cambodia a few days before the operations were launched. But this is dubious partly because of the continuing ethnic tensions between Cambodians and Vietnamese. During March and April, thousands of ethnic Vietnamese in Cambodia were massacred by Cambodian troops, and not surprisingly, Lon Nol might have been less than anxious to have ARVN operating in his country. Lowenstein and Moose noted in their postinvasion Senate report that in Phnom Penh "there was some evident and understandable uneasiness at the presence of large numbers of South Vietnamese on Cambodian soil, understandable in the light of historic Cambodian fears of Vietnamese aggressiveness.") In fact, Lon Nol was officially informed of it only hours *after* American units began moving into the Fishhook. State Department officials said later that communications difficulties prevented Washington from advising him earlier, but at best, it would have been a matter of hours; there certainly was no question of an actual consultation. American embassy officials in Phnom Penh learned of the Fishhook thrust from listening to Nixon's speech over the Voice of America.

Proof that the whole Cambodian operation was unrelated to any "call
. . . for assistance" from Phnom Penh was contained in a classified document, typed on White House stationery and titled "Points on the Cambodia Military Action," distributed to members of the president's senior
staff at a meeting in the Roosevelt Room shortly before the speech was
delivered. It stated: "It is a strike operation that is an integral part of our
operations in Vietnam. It is not in reply to any of Lon Nol's requests for
aid to Cambodia."

Addressing the nation, Nixon laid out what he called "three options,"
again relating the Cambodian situation to the safety of American troops
in Vietnam, something he regarded as a sure-fire argument. The first
option, he said, would be to do "nothing," but "unless we engage in
wishful thinking, the lives of Americans remaining in Vietnam after our
next withdrawal of 150,000 would be gravely threatened."

Again pointing to the map and the sanctuary area, the president
remarked that "if North Vietnam also occupied this whole band in
Cambodia, or the entire country, it would mean that South Vietnam
was completely outflanked and the forces of Americans in this area, as
well as the South Vietnamese, would be in an untenable military position." This, of course, was a specious military argument, as Nixon
must have known. The Communists had been in the sanctuaries for
years without making the situation in Vietnam any more untenable
than it already was. Neither militarily nor politically had anything
been learned by Washington about the Vietnam war. An expansion of
the conflict into Cambodia conceptually resembled the Westmoreland
"search-and-destroy" operations in pre-Tet days: it was the confused
notion that large-scale ground thrusts by an American *masse de manoeuvre* could break the back of the North Vietnamese armies. Likewise, Nixon was promising the impossible; inasmuch as he was placing
a sixty-day limit on the American presence in Cambodia and restrict-
ing the depth of American penetration to just over twenty miles, the
incursion could not conceivably have achieved the ambitious objectives he was outlining to his television audience. In short, he was attempting to convey the illusion of a victory on the cheap.

The second option before him, Nixon went on, was to provide "massive military assistance to Cambodia itself." But he immediately ruled it
out as impractical: "massive amounts of military assistance could not be
rapidly and effectively utilized by the small Cambodian Army against the
immediate threat. . . . The aid we will provide will be limited to the
purpose of enabling Cambodia to defend its neutrality and not for the
purpose of making it an active belligerent on one side or the other."

Nixon then moved to define the third option, the one he was selecting: "Our third choice is to go to the heart of the trouble. That means cleaning out major North Vietnamese and Vietcong occupied territories—these sanctuaries which serve as bases for attacks on both Cambodia and American and South Vietnamese forces in South Vietnam. Some of these, incidentally, are as close to Saigon as Baltimore is to Washington. . . . The Parrot's Beak [is] only 33 miles from Saigon."

Now Nixon paused, stared into the cameras, and let go with the announcement that indeed the war was being expanded into Cambodia:

> In cooperation with the armed forces of South Vietnam, attacks are being launched this week to clean out major enemy sanctuaries on the Cambodian-Vietnam border.
>
> A major responsibility for the ground operations is being assumed by South Vietnamese forces. For example, the attacks in several areas, including the Parrot's Beak . . . are exclusively South Vietnamese ground operations under South Vietnamese command with the United States providing air and logistical support.

That ARVN units with their American advisers and helicopters had gone into the Parrot's Beak was already known to the world. But the real news was that Americans were invading the Fishhook.

> There is one area, however, immediately above the Parrot's Beak, where I have concluded that a combined American and South Vietnamese operation is necessary. Tonight, American and South Vietnamese units will attack the headquarters for the entire Communist military operation in South Vietnam. This key control center has been occupied by the North Vietnamese and Vietcong for five years in blatant violation of Cambodia's neutrality.

Referring here to the elusive and mythical COSVN, Nixon created the impression that American troops were going to destroy the nerve center of the entire Communist force in Vietnam. And this was still another deception, for Nixon did not have the slightest idea whether COSVN really existed as a fully structured command. However, the president evidently felt that it was crucial to establish a specific target for the invasion, providing an easily understandable reason for the direct American involvement in the Fishhook, and he included the reference to COSVN—"the headquarters"—in his speech against the advice of his intelligence, military, and political experts, who seriously doubted COSVN's very existence.

(This is what the Lowenstein-Moose report for the Senate Foreign Relations Committee in June had to say about COSVN:

> When we were briefed at MACV on May 3, we were told that the combined ARVN and U.S. attack in the "Fishhook," called "Tuan Tang 43" or "Total Victory 43," was directed against "the main COSVN control headquarters for South Vietnam." And a senior U.S. field commander told us that he expected to find and destroy the "playhouse," as he called COSVN headquarters, and that he expected it to consist of an underground network of bunkers. Six days later, after the operations in Cambodia had been underway for nine days, a MACV briefing officer referred several times to the capture of "major enemy logistical complexes" but never mentioned COSVN. Thus, within a week, COSVN had disappeared from the area of the Cambodian border.)

Having proclaimed the invasion's apparent objective, the president hastened to offer assurances: "This is not an invasion of Cambodia. The areas in which these attacks will be launched are completely occupied and controlled by North Vietnamese forces. Our purpose is not to occupy the areas. Once enemy forces are driven out of these sanctuaries and once their military supplies are destroyed, we will withdraw."

The president also had assurances—as well as warnings—for the big Communist powers that he was simultaneously courting: "These actions are in no way directed to the security interests of any nation. Any government that chooses to use these actions as a pretext for harming relations with the United States will be doing so on its own responsibility, and on its own initiative, and we will draw the appropriate conclusions."

This was a neat piece of brinkmanship, but Kissinger had correctly calculated beforehand that neither the Soviet Union nor China would interpret the Cambodian adventure as a direct threat, or sacrifice long-term interests in steady big-power relationships for the sake of Cambodia's immediate fortunes. Nixon and Kissinger may not have understood the North Vietnamese mentality, but they had a sense of how far Moscow and Peking could be pushed with impunity.

For the balance of his speech, Nixon linked the invasion to the success of his program of withdrawing American forces from Vietnam. This was strictly for domestic consumption. Thus, "We take this action not for the purpose of expanding the war into Cambodia but for the purpose of ending the war in Vietnam and winning the just peace we all desire. We have made—we will continue to make every possible effort to end this war through negotiation at the conference table rather than through more fighting on the battlefield." Now it was Nixon, the tough president, addressing his nation as well as the enemy:

> The answer of the enemy has been intransigence at the conference table, belligerence in Hanoi, massive military aggression in Laos and Cambodia, and stepped-up attacks in South Vietnam, designed to increase American casualties. This attitude has become intolerable. We will not react to this threat to American lives merely by plaintive diplomatic protests. If we did, the credibility of the United States would be destroyed in every area of the world where only the power of the United States deters aggression. Tonight, I again warn the North Vietnamese that if they continue to escalate the fighting when the United States is withdrawing its forces, I shall meet my responsibility as Commander in Chief of our Armed Forces to take the action I consider necessary to defend the security of our American men.
>
> The action that I have announced tonight puts the leaders of North Vietnam on notice that we will be patient in working for peace; we will be conciliatory at the conference table, but we will not be humiliated. We will not allow American men by the thousands to be killed by an enemy from privileged sanctuaries. . . . If the enemy response to our most conciliatory offers for peaceful negotiation continues to be to increase its attacks and humiliate and defeat us, we shall react accordingly.

This was pure Nixon, bent on perceiving every foreign challenge to America's supremacy as an effort to humiliate us, the man who equated the United States' credibility in the world with its capability of exercising military power. And this was the speech that produced one of the most famous Nixonian phrases—a phrase that summarized his peculiar view of America's place in the world:

> If, when the chips are down, the world's most powerful nation, the United States of America, acts like a pitiful, helpless giant, the forces of totalitarianism and anarchy will threaten free nations and free institutions throughout the world. It is not our power but our will and character that is being tested tonight. The question all Americans must ask and answer tonight is this: Does the richest and strongest nation in the history of the world have the character to meet a direct challenge by a group which rejects every effort to win a just peace, ignores our warning, tramples on solemn agreements, violates the neutrality of an unarmed people, and uses our prisoners as hostages?

If we fail to meet this challenge, all other nations will be on notice that despite its overwhelming power the United States, when a real crisis comes, will be found wanting.

Could he have really meant that America's greatness hung in balance over the nation's support for the violation of the frontiers of a small and faraway Asian country, a country already grievously damaged over the years by the military might of the United States?

Even more startling was Nixon's reminder that "in this room," the Oval Office from which he spoke, Woodrow Wilson, Franklin D. Roosevelt, Dwight D. Eisenhower, and John F. Kennedy had made the great historical decisions ending great wars in their day or preventing new wars from starting. He explained that in terms of magnitude he was not really comparing the decisions of his predecessors with his decision on Cambodia, for "between those decisions and this decision there is a difference that is very fundamental." In the past, he insisted, "the American people were not assailed by counsels of doubt and defeat from some of the most widely known opinion leaders of the Nation." Nixon the politician was portraying himself as a selfless statesman and patriot, yet the tone was whining:

A Republican Senator has said that this action I have taken means that my party has lost all chance of winning the November elections. And others are saying today that this move against enemy sanctuaries will make me a one-term President. No one is more aware than I am of the political consequences of the action I have taken. It is tempting to take the easy political path: to blame this war on previous administrations and to bring all of our men home immediately, regardless of the consequences, even though that would mean defeat for the United States; to desert 18 million South Vietnamese people, who have put their trust in us and to expose them to the same slaughter and savagery which the leaders of North Vietnam inflicted on hundreds of thousands of North Vietnamese who chose freedom when the Communists took over North Vietnam in 1954; to get peace at any price now, even though I know that a peace of humiliation for the United States would lead to a bigger war or surrender later. I have rejected all political considerations in making this decision. Whether my party gains in November is nothing compared to the lives of 400,000 brave Americans fighting for our country and for the cause of peace and freedom in Vietnam. Whether I may be a one-term President is insignificant compared to whether by our failure to act in this crisis the United States proves itself unworthy to lead the forces of freedom in this critical period in world history. I would rather be a one-term President and do what I believe is right than be a two-term President at the cost of seeing America become a second-rate power and to see this Nation accept the first defeat in its proud 190-year history.

Chapter 10

Tragedy was swift in coming, both in Cambodia and in the United States. May 1, 1970, marked the start of a full-fledged war that steadily ravaged Cambodia for five years. The Cambodian government under Lon Nol was now fully engaged against the North Vietnamese and the Viet Cong as well as against the Khmer Rouge. Before May 1, the chief concern of North Vietnam and the Viet Cong had been to protect their sanctuaries and supply lines. But now a whole new set of forces was unleashed in Cambodia. Lon Nol's Phnom Penh emerged as a specific new Communist target.

In Peking, on May 5, Prince Sihanouk announced the formation of a government-in-exile to direct the warfare in Cambodia to be waged by FUNK (the acronym for the French term for the National United Front of Kampuchea [Cambodia], the political movement he headed before his overthrow). In the old days, Sihanouk and FUNK had fought the Khmer Rouge. Now the Khmer Rouge joined FUNK, at least in name; its two principal leaders, Khieu Samphan and Hou Yuon, became, respectively, minister of defense and minister of interior in the Sihanouk government.

Sihanouk, to be sure, was a figurehead, but a very useful one for the North Vietnamese and Chinese, who immediately recognized his "government" as Cambodia's legitimate regime. For complex reasons of Communist rivalries and Indochinese politics, the Soviet Union went on ignoring Sihanouk and maintaining diplomatic relations with Lon Nol. But for all practical purposes, a new force—hostile to the United States—emerged in Indochina. The administration had evidently never anticipated such a turn of events (since the White House planning for the invasion had been done in utter secrecy, it had been done without the benefit of advice from Indochina experts), and it went on refusing to take Sihanouk and his operation seriously until it was much too late. Sihanouk, meanwhile, spoke prophetically to the Cambodians over Peking radio:

I am convinced that with the protection and support of our Buddhist monks, all our compatriots who faithfully love the motherland and refuse to sell it out will rise and unite to fight and drive out of our beloved Kampuchea all the American archcriminal invaders and their no less criminal South Vietnamese lackeys, and to mercilessly overthrow the gang of traitors, sellers, and destroyers of the country and the nation, a gang headed by Lon Nol and Sirik Matak. Let these hideous devils go to hell and never return to haunt our people and the motherland. . . . Long live the People's National Liberation Army!

Having set in motion a new civil war in Indochina, as well as a new foreign war, the United States now moved to help expand and arm Lon Nol's armed forces to face all his enemies. This was in direct contradiction to Nixon's statement that large-scale military aid to Phnom Penh would be impractical. In truth, he wanted it both ways: to use the ARVN and United States troops to hit the sanctuaries, *and* to build up the Cambodian army. On April 30, the Cambodian army had 35,000 men; 100,000 more were called up in the next ten days. Cambodia had become an ally, and the United States was treating it accordingly. By May 8, Cambodia received 6000 captured Soviet and Chinese AK-47 automatic rifles with ammunition and 7200 United States M-2 carbines (even though Congress had still approved no military aid for Phnom Penh), and some 4000 ethnic Khmer Serei were moved to Cambodia to reinforce Lon Nol's army.

Legislative problems arising from the provision of military assistance in the absence of congressional appropriations were handled by Nixon *ex post facto* in a "presidential determination" issued on May 21, authorizing $7.9 million in "defense articles and services to Cambodia" for the fiscal year ending on June 30. Most of these funds had already been secretly expended, but Nixon, careful not to violate the law, invoked a special clause under which he was empowered to "find" that military aid to Cambodia "will strengthen the security of the United States and promote world peace." He also "found" that "the increased ability of Cambodia to defend itself is important to the security of the United States" and that military assistance to Cambodia "for fiscal year 1970 in an amount of up to $7.9 million is essential to the national interest of the United States." The president might have been in some difficulty in explaining why arms for Cambodia were important to "the security of the United States," but the still-trusting Congress did not challenge him on that point. The game plan, of course, was to handle the immediate arms deliveries through a "presidential determination," and then to request new military appropriations for Cambodia for fiscal year 1971, beginning on July 1. It was a typical Nixon way of doing business. The issuance of the "determination" was the first official admission that military aid had been secretly flowing to Cambodia.

Although Nixon specified that American forces could penetrate only 21.7 miles into Cambodia and promised that they would be out altogether by June 30, the reality was that the territory of Cambodia was irreversibly turned into a battlefield. Neither secrecy nor restraint was required any longer when it came to B-52 bombing runs over Cambodia.

Before the bombings became "official," on May 1, some 104,000 tons of bombs had already been dumped over Cambodia. Tactical air operations were now conducted openly. Within ten days, Washington officials began acknowledging that South Vietnamese forces might remain in Cambodia after the American withdrawal, perhaps indefinitely. For their part, the Communists—the North Vietnamese, the Viet Cong, and the Khmer Rouge—felt free to fight everywhere without constraint. This, in effect, was the price Cambodia was paying for having become an ally of the United States in the Indochina war, the war Nixon said would be *shortened* by his decision.

Perhaps the best summation of what had happened to Cambodia during May 1970 was provided in the Lowenstein-Moose report for the Senate Foreign Relations Committee. It rejected, by implication, the official line that was being fed from Washington.

> With U.S. and ARVN forces fighting North Vietnamese and Vietcong troops on Cambodian soil; with allied naval forces patrolling rivers and the southern Cambodian coast; with some Cambodians fighting in the Army, others in the Khmer Rouge and still others joining pro-Sihanoukist units fighting with enemy forces, Cambodia has become a theater of war. Virtually no one with whom we talked believed that it would not continue to be a theater of war after the U.S. forces leave. On the contrary, it was the view of almost everyone we met that Cambodia has now been linked inextricably to the war in Vietnam and that the terms of reference of that war have been permanently changed because its geographic area has been expanded.

Lowenstein and Moose concluded that the Cambodian venture would lengthen the Vietnam war. Quoting a "knowledgeable observer" of the Paris peace talks, they said,

> in all international negotiations the moment at which success can be achieved arrives when two conditions exist: . . . all the principal parties

must believe that they can yield and not have their concessions interpreted by others as having been made under pressure from a position
of weakness; [and] . . . the principal parties must be willing to forego
certain and important gains in order to reach a settlement. . . . As a
result of recent events in Cambodia, the moment when these two
conditions will exist lies even further in the future.

In this judgment, Lowenstein and Moose—who at the time knew
nothing about the secret Vietnam diplomacy—were more realistic regarding Cambodia's effect on the Paris negotiations than Kissinger,
whom William Safire quotes as estimating, "If we get through this, we
should have a negotiation by July or August." In Kissinger's parlance, "to
have a negotiation" meant engaging in a process likely to produce an
agreement. But Kissinger was a prisoner of his intellectual conviction that
the exercise of superior military power by the United States would inevitably force Hanoi to negotiate his kind of agreement.

Nixon evidently shared Kissinger's view. To his senior aides, he said
on May 3, "The diplomatic point is the most important of all: they have
to decide whether they want to take us on all over again. . . . In terms of
that pressure on them to negotiate, this was essential, but we'll know
more in two months."

Although the proclaimed objective of the allied offensive was the
destruction of Cambodian sanctuaries, in the first week of May American
aircraft carried out the heaviest attacks against North Vietnam since Lyndon Johnson had suspended the bombing on October 31, 1968. In four
separate raids, waves of United States planes—some consisting of 50
aircraft and some of up to 128—struck troop-staging areas, supply
dumps, and other military objectives deep in North Vietnam. There was
no official explanation for the raids although Ziegler at the White House
acknowledged that Nixon had given "overall authorization" for the attacks to be conducted "over a certain period of time." Some officials
suggested that the raids represented an application of the standing doctrine of "reinforced protective reaction"—the permission to air commanders to strike at North Vietnamese SAM batteries and antiaircraft
emplacements if American reconnaissance planes were fired upon. But
under this doctrine, invented by the Nixon administration, strikes had
been limited to antiaircraft batteries and supporting facilities.

In May, the planes went after all sorts of targets, plainly applying some
extra "pressure" on the North Vietnamese. That this was so with the
sudden new bombings seemed consistent with reports that neither
Rogers nor Laird was consulted in advance. Kissinger, on Nixon's orders,

transmitted direct secret instructions to the chairman of the Joint Chiefs of Staff. The State Department subsequently admitted under questioning that Rogers had been "informed" about the raids, which was different from being consulted.

At home, too, Nixon's actions brought violence and tragedy. In a manner far exceeding in scope and intensity even the worst fears of the Nixon administration, Americans exploded in protest against the Cambodian war. Four hundred forty-eight American universities and colleges declared themselves on strike. Riots swept the campuses. In Washington, police fought demonstrators with tear-gas and baton charges for two days while military units were deployed in reserve inside federal buildings. More than 100,000 protesters converged on the capital. The White House was under virtual siege for a day as the police drew up scores of municipal buses bumper-to-bumper, wagon-train fashion, around Lafayette Park, facing the executive mansion, to keep away the demonstrators. Pennsylvania Avenue and the streets behind the White House were cordoned off. Young Americans shouted their defiance from the Washington Monument grounds and the nearby streets while Nixon, locked in the White House, kept urging his aides to "hang tough."

The president himself gave an example of toughness, if that is what it was, when he went over to the Pentagon on the morning of May 1 to confer with his military chiefs. He stopped in a corridor to chat with a group of employees who had gathered to greet him. A question was asked about American troops in Vietnam, triggering an instinctive Nixonian reaction: "You think of those kids out there. I say 'kids.' I have seen them. They are the greatest. You see these bums, you know, blowing up the campuses. Listen, the boys that are on the college campuses today are the luckiest people in the world, going to the greatest universities, and here they are burning up the books, I mean storming around about this issue —I mean you name it—get rid of the war; there will be another one. Out there we've got kids who are just doing their duty. I have seen them. They stand tall, and they are proud. I am sure they are scared. I was when I was there. But when it really comes down to it, they stand up and, boy, you have to talk up to these men. And they are going to do fine; we've got to stand back of them."

A reporter accompanying Nixon taped on his recorder these somewhat incoherent remarks, and the next morning front-page war headlines in the newspapers included this one: "Nixon Calls Protesters 'Bums.' " The president's words only served to add fuel to the fire. (At a news conference Nixon later expressed regret that his use of the word "bums" was interpreted as applying to all dissenters, but he stood his ground in saying that when it came to students who burned buildings and "terrorized" others, " 'bums' is perhaps too kind a word." By that time, Nixon realized, a backlash reaction was developing against the widespread violence on the campuses, and his comments were calculated to support it.)

On May 4, a Monday, four students were shot to death by National Guard troops attempting to quell an antiwar riot on the campus of Kent State University on the outskirts of Akron, Ohio. Two of the dead were girls, two were boys. Eight other students were wounded when the guardsmen, themselves youngsters, fired a volley into the crowd of demonstrators, apparently because they thought they heard a sniper's shot. There was no sniper.

The Kent State tragedy stunned the nation. But Nixon's response, chilling in its insensitivity, was a brief statement read in his name by Ziegler at the regular briefing for White House newsmen. "This should remind us all once again that when dissent turns to violence, it invites tragedy. It is my hope that this tragic and unfortunate incident will strengthen the determination of all the Nation's campuses—administrators, faculty, and students alike—to stand firmly for the right which exists in this country of peaceful dissent and just as strongly against the resort to violence as a means of such expression."

Two more students were killed on May 16 in connection with antiwar protests at Jackson State College in Mississippi. This time Nixon, vacationing at Key Biscayne, responded with an equally short statement that was simply posted in the press room: "Mrs. Nixon and I are deeply saddened by the death of the two students at Jackson State College. In the shadow of these past troubled days, this tragedy makes it urgent that every American personally undertake greater efforts toward understanding, restraint, and compassion. I am confident that the Nation joins us in extending sincere sympathy to the families of these two young men, James Earl Green and Phillip L. Gibbs."

And Nixon wasted little time in facing his critics. On May 6, he received at the White House a delegation from the Senate Foreign Relations Committee and the House Foreign Affairs Committee. His immediate concern was to block the McGovern-Hatfield amendment to the military sales bill, then before the Senate, that in effect would ban the expenditure of funds for military operations in Vietnam by the end of 1970, unless Congress declared war, and insist on a scheduled withdrawal of American troops. This was known as the "end-the-war" amendment, and Nixon was in a fighting mood over it. He told New York's Senator

Jacob Javits, a liberal Republican, that it would be a "great mistake" for Congress to declare war—he did not want it as a means of securing funds for the Vietnam conflict. He acknowledged that Congress could, of course, cut off appropriations, but he shot this warning: "I will protect our men in Vietnam unless Congress hamstrings me. If it does that, then you will have to take the responsibility for American lives."

Pursuing the same theme, the president issued personal instructions the next day to all his cabinet members to go out and fight the McGovern-Hatfield amendment in the bluntest possible terms. Cabinet members were to tell congressmen: "Don't stab our men in the back while *they are fighting for this country in Vietnam.* . . . Don't take any actions on the floor of Congress which will give aid and comfort to the enemy and encourage that enemy to launch more offensives and kill more Americans." This was Nixon, the gut fighter: those who try to tie his hands in Indochina, he was saying, are traitors to America.

On May 8 at 10:00 p.m. (this was prime television time), Nixon held a news conference which, as he anticipated, was almost entirely devoted to Indochina and the consequences of the Cambodian incursion the previous week. But the president had resolved to hold his temper in check and to display statesmanship rather than anger. Asked whether he was surprised by the intensity of the protest against the Cambodian move and whether his policies would be affected by it, Nixon calmly replied that, no, he had not been surprised (which was not true).

> I realize that those who are protesting believe that this decision will expand the war, increase American casualties, and increase American involvement. Those who protest want peace. They want to reduce American casualties and they want our boys brought home. I made this decision, however, for the very reasons that they are protesting. As far as affecting my decision is concerned—their protests I am concerned about. I am concerned because I know how deeply they feel. But I know that what I have done will accomplish the goals that they want. It will shorten this war. It will reduce American casualties. It will allow us to go forward with our withdrawal program. The 150,000 Americans that I announced for withdrawal in the next year will come home on schedule. It will, in my opinion, serve the cause of a just peace in Vietnam.

This was a dexterous way of defusing the protest issue, identifying himself with the well-meant (but ill-expressed) motives of the protesters, and above all, assuming control of the discussion. It sounded right and it would make the right kind of headlines the next morning. In reply to a question about what he thought students were trying to say in their demonstrations, Nixon again sounded sympathetic:

> They are trying to say that they want peace. They are trying to say that they want to stop the killing. They are trying to say that they want to end the draft. They are trying to say that we ought to get out of Vietnam. I agree with everything that they are trying to accomplish. I believe, however, that the decisions that I have made, and particularly this last terribly difficult decision of going into the Cambodian sanctuaries which were completely occupied by the enemy—I believe that that decision will serve that purpose, because you can be sure that everything that I stand for is what they want.

But, Nixon added, he hoped students would understand what he wanted, and this was to bring Americans home from Vietnam. "I did not send these men to Vietnam," he pointedly reminded the television audience. Patiently, he went on to insist that there was no contradiction between his April 20 announcement of a new troop withdrawal in the light of the success of Vietnamization and his decision, ten days later, to send troops into Cambodia. Not about to disclose that the Cambodian operation had already been in an advanced planning stage when he spoke on April 20, he simply repeated his earlier assertion that during that ten-day period he had become aware of increased enemy action and, therefore, was forced to take strong action.

Answering other questions on the war, the president said he did not expect the North Vietnamese to cross the demilitarized zone into South Vietnam inasmuch as he had repeatedly warned Hanoi against such an action. He said that there were American Marines immediately below the DMZ and "I would certainly not allow these men to be massacred without using more force and more effective force against North Vietnam." But he did not mention that North Vietnam had already been heavily bombed in recent days even in the absence of any moves in the DMZ.

That excessive rhetoric and optimism are dangerous in war—something he should have learned from Kennedy's and Johnson's examples— was demonstrated anew in this assessment Nixon offered the newsmen gathered in the East Room:

> At the present time, I will say that it is my belief, based on what we have accomplished to date, that we have bought at least six months and probably eight months of time for the training of the ARVN. . . . We have also saved, I think, hundreds if not thousands of Americans. . . .

Rockets by the thousands and small arms ammunition by the millions have already been captured and those rockets and small arms will not be killing Americans in these next few months. And what we have also accomplished is that by buying time, it means that if the enemy does come back into those sanctuaries next time, the South Vietnamese will be strong enough and well trained enough to handle it alone.

One must assume, of course, that Nixon really believed that the "decisive" strike at the sanctuaries would alter the course of the war and, indeed, enable the South Vietnamese to defend themselves better. But if this was the case, then an immensely serious question arises concerning the quality of military advice the president was receiving from the Joint Chiefs of Staff and the commanders in Saigon.

The politics of the Cambodian decision—before and after the incursion—throw an interesting light on the inner workings of the Nixon administration and the personal attitudes of its key members.

Interestingly, Nixon never made the claim that his administration was wholeheartedly behind the Cambodian enterprise. This was uncharacteristic of him, but he must have been aware that word of Rogers's and Laird's reservations had already seeped out. When a reporter asked Nixon whether Rogers or Kissinger had opposed going into Cambodia, the president offered a skillful nonanswer that made him appear statesmanlike in the terrible loneliness of presidential decision-making:

Every one of my advisers, the Secretary of State, the Secretary of Defense, Dr. Kissinger, Director Helms, raised questions about the decision, and, believe me, I raised the most questions, because I knew the stakes that were involved, I knew the division that would be caused in this country. I knew also the problems internationally. I knew the military risks. And then after hearing all of their advice, I made the decision. Decisions, of course, are not made by vote in the National Security Council or in the Cabinet. They are made by the President with the advice of those, and I made this decision. I take the responsibility for it. I believe it was the right decision. I believe it will work out. If it doesn't, then I am to blame. They are not.

Cambodia split the administration, but these divisions never really weakened Nixon's position. None of the early inside critics ever "went public" with his doubts: they were, after all, team players, and they knew that open dissent would be politically suicidal. Nixon could not tolerate disloyalty, and as far as he was concerned, any public deviation from the official line was disloyalty. Secretary of the Interior Walter Hickel, an outspoken Alaskan, signed his political death warrant when he wrote to Nixon immediately after the Kent State incident suggesting that the president open lines of communication to America's young people and consider "meeting, on an individual and conversational basis, with members of your Cabinet." What annoyed Nixon most was that Hickel made public the text of his letter simultaneously with its delivery to the White House; by the end of the year Hickel was fired.

But Hickel's point about Nixon's maintaining more contact with his cabinet members was important. The president was operating almost exclusively with his senior staff and one or two cabinet officers he particularly liked. The cabinet met increasingly rarely, and its members, such as Hickel, had difficulties in obtaining Oval Office appointments. Attorney General Mitchell, who had been Nixon's law partner and now was one of his top political operators, had unlimited access to the president; he was totally loyal and on such matters as Cambodia he was properly hawkish. Labor Secretary George Shultz, very much his own man, had easy entrée because Nixon admired him intellectually; he was among the few to survive his association with the Nixon administration unscathed. But neither Hickel nor Shultz had any participation in foreign-policy decision-making.

The situation was much more serious with Rogers and Laird. Rogers, having been excluded from most of the early planning on Cambodia, attended the relevant NSC meetings—he was among the council's statutory members—and was called to the Oval Office a number of times, late in the game, to learn what Nixon was setting in motion. But he was never permitted to enjoy an intimate contact with the president despite their very long personal friendship (going back to the night in Los Angeles late in 1952, when Nixon slept at his house after delivering the famous "Checkers" television speech).

William Rogers, a pleasant man, had served as attorney general under Eisenhower, and the only possible reason for Nixon to name him secretary of state was that he was a trusted friend who would make no waves. Rogers was expected not to interfere; his task was to keep the State Department bureaucracy in line (or in the dark) and to act, when required, as the government's international lawyer. In fact, Rogers himself often remarked to friends that diplomatic negotiations were very much like labor-contract or corporate negotiations, of which he had conducted a great many in his career. Rogers's confusion between the formulation of foreign policy and the practice of law added, of course, to his impotence as secretary of state. He was one of the few secretaries of state in postwar history who had had virtually no prior exposure to foreign affairs —unlike, for example, Acheson, Dulles, Christian Herter, or Dean Rusk; his only experience was several months as an alternate delegate to the U.N. General Assembly in the 1950s. Still, Kissinger, never entirely secure, went on regarding him as a potential rival.

Rogers was too intelligent not to realize how utterly he had been neutralized (besides, he could read newspaper stories that said just that), but he was not a fighter—for himself or any cause. In conversations with friends during the Cambodian crisis, he put up a brave front, emphasizing his old friendship with Nixon, and pointing out that he did not have to measure his relationship with the president by how many times a week or a month he saw him face to face. Yes, he would say, it was true that Kissinger saw Nixon alone at least for the hour-long morning briefing, and frequently in the evening. But he, Rogers, would say, sometimes talked with Nixon on the telephone several times a day. None of this, of course, was very convincing. The truth, sadly, was that Rogers had abdicated to Kissinger from the very first day. He enjoyed the trappings of the office of the secretary of state—the social exposure, the limousines, the air force's VIP Boeing 707 that flew him around the world, and so on —and, clearly, he was not about to sacrifice it all by fighting the White House, even fighting Kissinger.

In the Cambodian situation, as before, he was the despair of his associates at the State Department because of his failure to stand up for his views. He did tell Nixon that he had deep reservations—and he also told many of his friends privately that he opposed the decision—but he stepped back when it became obvious that the president had made up his mind. Personal and institutional loyalty overcame his reservations. At a brief cabinet meeting on May 2, he praised Nixon for his "great courage"; he recognized that the need for surprise justified the absence of fuller consultations within the administration, and said that now the president needed the cabinet's "moral and verbal" support. On May 13, Rogers refused to tell newsmen publicly what advice he had given Nixon on Cambodia but quoted at length from comments he had made to student delegations; when some of the students admitted that Nixon could have been right, he told them "that it was the duty of all of us to support him during this interim period"—until the final results were known in July with the withdrawal of American troops from Cambodia. "We believe that it is going to work. . . . We believe it has worked. . . . We believe that the results will be very gratifying to the American people." Interviewed on a television program on June 7, Rogers said, "As you know, I support the Cambodian operation. . . . I think it's going to be very successful, and I think it is going to make the Vietnamization program a success."

In May, the State Department issued an internal paper "For Use by the U.S. Government—Not for Republication" on the American military action in Cambodia. This five-point paper provided officials with detailed answers to questions about the reasons for the American incursion—presumably when they were asked about it by Americans and foreigners with whom they came into contact. Thus Rogers and the State Department were effectively whipped into line.

Laird's relationship with Nixon was more complicated than Rogers's. He, too, had deep reservations about Cambodia—and made them known in no uncertain terms—but at the same time he had considerable involvement in military planning. Despite Kissinger's back-channel relations with the Joint Chiefs of Staff, Laird had an important constituency in the Pentagon, and he carried weight in Congress, where he had long served as a representative from Wisconsin. The White House had to handle Laird with kid gloves, negotiating with him almost as if he were a sovereign foreign power. Still, Laird had only limited access to the Oval Office, and his influence certainly was no match for Kissinger's.

As for Kissinger, his stand on Cambodia was both subtle and ambiguous. There is no doubt that he was actively encouraging the president to go into Cambodia—it was part of his concept of applying power in foreign policy—but there are also reasons to believe that he panicked, at least briefly, when the reaction against Cambodia swept the country. Kissinger, as his close associates often remarked, tended to panic and was often assailed by doubts. Basically, he believed that the Cambodian operation was necessary both as a military and as a political proposition. He took it for granted that the May attack would temporarily freeze his overall diplomacy, but correctly, he concluded that this gamble would pay off.

Not unexpectedly, the North Vietnamese and the Viet Cong for a while boycotted the weekly semipublic negotiating sessions in Paris, but they returned to the table after the Americans left Cambodia at the end of June, as Kissinger thought they would. His secret talks with Le Duc Tho were also interrupted for months in 1970—Le Duc Tho simply stayed away from Paris—but they were resumed in time. The brutal truth was that the Communists, just like the United States, were looking far down the road, past Cambodia.

China, to which Sihanouk's appearance in Peking was an unexpected bonus, went through the motions of denouncing Washington, but the Chinese evidently concluded that this was no reason to abandon altogether the nascent contact with the United States. American and Chinese envoys in Warsaw had originally scheduled their next meeting for May 20, but curiously, Peking waited until May 18, almost three weeks after the invasion, to cancel it.

Kissinger, then, was correct in his interpretation of the diplomatic consequences of Cambodia when he and Nixon weighed all the elements of the decision. But, it appears, there may have been another—and purely political—reason for Kissinger's espousal of the Cambodian invasion. An NSC official who worked closely with Kissinger at the time put it this way:

"I don't think that Kissinger would have dared at that stage in the game to appear in a posture which would have compromised him in the eyes of the president. It was very important that Henry establish at least one experience in which the president did something demonstratively unpopular, even unpopular in the bureaucracy, to which Laird and Rogers were opposed, which created a terrific storm in the country, which confirmed all of Nixon's paranoia about the media and about the rest of the government, all the things Nixon liked to talk about and to worry about—*and that Henry was on his side.* And Henry was willing to cut the ties as well with lots of his friends. I think that kind of credibility with Nixon when the going was tough—and Henry was there—was essential to everything else that Kissinger pursued. The one constituency that he could not afford to lose was Nixon. . . . He wasn't yet the superstar. He needed Nixon desperately. This was not a matter of principle, it was a demonstration of loyalty. The success of the invasion could be easily alleged and the thing was bound to come out—I think Henry understood it—as murky and indecisive, like everything else in Southeast Asia. In other words, Henry could survive it, the administration could survive it, but the demonstration of his fidelity, his staying power with the Nixon administration, would fortify him for some time to come, immunize him, as it were, against what he saw as a kind of basic distrust. It ingratiated him with Nixon, then it also strengthened him against the Haldemans and the Ehrlichmans, who felt that he had pacifist leanings, spent too much time in Georgetown, and was subject to pressures from outside. Cambodia is explained very much in terms of the politics of the White House. That was Kissinger's first triumph, the precondition of everything else he ever did; Cambodia was the turning point."

Nixon, to be sure, found as much genuine support among America's influential men for the Cambodian venture as he encountered opposition. Clark Clifford, who was Johnson's last defense secretary and an increasingly outspoken "dove," blasted Nixon in a highly emotional news conference. But Robert McNamara, his predecessor at the Pentagon and now president of the World Bank, called on Kissinger to offer him his support. Dean Rusk came up from Georgia to defend Nixon's Cambodian policies at a Washington symposium on international law. And Under Secretary of State Richardson, even years after the event, made no bones about admitting that he never changed his mind about the "wisdom" of going into Cambodia. But Richardson had no further role to play in foreign policy: he left the State Department in June to become Secretary of Health, Education and Welfare.

Only three men resigned from the government as a result of Cambodia—the NSC staffers Lake, Morris, and Watts. (Lake had been particularly close to Kissinger, who was deeply hurt by his move.) But Kissinger was now firmly established at the White House, even in the physical sense. Shortly before Cambodia, his office was moved from the basement of the West Wing to ampler and more elegant quarters on the ground floor. Now he was almost literally next door to the Oval Office, a psychological boost. A marine guard in full-dress uniform was posted for the first time at the door of the West Wing.

Richard Nixon craved approval as well as loyalty at crucial moments of his life. His basic insecurity, never conquered, went with his obsession over secrecy, his distrust of nearly everybody, and his suspicions that there were always conspiracies against him and his policies.

This craving for approval and acceptance was expressed, in the case of the Cambodian affair, in a series of curious personal acts the night of his May 8 news conference. He spent almost the entire night on the telephone, calling government officials, assistants, relatives, and friends (sometimes several times) to discuss his performance, practically inviting praise. He called Kissinger just forty minutes before the press conference, then called him again five minutes *after* to ask, "How did I do?" In all, according to the White House log, he spoke eight times with Kissinger that night, with the last call logged at 3:38 a.m. Of the fifty-one telephone conversations Nixon held during the night of May 8–9, only one was with Secretary Rogers, who called with congratulations right after the press conference; one was with Laird. But there were seven with Haldeman and two with his friend "Bebe" Rebozo. His last conversation ended at 3:50 a.m. Except for a short nap just before dawn, the president stayed up all night, playing classical records on his bedroom stereo when he was not on the phone.

Then he did a strange thing. Just before 5:00 a.m., he got dressed, ordered his limousine, and with his valet, Manolo Sanchez, took a five-minute drive to the Lincoln Memorial. Hundreds of young antiwar protesters were camping out on the memorial's steps and in the park surrounding it. The president got out of his car, went straight to the nearest group of startled youths, and struck up a conversation. This spur-of-the-moment foray was completely out of character. He embarked on an explanation that the intervention in Cambodia was really intended to bring a quicker end to the Vietnam war. At one point, he said that "I know that probably most of you think I'm an SOB, but I want you to know I understand just how you feel."

Almost with a touch of desperation, Nixon turned to reminiscences about his own youth, talked about travel, urging the young people around him to get to know the world. From the Lincoln Memorial, as the first light was breaking over Washington, Nixon ordered his driver to take him to the Senate building. The Senate doors were locked, so Nixon led his little party to the House building, where a custodian appeared with keys. In the House chamber, the president went to the seat he had occupied as a congressman a quarter of a century earlier. He told Sanchez, the valet, to sit in the speaker's chair and to make a little speech. The Cuban-born Sanchez spoke of being proud of being an American citizen. From this eerie, surrealistic scene in Congress, Nixon went to the Mayflower Hotel on Connecticut Avenue to breakfast on corned-beef hash and poached eggs. He wanted to walk back the five blocks to the White House, but the Secret Service agents talked him out of it. His limousine finally brought him home at 7:30 a.m., as the capital was starting work.

The sunrise expedition around Washington at a critical point in his presidency was one of Nixon's rare breakaways from the confines of the White House, even for a few hours. But back in the office, he was quickly retransformed into the tough, suspicious, and unforgiving commander in chief. And one of the things that was happening that week in the White House with his approval was the resumption of secret wiretaps against government officials and newsmen whom he distrusted. At that point, of course, nobody outside a small group around Nixon, Kissinger, and Hoover was aware of the wiretapping, and the president himself had gone out of his way at his May 8 news conference to assure the country that dissent and even violence would never lead to any form of repression in the United States.

This time around, leak plugging would not be much of an excuse because, as compared with 1969, there were very few serious leaks. The only important one had been in William Beecher's story in *The New York Times* late in April, reporting on secret deliveries to Cambodia of captured AK-47 assault rifles. The new wiretap program was designed chiefly to keep Nixon and Kissinger informed of what government officials may have been saying behind their backs. The wiretap pattern made this plain.

The first wiretaps in the new series were placed by the FBI on May 4, four days after the Cambodia invasion, on the home telephones of three senior officials and one newsman: the *Times*'s Beecher; Lieutenant General Pursley (Secretary Laird's military assistant, who had been wiretapped for two weeks in 1969); Richard Pederson (counselor of the State Department, who was extremely close to William Rogers); and William Sullivan, a deputy assistant secretary of state for East Asian and Pacific affairs. Sullivan, a former ambassador to Laos, was the head of the Interdepartmental Vietnam Task Force and State's principal officer concerned with Indochina on a day-to-day basis. But he had also been a protégé of Averell Harriman; this may have been one reason that the White House decided to have the FBI spy on him.

Then on May 13, wiretaps were placed on the phones of NSC aides Anthony Lake and Winston Lord. This made little sense. Lake had already submitted his resignation, and Lord was totally devoted to Kissinger. (Years later, Lord was named head of the highly influential New York Council on Foreign Affairs, which had been one of Kissinger's first sponsors.) But common sense was not the guideline. Morton Halperin, for example, had left the NSC long ago, but the tap on his phone remained. Later still, and for incomprehensible reasons, a wiretap was put on Sonnenfeldt, and on December 4, James McLane, a little-known White House aide, was wiretapped for equally mysterious reasons. Lord, Lake, Pederson, Sullivan, Pursley, and Beecher would remain under electronic surveillance until February 10, 1971, when, just as capriciously, all the FBI wiretaps were terminated. Despite numerous contradictions, there is every reason to believe that in 1970, just as in 1969, Kissinger was responsible for selecting the wiretap targets (with the probable exception of McLane, who worked outside the national-security apparatus). Along with Nixon, he read the intercept logs though neither man learned much if anything from this exercise.

Domestic political espionage was not, of course, new with the Nixon administration. President Johnson had a highly developed sense of political paranoia, and on his orders the Justice Department and the CIA

became involved in secret operations to track groups of dissenters at
home and search for possible overseas links. While the Justice Department set up a special committee to study the problem, the CIA on August
15, 1967, had launched its own program for collecting intelligence on
dissenters and militants (it was not terminated until 1974). The CIA
operation was run by the Special Operations Group headed by an agency
counterintelligence veteran named Richard Ober. Soon, the operation
was given the code name Chaos. In December, Attorney General Ramsey
Clark, an outstanding liberal, organized the Interdivision Information
Unit (IDIU) in the Justice Department, a secret group whose job it was
to pull together "all information . . . relating to organizations and individuals throughout the country who may play a role, whether purpose-
fully or not, either in instigating or spreading civil disorders or in preventing or checking them." IDIU developed working contacts with other
government agencies, including the CIA. In the agency's case, this was
legally a dubious proposition, inasmuch as the National Security Act
specifically prohibited the CIA from exercising police functions at home.

The CIA, to be sure, had been secretly—and illegally—involved in
counterintelligence work in the United States through a program, started
in the early 1950s, of intercepting and reading mail between addresses
in this country and Communist nations. The mail interception was conducted at major post offices handling overseas mail. Earlier in 1967 (and
again in 1968), the government used the Army Security Agency, a military
command specializing in cryptography and electronic intelligence associated with the top-secret National Security Agency (NSA), to monitor
the movements of antiwar demonstrators before and during manifesta-
tions. (In addition to performing more sophisticated worldwide electronic intelligence activities, the NSA had been eavesdropping for years
on international telephone traffic with the United States and intercepting
commercial Telex and cable traffic.) But it was IDIU and Operation
Chaos that really enmeshed the CIA—the principal foreign intelligence
agency—in domestic political espionage. This was a quantum jump from
illegal mail readings. And it is a reflection on the basically immutable
practices of succeeding American governments that the program was
devised by Johnson's liberal Democrats and expanded by Nixon's conservative Republicans.

In November 1967, the CIA gave Johnson a report on "International
Connections of the United States Peace Movement," which stated there
was little evidence of foreign involvement with antiwar groups and no
evidence of any significant foreign financial support for domestic peace

activities. Subsequently, the CIA presented other studies on worldwide "Demonstration Techniques" and on "Student Dissent and Its Techniques in the United States."

During 1968, the CIA expanded its activities; this was when Operation Chaos acquired its name. As the Rockefeller Commission (the Commission on CIA Activities within the United States) would report in 1975, "The CIA sent cables to all its field stations in July 1968, directing that all information concerning dissident groups be sent through a single restricted channel on an 'Eyes Only' basis to the Chief of Operation CHAOS. No other dissemination of the information was to occur." The agency took the view that this was a legitimate effort inasmuch as all the intelligence collection was being done abroad. But the line between the CIA's foreign and domestic operations quickly became blurred. Still in 1968, the agency prepared for Johnson a study on "Restless Youth," including a section on domestic antiwar and other activities. As the Rockefeller Commission summarized it, this study "concluded that the motivations underlying student radicalism arose from social and political alienation at home and not from conspiratorial activities masterminded from abroad." CIA Director Helms noted in a covering memorandum that "you will, of course, be aware of the peculiar sensitivity which attaches to the fact that the CIA has prepared a report on student activities both here and abroad."

Such was the internal secrecy surrounding Chaos that in May 1969 Helms, now in the Nixon administration, instructed Ober, the head of the operation, not to reveal his activities to his CIA superior, Counter Intelligence Staff Chief James Angleton. Ober was simply separated from the CI staff for an indefinite period; the secrecy and the compartmentalization in the CIA are so great that no questions were asked. This made Helms the man directly responsible for overseeing Chaos, along with his deputy director for plans (clandestine services), Thomas H. Karamessines. Later in 1969 other CIA deputy directors were apprised of Chaos as the operation expanded and required additional support.

The new administration was informed of CIA activities in this area almost at once. On February 18, 1969, Helms sent Kissinger a copy of the "Restless Youth" report, telling him even more explicitly than he had told Walt W. Rostow, Johnson's foreign-policy adviser, three months earlier that the CIA, in effect, had no business being involved in domestic politics: "In an effort to round-out our discussion of this subject, we have included a section on American students. This is an area not within the character of this Agency, so I need not emphasize how extremely sensitive this makes the paper. Should anyone learn of its existence, it would prove most embarrassing for all concerned."

There are no indications that Nixon's decision in May 1969 to wiretap government officials and newsmen was directly related to the wider domestic intelligence plan. It was more in the nature of an *ad hoc* move. But, almost spontaneously, all the pieces soon began falling into place as both Nixon and his national-security adviser were acutely aware.

On May 14, 1969, for example, Helms met with Attorney General Mitchell (nominal boss of the FBI) to discuss how best the administration could handle the question of intelligence concerning domestic dissidents. Mitchell expressed his unhappiness over the FBI's alleged failure to acquire domestic intelligence, and Helms agreed to have Ober, the head of Operation Chaos, establish liaison with the Justice Department's IDIU unit. The CIA would now assist IDIU by supplying information on the foreign travel and contacts of American citizens in whom the government had an interest and by advising on the organization and evaluation of intelligence information. This arrangement, however, was to be kept completely secret. Only Helms, his executive assistant, and Ober in the CIA; and Assistant Attorney General Jerris Leonard and James Devine, head of IDIU in the Justice Department, knew about it.

On June 18, Devine told Ober that IDIU was often unable to provide advance warning of incipient civil disorders because information was not available in time. He then turned over to Ober's Operation Chaos a computer listing of between 10,000 and 12,000 Americans classified as dissidents. The idea was that the CIA would check the Justice Department's list against Operation Chaos's own file on some 7200 dissidents to determine in what foreign travel these Americans might have been engaging. Again, only Helms, Ober, Devine, and a Chaos computer programmer knew that Justice Department files had been given to the CIA.

At the White House, meanwhile, Nixon was demanding more information on war dissenters. Tom Charles Huston, a young staff assistant, wrote Helms on June 20 that the president had ordered a report on foreign Communist support of revolutionary protest movements in the United States. Specifically, Nixon wanted to know what resources were being used to monitor foreign Communist support of "revolutionary youth activities" in this country, how effective these resources were, what gaps existed in the surveillance because of low attention priorities, and what steps could be taken to provide maximum possible coverage of the dissidents' activities.

Nixon, according to Huston, was particularly interested in the CIA's ability to collect this type of information. The CIA was given ten days to come up with the report, such was the urgency felt at the White House. On June 30, therefore, the CIA produced "Foreign Communist Support to Revolutionary Protest Movements in the United States," a study that concluded for the third time in three years that there was very little evidence of Communist funding or training of antiwar movements and none of Communist direction and control, even though Communists encouraged protest in the United States through propaganda and "exploitation of international conferences."

Nixon and Kissinger were concerned that the antiwar movement in the United States would weaken the American negotiating position in the Paris peace talks. They knew that Hanoi attached immense importance to the activities of peace groups in the United States; the North Vietnamese, indeed, considered war weariness in America a major factor in the overall diplomatic picture. This was an advantage Nixon was not prepared to grant his enemy. And he also feared that sooner or later Congress might be influenced by the antiwar militancy and start placing legislative obstacles in his way. Like Johnson, Nixon simply could not understand—and admit—that the antiwar movement was wholly indigenous. And this also went against Kissinger's assessment of the American propeace phenomenon. In the administration, only Rogers and Laird seemed to understand the motivations of the dissidents. As Laird put it bluntly at a White House meeting, the opposition to the war would end only when "flag-draped caskets stop arriving in Peoria, in Des Moines."

The administration persisted in its efforts to control the dissidents through all available means. On July 22, Attorney General Mitchell established—secretly—the Civil Disturbance Group (CDG), incorporating IDIU and the Intelligence Evaluation Committee (composed of representatives of the Justice Department, the Defense Department, and the Secret Service). The CIA was not formally included in the CDG, but three days after its creation Mitchell met with Helms to ask the CIA to investigate the adequacy of the FBI's intelligence-collection efforts in dissident matters and to persuade the bureau to turn its material over to the CDG. This was a most extraordinary request: asking one federal intelligence agency to investigate another federal intelligence agency, and it was a startling admission of how little control the attorney general had over Hoover and his FBI. Nixon was either unwilling or unable to put pressure on Hoover (although the FBI chief was most cooperative in the wiretap program) and left Mitchell in this bizarre position. He was evidently unaware that, for their own parochial reasons, the CIA and the FBI were on the verge of breaking all their working relations. The only help the CIA was able to provide to the new antidisturbance group was to establish contacts between the CDG and military-intelligence agencies.

Given the inability of Mitchell's CDG to cope with the intelligence aspects of its job, the CIA—quietly encouraged by the White House— took matters into its own hands. It assumed a major responsibility for surveillance activities against the "radical milieu" in the United States. And to do so, it vested virtually autonomous powers in Operation Chaos. This was spelled out in a memorandum Director Helms sent to his four deputy directors on September 6, 1969:

> I recently have reviewed the Agency's efforts to monitor those international activities of radicals and black militants which may affect the national security. I believe that we have the proper approach in discharging this sensitive responsibility. . . . I appreciate that there are several components in the Clandestine Service with a legitimate operational interest in the radical milieux. At the same time, it should be understood that Mr. Ober's Special Operations Group of CI [Counter-Intelligence] Staff has the principal operational responsibility for coordinating and developing operations to collect information on aspects of activities abroad which have a direct bearing on U.S. radical and black militant movements. I expect that area divisions and senior staffs will be fully cooperative in this effort, both in exploiting existing sources and in developing new ones, and that Mr. Ober will have the necessary access to such sources and operational assets. It is most important to ensure that Mr. Ober's Group has a small coterie of knowledgeable, effective officers. . . . If the right people are scarce and already ensconced in other activities, a select few nonetheless ought to be broken away for assignment to CI Staff.

Operation Chaos had thus acquired one of the highest priorities in the CIA; it was becoming a principal intelligence pillar in Nixon's campaign against antiwar dissidents. The Rockefeller Commission noted that "the increase in size and activity of the Operation was accompanied by further isolation and protective measures." The Chaos group, it said, "had already been physically located in a vaulted basement area, and tighter security measures were adopted in connection with communications of the Operation," but "these measures were extreme, even by normally strict CIA standards. . . . An exclusive channel for communication with the FBI was also established which severely restricted dissemination both to and from the Bureau of CHAOS-related matters."

Commenting on Helms's memorandum, the Rockefeller Commission concluded that "first, it confirmed beyond question the importance which Operation CHAOS had attained in terms of Agency objectives . . . second, it replied to dissent which had been voiced within the CIA concerning the Operation . . . third, it ensured that CHAOS would receive whatever support it needed, including personnel." Helms's upgrading of Chaos also led to a wholly new approach to domestic intelligence by the CIA. Prior to Helms's September review of the program, Chaos had collected most of its information from CIA field stations abroad and from the reports of other investigative agencies. Starting in October 1969, however, it recruited and "ran" agents directly and specifically for the operation, known in secret CIA files as Project 2. Under this procedure, Chaos case officers recruited individuals without actual affiliations with dissident groups and infiltrated them among the militants. The Rockefeller Commission described how it worked: "Individuals . . . after recruitment, would acquire the theory and jargon and make acquaintances in the 'New Left' while attending school in the United States. Following this 'reddening' or 'sheep-dipping' process (as one CIA officer described it), the agent would be sent to a foreign country on a specific intelligence mission."

Project 2 was formally approved by CIA headquarters in April 1970, but, for all practical purposes, it had become operational by late 1969. In the judgment of the Rockefeller Commission, the CIA's decision to dynamize Chaos and change its procedures was attributable to "first, and most important, an increasing amount of White House pressure." Another factor was a substantial increase in "the tempo of dissident activities." This was the period of the big antiwar moratorium demonstrations in Washington, when Nixon was extremely worried that his Vietnam policies were being undermined both at home and in the negotiations in Paris.

Thus the 1970 invasion of Cambodia and the consequent national uproar led to a still broader consideration of steps designed to control domestic dissidence. Now, the president took personal charge.

On June 5, Nixon presided over a White House meeting of the chiefs of the United States intelligence community convened to discuss domestic disorders: CIA Director Helms, FBI Director Hoover, National Security Agency Director Vice Admiral Noel Gayler, and Defense Intelligence Agency Director Lieutenant General Donald Bennett. The composition of the group was unusual, inasmuch as under the law neither the CIA, nor the NSA, nor the DIA were permitted domestic intelligence responsibilities. To be sure, all these agencies had, to a varying extent, been involved for quite some time in domestic spying activities, but never before had the situation been so formalized. The Rockefeller Commission described the meeting in these words:

> The President . . . made it plain that he was dissatisfied with the quality of intelligence concerning the extent of any foreign connections with domestic dissidence. The possible relationship of Black radicalism in the Caribbean to Black militancy in the United States was discussed, and the President directed that a study on the subject be prepared. Finally, the President said that Mr. Hoover was to organize the group to draft a plan for coordination of domestic intelligence.

The new group, composed of the directors of the four agencies, named Interagency Committee on Intelligence (Ad Hoc), held its first meeting on June 9, with Tom Charles Huston representing Nixon. The ICI started by setting up a subcommittee to draft a "Special Report." The CIA was represented on the subcommittee by Counter Intelligence Staff Chief Angleton, from whom Helms had kept secret the existence of Chaos; but Chaos had an "observer," his function unknown to anybody except Helms, attached to the subcommittee. While the full ICI was an *ad hoc* group, its subcommittee was formally made part of the U.S. Intelligence Board, which was headed by Helms in his capacity as director of Central Intelligence. But inasmuch as the U.S. Intelligence Board is subordinate to the National Security Council, this move had the effect of involving Henry Kissinger with domestic espionage; as the president's adviser on national security affairs, Kissinger controlled all the NSC committees and subcommittees.

The ICI's mandate was to assure "higher priority by all intelligence agencies on internal security collection efforts" and to assure "maximum use of all special investigative techniques, including increased agent and informant penetration by both the FBI and the CIA." Huston complained to the intelligence chiefs that "the president receives uncoordinated intelligence which he has to put together." Helms remarked later that "the heart of the matter" was "to get the FBI to do what it was not doing." But the most important point, as Huston explained it to the ICI, was that Nixon wanted the group to assume that all methods of gathering intelligence were "valid." According to Huston, the president took the view that whenever anything "obstructed" intelligence gathering, "everything is valid, everything is possible." This was another way of saying that no law should be allowed to stand in the way of the intelligence operators.

It took the ICI just over two weeks to produce a rather inconclusive forty-three-page report on internal-security threats posed by the domestic dissident groups and foreign organizations. The CIA contributed the section on "Definition of Internal Security Threat—Foreign," but it added virtually nothing to its earlier negative findings. Operation Chaos produced a separate report on possible relationships between black radicalism in the Caribbean and in the United States; Helms delivered it to Huston on July 6 to be handed to the president. This report, too, failed to provide any new light.

The principal content of the ICI's "Special Report" to Nixon was a series of distinctions it drew between legal methods of gathering intelligence and those that were subject to legal restraints or constitutional safeguards. Among the latter, it listed electronic surveillance (i.e., wiretapping), mail coverage, surreptitious entry (into foreign embassies in Washington, etc.), and development of intelligence sources on campuses. Covert mail coverage and surreptitious entry were specifically termed illegal. But the ICI refrained from any action recommendations on the subject: it simply discussed the benefits and drawbacks implicit in various methods and offered alternatives. It did recommend the establishment of a *permanent* interagency group for evaluating and coordinating domestic intelligence. Here, the lone dissenter was Hoover, who opposed any changes in existing domestic counterintelligence procedures as well as the creation of the permanent group. As much as anything else, Hoover probably feared that his own counterintelligence empire would be undermined by an interagency group. For some time, the FBI had been running its own secret program against radicals—it was known in the bureau as COINTELPRO—and Hoover wished no invasion of his turf.

But the White House wanted action—in a big way. After studying the ICI report, Huston on July 9 drafted his own recommendation to Nixon that virtually all the restraints on intelligence collection be relaxed. This was the famous "Huston Plan," later regarded as the prime seed of Watergate. Specifically, he favored break-ins into foreign embassies, presumably on the theory that they might yield evidence of foreign involvement in domestic dissent. In this, Huston had the support of NSA Director Gayler, whose agency was principally concerned with breaking foreign codes and ciphers and who hoped that code books and similar materials could be obtained. Late in 1975, the government admitted in a court deposition in connection with this writer's lawsuit over illegal wiretapping that United States intelligence agencies had recourse to every conceivable form of espionage—from satellite surveillance to a variety of clandestine means, including break-ins—in order to obtain information necessary for the formulation of American foreign policy. Thus, again, domestic espionage and the making of foreign policy were inseparable.

Nixon quickly accepted Huston's recommendations, as Huston was advised in a secret memorandum from Haldeman on July 14. Accordingly, Huston wrote the heads of the four intelligence agencies on July 23 that virtually all the restraints on intelligence collection at home had been lifted. The permanent intelligence committee was to start functioning on August 1.

Divisions and jealousies led, however, to a quick demise of the Huston Plan in its original form. For one thing, the White House had failed to inform Mitchell about it. When he learned of it on July 27—via Hoover, who complained to him about the memorandum—he told Helms that he opposed the Huston Plan, and on July 28 took his case to the president. He evidently succeeded in persuading Nixon that it was a serious error, for later that day the White House instructed the four agencies to return their copies of Huston's memorandum. Huston himself was shunted aside; John Dean, a counsel to the president, was put in charge of domestic intelligence on internal-security matters. Nixon later confessed that the only reason he rescinded the Huston Plan was Hoover's argument that the sensitivity of the measures proposed in it "would likely generate media criticism" in the event of public disclosure. Furtiveness was a characteristic trait of the president.

But the basic notion of expanding domestic intelligence remained very much alive. On September 17, Mitchell met with Helms, Karamessines, Angleton, and Ober at lunch at CIA headquarters to discuss how best to proceed. They agreed that the FBI lacked capability "for evaluation of domestic intelligence" and a new special unit should be established within the Justice Department to provide "evaluated intelligence from all sources" and "allow preventive action" to be taken in time. Later, Mitchell pursued this line of action with Dean at the White House. The upshot was that a *new* Intelligence Evaluation Committee was created on December 3, with the participation of the Department of Justice, the FBI, the CIA, the Defense Department, the Secret Service, the NSA, and the Treasury Department. The new IEC was headed jointly by Dean and Assistant Attorney General Robert C. Mardian.

Dean made it clear that while initially there would be no blanket removal of the restrictions on intelligence-gathering methods, certain restraints could be lifted *as required* to obtain intelligence on a particular subject. Also, all precautions were taken against public discovery of the

new committee. There was no presidential executive order creating the
IEC; Dean said that written directives should be avoided to sidestep
"problems of congressional oversight and disclosure."

Still, it was the CIA's Operation Chaos that proved to be the most
active under Nixon's domestic intelligence program. In addition to the
7200 separate personality files on Americans developed from 300,000
names in the Chaos computer index, the operation put together 1000
subject files on organizations, including Students for a Democratic Society (SDS), the National Mobilization Committee to End the War in Vietnam, Women's Strike for Peace, American Indian Movement, Student
Non-Violent Coordinating Committee (SNCC), Grove Press, women's
liberation movement, Black Panther Party, and Clergy and Laymen Concerned about Vietnam. The Chaos file also included reviews of the erotic
film *I Am Curious (Yellow)* because it was distributed by Grove Press, which
earlier had published a book by Kim Philby, the British intelligence agent
who defected to the Soviet Union. And Chaos operatives monitored
political activities at Boston, Brown, and Utah State universities, among
others.

As far as President Nixon was concerned, the Cambodian venture was
an overwhelming success from the first day to the last—when 18,000
American troops withdrew on schedule on June 30. During May and June,
an incessant stream of victory claims cascaded from the White House,
emphasizing the wisdom of the president's decision. The public simply
had to take the official word that the operation was developing beyond
all expectations. There was no possible corroboration of the claims, and
even correspondents in the field were unable to provide a satisfactory
picture of what was happening. On May 9, for example, the White House
announced that in the first nine days of the allied sweep in the sanctuaries, American and South Vietnamese forces had already captured more
enemy ammunition than the North Vietnamese and Viet Cong had ex-
pended in Vietnam in the first four months of 1970. This was one of those
impossible comparisons that could be neither proved nor disproved. The
figure given by the White House for captured ammunition during the
nine days was more than six million rounds, ranging from large rockets
to small arms rounds. And so it went, day after day, week after week. The
administration's propaganda machine was running in high gear.

Diplomatically, the administration had its hands full on all fronts. One
problem was whether any or all of the 43,000 South Vietnamese troops
operating in Cambodia should remain there after the departure of the

American forces or leave at the same time. From the military standpoint, the administration quietly favored an indefinite South Vietnamese presence in Cambodia; it was a tacit admission that the Cambodian war would be an open-ended affair regardless of how many thousands of guns, millions of ammunition rounds, and tons of supplies would be captured in the sanctuaries. To encourage Saigon to keep its troops in Cambodia to help shore up the Lon Nol regime, the Americans made it clear that they would continue to provide the ARVN with air support after the withdrawal of American ground units.

But the problem was political: while President Thieu was eager to keep fighting in Cambodia, where his soldiers seemed to be doing better than they were at home, Lon Nol's government was not so keen. There was considerable fear in Phnom Penh that with the ARVN firmly established in Cambodia, the South Vitnamese might in time develop territorial claims that would be impossible to resist. Instead, the Cambodians openly pressed Washington to let American forces stay beyond the June 30 deadline and to provide maximum military and economic aid.

Another variant examined by Washington was using Thai as well as South Vietnamese troops in Cambodia after June 30, though this would encourage an even greater expansion of the conflict; the Thais already had a 14,000-man division fighting in Vietnam, fully financed by the United States, and Thailand was a crucial staging area for American air operations in Indochina.

The effort to involve the Thais in Cambodia began in earnest when on May 27 the State Department let it be known that the South Vietnamese and Thai governments were free to transfer to Cambodia military equipment that the United States had supplied to them in the past. This was a way of quickly getting around the need for legislation to provide substantial military aid directly to Phnom Penh. All that was necessary was a presidential executive act authorizing the transfers under the provisions of defense treaties with South Vietnam and Thailand. Arms given by them to Cambodia would presently be replaced by Washington.

Appearing on a television program on June 7, Secretary Rogers said that "I think that it is possible that the [Cambodian] war will be fought in a different place, and it is possible that it will continue with South Vietnamese forces and even possibly Thai forces, fighting a common enemy." Then Rogers offered this extraordinary interpretation of the events in Cambodia: "After all, the Nixon Doctrine is to encourage Asian nations to handle Asian problems, and to cooperate with each other, and that is what they are doing." Some weeks earlier, Kissinger had put it more bluntly during a White House discussion of Indochina: "The Nixon Doctrine means that Asian boys will fight Asian boys."

As it turned out, however, other Asians took less kindly to the plans the United States had for them. Nixon discovered this when Indonesia's President Suharto visited him in Washington on May 26. Suharto was greatly admired in the United States government because he had helped to lead the military coup that in 1965 overthrew the increasingly pro-Communist regime of President Sukarno. But Indonesia was now a non-aligned country, and Suharto had sponsored a conference of the foreign ministers of eleven Asian nations in Djakarta ten days before coming to Washington. Nixon, who evidently misunderstood Indonesian motivations, described that conference as a "splendid example of Asian nations attempting to find solutions for Asian problems." But Suharto quickly set Nixon straight. In a toast at the White House dinner, he explained Indonesia's position:

> Instead of the peace we hoped for, the threat of a new war is spreading. Cambodia is now being engulfed in the fires of war. . . . What is at issue here is the threat against the sovereignty and integrity of a nation, a threat against the right of the Khmer people to maintain the neutrality they have chosen. We cannot afford just to wait; for the sake of peace and stability in Southeast Asia, all efforts should be taken to prevent the war from widening and to insure the preservation of Cambodia's right to sovereignty and neutrality, among other things, by effecting the withdrawal of all foreign forces from Cambodia. It was on the basis of those considerations that Indonesia, as a nonaligned state which pursues an independent and active foreign policy, had taken the initiative to convene a Conference of Foreign Ministers of Asian countries.

At first, the White House assumed that Suharto was speaking simply about the withdrawal of American forces from Cambodia (already under way and to be completed within a month). But in a speech the next day at the National Press Club, Suharto made himself unmistakably clear: he said that "other foreign troops" must be prevented from replacing the Americans after their departure. Indonesian diplomats hastened to explain that Suharto was specifically thinking of the possibility that South Vietnamese forces would stay behind after June 30 and that they might be joined by Thai troops. And Suharto reminded his audience that the Djakarta conference had recommended the departure of *all* foreign troops from Cambodia, the convocation of an international peace conference, and the reactivation of the International Control Commission set up in Geneva in 1954.

As a matter of reality, an international peace conference was out of the question because neither North Vietnam, nor the Soviet Union, nor China wanted it. The United States, official protestations notwithstanding, likewise lost interest in such a conference after committing its forces to the May invasion. Nixon and Kissinger took the view that the Cambodian situation could no longer be settled outside the context of the Vietnam war. In other words, this meant that a Vietnamese peace had to be negotiated before anything could be done in Cambodia and, for that matter, Laos.

On the evening of June 3, Nixon, who apparently saw Cambodia more and more as a domestic political problem, went on nationwide television with his first formal report on the new war. It was necessary to convince the American people—and Congress—that the results had justified his earlier decision.

The day before, however, the president had to turn his attention to the nagging oil problem as he received, at the White House, the president of Venezuela, Rafael Caldera. The Venezuelan complained that the United States was unfairly favoring Canada over his country in oil imports, and asked, "Is Canada a first-class friend? Is Venezuela a second-class friend?" It was one of those questions that American diplomats, always taking Latin America for granted, kept leaving unresolved. No one in the government seemed ready to imagine that Venezuela would before long become a power in OPEC and turn the tables on the United States; Washington tended not to think ahead, and it took major crises to shake it out of complacencies. Meanwhile, Nixon disposed of the Venezuelan problem with broad assurances and pleasantries. In the White House dinner toast, he managed to combine references to Simón Bolívar, Lafayette, Lincoln, and the Chicago White Sox and their famous Venezuelan shortstop Luis Aparicio. He was in a good mood.

And in his television address on June 3, he was euphoric. The past weekend, he had met in San Clemente with Laird, General Abrams, and other advisers to discuss Cambodia and, he said, "based on General Abrams's report, I can now state that this has been the most successful operation of this long and very difficult war." It was the usual Nixonian hyperbole: everything he did was the "biggest" or the most "successful," or, certainly, a "first." Thus he told his audience that "as of today . . . all of our major military objectives have been achieved. . . . Our combined forces have moved with greater speed and success than we had planned; we have captured and destroyed far more in war material than we anticipated; and American and allied casualties have been far lower than we expected."

Now for the first time Nixon disclosed the actual scope of the Cambodian operation: the use of 74,000 troops in the invasion, 31,000 of them
Americans. (Previously, the assumption was that the American contingent barely exceeded 20,000 ground troops.) In describing the achievement of "all of our major military objectives," Nixon never mentioned
COSVN (the very acronym had suddenly vanished from the official lexi-
con), but he announced that, "in the month of May, in Cambodia alone,
we captured a total amount of enemy arms, equipment, ammunition, and
food nearly equal to what we captured in all of Vietnam in all of last year."
Again, one had to take Nixon's word on faith—and trust in his visual
effects. A Defense Department film showing captured equipment was
flashed on a screen behind him, and in effect, the president now became
a voice-over narrator: "This is some ammunition you see. We have captured more than 10 million rounds of ammunition. That is equal to the
enemy's expenditures of ammunition for nine months. And here also you
see a few of the over 15,000 rifles and machine guns and other weapons
we have captured. They will never be used against American boys in
Vietnam." (Nixon's rhetoric at times turned surrealistic. Once he noted
that the "reality" that Communist weapons captured in Cambodia will
not kill American boys in Vietnam was "brought home directly" to him
when he was talking with a New York labor leader: "His son died in
Vietnam this past February. He told me that had we moved earlier in
Cambodia, we might have captured the enemy weapon that killed his
son." This was an almost cruel appeal for the sympathies of parents with
sons in Vietnam, an impossible identification of a specific weapon with
a specific death in a wide-ranging war.)

The president continued his narration:

And now you are looking at some of the heavy mortars and rocket
launchers and recoilless rifles that have shelled U.S. base camps and
Vietnamese towns. We have seized over 2000 of these along with
90,000 rounds of ammunition. That is as much as the enemy fires in
a whole year. Had this war material made its way into South Vietnam
and had it been used against American and allied troops, U.S. casualties would have been vastly increased. And here you see rice, more
than 11 million pounds of rice we have obtained. This is more than
enough to feed all the enemy's combat battalions in Vietnam for over
three months. But this rice you see will not be feeding enemy troops
now, rather the war refugees you saw a minute ago. . . . It will take
the enemy months to rebuild his shattered installations and to replace
the equipment we have captured or destroyed.

Nobody could deny that the Cambodian incursion was highly damaging to the Communists; obviously they lost arms, ammunition, and food. But Nixon's extravagant claims not only misled the American people, but may have affected the president's own judgment regarding the future if, indeed, he believed his own words. Thus his conclusions were that the invasion "eliminated an immediate danger to the security of the remaining Americans in Vietnam"; that "we have won some precious time for the South Vietnamese to train and prepare themselves to carry the burden of their national defense, so that our American forces can be withdrawn"; and that "one of the most dramatic and heartening developments . . . has been the splendid performance of the South Vietnamese Army."

All these conclusions, however, were wrong. Nixon was caught in a trap of his own making. He had a political commitment at home to continue the withdrawals of American forces from Vietnam; these withdrawals also were a bargaining element in his Paris negotiations with the Vietnamese. He knew that no matter what really happened he had to keep pulling out American soldiers—while relying on air power to keep Hanoi in line—or risk an impossible political situation. Public opinion would not tolerate an indefinite war. It was, then, necessary for Nixon to justify and rationalize the withdrawal program—and the "success" of Cambodia provided such a justification. The trouble, of course, was that Hanoi's strategy was to encourage the withdrawals, saving its own strength for what it hoped would be a knock-out offensive once the ARVN was pretty much on its own.

In any event, Nixon informed his audience on June 3 that "as a result of the success of the Cambodian operations, Secretary Laird has resumed the withdrawal of American forces from Vietnam" and that "50,000 of the 150,000 I announced on April 20 will now be out by October 15." He added: "As long as the war goes on, we can expect some setbacks and some reversals. But, following the success of this effort, we can say now with confidence that we will keep our timetable for troop withdrawals." Once more, there was the carrot-and-stick offer to Hanoi: "The door to a negotiated peace remains wide open. Every offer we have made at the conference table, publicly or privately, I herewith affirm. . . . However, if their answer . . . is to increase their attacks in a way that jeopardizes the safety of our remaining forces in Vietnam, I shall . . . take strong and effective measures."

While Nixon concentrated on these victory claims, there were thoughtful senior officials in his administration, particularly in the State

Department, who were increasingly concerned over the future of the Khmer kingdom.

They calculated—correctly—that the immediate Communist objective was to establish a permanent base in the northern Cambodian provinces, east of the Mekong. On June 5, for example, the Communists captured Lomphat, the capital of the northeastern Tatanakari Province. This became possible when the Communists secured supply routes from North Vietnam over the Se Kong and northern Mekong, after taking the town of Attopeu in southern Laos. The Communists assured themselves of this new route through Laos while the Americans and the ARVN were busy in the Cambodian sanctuaries to the south. At the same time, the Communists were establishing revolutionary cells in villages in central and southern Cambodia, preparing themselves for the protracted civil war that Nixon had triggered with his Cambodian policies. Rapidly, then, the Communists began turning their losses in the sanctuaries into long-range advantage throughout Cambodia.

Officials in Washington who had been kept out of the decision-making process during April and May now started to warn the White House that Sihanouk enjoyed widespread popularity in Cambodia. The realization that the United States faced an enlarged Indochina war as a result of the Cambodian invasion resulted in the quiet creation of a permanent Southeast Asia Task Force headed by Marshall Green, whom Kissinger finally brought into the planning of policy. Its immediate concern was to determine how best—or whether—the United States could support the Lon Nol regime beyond the maintenance of air operations.

With Nixon's emergency authority for $7.9 million in military aid to Cambodia expiring on June 30, the administration began preparing a request to Congress for expanded assistance in the new fiscal year. Congress, however, was not in a receptive mood. In fact, it was beginning to challenge the administration over the American involvement in Indochina. Nixon was already facing the McGovern-Hatfield amendment, and in mid-May, an amendment to the military sales bill introduced by Frank Church, the Idaho Democrat, and John Sherman Cooper, the Kentucky Republican, called for a ban on funds to finance any instruction of Cambodian forces. This would prevent the U.S. government from paying Thais or South Vietnamese for training Cambodians. The amendment also would ban further U.S. combat air activity over Cambodia. The Cooper-Church amendment became a major thorn in the side of the administration. Late in May, the Senate approved a section of the Cooper-Church amendment providing specifically that no funds could be expended for Cambodia after July 1, 1970, without congressional authorization. This blocked Nixon from having recourse again, as he had done during May, to presidential "determinations" that aid to Phnom Penh was in the national interest. On June 10, the Senate rejected a proposal authorizing him to send American troops back into Cambodia, if he deemed it necessary to protect American forces in Vietnam.

On June 22, the Senate voted overwhelmingly to terminate the so-called Tonkin Gulf Resolution it had passed in August 1964 on Lyndon Johnson's demand. That resolution had in effect given Johnson the power to send hundreds of thousands of American troops to Vietnam. Now even the legality of the war was in question. Three days later, however, the administration won a victory when the Senate rejected the McGovern-Hatfield "end-the-war" amendment. The senators were chipping away at Nixon's authority to continue the war, but they were not yet ready to tie his hands altogether. On Cambodia, however, they were obdurate. On June 29, the Senate rejected a proposal allowing the president to assist "other nations such as Thailand" in *their* support of Cambodia. The Nixon Doctrine of encouraging regional cooperation had been invoked in support of this maneuver, but the proposal was beaten by five votes, ruling out the plans for engaging Thai "volunteers" (many senators called them "mercenaries") in Cambodia at American expense. On June 30, the full Cooper-Church amendment was approved by the Senate. But the House, where the administration had more support, rejected it on July 7—which, among other things, made it possible for the United States to go on bombing Cambodia. The way was now also open for congressional approval of military assistance to Cambodia.

If any confirmation was needed that North Vietnam had decided to wage an Indochina-wide war as a result of the American intervention in Cambodia, it was provided by General Vo Nguyen Giap, in two articles appearing on May 31 and June 1 in *Nhan Dan*. Giap declared that Hanoi will "fight shoulder to shoulder with the fraternal peoples of Laos and Cambodia for genuine independence and freedom . . . and to lead the national liberation undertaking of the Indochinese people to complete victory." This suggested that Hanoi would consolidate the three Indochinese wars into one coordinated military effort, and it bore out the earlier predictions that the American attack in Cambodia would radically change the North Vietnamese priorities. Both the CIA and the State Department's intelligence bureau had argued from the outset that the Communists would no longer be content to regard Cambodia and Laos as secondary war theaters, but they had been overruled by the White

House, which had accepted the Pentagon view that most of the enemy forces in Cambodia would be used to defend the supply lines and border sanctuaries.

On June 30, as scheduled, American forces completed their withdrawal from Cambodia, ending the two-month operation. The military results of the sweep were at best uncertain, but the overall situation in Indochina had been totally altered. Undaunted, Nixon went on to claim success in a report issued from San Clemente on the day the operation was completed:

> Together with the South Vietnamese, the Armed Forces of the United States have just completed successfully the destruction of enemy base areas along the Cambodian–South Vietnam frontier. . . . The allied sweeps into the North Vietnamese and Vietcong base areas along the Cambodian–South Vietnamese border:
> —Will save American and allied lives in the future;
> —Will assure that the withdrawal of American troops from South Vietnam can proceed on schedule;
> —Will enable our program of Vietnamization to continue on its current timetable;
> —Should enhance the prospects for a just peace.

Nixon proceeded to explain at considerable length why the operation had been undertaken. He squarely blamed the Communists: "Not only the clear evidence of Communist actions but supporting data screened from more than six tons of subsequently captured Communist documents leaves no doubt that the Communists' move against the Cambodian government preceded the U.S. action against the base areas." He said nothing of American-supported South Vietnamese incursions into Cambodia during April nor did he relate that planning for the invasion of the sanctuaries had begun on the highest military level in Saigon and Washington within days of Sihanouk's fall from power.

The alternative to the sweep, according to Nixon, would have been that "the war would be a good deal further from over than it is today." And, "Had we stood by and let the enemy act with impunity in Cambodia, we would be facing a truly bleak situation." This was Nixon at his optimistic best, reporting to the nation that, yes, he had been right in what he had done—despite all the initial criticism.

Inevitably, Nixon had to make a political point as well:

> When the decision to go into Cambodia was announced on April 30, we anticipated broad disagreement and dissent within the society. . . . But the majority of the Americans supported that decision and,

now that the Cambodian operation is over, I believe there is a wide measure of understanding of the necessity for it. Although there remains disagreement about its long-term significance, about the cost to our society of having taken this action—there can be little disagreement now over the immediate military success that has been achieved. With American ground operations in Cambodia ended, we shall move forward with our plan to end the war in Vietnam and to secure the just peace on which all Americans are united.

The next day, July 1, Nixon announced that he was naming David Bruce, a highly respected American patrician who had served as ambassador to West Germany, England, and France, as chief of the American delegation to the Paris peace talks. Bruce's appointment was intended as a major gesture—there had been no chief American delegate in Paris for nearly six months—and Nixon was launching a diplomatic offensive. It was a skillful move, and the president stressed that Bruce "will have great flexibility in the conduct of his talks"; he failed to mention, of course, that Kissinger would remain the chief secret negotiator. But pointedly, he added that "we hope that this move on our part will be reciprocated by a similar move on the part of the North Vietnamese." It was a veiled invitation to Le Duc Tho to return to Paris.

In a televised conversation that evening with network correspondents, President Nixon was statesmanlike as he discussed the outlook, but at the same time, he reiterated the doctrine that there was a close relationship between negotiations and the situation on the battlefield. He also managed to tie diplomacy to domestic politics:

Put yourself in the position of the enemy. Also, put yourself in the position of an historian. . . . You will generally find that negotiations occur, negotiations which end war, only when the balance of power changes significantly, only when one party or the other concludes that as a result of the shift in the military balance they no longer have an opportunity to accomplish their goal militarily, and therefore, they had best negotiate. Now, I think one of the positive benefits of the Cambodian operation is that it has changed the military balance. How much it has changed in the minds of the enemy remains to be seen. I do not say it has changed it enough so that they will negotiate. I think it might help. Only time will tell.

But putting myself—again, looking at the enemy, I am convinced that if we were to tell the enemy now, the North Vietnamese, that within, as for example the McGovern-Hatfield resolution, that by the end of this year all Americans will be gone, well, I can assure you that the enemy isn't going to negotiate in Paris at all. . . . They are going to wait until we get out because they know that at the end of this year the South Vietnamese won't be ready to defend the country by themselves. But if, on the other hand, the enemy feels that we are going to stay there long enough for the South Vietnamese to be strong enough to handle their own defense, then I think they have a real incentive to negotiate, because if they have to negotiate with a strong, vigorous South Vietnamese government, the deal they can make with them isn't going to be as good as the deal they might make now.

There was a certain logic here, but a flawed logic. It was based upon the assumptions that the Cambodian invasion had really hurt Hanoi as badly as the president professed to believe, that South Vietnam would one day be able to handle its own defense, and that Saigon would negotiate anything at all in the event that it became self-sufficient. But to President Thieu, the war was not negotiable under any circumstances so long as the United States supported him. And Hanoi, of course, knew this.

Nixon's diplomatic offensive was wide-ranging. Just as the last American soldier left Cambodia, he dispatched Secretary of State Rogers to Asia with the mission of reassuring America's allies that the war had not been widened as a result of Cambodia, but that, on the contrary, the United States had acted to circumscribe it. The other message carried by Rogers—a more believable one—was that the United States would not abandon South Vietnam or any other ally. Rogers made these points at a ministerial conference of the Southeast Asia Treaty Organization in Manila, at a meeting in Saigon of countries contributing forces to the Vietnam war, and, finally, in Tokyo.

In Saigon, President Thieu told Rogers how well things were going in the Vietnam war since the invasion of the Cambodian sanctuaries. Then Rogers was flown to a village in the Mekong Delta to be briefed by local officials on the progress of pacification. At this Asian "Potemkin village" scene, well-scrubbed Vietnamese children waved flags and applauded, South Vietnamese and American colonels showed Rogers on multicolored maps how much of the delta territory was secure from the Viet Cong; huge water-filled vats kept bottles of Coca-Cola cool for the thirsty visitors. Colonel Michael Collins, the pilot of the first Apollo spacecraft to land on the moon and now assistant secretary of state for public affairs, stood up to tell the Vietnamese about the space program. With gunship helicopters protectively hovering overhead, it was a beautifully incongruous affair. But an American adviser, a battle-weary captain, offered a touch of reality. Sitting in his jeep, a beer bottle in his hand, he remarked to a passing newsman: "This is bullshit, man. . . . There's no pacification here. . . . At night, you wouldn't dare get in your jeep to drive ten miles down the highway. . . . The Cong would get your ass. . . . Why, I can't get my provincial forces platoon to move a step out of the village after dark. The guys know the Cong are all around; besides, I bet you that half of my provincials are Viet Cong themselves when night falls."

It was not considered wise for Rogers to visit Phnom Penh, but Marshall Green was dispatched to confer with Lon Nol. A man not easily impressed, Green returned to report that Lon Nol *was* impressive—a serious, Western-type leader who reminded him of President Suharto. Lon Nol, not surprisingly, had pleaded for urgent military and economic aid, and he sent his foreign minister, Yem Sambaur, to Saigon to have lunch with Rogers and press the case.

This marked the end of the 1970 phase of the Cambodian tragedy, a pathetic ending of what the Nixon administration had envisaged as a decisive turn in the Indochina war.

Chapter 11

Much as President Nixon was overwhelmed by the problems of Indochina and the domestic political reactions, his attention was distracted by a major crisis simultaneously developing in the Middle East. Soviet pilots were still flying combat missions to deflect Israeli penetration raids, Soviet-supplied SAM-3 antiaircraft-missile batteries were helping to turn the balance of power in the air against Israel, perhaps as many as 15,000 Soviet military personnel had been brought to Egypt, and the Russians were establishing a naval and air base at Alexandria. Moscow's rising military presence in the Middle East not only tended to destabilize the Arab-Israeli situation, but challenged American preeminence in the Mediterranean. In addition to the growing size of the Soviet Mediterranean fleet, Soviet long-range reconnaissance aircraft from Alexandria closely tracked the movements of the United States Sixth Fleet, often flying alongside American warships and carrier planes.

It was unclear, however, whether this jump in Soviet activities in the Middle East was a response to the deepening United States involvement in Indochina, simply represented new support for President Nasser, or was a combination of both. In any event, the Nixon-Kissinger hopes for policy linkages with the Kremlin were not working out, and the new round of Soviet-American talks on the Middle East was not producing results. Washington's concern over this situation was aggravated by the realization that, sooner or later, a decision would have to be made to resupply Israel with Phantoms and Skyhawks.

On April 29, just as he was putting the finishing touches on the Cambodia speech, Nixon had to turn his attention to the Middle East: he instructed Kissinger, Rogers, and Laird to undertake an "immediate and full" evaluation of the situation in that region. It was only five weeks since the last such evaluation, when Rogers had announced that deliveries of planes to Israel were being held "in abeyance." Although the State Department had been busy throughout April trying to develop a new peace plan for the Middle East—this paralleled Kissinger's resumed negotiations with Dobrynin—it was now obvious that things were getting out of hand. The Russians seemed to be playing a two-track game, but the administration was evidently late in understanding it. Only on May 1, the day American troops moved into the Cambodian Fishhook, did the United States ambassador in Moscow, Jacob D. Beam, finally present to senior Soviet officials expressions of "grave concern" over Middle Eastern developments.

The Russians ignored Beam's demarche. If anything, they quickened the rhythm of their military deliveries to Egypt. The United States, however, remained hesitant. The new peace plan was taking shape ever so slowly; it was still Rogers's baby, and neither Nixon nor Kissinger was showing much interest in it. Consequently, the "immediate and full" review of the Middle Eastern situation that Nixon ordered was bogging down in the bureaucracy. Nothing happened during May. The State Department was divided, as usual, between Arabists and pro-Israelis. The official line remained that the United States was pursuing an "even-handed" policy toward the Arabs and Israel, but it was uncertain how this related to the mounting Soviet support of the Egyptian cause and the continuing arms shipments.

On June 7, Rogers, appearing on a television program, said that a decision on Israeli requests for planes would be made "fairly soon," but he dampened Jerusalem's hopes by warning that the sale of the aircraft would be carried out in a "balanced and measured way so that we don't signal to the Arabs that we are so behind Israel that we'll support them no matter what they do." The standing Israeli request was for twenty-five Phantoms and a hundred Skyhawks, but Rogers was, in effect, telling them that they would not be given the whole lot, particularly if they persisted in their raids on Egypt. He was also linking the planes to his incipient peace plan, hinting that serious negotiations might begin in two or three weeks, and signaling to the Russians that he regarded their presence in Egypt as "a serious matter." But Rogers was all too vague. Ever careful, he remarked only that the Russians were flying "in patterns that would suggest operational patterns," adding that "we would hope that the Soviet Union responds favorably to discussions we've had, and that they desist from those operational flights, and that they don't inject any further Russian personnel into the area. . . . We don't know what their response is going to be."

Two days later, on June 9, an entirely different sort of Middle Eastern crisis erupted, this time in Jordan. Palestinian guerrillas identified with the radicalized Popular Front for the Liberation of Palestine (PFLP) had risen against King Hussein, a moderate Middle Eastern ruler, and a ferocious battle was raging throughout Amman, the capital. The main issue was Hussein's ban on the use of Jordanian territory by the PFLP guerrillas to stage raids against Israel; the raids had brought severe Israeli reprisals against Jordan, and Hussein was determined to put an end to this vicious circle. Besides, the king feared for his throne. Much of Jordan's population was made up of Palestinian refugees who had fled their homes when Israel became an independent state in 1948 and their descendants. The Palestinians, generally better educated than the Jordanians, were important in Jordanian society and in the civil service. The younger ones were gravitating toward liberation organizations such as the PFLP or the more moderate Palestine Liberation Organization (PLO), led by Yasir Arafat. All in all, they posed a danger to Hussein.

In Washington, the concern was that the well-armed guerrillas could either force Hussein to abandon his policy of preventing their anti-Israeli operations or overthrow him. Jordan was one of the few Arab countries with which the United States maintained diplomatic relations; in fact, the relationship was quite cordial.

Both the United States and Israel had an interest in keeping Hussein in power because he was a moderating influence. Despite the fact that Jordan lost the West Bank to the Israelis in the 1967 war, there were occasional secret contacts between Jerusalem and Amman, and as a practical matter the two governments had worked out a tacit live-and-let-live understanding. It was shattered only when Israeli planes hit Jordanian targets in retaliation for Palestinian guerrilla raids. Hussein had imposed his ban on the raids earlier in the year, using his army to patrol the Jordanian side of the border so that the guerrillas could be kept in check. But Hussein's fall or his capitulation to the guerrillas could unhinge the whole Middle Eastern situation.

From the United States viewpoint, the Jordanian crisis was compounded by the fact that the PFLP guerrillas, outspokenly anti-American, had taken over Amman's Intercontinental Hotel and made a group of Americans, including newsmen, their hostages. On the second day of the fighting, Major Robert P. Perry, assistant military attaché at the American embassy, was killed by the guerrillas, who fired automatic weapons through the locked doors of his house. There were 535 other Americans in Jordan, and there was fear in Washington over their safety. Many American homes in Amman were looted. On the morning of June 10, Harry L. Odell, the American chargé d'affaires, radioed, "We are now hearing tank fire and the chancery building itself has been hit by sniper fire."

On June 11, a Thursday, the Jordan crisis became the principal preoccupation in Washington. Nixon and Kissinger met for an hour at the White House to discuss possible civilian or military operations to rescue the Americans. Odell had decided against evacuating them by chartered airliner from Amman to Beirut because of the heavy fighting in the city; the road to the airport was insecure. Under State Department rules, it is the ambassador, or the chargé, who has the power to order an evacuation if he deems it necessary and reasonably safe. In this case, Odell did not think it safe, and he so advised Washington. The other option facing Nixon was a paratroop drop on the Amman airport, or the landing of airborne troops to secure it, and the opening of a corridor to the city to protect the evacuation. This occupied the attention of WASAG throughout the day. As part of "initial planning," the 82nd Airborne Division at Fort Bragg, North Carolina, was placed on alert. Likewise, consideration was given to ferrying marines aboard helicopters from the aircraft carrier *Forrestal,* cruising in the eastern Mediterranean, to the Amman airport. This, however, would have required the use of Israeli territory for refueling, something the administration preferred to avoid.

In the end, Washington was spared the decision. Hussein, whose bedouin army did quite well in battling the guerrillas though it had briefly lost the control of most of Amman, worked out an accommodation with the PFLP, the hostages were released, and the fighting ended. But the affair was far from over. The price Hussein paid for a truce and the release of the foreign hostages was the removal of two of his generals from their commands (the guerrillas had demanded the dismissal of four senior officials). And it was left unclear whether Hussein's army would go on preventing guerrilla raids against Israel.

The Jordanian crisis in June was the first major test involving Palestinian guerrillas. That Hussein was able to control them to some degree on that occasion was viewed with relief, but the main point—that the Palestinians were a force that could not be ignored forever—was overlooked by nearly everyone in the West and in Israel. As refugees and as an incipient political force, they had been forgotten by the world since the 1948 partition of the former Palestine mandate. Arab governments and politicians had used them for their own purposes—mainly as anti-Israeli propaganda—but without much tangible humanitarian concern. In Israel, only a few *sabra* leaders gave serious thought to the long-range aspects of the Palestinian question. And in Washington, the only senior official to take the Palestinians seriously at that point was Under Secretary of State Elliot Richardson, who had spent much time on Middle Eastern matters. When he left the State Department shortly after the Jordan crisis to become secretary of health, education and welfare, Richardson drafted a secret memorandum for Rogers suggesting that the United States devise ways to develop some form of communication with the Palestinians. "My last will and testament to the department on the Middle East was a paper which said in substance that the fallacy of the great-powers policy or of the involved powers in dealing with the situation from the establishment of the state of Israel to date had been the failure to recognize that the aggrieved party were the Palestinians," Richardson later explained. "They were a victim of the fact that they were stateless. I had been struck repeatedly at the State Department with the tendency on the part of the diplomatic process, internationally, to proceed on the assumption that a state is a state is a state. . . . Had the Palestinians been treated as if they were a sovereign state, even if they'd been reduced to the Gaza Strip or an enclave on the West Bank where they could have a capital and a flag, the situation might have been faced up to. It seemed to me we had blown chance after chance. . . . My argument was that we would never achieve a real settlement in the Middle East that did not deal with the situation of the Palestinians, and I thought we ought to find ways of exploring what the solutions could be. Although we had, by neglect, created a situation in which there were very few moderate Palestinians left to talk to, I thought that we ought to set about establishing some contacts and we should consider what the implications of this were—especially for Jordan."

Though there was no follow-up on Richardson's ideas about the Palestinians, U.S. policy *was* beginning to turn to the possibility of resuming U.N. mediation in the Egyptian-Israeli conflict. The idea was to bring Gunnar Jarring back into the picture. This was one of the elements of the new Rogers Plan on which Richardson and Sisco had been quietly working. On June 12, Sisco and Ambassador Dobrynin discussed it at some length at a lunch at Sisco's house. And the United States also kept pressing the Russians to reduce their aerial activities in Egypt as part of a broader effort to reduce Middle Eastern tensions, the American view being that diplomacy could not move forward so long as the danger of a clash between Soviet and Israeli aircraft existed. And for a while, progress was made. The Israelis, in part because of the losses they were taking from the SAM-3s, abandoned most of their deep-penetration raids. In mid-June, American intelligence officers reported that the number of sorties flown over Egypt by Soviet pilots had dropped substantially and current flights were mainly training missions. (The Russians were flying advanced MiG-23s with Egyptian markings.)

On June 25, encouraged by preliminary diplomatic results, the United States formally launched its new peace proposal for the Middle East. The plan for a temporary cease-fire of at least ninety days between Israel and Egypt and Jordan was unveiled at a news conference by Secretary Rogers. The basic concept was that a cessation of hostilities would allow Jarring to engage in a serious mediation effort. (Syria, which never accepted, even in principle, the 1967 U.N. Security Council resolution on a Middle East settlement, was not included in the American proposal. In fact, Israeli and Syrian forces had begun fighting heavy tank and artillery duels on the Golan Heights the day before.)

Prior to the public announcement, the main elements of the new United States plan were made known to the Israeli, Egyptian, and Jordanian governments as well as to the Soviet Union, Britain, and France. There was no prior *acceptance* by any of the parties to the conflict, but this had not been requested or expected.

The State Department realized, at the same time, that Israel might pose the most serious obstacle to a cease-fire. The Israelis might fear that a temporary truce would help the Egyptians consolidate their defenses and, with Soviet assistance, move to offensive operations. They might suspect that because of political considerations President Nasser in Cairo would not accept a cease-fire at all (Jerusalem was wary of premature one-sided commitments, although the Americans argued that the Israelis had nothing to lose by showing their goodwill). And, third and most important, there was Washington's last-minute decision to continue withholding new planes from Israel.

This decision was taken a few days before Rogers mounted the rostrum at the State Department to announce his peace plan. American policy-makers had concluded that the entire diplomatic effort would be undermined if they coupled the unveiling of the peace proposals with the announcement that additional aircraft would be supplied to Israel; it might induce Moscow to increase further its military deliveries to Egypt, and it might also create new problems for King Hussein. American officials carefully explained their reasoning to Yitzhak Rabin, the Israeli ambassador, who simultaneously was given private assurances that the United States would make aircraft available to Israel if a cease-fire could not be achieved within a reasonable time or if it broke down after going into effect. The Israelis refrained from public complaints but made it clear that they were not rushing into any cease-fire decisions.

What the United States had in mind diplomatically, after a cease-fire, was the so-called proximity talks among the parties. This was not a new idea, but there were no others at the time. Inasmuch as the Arabs still refused to sit down with the Israelis, the notion was that Jarring would shuttle among the three parties—possibly even in the same hotel in the same city—with specific proposals. The only really new element was the cease-fire.

Having launched its peace plan, the United States now went to work to win its acceptance. It made a point of disregarding a statement made by Nasser during a visit to Libya (on the day Rogers was making his announcement) that Egyptian forces would soon cross the Suez Canal, and that Israel must abandon the Golan Heights even before it left the Sinai Desert. The official State Department comment on Nasser's speech was that "we are waiting for a considered reaction to our initiative." And the responsibility for pushing the peace proposals was left to Joseph Sisco, inasmuch as Rogers soon embarked on a two-week world tour.

Two days after Rogers left, Nixon went out of his way to stress the dangers in the Middle East—and his rambling language was strikingly different in tone from Rogers's. In a televised meeting with correspondents of the three networks in Los Angeles on July 1, the president said:

> when we then look at it in terms of Israelis versus Arabs, moderate Arabs versus radical Arabs, and whoever would think that there would be somebody more radical than the Syrians, within the radical Arab states, *fedayeen* that are more radical, the superradicals—when we think of all these factors, we can see what a very difficult situation it is. . . . Once the balance of power shifts where Israel is weaker than its neighbors, there will be war. Therefore, it is in U.S. interests to maintain the balance of power, and we will maintain that balance of power. That is why as the Soviet Union moves in to support the U.A.R., it makes it necessary for the United States to evaluate what the Soviet Union does, and once that balance of power is upset, we will do what is necessary to maintain Israel's strength vis-à-vis its neighbors, not because we want Israel to be in a position to wage war—that is not it—but because that is what will deter its neighbors from attacking it. . . . Israel must withdraw to borders, borders that are defensible, and when we consider all those factors and then put into the equation the fact that the Russians seem to have an interest in moving into the Mediterranean, it shows you why this subject is so complex and so difficult.

·   ·   ·

Where Rogers tried to handle the Israeli military situation with utmost care, Nixon was openly promising the Israelis arms if the Soviets kept supplying Cairo. Where Rogers was being diplomatic about the Soviet role in the Middle East, Nixon was emphasizing the perilous nature of Russian moves into the region.

Then it was Kissinger's turn. The president's national-security adviser assembled White House reporters covering Nixon's stay at San Clemente to inform them that a goal of American policy was to "expel" the Russians from the Middle East. He did this in the form of a "backgrounder," a session with newsmen in which his remarks were not publicly attributed to him. Backgrounders are a standard Washington procedure—they are used by government officials who want to release information or opinion without having their names or affiliations publicized—and Kissinger was a master practitioner. It was a convenient way of making his views known without the encumbrance of being officially responsible for them. It was also a way of usurping Rogers's prerogatives as the ostensible American foreign-policy spokesman. However, it was no secret in the news profession or among State Department officials and foreign diplomats that Kissinger was the author of the White House foreign-policy backgrounders. He had not yet reached the point where he was allowed by the White House to speak on the record, but the backgrounders served their purpose.

Both Nixon and Kissinger, much more bluntly, were sending a message to the Soviet Union to watch its step in the Middle East. But Kissinger overdid it. Rogers learned of the remark when he received the text of the Kissinger briefing by radio-teletype aboard his plane over the Pacific. It was one of the few times when he became truly angry. Kissinger was torpedoing the peace proposals, he thought: not only were the Russians likely to break off the Washington negotiations, but the Egyptians themselves might become suspicious of the cease-fire if it meant that the United States was trying at the same time to deprive them of Soviet military assistance. Everybody on the secretary's plane was acutely aware of his fury; he immediately dispatched a top-secret telegram to Nixon.

Then, in London, Rogers had an opportunity to set *his* views on the record. At a news conference on July 11, the secretary remarked that the United States had "never thought of expelling" the Russians from the Middle East; Rogers was trying to establish a difference between expulsion, which could almost be construed as an act of force, and the American effort to lessen Soviet influence in the region as much as possible.

Still, Rogers and the White House were in agreement that Moscow was playing a dangerous game in the Middle East. In recent weeks, the Russians and the Egyptians had begun deploying SAM-3 batteries on the Egyptian side of the Suez Canal; heretofore these missiles had been stationed farther back, around Cairo, Alexandria, and the Aswan Dam. This forward movement suggested that the Egyptians wanted to cover the Suez area, effectively preventing Israeli aircraft from crossing the canal or even approaching it too closely; it gave the Egyptians an immediate military advantage if no cease-fire could be achieved, and it placed them in a better position should the truce be negotiated. What American diplomats did not realize was that the redeployment of the SAMs formed part of an intricate Soviet-Egyptian diplomatic and military strategy. Thus in Moscow, Kosygin was encouraging Nasser to accept the cease-fire under maximal Soviet protection. The Russians were convinced that this would make it impossible for Israel to attack Egypt from the air under any circumstances because, once deployed on the canal, the SAMs would not be withdrawn. The breakdown of a cease-fire would thus make no difference to the Egyptians. Besides, the SAMs provided a superb screen for Egyptian ground forces should Nasser ever decide to try to cross the canal. But at that stage all Rogers could say about the SAMs' movement was that "clearly, the situation is serious."

On July 20, Nixon called an unscheduled news conference at his White House office. There was still no answer from Cairo or Moscow on the cease-fire proposals. The president insisted that the strategic balance of power in the area had not *yet* been upset, but he made a point of saying that the continued flow to Egypt of Soviet arms and personnel to man them "causes us concern." Nixon repeated once more that a change in this balance of power could lead to war, then addressed himself to the Russians:

> As far as the Soviet Union . . . and the United States [are] concerned . . . we want to avoid a confrontation every place in the world. . . . An arms escalation, and particularly the insertion of troops, men, into the Mideast increases the risks of a confrontation. . . . That is why we are putting such emphasis on our peace initiative. That is why we have not announced any sale of planes or delivery of planes to Israel at this time, because we want to give that peace initiative every chance to succeed.

Next, the president took it upon himself to extricate Kissinger from the San Clemente indiscretion, but in so doing he only confused the issue further:

I know that there was some concern expressed about the use of the
word "expelled" in one of the backgrounders that was given. I read
the backgrounder and I support exactly what was said because what
we meant to say there was simply this: that in any peace settlement,
once a peace settlement is made, then there will be no need for the
forces of other nations to be in these countries. The use of the word
"expelled" was not with the idea of using armed force for that purpose but to negotiate any peaceful settlement, the removal of these
forces which if they remained there we believe might increase the
chance of a confrontation.

During the last week of July, both Egypt and Jordan agreed in principle to the American peace plan. The Egyptians did so partly on Soviet
advice, but also because the protracted war of attrition had been costly
to them. Israel had no real choice but to go along with the plan, and the
Israeli cabinet voted to accept the American proposals though with mis-
givings. The Israelis were not entirely wrong, for the hastily drawn-up
cease-fire contained major gaps, and American diplomats, rushing all
parties to proclaim the cease-fire, had failed to do their homework.

The idea was that during the ninety-day cease-fire, while diplomatic
mediation by Gunnar Jarring would be starting, both sides would refrain
from building up their forces in the thirty-two-mile truce zones on each
side of the Suez Canal. Nixon explained the situation at a news conference in San Clemente on July 30: "Some concern has been expressed by
Israeli government officials that if they agree to a cease-fire, that they run
the risk of having a military buildup occur during the cease-fire. We and
others have attempted to assure them that that would not be the case. If
there's a cease-fire, a natural proposition connected with that, a condition
with that, is that there will be a military standstill during that period."
And the next day he made the American position even more explicit: "It
is an integral part of our cease-fire proposal that neither side is to use the
cease-fire period to improve its military position in the area of the cease-
fire lines. All would have to refrain from emplacing new missiles or other
installations and from undertaking a military buildup of any kind in such
an area."

What Nixon did not reveal publicly was that the United States had
worked out a secret agreement with the three governments specifically
providing for a "standstill" cease-fire. The word "standstill," though
used by Nixon, did not appear in any of the official documents. Again,
Israel found itself in a position where it had to accept the American
assurances, including a private commitment that the United States would

be responsible for the verification of the agreement and the rectification of any violations that might occur. A senior Israeli diplomat who participated in the cease-fire negotiations later remarked, "For Israel, the main guarantee of the cease-fire was United States prestige. It was all done hurriedly, without a million documents, and no established verification procedures."

But even before the cease-fire took effect, there was a last minute "mini crisis." After U Thant, the secretary general of the United Nations, sent a letter to the Security Council early in August informing it that the three governments had accepted the peace formula, the Israelis demurred. They said they would be bound only by their own language contained in the formal reply to the United States, language that insisted on the inviolability of the cease-fire. They also wanted assurances that the Soviet Union would respect the agreement even though it was not a party to it. For a while, it seemed that the agreement was coming unglued. The Israelis were talking about ambiguities, about the uncertainty of the Soviet position. And when the United States moved to correct this situation, it committed two major errors: Rogers failed to obtain from Dobrynin an absolutely firm Soviet commitment on the inviolability of the agreement; and it pressed for an immediate cease-fire albeit it had not yet made the required surveillance arrangements to monitor the truce.

The cease-fire finally went into effect on August 7, 1970. But, unbeknown to the United States and Israel, Egyptian violations started at once. Nasser evidently had not had enough time to deploy all the SAM-3s he wanted in the truce zone before the cease-fire; he was able to move only between ten and sixteen batteries prior to the standstill order (each SAM battery usually consists of six missile launchers). On the nights of August 7 and 8, fifteen more batteries were deployed near the canal in a clear cease-fire violation. But the United States was unaware of this activity because in the rush of things it had failed to set its photographic reconnaissance operations immediately into motion. It took Washington more than a week of complex negotiations with Britain and Cypriot President Makarios (known as "Black Mac" around the State Department) to obtain permission for United States high-flying reconnaissance aircraft—the U-2s and SR-71s—to use the Royal Air Force base at Akrotiri on Cyprus for policing the truce. Likewise, there were delays in launching a space satellite in the proper orbit over the Middle East to supplement observation by the planes. It was three days after the cease-fire before the United States got the planes in the air.

Israeli intelligence, on the other hand, was very much in phase. Photographing the Egyptian truce zone at an oblique angle from planes flying over their side of the canal—a difficult task—the Israelis soon discovered that the Egyptians were steadily deploying SAM batteries in the forbidden area. Alarmed, they instantly informed the United States, which they regarded as a guarantor of the truce, of their findings, and demanded a rectification through the withdrawal of batteries emplaced after the cease-fire and an immediate halt to the violations. Their earlier fears about the cease-fire were being confirmed.

The American reaction was bizarre. Washington simply refused to believe that the Egyptians were violating the truce. Since the United States had no aerial photography from the pretruce period, it had no basis for comparison, yet American officials refused to accept Israeli "before-and-after" photography as proof of violations. It was a curious refusal to accept that the Russians (obviously involved in the Egyptian operation) were breaking their word. And, of course, Rogers was suddenly unsure whether or not Dobrynin had committed his government to help enforce the cease-fire. The Russians had, in effect, outmaneuvered the Americans over the ambiguities surrounding the truce agreement.

The Israelis were furious. In mid-August, Prime Minister Meir dispatched to Washington her foreign policy adviser, Simcha Dinitz, to assist Ambassador Rabin in presenting the Israeli case. But the administration still would not be convinced, even as intelligence officers studied aerial photographs submitted by the Israelis. On August 19, the State Department stated that there was "no conclusive evidence" of Egyptian violations as charged by Israel. After this body blow, Jerusalem began talking about denouncing the cease-fire unilaterally unless there was an Egyptian rollback. And Israeli anger immediately affected the second stage of the American peace proposal, the United Nations mediation.

This mediation process was begun when on August 25 Jarring met with Egyptian negotiators and then, separately, with Israeli diplomats at the United Nations in New York. But there was absolutely no progress. And the White House again added to the confusion. This was the day that Joseph Sisco chose to propose in a backgrounder that a joint American-Soviet peace-keeping force might be useful in guaranteeing a Middle East settlement. Interestingly, the backgrounder was held at San Clemente, where Nixon was vacationing, and it was quickly surmised that Sisco was expressing the president's—and Kissinger's—views. Sisco's trial balloon, if that is what it was, overshadowed Jarring's mediation efforts and caused deep resentment among the Israelis and Arabs. The next day, the White House disavowed Sisco, but the damage was done. Besides, the question remained whether Nixon and Kissinger were using Sisco for new devious diplomacy—six weeks after Kissinger had urged the "expulsion" of the Soviets from the Middle East. At the United Nations, Jarring met on August 26 with the Jordanian negotiating team, but again, there were no encouraging results. And the following day, the whole negotiating process crumbled as Israel recalled its chief negotiator on the grounds that no peace talks were possible so long as the Egyptians were violating the cease-fire.

On September 1, the State Department discovered that, after all, Israel had been right: the Egyptians *were* massively violating the truce. The CIA, for example, found that at least fifteen batteries of Soviet missile launchers were introduced in the truce zone between August 15 and 27. A formal State Department declaration said the United States was now "satisfied" on the basis of photographic and electronic evidence that Cairo had violated the standstill—an embarrassing reversal from the earlier position, and an admission of the inadequacies of American intelligence.

Now, the problem was how to salvage the Suez truce. In San Clemente, Nixon presided that same day over an emergency meeting on the Middle East. Rogers, Sisco, Helms, Kissinger, Admiral Moorer, and Vice President Agnew were in attendance. The group had before it U-2 and satellite pictures of the Suez area. No decisions were announced, but in Washington, the Senate overwhelmingly passed the Military Procurement Authorization Act with a clause granting Israel the right to receive nearly unlimited United States military aid on highly favorable terms to counter "past, present or future" Soviet arms deliveries to the Arabs. The administration had sought this authorization as part of its overall Middle East strategy.

The administration was sufficiently realistic by now to know that the Egyptians and the Russians would not withdraw the illegal missile batteries from the truce zone. In the face of this reality, the administration, now armed with congressional authority to supply Israel with arms, quickly concluded that the way to save the truce was to resume weapons deliveries to Jerusalem. It rushed specialized electronic equipment to Israel to help it to monitor the truce and to protect Israeli aircraft from SAM fire. This was ECM (electronic countermeasures) equipment of the type that had not been previously given to Israel. Also supplied were Shrike air-to-ground missiles designed to neutralize the SAMs.

Meanwhile, American diplomatic action centered on preventing new violations, keeping the truce going, and creating conditions under which

Jarring could resume his mediation. On September 3, notes were delivered to the Soviet Foreign Ministry in Moscow by Ambassador Beam and to the Egyptians by the senior American diplomat in Cairo, requesting both countries to halt the violations. The Israelis kept insisting that they would not meet again with Jarring until there was a missile rollback in the truce zone. It was a stalemate, but at that point, the Americans were willing to settle for the maintenance of the cease-fire and no more violations. If the administration had any hopes at all that Jarring's mediation could be resumed before too long, another Middle East crisis erupted suddenly early in September and forced new delays.

The year's second Jordanian drama began in earnest on Sunday, September 6, during the long Labor Day weekend in the United States, with Nixon, Kissinger, and Rogers resting at the Western White House in San Clemente. Palestinian guerrillas of the PFLP, moving with perfect synchronization, hijacked two jet airliners over Europe—a TWA plane and a Swissair plane—and forced them to fly across the Mediterranean to an abandoned RAF airfield in Jordan. The strip, twenty-five miles northeast of Amman and near the town of Zerqa, was known during the war as Dawson's Field. Now the Palestinians called it Revolution Field. However, the guerrillas had failed in their attempt to capture simultaneously an Israeli El Al jetliner shortly after its takeoff from London for Tel Aviv. In the fray, an Israeli security guard fatally shot one of the two Arab hijackers, a man, and subdued his female companion, Leila Khaled. When the airliner returned to London, Miss Khaled was arrested by British police. The next day, September 7, the Palestinians hijacked another plane, a British BOAC jet, forcing it also to fly to Revolution Field in Jordan. Now the guerrillas held three huge planes and 475 hostages, most of them Americans, British, and West Germans, on the sunbaked desert airfield.

The hijackers' specific demand was the release of all Palestinian and pro-Palestinian guerrillas and suspected guerrillas held in prisons in Israel, West Germany, Switzerland, and Britain. There were some 3000 of them in Israeli prisons alone. Leila Khaled was now the most important prisoner as far as the PFLP was concerned. The hijackers threatened to blow up the planes with the hostages if their conditions were not met. There were no Palestinian prisoners in the United States, but the PFLP must have reasoned that holding an American aircraft and American hostages would provide them with greater leverage. A seventy-two-hour deadline was set.

Much more was at stake politically than the ultimate fate of the planes and hostages. The hijackings were part of a broader plan devised by Palestinian organizations to prevent any settlement in the Middle East without their participation. The Palestinians had loudly and bitterly denounced Egypt and Jordan for their willingness to establish even a temporary cease-fire with Israel. In retaliation, Nasser shut down their Voice of Palestine radio in Cairo. Now the Palestinians were determined to show that they could effectively interfere with the truce. Their specific aim was to demonstrate that neither Egypt nor Jordan could control the situation within its own borders. Only a few weeks earlier, Egyptian security forces stood by helplessly when Palestinian terrorists blew up an empty Pan American World Airways jet at the Cairo airport. And in Jordan, the Palestinian guerrillas had resumed their defiance of King Hussein after the standoff that followed the June confrontation. Fighting increased between *fedayeen* units and the king's Arab Legion—so much so that the Jordanian Army was incapable of coming to the rescue of the hostages at Revolution Field, less than an hour's drive from Amman.

In Washington, it was instantly understood that the question of the hostages could not be separated from the larger context of the Middle East picture. Humanitarian concern for the hostages had to be weighed alongside fears over Hussein's ability to retain his throne. The British had been supplying Jordan with arms for some time, Centurion tanks for the army and Hunter Hawker jet fighters for the air force; now the United States began considering lifting the embargo, in effect since the 1967 war, on the delivery of American arms to the beleaguered king.

That the September hijackings coincided with renewed armed pressures on Hussein by the Palestinian guerrillas only served to reinforce Washington's view that no concessions of any kind should be made to the PFLP—and this included the situation at Revolution Field. Both the United States and Israel had long believed that to meet the demands of terrorists under any circumstances only invited more terrorism and blackmail; their standing policy was to risk the loss of lives, if necessary, rather than give in to terrorists. And in this particular instance—in Jordan in September 1970—Nixon was determined to remain absolutely firm on all fronts.

Diplomatic efforts to win the release of the hostages were launched at once. Early in the afternoon of Labor Day, Secretary Rogers (who had rushed back to Washington with the president and Kissinger the night before) met at the State Department with the representatives of the four other governments affected by the hijacking. It was a parade of worried men trooping through the holiday-empty halls: Israeli Ambassador

Rabin, British Ambassador John Freeman, West German Chargé Hans H. Noebel, and Swiss Chargé Charles Muller. Rogers had hoped for a joint Western policy toward the hijackers, but Muller told him that Switzerland had already released the three Palestinian guerrillas it had been holding. Noebel said the Bonn government was withholding a decision (no German airliners had been captured, but there were scores of Germans among the hostages). Only Britain seemed to side with the Americans and the Israelis—for the time being. The group agreed to request the International Committee of the Red Cross to act as intermediaries with the PFLP; the ICRC had done a superb job during the June fighting in Amman, and the Swiss men of the Red Cross seemed to have a way with the Palestinians.

Privately, American officials were thinking, as they had in June, that it might be necessary to use armed force to rescue the hostages on the desert as well as American citizens in Amman, where fighting between Hussein's troops and Palestinian guerrillas was reaching a danger point. Standby orders went out quietly to American commanders in the Mediterranean, West Germany, and Fort Bragg, home of the 82nd Airborne Division.

On September 8, Rogers turned to the Arab governments for support —he knew that none of them wanted to be identified with the guerrillas but hoped that they might have some leverage—and met with ten Arab envoys. Afterward, the Kuwaiti ambassador, acting as spokesman, told newsmen that hijackings of foreign airliners "do not serve the cause of the Palestinian people. . . . We will try to contact the guerrillas and convince them of this." However, he said, Arab governments did not have full control of the situation—which was precisely the point the PFLP had set out to make. The Israelis, refusing to make any deals over the hostages, kept insisting that no agreement should be made by the other governments that would exclude Israeli citizens among the captured passengers: they were the most vulnerable of all. Later in the day, Rogers drove to the White House to review the whole situation with Nixon. The tension in Washington was almost palpable.

Actually, the American judgment was that the guerrillas would not act rashly, that deadlines would probably be extended, and the West would do well to stand firm; the guerrillas had an interest in negotiating—they *did* want to have their prisoners released—and would not precipitate a tragedy. In this, Washington's instincts were correct. And Nixon, looking beyond the hijacking episode, was increasingly determined to display toughness in the crisis.

On September 9, the president took two steps that underlined the nexus between the hijacking drama and the larger Middle Eastern scene. He informed Israel that by the end of 1970 it would receive eighteen new Phantoms. It was a year since Mrs. Meir had first asked for new aircraft, but the official explanation now was that the planes were being given Israel to compensate it for the Egyptian-Soviet truce violations (Israel lost seven Phantoms just before the cease-fire) under the policy of maintaining the power balance in the Middle East. Simultaneously Nixon ordered six C-130 air force transports, carrying medical teams, to fly from bases in West Germany to the Turkish base at Incirlik, some 350 miles from Amman, to be ready to bring out the hostages. This was announced publicly.

Secretly, the United States was making other preparations. For the first time, official spokesmen refused to rule out direct American military action to rescue the hostages. Ronald Ziegler said ominously, "I cannot discuss other contingency steps that may or may not have been made." But it quickly became known that twenty-five U.S. Air Force Phantoms were also dispatched to Incirlik and the Sixth Fleet was steaming toward the Israeli and Lebanese coasts. On September 12, Secretary Rogers told a Senate committee that the United States planned to resume economic aid to Israel soon—for the first time in five years—and to increase military assistance. American "evenhandedness" in the Middle East had run its course—for the time being.

On the hostage front, deep differences developed between the United States and Britain. The British public, concerned over the fate of the 127 passengers aboard the BOAC jet, was pressing the government to release Miss Khaled, the new heroine of the Arab world, so that the guerrillas would spring the hostages loose. The British Foreign Office, in turn, was pressing Washington to agree to a common capitulation to the PFLP. It also wanted the United States to persuade Israel to release 450 Palestinians who had been arrested in the wake of the hijackings. But the White House was adamant, and, finally, Ambassador Freeman convinced the British Foreign Office that it was pointless to push this case.

The U.N. Security Council, responding to an Anglo-American request, met in New York and issued an appeal to all the parties concerned to help in the liberation of the hostages. On September 11, Nixon issued an order assigning armed guards—sky marshals—to all U.S. airliners and requiring all American airlines to install electronic surveillance equipment at American airports so that weapons that potential hijackers might be trying to carry aboard planes could be detected. In Jordan, the Red Cross continued negotiations with the guerrillas, who, as American experts had predicted, kept setting new deadlines. On September 12, however, the PFLP transferred all the hostages to a camp near Zerqa and blew up the three airliners. The planes were lost, but the hostages were spared. This led to a compromise: Israel agreed to set free 450 prisoners and the guerrillas started releasing the hostages—except for 55 Jewish passengers, who remained imprisoned until September 29. The British let Miss Khaled go on September 30.

The process of exchanging prisoners was still far from complete when another crisis erupted in Jordan. This time King Hussein deliberately triggered it. On September 15, he decided to take matters into his own hands and try to destroy his enemy. It was a bold decision because even Hussein's regular army, except for the Arab Legion and the air force, was heavily infiltrated by Palestinians. Still, the king had concluded that his offensive had to be a now-or-never proposition. The refugee camps were being used as guerrilla bases; they were a state-within-a-state.

The principal foreign news in Washington that day was Nixon's message to Congress outlining his proposed reforms in the foreign-assistance program, the result of long study within the administration and by a task force on international development chaired by Rudolph Peterson, former president of the Bank of America. The reforms were intended to bring some order to the chaos and overlapping of different foreign-aid programs, but the president also tied it to his Nixon Doctrine by creating a separate International Security Assistance Program designed primarily to handle military and related support assistance. As he put it, this new program would "help other countries assume the responsibility of their defense and thus help us reduce our presence abroad." Ironically, the message went to Capitol Hill just hours before Nixon was confronted with decisions about a possible new direct American involvement overseas. The other major reform proposed by Nixon was for the United States to channel most of its economic aid abroad through multilateral institutions, such as the World Bank, reducing bilateral arrangements.

The first word about Jordan came from London. Hussein had informed the British of his move before communicating with the United States. During the evening of September 15, a Tuesday, Prime Minister Heath had a top aide put in a transatlantic phone call to the White House to pass on the information. The call was taken by Colonel Haig. Kissinger was attending a black-tie dinner in honor of Defense Secretary Laird at Airlie House, a conference center in Virginia, about an hour's drive from Washington. Admiral Moorer, Deputy Defense Secretary David Packard, and State Department Middle East expert Joseph Sisco were also there.

Haig called Kissinger at Airlie House and simultaneously arranged for a helicopter to fly out to bring him back to the White House. Shortly after 9:30 p.m., Kissinger presided over a hastily assembled WASAG meeting in his office: a major emergency was developing in the Middle East.

Kissinger sensed that although the Jordanian affray was a civil war, its immediate implications were international. He argued that if the *fedayeen* succeeded in overthrowing Hussein, as they well might, there was the clear danger that Israel would invade Jordan at once; it could not tolerate, even briefly, a hostile Palestinian state along its unprotected eastern border. This, in turn, was certain to generate an overall war in the Middle East with a strong possibility of direct Soviet involvement. Inasmuch as the United States would not permit Soviet entry into the region, the feared superpower confrontation might then develop. Throughout the crisis, Kissinger related the Middle East situation to the respective positions of the United States and the Soviet Union. Then there were other potential complications. An Iraqi Army brigade had been stationed east of Amman since the 1967 war. Would it move in support of the Palestinians? And what about Syria? Would it intervene against Hussein in order to advance its anti-Israeli interests? Fresh intelligence reports indicated that Syrian tanks were advancing toward the Jordanian border. Thus another question: were the Soviets behind this movement? Soviet advisers were attached to Syrian units; therefore Moscow *must* have known what was happening.

The tentative conclusion at the WASAG meeting was that the United States must be prepared to become involved in Jordan, if necessary, to save Hussein. To some officials, it almost seemed preferable for the United States rather than for Israel to go into Jordan. Three principal elements emerged from the discussion. The performance of Hussein's forces was the first preoccupation—if the king could hold his own, the conflict would be confined for the time being. Israeli mobilization and readiness to go into Jordan and even Syria, if required by the circumstances, was the next step. And finally, the United States policy decision to prevent at all costs Hussein's collapse overshadowed all other considerations. Still, the idea of sending American troops to the Middle East just two-and-a-half months after the end of the Cambodian operation—and with the Vietnam war virtually stalemated—was obviously disturbing. This dilemma faced Nixon as he joined Kissinger and Sisco around midnight for another discussion after the full WASAG group had adjourned for the night. Secretary Rogers was inexplicably excluded from these deliberations. The president made no decisions, but he made it clear that he was prepared to go all the way.

The next day, September 16, Nixon flew to Chicago for a long-scheduled session with editors of Midwestern newspapers. He took Kissinger and Sisco along with him, presumably to have the benefit of their advice if the crisis deepened and urgent decisions had to be taken. En route to Chicago, the president stopped at Manhattan, Kansas, to deliver a Landon Lecture at Kansas State University. He made no reference to the Jordanian crisis, except for a mention of the hijackings, concentrating in his speech on campus unrest and on explaining once more his Vietnam policies. Still, in his special Nixonian fashion, he found a way of relating the hijackings in the Middle East to domestic unrest:

> When Palestinian guerrillas hijacked four airliners in flight, they brought to two hundred fifty the number of aircraft seized since the skyjacking era began in 1961. And as they held their hundreds of passengers hostage under threat of murder, they sent shock waves of alarm around the world to the spreading disease of violence and terror and its use as a political tactic. That same cancerous disease has been spreading all over the world and here in the United States. We saw it three weeks ago in the vicious bombing at the University of Wisconsin. . . . We have seen it in other bombings and burnings on our campuses, in our cities, in the wanton shooting of policemen, in the attacks on school buses, in the destruction of offices, the seizure and harassment of college officials, the use of force and coercion to bar students and teachers from classrooms and even to close down whole schools.

In Chicago later that day, Nixon as well as Kissinger and Sisco addressed the editors on a "background" basis with the Jordanian crisis very much on their minds. Messages from the White House Situation Room reaching the presidential party in Chicago told of heavy fighting in Amman between Hussein's army and the Palestinian guerrillas. In his talk, Nixon hinted strongly that the United States might have to use force in Jordan if the Syrians and the Iraqis threatened Hussein. Although the president was not speaking on the record, the *Chicago Sun-Times* published these remarks the next day. Marvin and Bernard Kalb wrote in their book, *Kissinger,* that the White House welcomed this violation of the rules because Nixon "wanted that implied warning to be heard in Moscow, Damascus and Baghdad."

On September 17, Nixon summoned Rogers, Kissinger, Laird, Helms, Moorer, and Sisco to the White House to decide what the United States and Israel should do if Syrian tanks invaded Jordan in support of the *fedayeen.* Fighting was now extremely heavy in Amman as well as in Irbid, a city in Jordan's northwest. Military experts in Washington believed that an outside force would be required to save Hussein, particularly if the Syrians intervened; and again, the question was whether it would be wiser to use Israeli or American forces to rescue the king.

On Friday, September 18, Israeli Prime Minister Meir met with Nixon and Kissinger at the White House. She was on a scheduled visit to the United States, a fortuitous occasion that allowed for instant American-Israeli consultations. However, Nixon was not yet prepared to push for a commitment. The situation was extremely fluid; information from Jordanian battlefields was uncertain and incomplete. There were reports from Jordanian sources that Syrian tanks had actually moved into Jordan, but there was no confirmation. Nixon, therefore, chose in his conversation with Mrs. Meir to confine himself to pleas for Israel to go on respecting the Suez Canal cease-fire. He wanted to be sure that Israel would not create a new Middle East crisis on the canal while Jordan was seemingly coming apart. Mrs. Meir gave the president her assurances that Israel would be restrained.

Later that day, the State Department received an urgent communication from Moscow advising the United States that the Russians were doing their utmost to prevent other countries from intervening in Jordan. This clearly referred to Syria, whose tank units were accompanied by Soviet advisers. The Soviet chargé d'affaires in Washington, Yuli Vorontsov (Dobrynin was home on leave), simultaneously assured Sisco that the Syrians were not moving. Kissinger was inclined to believe the Russians; Nixon was not so sure.

As it turned out, Nixon's instinct was right. On Saturday, September 19, at least three hundred Syrian tanks crossed the border into Jordan with Irbid as their first objective. At this point, the White House seriously expected a major war to break out in the Middle East at any moment. Kissinger grimly talked to his NSC aides about the immense danger of a Soviet-American confrontation. Then Nixon made two moves: he ordered a limited alert of American forces in the United States, Western Europe, and the Mediterranean, and he instructed the State Department to dispatch a short note to Moscow complaining that the Russians, contrary to their promise, had failed to stop the Syrians from invading Jordan. The military alert had a twofold purpose: to ready United States forces for action and, almost as important, to signal Moscow and the Arabs that Nixon meant business. Thus with maximal ostentation the 82nd Airborne Division at Fort Bragg and American airborne battalions in West Germany were placed in a high degree of readiness. The Sixth Fleet, its ships carrying marine detachments, steamed toward the Israeli coast. As Kissinger later told interviewers, "we wanted to get picked up" by Soviet surveillance. Independent of American preparations, Israel began openly to mobilize. Its tank units moved toward the Jordanian and Syrian borders; its air force was placed on alert.

It was an extraordinary exercise in brinkmanship by all sides, conducted with a great sense of control. Nixon and Kissinger were most uncertain about Soviet intentions, but several senior State Department officials were inclined to think that the Russians would not really allow the situation to "get out of hand," although it did look at one point as if this might happen. The judgment was that the Russians had not "masterminded" the Syrian attack but that, on the other hand, they did precious little to discourage it. The Soviet Union seemed to be gambling on the success of Syria's drive. She would have liked to see it succeed—and she did not want to lose her credibility with Damascus and Arab revolutionaries—but not at the risk of a major war. For one thing, Soviet advisers stayed behind when the Syrians went into Jordan—a fact that was immediately and strongly impressed on the United States.

The State Department, for its part, kept reading the riot act to Vorontsov, the Soviet chargé. He was told by Sisco that if the Syrians did not pull back, the Israelis might intervene and an American involvement could not be ruled out. These were no mere threats, but deliberate brinkmanship diplomacy: the United States was immensely anxious for Moscow to understand the dangers. Nixon and Kissinger thought this was the only way to deal with the Russians, whereas Secretary Rogers tended to favor pure diplomacy over saber rattling. Not surprisingly, he was overruled.

On Sunday, September 20, the situation worsened. Although Hussein was able to contain the first wave of Syrian armor, additional hundreds of Syrian tanks were pouring into Jordan. Hussein decided that the time had come to engage his small air force as the only way of stemming the Syrian advance, but he needed help. Calling the American embassy in Amman from his palace, the king asked the United States to pass on a message to the Israeli government that he would welcome air support from the Israelis. Mrs. Meir and Ambassador Rabin were at a fund-raising dinner in New York when Kissinger contacted them with the Jordanian request. Mrs. Meir's and Rabin's immediate question was whether the United States would assure Israel's safety from other directions if they agreed. Rabin relayed this question to Kissinger while Mrs. Meir urgently consulted with her cabinet colleagues in Jerusalem.

In the small hours of September 21, Rabin returned to Washington aboard an air force jet provided by Kissinger while Mrs. Meir took off for Tel Aviv on her El Al airliner. About the same time, word reached Washington that Irbid had been taken by the Syrians. In Jerusalem, where it was already late morning, the cabinet had agreed in principle to let the Israeli Air Force assist Hussein. Rabin so advised Kissinger, but the United States was not yet ready to give Israel the assurances of protection asked by Mrs. Meir.

During the day, Nixon, while pondering his reply to Israel, ordered additional military movements. United States infantry divisions in West Germany were placed on alert, and transport planes were assembled for an airlift to the Middle East. The Sixth Fleet, now augmented from two to five aircraft carriers with destroyer screens, moved closer to the Israeli coast. A small navy jet began flying an intelligence shuttle between the carrier flagship and Tel Aviv. The United States and Israel were ostentatiously coordinating their moves. Kissinger and Rabin, who had spent a virtually sleepless night, were in constant touch. At one point, Rabin told Kissinger that Israel was now considering engaging its own armor in Jordan against the Syrians; the command in Tel Aviv had concluded that a combined air-and-ground operation would be required to cope with Syria. Besides, there was concern about what the Iraqi units that had been stationed in Jordan since 1967 might do; so far they had stayed outside the battle. Late in the afternoon, Vorontsov arrived at the State Department with the message that the Soviet Union was pressing the Syrians not to send more tanks into Jordan and that it expected that the United States would counsel patience to the Israelis. This was the first break in the week-long tension, but the crisis was far from over.

On Tuesday, September 22, intelligence reports reaching the White House Situation Room told of more Syrian tanks crossing the Jordanian border. Hussein's armor and jet fighters were doing exceptionally well against the Syrians, but there was a limit to his resistance—especially if Damascus kept throwing fresh forces into the battle. It was at that point —sometime during the afternoon of Tuesday—that Nixon reached his decision. He instructed Kissinger to inform Rabin that the United States would intervene on Israel's behalf against both Egypt and the Soviet Union if it were attacked as a consequence of its involvement in Jordan.

What saved the day was the psychological effect on Hussein of this American-Israeli decision. Knowing that he could count on Israeli military backing, the king threw all his forces against the Syrians and the Palestinian guerrillas, and during the night of September 22–23 word came that Syrian armored columns were beginning to turn around and track their way back home.

Subsequent postmortems suggested several important conclusions to American diplomats. One was that whatever Moscow might have been thinking at the outset, it clearly "leaned" on the Syrians, as one American official put it, to avoid a confrontation with the United States. Nixon and Kissinger eventually decided that though Moscow was willing to take advantage of a promising situation, it was not willing to run intolerable risks. This proved the State Department right in its long-range perceptions of the Middle East. Solutions were possible only if they were based on the "dynamics of the area," as an official explained it later. Nixon and Kissinger went on believing for a long time that an overall settlement could come only in context of Soviet-American relations.

The other conclusion was that the Syrians lost the Jordanian war because their air force commander, General Hafez Assad, refused to commit his MiG jets to the fray, viewing the entire affair as a reckless adventure that he declined to support in defiance of his government's orders. The result of the Syrian military debacle was the fall of the Damascus regime and Assad's emergence as the new president.

The tensions over the Middle East abated so quickly that four days later, on September 27, Nixon was able to leave Washington on a nine-day European trip. This was his first major international foray of the year —he had gone for two days in August to Puerto Vallarta in Mexico for a meeting with President Gustavo Díaz Ordaz to complete a boundary agreement—and he was eager to hit the road again. For Nixon, foreign travel was one of the great joys.

The first stop was Rome, where the Nixons spent two days. On the second day, September 28, the president drove to the Rome airport to meet a group of thirty-two Americans who had been among the hostages in Jordan after their aircraft was hijacked. The group had stopped in Rome en route from Amman and Cyprus to New York, and Nixon went aboard the airliner for a chat. It was a typical Nixon conversation. He asked several persons from which states they hailed, then told them, "We were trying to help you without hurting you." When one of the men remarked that they were "so sick of that Red Chinese jam we had to eat," the president retorted improbably: "Is that what it was? It is a little better if you could mix some pineapple with it. That was the only way you could eat it." Afterward Nixon relayed to reporters his thoughts on how he had conducted matters during the Jordan crisis:

> I told them [the hostages] . . . that we were naturally terribly frustrated
> because we realized that if we did the wrong thing, it would cost them

their lives. . . . We had to show power and at the same time we had
to demonstrate restraint. They told me that that was exactly the right
policy, because they said that every day they had the feeling that their
captors might do something irrational in the event that we triggered
it, or somebody else triggered it. This, of course, bore out the wisdom
of our policy, and I am glad that we did show the proper restraint,
during this period while, at the same time, being very firm in our
diplomacy and firm in the demonstration of our military strength in
the event that that became necessary in that part of the world.

The perplexing thing about this Nixon account is that it was wholly
invented. The official White House transcript of the president's chat with
the ex-hostages does not show that *any* of them told him "that was exactly
the right policy" or *anything* about possible "irrational" acts. Why did
Nixon feel the need to invent this—since nobody in the United States
seriously questioned his policies in the first place?

Later in the day, Nixon lunched with Italian President Giuseppe Sara-
gat, then went to the Vatican for a meeting with Pope Paul VI in the Papal
Library. Nixon's emphasis on his temporal power seemed bizarre as he
formally addressed the pontiff: he told him he would be visiting the Sixth
Fleet after leaving the Vatican, and "I will be flying to sea and there I shall
see the mightiest military force which exists in the world on any ocean.
Today, here in this room, we have had the opportunity to hear expressed
a different kind of power—the spiritual power which moves nations and
moves men."

The same theme emerged minutes later as he spoke to students from
the Vatican's North American College, in the beautiful Clementine Hall:

> As I pointed out to His Holiness, I am going to be visiting in a very
> short time the mightiest fleet that has ever been assembled in the
> history of the world. When we think of that great power that I will see
> there, I suppose the pragmatists—those who are pragmatists without
> being idealists—the pragmatists would say what really matters only is
> the power, the power that can be mounted there, militarily, main-
> tained by the United States, supplemented by its allies. I know, how-
> ever . . . that there is another power in the world, a power that
> transcends material factors, a power that transcends also even the
> great military strength that we may have, or other nations may have.
> It is the power of the spirit.

When Nixon boarded the aircraft carrier U.S.S. *Saratoga* in the evening of September 28, he learned that Egyptian President Nasser had just
died of a heart attack in Cairo at the age of fifty-two. The news came as

a shock to Nixon, and his formal statement saying so was not exaggerated, nor was his remark that "this tragic loss requires that all nations, and particularly those in the Middle East, renew their efforts to calm passions, reach for mutual understanding, and build lasting peace."

Concern over future developments in Egypt led to a quick White House decision for high-level United States representation at Nasser's funeral. Inasmuch as Egypt and the United States had no diplomatic relations, protocol problems prevented Nixon or Rogers from going to Cairo, and the choice then fell on Elliot Richardson, secretary of HEW, who as under secretary of state until the past June had been deeply involved in Middle Eastern diplomacy. Since the Soviet Union was represented by Premier Kosygin, Richardson was instructed to seek a private meeting with him, and this was arranged, as was a conversation between Richardson and Acting President Anwar el-Sadat. The White House was eager to learn all it could about the man who was expected to lead Egypt, and Sadat was a completely unknown political quantity. There were reports in Washington that the Soviets were considering a new diplomatic initiative in the Middle East, and it was Richardson's mission to find out what was on Kosygin's mind and how Sadat might react to it.

Nasser's death coincided with assurances from Congress to Israel that the arms it might buy from the United States on highly favorable credit terms would specifically include aircraft as well as tanks and missiles. A House-Senate conference report on the new military procurement bill guaranteed that there would be no cost or quantitative limits on Israeli military credit purchases. This was the most open-ended arms-buying program offered any country by the United States. Israel now could feel quite secure, or so it seemed, in the face of new Middle Eastern uncertainties resulting from Nasser's death.

From the *Saratoga,* Nixon flew to the cruiser *Springfield,* the flagship of the Sixth Fleet, for a conference on general strategic problems with all U.S. and NATO commanders in the Mediterranean. The new Egyptian situation was one of the topics. In Naples, later in the day, Nixon told newsmen that the United States would like to have good relations with Cairo and that "we believe that the new government, whoever it is, will see that its interests will be served by continuing the cease-fire, and, we trust, then going on to talks." With the Jordanian crisis resolved, the administration's policy was to try again to resume peace talks between Egypt and Israel through the United Nations mediator.

On September 30, Nixon was in Yugoslavia—it was the second Communist country he visited—to confer with President Tito. A special relationship had existed between Yugoslavia and the United States ever since 1948, when Tito first broke with the Soviet Union: American arms were sold to the Yugoslavs, the United States offered Tito a defense commitment following the Soviet invasion of Czechoslovakia in 1968, and Tito had twice visited America. The Belgrade visit probably annoyed the Soviet Union, but Nixon's policy included a cultivation of the "independent" Communist states. For Nixon, it was a highly useful visit, a sign of the acceptance of his "generation of peace" policies by one of the most influential leaders in the nonaligned world. It served to convince him that neither Vietnam nor Cambodia—nor America's support of Israel in the Middle East—needed to interfere with his grand policy designs. Men like Tito, Nixon reasoned, were too pragmatic and realistic to make an issue of how the United States coped with its Asian or Middle Eastern problems. Happily away from domestic protest over his Indochina wars, Nixon had a sense of vindication.

His two-day visit to Madrid—on October 2 and 3—further increased his satisfaction with the trip. The president's presence in Spain and his cordiality toward Generalissimo Francisco Franco irritated the West Europeans, as it did American liberals, who took a dim view of the unflagging United States government support of the Spanish dictatorship. But to Nixon, Spain was a partner in Western defense—even though Franco remained a pariah in the eyes of most of NATO—and Washington attached considerable importance to the air and naval bases on the Iberian Peninsula. Besides, Nixon felt there was a certain evenhandedness in visiting Yugoslavia and Spain on the same trip: a leftist and a rightist dictatorship.

The president's final stop on his European tour was Ireland, where his three-day visit took him to Limerick, Drumoland Castle in County Clare, Timahoe, and Dublin. A reception at Drumoland Castle gave Nixon an opportunity to summarize for newsmen his impressions of the trip, with special emphasis on the Middle East after the Jordanian crisis. It was the nearest thing to a policy speech. But Nixon did not tell the newsmen that he was planning new peace proposals for Indochina. Work on these proposals had been proceeding in Washington for weeks—even at the height of the Jordanian crisis—and the final touches were applied by Nixon, Kissinger, and Rogers during the president's European tour. In Ireland, Nixon set time aside for final consultations with David Bruce, the chief American delegate to the Paris peace talks, and Philip Habib, his deputy.

Chapter 12

To Richard Nixon, diplomacy was theater. And the best of theater is timing. At 11:15 a.m. on October 6—fifteen hours after returning to Washington from his European trip—the president suddenly appeared in the White House press briefing room. The place was still littered with the morning newspapers full of Nixon European-voyage stories. Standing behind the briefing lectern, the president smiled, cleared his throat, and announced that the following evening he would address the nation. It would be a "major statement" on new American peace proposals for Southeast Asia, he said. He added that his speech would be "the most comprehensive statement ever made on this subject since the beginning of this very difficult war" and "comprehensive geographically—it will not be limited to Vietnam; it will cover all of Southeast Asia." And, Nixon said, it would not be a "propaganda gimmick."

The preparations for the launching of the Nixon proposals were unprecedented: the president himself would brief the cabinet and, separately, bipartisan legislative leadership in the late afternoon of October 7. Secretary Rogers would spend the day briefing "foreign governments . . . who have interest in the area." And finally, Kissinger would hold separate background briefings for the writing press and the television press several hours before the president went on the air to explain in considerable detail the meaning of the proposals.

What the nation was being shown was Nixon the dynamic and tireless leader in foreign affairs, successfully presiding over the solution to the immensely dangerous Middle East crisis, then touring Europe and the Mediterranean to preach his doctrine of the "structure of peace" based upon American strength overseas, and finally stunning the world with his "most comprehensive statement ever made" on Indochina—all within a matter of weeks. The image was one of a superbly organized presidency, capable of dealing smoothly and efficiently with many international problems and crises all at the same time, while keeping a steady hand on domestic affairs (between his return from Europe and the Indochina speech, Nixon managed to send Congress a study on ocean pollution, criticize a $1-billion bill on the construction of sewer and water lines as inflationary, and issue a statement on National Newspaperboy Day).

In fact, Nixon was doing even more than he cared to tell the country at that point: for example, he was directing the CIA in its secret efforts to organize a military *coup d'état* in Chile to prevent Allende, the Socialist president-elect, from taking office. It was one of Nixon's pet personal projects, and it is difficult to resist the temptation of recalling his words in Belgrade, when the Chilean operation was already well under way, that the United States did not accept doctrines "by which one power purports to abridge the right of other countries to shape their own destinies and to pursue their own legitimate interests."

From an international viewpoint, both Kissinger and Nixon realized that, particularly after Cambodia, the United States could not let the diplomatic negotiating process lapse altogether. Relations with the Soviet Union and China hinged to an important degree on the pace of negotiations with North Vietnam. There was a tacit understanding in the Communist capitals that progress toward improved relations with the United States had to be synchronized to some extent with progress toward peace in Vietnam. There had to be a decent interval after the Cambodian intervention: early October seemed like the right time for renewed diplomacy.

Purely military considerations were intertwined with domestic politics. It was clear to Nixon that for reasons of domestic peace (as Laird kept reminding him), he had to continue phased withdrawals of American troops from Vietnam even though the battlefield situation was far from satisfactory; the White House was willing to accept the fiction of successful Vietnamization. The military risks implicit in such a policy were perfectly well understood, and the president kept assuring General Abrams and the Pentagon that in an emergency he would authorize unlimited use of American air power to prevent a collapse in South Vietnam. New antiwar moratoriums were being planned for October and November, and the president believed he needed to make a major gesture toward the peace movement.

Finally, the mid-term congressional elections were approaching, and Republican candidates were in trouble. Nixon would later reject the suggestion that the elections affected his timing: "If we had intended it for that, I am politically enough astute to have done it just about four days before the election. . . . Then we would not have known what the result would have been and people would have voted their hopes rather than the realities." But the flaw in this argument was that the presentation of peace proposals four days before the elections would have been *so* obvious and transparent as to be damaging. The November elections *were* a third major element.

Nixon and Kissinger had begun planning for the new diplomatic initiative early in August. As usual, the rest of the government was cut out of these deliberations; presently, Kissinger instructed the NSC staff to undertake an urgent but systematic study of the entire Indochina situation and its ramifications. As was his custom, he asked for a variety of options.

On August 17, the NSC staff submitted to Kissinger the completed study entitled "Southeast Asia Strategy," NSSM–99. Kissinger reviewed it in San Clemente, where he was spending part of the summer with Nixon, and gave it to the president. When Ambassador Bunker arrived from Saigon for conferences with Nixon, Kissinger, and Rogers (the last having now been included in the secret deliberations), he was asked his opinion about various options in the NSC paper. Later, his job would be to sell the new plan to President Thieu. American ambassadors in Laos and Cambodia, not brought in on the preliminary consultations, would in time receive similar assignments in dealing with the governments to which they were accredited.

Early in September, before the Jordanian crisis reached explosive proportions, Kissinger flew twice to Paris for secret sessions with Xuan Thuy, who had just returned from Hanoi after an absence of several months. Essentially, Kissinger was trying to pick up the threads of the private negotiations where he left off in April. He did not tell Xuan Thuy that the United States was about to spring major new proposals; instead, he tried to determine how Hanoi's attitude had changed during the past five months. There was nothing encouraging in Xuan Thuy's responses —the North Vietnamese, in fact, made a new public proposal on September 17, defining the coalition regime they wanted to see established in Saigon—but Kissinger nevertheless concluded that the "major initiative" should be pursued. He hoped it might move Hanoi off dead center. He so advised Nixon, and before he left on the European trip, the president approved the latest Indochina strategy.

As Nixon told newsmen on October 6, the final step was the meeting with Bruce and Habib in Ireland. The idea was for Bruce to present the Nixon plan formally to the North Vietnamese and Viet Cong delegations in Paris at the regular weekly Thursday semipublic session.

Nixon's "major new initiative for peace," as he explained it, was a blend of new and old ideas. For the first time he proposed an internationally supervised cease-fire in place—a standstill cease-fire—in Vietnam as well as in Laos and Cambodia. Given the reality of a large North Vietnamese presence in the three Indochinese states, Kissinger thought this proposal would be tempting to Hanoi. The United States no longer demanded a commitment to a mutual withdrawal of foreign forces from these countries as a precondition for the cessation of hostilities. Moreover, Nixon was urging a cease-fire in *all* Indochina. Nixon then proposed that the standstill cease-fire be submitted to immediate negotiations in Paris, and that the truce be supervised by "international observers, as well as by the parties themselves."

> A cease-fire should not be the means by which either side builds up its strength by an increase in outside combat forces in any of the nations of Indochina. And a cease-fire should cause all kinds of warfare to stop. This covers the full range of actions that have typified this war, including bombing and acts of terror. A cease-fire should encompass not only the fighting in Vietnam but in all of Indochina. Conflicts in this region are closely related. The United States has never sought to widen the war. What we seek is to widen the peace. Finally, a cease-fire should be part of a general move to end the war in Indochina. A cease-fire-in-place would undoubtedly create a host of problems in its maintenance. But it's always been easier to make war than to make a truce.

Still, the crux of the negotiating situation was the question of the withdrawal of foreign forces, especially from Vietnam. A number of diplomatic observers were struck initially by the fact that Nixon—for the first time—failed to use the expression "mutual withdrawals" in addressing Hanoi, and interpreted it as a sign that the United States was abandoning its insistence on this point. But a close reading of Nixon's text reveals that he added that "we are prepared to withdraw all our forces as part of a settlement based on the principles I spelled out previously and the proposals I am making tonight." And one of the principles *previously* mentioned by Nixon was mutual withdrawal. The next day, talking to newsmen at Skidway Island, off the coast of Georgia, the president confirmed that ostensible American policy had not changed in this particular. He said: "We offered a total withdrawal of all of our forces, something we had never offered before, if we had mutual withdrawal on the other side."

Nixon's second important point was the convocation of an Indochina peace conference. But this idea was a nonstarter, and it was curious that Nixon was proposing it. It took no great foresight to realize that neither the Soviet Union nor China wished to be drawn into a major international conclave to decide the fate of Indochina. Presumably, Nixon was keen on giving his overall proposals the most sweeping character possible.

Another point in Nixon's speech dealt with a political settlement in South Vietnam. Hanoi had for years demanded that a coalition regime be established in Saigon—and Thieu and others expelled—before it would consider a broad agreement. Its September 17 proposal repeated this view. On this score, Nixon offered no new ideas, simply restating the long-standing American position.

The president's final point was "the immediate and unconditional release of all prisoners of war held by both sides." The question of American POWs in North Vietnam was becoming increasingly important in the Paris negotiations. To Hanoi, American war prisoners were an issue that gave it powerful leverage. At no time, however, had it evinced any interest in mutual release of prisoners; the North Vietnamese took the view that such an exchange, like all other things on the negotiating table, should be included in a general settlement accord. But in Nixon's eyes the release of all prisoners, aside from being "a simple act of humanity," could "serve to establish good faith, the intent to make progress, and thus improve the prospects for negotiations."

Nixon's speech was unusually conciliatory. He refrained from warning the North Vietnamese of the usual dire consequences if they threatened the security of American troops, and clearly he was optimistic that Hanoi would consider his new proposal carefully and, perhaps, positively. Kissinger thought that a breakthrough might not be far off.

While most domestic and international reaction to Nixon's speech was extremely good, North Vietnam was another story. Hanoi's delegation in Paris, formally given the proposals by Bruce at the negotiating session on October 8, dismissed them as "a maneuver to deceive world opinion." So did the North Vietnamese press and radio. Yet Hanoi accurately reported Nixon's proposals to its own population, and this was regarded in Washington as mildly encouraging.

The truth was that the administration was most reluctant to accept the first North Vietnamese response as a rejection. Thus Secretary Rogers told a hastily summoned news conference on October 9 that while the United States had expected an initial "knee-jerk" rejection by Hanoi, it had a feeling that a secret acceptance and private talks in Paris might follow. On the same day, Deputy Defense Secretary David Packard said that the North Vietnamese would move toward a cease-fire because they were losing ground militarily. As part of the administration's campaign to persuade Hanoi to take up the new proposals, Rogers offered an additional sweetener: "We are making the proposal at this time because we feel sure that the Vietnamization program will succeed and that we will have American forces out of combat in Vietnam by May 1." The explanation was that at the rate U.S. troops were leaving Vietnam, the forces still there in the spring of 1971 would be confined to logistical, support, training, and advisory missions—they would no longer be fighting. Still, Rogers was talking of upward of 350,000 Americans remaining in Vietnam in spring 1971, which made his argument less than convincing.

The problem was that Hanoi was not seeing *any* of it in the same way as Washington. Gareth Porter, a student of the Vietnam negotiating history and a man with good Hanoi contacts, summed up the reasons for the North Vietnamese rejection of the Nixon plan in his book *A Peace Denied:*

> Such a cease-fire would have left the PRG [Provisional Revolutionary Government] with a choice of a political settlement along the lines of the "territorial accommodation" plan . . . or no settlement at all. As Kissinger had written in 1968, "a formal cease-fire is likely to predetermine the ultimate settlement. . . . Cease-fire is thus not so much a step toward a final settlement as a form of it." Not only did the October 1970 proposal freeze the PRG legally into a diminished zone of control *without* a political settlement at the central government level, it also demanded cease-fires in Laos and Cambodia, where the left-wing forces were on the offensive despite heavy US bombing. Again, this Indochina-wide cease-fire was to take place without any negotiations involving the Pathet Lao and Sihanouk's Royal Government of National Union in Cambodia. In other words, the principle of cease-fire without political settlement was extended throughout Indochina.

Put simply, Hanoi saw the American cease-fire proposal as a trap that would rob it of the kind of political settlement it had in mind. Another consideration was that as the numbers of American troops diminished in Vietnam, the North Vietnamese had a better chance, in the long run, to win militarily. Hanoi was patient and it believed in its "protracted war" concept. Besides, it was far from hanging on the ropes.

The correctness of the North Vietnamese analysis was shortly confirmed by Nixon himself when on October 12 he issued a brief announcement that the ceiling of American forces in Vietnam would be reduced by 40,000 men by Christmas. This was part of the 150,000-man reduction Nixon had announced on April 20 to be completed by spring 1971. The withdrawal of 50,000 men under this program was achieved in October; what Nixon was doing at this point was speeding up the departures. As he put it, "there will be authorized 205,500 fewer Americans in Vietnam by Christmas of this year than when I took office." That would leave 384,000 troops in Vietnam. Nixon's plan was to order further withdrawals in mid-1971.

With Vietnam a major election issue, Nixon was unabashedly using it in campaigning for Republican candidates. Speaking in Burlington on behalf of Vermont's Senator Winston L. Prouty, who was seeking reelection, the president went right to the point:

> We have implemented a plan to bring Americans home, and during the spring of next year half of the men that were in Vietnam when we got there will be coming home. . . . We have cut American casualties to the lowest level in four and a half years. . . . We have presented to the North Vietnamese, over national television . . . a far-reaching peace plan. . . . I can say confidently the war in Vietnam is coming to an end, and we are going to win a just peace in Vietnam. . . . Let us work for what all of us want, not just peace for the next election, but peace for the next generation.

The Vietnam theme was repeated by Nixon as he campaigned in New Jersey ("We want peace . . . not just for the next election. Nelson Gross stands for that"), and it was emphasized in speeches in Lancaster, Pennsylvania, and Green Bay, Wisconsin. In fact, Nixon even brought up Vietnam in a speech at a testimonial reception for Bart Starr, the Green Bay Packers quarterback; no American statesman has ever matched Nixon's talent for mixing football with foreign policy. Then, the president kept up the Vietnam war issue, obviously convinced that it was now working for him, in appearances in Ohio, North Dakota, Missouri, Tennessee, North Carolina, Indiana, Maryland, Florida, Texas, Illinois, Minnesota, Nebraska, California, Arizona, New Mexico, Nevada, and Utah, as he endorsed Republican senatorial candidates in a breathless two-week tour of the country.

Nixon's stance was evidently as unconvincing to the American electorate as it was to Hanoi. Many of the Nixon-backed Senate candidates were defeated—the Republicans remained in a 55–45 minority—and the president suffered the indignity of being stoned by demonstrators after a campaign speech in San José four days before the elections. No American president before Nixon had ever been thus attacked by a crowd.

Nixon interrupted his campaigning on October 23 to come to New York to address the General Assembly on the twenty-fifth anniversary of the United Nations. There, his theme was world peace and, to an overwhelming extent, the state of Soviet-American relations.

Nixon's comments on Soviet-American relations were motivated by a certain amount of disenchantment with Moscow's policies since, as he put it, "I announced, on taking office, that the policy of the United States would be to move from an era of confrontation to one of negotiation." There was annoyance over the Soviet role in the summer crisis in the Middle East, the virtual stalemate in the SALT negotiations since they began, nearly a year earlier, and what Nixon regarded as Moscow's reluctance to be helpful in the Vietnam peace negotiations. At the same time, however, the president was attempting to encourage the Russians to join the United States in more promising negotiations. It was the first time that Nixon had used the word "détente" in a major policy speech. While the Russians wanted a Brezhnev-Nixon meeting, the White House believed that it must be preceded by more progress in specific negotiations. Both the president and Kissinger felt it was premature to think in terms of "summitry" with Brezhnev, and Nixon said so. In this, of course, Nixon and Kissinger were entirely right. Then, the president summed up his foreign policy: "What we seek is not a Pax Americana, not an American Century, but rather a structure of stability and progress that will enable each nation, large and small, to chart its own course, to make its own way without outside interference, without intimidation, without domination by ourselves or any other nation."

Still, this structure of stability kept eluding Nixon. Hanoi had rejected his October peace plan, and the battlefield situation in both Vietnam and Cambodia kept deteriorating. On November 10, the president learned that General de Gaulle had just died, and this seemed to provide a new diplomatic opportunity. As many other heads of state did, Nixon flew to Paris two days later to attend memorial services at Notre Dame Cathedral for de Gaulle. Afterward, he met with President Georges Pompidou to discuss Indochina. The French, of course, had been active in the secret peace diplomacy, but this time not even Pompidou had any fresh ideas on how to deal with the intractable Indochina problem. Nixon returned home with a growing sense of futility.

In mid-October, as the dry season was beginning, North Vietnam launched a major troop infiltration effort into the South. This was one form of response to Nixon's peace proposals, although the new south-ward movement had been planned for some time. In fact, Hanoi's defense minister, Vo Nguyen Giap, had said in a September report to the All-Army Conference on the Military Situation that "the present struggle to liberate the South has raised striking and complicated problems, which must be solved in time in order to frustrate the enemy's new schemes and tricks." Giap may well have been referring to Cambodia. In any event, intelligence reports reaching Washington in mid-November indicated that the infiltration rate in the 1970 dry season was twice that of the previous year; estimates spoke of 200,000 men during the 1970–71 dry season if the rate were maintained. In short, Hanoi was putting fresh North Vietnamese troops into Indochina in numbers exceeding American withdrawals from Vietnam. The North Vietnamese units appeared to be headed for southern Laos, the Central Highlands in South Vietnam, and Cambodia, presumably to make up for the losses suffered there in the spring. It was estimated that three months might elapse before all these new troops emerged from the pipeline and became combat ready.

Nixon struck immediately. On November 21, 200 American fighter-bombers hit targets across North Vietnam, and they hit again on November 22. This bombing, the most extensive since the May raids timed with the Cambodian incursion, ranged from the Hanoi-Haiphong area to military supply depots, highways, bridges, and strategic mountain passes at the northern entrance to the infiltration trails. Simultaneously, raids were carried out against objectives in Laos and Cambodia. The United States denied, however, that the Hanoi area had been attacked.

The administration never made it entirely clear, despite lengthy congressional testimony by Laird, Rogers, and other senior officials, why precisely these raids were undertaken. The decision was made personally by Nixon after a series of meetings with WASAG and then a session of the full National Security Council on November 19. Among the reasons invoked was the downing on November 13 of an unarmed American reconnaissance plane monitoring the North Vietnamese infiltration movements, so the strikes could be construed as what Laird called "reinforced protective reaction," but it seemed rather unlikely that the United States would have responded so violently to the loss of a single aircraft —and eight days after the event. Another reason suggested by official spokesmen was that Saigon and Hue had recently been shelled by Viet Cong forces, which the U.S. government interpreted as a violation of the unwritten 1968 agreement under which the United States declared the bombing pause and Hanoi promised not to shell South Vietnamese cities and to refrain from sending troops south across the demilitarized zone. Laird told a Senate committee on November 24 that he would recommend the resumption of full-scale air attacks on North Vietnam if Hanoi engaged in "major violations of these [1968] understandings."

Privately, however, senior officials said that there was no question that the deep raids on November 21–22 more simply represented a warning to Hanoi to desist from new military buildups in the three Indochina states. The North Vietnamese rejection of the president's October 7 cease-fire proposal also appears to have been a factor. Nixon, in short, was furious with Hanoi. The more cynical among Washington observers went further: Nixon, they argued, was applying air power in support of his diplomacy; the air strikes were intended to force Hanoi to change its mind about rejecting his peace proposals.

Another event had coincided with the weekend air strikes, adding to the confusion. At 2:00 a.m. November 21, Hanoi time, a task force made up of volunteers from the U.S. Army's Special Forces and the Air Force's Special Operations Force landed at the North Vietnamese prisoner-of-war camp at Sontay, twenty-three miles west of Hanoi, in a daring but futile attempt to liberate the 70 to 100 American POWs who were believed to be held there. The attempt was futile because when the task-force helicopters landed at Sontay, the camp was empty: unknown to American commanders, the prisoners had been removed (though apparently not very far) shortly before. This was a highly embarrassing intelligence failure, inasmuch as the operation had been long and carefully planned, with life-size mock-ups of the Sontay buildings erected at the Eglin Air Force Base in Florida, and so on. The timing of the raid had related to Nixon's wish to have the liberated prisoners home for Thanksgiving. But the best the helicopter force could do was to land at Sontay, determine that there were no prisoners to free, and extricate itself after a firefight with North Vietnamese guards.

For two days, no government sources in either Washington or Hanoi reported the Sontay raid. Laird said later that he was not planning on announcing it at all because it had failed. As for Hanoi, its silence was evidently due to embarrassment that American helicopters had so easily penetrated its air defenses.

On November 27, the Defense Department admitted aircraft flying cover for the American helicopter commandos had attacked North Vietnamese SAM and antiaircraft emplacements near Hanoi; this action had included the use of guided Shrike bombs designed to neutralize the SAMs. A few days earlier, Laird had told a congressional committee that the only "diversionary" activity during the Sontay raid was flares dropped by navy planes to deflect North Vietnamese radar. The administration kept insisting that the air strikes against North Vietnam on that November weekend—strikes intended to disrupt Hanoi's military preparations for a possible offensive in the South—were distinct from the air support around Hanoi given the helicopter "mercy mission."

In general, the state of affairs in Indochina was discouraging as 1970 drew to an end. The October peace initiative had failed, the North Vietnamese were stepping up infiltrations, and the situation in Cambodia remained so uncertain that Nixon asked Congress in a special message on November 18 for supplemental funds for the Lon Nol regime for the balance of the fiscal year. This was part of his broader request for supplemental foreign-aid appropriations throughout the world for the next seven months.

For Cambodia, Nixon asked $155 million in new funds—$85 million for military assistance, mainly in the form of ammunition—as well as $100 million to restore funds taken from other foreign appropriations during the year to help the Cambodians. But while the president claimed that American activities in Cambodia were confined to supplying military and economic aid, a report by investigators for the Senate Foreign Relations Committee, issued in December, charged that U.S. aircraft were providing "close air support" for the Cambodian Army and performing other combat missions under the "camouflage" of preventing Communist infiltrations from North to South Vietnam. The conclusion was that American operations in Cambodia were inextricably related to the Vietnam war. This situation seemed to violate a provision in the legislation approving new aid for Cambodia that such assistance should not be considered as a U.S. commitment to defend the Lon Nol regime. The Nixon administration was living from deception to deception.

(There also was quite a bit of self-deception in Washington's appreciation of the situation in Vietnam. For example, Nixon frequently claimed in public that areas held by South Vietnamese and American forces were increasingly secure from Viet Cong penetration, but a classified survey conducted in late October in 242 hamlets in 35 South Vietnamese provinces under the Pacification Attitude Analysis System [PAAS] showed that 59 percent of the respondents said that "small to medium-size [Viet Cong] forces can enter their hamlet at night"; 62 percent said that hamlets are not "secure enough to take down fortifications." This PAAS survey, like all others, was sent to the State Department by the Saigon embassy in a confidential telegram.)

On December 10, the president undertook to explain at his news conference the November bombings of North Vietnam as well as to warn that new air strikes would be ordered if Hanoi continued to challenge the United States. The November raids, he said, were in response to North Vietnamese ground fire against unarmed reconnaissance planes. Hanoi's denials notwithstanding, he said, an understanding existed since 1968 that American reconnaissance aircraft over North Vietnam would not be fired upon; this was part of the price for the bombing pause ordered by Lyndon Johnson.

Discussing the negotiating scene in Paris, the president announced that earlier in the day the American delegation had proposed the exchange of 8200 North Vietnamese war prisoners held by American and South Vietnamese forces for 800 American and other allied POWs in Hanoi's hands. But his earlier optimism over progress in negotiations had now vanished. His tone suggested that diplomatic prospects were bleak and the United States had no choice but to center again on the battlefield. Asked whether the war might end by 1972—and how many Americans would be in Vietnam by 1972—the president replied:

> I am not going to indicate the rate of withdrawal of Americans as long as we are still negotiating in Paris. Indicating the rate of withdrawal, indicating when the Vietnamization program would be concluded, would completely destroy any reason to continue the Paris negotiations. The Paris negotiations have not produced results. We do not have great hopes for them at this time. But we are going to continue to try in that line, and as long as we are negotiating there, I am not going to indicate a withdrawal schedule.

A letter Nixon sent on December 26 to the families of the POWs further emphasized his gloom:

> Hanoi . . . has so far rebuffed every effort to obtain release of our men or to verify the conditions of their treatment. This attitude violates not only the Geneva Convention, which Hanoi had pledged to observe, but all common standards of human decency. It is barbaric. It has been universally and justifiably condemned.

Despite the stalemate between Washington and Hanoi, there was some reason for hope about U.S.–China relations. The Cambodian intervention in May had interrupted the ambassadorial-level talks between the Americans and the Chinese in Warsaw, but the White House received hints throughout the summer and early fall through friendly governments that Peking continued to be interested in improving relations. It was only a question of time—and opportunity—before the dialogue would be taken up again.

Kissinger set his NSC staff and the State Department to work on new China position papers. Two interdepartmental working groups were organized to pull together all the knowledge on China available to the United States government in the form of two massive studies. Aside from the NSC, the center of this activity was the State Department's Office of Chinese Communist Affairs. A senior official who took charge of this effort in the summer of 1970 recalled later, "We were producing papers in great tonnage, reviewing China policy with all of its conceivable options: what would happen if we did this or didn't do that, and what would happen to our interests in the rest of the world if we did it or didn't." As usual, the White House offered no particular explanation as to why it desired such massive studies on a crash basis. But "from the magnitude of these China studies, we definitely assumed that a major policy effort was under way, though we didn't know the exact chapter and verse as to how the president planned to execute such an approach." NSSM–106 was completed on November 19.

Nixon's approach was executed in October through the presidents of Pakistan and Romania when they visited the United States for the celebration of the twenty-fifth anniversary of the United Nations. (In Ceauşescu's case, it was also a two-week state visit to the United States, returning Nixon's visit to Bucharest the year before.)

Knowing that Yahya Khan was en route to Peking after his American visit, Nixon asked him to convey to the top Chinese leaders a message couched in general terms about the desire of the United States to establish a relationship with China. The two presidents then agreed that Yahya Khan would relay back to Washington whatever messages he might receive from the Chinese. This was when the principal secret channel between Washington and Peking was set up. Both Nixon and Yahya Khan felt that such a secret channel was necessary because the Warsaw ambassadorial talks were too visible, too cumbersome, and involved too many people.

But the White House also wished it to be *publicly* known that the United States was pursuing contacts with China. Ron Ziegler told newsmen that in his meeting with Yahya Khan, Nixon "indicated that the United States is continuing the understanding of Pakistan's independent foreign policy of maintaining warm relations with the major powers." Then this brief dialogue ensued:

Reporter: Was the president of Pakistan's proposed visit to China . . . or relations with China, touched upon?

Ziegler: I would think it would have been. President Yahya, of course, has just returned from Moscow and is planning a visit to China. President Nixon no doubt conveyed to President Yahya his general feelings about China.

Reporter: Was President Yahya given a message to the Chinese?

Ziegler: No formal message as such, no.

By coincidence, Nixon met later that same day with Nationalist China's premier, C. K. Yen, also visiting the United States for the United Nations anniversary, but nothing was said concerning the emerging American policies toward Peking.

Two days later, on October 26, Nixon received Ceaușescu at the White House. In this instance, Nixon's hope was that the Romanians would pass on his views to Peking through their own channels, and there was no suggestion that Bucharest act as a full-time intermediary. His public signal to Peking came in a toast to Ceaușescu at the White House dinner that evening: "There are times when the leader of one nation does not have adequate communication with the leader of another. But as I was saying to the president earlier today, he is rather in a unique position. He heads a government which is one of the few in the world which has good relations with the United States, good relations with the Soviet Union, and good relations with the People's Republic of China." This was the first time that an American president had publicly referred to the Peking government as the "People's Republic of China." In fact, it was a major policy decision to employ that name, inasmuch as in the subtle language of diplomacy it conveyed a form of acceptance of the existence of the Peking government. Nixon's choice of language received scant attention in the United States, but it was immediately noticed on the highest levels in Peking.

Nixon then added, "It is extremely valuable for the president of the United States to have the opportunity to speak to the president of Romania to discuss . . . these broader world problems in which Romania . . . can make a very constructive contribution to the eventual peaceful world we all want to share together." This was more than formal politeness. Their two-hour conference at the White House that morning had been extremely useful, and, a White House official remarked afterward, Nixon learned twice as much from Ceaușescu about how the leaders of the Communist world thought than from an earlier conversation with Soviet Foreign Minister Gromyko.

Events in Chinese-American relations began to move with a certain speed. Yahya Khan relayed Nixon's message to Chairman Mao Tse-tung and Premier Chou En-lai, discussed the subject at some length with Chou, and received what he considered an encouraging, if vague, response. Back in Islamabad, he entrusted Foreign Secretary Sultan Khan, a career diplomat who had served for five years as ambassador in Peking, with personal responsibility for acting as the channel between the United States and China. Sultan's first act was to pass on to Washington the Chinese reaction to Nixon's overtures.

To assure maximum secrecy, Sultan was the only Pakistani official in Islamabad besides President Yahya to be aware of this system. Here is how it worked: Chinese messages to the United States were delivered personally by Chinese diplomats to the foreign secretary, then he relayed them in cipher or by pouch to his ambassador in Washington, Agha Hilaly, who in turn took them personally to Kissinger at the White House. It worked the same way in reverse. Sultan, however, took upon himself the additional role of *interpreting* the American messages for the Chinese ambassador in Islamabad. He made recommendations and, when he deemed it necessary, offered advice. As he explained, "because of so many nuances, messages in cold print might have delayed the dialogue or even caused misunderstandings." Because of his long experience in Peking, the foreign secretary was fully trusted by the Chinese, who sought his opinions on a whole range of matters pertaining to the United States: Nixon's personality, the role of Kissinger, the attitudes of Congress, the views of the American press, and so on. Completely unfamiliar with the American scene as they were, they came to depend heavily on Sultan Khan.

The Nixon administration was not yet ready, however, to make an open diplomatic commitment to Peking at the expense of the Chinese Nationalists, with whom the United States maintained cordial if occasionally strained relations. Taiwan was America's ally in the strictest sense, with American troops and aircraft stationed on Generalissimo Chiang Kai-shek's island. For this reason, Washington kept up its opposition to Peking's seating in the General Assembly when the perennial question of Chinese representation came up at the 1970 fall session. For years, the United States was able to prevent this issue from coming to a formal test through the stratagem of having the assembly declare that Chinese representation was an "important question" under the provisions of the United Nations Charter, requiring a two-thirds majority for an affirmative decision to seat Peking. The vote to declare it an "important question" required a simple majority, which the United States was always able to marshal. Each year, however, the winning margin narrowed—as more and more nations established diplomatic relations with Peking and broke with Taiwan. Peking, insisting that there was only one China, refused to enter relationships with countries that kept ties with Taiwan.

In 1970, the United States felt compelled to fight again for Taiwan, although the State Department knew that this was probably the last year it could win a majority. Nixon nevertheless decided to proceed on the grounds that domestic public opinion was not yet ready for a sudden switch to Peking (and this was an election year) and the secret diplomacy had not yet progressed sufficiently. (In the end, Peking's backers once more lost the General Assembly battle.) The Chinese evidently understood Nixon's situation and, philosophically, chose to ignore the United States stand on the representation issue. They knew it was only a matter of time, perhaps no more than a year, before they gained full membership in the United Nations. They had also noted the American hints of a two-Chinas policy.

In mid-December, Premier Chou En-lai told Gheorghe Rădulescu, a deputy premier of the Romanian Council of Ministers, that China was interested in a relationship with the United States if the Americans "could find a solution for Taiwan." Receiving Rădulescu's report, Ceauşescu summoned his ambassador in the United States, Corneliu Bogdan, to Bucharest on an urgent and secret basis to acquaint him with the Peking conversation. He instructed Bogdan to pass Chou's message on to Kissinger. When the two men met in Washington, Kissinger asked Bogdan whether Chou meant that the United States must end its ties with Taiwan as a precondition for any relationship with Peking; Bogdan replied that while he could not interpret Chou's thoughts, his own impression was that the Chinese premier was, in effect, suggesting that the White House elaborate a mutually acceptable compromise formula—without trying to tell the United States what to do. The Romanian message was a major milestone in this secret diplomacy.

Other signals, perhaps even more important, started coming from Chairman Mao. On October 1, China's National Day, Mao invited Edgar Snow, the American writer he had known for thirty-five years, to join him in reviewing the parade in T'ien An Men Square. This was an unusual gesture toward an American; Nixon recognized it as such. On December 18, Mao was interviewed at length by Snow. When Snow raised the question of Americans being allowed to visit China more freely, Mao came up with this surprising answer, subsequently paraphrased by Snow:

The Foreign Ministry was studying the matter of admitting Americans from the left, middle and right to visit China. Should rightists, like Nixon, who represented the monopoly capitalists, be permitted to come? He should be welcome because, Mao explained, at present the problems between China and the USA would have to be solved with Nixon. Mao would be happy to talk with him, either as a tourist or as President. . . . Discussing Nixon's possible visit to China, the Chairman casually remarked that the presidential election would be in 1972, would it not? Therefore, he added, Mr. Nixon might send an envoy first, but was not himself likely to come to Peking before early 1972.

These comments were not published until April 1971, but their essence was quickly communicated to the White House. The conclusion was that Mao was responding in the most direct possible way to the suggestion that a high-level American emissary be sent to Peking to upgrade the new dialogue. The idea that *Nixon himself* might visit China was wholly unexpected; it had not occurred to anybody in Washington. But now this long-range plan outlined by Mao became plausible. If Kissinger could, indeed, elaborate a formula skirting the Taiwan issue, as Chou had hinted, then he could go to Peking as the "envoy" Mao had suggested. Things were moving more rapidly than Nixon and Kissinger would have dared to imagine.

Pleased as Nixon was with the progress in his overtures to China, business with the Soviet Union was excruciatingly slow. Obviously, the two situations were not comparable: with China, the United States was involved in no more than preliminary diplomacy; with the Soviet Union, there were major substantive issues under negotiation. Still, the president and Kissinger felt that the Russians should be more responsive along the whole spectrum—SALT, the Middle East, Berlin, and Indochina.

Answering a question at his December 10 news conference, the president remarked about Soviet-American relations that "sometimes they're warmer and sometimes they're cooler." He added:

The significant thing is that we are negotiating and not confronting. We are talking at SALT. We are very far apart because our vital interests are involved, but we are talking, and our vital interests . . . require that we have some limitation on arms, both because of the cost and because of the danger of a nuclear confrontation. And so it is with Berlin, so it is with the Mideast. I am not suggesting that we are going to find easy agreement, because we are two great powers that are going to continue to be competitive for our lifetime.

Late in December, Secretary Rogers and Soviet Ambassador Dobrynin discussed the possibility of a resumption of Middle East peace talks under the aegis of Gunnar Jarring. Since the talks had broken down in August after Egypt and the Soviet Union had moved the SAM batteries into the Suez Canal truce zone—the Israelis refused to negotiate until the violations were "rectified"—Rogers was now seeking assurances from Dobrynin that there would be no further interference with the cease-fire. The State Department declared that while there was no "direct" understanding on truce violations, "the Soviets understand that we expect, we hope that the cease-fire will be maintained and that there will be no other military violations." (Just before the end of the year, Israel agreed to go back to the Jarring mediation. Congress had recently approved an additional $500 million in military assistance to Israel, and this evidently influenced Jerusalem's unenthusiastic decision to give the diplomatic process another try.)

But in light of the reality of the nuclear stalemate, President Nixon was prepared—indeed eager—to negotiate with the Soviet Union on a whole range of world issues, as well as to seek special relationships likely to benefit both countries. He busied himself improving relations with Eastern Europe as part of wider policies toward the Soviet Union. In these policy endeavors, ideological questions were wholly irrelevant. In this sense, Nixon's personal and deeply ingrained anti-Communism—and Kissinger's own version of it—was unrelated to the global policies they were pursuing. It was not a "new Nixon" who emerged from the 1968 elections to champion negotiation over confrontation with the Communist superpowers; it was a coldly calculating strategist who perceived the finite limits of United States power in the nuclear world—but not necessarily in nonnuclear situations—and truly believed that a "structure of peace" had to be hammered together with the Russians and the Chinese to defuse the nuclear dangers.

But it was also part of this pragmatism to keep fighting the Indochina war in the cause of anti-Communism—for this remained the fundamental tenet of American foreign policy—and to checkmate the Soviets in the Middle East and elsewhere. In other words, Nixon and Kissinger dealt with world Communism on two levels: working for a relaxation of global tensions with the nuclear superpowers while combating Communism regionally. They feared more the emergence of regional Communist focuses, where they could be hard to control and become contagious, than the Communist power status quo as represented by Moscow and Peking. With the latter, they assumed, rational negotiations were both necessary and possible because the Russians and the Chinese had to behave as responsible world powers.

This approach was not merely an expression of Nixon's conservative anti-Communism. It was a basic strain in postwar American policy, and it had guided conservatives and liberals alike. Kennedy and Johnson had engaged America in the Vietnam war in the name of anti-Communism; like Nixon later, they had claimed that the United States could not abandon its allies. It was Kennedy who committed American prestige to the Bay of Pigs invasion to wrest Cuba away from Communism and who allowed the CIA to conduct a clandestine war against Fidel Castro. And it was Johnson who ordered American military intervention in the Dominican Republic's civil war in 1965, convinced that he was saving the Dominicans from Communism. It was also under Johnson's administration that the United States covertly poured resources into Chile to prevent the election of a Marxist president. This was the ideological and political background against which Nixon and Kissinger launched an intervention into the internal affairs of Chile in 1970.

The United States had been using the CIA from the outset of the cold war to influence events around the world covertly—and often violently. It had become part of the American political ethos. But aside from long-range military-type operations, the CIA had never been used as systematically to affect the affairs of a foreign nation as it was called upon to do in Chile over a period of years.

The target of this CIA intervention in Chile—in 1964 as in 1970 and subsequently—was Salvador Allende Gossens, a Socialist politician (a physician by profession) with views that were fairly radical by Washington's standards, and something of a personal friendship with Fidel Castro, whom he had visited on a number of occasions. Allende was the leader of a leftist coalition that included his Socialist Party, the Communists, the left-wing faction of the Radical Party, and various Marxist splinter groups. Though certainly a Marxist, Allende never espoused the Communist orthodoxy. He first ran for the presidency of Chile in 1958, but was badly beaten by the conservative candidate, Jorge Alessandri. In 1964, he reappeared as a much more formidable contender in a race against Eduardo Frei Montalvo, the leader of the Christian Democrats, a man with rather progressive positions on such issues as land reform and even the nationalization of Chilean copper mines, most of them owned by American companies.

The United States' support of Frei started in 1962, two years before the actual elections, when John Kennedy's White House approved $180,-000 in covert funds to be funneled to the Christian Democrats via a third country. By September 1964, when the Chileans went to the polls, the CIA had spent $3 million. In the words of a subsequent study by the Senate Select Committee on Intelligence Activities (the Church committee),

> a total of nearly four million dollars was spent on some fifteen covert action projects, ranging from organizing slum dwellers to passing funds to political parties. . . . In addition to support for political parties, the CIA mounted a massive anti-Communist propaganda campaign. Extensive use was made of the press, radio, films, pamphlets, posters, leaflets, direct mailings, paper streamers and wall paintings. It was a "scare campaign," which relied heavily on images of Soviet tanks and Cuban firing squads and was directed especially to women. Hundreds of thousands of copies of the anti-communist pastoral letter of Pope Pius XI were distributed by Christian Democratic organizations. . . . "Disinformation" and "black propaganda"— material which purported to originate from another source, such as the Chilean Communist Party—were used as well. . . . The CIA regards the anti-communist scare campaign as the most effective activity undertaken by the U.S. on behalf of the Christian Democratic candidates.

Frei obtained a clear majority over Allende in the 1964 elections, and a CIA study concluded that the U.S. intervention had made the difference. The report also noted that "a group of American businessmen in Chile offered to provide one and a half million dollars to be administered and disbursed covertly by the U.S. government to prevent Allende from winning. . . ." The 303 Committee, the White House group in charge of coordinating covert-intelligence operations, turned down this offer because, according to the Senate report, this was "neither a secure way nor an honorable way of doing business. . . . However, CIA money, represented as private money, was passed to the Christian Democrats through a private businessman."

Frei's election did not mark the end of covert American activities in Chile. In 1965, the White House approved $175,000 in covert funds for the CIA to support candidates it favored in Chilean congressional elections. This helped to elect nine pro-American candidates and defeat thirteen candidates of the Allende coalition. In July 1968, $350,000 was authorized to support anti-Allende candidates in the March 1969 congressional races. The United States was being farsighted: it began working against Allende's expected candidacy in the 1970 presidential election as soon as the 1964 election was over. The Senate committee's report said that "the CIA spent a total of almost two million dollars on covert action in Chile" between the two elections.

What the Nixon administration proceeded to do was to continue and increase covert operations in Chile as the new elections approached. The White House took the first high-level look at Chile when the Forty Committee considered the Allende problem at an April 17, 1969, meeting. (The Forty Committee had replaced the 303 Committee in the NSC apparatus as the decision-making body for major covert-intelligence operations. It was chaired by Kissinger, and its members were the director of Central Intelligence, the chairman of the Joint Chiefs of Staff, the deputy secretary of defense, and the under secretary of state for political affairs. From the outset, however, Kissinger was the key figure on the committee. Forty Committee meetings were always held in utmost secrecy and virtually no records were kept on them in the NSC except for dates and sometimes topics. The group's permanent secretary was a CIA official detailed to the NSC.)

At the April meeting, no new decisions were taken although Helms, the director of Central Intelligence, offered the opinion that a Chilean election operation would not be effective unless it started early. Kissinger had not yet focused on Chile. He knew very little about Latin America and was not particularly interested in it. The exception was Cuba because it had already become a Communist state, and Kissinger looked at it from the viewpoint of Soviet-American relations. According to his NSC aides, Kissinger was constantly urging Helms—from the very beginning—to infiltrate more CIA agents into Cuba so as to gather intelligence on Soviet activities there and create problems for Castro. Helms resisted this on the grounds that Cuba was rather low on the CIA's list of priorities and he had a shortage of agents.

Meanwhile, Chilean politics produced a three-way race for the 1970 presidential election. Allende was the candidate of Unidad Popular (UP, Popular Unity), the reorganized leftist coalition; Radomiro Tomič, a left-wing Christian Democrat, was supported by Frei, but his candidacy was ideologically preempted by Allende. Finally, the conservatives put up former President Alessandri. Clearly the race was going to be between Allende and Alessandri, and just as clearly, as far as the United States was concerned, Allende was the man to beat. He stood for the nationalization of the copper industry (although the Chilean Congress under Frei had already taken the first step in that direction, through a "Chileanization" law providing for a gradual transfer of the mines to the Chilean state), stepped-up land reform (it was Frei who had started it), control of many sectors of the economy, a vast housing program, higher wages, social programs, and independence in foreign policy.

Allende's candidacy alarmed the American business community in Santiago, as it did the American embassy. Ambassador Edward Korry, a former newspaperman whom Kennedy had brought into the diplomatic service, took a rather conservative view of his host country; he even had problems with the Christian Democrats. In December 1969, Korry and the CIA station chief in Santiago, receptive to American businessmen there, drafted a plan for a covert anti-Allende campaign resembling the 1964 operation, but Washington was not yet prepared to authorize it, for Rogers and Charles Meyer, the assistant secretary for inter-American affairs, had doubts about the wisdom of such an American involvement. Rogers was not an interventionist, and Kissinger had not yet appropriated Chile as an area of his special interest.*

On March 25, 1970, the Forty Committee again examined Chile. It made a partial decision: to oppose Allende actively but to support neither Alessandri nor Tomič for the time being. In this, the Forty Committee was, in effect, acting on the basis of a National Intelligence Estimate (NIE) produced in late 1969. A NIE is an agreed estimate reflecting the views of all the intelligence agencies in Washington. As summarized by the Senate committee's report, this NIE predicted that "whoever succeeded Frei in the presidency was likely to continue to stress Chilean independence, to be less cooperative with the U.S. than Frei had been, and to explore somewhat broader relations with Communist countries. . . . Were Allende to win, his administration would almost certainly take steps aimed at moving Chile away from the U.S. . . . Steps toward either government participation in or outright nationalization of U.S. copper holdings in Chile were inevitable."

Actually, Frei had ceased to be the darling of Washington sometime earlier because of his views on copper and his increasingly independent foreign policy. Korry blamed Frei's foreign minister, Gabriel Valdés, for this trend. But in any event, the United States could not back Tomič because he was to the left of Frei. The CIA felt that the United States should support Alessandri, the candidate of the National Party. Accord-

---

*In 1977, Korry brought suit in federal court against ITT and Geneen, alleging that false and misleading testimony had been given to various congressional committees, that responsibility had been foisted on him for their own covert political actions in Chile, and that he had not heard of Track II (see below, pp. 362ff.) until June 1975.

ing to the Senate committee, the CIA "believed that Alessandri, the apparent front runner, needed more than money; he needed help in managing his campaign." While the Forty Committee had resolved in March not to provide assistance to any candidate—the CIA's recommendations notwithstanding—it did authorize $135,000 for covert "spoiling" operations *against* Allende. The agency proposed this course of action after its pro-Alessandri recommendations were turned down.

On June 18, Korry presented the State Department and the CIA with an updated plan: it called for an increase in support for the "spoiling" anti-Allende campaign and for a $500,000 contingency fund to be used to swing votes in the Chilean Congress should neither Allende nor Alessandri win a clear majority. (Under the Chilean constitution, the Congress elects the president if neither of the two leading candidates garners more than 50 percent of the popular vote.) Korry was evidently the most respectable spokesman for the "hard-line" position against Allende—the CIA was simply *expected* to take such a stand—but his State Department superiors remained cautious. As the Senate report put it, "In response to State Department reluctance, the Ambassador responded by querying: if Allende were to gain power, how would the U.S. respond to those who asked what actions it had taken to prevent it?" This smacked of the old "Who lost China?" and "Who lost Cuba?" arguments of the past—and it did produce some results. Ambassador Korry flooded the department with Cassandra-like dispatches ("Korrygrams") and, several times, he predicted that Allende's victory would be worse than Castro's.

Consequently, when the Forty Committee discussed Chile on June 27, it agreed to authorize an additional $300,000 for the anti-Allende campaign. The Senate report noted that "State Department officials at the meeting voted 'yes' only reluctantly." They also opposed Korry's "contingency plan" and action on this point was deferred until after the elections. The final decision was to fight Allende, but not to provide actual support for Alessandri.

But that rightist candidate, as it turned out, found other angels: the International Telephone and Telegraph Company—which held a $100-million controlling interest in the Chilean telephone company and was determined at all costs to prevent Allende's victory—and some of its fellow American corporations. ITT's board of directors, at a special meeting in New York in June to assess the Chilean situation, decided to engage its own resources against Allende. It also developed the notion that the ITT should work hand in hand with the CIA. One of its directors, John McCone—a former CIA director and still a consultant to the agency—was delegated to establish this liaison. During late June and July, McCone met several times with Helms, and a working relationship between the agency and the corporate giant was presently set in motion. It seemed to confirm the worst Marxist demonological dreams about government and big business jointly formulating American foreign policy. On July 16, ITT president Harold Geneen told the head of the CIA's Western Hemisphere Division, William Broe, that ITT had earmarked $350,000 to support Alessandri and suggested that the CIA handle the disbursements. Broe, on instructions from Helms, told Geneen that the CIA could not handle private funds, but he offered the CIA's assistance on how best it could be done. (Helms denied this cooperation when he testified before a Senate committee in 1973. In 1977, he pleaded "no contest" on charges of lying to the senators. He was allowed this plea by the Justice Department to avoid a trial at which CIA secrets might have been revealed.) ITT was not the only American corporation to invest in the elections. The Senate report told the story:

> Some $350,000 of ITT money was passed to Alessandri during the campaign—$250,000 to his campaign and $100,000 to the National Party. About another $350,000 came from other U.S. businesses. According to the CIA documents, the Station Chief informed the Ambassador that the CIA was advising ITT in funding the Alessandri campaign, but not that the Station was aiding ITT in passing money to the National Party.

The Anaconda Company, the owner of copper mines, offered $500,000 to help beat Allende.

The extent of the CIA intervention in Chilean politics during the 1970 presidential campaign is best described in the report of the Senate select committee:

> The "spoiling" operations had two objectives: (1) undermining communist efforts to bring about a coalition of leftist forces which could gain control of the presidency in 1970; and (2) strengthening non-Marxist political leaders and forces in Chile in order to develop an effective alternative to the Popular Unity coalition in preparation for the 1970 presidential election. In working toward these objectives, the CIA made use of half-a-dozen covert action projects. These projects were focused into an intensive propaganda campaign which made use of virtually all media within Chile and which placed and replaced items in the international press as well. Propaganda placements were achieved through subsidizing right-wing women's and "civic action"

groups. A "scare campaign," using many of the same themes as the 1964 presidential election program, equated an Allende victory with violence and Stalinist repression. . . . The CIA's effort prior to the election included political action aimed at splintering the non-Marxist Radical Party and reducing the number of votes which it could deliver to the Popular Unity coalition's candidate. Also, "black propaganda" . . . was used in 1970 to sow dissent between Communists and Social-ists, and between the national labor confederation and the Chilean Communist Party. . . . During the 1970 campaign [the CIA] produced hundreds of thousands of high-quality printed pieces, ranging from posters and leaflets to picture books, and carried out an extensive propaganda program through many radio and press outlets. . . . A newsletter mailed to approximately two thousand journalists, academicians, politicians, and other opinion makers; a booklet show-ing what life would be like if Allende won the presidential election; translation and distribution of chronicles of opposition to the Soviet regime; poster distribution and sign-painting teams. The sign-paint-ing teams had instructions to paint the slogan *"su paredón"* (your wall) on 2,000 walls, evoking an image of communist firing squads. The "scare campaign" exploited the violence of the invasion of Czecho-slovakia with large photographs of Prague and of tanks in downtown Santiago. Other posters . . . portrayed Cuban political prisoners be-fore the firing squad, and warned that an Allende victory would mean the end of religion and family life in Chile.

The next time the Forty Committee met on Chile was on August 7, mainly to bring itself up to date. No decisions were taken, but the empha-sis was on what American policy should be in the event of Allende's victory. Korry's earlier optimism that Alessandri would win was now being seriously questioned. On July 24, Kissinger had ordered the NSC to produce a special study on Chile—he wanted policy alternatives if Allende won—and a paper based on its conclusions was circulated to Forty Committee members on August 13. NSSM–97, approved on Au-gust 18 by the NSC's Interdepartmental Group (IG), contained four options ranging from the possibility of normal relations with Chile under Allende to the suggestion that covert action be undertaken with the greatest intensity to bring about his fall—or even to prevent him from taking office. The IG favored maintaining minimal relations with Allende, but the NSC's Senior Review Group, headed by Kissinger, resolved to await the elections just a few weeks away. The State Department was still fighting a rearguard action against full-blown intervention in Chile; the White House, the Defense Department, and the CIA favored it.

This majority view was supported by the NIE on Chile issued late in

July. This NIE was quite pessimistic about Chilean-American relations under Allende.

> [It] stated that if Allende were to win the election, he would almost certainly take harsh measures against U.S. business interests in Chile and challenge U.S. policies in the Hemisphere. . . . [It] cited several foreign policy problems an Allende regime would pose for the U.S., including recognition of Cuba, possible withdrawal from the Organization of American States, the deterioration of relations with Argentina, and anti-U.S. votes in the United Nations. . . . [It] predicted, however, that Allende would probably not seek a break with the United States over the next two years.

The NIE also argued, in the words of the Senate committee, that Allende "would proceed as rapidly as possible toward the establishment of a Marxist-Socialist state," which "would be a Chilean version of a Soviet-style East European Communist state." The intelligence document took the view that Allende expected progress on "basic bread and butter issues," helping him to win the 1973 congressional elections and thus impose a "Socialist state of Marxist variety by the *vía pacífica* [peaceful road]." The CIA and Korry, whose views were reflected in the NIE, talked of the imposition of a "classic Marxist-Leninist regime in Chile." Again, the State Department, speaking through its Intelligence and Research Bureau, dissented from such stark evaluations. But as far as the majority in the administration was concerned, Chile was a "worst case" situation.

On September 4, 1970, Allende won a small plurality but not a majority in the presidential election. (He had 36.3 percent of the vote; Alessandri was 1 percentage point behind with 35.3 percent. Tomič and minor candidates wound up with 28.4 percent. Allende had defeated Alessandri by 39,000 votes out of a total of 3 million ballots.) Allende emerged in this narrowest of victories with just a little over one-third of the national vote. But if the issue was couched in terms of whether the Chilean electorate in general was swinging leftward, the answer was affirmative inasmuch as Tomic also represented left-of-center views, and the Christian Democrats gave him nearly 28 percent of the vote. Ideologically, then, it could be argued that the *antirightist* vote by Allende's and Tomic's supporters totaled around 64 percent.

But Washington was not interested in such subtleties. Nor did it care for the sanctity of the democratic process—if it went against its interests. There was no awareness that the Chilean election represented a new current in history—Allende, after all, won in a free election—just as there was no awareness that new ideas and forces were coming to the fore in the so-called third world. In the case of Chile, what mattered was that the detested Allende, perceived by the majority of responsible officials as a tool of Communism (although nobody had proof of it then—or later), had been elected despite the best efforts by the CIA and American corporate interests. The next step, therefore, was to keep him from taking office in November. The Chilean Congress was to vote on October 24 between Allende and Alessandri, and the immediate objective was to make sure that it went Alessandri's way.

But there were enormous contradictions in Washington's position. Despite all the earlier cries about the awesome perils of Allende's victory, the CIA suddenly reached the conclusion that it was not all quite that catastrophic. A CIA intelligence memorandum, a top-secret document issued immediately after the elections, summarized the conclusions reached by the Interdepartmental Group after studying NSSM–97. This is how the Senate committee told it: "The Group . . . concluded that the United States had no vital interests within Chile, the world military balance of power would not be significantly altered by an Allende regime, and an Allende victory in Chile would not pose any likely threat to the peace of the region. The group noted, however, that an Allende victory would threaten Hemispheric cohesion and would represent a psychological setback to the U.S. as well as a definite advance for the Marxist idea."

Nevertheless, the administration decided to intervene in Chilean affairs because, to put it bluntly, it was running scared of history. If Allende's election was a "psychological setback," it was because the United States made it so by its preelection attitudes. The administration, then, went after self-fulfilling prophecies. And the business community was pressing: John McCone went as far as to offer $1 million to Kissinger and Helms for CIA operations. He received no answer.

The Forty Committee met on September 8 and again on September 14 to make plans for action designed to prevent Allende from being confirmed by the Chilean Congress. At the second meeting, the group came up with this stratagem: if the Chilean Congress could be made to elect Alessandri, he would immediately step down so that special elections could be held with ex-President Frei legally running for office. This wild idea became known as the "Frei gambit." The notion was that Chilean congressmen could be bribed to vote for Alessandri, and the Forty Committee approved $350,000 in covert funds to be handled by Ambassador Korry to win the support of the moderate faction of the Christian Democrats for Alessandri on October 24.

But Nixon and Kissinger did not trust this operation; they preferred immediate and conclusive action. Chile seemed so urgent to the president that he found time to deal with it in the midst of the Jordan crisis. On September 15, Nixon met with Kissinger, Helms, and John Mitchell. According to the Senate committee report, Nixon ordered the CIA, acting in absolute secrecy, to organize a military *coup d'état* in Chile. Thus:

> Nixon informed CIA Director Richard Helms that an Allende regime in Chile would not be acceptable to the United States and instructed the CIA to play a direct role in organizing a military coup d'état in Chile to prevent Allende's accession to the Presidency. . . . This effort was to be conducted without the knowledge of the Departments of State and Defense or the Ambassador. . . . [It] was never discussed at a Forty Committee meeting. . . . It quickly became apparent to both White House and CIA officials that a military coup was the only way to prevent Allende's accession to power.

Actually, the CIA had been thinking all along in terms of a military coup. As early as July 1969 the CIA station in Santiago had received approval from headquarters for a covert program "to establish intelligence assets in the Chilean armed services for the purpose of monitoring coup plotting." This program existed for four years, and "it involved assets drawn from all three branches of the Chilean military and included command-level officers, field- and company-grade officers, retired general staff officers and enlisted men." The CIA was encouraged by a revolt on October 21, 1969, by a military unit at Tacna, in northern Chile, led by General Roberto Viaux, a rightist officer—even though it failed—for the agency thought it indicated that forces within the Chilean military establishment were prepared to move against Allende when the time came.

From that point on, American policy toward Chile operated on what was known to top White House and CIA officials as Track I and Track II. Track I consisted of all the covert activities authorized by the Forty Committee designed to keep Allende out of office. It included the "Frei gambit" and the whole spectrum of political, economic, and propaganda activities. Track II was the planning for a military coup.

In sworn written answers to questions submitted to him by the Senate select committee in 1975, Nixon denied that he had specifically ordered the CIA to carry out a military coup in Chile. "I . . . informed Mr. Helms that to be successful, any effort to defeat Mr. Allende would have to be supported by the military factions in Chile. I do not recall discussing

during the September 15, 1970, meeting specific means to be used by the
CIA to prevent Mr. Allende from assuming the Presidency of Chile."
This, however, conflicted with Kissinger's and Helms's testimony. Kissinger said, "There was work by all of the agencies to try to prevent
Allende from being seated, and there was work by all of the agencies on
the so-called Track II to encourage the military to move against Allende.
. . . The difference between the September 15 meeting and what was
being done in general within the Government was that President Nixon
was encouraging a more direct role for the CIA in actually organizing
such a coup." Helms's testimony was even more explicit: "This was a
pretty all-inclusive order. If I ever carried a marshal's baton in my knap-
sack out of the Oval Office, it was that day." But Nixon also swore that
his reasons for acting against Allende in 1970 were based on "the same
national security interests which I had understood prompted Presidents
Kennedy and Johnson to act from 1962 to 1964" against the Castro
regime in Cuba.

On September 16, Kissinger offered a public rationale for the administration's opposition to Allende although he revealed nothing of the
subversion against the Chilean president-elect. He did it in the form of
a background briefing for the press when he accompanied Nixon to
Chicago for a meeting with Midwestern editors. It is worth recalling
because it demonstrated his utter ignorance of the Latin American political scene at the time he was engaged in making major decisions about the
fate of Chile, as well as his ideological perception of the world as a whole:

> Now it is fairly easy for one to predict that if Allende wins, there is a
> good chance that he will establish over a period of years some sort of
> Communist government. In that case you would have one not on an
> island off the coast which has not a traditional relationship and impact
> on Latin America, but in a major Latin American country you would
> have a Communist government, joining, for example, Argentina,
> which is already deeply divided, along a long frontier; joining Peru,
> which has already been heading in directions that have been difficult
> to deal with, and joining Bolivia, which has already gone in a more
> leftist, anti–U.S. direction, even without any of these developments.
> So I don't think we should delude ourselves that an Allende takeover
> in Chile would not present massive problems for us, and for demo-
> cratic forces and pro–U.S. forces in Latin America, and indeed to the
> whole Western Hemisphere. What would happen to the Western
> Hemisphere Defense Board, or to the Organization of American
> States, and so forth, is extremely problematical. . . . It is one of those
> situations which is not too happy for American interests.

But as the Senate committee remarked in its report, "the more extreme fears about the effects of Allende's election were ill-founded; there never was a significant threat of a Soviet military presence; the 'export' of Allende's revolution was limited, and its value as a model more restricted still. . . . Nevertheless, those fears, often exaggerated, appear to have activated officials in Washington."

It is necessary to open a parenthesis here to deal with a still mysterious crisis that coincided with the civil war in Jordan and Allende's election in Chile. It had to do with Cuba and the Soviet Union, and it may have had a bearing on how Nixon and Kissinger handled the other two, larger situations.

Sometime around September 10, Kissinger brought to Nixon's attention aerial photographs taken by a U-2 plane on a recent routine pass over Cuba and developed by CIA photo interpreters. The photographs showed that new barracks, communication towers, and antiaircraft sites were being constructed near the naval base of Cienfuegos in southern Cuba. Also appearing on the photographs was a soccer field. Inasmuch as soccer is not a game normally played in Cuba, the CIA's conclusion was that this field was being prepared for Russians, who do play it. Simultaneously, intelligence reports indicated that a Soviet submarine tender, a 9000-ton *Ugra*-class vessel, was in the vicinity of Cienfuegos. She was accompanied by two towed barges that, intelligence experts believed, served as storage for radioactive wastes from reactors aboard nuclear submarines. Finally, a Soviet nuclear submarine was reported in the general area of Cuba.

According to subsequent published accounts—by the Kalb brothers in *Kissinger* and by Henry Brandon in *The Retreat of American Power*—Nixon and Kissinger concluded that the Soviet Union was in the process of establishing a nuclear-submarine base in Cuba. If so, this would be a clear violation of the Soviet-American agreement that had followed the 1962 missile crisis, in which the Russians had committed themselves not to place offensive nuclear weapons in Cuba. Now Nixon and Kissinger were wondering whether Moscow was attempting a *fait accompli*, taking advantage of the distraction of the United States over the Middle Eastern affair. It would not be out of character, of course, for the Russians to be doing so—and Nixon again felt himself tested.

The official version of the events is that Nixon instructed Kissinger to warn the Soviets privately as well as publicly to desist from nuclear mischief in Cuba, and this was described as "preventive diplomacy." The same version has it that suspicious construction at Cienfuegos was spotted only in early September. But the record shows contradictions. The question of a possible Soviet nuclear-submarine base in Cuba came up during closed hearings before the House Subcommittee on Inter-American Affairs *between July 8 and August 3*. Even the heavily sanitized transcript of these hearings shows that both Admiral E. P. Holmes, commander in chief of the Atlantic Fleet, and G. Warren Nutter, assistant secretary of defense for international security affairs, had expressed concern over Soviet submarine bases in Cuba. Nutter remarked that the establishment of such Soviet bases "cannot be discounted as long as Castro's hostility to the United States persists." The rest of his and Admiral Holmes's remarks were deleted from the transcript.

If the United States was aware of these Soviet efforts as early as July, the U-2 photographs taken in September would have simply *added* to the evidence. The first unanswered question, therefore, is why Nixon and Kissinger waited until September before engaging in "preventive diplomacy" with Moscow. The other puzzling question is why Kissinger kept the entire State Department, including Secretary Rogers, out of his sudden diplomacy over Cuba. The official explanation was that the White House wanted to avoid a public confrontation with the Russians on the subject of Cienfuegos at the time of the Jordan crisis. But this does not fully explain it, and it is, further, contradicted by the fact that Kissinger himself made part of the story public on September 16.

He did so after summoning Ambassador Dobrynin to the White House and "confronting" him with the photographic evidence. Dobrynin, according to the official version, turned "ashen" and promised to seek clarifications in Moscow. Kissinger addressed himself to this topic in general terms in the same press background briefing in Chicago in which he warned the Russians about their Middle East policies and spoke of the Communist dangers posed by Allende's victory in Chile:

If they [the Soviets] start operating strategic forces out of Cuba, say, Polaris-type submarines, and use that as a depot, that would be a matter we would study very carefully. . . . If we put the Polaris submarine into the Black Sea . . . there are many newspapers who would say that this is a provocative thing to do. Why operate so close to the Soviet borders? . . . Therefore, both sides have to decide whether they want to restrain measures which they have a legal right to take. We are watching these events in Cuba and it isn't yet clear what, exactly, the Soviet Union is doing there. The fleet is rotating in and out, and we are watching events very carefully.

Kissinger did not explain what "these events in Cuba" were, and he dropped the subject there. But he knew, of course, that the Soviets would read his words.

On September 25, *New York Times* columnist C. L. Sulzberger broke the story in an article written from Washington, where he happened to be visiting. By noon, the Pentagon rushed to confirm it. Later in the day, Kissinger said that the president would regard as a "hostile act" any Soviet attempt to build a nuclear-submarine base in Cuba.

The Cienfuegos affair thus became public at the time of Kissinger's choosing. The State Department was caught completely by surprise, and its senior officers privately and in at least one background briefing expressed skepticism over Kissinger's "Cuban crisis." One theory they advanced was that Kissinger—whose information about Cienfuegos they described as dated and dubious—was using the Cuba issue to put pressure on Moscow in the context of the Middle East crisis and, for the benefit of American public opinion, to relate the dangers inherent in Communist Cuba to the dangers in Chile if Allende were confirmed as president. To some, it sounded like part of the Track I operation in Chile. The doubts expressed by State Department officials over Kissinger's Cuban diplomacy were summarized in an article I wrote for *The New York Times.* Kissinger read it in Madrid, where he was accompanying Nixon, and angrily denounced it as an "act of treason."

Just before the departure for Europe, Dobrynin had informed Kissinger that the Soviet Union was not building military installations in Cuba, but the White House was less than satisfied. On October 5, just as Nixón and Kissinger returned from their journey, Dobrynin repeated his earlier statement. Soviet Foreign Minister Gromyko did likewise with Secretary Rogers at a dinner at the Soviet mission to the United Nations in New York. On October 13, the Soviet news agency, Tass, issued a communiqué declaring that the Soviet Union "has not been and is not building its own military base" in Cuba. This marked the end of the Cienfuegos affair. There is no question that the Russians were involved in some form of peculiar activities in Cuba in the late summer of 1970, and it still remains unclear what they were doing. For Kissinger, this whole episode became a personal diplomatic victory.

Meanwhile, the Nixon administration kept up its efforts to prevent Allende's confirmation by the Chilean Congress. On September 29, the Forty Committee met in Kissinger's absence—he was in Europe with the president—but he left behind careful instructions. The group decided to drop the "Frei gambit" because the former president, finally apprised of the plan, refused to cooperate. The "second-best option"—the resignation of the Frei cabinet and the establishment of a military cabinet—was also abandoned for the same reason. The Forty Committee turned to other options under Track I; it was, of course, unaware of Track II—the military coup.

The report of the Senate committee said:

> The point was then made that there would probably be no military action unless economic pressures could be brought to bear on Chile. It was agreed that an attempt would be made to have American business take steps in line with the U.S. Government's desire for immediate economic action. The economic offensive against Chile, undertaken as part of Track I, was intended to demonstrate the foreign economic reaction to Allende's accession to power, as well as to preview the future consequences of his regime. Generally, the Forty Committee approved cutting off all credits, pressuring firms to curtail investments in Chile and approaching other nations to cooperate in this venture. These actions of the Forty Committee, and the establishment of an inter-agency working group to coordinate overt economic activities towards Chile (composed of the CIA's Western Hemisphere Division Chief and representatives from State, the NSC, and Treasury), adversely affected the Chilean economy: a major financial panic ensued.

The CIA, meanwhile, was busy with the Track II encouragement for a military coup. Between October 5 and 20, the agency made twenty-one contacts with key military and Carabinero (national police) officials in Chile. The Senate report said that "those Chileans who were inclined to stage a coup were given assurances of strong support at the highest levels of the U.S. Government, both before and after the coup." Ambassador Korry was authorized by the White House to inform his Chilean military contacts, directly or through American military attachés, that the United States would cease providing military assistance to Chile if Allende were seated. He was also instructed to tell the Chilean military leaders that the United States was suspending all military sales and deliveries pending the outcome of the October 24 congressional vote; the Chilean generals were also told that American military aid would be increased if Allende was kept out of the presidency.

The CIA's contacts with anti-Allende military groups revealed that in each case the scenarios called for the abduction of General René Schneider, chief of staff of the Chilean army. Schneider was known as a firm supporter of the constitutional process in Chile, and the plotters' idea was to blame the planned kidnaping on leftists so that the armed forces would rise against Allende. One of these groups received three submachine guns and tear gas from the CIA, apparently to be used in the abduction, but the equipment was returned unused. For reasons that remain unclear, the CIA withdrew its support from another group of military conspirators on October 15.

It was this latter group that carried out the kidnaping on October 22 as Schneider was leaving his Santiago home for the Defense Ministry. In the affray, the general was shot and killed. But this event had an adverse effect on the plotters' plans: Chileans immediately concluded that the killers were connected with right-wing groups because Schneider was expected to guarantee Allende's inauguration. The armed forces closed ranks behind the constitution—at least for the time being. The extent of White House awareness of the plot against Schneider is uncertain; in all probability it did not want to see him dead. But the Senate committee concluded that "there is no doubt that the U.S. government sought a military coup in Chile."

On October 24, the Chilean Congress confirmed Salvador Allende as president. All the efforts of the Nixon administration and its corporate friends turned out to have been in vain. On November 3, Allende was sworn in, and Frei passed him the presidential sash at the inauguration ceremony. The United States showed its displeasure by dispatching only Assistant Secretary of State Meyer to the inauguration. Other countries, including most of those in Latin America, sent foreign ministers. The Soviet Union, quick to assess the situation, was represented by a vice president of the Supreme Soviet.

As for Allende, he was extremely anxious to establish good relations with the United States. He knew the dangers inherent in a bad relationship, though he did not suspect to what extent Washington had been conspiring against him. He made a point of receiving Meyer at a special audience and assured him of his friendship for the United States.

The Nixon administration was more determined than ever to make life unbearable for Allende. Its policy had been established by Nixon on September 15: Helms's notes from his meeting with the president that day include the phrase, "Make the economy scream. . . ." During September, Korry informed the Frei government that "not a nut or bolt would be allowed to reach Chile under Allende." And now that Allende was in office, the United States began drawing up plans for a virtual economic blockade.

In mid-November, the White House issued NSDM–93 setting forth the anti-Allende economic policy. The Senate report summarized it as follows: "All new bilateral foreign assistance was to be stopped, although disbursements would continue under loans made previously. The U.S. would use its predominant position in international financial institutions to dry up the flow of new multilateral credit or other financial assistance. To the extent possible, financial assistance or guarantees to U.S. private investments in Chile would be ended, and U.S. businesses would be made aware of the government's concern and its restrictive policies." And the Track II policy was kept alive too, though more discreetly. For one thing, the collapse of the plotters' groups in the wake of General Schneider's assassination left the CIA station in Santiago with virtually no assets among the military. The immediate task was to rebuild these contacts.

The Forty Committee was wasting no time. On November 13, it approved $25,000 for support of Christian Democratic candidates in next year's municipal elections. On November 19, it approved $725,000, a whopping sum, for a general covert-action program against Allende. This raised the total of all moneys secretly authorized for subversion in Chile to $1.5 million for the year 1970. Nixon and Kissinger had declared a secret war against Allende's government. They lost the battle in 1970, but they were gearing up for a "protracted war" against Chile, the colossus of the North marshaling its power against a small functioning democracy in Latin America. By the end of the year, the Nixon administration felt somewhat vindicated: on December 21, Allende proposed a constitutional amendment establishing state control of the large copper mines and authorizing expropriation of all foreign firms working them. It was not an outright grab—it was being done through the constitutional process (unlike in Cuba after Castro's advent to power)—but to Nixon and Kissinger this made no difference. The word was that Allende must go.

BOOK THREE

1971

The Year of Shocks

Chapter 13

The third year of Richard Nixon's administration was a period of major transition in America's relations with friend and foe. The president so described it in his "State of the World" report to Congress on February 25, 1971: "The transition from the past is under way but far from completed. . . . Adjustments in our policies surely will be required, but our experience in 1970 confirmed the basic soundness of our approach. We have set a new direction. We are on course."

What Nixon had primarily in mind was American diplomacy aimed at détente with the Soviet Union and an opening to mainland China. The foundations for these policies were laid in 1969 and 1970, and the new year would serve to expand these relationships beyond all expectations. In the process of all his policy "adjustments," however, Nixon would produce major international shocks, principally affecting America's allies. In one section of the 235-page message, Nixon dealt with China, telling Peking what the United States was prepared to do:

> The People's Republic of China is making a claim to leadership of the less-developed portions of the world. But for that claim to be credible, and for it to be pursued effectively, Communist China must expose herself to contact with the outside world. Both require the end of the insulation of Mainland China from outside realities, and therefore from change. The twenty-two-year-old hostility between ourselves and the People's Republic of China is another unresolved problem, serious indeed in view of the fact that it determines our relationship with 750 million talented and energetic people. . . .
>
> We are prepared to establish a dialogue with Peking. We cannot accept its ideological precepts, or the notion that Communist China must exercise hegemony over Asia. But neither do we wish to impose on China an international position that denies its legitimate national interests. The evolution of our dialogue with Peking cannot be at the expense of international order or our own commitments. . . . We will continue to honor our treaty commitments to the security of our Asian

allies. An honorable relationship with Peking cannot be constructed at their expense. Among these allies is the Republic of China. . . . Our present commitment to the security of the Republic of China on Taiwan stems from our 1954 treaty. The purpose of the treaty is exclusively defensive, and it controls the entire range of our military relationship with the Republic of China. . . . I do not believe that this honorable and peaceful association need constitute an obstacle to the movement toward normal relations between the United States and the People's Republic of China. . . . I wish to make it clear that the United States is prepared to see the People's Republic of China play a constructive role in the family of nations. The question of its place in the United Nations is not, however, merely a question of whether Peking should be permitted to dictate to the world the terms of its participation. For a number of years attempts have been made to deprive the Republic of China of its place as a member of the United Nations and its Specialized Agencies. We have opposed these attempts. We will continue to oppose them.

This section, drafted with extraordinary care, was meant for Peking's benefit—supplementing the secret exchanges—as well as for that of Nationalist China and other American allies in Asia. It was likewise intended to be read in Moscow. And, just as important, it was an effort to educate and prepare public opinion in the United States. Nixon and Kissinger were publicly trying out the two-Chinas concept, the idea that it might be possible for *both* Peking and Taiwan to be represented for a time in the United Nations and for the United States to enter into a relationship with the People's Republic without severing all ties with the Nationalists.

But on the first point, the White House must have known that it was proposing the impossible. Peking had made it clear on numerous occasions that it wanted *the* China seat—in the Security Council, the General Assembly, and other United Nations organs—or nothing. It was prepared to wait indefinitely to achieve what it considered an absolutely vital objective. Washington seemed to be measuring public-opinion responses to a two-Chinas policy, and making it a matter of record that it would resist Taiwan's expulsion though it was unquestionably clear that it could no longer marshal enough votes in the General Assembly to save the Nationalists.

There was more plausibility in the two-Chinas policy in bilateral relations with the United States. Chou En-lai himself had hinted at this possibility, and the Chinese were aware that Nixon could not simply ditch Taiwan. They were therefore prepared to be flexible. And Peking's signals, sent through secret channels, did not, as Nixon and Kissinger discovered with interest, contain any hostile references to American treaty relationships with other Asian allies—such as Japan and South Korea. Likewise, Peking was not pushing Washington on Vietnam. The Chinese were being more realistic than Nixon and Kissinger had ever thought possible.

Strictly speaking, the president's portrayal in his report of the diplomatic situation on Indochina was accurate. The United States had made new proposals, and North Vietnam had rejected them. And just as correctly, Nixon diagnosed the "fundamental question" as being the allocation of political power in Saigon. But having so diagnosed it, he persisted in his refusal to understand that the North Vietnamese were fighting precisely to attain this political objective—and that no amount of American military and diplomatic pressure would dissuade them.

Another area of United States foreign policy upon which Nixon touched at some length, wholly misleading the nation and the world, was Chile. Americans were, of course, totally unaware of the CIA's vast subversive operations in Chile as they read Nixon's pious declaration that

> the United States has a strong political interest in maintaining cooperation with our neighbors regardless of their domestic viewpoints. We have a clear preference for free and democratic processes. We hope that governments will evolve toward constitutional procedures. But it is not our mission to try to provide—except by example—the answers to such questions for other sovereign nations. We deal with governments as they are. Our relations depend not on their internal structures or social systems, but on actions which affect us and the inter-American system.

Nixon then proceeded to deliver an outright lie:

> Our bilateral policy is to keep open lines of communication. We will not be the ones to upset traditional relations. We assume that international rights and obligations will be observed. We also recognize that the Chilean government's actions will be determined primarily by its own purposes, and that these will not be deflected simply by the tone of our policy. In short, *we are prepared to have the kind of relationship with the Chilean government that it is prepared to have with us* [italics added].

In truth, the United States was *not* prepared simply to respond to Chilean attitudes toward it. In the four months that Allende had been in power, he had done nothing to antagonize the United States except to lay plans to nationalize the copper industry owned by American interests. But expropriations were nothing new in Latin America—Peru and Bolivia nationalized some American properties during the same period without becoming targets for all-out CIA subversion. And Chile's new ties with Cuba were not exactly a challenge to the inter-American system: Mexico, which had close relations with Washington despite its independent foreign policy, had refused to observe the OAS decision in 1964 to break diplomatic relations with Havana.

Secrecy, cover-ups, and lies formed an integral part of the Nixon-Kissinger foreign policy during 1971. Presently, this White House approach became contagious, poisoning the very presidency and the American body politic.

The notion still held in Saigon and Washington that the Indochina war could be won by a slashing thrust at the jugular of the North Vietnamese logistics system—the Ho Chi Minh infiltration trails—resulted in a tragically ill-planned invasion of the Laos panhandle in February 1971. This was a repetition on a smaller scale of the 1970 Cambodian incursion, with the difference that no American combat troops were involved, although ARVN forces were ferried by U.S. helicopters and U.S. aircraft provided tactical and strategic support.

Hatched by General Abrams's MAC/V command and the South Vietnamese general staff in Saigon—and approved by the White House and the Joint Chiefs of Staff—this operation, known as Lam Son 619 (Total Victory 619), was designed to sever Hanoi's main line of supplies and communications running from North Vietnam to the southern section of Laos. The panhandle area lies just above the terminus of the Ho Chi Minh Trail complex; from there the main-force North Vietnamese units and their supplies were fed into South Vietnam and Cambodia. American B-52s had been mercilessly pounding the panhandle for years but it never seemed to make much difference. North Vietnamese engineer battalions repaired the jungle roads almost as soon as the B-52s completed their bombing runs. Traffic was detoured to secondary roads; when North Vietnamese trucks were delayed by bomb craters along the roads, men carried supplies on their backs—on foot or on bicycles—until repairs were completed.

Lam Son 619 was formally launched on February 8 and announced simultaneously in Saigon and Washington, although Laotian Communist spokesmen had reported two days earlier that South Vietnamese units had already penetrated the panhandle, reaching the town of Tchepone, twenty miles inside Laos. The operation was planned in conjunction with parallel ARVN thrusts into the Cambodian sanctuaries area—the latter were chiefly search-and-destroy missions—and it was preceded by saturation B-52 bombing strikes against North Vietnamese positions in north-west South Vietnam to smooth the way for the forces invading the Laos panhandle.

There was considerable optimism in Saigon over Lam Son 619 (although Kissinger privately remarked in Washington that the South Vietnamese had acquired the habit of code-naming most of their operations "Total Victory"); probably for the first time in the long war there was something of a gung-ho spirit in the ARVN. The South Vietnamese had performed reasonably well in the 1970 Cambodian campaign (they had American advisers and American combat troops fighting alongside) and now they had become confident that, as General Abrams imprudently cabled Nixon, they could "hack it" alone in Laos. Their confidence had reached such proportions that President Thieu began pressing Washington for clearance to invade North Vietnam as his next major operation. An invasion of North Vietnam by the ARVN was the last thing Nixon desired—it would have created untold political and diplomatic problems and even American commanders had serious doubts about the success of such an enterprise—but Thieu's palace kept generating rumors that it was in the offing.

At first, the invasion of Laos seemed to be going rather well. The Saigon-designed plan was to cause maximum damage to the infiltration trails and to destroy whatever caches of arms and supplies the North Vietnamese had there, and it was hoped that Lam Son 619 could fulfill its objectives within five to eight weeks. It would last five weeks if the North Vietnamese were able to mount a serious counteroffensive; eight weeks if the ARVN was not pressed too hard. This, in any event, was what General Abrams told Defense Secretary Laird as the operation got under way.

But Washington had underestimated the difficulty of severing the Ho Chi Minh Trail. Contrary to popular assumptions, the trail was not a single route, but a labyrinth of parallel and criss-crossing roads covering an area some five miles wide and nearly a hundred miles long. In the Laos panhandle, the South Vietnamese were attempting to block about thirty miles of the trails at a depth of four to five miles. Given the rough terrain and the uncertainty over North Vietnamese reactions, Lam Son 619 was a much more complex undertaking than Nixon seemed to realize when he discussed it with newsmen in the Oval Office on February 17, nine days after the offensive had started. The president was of good cheer.

> Laos would not have been possible had it not been for Cambodia. Cambodia cutting off one vital supply line and thereby practically bringing enemy activity in the southern half of South Vietnam to an end released the South Vietnamese forces—who, by this time, had not only gained confidence in Cambodia, but also had additional strength —released them for undertaking what they could not have undertaken even eight months ago: an incursion on their own into Laos with only U.S. air support. . . . The decision to do it now was that based on the fact that the South Vietnamese, because of their confidence, the training they gained as a result of their actions in Cambodia, the South Vietnamese felt that they were able to undertake it. Our commanders agreed.

The president's confidence was based on information he was getting from General Abrams:

> The operation—and I read a complete report from General Abrams this morning—the operation has gone according to plan. The South Vietnamese have already cut three major roads . . . which lead from Tchepone down into Cambodia and, of course, South Vietnam. The South Vietnamese have run into very heavy resistance on the road going into Tchepone. We expected that resistance. . . . The Cambodian action in May and June cut one lifeline, the lifeline from Sihanoukville into the southern half of South Vietnam. This action would either cut or seriously disrupt the other pipeline or lifeline coming . . . down through Laos, the Ho Chi Minh Trail, into the northern half of South Vietnam. . . . Finally, I think it is quite important to note General Abrams's evaluation, which I specifically asked him to give me by cable just a few days ago, of how the South Vietnamese are conducting themselves. They are fighting, he said, in a superior way. . . . They are proceeding in a way that he believes is in accordance with the plan and holding their own against enemy attack. And he also pointed up another fact that, of course, has been overriden by the Laotian activity: that the operation in the Chup Plantation [in Cambodia] led by [Lieutenant] General [Do Cao] Tri is going along in a fashion much better than was expected, with a great number of enemy casualties and, as General Abrams put it, excellent performance on the part of those groups.

And Nixon's optimism about the Laotian operation extended to his political plans for further withdrawals of American troops from Vietnam. This was part of Nixon's political balancing act: Americans had to be convinced that the war was winding down, and Hanoi had to be shown that the United States was really getting out of Vietnam; it had to be persuaded that it could get better peace terms from the United States than from the Saigon regime. But Nixon was out on a very long limb if he really assumed that the ARVN could, within the foreseeable future, take over the defense of South Vietnam. (Actually, he was aware of the dangers ahead, for he told the newsmen that "next year will be a year when the Vietnamization program's very success creates the point of greatest danger, because then the number of ground combat troops that we will have in South Vietnam will be lower.")

Laos was especially cruel for the South Vietnamese soldiers who were placed there by their own commanders—and by American commanders—in untenable positions. It was cruel as well to the South Vietnamese and Laotian men, women, and children in the operational area on both sides of the border; again people were killed, maimed, and forced to flee their homes. But this did not count. What counted were military results, although from the American and South Vietnamese viewpoint these results were disastrous. In less than five weeks of fighting, the North Vietnamese crushed the ARVN—and with it the ARVN's incipient self-confidence—inside the Laos panhandle. This was an outcome that General Abrams had never anticipated. The North Vietnamese were expected to fight back, certainly, but never on the scale they actually did. Neither were they expected to engage tanks in a massive fashion against the ARVN. They had never used armor in the past. When the first Soviet-built tanks appeared near Tchepone, incredulity quickly changed to concern and then to panic.

Despite heavy B-52 bombings of the trails, the North Vietnamese were able to move several regiments of crack troops as well as tanks to the panhandle area during the third week of the ARVN operation. For a week or so, the South Vietnamese withstood the counterassault. By March 1, they started pulling back. Around March 15, the ARVN lines broke and the invading army was swept by panic. The retreat became a rout. Men died or surrendered. Others tried to flee. Desperate South Vietnamese troopers, members of Thieu's elite units, fought their way aboard American and South Vietnamese helicopters to be flown out of the hellish battlefield. Some clung to the choppers' skids, falling to the ground when they could no longer hold on. Americans at home could see it on their television screens and in photographs on the front pages of their newspapers.

Incredibly, the U.S. government kept insisting that the Laos catastrophe was an "orderly retreat" and that the gains in the operation still outweighed the losses. Vice President Agnew argued forcefully on March 18 that what Americans were witnessing "was not a rout—this was an orderly retreat." However, the administration was unable to explain *why* the South Vietnamese were suddenly retreating, let alone being routed, ahead of schedule. There was no explanation for the atrocious intelligence failures, the inability to predict accurately the North Vietnamese response and, especially, the appearance of tanks. No administration official could say how the North Vietnamese not only mauled the ARVN in the Laos panhandle, but were able, at the same time, to mount a major artillery attack against the American fire base in Khe Sanh on the South Vietnamese side of the border.

Washington's reactions were a mix of bafflement, self-justification, deceit, and new military action. On March 20 and 21, for example, U.S. aircraft resumed strikes in North Vietnam against antiaircraft-missile batteries in what Secretary Laird described as "protective reaction." Laird also made it clear that the United States might launch a new wave of raids against North Vietnam: "That question," he said, "will be answered on the basis of what happens from now on."

As for the president, he also tried to create the impression that, all things considered, the Laos operation was not a total loss. At a March 4 news conference, he was still serenely optimistic about the fighting in the panhandle:

> The disruption of the supply lines of the enemy through Laos, which has now occurred for three weeks, has very seriously damaged the enemy's ability to wage effective action against our remaining forces in Vietnam. . . . I just had a report from General Abrams today with regard to the performance of the South Vietnamese. . . . General Abrams tells me that in both Laos and Cambodia his evaluation after three weeks of fighting is that—to use his terms—the South Vietnamese by themselves can hack it, and they can give a better account of themselves even than the North Vietnamese units. . . . The decision to go into Laos, I think, was the right decision. It will reduce American casualties. . . . I checked the flow of supplies down the trails from the area in which the North Vietnamese and the South Vietnamese are engaged. General Abrams reports that there has been a 55 percent decrease in truck traffic south into South Vietnam.

Nixon was considerably more sober in discussing this situation in a televised interview with Howard K. Smith, of the American Broadcasting Company, on March 22.

> *Smith:* Now, you also said that the Laos operation showed that the South Vietnamese could hack it by themselves. Now, that seems partly

so, but it has to be added that they do that to that degree only with tremendous U.S. air support, 40,000 helicopter sorties, against an adversary that has no air power at all. . . .

Nixon: We found that the South Vietnamese went in with forces that numerically were very inferior to the forces they found. As a matter of fact, the North Vietnamese had twice as many ground forces in the area of southern Laos as South Vietnam had. South Vietnam had, of course, to have support, firepower support, through our air power, which would equalize that difference. . . . They fought extremely well. Now they are withdrawing. They are having all the problems of an army withdrawing. Some of their units have not done so well. But eighteen out of the twenty-two battalions, as General Abrams has pointed out, are doing extremely well and, he says, will come out with greater confidence and greater morale than before.

The next day, March 23, the Pentagon admitted that, in effect, the ARVN had retreated from Laos earlier than planned. An official spokesman put it this way: "If the enemy had not reacted, they might have stayed longer. If the enemy had reacted stronger than he did, it might have moved to the shorter end of the parameter. Obviously the enemy influences the course of battle."

The Laos campaign certainly served to compound and expand human suffering in Indochina. A great part of this suffering was borne—increasingly—by millions of refugees in Vietnam, Laos, and Cambodia who were continuously uprooted and rendered homeless by advancing and retreating armies in the unending flux of battle. The fate of the refugees, especially in Vietnam, was one of the most bitter if generally unnoticed tragedies of the war.

The administration's own estimates in mid-March showed that the number of refugees in South Vietnam had risen dramatically, perhaps by as many as 150,000, since American and South Vietnamese forces launched new operations late in 1970. (The cumulative refugee total since 1965 was 5 million, most of them absorbed in one fashion or another in Vietnamese cities and rural communities.) Between October 1970 and February 1971 the monthly number of new refugees had increased more than five times.

This dislocation was caused by the action of American and ARVN forces in clearing out big swaths of territory preparatory to offensive actions against the Viet Cong, North Vietnamese regulars, or the infiltration trails in Laos. Entire villages were emptied without notice, their inhabitants dispersed in various directions. Civilians get in the way of large-scale military operations. Another reason was concern that there might be Viet Cong infiltrators in these villages who could turn against the allied forces. Thus 40,000 members of the Bru tribe of *montagnards* were evacuated from Cambodian and Laotian border areas—they were moved east to Kontum and Pleiku provinces—in anticipation of ARVN thrusts into Cambodia and Laos. Although the Mekong Delta was officially considered to be pacified, some 38,000 people were evacuated from the U Minh forest area there between December and February to clear the way for B-52 strikes against suspected North Vietnamese and Viet Cong concentrations.

These mass evacuations antagonized the South Vietnamese villagers and, in many instances, influenced them in favor of the Viet Cong. In this sense, American and ARVN military operations were undermining the pacification program. Highly classified surveys of public attitudes by joint American–South Vietnamese teams showed that "only a minority" of refugees in the camps supported the Saigon regime. Most of them were "politically neutral," according to the secret survey, and "large numbers" were Viet Cong sympathizers.

A secret report from the Refugee Division of the Civil Operations and Rural Development Support (CORDS) organization, which was in overall charge of pacification, said that it is "sometimes only after relocations have been completed or are well under way that they come to the attention of the CORDS staff." A classified survey by teams of the Pacification Attitude Analysis System in twelve refugee camps in northern South Vietnam observed that "there was a clear correlation between forced relocation and a high degree of pro-Communist sympathies." It added: "Most refugees are disgruntled and the Government of Vietnam apparently cannot aid them economically or protect them militarily. . . . Viet Cong cadres operate [in refugee camps] with few checks placed upon them by the Government of Vietnam."

While pacification was so obviously failing, CORDS found itself involved in aiding the Saigon regime to erect new maximum-security prison facilities on the notorious Con Son island, the home of the "tiger cages" in which President Thieu's opponents were jailed. Early in January 1971, the South Vietnamese "Naval Facilities Engineering Command, Contracts" let a $400,000 contract to a California contractor to build a new penal installation on Con Son. It was never made clear, as a matter of morality or practical need, why the United States was involved in improving South Vietnamese prisons, but an official memorandum, describing CORDS as the project sponsor, stated that "the Scope of Work is the completion of three cell blocks, each partitioned into ninety-six isolation cells; an outer compound wall of concrete block; a barbed wire perimeter fence with security gates; kitchen; and dispensary. Construction is to be similar to the isolation cell block currently under construction as a self-help project."

The International Committee of the Red Cross, whose representatives visited the new Con Son facilities in 1971, reported that "the new isolation cells which have been built to replace the 'tiger cages,' while of slightly different dimensions than the 'tiger cages,' are actually smaller; 'tiger cages': 55.1 square feet; new cells: 52.9 square feet." The committee also found "the use (on a large scale) of shackles (presumably irons) for 'troublemakers' from last summer until January 26, 1971." It added that "all of the inadequacies described . . . above are violations of the Geneva Convention insofar as they pertain to the POWs at Con Son." Now South Vietnamese prison administrators were "advised" by a mission from the Public Safety Division of the U.S. Agency for International Development. In this manner, the United States was struggling for the "hearts and minds" of the South Vietnamese. It ran the Phoenix program to catch Viet Cong sympathizers, and it helped to operate the prisons to which they were sent.

There was no question that Vietnam—a cruel sideshow—was complicating the general conduct of United States foreign policy. The White House seemed to have no time to concentrate on any number of important issues—Kissinger, for example, tended to pay attention to the Middle East only when a new crisis was at hand—and this state of affairs was disturbing to the diplomats at the State Department. Thus Secretary of State Rogers summarized this sentiment in his introduction to the department's biennial report to Congress on foreign policy when he observed that "national preoccupation with Vietnam has pre-empted our attention from other areas of concern. By ending our involvement in the war we will restore perspective; by altering the character of our involvement in the world we will re-establish a balance in the conduct of our relations."

In any event it was up to Rogers and his experts to pursue Middle Eastern diplomacy. The United States was eager to convince Israel, Egypt, and Jordan to resume peace talks through Gunnar Jarring. In January, Israel, under heavy American pressure, agreed; so did Egypt. The United States was pushing for a new "interim agreement" between Israel and Egypt, a follow-up on the Suez Canal truce.

But Rogers had to conduct this Middle Eastern diplomacy almost single-handed. Elsewhere, significant policy issues were relegated to the background: the United States still lacked a coherent foreign economic policy (although a special council to look after these matters was formed at the White House in January); it was inattentive to the fact that a major petroleum crisis was brewing in the Middle East; it was hardly aware of matters concerning the third world; and nobody thought very hard about Latin America or Africa.

Meanwhile, the Indochinese diplomacy that so preoccupied the White House was faltering. Nixon and Kissinger were beginning to realize only very belatedly that the fate of the some 1600 Americans held as war prisoners in North Vietnam or missing in action was being turned into a major point in the peace negotiations. It had been North Vietnam's policy all along to provide virtually no information about the prisoners —Hanoi, like Saigon, had a peculiar view of the Geneva Convention on POWs—and there was no way of knowing how many men were actually imprisoned and how many were missing. (The great majority were crews of American aircraft shot down over North Vietnam or areas in South Vietnam under revolutionary control.) On March 13, Nixon issued a formal statement on this subject: "Let us give our continued dedication and continued public understanding, for the sake of the prisoners, for the sake of their families, and for the sake of human decency." And he proclaimed March 21–27 National Week of Concern for Americans Who Are Prisoners of War or Missing in Action. But this changed nothing.

On the battlefield, the situation worsened. Intelligence reports reaching Washington early in April showed that the North Vietnamese were moving some 100,000 fresh troops close to the DMZ; new units were also observed entering South Vietnam, Laos, and Cambodia from the Ho Chi Minh Trail complex. These reports ignited a controversy within the administration as to the reasons for this latest North Vietnamese military activity; this, in turn, reopened the festering argument over the quality of intelligence upon which President Nixon had based his decision to support the Laos operation.

The White House and the Pentagon insisted that the new moves by Hanoi—including a rash of hit-and-run operations throughout Indochina —were simply an attempt to "show the flag" and hide the extent of losses it had suffered in Laos. The CIA and the State Department's intelligence experts, however, thought that the North Vietnamese had not been badly hit at all, and that they were now engaged in an effort to keep Saigon and the United States off balance in all three Indochina theaters. The CIA cautioned that, once more, the capabilities of the North Vietnamese were being underestimated. Civilian intelligence specialists went out of their way to call the attention of top policy-makers to the fact that the North Vietnamese were busily streamlining their political and economic institutions as part of what appeared to be plans for an indefinite pursuit of the war. The full meeting of the Central Committee of the North Vietnamese Workers' (Communist) Party held in January, the first such publicly announced meeting since 1964, issued directives stressing that the war had priority over economic development. On April 2, Hanoi set up a special government department to supervise agriculture and to push for higher rice production. North Vietnam's 1970 rice harvest was the best in years, but Hanoi evidently was aiming at self-sufficiency in food—and the end of its dependence on Chinese and Soviet shipments. In an Asian war, rice is a major weapon, as the Hanoi leadership always understood.

It developed that the Laos operation had been cleared at the top in Washington without an agreed-upon National Intelligence Estimate, and with the White House relying entirely on Pentagon intelligence and General Abrams's views. When CIA and State Department officials raised "devil's advocate" arguments over the plausibility of the Laotian enterprise, their views were largely disregarded. Here it appears that Kissinger was the chief culprit. Having turned his NSC staff—and especially his own office—into the principal channel for the flow of all intelligence to the White House, he now simply turned aside intelligence views with which he was in disagreement. This was an immensely dangerous way to deal with the intelligence product.

Following the Laos operation, civilian intelligence specialists began warning the White House that the new pattern of North Vietnamese attacks—it included the shelling of civilian and military targets as well as the burning of the district capital of Ducduc at the end of March—was part of a long-range effort to interfere with the pacification program in South Vietnam. This effort, in the judgment of the experts, was aimed at causing maximal havoc in the country prior to parliamentary elections scheduled for August and presidential elections set for October, in which President Thieu was a candidate to succeed himself.

The American response was to act exactly as it had acted in the past —except more so. A case in point was the launching on March 1 of what was the most ambitious and costly pacification program in the history of the Vietnam war. This was the 1971 Community Defense and Local Development Plan, formulated jointly by the American command in Saigon and the South Vietnamese government, and costing $1 billion. Its top priority, as described in the 304-page classified plan, was the "neutralization" of the Viet Cong underground network in South Vietnam.

This new plan was the latest version of many past programs, and as in the past it assumed that it was indeed possible to extirpate the Viet Cong and marshal South Vietnamese populations under Saigon's flag. And again Washington turned for advice and help to Sir Robert Thompson, the British police expert who over three administrations had acted as a private counterinsurgency counselor to the White House. Shortly after the pacification plan was launched—it was done in utter secrecy and the administration confirmed its existence only after I was able to publish its highlights in *The New York Times*—Thompson claimed that South Vietnam's ability to control subversion "has steadily improved all the time."

To achieve its objectives, the pacification plan proposed to eliminate, by death or capture, 14,400 Viet Cong agents during a twelve-month period starting in March. This was the responsibility of the CIA-run Phoenix program. The Viet Cong elimination effort was to be supported by an elaborate "people's intelligence network" to inform on "enemy activity." And although the South Vietnamese army was already 1 million men strong, the plan called for expanding the People's Self-Defense Force in rural areas from 500,000 to 4 million members. Women were to be enlisted in combat units in the PSDF; children of both sexes over the age of seven were to be recruited for supporting units.

On April 7, Nixon went on nationwide television to announce that an additional 100,000 American troops would be brought home from Vietnam between May 1 and December 1. Under this repatriation schedule, Nixon would have returned 365,000 men to the United States from Indochina by the time his third year in office ended. There were 540,000 Americans in Vietnam when he was inaugurated in 1969; at the start of 1972, there would be only 175,000 men directly engaged in the war on the ground, not counting air force personnel in Thailand and Pacific bases or navy units supporting the military effort.

Nixon's new announcement came as no surprise. He and his senior administration officials had been suggesting that new withdrawals would be made known in the spring. In fact, the announcement was made earlier than originally planned for reasons relating to new diplomatic moves in Paris. Exchanges through the Paris channels late in March, initiated by Kissinger, brought strong hints that the North Vietnamese were interested in resuming secret negotiations before too long. The White House may have wished to give Hanoi as much time as possible to ponder the implications of the new withdrawals.

The important thing about cutting back American forces in Vietnam to roughly 175,000 men by 1972 was that, for all practical purposes, U.S. troops would no longer be able to play a meaningful combat role. Out of this American troop total destined to remain behind in 1972, no more than 75,000 men formed actual combat units; the other 100,000 were headquarters, logistics, and security personnel. Obviously, this small combat force would be unable to act decisively if Hanoi decided to launch an important offensive. Whether the ARVN could defend itself alone was, at best, a moot point.

The Laotian campaign had no particular bearing on Nixon's announcement. The decision had been made before the February incursion —and before the subsequent North Vietnamese buildup north of the DMZ—and, in a sense, Laos was the last hurrah of the war.

Nixon's and Kissinger's view was that American air power would be a sufficient guarantee of Saigon's survival, and the president's April 7 speech marked the end of the phase of full-fledged U.S. ground combat involvement in the Vietnam war. The White House remained convinced that an unlimited application of air power—including, if necessary, blanket bombings of Hanoi and the rest of North Vietnam—would hold the North Vietnamese in check as long as necessary. Neither Nixon nor Kissinger was averse to saturation bombing raids.

Nixon continued to refrain from threatening Hanoi with awesome reprisals if the North Vietnamese took advantage of American withdrawals, and he ignored the reports on the buildup above the DMZ. The highly conciliatory tone was evidently a prelude to Kissinger's new diplomatic initiative: "The day the South Vietnamese can take over their own defense is in sight. Our goal is a total American withdrawal from Vietnam. We can and will reach that goal through our program of Vietnamization if necessary. But we would infinitely prefer to reach it even sooner—through negotiations. . . . Tonight I again call on Hanoi to engage in serious negotiations to speed the end of this war."

On April 16, at the annual convention of the American Society of Newspaper Editors, in Washington, President Nixon spelled out the strategy of maintaining air power and a residual ground force in Vietnam until a peace settlement made a total American withdrawal possible.

We do not have as a goal a permanent residual force such as we have in Korea. . . . But it will be necessary to maintain forces in South Vietnam until two important objectives are achieved: one, the release of the prisoners of war held by North Vietnam in North Vietnam and other parts of Southeast Asia; and two, the ability of the South Vietnamese to develop the capacity to defend themselves against a Communist take-over—not the sure capacity, but at least the chance.

The president refused to be drawn by the editors into a discussion of when a total withdrawal would come but he did say that the next announcement on American troop withdrawals was planned for October. "I will then analyze the training of the South Vietnamese forces and particularly their air force at that time" and "analyze enemy activity and, also, any progress in negotiation, particularly in negotiation with regard to prisoners."

This was the first time that Nixon publicly indicated that the release of the POWs was a condition *sine qua non* for complete withdrawal from Vietnam. It was also the first time he said in so many words that American air power might be used against North Vietnam to secure the prisoners' freedom. The United States negotiating stance was toughening.

But again, the White House was misreading Hanoi. It may have seemed logical to Nixon that the North Vietnamese should agree immediately to release the American POWs in order to remove the threat of heavy air retaliation. But to Hanoi the prisoners were a major negotiating trump card, and they were not about to give it up *only* to win Nixon's commitment that they would not be bombed any more. The more Nixon insisted on the release of the POWs, the more Hanoi was determined to hold on to them. Besides, as a Hanoi diplomat remarked later, North Vietnam had no real guarantee that Nixon would not think up another reason to resume or increase bombings even after the POWs were set free.

On April 29, the president held another news conference just as tens of thousands of antiwar demonstrators were gathering in Washington for a planned May Day manifestation. Nixon appeared serene about the demonstrations and certain of the correctness of his course: "I think they [the demonstrators] will judge me very harshly for the position that I take now. But I think what is important is how they judge the consequences of the decisions that I make now, which I think are in their best interests and in the best interests of our children."

And, once more, the president strongly linked the POW question with the ultimate American withdrawal from Vietnam. The Hanoi delegation in Paris had indicated its willingness to *discuss* the release of American POWs, but Nixon took the view that this was no longer good enough.

At that point, the Paris diplomatic effort remained completely deadlocked. Nixon's continuing hope was to obtain a negotiating breakthrough, however, and new instructions were prepared for Kissinger in the greatest secrecy. Likewise, the administration offered minor gestures toward North Vietnam: at the semipublic session in Paris on April 29, some hours before Nixon spoke to the press at the White House, the American and South Vietnamese delegations offered unilaterally to free 570 sick and wounded North Vietnamese prisoners and to send to a neutral country 1200 North Vietnamese captives who had been prisoners in the South for four years or longer.

On May 3, a sunny Monday, masses of antiwar militants descended on Washington for a demonstration intended to "shut down" the capital. With their bodies, they tried to block commuter access routes to the city as well as the bridges over the Potomac River leading to Washington from Virginia. Inasmuch as huge numbers of people working in the capital live in the suburbs, the demonstrators' idea was to prevent them from reaching their places of employment and thereby paralyze the government for the day. Other thousands of demonstrators roamed the city's streets shouting slogans, stopping traffic, breaking windows, and all in all, facing Washington with one of the worst riots in its history.

The administration took the view that no government could tolerate this kind of defiance, and it responded with a formidable show of strength. In addition to the metropolitan police and its tactical squads, Washington was "defended" by National Guard and 82nd Airborne Division units brought from the outside. Marines were held in reserve. Army and National Guard troopers were deployed along the bridges and freeways leading to the city. It was the task of the police to control the situation inside the city, and Jerry Wilson, the metropolitan police chief, decided to cope drastically. Crowds were broken up with tear gas and baton charges. In successive sweeps, the police rounded up and arrested virtually everybody in downtown streets. It soon became impossible to charge individuals with specific offenses, and by the end of the day, nearly 12,000 citizens were in detention—and, then, nobody seemed to know what to do with them. Magistrates in Washington courts were unable to handle the numbers brought before them; besides, they were reluctant to act because of the arbitrary manner in which the detentions were carried out. By next morning, therefore, the vast majority of the detainees were released. Later, when the case was made that the actions of the Washington police might have violated the constitutional rights of thousands of citizens, the courts decided to expunge the charges from the criminal records of those who had actually been arraigned.

As for President Nixon, he sat out the demonstration at his home in California. Two days before, he had held another news conference there. (The frequency of his news conferences had become startling for a president reluctant to meet with the press: this was the third one in two weeks.)

One of the first questions asked of him on the lawn in San Clemente was whether he would be intimidated by antiwar demonstrators. The May Day demonstration was two days away, and some of the antiwar groups had been invading congressional and government offices during the week. The previous week, there were minor and reasonably peaceful acts. Nixon said:

> When I say that I will not be intimidated, and that the Congress will not be intimidated, I am simply stating the American principle that while everybody has a right to protest peacefully, that policy in this country is not made by protests. Those who make policy must, of course, listen, and then they must weigh all the other facts and then do what they think is right. . . . I should point out that while the demonstrations a week ago were peaceful demonstrations for the most part, this week we had some incidents at several departments where it was necessary to arrest those who were breaking the law. If this kind of illegal conduct continues next week, as some say it will, we are prepared to deal with it. We will arrest those who break the law. . . . The right to demonstrate for peace abroad does not carry with it the right to break the peace at home. . . . We are going to see to it that the thousands of government workers who have a right to go to work peacefully are not interfered with by those militants, those few militants, who in the name of demonstrating for peace abroad presume that they have the right to break the peace at home.

The president returned to the White House on May 4, just as Washington courts began releasing the thousands of demonstrators arrested on Nixon's orders. He had "proved" that he would not be "intimidated" by domestic protest and his Vietnam policies would not be affected by outcry or riot.

Most of May in the White House was spent preparing new secret American proposals for the North Vietnamese and working out dates for the next Kissinger–Le Duc Tho session in Paris. Finally, the date was set for May 31, the Monday of the long Memorial Day weekend, and Kissinger left Washington surreptitiously on Sunday night, after attending an evening party at a friend's. Nixon had flown to Camp David by helicopter that same afternoon. It was a relaxed holiday weekend, and none of the Kissinger watchers in the press corps had the slightest suspicion that the presidential adviser had eluded them.

In Paris the next day, Kissinger and Le Duc Tho met at a villa belonging to the French Communist Party. The two men had not seen each other for more than half a year; they greeted each other cordially. Kissinger was unusually optimistic that the new plan he was submitting to Le Duc Tho would be more acceptable.

For one thing, the plan no longer specifically required the withdrawal of North Vietnamese troops from South Vietnam. Nixon had been vague about this in October, but had subsequently explained that the United States indeed still did insist on mutual withdrawals. This time, Kissinger made a point of telling Tho in so many words that Washington would not make an issue if the North Vietnamese remained where they were the moment a truce in place was declared. This went far to meet Hanoi's desires. Moreover the United States would be ready to agree on a specific deadline for the departure of all its forces from Vietnam in exchange for the release of the American POWs. This deadline, Kissinger explained, would be negotiated as soon as the North Vietnamese accepted the principle of freeing the prisoners.

In linking an American pullout date to the release of the prisoners, Kissinger knew he was running a serious diplomatic risk. If Le Duc Tho accepted the proposal, the United States might find itself in a "trap," because Nixon would then be forced to do what he had resisted for more than two years: establish a deadline for the total pullout of American troops. Still, Kissinger thought the risk was worth taking. He was "amazed" that Le Duc Tho immediately turned him down. After the meeting, Kissinger remarked to his aides that the North Vietnamese had lost a major chance to advance their negotiating cause.

But that is not what Le Duc Tho thought he had done. That the United States no longer demanded the departure of North Vietnamese troops from the South was fine, but it was not enough. In the first place, the cease-fire proposal implied strongly that hostilities would cease *before* the question of political control in Saigon was decided. And a political agreement on the future situation in Saigon was the touchstone of Hanoi's negotiating position. Second, the United States still demanded that the date for a complete American withdrawal be set *following* the cease-fire and Hanoi's agreement to free the POWs. In other words, the new plan represented twin dangers to North Vietnam: that it be forced to accept the indefinite presence of President Thieu in Saigon; and that it be forced to give up prematurely the trump card represented by the POWs. Therefore Le Duc Tho said no. The South Vietnamese political situation was the crux of the continuing deadlock: Thieu was facing a reelection campaign in October and the North Vietnamese could not rule out the possibility, faint as it was, that he might be pushed aside by a "peace" candidate. Playing on this situation, they spread the word that almost anybody would be acceptable to them in Saigon except Thieu.

Kissinger reported his failure to Nixon on June 1, and the two men agreed that the rejected peace proposal should remain secret. (Kissinger had the same secrecy understanding with Le Duc Tho.) Under these circumstances, the president had little new to say about Vietnam when, hours after Kissinger's return to Washington, he held yet another news conference.

In mid-June, word reached Kissinger that the North Vietnamese wished to make a counteroffer to his May 31 proposal. Accordingly, he flew to Europe on June 24. He spent two days in London, completely visible as he lunched with Prime Minister Edward Heath and conferred with other British officials. Then, on Saturday, June 26, he vanished from sight. The general assumption was that he was resting and working at the American embassy residence in London. But what he did was to board a U.S. Air Force plane at a nearby RAF base for the short flight to a French Air Force base outside of Paris, whence he was driven to the meeting with Le Duc Tho.

The North Vietnamese Politburo member proceeded immediately to submit a nine-point peace plan. In essence, it was an offer to release all American military and civilian war prisoners simultaneously with the withdrawal of all U.S. forces from Vietnam. The two actions would be completed on the same date. But Tho's proposal carried several catches. It demanded, for example, that an Indochina cease-fire should be negotiated by the United States and the pro-American factions in the three countries with all the parties concerned on the Communist side—i.e., the Provisional Revolutionary Government (Viet Cong) in South Vietnam, the Pathet Lao in Laos, and Sihanouk's exiled Cambodian government. This, of course, implied United States recognition of the three rebel groups (the PRG had already been represented at the Paris talks since early 1969), and it conjured up a diplomatic nightmare. Last, Le Duc Tho's proposal went beyond a simple demand for Thieu's removal in Saigon, urging instead that the United States "stop supporting Thieu-Ky-Khiem so that there may be set up in Saigon a new administration standing for peace, independence, neutrality and democracy." This new nuance was related to the approaching presidential elections.

Kissinger decided not to reject the proposal out of hand. He concluded that there were negotiable elements in Hanoi's plan, and there was enough vagueness in it to appeal to his nimble mind. His own diplomatic technique was based on the theory that vague notions can, with patience, be reduced to specific ideas. What he abhorred were hard positions that appeared to leave no room for negotiation. Besides, Kissinger liked to separate issues and deal with them one by one. He told Le Duc Tho that the United States was willing to take the proposal as the "basis" for further negotiations. As he explained later to the Kalb brothers, "From then on, every American proposal followed the sequence and the subject matter of the nine points."

On July 1, however, Kissinger had a major shock. The PRG delegation in Paris publicly issued a seven-point peace plan of its own that differed substantially from Le Duc Tho's nine points of five days earlier. It called for a date for the American withdrawal from Vietnam and Thieu's deposition, and urged the United States to "stop all maneuvers, including tricks on elections, aimed at maintaining the puppet Nguyen Van Thieu." Mrs. Nguyen Thi Binh, the PRG foreign minister, brought up the POW question, but somewhat differently from the proposal in the Hanoi plan. She said American prisoners would be released gradually during 1971 if all U.S. forces were withdrawn during the same period. Under Hanoi's formulation, the two actions would be completed simultaneously—without any ifs.

Complicating the situation was the fact that Kissinger was apprised of the PRG plan only hours before he left Washington again, this time for Asia and Europe. The real purpose of this travel was a secret side trip to Peking, but now, as he flew over the Pacific, Kissinger had to ponder the Paris diplomatic crisis simultaneously with his last-minute preparations for the meetings with Premier Chou En-lai.

What troubled Kissinger was that he could not understand why the PRG had made a public proposal so much at variance with Le Duc Tho's private ones. He could not believe that Hanoi and the Viet Cong had suddenly developed separate policies. The confusion was compounded by an interview granted by Le Duc Tho to a *New York Times* correspondent on July 6, in which he suggested that the POW question was "separable" from other aspects of the settlement. Finally, Kissinger—then spending a day in New Delhi—instructed David Bruce, the chief American delegate in Paris, to ask Le Duc Tho whether Hanoi's proposal of June 26 still stood. Bruce saw Tho and cabled back in the affirmative.

Kissinger's private conclusion was that Hanoi and the PRG had decided for Vietnamese political reasons to pursue two negotiating tracks. He assumed that the more belligerent tone of the PRG was related to the Saigon elections in October; the Viet Cong, as Kissinger knew from intelligence reports, had instructed its followers to vote for the candidate running against Thieu rather than abstain, as had been done in 1967. The

CIA, in an analysis in its classified daily bulletin for July 2, speculated that the PRG proposal was designed to embarrass the United States "both at home and overseas" and to encourage Thieu's domestic opponents. The agency's analysts, unaware of Tho's private proposals to Kissinger, found at the same time that while the PRG "softens" their stance on the POWs, they "may also believe that their political proposals will appeal to many in the United States who are looking for a face-saving way out of the war. . . . They probably are also hoping that the new proposal will fuel worries in Saigon about Washington's longer-term support."

Under the circumstances, the administration refrained from making an immediate public reply to the PRG. Nixon and Kissinger—who were in constant communication while Kissinger traveled across Asia—felt that another secret meeting with Tho was required before the United States could take a public position on the negotiations. The president ordered a full-fledged policy review on Vietnam in the meantime. This review would be held in San Clemente, where Nixon flew on July 6, with Secretary Rogers, Helms, and Kissinger's deputy, Alexander Haig. Kissinger, it was explained, would join the group on his return from meetings with Thieu in Saigon and Le Duc Tho in Paris.

But Kissinger's trip for consultations with the South Vietnamese in Saigon and the North Vietnamese in Paris had become essentially a cover for the most secret of all his secret trips.

Chapter 14

Henry Kissinger's trip to Peking in July 1971 to meet with Premier Chou En-lai marked the great breakthrough in Nixon's efforts to establish a working relationship with China. It is an interesting reflection on Nixon's and Kissinger's policy instincts that it was the president who personally pressed from the very outset for this new attitude toward China while Kissinger was unconvinced in the beginning of its wisdom and feasibility. China was one of the few examples in the Nixon-Kissinger relationship where the two men had substantial conceptual differences. Even in 1969, when he was already ensconced at the White House, Kissinger continued to perceive basic world-security relations along the Washington-Moscow axis, reasoning that policy linkages between the two nuclear superpowers formed the principal guarantee of peace. As for China, his principal worry was the threat of an armed confrontation between it and the Soviet Union. Nevertheless Kissinger went along with Nixon's increasing fascination over the possibilities inherent in an active China policy, harnessing his diplomatist's talents to its execution.

(Discussing his foreign policy in television interviews with David Frost in 1977, Nixon said: "I do not know when Dr. Kissinger may have conceived of the possibility of an initiative toward China. I do know that I conceived it before I ever met him and that I pushed it very, very hard from the first days of the administration. I was the one, as he of course agrees, who raised the issue and kept pressing the issue, but he pursued it with enormous enthusiasm.")

Although the secret diplomatic channel through Pakistan seemed to be functioning satisfactorily in the opening months of 1971, the Chinese were less than forthcoming in revealing their long-range thoughts. The written communications from Peking were generally vague, which was exactly what was expected in Washington, and the Nixon-Kissinger judgment was that not too much of significance would happen in the course of the year. It was decided that the United States should pursue its efforts regardless of Chinese responses. In fact, Nixon thought that these efforts should be accelerated so as to create a visible rhythm in the policy. He had been encouraged by Mao Tse-tung's comments to Edgar Snow that he would be welcome in Peking, and for the first time, he and Kissinger began thinking seriously in terms of a presidential visit while Nixon was still in office.

Nixon lost no public opportunity to send "signals" to the Chinese about his desire for an improved relationship. He knew that Washington newsmen were becoming aware of his changing policy toward China; presidential news conferences thus became an excellent forum to express thoughts on the subject. The correct assumption was that the Chinese leaders read his every word with utmost attention.

At his March 4 news conference, entirely dedicated to foreign policy, Nixon gently nudged Peking to start responding to his courtship while, at the same time, explaining once more that he would not sacrifice American commitments to Taiwan. "We would like to normalize relations with all nations in the world. There has, however, been no receptivity on the part of Communist China. But under no circumstances will we proceed with a policy of normalizing relations with Communist China if the cost of that policy is to expel Taiwan from the family of nations."

Here, however, Nixon was holding back. China *was* showing a certain "receptivity" to the United States by keeping open the secret Pakistani channel, but the president of course could not allude to this in public. He reasoned that even if Taiwan were expelled from the United Nations in 1971, the United States was not obligated to break relations with the Nationalists. This was the real meaning of the two-Chinas policy, a response to Chou En-lai's intellectual challenge to invent a formula allowing both sides to skirt the Taiwan issue.

On March 15, the United States took another public step in the direction of Peking, lifting the twenty-year ban on travel by Americans to the mainland. Theretofore the State Department had had to validate passports of Americans wishing to go to China if the purpose of the proposed trip was considered "legitimate." Actually the validations were not hard to obtain—quite a few thousand of them had been granted since 1970 when Nixon authorized the procedure—and the problem resided in China's reluctance to give Americans entry visas. For example, only *three* visas had been authorized by Peking in the previous eighteen months. This may have been due to the fact that the Chinese resented the formal travel ban; the idea behind lifting it was to encourage new contacts. The State Department, in announcing the decision, said it had been taken in line with Nixon's promise in his February message to Congress "to create broad opportunities for contacts between the Chinese and American people." But as officials freely conceded that day, no rapid response from Peking was anticipated.

Nixon was resting at Key Biscayne when the State Department announced the travel-ban suspension. But the White House was not left out of the picture. Ziegler made a point of telling newsmen that "it is the president's policy to carefully examine further steps we may take for broader contacts between Red Chinese and Americans and it is his intention, wherever possible, to remove needless obstacles to the realization of these opportunities." This was a signal to Peking that the United States would soon move beyond the lifting of the travel ban no matter what the Chinese did. "We hope for, but will not be deterred by lack of, reciprocity," Ziegler said.

The administration also felt that the time had come for more direct diplomacy. The secret exchanges through Pakistan were encouraging, but not wholly satisfactory. Nixon, for one, believed that the discussion should be elevated to a more personalized level. Not knowing precisely what other venue would be acceptable to the Chinese—or, for that matter, how quickly they were prepared to move—the White House turned to the idea of reviving the Warsaw ambassadorial talks interrupted nearly a year earlier. Early in March, the suggestion for doing so was made to Peking via the Pakistani channel. Again, the administration expected no immediate reply—and again, it was wrong. The Chinese were approaching a major decision—and Premier Chou En-lai was its prime advocate.

This breakthrough, just three weeks after the United States lifted the travel ban, was executed in an artful Chinese fashion. And it happened in, of all places, Nagoya, Japan, where American and Chinese players were among the teams participating in an international Ping-Pong tournament. For days, the Chinese had ignored the Americans socially. Then, on April 6, as the competition was ending, the Chinese team suddenly approached the Americans, and all smiles, invited them to come to play in China as soon as the Nagoya games were over. It was a stunning move. Clearly, the Chinese players could not have issued the invitation without instructions from the very top in Peking; no American group had *ever* been invited to Communist China.

Graham B. Steenhoven, the president of the United States Table Tennis Association and the leader of the American team in Nagoya, thanked the Chinese for the invitation, but delayed acceptance. Aware of the immense political implications of the Chinese approach, he grabbed the telephone to call the American ambassador in Tokyo, Armin H. Meyer, to ask for advice. Meyer sent a top-priority telegram to the State Department requesting instructions. Since the travel ban to China had already been lifted, there was no actual need for the embassy in Tokyo to validate the passports of the American players. But Meyer believed that Washington had to be given the opportunity to encourage or discourage the proposed trip. The moment he received Meyer's dispatch, Secretary Rogers contacted the White House to inform the president and Kissinger. There was not a moment's hesitation: Meyer was told that the Ping-Pong players should by all means go to Peking.

While Steenhoven in Nagoya was advising the Chinese that his team would be "delighted" to accept the invitation, the president in Washington was convoking the National Security Council to debate the overall China policy in the light of the Ping-Pong *coup de théâtre*. It was obvious to Nixon, Kissinger, and Rogers that the invitation to the table-tennis team was a subtle but unmistakable response to the patient United States overtures of the last two years. They were convinced that the invitation was not an isolated episode—the Chinese did not operate that way—but the long-awaited start of a serious diplomatic process.

There had been hints from West European diplomats for several months that Chou En-lai was increasingly interested in opening a dialogue with the United States. A similar report came from Romania's Deputy Premier Gheorghe Rădulescu, who saw Chou on March 22. The Pakistani channel was spewing vague but intriguing thoughts. In March, for example, there was a general exchange of ideas about the possibility of a senior American official visiting Peking. But a formal confirmation of Chinese interest had been lacking. Now it was given through the Nagoya invitation. The administration had been planning an announcement of additional goodwill gestures toward China, but Nixon now told the NSC that he was ordering the bureaucracy to move on this as soon as possible. He did not want to waste any time.

Neither, as it turned out, did Peking. Chinese visas were issued not only to the nine members of the Ping-Pong team, four team officials, and two of their wives, but also to three American newsmen—the last all "old China hands." The American group arrived in Peking on April 10, and was given red-carpet treatment. The Chinese were clearly determined to turn the Ping-Pong visit into a major political occasion. On April 14, after the first exhibition game (the Chinese players, being the best in the world, easily but cordially trounced the Americans), Chou En-lai invited the visitors to a reception at the Great Hall of the People, an honor not usually accorded foreign sports teams. There, he delivered his central message with utmost clarity: "You have opened a new page in the relations of the Chinese and American people. I am confident that this beginning again of our friendship will certainly meet with majority support of our two peoples." Steenhoven replied in kind, inviting the Chinese team to visit the United States. Chou indicated that the Chinese would accept.

Chou's words were instantly transmitted to the United States by the three American reporters; Peking saw to it that proper communications were available to them. Nixon, Kissinger, and Rogers studied the text, and quickly decided that the announcement of new measures easing up contacts with China would be issued at once. Accordingly, the White House, at noon, made public a statement in Nixon's name authorizing American visas for Chinese visitors and lifting a wide range of economic restrictions. The president chose to couch this historic statement in formal terms:

In my second annual Foreign Policy Report to the Congress on February 25, 1971, I wrote, "In the coming year I will carefully examine what further steps we might take to create broader opportunities for contacts between the Chinese and American peoples, and how we might remove needless obstacles to the realization of these opportunities."

I asked the Under Secretaries Committee of the National Security Council to make appropriate recommendations to bring this about. After reviewing the resulting study, I decided on the following actions, none of which requires new legislation or negotiations with the People's Republic of China:

—The United States is prepared to expedite visas for visitors or groups of visitors from the People's Republic of China to the United States.

—U.S. currency controls are to be relaxed to permit the use of dollars by the People's Republic of China.

—Restrictions are to be ended on American oil companies providing fuel to ships or aircraft proceeding to and from China except on Chinese-owned or Chinese-chartered carriers bound to or from North Vietnam, North Korea, or Cuba.

—U.S. vessels or aircraft may now carry Chinese cargoes between non-Chinese ports and U.S.–owned foreign flag carriers may call at Chinese ports.

—I have asked for a list of items of a nonstrategic nature which can be placed under general license for direct export to the People's Republic of China. Following my review and approval of specific items on this list, direct imports of designated items from China will then also be authorized.

After due consideration of the results of these changes in our trade and travel restrictions, I will consider what additional steps might be taken. Implementing regulations will be announced by the Department of State and other interested agencies.

Two days later, on April 16, Nixon took a much warmer public stance toward Peking—including a strong hint that he might visit China while still in office:

The other day was Easter Sunday. Both of my daughters, Tricia and Julie, were there—and Tricia with Eddie Cox . . . and Julie and David Eisenhower. And the conversation got around to travel and also, of course, with regard to honeymoon travel and the rest. They were asking me where would you like to go? Where do you think we ought to go? So, I sat back and thought a bit and said, "Well, the place to go is to Asia." I said, "I hope that sometime in your life, sooner rather than later, you will be able to go to China to see the great cities, and the people, and all of that there." I hope they do. As a matter of fact, I hope sometime I do. I am not sure that it is going to happen while I am in office. I will not speculate with regard to either of the diplomatic points. It is premature to talk about recognition. It is premature to talk about a change in our policy with regard to the United Nations. However, we are going to proceed in these very substantive fields of exchange of persons and also in the field of trade. That will open the way to other moves which will be made at an appropriate time.

Actually, the way to "other moves" was opened almost immediately by Peking—and the "appropriate time" suddenly became now. On April 16, the president had told newsmen that he did not know whether the Chinese were interested in resuming the talks in Warsaw, but within days it developed that Peking was interested in much more than that—and very quickly. The White House had hardly recovered from the "Ping-Pong diplomacy" when the Chinese came through with something else.

This time it was the extraordinary proposal from Chou En-lai personally that Nixon dispatch a high-level emissary to Peking to discuss the developing Sino-American relationship with the Chinese leaders. The notion of sending an American envoy of senior rank to China had of course been broached by Ambassador Stoessel in Warsaw more than a year before. Now Pakistani Ambassador Hilaly delivered to Kissinger at the White House a communication from Peking suggesting that either Kissinger or Rogers come to Peking for top-level talks. The implication was that the American envoy would visit the Chinese capital secretly.

(Nixon reminisced later that "the message was . . . very conciliatory, very warm. . . . The other messages had been more at the ambassadorial or lower levels, or quoting Chou En-lai. But this was a message directly from Chou En-lai . . . to me as President. . . . With a nice grace note, which was so typical of Chou En-lai, one of the most sophisticated and subtle diplomats in world history, he said, 'This is the first time in history when a message has been sent from a head through a head to a head.' He had pointed out incidentally that he was sending this message with the knowledge and approval of Mao Tse-tung and also Lin Piao.")

Kissinger received the Chinese invitation early in the evening; Nixon was presiding over a state dinner and could not be disturbed until after midnight. Only then could the two men spend several hours in the Lincoln Sitting Room discussing the Chinese initiative. They were surprised by the alacrity and intensity of Peking's responses to the gradual American gestures. But there was no question in Nixon's mind that an envoy should go to Peking as soon as practicable. His first reaction was that it should be Kissinger rather than Rogers: the prestige of the office of the secretary of state should not be engaged in a secret mission that could conceivably fail, and Nixon had more confidence in Kissinger's diplomatic talents than in Rogers's. Still, the secretary was the only other member of the administration to be apprised of the Chinese proposal, and he accepted Nixon's reasoning that Kissinger should be the envoy. (Nixon said subsequently that Kissinger had opposed informing Rogers: "We had quite an argument about that. . . . I said, 'Rogers has gotta know.' And he said, 'Well, he'll leak . . . or he'll object to it." I said, 'You cannot have the Secretary of State not be informed.") A few days later, Kissinger handed the Pakistani ambassador a written American reply expressing the decision to come to Peking. Only the date remained to be set; the White House was aiming tentatively for July. The message also included a guarded suggestion that the president might wish to visit China himself sometime in 1972.

Like all the messages moving through the secret channel, this, too, was addressed to Pakistani President Yahya. (It was signed by Nixon.) It was taken to Islamabad by a Pakistani diplomatic courier in a sealed envelope (all the communications between the White House and Yahya were in the form of sealed letters although on a few urgent occasions messages were exchanged in cipher), as was the case with all the Chinese-American diplomatic traffic. The Pakistanis chose this delivery method because too many trips by senior diplomats to Washington might have aroused suspicions. In Islamabad, Yahya turned Nixon's letter over to Foreign Secretary Sultan Khan; Yahya and Sultan then called in the

Chinese ambassador, Chang Tung, and read to him from Nixon's letter; Chang Tung relayed the information to Peking.

Several days later, Chang Tung informed the Pakistanis that a final answer was forthcoming. Sultan wrote Kissinger directly to advise him. The following week, Yahya received a formal Chinese reply. He sent Nixon a sealed letter that was taken to Washington by a hand-picked Pakistani diplomat at the end of April. All that was left to arrange were the final details.

The months of May and June had been enormously busy in Washington in terms of secret and overt diplomacy on at least four major fronts. It was probably the most actively creative period in foreign policy since Nixon had taken office. Kissinger—with the president's support—was working on the Vietnam negotiations and making the secret trips to Paris. Also in May, the United States and the Soviet Union reached an accord in principle on SALT that Kissinger had been secretly negotiating for months with Ambassador Dobrynin, parallel with the talks conducted by the two delegations in Helsinki and Vienna. This, too, was immensely time-consuming as Kissinger had to consult with the White House Verification Panel and the Pentagon. Then Nixon and Brezhnev completed the deal through secret exchanges.

From early April, China had become a top priority for the White House, and still more staff work was needed in addition to the secret after-hours exchanges between Nixon and Kissinger in the Lincoln Sitting Room. And in the Middle East, Secretary Rogers was seeking to reactivate Egyptian-Israeli negotiations while, at the same time, making secret preparations to arm Jordan's King Hussein against a new flare-up of Palestinian rebellions. Nixon also had to play host to Saudi Arabia's King Faisal, a very important visitor, in late May, and to West German Chancellor Willy Brandt, who visited him in June to discuss the status of Berlin. The completion of negotiations with Japan on the reversion of Okinawa and a host of lesser foreign-policy problems required Nixon's attention in varying degrees.

Nixon and Kissinger were thriving on this filling diplomatic diet. The president was absorbing it all and making decisions as he went along. Kissinger was working his NSC staff to death: his temper kept exploding, he had staff papers rewritten over and over again, and some of his aides began to experience something akin to battle fatigue. But there he was in the center of decision-making, juggling a half-dozen foreign-policy balls in the air, planning policy linkages, anticipating reactions from Hanoi, Moscow, and Peking on a whole set of problems, and striving to fit it all—if possible—into coherent American foreign policy.

As for the China question, public events remained intertwined with secret diplomatic moves, for China was increasingly dominating public attention. On the whole, there was remarkable support in the administration for the new China policy—a notable exception was Vice President Agnew, who infuriated Nixon by criticizing it at a private session with a group of newsmen—as there was among the public. Only a few conservative voices were heard in opposition, but Nixon, the arch anti-Communist, simply ignored them. He had decided that Americans were ready to support him and that he, a Republican president, could make it work. He was also earning the approval of liberals who so vocally chastised him over Indochina, and this was a political bonus.

There were new headlines almost every day. On April 26, a special presidential commission recommended that the United States support "as early as practicable," the admission of Peking to the United Nations, but without the expulsion of Nationalist China. Americans were beginning to accept the two-Chinas concept—if such conservatives as Henry Cabot Lodge (the commission's chairman), Cardinal Cooke, Dr. Norman Vincent Peale, Senator Robert Taft, Jr., and Senator Bourke B. Hickenlooper were willing to give it credence.

Two days later, on April 28, the State Department took another step that was bound to please Peking. Under intensive questioning by newsmen, the department's spokesman, Charles W. Bray III, expressed the opinion that one way to solve the Taiwan problem would be through negotiations between the Communists and the Nationalists. This was a subtle departure from earlier policy: Washington was no longer saying that the Nationalists on Taiwan *necessarily* held legitimacy over the island, but, rather, that "sovereignty over Taiwan . . . is an unsettled question subject to a future international resolution."

China was again a major topic when Nixon held a news conference at the White House on April 29. This was the day the latest communication had come from Peking. Although—unbeknown to the public—Washington and Peking had already agreed that Henry Kissinger would soon visit China, the president chose to be cautious, and refused to discuss the position his administration would ultimately take on the question of China's representation in the United Nations. "Progress," he said, "is not helped in this very sensitive area by speculation that goes beyond what the progress might achieve." But he could not resist the temptation to tantalize his audience a bit—and at the same time, of course, send another signal to the Chinese:

What we have done has broken the ice; now we have to test the water to see how deep it is. . . . I would finally suggest that—I know this question may come up if I don't answer it now—I hope, and, as a matter of fact, I expect to visit mainland China sometime in some capacity—I don't know what capacity. But that indicates what I hope for the long term. And I hope to contribute to a policy in which we can have a new relationship with mainland China.

On May 7, the United States took still another step toward this "new relationship" when the Treasury Department formally removed all controls on dollar transactions with Peking. This move effectively cleared the way for a full-fledged resumption of trade with China for the first time in twenty-one years. In December 1950, after the Chinese entered the Korean war, the Treasury Department had banned the use of dollars in all dealings with the mainland, making it illegal for Americans to trade there. Now the Treasury issued a "general license" on the use of American currency in the China trade. It was a necessary prerequisite for the next planned initiative, the designation of specific items that could be exported to China and the freeing of all imports from there. On Nixon's instructions, a five-agency group busied itself drafting the list of nonstrategic goods that could be sold to the Chinese.

The list was announced on June 10 at the White House, completing the twin package on travel and trade that the United States was prepared to grant China in the first phase.

As I recall [the president said], there is a Chinese proverb to the effect that a journey of a thousand miles begins with a single step. We have taken two steps, but the important thing is that we have started the journey toward a more normal relationship with mainland China; and eventually—and this is vitally important—ending its isolation and the isolation of 700 million people from the rest of the people of the world. This we think is a goal well worth pursuing.

The third American step in the "journey of a thousand miles"—and this time the description was an understatement—began on July 1, when Henry Kissinger left Washington on a trip to Asia and Europe. Ostensibly, the purpose of this expedition was to confer with President Thieu in Saigon and with the North Vietnamese in Paris.

Between Saigon and Paris, Kissinger was to stop in India and Pakistan to see what he could do to arrest the rising momentum toward a war between them over the fate of East Pakistan (Bangladesh), the Bengali region seeking independence from the Pakistani state. Obviously unknown—it was the best-kept secret of the administration—was that Kissinger's real schedule included three days to be spent surreptitiously in Peking in meetings with Premier Chou and in travel to and from the Chinese capital.

Actually, the decision on the dates Kissinger would visit Peking—July 9 to 11—was made only one week before he left. Until the last week of June, while Kissinger was in Europe for the secret June 26 meeting with Le Duc Tho, there was uncertainty about the timing. But finally, the Peking message accepting the dates proposed by the White House was received in Washington through the Pakistanis—and Kissinger was all set to go.

On July 2 and 3, Kissinger was in Saigon—highly visible—conferring with President Thieu about Vietnam peace proposals. On July 4, he was in Bangkok. On July 6, he arrived in New Delhi. At the airport, he was greeted by demonstrators protesting covert shipments of military spare parts to Pakistan in violation of the standing United States embargo on sales of arms to both the Pakistanis and the Indians. The secrecy over these shipments had been shattered by a *New York Times* story reporting that at least one vessel was en route from New York to Karachi with spare parts for American equipment long held by the Pakistani armed forces.

Officially, the United States was following an "evenhanded" policy. Much world opinion was against Pakistan because of the brutalities perpetrated by President Yahya's army in trying to stamp out the Bengali rebellion, but Washington took the view that nothing would be solved by suspending the economic aid provided to the Pakistanis through an international consortium in which the United States participated. (The World Bank, which acted as consortium manager, favored suspension.) The American view was that war between India and Pakistan had to be averted, but the administration opposed drastic pressures against Yahya. Privately, Nixon and Kissinger shared a dislike of India's ruling politicians—they were much more at home with the Pakistanis—but there is no proof that this sentiment affected the administration's policies in the subcontinent conflict. Political ties with Pakistan—which had an alliance with the United States, whereas India had always studiously pursued neutralist policies and now was inclining toward a special relationship with the Soviet Union—were much more to the point. And presumably, Yahya's contribution to the China policy was a major factor.

Kissinger's discussions in New Delhi had no particular effect on Indian attitudes toward Bangladesh. Indira Gandhi, the prime minister, had evidently made up her mind that a partition of Pakistan would be a desirable outcome of the Bengali revolt. With 5 million Bengali refugees in India in June, pressures for Indian intervention were mounting. Bangladesh guerrillas were training on Indian soil. Kissinger left New Delhi highly pessimistic: a war in South Asia would destabilize superpower relationships. If there were a subcontinent war, however, his inclination was to side with Pakistan.

On July 8, Kissinger arrived at the Rawalpindi airport, which serves the nearby capital of Islamabad. He was expected in Peking the following day, and presently, the great deception, carefully prearranged by Yahya and Sultan, was set in motion by Kissinger's Pakistani hosts. It was a perfect *mise-en-scène*. First, Kissinger paid a courtesy call on Yahya. They spent ninety minutes together, discussing the final details for the Peking flight as well as the situation in the subcontinent. Next, Kissinger went to his quarters at the government guest house to rest before a dinner there that evening; ninety guests had been invited to attend. But according to plan, it was canceled at 5:00 p.m., when calls went out from the Foreign Ministry to advise the prospective guests that the American visitor had suddenly been taken ill. So that the cover would not be blown, the Pakistanis went to the extent of actually having a dinner for ninety cooked—although there was never any intention of having guests to eat it. Sultan was concerned that newsmen might telephone the chef during the afternoon to check on the menu, and he wanted him to be able to answer truthfully. The Pakistani foreign secretary's fears of an accidental disclosure of the secret plan were not exaggerated, and he overlooked no detail. In fact, a newsman *did* call the chef at 4:00 p.m.

Later in the evening, word went to the press that Kissinger was suffering from a stomach "indisposition"—not an unusual occurrence for Westerners in Asia—and that his doctor had suggested a short rest in the mountain resort of Nathia Gali, away from Islamabad's heat, before he continued his trip on to Paris. Kissinger was to be driven to the mountains the next morning. Some newsmen covering Kissinger's visit easily accepted the official explanations. Others speculated that the proposed stay at Nathia Gali was intended as a cover for a quick dash to East Pakistan to try to mediate the rebellion there. But even this speculation died down quickly. That Kissinger might be going to China simply never crossed anybody's mind.

Sultan's precautions were absolutely foolproof. The plan was for Kissinger to fly to Peking aboard a Boeing 707 airliner of Pakistani International Airlines (PIA) on a special flight. When Sultan asked top PIA officials for the plane a week earlier, he simply told them that it was for a very secret and important "national security" mission that could not be explained beforehand. PIA assumed that it was President Yahya who would be the passenger; they asked no further questions. The assigned PIA pilots were told that their special flight on July 9 would take them to Peking over an unusual Himalayan route, but they were not told why. Three days earlier, two Chinese air force navigators quietly slipped into Rawalpindi on a scheduled PIA flight from Peking; they were needed because the Kissinger flight would be routed over an area Pakistani pilots knew little. Scheduled PIA flights to Peking normally made stops in Dacca, in East Pakistan, Canton, and Shanghai. But these stops could unmask the secret voyage. Besides, there were Indian radar stations in Indian-held portions of Kashmir, as well as Soviet radar on the Soviet side of the Pakistani border, that could have tracked a PIA jet on its accustomed route, and New Delhi and Moscow would have wondered about an unscheduled flight.

At 2:30 a.m. on Friday, July 9, Sultan, a tall, distinguished man, drove up to the guest house at the wheel of his Japanese-built car to take Kissinger to the Rawalpindi airport. Another car picked up Kissinger's aides and his two Secret Service men. The PIA airliner was parked at the far side of the field. Sultan led Kissinger aboard. Only then did he inform the pilots and the cabin crew who their passenger was. He told them that they were involved in a secret mission in the interest of peace, that they were not to address Kissinger by name, and that they were to maintain the secrecy until such a time as an official announcement was made. "It worked on the basis of the honor system," Sultan explained in a subsequent interview.

Awaiting Kissinger aboard the plane were four Chinese Foreign Ministry officials who had arrived in Rawalpindi earlier in the week to escort their visitor to Peking. On the American side, only Kissinger's three aides had known ahead of time about the China trip. They were John Holdridge, the NSC's China expert; Richard Smyser, an Asia specialist; and Winston Lord, Kissinger's personal assistant. The two Secret Service men knew nothing until they boarded the jetliner and saw the Chinese officials and navigators.

Just as surprised, when he found out about the trip a few days later, was Navy Yeoman Charles E. ("Chuck") Radford, a noncommissioned officer attached since 1970 to the Joint Chiefs of Staff liaison office at the White House. Radford, a clerk and stenographer, often traveled on secret diplomatic missions with Kissinger to handle the paper work. Kissinger preferred to rely on the young yeoman rather than on regular NSC secretaries. For one thing, a secretary might accidentally be spotted in Paris or elsewhere by an alert newsman acquainted with the NSC staff, and would thus signal Kissinger's presence. An unknown yeoman in civilian clothes, on the other hand, called no attention to himself. What Kissinger, the most secretive official in Washington, did not suspect at the time was that Radford made it a practice to pass copies of his most secret papers surreptitiously to the Joint Chiefs.

But this was part of the miasma pervading all parts of the Nixon administration. Radford was acting on the instructions of Admiral Robert O. Welander, his boss at the JCS liaison office at the White House, to whom he passed Kissinger's documents; Welander in turn delivered them to Admiral Moorer, JCS chairman. Moorer was a member of the National Security Council, and at least in theory he should have had direct access to all top-secret information on foreign policy and defense generated in the White House. In practice, however, Nixon and Kissinger had a way of holding back from the council what they considered to be too sensitive to be known even in that top-level policy organ. Moorer, therefore, short-circuited this system. But there is nothing to indicate that he shared his purloined information with Defense Secretary Laird, whose telephone conversations with his military assistant were tapped by the FBI on White House orders. Nearly everybody high in the Nixon administration, it seemed, was spying on everybody else.

Kissinger left Radford behind in Islamabad when he flew to Peking on July 9, but the yeoman knew all about it three days later when Kissinger dictated to him his lengthy report to Nixon on the China visit. Moorer already had a copy when Kissinger returned home.

Despite all the precautions, the secrecy surrounding Kissinger's departure for Peking was nearly blown at the last moment. A Pakistani stringer for the London *Daily Telegraph* happened to be at the Rawalpindi airport during the night when he saw several cars heading across the tarmac toward the PIA jetliner. He walked over to the plane and, to his enormous surprise, thought that he recognized Kissinger in the rotund figure boarding the plane. He asked a PIA official if he had seen it right; the airline official, who had somehow escaped being sworn to secrecy, confirmed it. Answering the follow-up question, he told the stringer that Kissinger was leaving for China. The reporter raced back to town and filed an urgent dispatch to London that Kissinger was en route to Peking. *Daily Telegraph* editors refused to believe it and killed what was easily the scoop of the year.

The American ambassador in Islamabad, Joseph S. Farland, was among those in the Pakistani capital who were kept in the dark about the Kissinger mission. It was, to be sure, par for the course for Kissinger to conceal his secret diplomacy from American ambassadors in the capitals where he happened to be operating. What remains unclear is how Kissinger explained his three-day absence from Pakistan and the Nathia Gali cover-up to Farland. The ambassador had to know that the "real" Kissinger was not at the mountain resort—he too went up there with the official party—and he had to play his part in the deception. But, it appears, Farland had no idea why the charade had been mounted. Sultan remains convinced that Farland learned about Kissinger's side trip to China only when the official announcement was made.

After the PIA plane took off from Rawalpindi, at 3:30 a.m., Sultan drove back to Islamabad to engage in the next phase of the cover-up. At 6:00 a.m. he was again at the guest house, this time as ostentatiously as possible. He and Farland led the five-car motorcade that, supposedly, was taking Kissinger up to Nathia Gali. Pakistani police kept the curious away from the guest house area so that nobody would notice that instead of Kissinger, a Secret Service agent sat in Sultan's official limousine, which flew American and Pakistani flags as it left the capital escorted by motorcycle outriders.

At Nathia Gali, the news given the press was that Kissinger would stay there for several days to recover. Many senior Pakistani officials, not informed of the cover-up, went up to the health station to pay courtesy calls on "Kissinger." However, Sultan diverted them by telling them sadly that his guest was not well enough to see visitors.

Kissinger's PIA airliner landed precisely at noon at a military airfield near Peking after a smooth five-and-a-half-hour Himalayan flight from Rawalpindi over some of the world's most spectacular mountains. Remaining awake throughout the flight, Kissinger again studied his black-bound briefing books on China, which, among other material, contained "talking points" he planned to use in his meeting with Chou En-lai. Nixon had approved them shortly before Kissinger left on his trip, but as a practical matter, the president had to give him considerable negotiating latitude. The two men had tried to anticipate what Chou might say; still surprises could not be excluded and Kissinger had no way of consulting Nixon from Peking through secure communication channels. In this sense, then, Kissinger was in China as an envoy plenipotentiary.

At the airport, Kissinger was greeted by Marshal Yeh Chien-ying, acting foreign minister, and Huang Hua, a senior diplomat who had accompanied Chou En-lai to the Geneva conference in 1954. That was when John Foster Dulles humiliated Chou by refusing to shake hands with him. Now, seventeen years later, Chou and Kissinger were to meet as equals, with the premier playing the gracious host and the American envoy the perfect guest. Still, the diplomatic game was being played on Chinese terms: it was the American emissary who had come to Peking, and not the other way around, and it was China that issued the invitation for the visit in the old tradition of foreign ambassadors being permitted to call on the Chinese court. In 1651, the first Russian ambassador to China was refused an audience with Emperor Shun Chih and summarily sent home because he would not kowtow before him. In 1816, the British ambassador, Lord Amherst, had been accorded similar treatment when *he* declined to kowtow before Emperor Kia K'ing. In 1971, Henry Kissinger was not expected to kowtow—not even politically. Chou was too wise and sophisticated to try to exact vengeance from the Americans for the 1954 slight in Geneva. Nonetheless, it was clear from the start that the Chinese premier was setting the tone for the dialogue.

The first session between Chou and Kissinger, starting four hours after the Americans landed in Peking and lasting eight hours, was held at a Chinese government guest house where Kissinger was staying. Chou made a point of calling on Kissinger, the guest, rather than having the American visit him first, even though his official rank was ever so much higher than Kissinger's. It was part of the exquisite Chinese politeness— almost cordiality—that the premier wished to accord the Americans.

Chou and Kissinger immediately developed a superb personal relationship—they admired each other from the outset—and this helped to ease the negotiating process. It was the mutual admiration of two intellectuals whose minds were remarkably akin in their analytical processes, particularly in the ability to center instantly on fundamental issues and skirt secondary matters. Chou was not trying to strike hard bargains or force the United States into unacceptable positions. Instead, he engaged Kissinger in a series of *tours d'horizon* on world politics, making clear what was vital to China and what was less essential in immediate terms. Unlike negotiators from the Soviet Union, Chou was not interested in scoring specific points on every issue that came under discussion or seeking American commitments over a whole spectrum of problems. In other words, there was no confrontation and no attempt to nail down hard solutions. Showing himself astoundingly well informed about American policies—the Chinese had been studying them down to the most minute detail—the premier had an appreciation of United States commitments in Asia and of the Nixon administration's present limitations on how far it could move, domestically and internationally, to meet Chinese views and wishes.

At the same time, Chou gently explained to Kissinger Peking's minimal requirements before it could embark on even a tentative relationship with the United States. They posed no great problems for Kissinger. Chou wanted recognition by the United States that Taiwan was part of China and that its future fate should be settled by the Chinese rather than remain an international issue. This was easy: the State Department had, in effect, accepted this interpretation of Taiwan's status as far back as April. Kissinger thus simply confirmed for Chou's benefit that the United States had already changed its policy on this point. To Chou, this was a matter of principle, and he was satisfied with Kissinger's statement. He indicated that Peking expected that in time Washington would sever diplomatic relations with the Nationalists, but he suggested no date and did not precondition further steps. Likewise, he made no special issue of the continued presence of American forces on Taiwan, reduced as they already were.

Kissinger for his part explained to the premier that the Nixon administration would not in the immediate future contemplate a break with Chiang Kai-shek. He said he understood full diplomatic relations with Peking were out of the question under the circumstances, but he suggested that an intermediate formula might be devised. Chou nodded, saying that the important thing was to maintain the new contacts. The Chinese were strikingly reasonable, and Kissinger concluded that they were so interested in a viable relationship with the United States that they were prepared to be infinitely patient and flexible so long as understandings existed in principle.

Likewise, Chou and Kissinger worked out a compromise of sorts on the question of Chinese representation at the United Nations. Chou stated Peking's all-or-nothing position, and Kissinger tried to explain that the United States still favored continued membership for the Nationalists while supporting the parallel entry of Peking. He stayed away from the insoluble question of the Chinese Security Council seat (the 1945 Charter provided for five veto-wielding permanent council members, one of them China, and obviously, neither could the council be enlarged nor could the Chinese seat be split in two), but this point was academic so long as Peking refused to join the U.N. altogether until Taiwan was expelled. There also was an unspoken understanding, or presumption, that it was most likely that Taiwan *would* be expelled in the fall 1971 session of the General Assembly.

All of this was a measure of the conciliatory diplomacy Kissinger and

Chou chose to pursue. Both sides, aware as they were of all problems, saw no point in fighting over them. The crux of their diplomacy was the fundamental decision to arrive at a general policy understanding. Kissinger was mildly surprised that Chou made no major issue of formal military-treaty ties between the United States and its principal Asian allies —Japan, South Korea, Taiwan, Thailand, and the Philippines—and of the presence of nuclear-armed American forces in some of these countries. Chou merely referred to this in a general way as something to be addressed in the future. The American delegation began to suspect that, all things considered, Peking perhaps was not all that keen on the removal of an American military presence in the Pacific altogether. Chou had said enough about the Soviet Union to let Kissinger conclude that, in a sense, the Chinese almost welcomed the Americans in Asia as a deterrent to what they saw as Soviet expansionism. Kissinger commented in one of his reports to Nixon that concern over Soviet policies was the common denominator in American and Chinese views of the world.

China's evident desire to gain formal recognition as a world power was demonstrated in a curious fashion during Kissinger's stay. Chou asked his visitor to what extent the United States *really* saw China as part of a new pentagonal world power equation. Whether by coincidence or design, Nixon had made the central point—in the course of a policy briefing for Midwestern editors in Kansas City on July 6, just three days before the secret meetings began in the Chinese capital—that "five great power centers" were emerging in today's world economically: the United States, Western Europe "with Britain in the Common Market," Japan, the Soviet Union, and mainland China.

> In terms of its economic capacity at the present time, a pretty good indication of where [China] is, is that Japan, with 100 million people, produces more than mainland China, with 800 million people. But that should not mislead us, and it gives us, and should give none of the potential competitors in world markets of mainland China, any sense of satisfaction that it will always be that way. Because when we see the Chinese as people . . . they are creative, they are productive, they are one of the most capable people in the world. And 800 million Chinese are going to be, inevitably, an enormous economic power, with all that that means in terms of what they could be in other areas if they move in that direction.
>
> That is the reason why I felt that it was essential that this administration take the first steps toward ending the isolation of mainland China from the world community. We had to take those steps because the Soviet Union could not, because of differences that they have that at

the present time seem to be irreconcilable. We were the only other power that could take those steps. . . . What we have done is simply opened the door—opened the door for travel, opened the door for trade. . . .

But mainland China, outside the world community, completely isolated, with its leaders not in communication with world leaders, would be a danger to the whole world that would be unacceptable, unacceptable to us and unacceptable to others as well. So consequently, this step must be taken now . . . But . . . the very success of our policy of ending the isolation of mainland China will mean an immense escalation of their economic challenge not only to us but to others in the world. . . . Eight hundred million Chinese, open to the world, with all the communication and the interchange of ideas that inevitably will occur as a result of that opening, will become an economic force in the world of enormous potential. . . . What we see as we look ahead five years, ten years, perhaps it is fifteen, but in any event, within our time, we see five great economic superpowers: the United States, Western Europe, the Soviet Union, mainland China, and, of course, Japan.

Did the United States, indeed, see such a pentagonal world with China as one of its pillars? Kissinger had not read Nixon's text, but the concepts in it were naturally familiar to him. Yes, he told Chou, this was the way the United States saw the changing world, and this was why he, Kissinger, was in Peking that moment hoping to help the Chinese out of their isolation.

That Chou (who consulted closely with Mao Tse-tung between his meetings with Kissinger) was satisfied with how the talks were going became clear when he issued a formal invitation to Nixon to visit China. He did it toward the end of their second session, held at the premier's office in the Great Hall of the People, the evening of Saturday, July 10. Kissinger, who was prepared for the possibility of the invitation, promptly accepted in the name of the president. The Chinese proposed that the visit take place sometime during 1972; Kissinger agreed, but stressed that it should occur before the summer and the presidential nominating conventions. He wanted to be careful to avoid any charges that the administration might be using a foreign-policy breakthrough for the purpose of electoral politics. This, Chou said, made sense. Now that Kissinger's presence in Peking had established a direct contact between the two governments, it was decided that the Pakistani channel was no longer required. Instead, Kissinger and Chou agreed, all communications would flow through the American and Chinese embassies in Paris.

The Kissinger-Chou conversations had by and large gone according to plan. If Kissinger ran into foul diplomatic weather at all in Peking, it was over the Vietnam war, a topic he discussed fully with Chou. The Chinese premier felt strongly that the war should end as soon as possible with a total American withdrawal from Indochina, but, again, he did not make this a prerequisite for an invitation to Nixon or other aspects of the developing relationship. From Kissinger's explanations—and, presumably, from their own sources in Hanoi—the Chinese must have realized that the war was unlikely to abate during 1971. In other words, Peking was willing to receive Nixon even with the war still going on. In terms of Communist international politics, this was a daring decision. Kissinger sought some commitment from Chou, most delicately, for Chinese assistance in his efforts to negotiate a peace settlement. Chou, just as delicately, sidestepped the suggestion.

It remains unclear whether Kissinger had told Chou that Nixon was also hoping to visit Moscow in 1972. The Chinese knew, of course, that SALT negotiations were progressing reasonably well—the Russians and Americans had announced an agreement in principle seven weeks before Kissinger went to Peking—and they could draw their own conclusions; it is possible that this agreement led China to accelerate the diplomatic process with the United States. Conversely, it is just as possible that Nixon and Kissinger calculated that a decision about a presidential journey to China would force the Russians to be even more forthcoming on SALT and détente. For the moment, at least, Washington was in a superb position toward both China and the Soviet Union. Nixon, as he read Kissinger's reports some days later, felt vindicated in his belief that the Vietnam war was not an obstacle to broader diplomatic moves by the United States.

Kissinger and his party left Peking aboard the PIA airliner around 1:00 p.m. on Sunday, July 11, after a final morning meeting with Chou when the two men agreed on the text of the public announcement of Nixon's planned visit to China to be issued simultaneously by the two governments four days later. Kissinger had spent just forty-eight hours in Peking.

Marshal Yeh Chien-ying saw Kissinger off at the military airport near Peking, and Sultan Khan was at the Rawalpindi airport to receive him when the plane landed at 2:30 p.m., local time. The airliner stopped on an isolated runway, near the hangars, in order to attract no attention. Kissinger transferred to Sultan's car for the drive to the Islamabad guest house. President Yahya met him there, and Kissinger provided his host with a fairly full account of his Peking discussions. At one point, Kissinger asked Yahya about the steadily deteriorating situation in Bangladesh. Yahya replied: "What you are doing is more important; you shouldn't be distracted."

The official word was that Kissinger had returned from Nathia Gali during the morning, and nobody seemed to question the cover story. After meeting with Yahya, Kissinger returned to the Rawalpindi airport —this time openly—and boarded his air force Boeing 707 for the long flight to Paris. For the Pakistanis, too, the Kissinger trip to Peking represented a major success.

Kissinger reached Paris late on July 11. Although his presence there was well publicized, he managed to keep secret the fact of his short meeting with Le Duc Tho the next day. Newsmen assumed that he simply attended a routine semipublic negotiating session with the North Vietnamese. He left for the United States that same evening, arriving in San Clemente, where Nixon was awaiting him, on July 13. He spent a long evening with the president, giving him virtually a moment-by-moment account of his Peking visit. Nixon was overjoyed. The breakthrough in relations with China was accomplished.

On July 14, Kissinger spent more time alone with Nixon. Then the president brought in Secretary Rogers, Helms, and Haig. As far as the press was concerned, it was the long-planned Vietnam policy review meeting.

Thursday, July 15, was ostensibly a day of relaxation. To preserve secrecy, the networks were not notified until the afternoon that the president would be requesting time for a major statement. Nixon spent much of the morning at his swimming pool and, after lunch, received the British journalist Henry Brandon and his wife at the Casa Pacifica study. Kissinger, who had invited the Brandons to San Clemente, was along as Nixon chatted about politics and foreign policy with his visitors. Brandon later wrote in his book *The Retreat of American Power* that "despite his most courteous manner and the impression he created that he had all the time in the world to spend with us, I couldn't help sensing that both he and Kissinger were anything but relaxed." Nixon and the Brandons were standing by the window of the study when the president suddenly turned to Brandon, saying "with an underlying excitement in his voice" that "we shall have a very important announcement to make this evening. Just remember this room and this view when you hear it."

The networks were presently notified that Nixon wanted about five minutes of air time at 7:00 p.m., California time, to make an announcement. Arrangements were made for the president to fly to Burbank, outside of Los Angeles, to deliver a brief address from the NBC studios there. While Nixon was en route to Los Angeles, the task of informing foreign governments slightly ahead of the presidential statement fell on Secretary Rogers.

One of his first calls from San Clemente was to Marshall Green in Washington. Green had strongly suspected that something along these lines was afoot—he said later that he had worked it out by "deduction" —but it had not occurred to him that Nixon was about to announce a *trip* to China. Recovering from the surprise, Green's first concern was Japan. He judged correctly that the announcement would come as a shock to the Japanese and that they would deeply resent having been kept in the dark about Kissinger's Peking expedition. He knew that Kissinger disliked the Japanese (in the same way in which he disliked Indians), but he persuaded Rogers to let him send a telegram to Ambassador Armin Meyer in Tokyo, telling him enough so that he could explain it to the Japanese Foreign Ministry as soon as the announcement was made.

(Green failed to reach Meyer in time. Instead, the ambassador learned about the Peking trip when he heard Nixon's voice on an Armed Forces Radio broadcast while having a haircut in his office. As Meyer recounted it later in his book, *Assignment: Tokyo,* he first thought it was a Nixon slip of the tongue, so unbelievable was the news. His second reaction was that the announcement would have "seismic impact" on Japan—as it did. His third reaction was of deep annoyance: the White House had once more made its ambassador in Tokyo lose face by keeping him in the dark about major policies.

Meyer had never conferred with Nixon during his three-year tenure in Japan because the president, with rare exceptions, did not believe in substantive discussions with American ambassadors. He regarded them as messengers not to be trusted with important matters, preferring to deal himself, or through Kissinger, with foreign chiefs of state. When Nixon and Kissinger met in 1969 with Prime Minister Eisaku Sato, the ambassador was excluded from the conferences; this routine Nixon-Kissinger practice proceeded in complete indifference to the harm done to the ambassadors and to normal diplomatic relations. Similarly, the Tokyo embassy was never informed about what White House emissaries were doing during the long, complex textile-trade negotiations, and Meyer usually discovered it from Japanese officials or, worse, the Japanese press.)

An hour before Nixon went on the air, Rogers began telephoning a selected group of foreign ambassadors: the Japanese, Nationalist Chinese, and Russian, to begin with. All of them were taken aback by the news, but none offered Rogers immediate comment nor did he ask for any. Ambassador Shen told inquiring newsmen later that evening that the Nationalist Chinese viewed Nixon's proposed trip as a "shabby deal."

At 7:00 p.m. (it was 10:00 p.m. in Washington), Nixon faced the television cameras. He knew he was making history.

> Good evening.
> I have requested this television time tonight to announce a major development in our efforts to build a lasting peace in the world.
> As I have pointed out on a number of occasions over the past three years, there can be no stable and enduring peace without the participation of the People's Republic of China and its 750 million people. That is why I have undertaken initiatives in several areas to open the door for more normal relations between our two countries.
> In pursuance of that goal, I sent Dr. Kissinger, my assistant for National Security Affairs, to Peking during his recent world tour for the purpose of having talks with Premier Chou En-lai. The announcement I shall now read is being issued simultaneously in Peking and in the United States:
> "Premier Chou En-lai and Dr. Henry Kissinger, President Nixon's assistant for National Security Affairs, held talks in Peking from July 9 to 11, 1971. Knowing of President Nixon's expressed desire to visit the People's Republic of China, Premier Chou En-lai, on behalf of the Government of the People's Republic of China, has extended an invitation to President Nixon to visit China at an appropriate date before May 1972. President Nixon has accepted the invitation with pleasure.
> "The meeting between the leaders of China and the United States is to seek the normalization of relations between the two countries and also to exchange views on questions of concern to the two sides."
> In anticipation of the inevitable speculation which will follow this announcement, I want to put our policy in the clearest possible context.
> Our action in seeking a new relationship with the People's Republic of China will not be at the expense of our old friends. It is not directed against any other nation. We seek friendly relations with all nations. Any nation can be our friend without being any other nation's enemy.
> I have taken this action because of my profound conviction that all nations will gain from a reduction of tensions and a better relationship between the United States and the People's Republic of China.
> It is in this spirit that I will undertake what I deeply hope will become a journey for peace, peace not just for our generation but for future generations on this earth we share together. Thank you and good night.

It was a fantastic *coup de théâtre*. As the world began to assess the meaning and the implications and ramifications of Nixon's announcement, the president went to celebrate. With Kissinger and several close advisers, President and Mrs. Nixon drove from Burbank to a favorite restaurant in Beverly Hills for a celebration dinner. A bottle of 1947 vintage French red wine was opened, festively.

Chapter 15

The eyes of the world were on China in mid-1971, what with President Nixon's July announcement, but just as important, the administration was busy working on a strategic-arms–control agreement with the Soviet Union. The SALT negotiations, now halfway through their second year, were aimed at limiting both the quantitative expansion and the qualitative development of nuclear arsenals on the two sides. This was to be the crux of détente.

However, the progress in the talks was painfully slow. At the outset of the year, neither Washington nor Moscow was prepared to abandon its basic views: the American stance that a strategic agreement should cover offensive as well as defensive arms and the Soviet belief that a pact on defensive-weapons systems should come first. And Nixon and Kissinger still thought that the policy of linkages, or tradeoffs, with the Russians would work in the end. Nixon, the politician, believed that the Russians, likewise acting politically, would see mutual advantages in tradeoffs. As a White House aide explained it, "Nixon figured that Brezhnev understood this business of 'I'll do this for you, if you do that for me.' " Kissinger, on the other hand, was convinced that the Soviet Union —still militarily and economically weaker than the United States—would be amenable for purely pragmatic reasons to a system of interlinked policy understandings. Kissinger thought that Moscow would be interested in living up to linkage commitments because of his underlying view that the Russians, embroiled as they were in a perilous dispute with China and clearly in need of exports of American food and technology, desired détente even more than the United States. Together, then, Nixon and Kissinger evolved the notion that the Soviets would agree to a general relaxation of tensions with the United States as the political price for trade and all that went with it. "We have reversed the old idea that trade paves the way to peace," Nixon remarked to a visitor early in 1971.

SALT negotiations in 1971 and related events were an excellent example of the Soviet strategy. Whereas in 1969, Nixon was reluctant to enter into strategic-arms–limitation talks with the Russians, largely because of Pentagon opposition, his stance had shifted dramatically by 1971. The success of Nixon's new China policy required that for reasons of political symmetry there should be an American-Soviet rapprochement as well.

The Soviets, to be sure, also wanted a form of détente—the implications of the American opening to China were not lost on them—but they remained realistic and did not allow themselves to be carried away. Nixon, to whom détente became in his mind's eye a ticket to reelection the following year, *was* carried away.

Arms control—through SALT and other means—was the *sine qua non* of a serious relationship with the Soviets. The White House saw it as the centerpiece of the linkage concept, assuming that all else would flow from it in terms of policies and agreements, including cooperation in the Middle East, help in the Vietnam negotiations, and so on.

What the United States and the Soviet Union were seeking was "essential equivalence" in strategic forces. This was the only possible basis for an agreement that, by definition, had to concern itself with quantitative as well as qualitative limitations. "Essential equivalence" means, of course, that each side admits that the other has a "second-strike capability," i.e., is capable of retaliating in a devastating manner even *after* the enemy has delivered a surprise first strike. In the SALT negotiations, Washington and Moscow started from the premise—or accepted this premise during talks in 1970—that the United States had the *qualitative* edge resulting from the MIRV while the Soviet Union had the *quantitative* advantage in the actual number of weapons and in the superior throw-weight of individual missiles. In other words, American land-based Minuteman and submarine-launched Poseidon missiles were more accurate because of their clustered, independently targeted warheads, while the Soviet weapons carried a bigger nuclear payload, propelled by greater launching thrust.

The principal reality underlying the 1970–71 negotiations was that neither side was prepared to give up its MIRV freedom. This obviously affected in the most fundamental manner the kind of agreement on offensive weapons that would be possible: it ruled out a mutual MIRV test or deployment ban. As early as 1970, the United States made the decision that a qualitative limitation accord, which meant any MIRV restraint, was neither desirable nor possible, and this certainly did not displease Moscow. In April 1970, MIRVed Minuteman III missiles had been deployed in North Dakota, the principal launching site in the United States, and MIRV-warheaded missiles had been fitted aboard Poseidon submarines. In July, Nixon personally amended the option that provided for a MIRV ban—one of nine in the package of United States proposals prepared by the NSC staff and the Verification Panel—by including a requirement for on-site inspection. The president did so in full knowledge that this would be unacceptable to the Soviets; the United States, in fact, never formally proposed a MIRV test or deployment ban to the Russians.

Nixon's move was related to a more fundamental decision that he had reached on the whole question of SALT: the policy would be to go for a "low" pact on ABM systems—the antimissile deployments—and for the "freeing" of the MIRV. However, the White House still wanted a formal accord on offensive weapons—quantitatively—that would be linked to an ABM treaty. The reason for a "low" agreement on ABMs was the administration's judgment that unless each side deployed at least 1000 ABM launchers, it would be meaningless strategically. The other part of this argument, stated by Nixon early in 1969, was that through an ABM saturation both sides might be inviting a first-strike attack, the assumption being that one would invest heavily in a defense system only in the context of preparations to launch a nuclear offensive. This perception was fully shared by the Soviets.

No meaningful progress was achieved in the SALT talks during 1970, mainly because Moscow opposed a comprehensive agreement on offensive weapons linked to an ABM treaty. It insisted on a separate deal on ABMs and some vague statement of principles on offensive arms. Some experts believe that the Russians wanted maximal freedom to keep developing the MIRV without having their hands tied on the expansion of their ICBM arsenal. They were adding some 200 ICBMs a year, building a numerical superiority over the United States.

In 1971, however, new movement appeared in the whole area of military negotiations. In fact, there was a palpable sense of relaxation— and promise—in dealing with the Soviet Union, more so than at any time since Nixon had taken office. To be sure, the Russians were certainly not withdrawing from overall competition with the United States—friendship treaties with Egypt and India were signed during 1971, expanding Soviet influence in the Middle East and South Asia—but just as clearly they wanted to compose many of their differences with the United States, particularly in bilateral and European situations.

This new scenario began to develop with the signing in Washington, Moscow, and London on February 11 of the Seabed Arms Control

Treaty, under which the major nuclear powers agreed not to place weapons of mass destruction on the ocean floor. This was intended to eliminate the threat that nuclear-missile launchers might be installed in fixed positions on the bottoms of oceans and seas. Inasmuch as these waters cover 70 percent of the earth's surface, the treaty was considered a useful first step in the control of strategic arms. Although the United States and the Soviet Union were obviously the most important adherents to the treaty, it was a multilateral instrument negotiated in the United Nations Disarmament Committee in Geneva, and some eighty states (but not France and China) presently signed it.

When the two SALT delegations reconvened in Vienna on March 15, however, the main deadlock was unbroken. Nixon and Kissinger decided that top-level secret diplomacy was required if any progress was to be made in the predictable future. The delegations in Vienna were simply bypassed, and Kissinger went back to his direct dealings with Ambassador Dobrynin. After several preliminary meetings, both governments agreed that the level of secret negotiations had to be raised even higher. By the end of March, Nixon and Brezhnev began to exchange secret personal letters through the Kissinger-Dobrynin back channel. Nixon claimed later that he initiated the direct exchanges with Brezhnev, but there are reasons to believe that this idea emerged simultaneously on the Russian side.

Actually, the SALT back channel in 1971 started functioning as early as January 9, when Nixon handed Dobrynin a private letter to Premier Kosygin urging new efforts in the strategic-arms negotiations. At that time, the White House still tended to regard Kosygin as the principal Soviet spokesman on Soviet policy. Although the premier did reply in a vaguely encouraging fashion, the correspondence with the Russians became serious only when Brezhnev assumed undisputed command of the Kremlin's foreign policy after the Twenty-fourth Congress of the Soviet Communist Party in March. From then on, Brezhnev replaced Kosygin as Nixon's secret pen pal.

One of the main obstacles in SALT was the American insistence on linking defensive- and offensive-arms agreements as opposed to the Soviet view that the negotiations should center on an ABM pact. Another complex problem was the definition of actual weapons that should be subject to limitation—this was particularly true in the offensive-systems area on both sides—as well as the fact that the United States and the Soviet Union were at that point at different stages in the development and deployment of vital weapons programs.

The United States, having MIRVed its Minuteman III and Poseidon missiles, ceased deploying additional ICBMs in 1970 on the theory that its arsenal was adequately stocked with current-generation weapons. Likewise, no new ballistic-missile submarines had been built since 1967. This, however, was not a voluntary unilateral restraint; the Pentagon had simply decided that there was no sense in expanding systems that would soon become obsolescent. Instead, the American military preferred to await the development of new systems, including the Trident submarine.

The Soviets, on the other hand, were playing catch-up ball. They were constantly increasing their ICBM force and, since 1969, accelerating their submarine-building program. In December 1970, with the aid of satellite photography, United States intelligence spotted what it considered to be a new pattern of Soviet offensive-arms deployment. The new sites—five clusters stretching from the Polish border to the Chinese frontier—comprised holes large enough to accommodate the giant Soviet SS-9 missile, the largest in the world. Washington thought that this new effort was related to the Soviet MIRV program; some analysts predicted that MIRVed SS-9 missiles in the new emplacements would be operational by mid-1972. Though Nixon had no intention of asking for a MIRV ban, the scope of Soviet construction increased the urgency for some sort of SALT agreement. In the course of the first year of SALT talks, the Soviets had increased their land-based ICBM launchers by nearly one-fourth and submarine launchers by nearly one-half. Strategic parity with the Soviet Union, for the first time ever, was imminent, and this was recognized in Washington.

But the SALT talks in 1970 and early 1971 were tough going. Not only did Washington and Moscow disagree on the ultimate objectives of the negotiations, but in the case of offensive weapons, they differed on what should be covered. The Americans felt that *all* offensive weapons—including heavy bombers, as well as antiballistic missiles and radars in the defensive field—should be subject to limitation. The Russians argued instead that U.S. nuclear-armed aircraft and warships and medium-range nuclear weapons stationed in Europe and in European waters—the so-called Forward Based Systems (FBS)—be added to the package. FBS deployments in Europe were meant to match medium-range missilery in the Soviet Union and Eastern Europe, but Moscow took the view that its medium-range missiles were not "strategic" and thus not subject to SALT controls.

In light of these problems, Nixon decided that further SALT negotiations should be based on four "principles" that formed the new American position. He listed them as follows:

First, the strategic balance would be endangered if we limited defensive forces alone and left the offensive threat unconstrained. An essential objective of the negotiations would be defeated by unchecked deployment of offensive systems. For example, with only defensive forces limited by an agreement, the continued expansion of Soviet offensive forces, especially the large SS-9 ICBMs if armed with multiple warheads, could eventually give the U.S.S.R. a capability for seriously threatening our land-based strategic forces.

Second, it would be dangerous if, while constraining offensive forces, strategic defenses were allowed to increase without limit. In sufficient numbers and sophistication, ABM systems deployed to defend cities can reduce capabilities to retaliate. Thus, unlimited ABM expansion ultimately would force an offensive buildup.

Third, if we could not devise satisfactory formulas for limiting all major weapon systems, we should concentrate on those of primary importance in the strategic balance which if unchecked would become most threatening to overall strategic equilibrium.

Finally, if we could not find technical solutions for limiting systems that already differed in numbers and capabilities, an interim step might be a freeze at current levels on deployments of the most destabilizing offensive weapons.

Nixon was now clearly going for a compromise over SALT. He and Kissinger concluded that inasmuch as linked and comprehensive treaties on offensive- and defensive-weapons systems were unattainable, there was merit in accepting a full-fledged ABM treaty and an *interim* agreement on offensive arms. The interim-agreement concept, devised largely by Kissinger, was intended to break the logjam by granting the United States at least a temporary freeze on deployments of the Soviet SS-9, soon to be MIRVed, without forcing Moscow into a comprehensive long-range commitment on limiting its entire offensive-arms program.

To sell the idea of such a compromise became the basis of Nixon's secret diplomacy with Brezhnev. As he noted later, "Recognizing that only by establishing a political commitment at the highest level could we make significant progress on the range of technical issues that still confronted the negotiators, I attempted to create a new negotiating framework in which both sides could proceed."

Brezhnev was encouraging in his first responses, and the secret exchanges continued throughout April and early May. For one thing, the Soviet leadership was in a rather conciliatory mood. The Soviet Communist Party held its Twenty-fourth Congress late in March, and both Brezhnev and Foreign Minister Gromyko delivered speeches that Washington found constructive. When the Soviet leader began showing interest in

Nixon's SALT compromise ideas, the exchanges quickened. Then the Soviets suddenly agreed to a convention outlawing biological weapons, a topic they had been ignoring for a long time. And on May 14, Brezhnev, speaking in Tiflis in Soviet Georgia, surprised the West by declaring interest in standing NATO proposals for a mutual balanced reduction of forces in Europe between the Western alliance and the Warsaw Pact. Until then, MBFR, as it was known, seemed to command no attention on the part of the Russians. NATO had first proposed it in 1968. By May 15 the White House knew it had a SALT deal with the Kremlin.

Although Nixon was heartened by all these signals, public and private, he remained cautious in discussing the situation. At a news conference on April 29, he had remarked that "we are seeking good relations with the Soviet Union, and I am not discouraged by the SALT talk progress. I can only say that we believe that the interests of both countries would be served by an agreement there." But on May 20, he was ready to announce a "breakthrough" in SALT. Appearing without advance notice in the White House press briefing room exactly at noon, he stunned newsmen with this statement:

> As you know, the Soviet-American talks on limiting nuclear arms have been deadlocked for over a year. As a result of negotiations involving the highest level of both governments, I am announcing today a significant development in breaking the deadlock. The statement that I shall now read is being issued simultaneously in Moscow and Washington: Washington, 12 o'clock; Moscow, 7:00 p.m.
> "The Governments of the United States and the Soviet Union, after reviewing the course of their talks on the limitation of strategic armaments, have agreed to concentrate this year on working out an agreement for the limitation of the deployment of antiballistic missile systems (ABM). They have also agreed that, together with concluding an agreement to limit ABMs, they will agree on certain measures with respect to the limitation of offensive strategic weapons. The two sides are taking this course in the conviction that it will create more favorable conditions for further negotiations to limit all strategic arms. These negotiations will be actively pursued."

The compromise had dangerous built-in weaknesses, however. Nixon had allowed a situation to develop in which his "certain measures" on offensive weapons would have to be negotiated under the gun in 1972. By saying that the ABM pact and the interim agreement on offensive arms would be concluded simultaneously, Nixon, in effect, forced himself into a corner. He would have no choice but to sign an interim agreement that was at best controversial in order to salvage the entire SALT package—a major consideration with the approach of the presidential elections. Finally, he may have prematurely weakened the American negotiating position by agreeing in the May 20 compromise to concentrate on the offensive systems with the major impact on the strategic balance. This opened the door to no end of ambiguities in the future.

Curiously, Nixon and Kissinger concealed from the public the knowledge they possessed at the time of the SALT announcement that the Soviet Union had secretly developed an entirely new offensive system: the Backfire intercontinental supersonic bomber. The president obviously excluded the Backfire because a White House release that same day on comparative strengths of Soviet and American strategic forces made no reference to it, and there is nothing to suggest that American negotiators raised the question of the Backfire in the 1971 and 1972 SALT talks.

This inexplicable omission was to haunt the United States in the years ahead. The administration at the highest levels knew as early as March 1971 that the Soviets had successfully tested the swing-wing Backfire, the first supersonic intercontinental bomber in existence. NATO military intelligence had reported sighting the Backfire in the area of the Ramenskoye test center near Moscow early in the year. Inasmuch as the only intercontinental bomber in the American arsenal was the slow, twenty-year-old B-52, there could be no question that the Backfire could deeply affect the strategic balance. The B-1, the United States version of a supersonic intercontinental bomber, was in preliminary development stages in 1971 and could not become operational before 1978 at the earliest.

The existence of the Backfire—and the administration's awareness of it—was publicly disclosed in *The New York Times* in an article by this writer on September 5, 1971, based on a secret, very detailed CIA study of the bomber. It was accompanied by a drawing of the Backfire, reproduced from the CIA report. However, Defense Department officials refused to discuss the Backfire because it was a "sensitive intelligence matter."

The SALT compromise in May was like the uncorking of a bottle. Along with it came Soviet concessions on European problems as well. This was highly encouraging to the Nixon administration: the view from the White House was that with China opening and the progress in relations with Moscow, a "new era" was dawning.

However, just as in the linkage concept, there was a profound flaw in Washington's overall optimistic analysis of developing events in 1971. This flaw was Washington's almost total ignorance of internal political processes in the key Communist capitals. In terms of major policy trends, the United States was an open book: these could be observed, documented, analyzed, and even understood by the Communist governments. Dealing with an open society—the superabundance of public debate and controversy, congressional hearings, presidential speeches and press conferences, critical pronouncements by opposition spokesmen, and the very existence of the antiwar movement—Communist leaders could draw conclusions about the United States and tailor their own policies accordingly.

Washington, on the other hand, lacked this advantage. The best American experts could do was to give the White House intelligent guesses and estimates—but only that. Public speeches and other official materials were almost all they had to go on. To say simply that China was responding affirmatively to the American courtship because of her fear of the Soviet Union and that Moscow was more accommodating in the light of American overtures to Peking was, of course, easy; there must have been far more complex reasons for all these attitudes, reasons unknown to the American government.

Given Richard Nixon's personal propensity for claiming triumphs, victories, and breakthroughs in his diplomacy, there was a serious danger that he would overinterpret the positions adopted by the Soviet Union in a manner favorable to his own interest. And indeed, Nixon and Kissinger could never quite distinguish between Moscow's strategy and its tactical feints. Still, all the signs in 1971 suggested that the Soviet Union wanted to eliminate long-standing irritants in its relations with the West.

The most important of these troublesome issues was the question of Berlin. Under quadripartite military rule since the end of World War II, Berlin had remained an unresolved problem between the Western allies and the Soviet Union for over a quarter of a century. There had been the Soviet blockade in 1948, broken by the American airlift; the erection by the Communists of the Berlin Wall, between the city's Eastern and Western sectors, in 1961; and an interminable series of harassments of traffic in and out of West Berlin, a Western island in the middle of the sea of East Germany.

For years, the question of Berlin had been under negotiation in a desultory way between American, British, and French diplomats on one side and Soviet representatives on the other. Occasional crises led to somewhat more urgent efforts to resolve the impasse, but it persisted. The situation began changing slowly in 1969, after Nixon had made the ritualistic pilgrimage to West Berlin and, perhaps more important, after the Russians had begun to realize that he was serious about a new "era of negotiation." Coincidentally, Soviet-Chinese relations were sinking to their lowest point in 1969, and Moscow may have decided that it needed to protect its western flank. In February 1970, all parties agreed to initiate ambassadorial-level meetings concerning Berlin on a systematic basis.

The new negotiations, which began in March 1970 at the Allied Control Council building in the American sector of Berlin, continued nearly seventeen months before the ambassadors worked out an agreement. The principal reason for the slow pace was that the Russians were still dragging their feet on the question of free access to West Berlin and insisting that the interests of East Germany be extensively taken into account in any accord; the latter point tended to create complications with West Germany, whose interests, for their part, the Allies had to consider.

These protracted Berlin talks were an excellent example of the Soviet diplomatic pattern: Moscow may have wished to be actively engaged in a series of negotiations with the United States, but it was in no hurry to get an agreement except on its own terms. It soon became clear to the American side that real movement in a negotiation would be possible only if the Soviets wanted something else badly enough to compromise in any given area.

This was what happened in 1971. In the case of Berlin, and aside from general considerations, the Soviets decided on a tradeoff. For some time, the Russians and their East European "clients" in the Warsaw Pact had been pressing for a European security conference (ESC) that would, in effect, confirm the postwar borders. Foreign Minister Gromyko broached the subject again with Nixon during a White House visit in October 1970, but was told that the United States would not even consider it unless the Berlin problem was solved and the Warsaw Pact agreed to negotiate with NATO a mutual reduction of forces in Europe. This set in motion a new chain of events.

Thus in the speech in Tiflis on May 14 Brezhnev accepted the principle of MBFR negotiations. Almost simultaneously, Western negotiators in Berlin began reporting a change in Soviet attitudes there, and Dobrynin told Kissinger that his government would like to wrap up the Berlin talks as soon as possible. This was quickly followed by the SALT compromise. Now there was optimism in the air. When West German Chancellor Willy Brandt visited Washington, on June 15, he devoted most of his time with Nixon and Kissinger at the White House to the questions of Berlin and MBFR.

The next day, Secretary Rogers conferred with Dobrynin to determine how soon the Russians wanted to open NATO–Warsaw Pact talks on mutual troop reductions. He assured him, although this was not made public, that the United States would regard with sympathy the idea of a European security conference as soon as understandings could be reached on Berlin and MBFR. Simultaneously, Brezhnev, speaking in East Berlin at the Communist Party's congress, went out of his way to say that at the Berlin talks the four parties were examining "concrete proposals on the content of a possible agreement" and the Soviet Union was "prepared to make efforts to bring this matter to a successful completion."

July and August were spent in home-stretch diplomacy. On the American side, negotiations were coordinated by a State Department–based Berlin Task Force (originally established in 1958) working closely with Kissinger's NSC staff. And on major points, Kissinger consulted with Nixon, who developed an intense interest in the Berlin negotiations. In Bonn, the American, British, and French ambassadors coordinated the Western stance; then in Berlin they acted as a team in negotiations with the Soviet delegation. (There also was permanent liaison in Bonn with West Germany.) It was one of the most successful instances of Western diplomatic collaboration.

On September 3 (which happened to be the thirty-second anniversary of Britain's and France's entry into the war against Nazi Germany), the Western allies and the Soviet Union signed the Quadripartite Agreement on Berlin. In the absence of a formal peace treaty with Germany and Germany's division into two states, there never was a question of changing the city's legal status, and the four-power rule over Berlin was maintained. But the Soviet Union for the first time formally committed itself to guarantee that all forms of traffic to and from West Berlin would henceforth be "unimpeded." West Berliners would be authorized to visit East Berlin and East Germany for a total of thirty days annually. East Berliners, of course, were free to enter the Western sectors, but East Germany retained control over departures of its citizens. The Western concession to the Soviets—and East Germany—was to "confirm" that Berlin's Western sectors were not "a constituent part" of West Germany and would not "be governed by it." Specifically, the allies agreed that the West German parliament would no longer meet in West Berlin, as it had in the past, to elect the president of the German Federal Republic or for other purposes. (For years this had been a sore point with East Germany.)

The full Berlin agreement was completed when East Berlin and West

Germany signed their accords to it on December 17, and the West Berlin government and East Germany signed theirs on December 20. One of the main East-West irritants had finally been eliminated.

The Berlin agreement made it possible for the United States to offer formal support for the European security conference that the Warsaw Pact countries had been urging since the late 1960s, although the West still had another condition. But Berlin was the touchstone of the whole diplomatic situation. American and Canadian participation in the proposed conference was essential because both countries had troops stationed in Europe. As Secretary Rogers stressed, the United States felt strongly that a European conference, to be worthwhile, must "emphasize substance over atmosphere" and, most important, "encourage the freer movement of people, ideas, and information beyond the traditional patterns of cultural exchanges" between Eastern and Western Europe. The American view was that so long as the conference was held, it should, in effect, help to pierce the Iron Curtain. On October 2, the administration began preparing quietly for the conference as Kissinger instructed his staff to prepare a special options study on it—NSSM–138.

The other NATO condition for the European security conference was an agreement to proceed with MBFR. Although Brezhnev had indicated in May that he was interested in negotiating reductions in forces, something happened in Moscow after the signing of the Berlin agreement— it was never clear just what—to freeze the Soviet position on this point. In October, NATO instructed Secretary General Manlio Brosio to go to Moscow to explore the possibilities of a MBFR conference. But the year ended without Brosio being able to do this: the Russians would not receive him.

In bilateral relations with the United States, on the other hand, the Soviet Union was prepared to move ahead. The SALT breakthrough in May was followed on September 30 by two related agreements. The first set forth a series of specific measures that each nation would adopt to reduce the risk of nuclear war occurring as a result of an accident or "unauthorized acts."

One of the nightmares of the nuclear age is that a nuclear missile might be launched from a land base, submarine, or aircraft in a purely accidental fashion—a technical malfunction or a communications breakdown or misunderstanding—or that a senior civilian or military official or field commander might push the button in an act of insanity. What the new agreement meant, in effect, was that the side under such attack could ascertain, or at least try to ascertain, whether the missile launching was deliberate or accidental. If it was the latter, retaliation and the triggering of an all-out nuclear war might be averted. Admittedly, neither side could know how it would react if it was accidentally hit by one or more nuclear devices of high megatonnage, but the agreement was an effort to strengthen "fail-safe" controls.

The second agreement provided that the existing "hot line" between Washington and Moscow be switched to satellite communications to make it less vulnerable to disruptions caused by an accidental nuclear launch. The old hot line was a land-line and radio-teletype link. The idea was that American and Soviet leaders could consult instantly and safely in the event of a nuclear accident.

Along the same lines, the United States and the Soviet Union in October reached a preliminary understanding on measures to prevent incidents between their warships on the high seas. This was an American idea, personally encouraged by Nixon, and it stemmed from fears raised by the frequent physical proximity of American and Soviet ships, particularly in the Mediterranean. There, the two navies had developed the practice of shadowing each other's vessels and buzzing them with aircraft. This, too, had the potential for an accidental triggering of a war.

Everything was now ready for the next logical step in the new dynamics of Soviet-American relations. On October 12, the two governments announced that Nixon would visit the Soviet Union in May of the next year to meet with Brezhnev. Since the July announcement of the president's forthcoming journey to China in the early part of 1972, this second trip had become virtually inevitable, and Nixon, who had been skeptical of the wisdom of meeting with Brezhnev, was now eager for it. The SALT compromise, the Berlin agreement, and the other accords made it plausible.

The president was cautious, however, in his comments to reporters as to whether he would be able to sign a SALT agreement while in Moscow. He noted that progress was being made "toward that goal," adding that "if the goal can be achieved before May of 1972, we will achieve it, and that, incidentally, is also the view of the Soviet Union." But, he said, "if it is not achieved, certainly that would be one of the subjects that would come up" in Moscow.

Asked about other potential agenda subjects at the summit, Nixon listed the Middle East, Southeast Asia, and Cuba as a "peripheral area." He drew a distinction between Soviet-American bilateral topics, such as SALT, and the other ones. He insisted that Peking and Moscow were "independent trips," stressing that "neither trip is being taken for the

purpose of exploiting what differences may exist between the two nations; neither is being taken at the expense of any other nation." And the
president made the point that Peking had been informed in advance
about his trip to the Soviet Union.

American evenhandedness in relations with Communist countries was
stressed again two weeks later when Nixon played host at the White
House to Yugoslavia's President Tito. Although, according to the joint
communiqué issued at the conclusion of his visit, Tito "expressed his
great interest in the foreign policy initiatives of the United States government," both presidents avoided referring publicly to Nixon's forthcoming trips. They had, of course, discussed them in private, but it was a
measure of diplomatic discretion to maintain public silence on the subject
while Tito, the pioneer of controversies within the international Communist movement, was being received in Washington.

The Middle East was one of the best illustrations of the Nixon administration's self-delusions about a global policy of linkages with the
Soviet Union. Nixon and Kissinger, becoming captives of their own concepts, tended to confuse specific tradeoffs with broader relationships with
the Soviet Union. The basic thrust of Soviet policy was essentially similar
to American policy; the main distinction was that the Soviet Union, in a
different stage of power development, endeavored to *expand* its worldwide influence while the United States strove to *retain* its influence. Because the United States was on the defensive to a greater extent than
Nixon would admit (although this is why he fought' in Indochina and
conspired in Chile), the government believed that linkage would control
Moscow's ambitions in such areas as the Middle East. The Nixon-Kissinger theory was that the Soviet Union would restrain itself from overex-
tending its influence in exchange for a general détente with the United
States. In its most profound sense, this Nixonian idea of détente retained
strong elements of earlier postwar containment policies. From the Soviet
viewpoint, however, the movement toward détente did not imply the
abdication of power interests in the Middle East, South Asia, or other
contested regions. The Russians sought rapport with the United States
in selected situations simply because it was advantageous to them.

That the Soviet Union was building up political and military positions
in the Middle East, capitalizing on its support of the Arabs in the conflict
with Israel, was not especially diabolical. It was simply inherent in the
reality of its competition with the United States in that part of the world.
Washington had traditionally played the Israeli card; Moscow chose to
play the Arab card (particularly after John Foster Dulles, when Nixon was

vice president, had wholly unnecessarily antagonized Nasser in the 1950s, thereby forfeiting American influence in Cairo). The same applied to South Asia and the Indian Ocean, where the Russians also chose to be present for obvious strategic reasons. Since the United States was backing Pakistan in subcontinental disputes and Pakistan also had a close relationship with China, the Russians swung behind India, which had a neutralist tradition, resented the United States, and had fought a war with China in 1962.

Natural or not, all these Soviet policies were highly disturbing to the United States. The Nixon administration felt that the growing Soviet military presence in the Middle East was further complicating an already explosive situation. It was the Soviet Union that had armed Egypt and Syria for the 1967 war and rearmed them after the defeat in the Six-Day War. Iraq, too, was armed by the Russians. In 1969 and 1970, the Russians had equipped the Egyptian army with artillery, then provided sophisticated air-defense systems, and were in cahoots with the Egyptians when SAM emplacements were moved forward in the Suez Canal zone in violation of the truce. That the Soviets apparently dissuaded Syria from pursuing the invasion of Jordan in 1970 was due more to a fear of Israeli and even American involvement than to any lessening of their desire to remain influential in the area. American intelligence agencies calculated that there were 12,000 Soviet military personnel in Egypt, including thousands of officers and men operating SAM-2 and SAM-3 missile batteries. About 200 Soviet-manned SAM sites were in the Suez Canal zone. Soviet experts were in direct or indirect charge of the Egyptian air-defense system. Soviet pilots flew MiGs with Egyptian markings. Some 3000 Soviet instructors were training the Egyptian armed forces. Finally, there were Soviet security units—combat troops—protecting the detachments manning the missile sites. In his review of the world situation in 1971, Nixon said that SAM-6 mobile missiles were also introduced along with Foxbat (MiG-23) jets, the most advanced in the Soviet arsenal, and Tu-16 bombers equipped with long-range air-to-surface missiles.

While all these Soviet units and sophisticated equipment in Egypt were primarily intended to bolster Cairo's position vis-à-vis Israel, the United States observed with rising concern that the Russians were also establishing their *own* bases there, presumably for other purposes. The Soviet navy established facilities in Alexandria in support of a growing Mediterranean fleet. Long-range reconnaissance aircraft, employed to track the movements of the United States Sixth Fleet, were based at Egyptian airfields.

Still, 1971 was a year of intricate Middle Eastern diplomacy by all sides rather than one of new confrontation. Under American pressure, Israel had agreed on December 28, 1970, to let Gunnar Jarring, the United Nations mediator, resume his peacemaking mission, which had broken down four months earlier.

Early in January 1971, Jarring went to Jerusalem, where the Israeli government handed him a document setting forth its views on the "essentials of peace," and then went to Cairo and Amman to receive in writing Egyptian and Jordanian statements of position. He was sufficiently encouraged by these preliminary contacts to make it possible for U.N. Secretary General U Thant to report to the Security Council on February 2 that there were grounds for "cautious optimism."

In Washington, there was some satisfaction when Egypt advised the United States on February 3 that the Suez Canal truce, due to expire on the fifth, would be extended by a month. The administration felt that the Egyptians had agreed to this as a result of three consecutive messages from Secretary Rogers to Foreign Minister Mahmoud Riad. The third of these secret oral messages, delivered by Donald C. Bergus, the senior American diplomat in Cairo (Bergus, heading the "American interests" section of the Spanish embassy, was a *de facto* ambassador), had said that Israel would present "substantive ideas" for a peace settlement after the extension of the cease-fire. Still, it was disappointing that Cairo was willing to add only thirty days to the truce, not three or six months as the United States had hoped. (Israel, of course, wanted the cease-fire to be indefinite.)

The main reason President Sadat insisted on a short extension was that he wanted Jarring to work under deadline pressure in his shuttle diplomacy—and this the Americans considered to be very foolish. But State Department analysts believed that Sadat had planned on extending the cease-fire all along and needed only a domestic political justification for so doing. On February 4, the Egyptian president also proclaimed that he would allow the reopening of the canal to international traffic (the waterway had been closed since 1967, with dozens of ships trapped in the canal) if Israel withdrew its troops from the eastern bank of the canal during the thirty-day period of the new truce. Sadat knew Israel would not pull back from the canal, but he was establishing a bargaining position that would limit the likelihood of new hostilities. The belief in Washington was that Sadat, a shrewd trader, was not prepared or willing to resume the war but had to take this position as a matter of political necessity. To help him, the United States, in a policy shift, met Sadat's request that the Middle Eastern question be taken up again in the Big

Four forum in New York, where the Soviet Union was represented. There was no serious expectation that *these* meetings, interrupted late in 1969, would have any results, but it was a worthwhile political concession. For one thing, it gave an excuse for the Egyptians to extend the truce once more in March on the grounds that a quadripartite diplomatic process was under way. And it removed pressure from Jarring.

On February 8, three days after the truce extension, Jarring sent *aides-mémoire* to the three governments seeking what he called parallel and simultaneous commitments on the terms of a peace accord. Israel was asked to evacuate occupied Egyptian territories back to the preindependence lines of 1948 (not merely the 1967 lines) in exchange for the establishment of demilitarized zones, "practical security arrangements" in the Sharm al-Sheikh area to guarantee freedom of navigation through the Strait of Tiran, and freedom of navigation through the Suez Canal. Egypt was requested to commit itself to enter into a peace agreement with Israel by terminating all Egyptian claims of belligerency and acknowledging Israel's sovereignty, territorial integrity, and political independence.

This was not a very realistic set of proposals, as quickly became obvious. The Israelis said they were ready to enter negotiations if Egypt agreed to "secure, recognized and agreed boundaries," but they had their own notion of such boundaries, and told Jarring they would not pull back to the 1967 lines—let alone the 1948 ones.

Egypt in principle accepted Jarring's proposals, but it demanded an Israeli commitment to withdraw from the Gaza Strip, which adjoins Israeli territory on the Mediterranean coast, and to pull back from all of Sinai. Sadat also wanted demilitarized zones astride the new borders (which would encroach on Israeli territory) and a U.N. peace-keeping force. The only point on which the two sides agreed was the reopening of the Suez Canal.

Not only were the two basic positions irreconcilable, but Jarring compounded the problem by his ill-advised decision to make these exchanges public. Irked, Israel notified Jarring that it was no longer interested in his mediation. His diplomatic enterprise—and any serious United Nations role in the entire peace-keeping effort—had come to an end.

At this stage, the United States decided to take over Jarring's responsibilities and resume its direct mediatory involvement for the first time in more than a year. But Nixon was not yet ready to engage White House prestige in this undertaking; besides, he and Kissinger were busy with Indochina, China, and SALT. Secretary Rogers was therefore assigned the Middle East mission.

Rogers began with a statement at a news conference on March 16 that "the climate has never been better for a settlement in the Middle East, and if we don't make a settlement now, we are going to plant seeds that will lead to future war." Rogers was right that the diplomatic situation lent itself to a potential settlement—at that point the Arabs were clearly not ready for war—but he was also right that a prolonged stalemate would inevitably produce future wars.

Pledging the United States to efforts to overcome the latest "impasse" and to "work behind the scenes" to that end, Rogers nevertheless chose the policy of leaning on Israel to produce concessions that would induce Egypt to accept a peace agreement. This was part of an immensely intricate diplomatic plan designed to gain influence with the Arab states in order to make the United States a credible mediator and to reduce Soviet leverage in the region.

What Rogers was proposing was, in fact, a combination of the Jarring plan and some of Sadat's ideas with a number of American modifications. He urged Israel to withdraw to the 1967 lines and, in exchange, offered "adequate, satisfactory" arrangements over Sharm al-Sheikh and the Sinai, with an international force guaranteeing peace. (Sharm al-Sheikh, in southeastern Sinai, was absolutely vital to Israel because it controlled the entry to the Strait of Tiran and thence to the Gulf of Aqaba and the Israeli Red Sea port of Elath; Nasser's blockade of the Strait of Tiran had contributed to Israel's decision to wage the 1967 war.) Rogers's argument was that a combination of a "contractual agreement" with Egypt, special arrangements on Sharm al-Sheikh and the Sinai, and the presence of an international force, including United States troops, "is the most adequate possible guarantee that you can conceive of in modern life."

The idea of an international peace-keeping force in the Middle East had first been raised by the State Department in 1970 as a joint Soviet-American operation, but this was quickly shot down. In suggesting a peace-keeping force that would include American troops, Rogers was in effect returning to that concept; the intriguing question was why the administration was suggesting a situation in which the Soviet military presence in the Middle East would be legitimized?

Not surprisingly, the Israeli reaction to Rogers's proposals was fulminatingly negative. Israel "cannot trust Rogers's offer, even if it is proposed in good faith," Mrs. Meir said. The State Department began obfuscating, and Israeli Foreign Minister Abba Eban buried this new phase of diplomacy in the Middle East with the public declaration that his country would never withdraw to the 1967 lines as the price for a peace treaty with

Egypt. Some elements of national security, he said, are "so vital to us that we will, if necessary, uphold and defend them alone." Eban is a celebrated phrasemaker, an eloquent diplomat: "A nation must be capable of tenacious solitude," he explained.

The Middle East situation remained deadlocked through April and much of May. The Americans began to worry again about Jordan, where Palestinian guerrillas were regrouping against King Hussein. On March 7, King Hussein, bypassing the State Department, wrote a letter to Defense Secretary Laird outlining his military needs; Laird replied in a top-secret telegram on April 5 that the United States was prepared to increase its military assistance to the Jordanians, including the supply of M-16-A-1 tanks, the most modern in the American arsenal, which the king had requested; he also told Hussein that the United States was prepared to discuss the possibility of providing Jordan with C-130 transport aircraft and M-16 rifles. (Self-propelled howitzers and F-5E jet fighters—also mentioned in Hussein's letter—were not immediately available.) The administration was willing to ask Congress for $45 million in military aid to Jordan.

Actually, Hussein was able to beat down the new challenge by the guerrillas even before the delivery of the American weapons. After months of intermittent fighting, some of it in and around Amman, the rebellion was put down at the end of July.

In the first week of May, Secretary Rogers flew to Saudi Arabia, Jordan, Lebanon, Egypt—and Israel. In Egypt and Israel, Rogers discussed the possibility of an *interim* agreement, mainly covering the Sinai, as a step to a broad peace settlement.

Sadat and Foreign Minister Riad told Rogers an interim agreement would have to be along the lines of their position as outlined in the Egyptian memorandum to Jarring in February—which of course was unacceptable to Israel. But they urged the United States to pursue its mediation. In Israel, too, Rogers found inflexibility. A State Department document succinctly summed up this situation in a remarkable understatement: "major differences existed in the positions of the two states on many issues."

On May 27, Nixon played host at the White House to Saudi Arabia's King Faisal ibn Abd al-Aziz. It was an important visit for several reasons, but Nixon did not take advantage of all the opportunities it presented. This was especially true insofar as oil was concerned. Saudi Arabia was the world's largest producer and exporter of petroleum, working through Aramco (Arabian-American Oil Company), the conglomerate owned by four of the biggest United States oil companies, which held Saudi concessions; and it was a key member of OPEC. In 1971, new trends were beginning to develop in OPEC, but this was something the U.S. government, as well as the big oil companies, had not yet faced. In 1951, America had to import 10 percent of its petroleum requirements. In 1971, imports accounted for 25 percent of consumption, which had nearly tripled in these twenty years. As American petroleum reserves became more and more depleted, the growth in domestic production ceased in 1970. New oil had been discovered in Alaska, but it would take years before pipelines could be constructed and Alaskan petroleum could start flowing.

The stark reality was that the United States was caught between its no longer adequate production and OPEC's power in the seller's market that was developing in petroleum. Yet, the Nixon administration—as well as the oil industry—took an extraordinarily cavalier view of the situation. Regarding OPEC, the judgment was that the companies could handle the emerging problems alone although the State Department did provide some diplomatic support during 1971. It was a dramatic case of underestimating the strength of OPEC's position. The administration, particularly the White House, felt that agreements signed early in 1971 between the companies and Middle East producers would guarantee price stability for the five-year period stipulated in the new contracts. It just did not occur to the president and his top advisers that the situation could, and would, change drastically within a short time.

Thus, rather incredibly, Nixon's foreign-policy report to Congress for 1971, issued in February 1972 (and drafted by Kissinger and his staff), did not contain a single word about oil and OPEC. Its section on "International Economic Policy" concentrated only on monetary and trade issues. The State Department, on the other hand, was much more aware of the gathering dangers.

The key to the changing situation was Libya, a major producer of some of the world's best and cheapest crude oil. After Saudi Arabia, Libya was one of the most important sources of oil for the United States. In 1970, experts in the State Department's Office of Fuels and Energy—and especially its director, James Akins—became concerned about Libya's political stability. They thought they were detecting signs that King Idris, presiding over Libya's enormous new wealth and equally enormous corruption, was in trouble. At a State Department meeting in April, Akins argued against American overreliance on Libya, suggesting that the oil companies reduce production there and increase it elsewhere. However,

David Newsom, the assistant secretary for Africa, refused to take Akins's warnings seriously. There was good CIA "penetration" in Libya, he said, and the agency saw no danger of a revolution. There was no reason to press the oil companies to change their production patterns. Nothing was done.

In September, a group of young Libyan officers took over the government, and King Idris, who was then visiting Athens, was ousted from power. Instantly, Libya changed her oil policies. The xenophobic young officers demanded an increase in the oil price and a review of all the concession agreements with foreign companies. In the latter endeavor, the Libyan technique was to pit one foreign company against another in order to win the best possible terms. Even more important, the Libyans started talking to their OPEC partners about forming a united front in pricing oil. Under Secretary of State John Irwin raced to the Persian Gulf early in 1971 to press the producers to keep the price line intact, but he achieved nothing.

By May 1971, when King Faisal came to Washington, the State Department's petroleum specialists, led by Akins, were deeply preoccupied with the new trends in OPEC. Iran, the principal producer in the Persian Gulf, was showing signs of siding with Libya in her demands for higher prices. But how would Saudi Arabia respond to this? Akins and his colleagues hoped that Nixon would take up this question with King Faisal, but the president did not.

As to Faisal, the problem that concerned him most was Israel, and this is what he wanted to discuss with Nixon. A deeply religious monarch, Faisal had sworn that he would pray at Al-Aqsa mosque in Jerusalem before he died, and his opposition to Israel was even more intransigent than Egypt's or Syria's, particularly since Israel had occupied East Jerusalem with its Islamic shrines in the 1967 war. At the same time, however, Faisal was fanatically anti-Communist and anti-Soviet, and this was the basis of his close relations with the United States.

But Nixon did not consider Faisal a vital interlocutor in the Middle East. Saudi Arabia had been providing financial assistance to Egypt and Jordan, but this was a minor matter. The conventional wisdom was that, no matter what, the Arabs had to keep on selling their oil to the West.

On the day Nixon was meeting with King Faisal, U.S. policy in the Middle East suffered a major blow. An announcement from Cairo and Moscow on May 27, 1971, revealed that Egypt and the Soviet Union had signed a treaty of friendship and cooperation, a virtual alliance. The immediate—and correct—assumption in Washington was that the Russians would further increase their military assistance to Egypt as a result. The treaty's Article 8 expressed the Soviet commitment to keep developing cooperation in the "military field" to help Egypt "stand up to aggression."

Early in July, intelligence reports showed that between September 1970 (right after the Suez Canal truce went into effect) and June 1971, Egypt had received about 100 MiG-21 jet fighters, 8 of them during June. (Only 90 had been received between the end of the 1967 war and mid-1970.) Similarly, the Egyptians received 16 MI-8 troop-carrying helicopters in June for a total of about 80 since 1970. Syria acquired 21 MiG-21s between April and June, as well as some older-model fighters and fighter-bombers plus 22 MI-8 helicopters. The question in Washington was whether Egypt and Syria were preparing for a new war with Soviet backing. And had the Egyptians decided to cast their lot entirely with the Soviet Union?

Simultaneously, new problems developed with Israel. The Israeli government charged that the United States was holding back on deliveries of warplanes because of Arab pressures, and relations between the two countries soured again—a recurring pattern. But unpromising as the situation looked, the Nixon administration was determined to press on. In July, Kissinger, becoming personally active in the negotiations, sent a secret memorandum to Sadat through Donald Bergus, offering several options for an interim agreement, including the proposal that 500 Egyptian soldiers be symbolically stationed on the east bank of the Suez Canal in an area from which the Israelis would withdraw. Kissinger proposed this in the context of a possible agreement on the reopening of the Suez Canal—a first step toward breaking the overall stalemate. This approach to the question failed, however, when his memo was leaked to American newspapers; the Israelis were indignant when they realized that Kissinger was, in effect, urging them to abandon the fortified Bar-Lev Line along the canal.

Late in July, Assistant Secretary of State Joseph Sisco and his deputy, Alfred Atherton, were dispatched to Jerusalem to discuss again an interim agreement starting with the reopening of the canal, a simultaneous Israeli pullback from the waterway, and guarantees over Sharm al-Sheikh. But in meetings with Mrs. Meir, Deputy Prime Minister Allon, Defense Minister Dayan, and Foreign Minister Eban, they found themselves "stonewalled," as an American official described it later. Sisco tried to improve the atmosphere at the first meeting at Mrs. Meir's house by telling the Israelis a long story about his friendship with a Jewish family when he was growing up in Chicago: his best friend, he said, was a Mrs. Goodman, who often fed him—the son of an Italian family—bowls of chicken soup. But this made little impression. An Israeli official who attended the meeting commented afterward that "Sisco was trying to trade Mrs. Goodman's chicken soup for pullback from Suez."

Besides, to the Israelis the foremost subject was the resumption of aircraft deliveries, especially the Phantoms. They seemed to want a *quid pro quo:* assurances of immediate plane deliveries in exchange for a possible agreement to pull back from the Bar-Lev Line. But they opposed even a symbolic Egyptian presence on the east bank. General Bar-Lev himself, the Israeli chief of staff, took Sisco and Atherton on a tour of the fortified line named after him. Then, making his farewells to the Americans, he said: "I hope to see you again, *right here.*"

In September, Secretary Rogers resumed his peacemaking attempts with the Israeli and Egyptian foreign ministers, who were in New York for the U.N. General Assembly. He suggested the idea of conducting Israeli-Egyptian negotiations through an American mediator (presumably Sisco) shuttling between rooms in a New York hotel. Rogers also discussed the "hotel formula" with Gromyko, but no headway was made. The Big Four meetings had been abandoned on September 9, and now Gromyko as well as the British and French foreign ministers told Rogers that the interim agreement was unattainable at this time. The situation was "bleak."

The Americans were still not giving up. In a speech to the General Assembly on October 4, Rogers outlined six principal areas in the negotiations and urged renewed efforts for an interim agreement.

By December, there had still been no progress. Nixon was finally persuaded, however, that indeed the balance of power in the Middle East was turning against Israel. After more than a year, the U.S. government agreed to resume the deliveries of Phantoms and other aircraft and military equipment to Israel. The Israelis breathed easier, but peace in the Middle East seemed more elusive than ever.

This was true in Southwest Asia as well. And there, too, the Nixon administration saw the Soviet Union taking advantage of the situation. The Bangladesh rebellion was increasing, despite Pakistani military efforts to stamp it out, often in an immensely cruel fashion, and now ranked as a full-fledged civil war in which India was openly assisting the rebels. India, in turn, enjoyed the support of the Soviet Union, which had supplied it with $730 million in arms since the 1965 Indo-Pakistani war. Tanks and other weapons, as well as engines for MiG jet fighters, were produced in India under Soviet licenses.

When on August 9, the Soviet Union and India signed a twenty-year treaty of peace, friendship, and cooperation, fairly similar to the May pact between the Russians and the Egyptians, it came as a considerable and unpleasant surprise to the United States.

Both Moscow and New Delhi hastened to assure the United States that their pact was not aimed against any other country and, in fact, would help peace in South Asia. But Washington was wholly unconvinced. The White House, the Pentagon, and the State Department began contingency planning for the possibility of an Indo-Pakistani conflict over Bangladesh and its probable escalation. Nixon and Kissinger immediately asked what the United States could and should do if the Indians turned against *West* Pakistan. Considering West Pakistan's strategic location on the Indian Ocean on the south and bordering Iran on the west, its defeat by India would, in the administration's judgment, affect U.S. interests from the Persian Gulf to Malaysia.

On November 12, Secretary Rogers expressed the apprehension of the United States over the buildup of military forces in India and Pakistan and an increasing number of incidents. These clashes, he said, "might lead to an outbreak of hostilities in the days ahead." But diplomacy failed totally. War between India and Pakistan broke out on December 3.

In short order, the overwhelmingly superior Indian Army defeated the Pakistanis. Indian forces supporting the Bangladesh guerrillas captured what had been East Pakistan, trapping over 90,000 Pakistani troops. In the west, they crossed the Pakistani border in disputed Kashmir, taking some territory. The fighting ended on December 17, but during the two weeks of the war, the Soviet Union vetoed three resolutions in the U.N. Security Council calling for an immediate truce and the withdrawal of all foreign forces.

There is no question that the United States favored Pakistan in the conflict—as much as anything else out of concern that India would deal a mortal blow to the Pakistanis in the west, which would have been an immense gain for the Soviet Union. Minutes of secret meetings of WASAG showed that the president wanted a "tilt" toward Pakistan, and this implied a scrapping of the formal American commitment to remain neutral in the subcontinent. Nixon later explained:

> During the week of December 6, we received convincing evidence that India was seriously contemplating the seizure of Pakistani-held portions of Kashmir and the destruction of Pakistan's military forces in

the west. We could not ignore this evidence. Nor could we ignore the fact that when we repeatedly asked India and its supporters for clear assurances to the contrary, we did not receive them. We had to take action to prevent a wider war. . . . We could take a stand against the war and try to stop it, or we could maintain a "neutral" position and acquiesce in it. . . . Acquiescence had ominous implications for the survival of Pakistan, for the stability of many other countries in the world, for the integrity of international processes for keeping the peace, and for relations among the great powers. These risks were unacceptable.

The actions taken by the Nixon administration ranged from urgent diplomatic efforts at the United Nations to a series of military steps, some covert, some overt. But publicly, even after December 6, Nixon was proclaiming total American neutrality although he had already set in motion a different policy. In secrecy, the United States persuaded Jordan and Iran to transfer a number of F-5 jet fighters to the Pakistani air force, which had only obsolete F-86 jets of Korean war vintage, an F-104 squadron, and some Mirages. Washington assumed the responsibility for replacing these planes. Overtly, Nixon ordered a navy task force from the Seventh Fleet, led by an aircraft carrier, to cross the Strait of Malacca into the Indian Ocean and head toward the Bay of Bengal. This was meant as a signal to India as well as the Soviet Union that the United States would not stand still in the event of a massive attack on West Pakistan. The administration never said publicly what the mission of the naval task force was, but Pentagon sources deliberately obliged newsmen by providing daily "backgrounders" on the location of the warships. Nixon and Kissinger wanted New Delhi and Moscow to know exactly what the fleet was doing, but they kept them guessing as to its ultimate mission. They did nothing to discourage speculations ranging from reports that the task force would protect the evacuation of American citizens from East Pakistan to predictions that it would intervene if the Indians struck West Pakistan.

It *is*, however, known that Nixon was prepared to engage carrier-based aircraft in the defense of West Pakistan. He felt that the United States had to take drastic action to prevent a wider war. It remains unclear what Nixon proposed to do in the long run if the Indians did not desist from invading West Pakistan, if this is really what they had in mind. (Nixon never explained what the "convincing evidence" was.) Carrier air strikes would obviously be insufficient. And what with the Indochina war still very much in progress, the president would have faced strenuous opposition in Congress and from public opinion to a new American involvement in Asia. As it was, the deployment of warships in the Indian Ocean resulted in strident criticism: the American people saw Bangladesh as the victim of West Pakistani violence, and sympathies were on the side of the rebels and India.

Nixon's enormous calculated risk in the Indian Ocean seems to have worked. Rightly or wrongly, the president and Kissinger were convinced that the threat posed by the navy task force had persuaded India to bring the hostilities to an end. If so, it was another case of the superpowers edging away from confrontation, as they have repeatedly done in the Middle East and elsewhere. The theory in the White House was that Moscow had prevailed on the Indians to give up their ambitions in West Pakistan. But Nixon refrained from saying so publicly: there was no point in embarrassing the Russians. The United States also had to invoke the Indian-Soviet threat to force President Yahya to accept the cease-fire. Yahya, having lost all sense of reality, wanted to go on fighting in Kashmir.

In 1971, Britain formally abdicated her defense responsibilities in the region "east of Suez." The immediate American response was to turn Iran into a major military power in the Middle East; the worry was that otherwise the Russians would try to fill the vacuum in the Persian Gulf.

The new policy was stated by Secretary Rogers in his annual report on foreign affairs:

> The year 1971 was an historic year in the Persian Gulf. The long-standing protective treaty relationship between the United Kingdom and the nine small sheikdoms along the eastern coast of the Arabian peninsula was terminated. By early December, the British had ended their special role in the Gulf under arrangements promising future cooperation among both the Arab states and Iran. Three new and independent states emerged, Bahrain, Qatar, and the United Arab Emirates. Throughout these developments, the U.S. interest was to encourage all parties to cooperate for the future welfare and stability of the region. . . . The U.S. objectives in Iran are . . . to assist Iran, in accordance with the Nixon Doctrine, in attaining economic and military self-reliance. . . . We now provide Export-Import Bank loans to assist Iran in purchasing both military and commercial equipment and services in the United States.

Rogers, however, failed to spell out the extent of the military programs being envisaged for Iran. Key officials in the administration were apprised of it in a secret CIA study circulated on July 20. What this study revealed was that the United States and Britain were quietly underwriting an initial $1-billion program to build Iran into the leading military power in the Middle East. The United States, the CIA paper said, was covertly providing Iran with Phantom jet fighter-bombers, Chinook helicopters, and other weapons systems. Britain was selling the shah hundreds of Chieftain tanks, scores of missile-equipped frigates, and large armored hovercraft for troop transport in the Persian Gulf. Although Rogers had acknowledged Export-Import Bank credits for Iranian purchases of military equipment, he offered no hint of their magnitude. The bank itself refused to discuss military credits to Iran. It was left to the CIA to disclose that $220 million in loans to Tehran had paid for purchases of Phantoms, F-5s, and other equipment in 1970 and 1971. By 1971, Iran had 100 Phantoms—more than Israel. Other American credits helped to complete a plant south of Tehran, where 850 American-made M-47 medium tanks were being retrofitted with more powerful engines and new guns; U.S. loans made possible the expansion of the port of Bandar Abbas, where a new naval base and an airfield were added. (Bandar Abbas controls the Strait of Hormuz, connecting the Persian Gulf with the Gulf of Oman and thence the Indian Ocean. This is the tanker route from the Persian Gulf.)

Credits were necessary in 1971 because Iran had not yet developed adequate financial sources of its own. This would come with new oil revenues in the years ahead. But the foundations for the transformation of Iran into the greatest arsenal in the Middle East were laid through these secret policies. More such programs would later come as the United States proceeded with a plan to create a surrogate military power in Iran.

Chapter 16

For many decades, the United States—the world's greatest economic power—has been devoid of a comprehensive foreign economic policy. When the need arose in specific situations, policies were developed—the creation of the postwar monetary system at Bretton Woods, the Marshall Plan, foreign aid, the negotiation of the Kennedy Round of tariff agreements in the 1960s, international commodities accords, or bilateral agreements, such as on Japanese textiles—but often these policies did not relate to each other. There was no centralized planning or thinking in the United States government on *all* these subjects.

Perhaps precisely *because* the United States was the dominant economic power in the world, the tendency had developed to do without a comprehensive global economic policy. Frequently the White House merely approved the recommendations of one or more departments or agencies; occasionally it arbitrated their differences and arrived at the lowest common denominator in policy. There were entrenched bureaucratic fiefdoms when it came to foreign economic policy: in the Treasury, State, Commerce, Agriculture, and even Defense departments, and in agencies such as the Office of Management and Budget, the Council of Economic Advisers, the Federal Reserve Board, the Federal Power Commission, the Civil Aeronautics Board, the Export-Import Bank, and so on. Each tended to defend its own biases and interests or those of its constituencies.

Richard Nixon remembered John Foster Dulles's telling him, toward the end of Eisenhower's second term, that international economic problems were far in the future, that there was nothing to worry about. Nixon, like so many others, placidly accepted Dulles's views, which exemplified a widespread attitude.

When Nixon took office in 1969, it was business as usual in foreign economic policy. Inflation within the United States was increasing, trade deficits were beginning to pile up abroad, and petroleum was becoming a problem, but the Nixon administration paid virtually no attention to foreign economic policy during its first two years. The president and Kissinger were chiefly preoccupied with Indochina and their "double détente," plus the management of crises in the Middle East, Southwest Asia, and elsewhere. Rogers was "passive and benign," in the words of one of his subordinates, although the State Department had a very competent Bureau of Economic Affairs. Yet it was puzzling that the White House proposed to create an entirely new foreign policy for the United States without taking economic affairs seriously into account.

The trouble was that the makers of foreign policy had little sense of economics, and the government economists cared little about pure foreign policy. The conventional view was that if the United States simply continued its normal policies—or lack of a comprehensive policy—all would be well. Around the White House, the "religious view," as one official put it, was that "first-class minds don't worry about economics"; they "worry about war and peace, nuclear weapons, and that sort of thing." Surely this tone was set by Kissinger. His staff did include a professional economist, Fred Bergsten, but during 1969, the NSC apparatus turned out only four studies on foreign economic problems out of a total of eighty-five. Three of these National Security Study Memoranda, in February and March, dealt with trade policies, one on "International Monetary Policy"—a topic of immense importance, as the administration soon found out. In 1970, there was a total of twenty-six NSSMs, but only one on economic affairs: a study on "Preferential Trade Agreements." Then, in January 1971, the Kissinger machine produced a study on oil. In June, it came up with one on "United States Foreign Investment."

Peter G. Peterson, the chairman of the board of Bell & Howell, was brought to Washington early in 1971 to try to coordinate foreign economic policy when it finally dawned on Nixon that the situation was getting out of hand; he was appalled by what he found. "A global view was needed," he said later, "but in Washington, there was no system of information. Government departments were turning out reports by the ton, but with only ounces of analysis." He discovered "remarkably different perceptions on economics" in the bureaucracy. In the top echelons of the administration, "nobody seemed to care." Elsewhere in the government, however, there was concern that, what with high production costs and an overvalued dollar, American goods were no longer competitive in foreign markets. There was talk of import quotas by protectionist-minded industry and labor lobbies—although this would violate the American tradition of free trade and could result in trade wars. As Peterson said, "it wasn't clear if there was a problem, and if so, what it was."

It was Nixon himself who intervened personally to do something about this sorry state of affairs. He had read with deep interest a report by a task force headed by Roy Ash, president of Litton Industries, making the point that international foreign policy was falling between stools in the government. Nixon was also aware of monetary and trade problems and the threats they were posing to Western stability; 1971 would be the first year since 1893 when the United States had a trade deficit, although it had been running a tolerable balance-of-payments deficit since 1950.

On January 19, 1971, Nixon announced the establishment of the Council on International Economic Policy (CIEP) to pull together all the strands of economic policy-making in the foreign area. This was the first step in what would later in the year turn into another "Nixon shock" applied to America's allies. The president was the chairman of the new council, and Rogers was designated to preside over meetings in his absence. The secretaries of treasury, agriculture, commerce, and labor, the director of the Office of Management and Budget, the chairman of the Council of Economic Advisers, the assistant to the president for national security affairs (Kissinger), the executive director of the Domestic Council (Ehrlichman), and the president's special representative for trade negotiations were the other members of the CIEP. Peter Peterson became the council's executive director and assistant to the president for international economic affairs. This, at least in theory, made him coequal with Kissinger, and Peterson told friends self-confidently, "Now Henry and I will split up foreign policy: he'll run the politics and I'll run the economics." It was not long before Peterson discovered that Kissinger did not gladly "split up" foreign policy with anybody—as Rogers had found out two years earlier. Likewise, John Connally, the enormously assertive treasury secretary, was not about to share his authority or wholly subordinate himself to the new council. Then there was Peter M. Flanigan, an assistant to the president who had heretofore handled, in the White House, some of the most delicate international economic problems and was not about to abandon his prerogatives.

The concept of the CIEP was, of course, laudable, but, in practice it never had a chance of surviving the savage politics of Nixonian Washington. The president, as was his inclination, went on making his decisions in a narrow circle of trusted advisers, often in total secrecy, and the council failed in the end to fulfill its function. Although the State Department was placed in charge of an "operations group" in the council, its input into foreign economic policy was limited.

Nixon's appointment, in November 1971, of Earl L. Butz as secretary of agriculture to replace Clifford M. Hardin, a rather passive figure, further diminished the CIEP's importance. Butz, an imperious personality with very strong views on farm policies, quickly turned U.S. agricultural policy into his undisputed domain. Given the scope of American agricultural exports and foreign food-assistance programs, Butz could play a major role in foreign economic policy, but he seldom sought opinions from his cabinet colleagues. Yet this was at a time when economic relations between the United States and Western Europe were breaking down over agricultural policies: the Americans resented the Common Market's efforts to limit their European sales, and also such practices as the West German subsidies to farmers to make their products competitive with American ones; the Europeans feared that the United States was undermining their farm economies. In 1970, Olivier Long, director general of the General Agreement on Tariffs and Trade (GATT), warned that "the situation now seems to have reached alarming proportions and to be already out of control." Butz, closely allied with big American farm exporters and playing domestic farm politics, was determined to sell as much as possible abroad; he was oblivious of wider foreign-policy considerations.

The council nevertheless had a certain educational value in the government. Nixon's directive to "achieve consistency between domestic and foreign economic policy," "provide a clear top level focus for the full range of international economic policy issues . . . as a coherent whole," and "consider the international economic aspects of essentially foreign policy issues, such as foreign aid and defense, under the general policy guidance of the National Security Council" at least served to call the attention of the bureaucracy to the need to coordinate various economic policies. The president's main injunction to the CIEP was to "maintain close coordination with basic foreign policy objectives."

When he announced Peterson's appointment to manage the council, Nixon offered examples of problems requiring coordination by the council:

> Over the past four days either personally or by phone we have been discussing matters in the field of this Council which were of great concern to the Nation. For example, you read of the oil crisis in the Middle East. You also read of the decision of the Tariff Commission . . . with regard to a shoe import [quota] for shoes. And you, of course, have been following the situation with regard to possible British entry

into the Common Market and what decisions that may require, what impact it may have on our policies. In all of these areas we have direct examples of matters that cut across foreign policy and domestic policy.

Of Peterson, the president said that he "will bring some new ideas and, more important than that, some form, some central direction to a number of areas that have simply been handled on an *ad hoc* basis due to the fact that they cut across so many departments." A man of vast enthusiasm, Peterson indeed set out at once to establish the "central direction" Nixon had mentioned. As he recalled later, he wanted to "energize people, to get them into agreement." But bureaucratic realities quickly asserted themselves. "In terms of Washington politics, it was that you had to invent a problem in order to get an answer."

Peterson proceeded to put together a massive report on U.S. foreign economic policy, and Nixon had him deliver a two-hour briefing based on it (although he had not yet read it himself) to the full council gathered in the Cabinet Room. Nixon, typically, told Peterson that it was "the most important briefing I had as president." Peterson thought Nixon was "exercised about the situation; he wanted new routes." Kissinger mysteriously remarked that Peterson had "never told me anything like this." Still, it took a series of crises for the United States to embark on "new routes."

The immediate problem, if not quite yet a full-blown crisis, was petroleum and the OPEC price revolution. When James Akins, the State Department's expert on fuels and energy, proposed in a special report in mid-1971 that the administration consider enforcing oil-conservation measures, a rather logical recommendation, the White House rejected it. John Ehrlichman, the head of the Domestic Council (and a CIEP member), commented in a memorandum to presidential assistant Peter Flanigan (who favored the proposed measures), "Conservation is not in the Republican ethic."

Nonetheless Nixon could not altogether ignore the energy problem. On June 4, he sent Congress a "Special Message on Energy Resources," emphasizing that the United States must find "new sources of energy to fuel the economy" that "will not pollute the environment." It made no mention of conservation (though Nixon urged a more efficient use of energy) and it did not address itself to the international petroleum situation (except for a reference to imports from Canada).

As noted earlier, the administration (except for the State Department) had allowed itself to be lulled into a false sense of security when Libya and the Persian Gulf producers committed themselves, after signing new pricing agreements with the companies in the winter of 1971, to maintain this price level for five years. The commitment was made to Under Secretary of State Irwin, a man with no experience in oil policies and no time to prepare his mission, when he rushed to Tehran and other Persian Gulf capitals in mid-January 1971, to tell the governments concerned that the freezing of prices was in United States national interest and that if the agreements with the companies were not honored, Washington would regard it as an "unfriendly act."

This was the first time that the United States government had formally intervened with OPEC producers on behalf of the companies. In the past, the industry had opposed any government involvement, but this time the big companies became scared and persuaded the administration to dispatch Irwin on his mission. Late in 1970, they had been shaken by their experience at the hands of the producers. After a first agreement for higher prices with Libya (the price at the wellhead had gone up from less than $1.00 to $1.40, something that the companies found outrageous), they had to sign an accord for still higher prices with the Persian Gulf countries. Then, Libya obtained a renegotiation to match the Persian Gulf levels. It was at that point, when the industry finally realized that it was being played like a tennis ball by the producers, that it asked for the Irwin mission.

The Nixon administration, as close as ever to the companies, was happy to oblige. A few months earlier, the White House authorized the Justice Department to lift antitrust controls over the industry so that the big American companies could negotiate as a group (it became known as the London Group because it included British companies with interests in the Middle East) with the producers. Otherwise, they feared, they would be picked off by the producers one by one. Under the same authority, the companies worked out among themselves a "safety net" agreement providing for the sharing of oil and money in the event one of them was cut off from production by a local government. In other words, the OPEC monopoly was now faced by an industry monopoly.

Irwin, who visited Iran, Saudi Arabia, and Kuwait, did get assurances that the 1971 prices would be kept until 1976. The official position of the Nixon administration was to "take the word" of the producers although the shah warned Irwin that Iran would keep the oil flowing only if prices were satisfactory. Otherwise, he said, Iran might take over the companies altogether. The State Department—and, particularly, Akins—was less optimistic about the future. It thought there was great uncertainty in the whole picture. Its experts correctly foresaw that the next step by OPEC would be demands for direct participation by its governments in the equity of the producing companies and a voice in decisions on output, marketing, and so on. They were already detecting these signs in Libya and in the shah's remarks to Irwin. But as usual, neither the White House nor the companies paid heed.

In the meantime, the United States was piling up balance-of-payments deficits, as its imports increasingly exceeded exports, and the great trading nations like West Germany and Japan accumulated huge dollar surpluses. American private capital investments were increasing foreign-held dollar balances; the dollars were staying in Europe and Japan. Fears were developing in Washington that United States dollar reserves simply would not withstand the outflow pattern. The directions of world trade were being rapidly distorted as importers and exporters—as well as governments—were caught in the uncertainty of dealing with overvalued currencies (the dollar and the British pound) and undervalued currencies (the West German mark, the Japanese yen, and the French franc).

The United States was coming under growing pressure to devalue the dollar by severing its link to the official price of gold, which had been held since the 1930s at $35 per ounce, no longer a realistic ratio. Confidence in the dollar as an international reserve currency had already slipped to the point where the International Monetary Fund (IMF) had devised a special currency equivalent for use in international financial transactions; it was known as Special Drawing Rights (SDRs), a composite of the value of principal currencies. By 1971, American payments deficits combined with inflation had further eroded the dollar's real value. Very clearly something had to be done to avert a breakdown in the world monetary system. By May, a veritable dollar war had developed, fueled by speculators, and the United States government had to dump additional dollars on the exchange markets to support the value of the no longer wanted American currency.

Nixon's reaction to this was at first to fight for the preservation of the dollar's current value. On political and psychological grounds he rejected the idea of devaluing the dollar, his view being that America's power image would be harmed. Likewise, he opposed freeing the price of gold because this would inevitably lead to a *de facto* devaluation, one the United States could not control. (General de Gaulle had tried in the 1960s to free the gold price, but the United States fought him tooth and nail, suspecting that he was simply conducting a kind of monetary guerrilla war to weaken the American position in the world. It had not occurred to American policy-makers and financial experts at the time that de Gaulle might have been prescient about the changing nature of the international monetary system, rather than just ornery.)

Rather than devalue the dollar, the Nixon administration began pressing the West Germans and the Japanese to revalue the mark and yen upward; this would make their exports more costly and less competitive; there would be fewer dollars flowing out and more coming back. But neither Bonn nor Tokyo was prepared to accommodate the United States. (In May, West Germany let the mark float upward, but would not formally revalue it.) Nixon saw it all as a ghastly irony: American postwar aid had made possible the reconstruction of Western Europe and Japan, and now the recipients of this largess were undermining the American dollar. He was also annoyed with America's allies for their reluctance to renegotiate trade agreements in the absence of a monetary reform. The drop in U.S. exports meant fewer jobs at home, and the administration began to worry about unemployment and a recession.

During June and July, the president's top advisers—chiefly Shultz and Connally—became convinced that some action must be taken to arrest the economic deterioration in the United States: they started thinking in terms of price and wage controls and associated measures. They had not yet seen that domestic measures would have to be taken in conjunction with new international policies.

It was Peterson who first realized that the establishment of a surtax (probably temporary) on all U.S. imports could be the nexus between the domestic and foreign fields. He thought that such a tax—at first he was talking about 15 percent—would restore some balance to trade and monetary situations, probably encouraging the Europeans and the Japanese to undertake serious trade negotiations. Sometime in June, Peterson told Nixon the United States had to take urgent action to preserve its international credibility. But Rogers demurred, taking the unrealistically optimistic view that in effect the question of United States reserves would take care of itself. (Kissinger, caught up in his Paris shuttle on the Vietnam peace talks and his secret trip to China, was totally out of the picture.) The administration was still incapable of relating economics to foreign policy: even Peterson was not thinking of the international political effects of the steps he was proposing.

Early in August, a new financial crisis erupted as international speculators (and, possibly, some foreign governments) launched a new assault on the dollar. This time Nixon decided that action could no longer be

delayed. On August 10, George Shultz, acting as White House coordinator in the crisis, advised the principals that the president wanted to hold
a meeting at Camp David to decide on a policy. On Friday, August 13,
the men began gathering at Camp David: Shultz, Connally, Rogers, Peterson, Flanigan, Chairman Paul McCracken of the Council of Economic
Advisers, Federal Reserve Board Chairman Arthur Burns, Commerce
Secretary Maurice Stans, and their advisers. Kissinger, in the words of a
participant, was not "part of the program." For one thing, he was about
to fly to Paris for another secret meeting with the North Vietnamese.

A major debate raged during the hot summer weekend at Camp
David. A devaluation of the dollar or tampering with the price of gold was
never considered. With Connally and Shultz acting as principal advo-
cates, and McCracken and Burns concurring, the group quickly agreed
on a package of purely domestic measures ranging from a ninety-day
wage-and-price freeze to a series of steps—tax breaks and job incentives
—designed to stimulate economic recovery without deepening inflation.
But the big argument came over action in the international field.

A 10-percent cut in foreign aid was accepted easily. So was Connally's
proposal temporarily to suspend the dollar's convertibility into gold or
other reserve assets. The question of a surtax on imports became the
central issue. Peterson thought of it as leverage for monetary and trade
negotiations, arguing that if gold were to be a negotiating weapon, the
United States had better hold on to its reserves. "If we have no gold left,
we have no leverage," he commented at one point. The surtax, Peterson
kept saying, would be a symbol to the world that the United States was
prepared to act seriously to restore international economic equilibrium;
what he saw in the world at that juncture was "a sense of despair, drift,
and protectionism." But he felt the surtax should be temporary. Connally, who supported the surtax fully, was more interested in its *domestic*
political implications. He wanted the surtax to stay on indefinitely, for it
would protect American jobs through a decrease in imports and thus
bring the administration valuable political advantage as the 1972 presidential election approached. Burns opposed the surtax altogether; he did
not think it would be a real solution. Shultz, the man who probably best
understood the situation and all its ramifications, favored floating rates
for currencies, an idea Nixon was not ready to accept.

Connally was enraged with the "foreigners," having heard the rumor
that the British and the Dutch were preparing an assault on the gold
price; it was the sudden weakness of the Dutch currency that had precipitated the August financial crisis. This clinched the argument for "closing

the gold window," i.e., suspending the dollar's convertibility. But he still wanted an import surtax of indefinite duration. Most of the discussion was couched in domestic political terms: Connally and most of the others attached relatively little importance to the international implications. The notion of the surtax as a negotiating instrument rather than an end unto itself seemed somewhat arcane. As one of the participants recalled it, "Connally's view was that we should strongarm the world. His argument was that the foreigners have been screwing us for twenty-five years, so let's keep the surtax until the 1972 elections and tell the foreigners to go to hell. So what started as a reform move became Connally's domestic politics. He kept making domestic linkages."

Having a better sense of foreign affairs than most of his cabinet and advisers, Nixon realized that the indefinite surtax would have a deeply adverse impact worldwide. Any import surtax would have to be temporary, would have to be kept down to 10 percent, and would have to be applied as an instrument to force the Europeans and Japan to negotiate on trade and a monetary reform. Most of Sunday, August 15, was spent drafting the speech Nixon would deliver that night to announce the "new economic policy." In the afternoon, the president boarded his helicopter for the White House. Another "Nixon shock" was in the works.

When the president spoke at 9:00 p.m. on nationwide radio and television from his Oval Office, the words were rich in Nixonian drama and hyperbole:

> America today has the best opportunity in this century to achieve two of its greatest ideals: to bring about a full generation of peace, and to create a new prosperity without war. . . . Prosperity without war requires action on three fronts: We must create more and better jobs; we must stop the rise in the cost of living; we must protect the dollar from the attacks of international money speculators.
>
> We are going to take that action—not timidly, not halfheartedly, and not in piecemeal fashion. . . . The time has come for a new economic policy for the United States. Its targets are unemployment, inflation, and international speculation.

Nixon was unable to resist the temptation of blaming the previous administration and its Vietnam war for inflation: "In the four war years between 1965 and 1969, your wage increases were completely eaten up by price increases. Your paychecks were higher, but you were no better off." He announced a wage-price freeze, and then explained the temporary suspension of the dollar's convertibility and the 10 percent import surcharge. As to the former, Nixon said he wanted to "lay to rest the bugaboo of what is called devaluation" because "the effect of this action . . . will be to stabilize the dollar"; as for the latter, it was "a better solution for international trade than direct controls on the amount of imports."

> This import tax is a temporary action. It isn't directed against any other country. It is an action to make certain that American products will not be at a disadvantage because of unfair exchange rates. When the unfair treatment is ended, the import tax will end as well.
>
> At the end of World War II the economies of the major industrial nations of Europe and Asia were shattered. To help them get on their feet and to protect their freedom, the United States has provided over the past twenty-five years $143 billion in foreign aid. That was the right thing for us to do. But now that other nations are economically strong, the time has come for them to bear their fair share of the burden of defending freedom around the world. The time has come for exchange rates to be set straight and for the major nations to compete as equals. There is no longer any need for the United States to compete with one hand tied behind her back.
>
> To our friends abroad, including the many responsible members of the international banking community who are dedicated to stability and the flow of trade, I give this assurance: the United States has always been, and will continue to be, a forward-looking and trust-worthy trading partner. In full cooperation with the International Monetary Fund and those who trade with us, we will press for the necessary reforms to set up an urgently needed new international monetary system. Stability and equal treatment is in everybody's best interest. I am determined that the American dollar must never again be hostage in the hands of international speculators.

As Nixon had fully expected, the world reacted with shock to his "new economic policy," especially to the import surcharge. Latin American countries that were not involved in the wars over exchange rates and major trade disputes felt discriminated against. Western Europe was mortified because Washington had not given advance notice about the new policy. And the Japanese, who had not yet recovered from the shock of China, took it the hardest, and relations between Washington and Tokyo hit their lowest point since the war.

Nixon would later acknowledge that the "unilateral" steps he had taken were "harsh," and yet he believed there was no other way of forcing the other industrialized nations to face the need for immediate reforms in monetary arrangements. As Peter Peterson remarked, "Europe was preoccupied with her own problems, and she didn't want to go into negotiations; Japan was in a dandy position building up trade surpluses." Hence the surgical approach.

The president's weakness was his rhetoric and penchant for exaggeration. The "new economic policy" was not a policy in the full sense of the word: it was a package of emergency measures of limited duration that were intended to serve only during an interim period. They may have averted an even worse situation, but they certainly did not launch America on a "new prosperity" or provide the economic basis for Nixon's promised "generation of peace."

The period between August and December was a transitional time during which, the administration hoped, world trading and monetary systems could be put in a semblance of order. It was also a time to mend political fences in Japan.

The "new economic policy" offered another example of how the White House gave an ambassador in a key post—in Tokyo—absolutely no information on what was being planned, leaving him unable to clarify the policy to the government to which he was accredited. Just as had happened in July, the hapless Ambassador Meyer heard on the radio about Nixon's latest surprise. This time the broadcast simply reported that the president would make a major statement on economic policy within a matter of hours. Meyer, who had learned his lesson, quickly telephoned the State Department, but it was Sunday afternoon in Washington and there was nobody on hand to brief him, and in any case, only Rogers knew what Nixon would say. (According to Meyer's own account, the State Department called him back twenty-five minutes before the president was to go on the air to arrange for Prime Minister Sato to telephone Rogers at once. Meyer passed on the request to Sato, but inasmuch as the prime minister spoke no English, precious minutes were wasted before an interpreter could be located. By the time Sato and Rogers were able to communicate, Nixon was beginning his speech, thereby rendering this effort at "advance notice" pointless.)

The entire year 1971 had, in fact, showed ups and downs in American-Japanese relations. In March, a major dispute had flared over the question of Japanese textile exports to the United States, which the two governments had been trying for years to settle. Suddenly, the Japan Textile Federation's representatives in Washington made a private deal with Representative Wilbur Mills, then chairman of the House Ways and Means Committee (the panel responsible for trade legislation), for a unilateral limitation of exports. The Japanese government followed it up with a public statement of endorsement, thus terminating negotiations with the Nixon administration. The president, livid over this procedure and convinced that the private agreement was unsatisfactory, hit back on March 11 with a tight-lipped statement that "the maneuver of the Japanese industry, now apparently ratified by the Government of Japan, has effectively precluded further meaningful government to government negotiations, the resumption of which this country would welcome."

But textiles were only a part of the problem with Japan, and in this instance the president was really acting in defense of the domestic textile industry; later he announced that he would support legislation to impose textile import quotas. The essential difficulty was the tremendous imbalance in Japanese-American trade; the United States trade deficit with Japan would reach $3 billion in 1971, twice the 1970 figure. Not only did the Japanese avoid an acceptable textile agreement and refuse to increase the value of the yen, but they also maintained import quotas on American goods and strict controls on American investments. Finally, Tokyo was subtly given the hint that the signing of the treaty for the reversion to Japanese sovereignty of Okinawa and the other Ryukyu Islands might be delayed pending resolution of the trade disputes. Nixon and Sato had agreed in 1969 on the principle of reversion, but negotiations had dragged on. Now the prime minister, eager for domestic political reasons to have the treaty signed, was vulnerable to such pressures. On June 4, his government announced an eight-point plan covering all the areas of economic cooperation in which the United States was interested, and on June 17, the Okinawa treaty was ceremoniously signed in Washington and Tokyo; the actual reversion was to take place on May 15, 1972. These two events in June seemed to improve Japanese-American relations, but then the two Nixon shocks in July and August sent them plummeting.

Tokyo's initial response to the "new economic policy" was that it represented a protectionist policy injurious to Japan. But twelve days later, the Japanese accepted the inevitable and allowed a controlled float of the yen, to permit it to appreciate in value in relation to the dollar. Now it was the turn of the United States to embark on gestures toward Japan. Having learned that Emperor Hirohito and his empress were to fly to Europe in September—the first time a Japanese emperor was leaving his country—Nixon arranged to meet him in Anchorage, Alaska, during the refueling stop. Nixon added, of course, that the meeting would also "mark the first time that an American president in office and a reigning Japanese emperor have met."

The new warmth in relations continued when Foreign Minister Takeo Fukuda visited Washington for economic talks and to coordinate policy with the United States in connection with the impending General Assembly debate on Chinese representation. On September 21, Nixon sent the Okinawa reversion treaty to the Senate for ratification, pointedly enclosing Japanese government letters concerning "treatment of foreign nationals and firms." The White House was aware that the Senate might weigh Japanese-American economic relationships as it proceeded with the ratification of the Okinawa treaty.

President and Mrs. Nixon arrived in Anchorage on September 26 to meet the emperor and empress of Japan. (This was the northernmost point on a quick trip that took the Nixons to Michigan, Montana, Oregon, and the state of Washington. Before the Japanese party landed, the president found time to issue a statement declaring that "I do not believe that the apparent conflict between oil and the environment represents a permanent impasse." The reference, of course, was to the battle waged in the courts by environmentalists against the building of the Trans-Alaska pipeline that was to bring new oil from the North Slope to Valdez, the port in southwest Alaska where it could be loaded aboard tankers. The argument had been going on for two years, preventing the start-up on the pipeline, and the administration was concerned over the delays in new domestic production of oil.)

It was well after 10:00 p.m., but still daylight, when Nixon stepped forward at Elmendorf Air Force Base to greet Hirohito. He delivered a brief, formal statement of welcome, describing the meeting as a "historic" one, although it lasted not quite an hour. Hirohito responded with expressions of Japan's gratitude for American assistance since the war. Then Nixon issued an additional statement, quoting from the Nobel Prize citation to the Japanese novelist Yasunari Kawabata (White House speech-writers were always on the *qui vive* for pertinent literary allusions) that he had built "a spiritual bridge spanning between East and West." Now Japanese-American relations were back on the right track. On October 15, the deadlock over Japanese exports of synthetic textiles was finally broken when the two governments worked out a three-year agreement meeting United States requirements. Though the credit for the breakthrough belonged to David M. Kennedy—former treasury secretary and in 1971 ambassador at large, who patiently put all the negotiating pieces back together again after the March fiasco—he was given none publicly.

The Nixon administration's central motive in applying the August "shock" internationally was to force a reform in the monetary system as far as the industrialized countries were concerned. The dollar had to be defended, as Nixon said, and the statistics the administration was getting in July helped to make his point: U.S. holdings of all reserve assets (gold, foreign currencies, SDRs, and the quota in the IMF) had dropped from $17 billion at the end of 1969 to $12 billion by mid-1971, and the downward trend was gaining momentum. U.S. dollar liabilities to foreign official institutions not only exceeded its reserves, but were snowballing: they rose from $12 billion at the end of 1969 to $20 billion at the end of 1970, and doubled in the first six months of 1971 to $41 billion.

The truth was that the United States was broke in terms of its international financial accounts, a fact that American public opinion did not realize at the time. Very few people study international financial accounts, and the president chose not to be alarmist, preferring to emphasize the "new prosperity" he said his new policies would bring. A State Department study added:

Our major immediate objective was a realignment of exchange rates. . . . [The] competitive position [of other industrial countries] on world markets improved sharply; their balances of payments moved out of deficit into surplus; and they accumulated large, if not excessive, amounts of monetary reserves. Yet, these changes had not been reflected in the rates of exchange between the dollar and the currencies of the other industrial countries. Clearly, a realignment of exchange rates was overdue. There was little the United States could do about it unilaterally. We could increase the price of gold. But this would not affect the exchange rate unless other countries agreed to permit their currencies to appreciate against the dollar. Few of these countries were willing to revalue their currencies, despite the real economic benefits which would accrue to them and the contribution this would make to international monetary stability. . . . Countries were afraid to act alone, exposing their economies to competition from others besides the United States; they would more readily appreciate their currencies against the dollar if other countries would do likewise. . . .

The August 15 measures were the first step in a realignment of exchange rates. But it took nearly four more months of frantic negotiation and maneuvering—on the international scene as well as within the Nixon administration—before the crucial monetary problem was finally resolved. When the governors of the World Bank and the International Monetary Fund gathered gloomily for their annual meeting in Washington on September 29, Nixon put on more pressure. He cited Mark Twain's description of a banker as someone "who will loan you his umbrella when the sun is shining and ask for it back when it's raining," adding that "we understand that at this particular period there will be hard bargaining between bankers representing other countries and our own. And that is all to the good. I think a banker does no favor to a borrower by making a bad loan. It appears that it is a favor, but in the end the banker is right in insisting on responsibility and the ability to pay."

Of the greatest concern to the world community was how long the American "temporary measures" would be maintained—and this was also the subject of lively controversy within the administration. Nixon, maintaining the pressure, chose to be noncommittal: "How long 'temporary' is depends upon what we want to come up with. If we want to go to another temporary system, it would be very, very short; but if we want to build permanently for the future and build well, then we must have that kind of discussion in which all sides bargain hard in their own interest . . . and then have an understanding which is in all of our mutual interest. It can be done, and it will be done."

Connally was so uncompromising in his insistence on indefinitely prolonging the surcharge on imports that Peterson decided to seek support from Kissinger. He told him, "You are going to China and to Moscow, but you also need a foreign policy for our allies. . . . As things stand now, you'll be burning your bridges to the West." Arguing for the lifting of the surtax after a monetary agreement was reached, Peterson insisted that a positive policy toward the Western allies was essential even in domestic terms because the United States had no need to expose itself to economic retaliation. Peterson also was one of the few Nixon advisers who felt that the United States had to devalue the dollar; he believed that the Europeans simply could not be expected to "cave in" on all fronts.

Peterson seemed to have convinced Kissinger, who was now taking a growing interest in the economic situation, and Kissinger, in turn, prevailed on Nixon to reject Connally's position. Thus in a message to Congress on trade agreements on December 1, the president commented that "with the cooperation of other major economic powers, I am confident that the deterioration in our merchandise trade balance . . . which reached intolerable proportions in the spring of 1971, will be sufficiently improved that the present U.S. surcharge on imports can be removed."

By the end of November, negotiations with West European governments and Japan reached the point where it was judged that the overall problem could be settled at a summit meeting. Instead of a complex conference with many heads of state, it was decided that Nixon would represent the United States and France's President Pompidou would act as the authorized spokesman for the other industrialized countries, and a Nixon-Pompidou meeting was set for December 13 on the island of Terceira in the Portuguese Azores. To avoid a sense of confrontation, the White House explained that one of the reasons for the meeting was Nixon's desire to consult with Pompidou before his planned trips to China and the Soviet Union in the early part of 1972.

But the choice of the Azores as the site of the conference made it necessary for the United States to negotiate quickly a new five-year treaty with Portugal covering the use of air and naval facilities on the archipelago. The previous treaty had expired three years earlier and the United States had gone on operating the Azores bases under a "gentlemen's agreement" with Lisbon. In the past, Portugal had not charged the United States a cent for these bases, but this time, to speed up the process, it was agreed that the Portuguese would receive up to $400 million in Export-Import Bank credits for the development of their impoverished economy. The long colonial war in Africa had further weakened the Portuguese economy, and now Lisbon wanted aid. Just before the Azores meeting, Secretary Rogers signed the new agreement with Portuguese Foreign Minister Rui Patrício.

Nixon landed at the American-operated Lajes Air Force Base on Terceira Island in the late afternoon of Sunday, December 12, bringing along Connally, Rogers, and Kissinger aboard *Air Force One*. Pompidou, upstaging Nixon, flew from Paris aboard a supersonic Concorde. Nixon, whose legislation for the development of an American supersonic transport had been defeated in Congress in March, wistfully watched the Concorde sitting on the tarmac as his Boeing 707 landed. Nixon and Rogers spent hours in the middle of the night listening to a radio broadcast of a Redskins football game.

When Nixon and Pompidou met the following morning at the lovely palm-fringed government mansion at Angra, they failed to make any progress on the central question of gold price and dollar devaluation. Pompidou made it a virtual condition for an agreement; Nixon, strongly supported by Connally, resisted it. Following the presidential meeting, Connally had a private conference with French Finance Minister Valéry Giscard d'Estaing, where the two men clashed severely. Then at one o'clock in the morning, after a state dinner, Connally burst into the press room at Lajes Air Force Base. In the course of a chaotic news conference, he painted a situation of total deadlock, claiming that the French were intransigent and hinting that probably no agreement would be reached.

Nixon, however, had his own game plan; he had arranged for Kissinger to bring secret diplomacy into play. Accordingly, Kissinger drove the next morning to a discreet breakfast with Pompidou at the French president's villa on the other side of the island. He was able to work up the outlines of an agreement in less than two hours of discussions with Pompidou and Giscard. Connally was left out of the picture, and Kissinger scored a major coup for the cause of rational foreign policy.

The two presidents met again in midmorning for three hours, while Secretary Rogers and French Foreign Minister Maurice Schumann, having completed their foreign policy talks early, strolled through the town's narrow streets. Nixon and Pompidou, looking tired, appeared together in the rose garden of the government mansion at 1:38 p.m. to announce an historic agreement on the devaluation of the dollar and the upward revaluation of other currencies. All the currencies, their statement added, would be allowed to float in "broader permissible margins" around the newly established exchange rates. And the European Community committed itself to extensive trade negotiations with the United States—a point of extreme importance to the Americans. Nixon had accepted the dollar's devaluation, which implied a change in the price of gold, despite his early strong opposition to it. (The joint communiqué did not specify the extent of the devaluation, but newsmen were told it would be around 8 percent.) But he could not let well enough alone: Ron Ziegler went around the press room telling reporters that the decision to devalue the dollar was a Nixon "victory."

The "Group of Ten" (the major financial nations of Western Europe, plus Canada, Japan, and the United States), with Connally representing the United States, met on Friday, December 17, at the "castle" building of the Smithsonian Institution in Washington to formalize the Azores pact and agree on all the monetary details. But Connally was still fighting a rearguard battle. Nixon once more brought Kissinger into action, having him advise Connally that a "tough line" toward America's partners was no longer desirable. As one of Connally's colleagues remarked privately at the time, "He was a chauvinist; he was not strategic in what he was doing." In any case, the Group of Ten came up with a full-fledged agreement late on Saturday, and Nixon made a point of driving over to the Smithsonian to announce it personally in the Commons Room of the castle.

It is my very great privilege to announce on behalf of the Finance Ministers and the other representatives of the ten countries involved, the conclusion of the *most significant monetary agreement in the history of the world.* . . . The fact that these gentlemen . . . have reached agreement on the realignment of exchange rates is, indeed, the *most significant event that has occurred in world financial history.* . . . What has happened here is that the whole free world has won, because as a result of this agreement, we will have, from a financial and monetary standpoint, a more stable world. . . . We will have a world in which we can have more true prosperity than would be the case if we continue to have an alignment which was inevitably doomed to fail because of the instability [italics added].

The crux of the Smithsonian Agreement was the restoration, through the realignment of currencies, of a monetary balance in the West and the creation of a framework for longer-term reforms. The United States agreed to propose to Congress a dollar devaluation as soon as trade-expansion proposals could be ironed out, and it also agreed to end the nonconvertibility of the dollar and to lift the import surcharge. This latter was done two days later.

The immediate practical effect was a 9-percent devaluation of the dollar (the final figure) as the price of gold was raised by the United States from $35 to $38 per ounce. Japan revalued the yen by 17 percent, West Germany the mark by 13½ percent, and France the franc and Britain the pound by 8½ percent.

Chapter 17

Richard Nixon's foreign policy, as the president himself saw it, had to be protected at all costs. It had to be protected from open opposition, as in the case of the Vietnam war, and it had to be protected in its diplomatic secrecy from the prying eyes of bureaucrats, congressmen, newsmen, and the public at large. To be successful, Nixon (and, with him, Henry Kissinger) believed, foreign policy *had* to be swathed in secrecy until the architects themselves were ready to unveil the results. Opposition and attempts to breach this secrecy were intolerable. During 1971, as Nixon was deeply enmeshed in complex moves toward a double détente, Vietnam peace negotiations, settlements in the Middle East and Southwest Asia, and a whole variety of other undertakings, he believed that defensive action must be taken in the name of a greater good—he called it national security—and he was prepared to take it.

Developments of this nature tend to take shape gradually as one act begets the next. And to be sure, other forces were in play: the autonomous intelligence agencies, whose vested interests happened to coincide with those of Nixon and the White House palace guard bent on overprotecting him, and of course Henry Kissinger.

Nixon's subjective state of mind was well expressed when he remarked to newsmen at a press conference on April 16:

> I believe the nation's press has a responsibility to watch government —to see that "Big Brother" isn't watching. I don't want to see a police state. . . . I feel strongly about the right of privacy. But let's also remember that the president of the United States has a responsibility for the security of this country and a responsibility to protect the innocent from those who might engage in crime or who would be dangerous to the people of this country. In carrying out that responsibility, I defend the FBI in this very limited exercise of tapping. . . . What I am simply saying is this, my friends: There are police states. We don't want that to happen in America. But America is not a police

state, and as long as I am in this office, we are going to be sure that not the FBI or any other organization engages in any activity except where the national interests or the protection of innocent people requires it, and then it will be as limited as it possibly can be. That is what we are going to do.

But that was *not* what the Nixon administration was going to do. The year 1971 saw the beginning of a new series of domestic-intelligence programs along with the maintenance of wide-ranging surreptitious activities inherited from previous administrations. All of it would be in the name of national security as defined by the president and his associates.

Already when Nixon took office, the FBI was running a massive Counter Intelligence Program (COINTELPRO) within the United States. This was aimed at groups ranging from the civil-rights movement (one of COINTELPRO's projects was to discredit Dr. Martin Luther King, Jr.) to the Black Panthers, the antiwar movement in general, Students for a Democratic Society (SDS), the Ku Klux Klan, the Socialist Workers Party, the "new left," and "rabble rousers" and "agitators." Aside from spying, the FBI engaged in massive burglaries of homes and offices of radicals and dissidents to photograph files and install bugs. And the CIA had its top-secret Operation Chaos. Simultaneously, the CIA had been engaged since 1967 in Project Merrimack and Project Resistance, allegedly intended to safeguard the agency's facilities, recruiters, and contractors at home from "demonstrators." However, according to the conclusions of the Senate Select Committee on Intelligence Activities, Merrimack's "collection requirements were broadened to include general information about the leadership, funding activities, and policies of the targeted groups," and Resistance "was a broad effort to obtain general background information about radical groups across the country, particularly on campuses. . . ." Chaos itself, "in addition to collecting information on an excessive number of persons, [acquired] information . . . wholly irrelevant to the legitimate interests of the CIA or any other government agency. . . . One CIA agent . . . submitted detailed accounts of the activities of women who were interested in 'women's liberation.' " Together, the CIA and FBI opened and photographed nearly 400,000 first-class letters to and from American citizens between the late 1940s and 1973 (when this totally illegal effort was finally ended), and the CIA produced "a computerized index of nearly one and one-half million names" from the mail intercept.

The National Security Agency (NSA) was just as deeply involved in domestic intelligence. Under Operation Shamrock, initiated in 1945 by the army (before the NSA was created), the NSA received over the next thirty years copies of millions of international telegrams and Telex messages sent to or from the United States. "This was the largest governmental interception program affecting Americans, dwarfing CIA's mail opening program by comparison. Of the messages provided to NSA by the three major international telegraph companies, it is estimated that in later years approximately 150,000 per month were reviewed by NSA analysts," the Senate committee reported. This program continued until mid-1975, having been sharpened in 1969 (after Nixon took office) through the addition of the top-secret Project Minaret, which covered not only communications between Americans but also those *in which United States citizens were mentioned.* Special "watch lists" were developed with the names of thousands of Americans to whom the NSA paid special attention. The NSA also annually monitored and recorded millions of international telephone conversations to and from the United States. This agency then supplied the FBI, the CIA, and others with its information. Under Minaret, special precautions were taken to disguise the NSA's role in these illegal intercept programs. And of course the private telegraph companies, in supplying copies of all their traffic to the NSA, violated laws protecting the privacy of communications.

The Senate committee also noted that "the names of Americans submitted to NSA" by other intelligence agencies "for the watch lists ranged from members of radical political groups, to celebrities, to ordinary citizens involved in protests against their Government. Names of organizations were also included; some were communist-front groups, others were non-violent and peaceful in nature." Besides these, Nixon kept his own "enemies list" at the White House.

All the military- and civilian-intelligence agencies were vitally interested in information from the NSA and elsewhere concerning antiwar and civil-rights activists. The official paranoia inspired by first the civil-rights movement and then the opposition to the Vietnam war created, in the words of the Senate committee, "the overriding fear that the nation was being undermined internally and externally." This was perfectly expressed in a memorandum from Hoover to NSA Director Noel Gayler, on November 6, 1970:

> There are both white and black racial extremists in the United States advocating and participating in illegal and violent activities for the purpose of destroying our present form of government. Because of

this goal, such racial extremists are natural allies of foreign enemies of the United States. Both material and propaganda support is being given to United States racial extremists by foreign elements. The Bureau is most interested in all information showing ties between United States racial extremists and such foreign elements.

Of course, as both the Rockefeller Commission in 1975 and the Senate committee in 1976 demonstrated, neither the FBI nor the CIA could ever establish the existence of any links between American dissidents and foreign governments or groups.

There can be no question that Nixon knew about most, if not all, of the government's domestic-espionage programs—both the ones he inherited and those that were refined or created while he was in office. The Senate select committee found that domestic political-intelligence operations were greatly augmented under Nixon, particularly during 1971.

That he had withdrawn his approval for the "Huston Plan" for illicit domestic intelligence a few days after authorizing it in July 1970 made no practical difference. For one thing, some aspects of this plan would have simply sanctioned what already was being done anyway—such as the NSA's intercepts of electronic communications and the CIA's mail intercepts—and these operations just went on as before. As the Senate committee concluded, the "idea of a central domestic intelligence body had taken root."

Efforts to improve the collection of domestic intelligence continued. In March 1971, Attorney General Mitchell, CIA Director Helms, FBI Director Hoover, and NSA Director Gayler met (according to a Hoover memorandum) to discuss "a broadening of operations, particularly of the very confidential type in covering intelligence both domestic and foreign." The conference had been called by Helms (in another violation of the CIA's own charter prohibiting domestic activities by the agency), and separately, Gayler sent a memorandum to Mitchell and Defense Secretary Laird on the NSA's "Contribution to Domestic Intelligence."

As far as the FBI was concerned, changing conditions—including congressional repeal in mid-1971 of the Emergency Detention Act of 1950, which was one of the foundations of the bureau's investigative authority—forced it to modify its methods. It had abandoned the COINTELPRO operation earlier in the year because of public disclosure and attendant adverse publicity. But modifications did not lessen the bureau's activities; on the contrary, they were augmented in new contexts. As a senior FBI official testified, the bureau was "getting a tremendous amount of pressure from the White House" to expand its programs.

Thus it accepted a recommendation in the Huston Plan to lower the age of campus informants from twenty-one to eighteen. This made it easier to carry out a directive to all bureau field offices to investigate members of "militant New Left campus organizations" even if they were not "known to be violence-prone." The idea was to identify "potential" as well as "actual extremists." The FBI also began a Key Black Extremist Program, under which field offices were ordered to launch at least 10,500 new investigations, including ones of all black student groups "regardless of their present or past involvement in disorders."

The repeal of the Emergency Detention Act simply meant that the FBI shifted its investigatory procedures from the use of its "Security Index" —a list of potentially dangerous American citizens to be arrested in a national emergency—to what Hoover called the "Administrative Index" (ADEX). The "Security Index" and its companion "Agitator Index," a supersecret list, were abandoned when the FBI satisfied itself that the ADEX could serve as the basis for a new detention program. As Hoover explained to Mitchell on September 30, "We . . . feel that it is absolutely incumbent upon the FBI to continue investigations of those who pose a threat to the internal security of the country and to maintain an adminis-trative index of such individuals as an essential part of our investigative responsibility."

Curiously, Mitchell decided at that point that the Justice Department would no longer review the names on FBI lists, as it had done in the past, so from 1971 on, the bureau, in the words of an FBI official, was "in a position to make a sole determination as to which individuals should be included in an index of subversive individuals." Previously, the Justice Department had "frequently removed individuals who in the strictest legal interpretation should not be considered for arrest and detention." Now the FBI could make its own "determination based not on arrest and detention but rather on overall potential for committing acts inimical to the national defense interest." The ADEX did not stress "membership in or affiliation with old-line revolutionary organizations," such as the Communist Party; it concentrated, instead, on the "new breed of subversive individual." An internal FBI document of 1971 explained:

He may adhere to old-line revolutionary concepts but he is unaffiliated with any organization. He may belong to or follow one New
Left–type group today and another tomorrow. He may simply belong
to the loosely knit group of revolutionaries who have no particular

political philosophy but who continuously plot the overthrow of our Government. He is the nihilist who seeks only to destroy America. On the other hand, he may be one of the revolutionary black extremists who, while perhaps influenced by groups such as the Black Panther Party, he is also unaffiliated either permanently or temporarily with any black organization but with a seething hatred of the white establishment will assassinate, explode, or otherwise destroy white America.

The Senate committee noted that the 1971 ADEX included "teachers, writers, lawyers, etc., who did not actively participate in subversive activity but who were nevertheless influential in espousing their respective philosophies. . . . The total case load increase under the ADEX [was] in excess of 23,000 cases the first year."

Besides actual "revolutionaries," affiliated or not, and radical leaders on all levels, FBI headquarters instructed its field offices to list in the ADEX the following: "An individual who, although not a member of or participant in activities of revolutionary organizations or considered an activist in affiliated fronts, has exhibited a revolutionary ideology and *is likely to seize upon the opportunity presented by national emergency* to commit acts of espionage or sabotage, including acts of terrorism, assassination, or any interference with or threat to the survival and effective operation of national, state, and local Governments and of the defense effort" (italics added).

As for the CIA, Nixon's White House wanted it, too, to intensify its domestic intelligence efforts. The agency was "instructed to broaden its targeting criteria" and told that "foreign Communist support" should be "liberally construed." A White House memorandum declared that "it appears that our present intelligence collection capabilities in this area may be inadequate."

Clearly, the intelligence agencies had all along been violating laws that protect the rights of Americans from the government's political espionage. But, as Tom Huston testified before the Senate select committee, the legality or the constitutionality of the White House recommendations contained in the Huston Plan was never discussed in all the meetings on the subject. William C. Sullivan, at the time the FBI's assistant director for intelligence, explained in 1975, "We never gave any thought to this realm of reasoning, because we were just naturally pragmatists. The one thing we were concerned about was this: Will this course of action work, will it get us what we want, will we reach the objective that we desire to reach? As far as legality is concerned, morals, or ethics, [it] was never raised by myself or anybody else. . . . I think this suggests really in government that we are amoral. In government—I am not speaking for everybody—the general atmosphere is one of amorality."

But President Nixon devised a most extraordinary doctrine to justify his administration's actions. In answer to a Senate interrogatory in 1976, he put it this way:

> My approval [of the Huston Plan] was based largely on the fact that the procedures were consistent with those employed by prior administrations and had been found to be effective by the intelligence agencies. . . .
>
> It is quite obvious that there are certain inherently governmental actions which if undertaken by the sovereign in protection of the interest of the nation's security are lawful but which if undertaken by private persons are not. . . . It is naive to attempt to categorize activities a President might authorize as "legal" or "illegal" without reference to the circumstances under which he concludes that the activity is necessary. . . . In short, there have been—and will be in the future —circumstances in which Presidents may authorize lawfully actions in the interests of the security of this country, which if undertaken by other persons, or even by the President under different circumstances, would be illegal.

The Senate committee was outspoken in its response to this line of reasoning: "The dangers . . . are clear, for it permits a President to create exceptions to normal legal restraints and prohibitions, without review by a neutral authority and without objective standards to guide him."

Still, Nixon kept pressing for more and more domestic intelligence. The Senate committee commented that his "misuse" of the FBI "had progressed by 1971 . . . to the use of a full array of intelligence operations to serve the political interests of the administration." In the end, the president was dissatisfied with the FBI's and the CIA's performance. "The final irony," the committee wrote, "was that the Nixon administration came to distrust Director Hoover's reliability and, consequently, develop[ed] a White House–based covert intelligence operation." This was the White House "Plumbers Unit," which, in the words of the House Judiciary Committee, "led inexorably to Watergate."

On June 13, 1971, *The New York Times* began to publish texts of secret Vietnam war documents taken from a multivolume compendium that had been prepared in the Department of Defense and that became known as the Pentagon Papers. The Pentagon Papers told the story of American

involvement in Vietnam up to the end of the Johnson administration—
they included *nothing* after 1968—but their publication caused alarm
bordering on hysteria in the Nixon administration.

The fear in the White House was that this unauthorized publication
of the Pentagon Papers (the materials in them were highly classified)
might be only the first step, the next one being leakage of *current* diplomatic secrets. These fears were irrational, because it quickly became
known that the *Times*'s source for the papers had been Daniel Ellsberg,
the Vietnam expert from the Defense Department who had briefly
worked for Kissinger's NSC staff in early 1969, helping to draft NSSM–1
on the war. Ellsberg had then left the government and spent some time
with the RAND Corporation, in California. It was during the closing
period of his relationship with RAND that Ellsberg and one or two associates painstakingly Xeroxed the Pentagon Papers. His motive, as he frequently explained afterward, was to acquaint American opinion with the
deeply disturbing secret history of the United States intervention in Vietnam in the 1960s. RAND, to be sure, was working all along on classified
projects under Defense Department funding, but Ellsberg (or RAND) did
not have access to secret White House materials during that spring-
summer of 1971.

Nixon and Kissinger, however, were more stunned by the publication
of the Pentagon Papers than they could publicly explain at the time.
Kissinger was getting ready to leave on his trip to China; he and Nixon
became suspicious that Ellsberg and others inside or outside the government might have knowledge of this expedition and the story might break
prematurely. Likewise, the White House was actively engaged in the
secret peace negotiations in Paris and in the formulation of new SALT
proposals following the May "breakthrough." General Haig made matters worse when he expressed the opinion at a White House meeting that
hundreds of other top-secret documents might be floating around—and
that they could find their way into print.

All these considerations led the administration to seek restraining
orders from the courts to force the *Times* and other newspapers (Ellsberg
was now arranging to make copies available to a number of publications)
to halt the printing of the Pentagon Papers. The official argument was
that publication would complicate the conduct of relations between the
United States and foreign countries. Inasmuch as the White House could
not mention its China, Vietnam, and SALT secrets before the courts, the
judges found the administration's justification for prior restraint of the
newspapers to be unconvincing. The Supreme Court upheld the rulings

of lower courts in refusing to issue restraining orders, and rejected the argument that the future of American foreign policy might be endangered by revelations from the past.

The White House, therefore, took matters into its own hands. This time the FBI was cut out from the antileak operations. The White House was of two minds about the CIA, but it seemed like a bad idea to involve the agency in additional illegal domestic police functions, so the idea, then, was to set up a White House secret police that, if needed, might draw to some degree on CIA resources.

On July 2, 1971, the White House organized its Plumbers Unit; the nickname was appropriate because its task was to act as plumbers in plugging leaks. John Ehrlichman, H. R. Haldeman, Charles Colson, and John Dean were all aware of the birth of this secret unit. So were the president and Kissinger, although it remains unclear how much they knew of the details. The chief of the Plumbers was David Young, a close Kissinger associate who had been released from his NSC staff duties to run the new unit. Kissinger later said that he did not really know why Young was borrowed from him—a rather unlikely situation, given Kissinger's jealous protection of his staff and operations.

The other recruits for the Plumbers operation, which was overseen by Colson, were rather bizarre. One of them was G. Gordon Liddy, a tough ex-FBI agent and ex-district attorney from upstate New York, who happened to be on the White House payroll already. Another was White House aide Egil Krogh, Jr. The third was E. Howard Hunt, Jr., a career CIA undercover-operations specialist who had resigned from the agency on April 30 after twenty years of service, and the next day joined the staff of Robert R. Mullen & Company, a Washington-based public-relations firm that served as a CIA front organization (and also held a Howard Hughes account). Hunt, a prolific writer of mystery books and a man of high imagination trained in the CIA's cold war conspiracies, happened to be Colson's neighbor in suburban Potomac and the two men were pleasantly acquainted. They had both gone to Brown University, an additional bond. After Hunt joined the Mullen company, Colson saw him rather frequently. When the White House was ready to form the Plumbers Unit, early in July, he tapped Hunt for the job. Hunt started work July 6. For security reasons, Hunt retained his association with Mullen, and became a paid White House consultant secretly.

Hunt's postretirement connections with the CIA were never satisfactorily explained. Two years later, when James R. Schlesinger became CIA director, he had not been completely briefed about what he called in testimony "this whole set of relationships" between Hunt and the CIA. But it stands to reason that the CIA, which had a full-time case officer attached to the Mullen company, had to be aware that Hunt was spending his "spare time" at the White House.

The White House's anxiety about "leaks" grew on July 23 when *The New York Times* published a front-page story reporting that "American negotiators have proposed to the Soviet Union an arms control agreement that would halt construction of both land-based missiles and missile submarines." This was an accurate description of Kissinger's idea for the first step toward an agreement on offensive weapons under SALT. The same story revealed that the United States had proposed to the Russians that each country be allowed up to 300 ABM missile launches to protect the launching pads for its offensive weapons. Kissinger's notion was to link defensive- and offensive-weapons agreements. Nixon's impeachment hearings in 1974 would demonstrate that it was this *Times* article that led to a specific White House authorization to the Plumbers to undertake active investigations into national-security news leaks. Prior to that, the unit had spent its time wondering what it should do; Hunt, for one, occupied himself reading up on the story of the Chappaquiddick incident in 1969 involving Senator Edward M. Kennedy.

Another thing Hunt did during this interval was to visit the CIA's deputy director, General Robert Cushman (Helms was out of town), to ask for false documentation and disguises for a "highly sensitive mission" for the White House. This was on July 22, the day *before* the *Times* story was published. Cushman agreed, presumably because he had received a call from Ehrlichman on July 7, requesting the CIA's assistance in the fulfillment of a national-security mission. Cushman, who assumed that Ehrlichman was speaking in the president's name, promised cooperation, and he assumed that Hunt's visit two weeks later was related to this call. He told Hunt the CIA would give him what he needed.

The Ehrlichman-Hunt-Cushman relationship suggests that the White House was prepared to draw the CIA into its new secret operations—Cushman could hardly have refused Ehrlichman's request—and that these had little to do with plumbing leaks and more to do with a planned vendetta against Ellsberg. With Ellsberg's trial approaching—he was charged with a felony for releasing the Pentagon Papers—the White House decided to denigrate him as much as possible. After Dr. Lewis J. Fielding, Ellsberg's psychiatrist in Los Angeles, refused to turn over his files to the FBI, David Young, the Plumber borrowed from Kissinger's staff, asked the CIA to prepare a psychological profile of him. The agency, not known to work on profiles of Americans though it does it routinely on foreigners, reluctantly produced a study. Young found it unsatisfactory because it concluded that Ellsberg had been motivated by "what he deemed a higher order of patriotism" in publicizing the Pentagon Papers.

Young's next move was to get Ehrlichman's permission for a "covert operation" to obtain and examine Ellsberg's medical files from the period when he was undergoing psychoanalysis with Dr. Fielding. Hunt and Liddy were assigned this task. First, however, Hunt flew to Miami to recruit Bernard ("Macho") Barker, a Cuban-American who had worked for him in 1960 and 1961 in preparing the Bay of Pigs invasion. (Hunt had served as a CIA case officer for the invasion.) Barker agreed to join Hunt's new operation and to provide additional ex-CIA Cuban exiles for special missions. On August 25, Hunt and Liddy went to Los Angeles to "case" Dr. Fielding's office building. Hunt took some photographs; he turned them over for processing to two CIA agents on his return to Washington.

The CIA advised Hunt on August 26 that it would no longer assist him, but this did not discourage the Plumbers. On the evening of September 3, during the Labor Day weekend, Hunt, Liddy, Barker, and two Cubans named Eugenio R. Martinez and Felipe DeDiego flew to Los Angeles to raid Dr. Fielding's office. They broke in and photographed medical files, but to the dismay of the White House, the burglars' films did not include Ellsberg's files. Dr. Fielding may have removed them. Ehrlichman, however, refused to authorize a second break-in. Instead, the CIA was asked for another Ellsberg profile; it was as unsatisfactory as the first one.

The Plumbers' only other known activity in 1971—and this one showed how pathetic the White House secret-police enterprise was—was Hunt's attempt, in conjunction with Colson, to forge top-secret State Department telegrams to prove that President Kennedy had specifically authorized the assassination of the deposed South Vietnamese President, Ngo Dinh Diem, and his brother, Ngo Dinh Nhu. The idea was to leak these forgeries to *Life* magazine. Instead of plugging leaks, the Plumbers were trying their hand at burglaries to discredit earlier leakers, and at forgeries to leak on their own.

That Hunt and his friends had violated the law in raiding Dr. Fielding's office—and that the White House had had no right to order it— was emphasized in a subsequent ruling by United States District Court Judge Gerhard Gesell: "The search of Dr. Fielding's office was clearly illegal under the unambiguous mandate of the Fourth Amendment.

. . . The Government must comply with the strict constitutional and statutory limitations on trespassory searches and arrests even when known foreign agents are involved. . . . To hold otherwise, except under the most exigent circumstances, would be to abandon the Fourth Amendment to the whim of the Executive in total disregard of the Amendment's history and purpose." But the Fourth Amendment seemed to be of little concern to the White House. Henry Kissinger's special wit addressed itself to this point in a widely publicized remark he made at a party: "The illegal, we do right away; the unconstitutional takes a little longer." Sophisticated Washington smiled knowingly, though nobody, perhaps not even he, realized the truth of his words.

The White House's abuse of the intelligence agencies in involving them in domestic espionage programs—and its tolerance of illegal programs already under way—did little to help the quality of *foreign* intelligence that they were supposed to be collecting. Subsequent investigations pointed to many weaknesses in the United States intelligence-gathering process as well as in the use of this intelligence by the White House. In this, Henry Kissinger was one of the major culprits.

What happened was that, starting in 1969 and culminating in 1971, Kissinger became the *de facto* chief of United States intelligence. The intelligence agencies were in a state of considerable bureaucratic disarray, and Richard Helms, wearing his two hats as director of Central Intelligence (the position from which he was supposed to coordinate the activities of all civilian and military intelligence agencies) and director of the CIA (only one of the many), was basically a weak man, easily bushwhacked in top-level political infighting. He was invited less and less to the White House and was soon no longer principal intelligence adviser to the president. As the Senate Select Committee on Intelligence Activities summarized it:

It was Kissinger rather than Nixon who maintained regular contact with . . . Helms . . . and in effect, it was Kissinger rather than the DCI who served as Nixon's senior intelligence advisor. Under Kissinger's direction the NSC became an intelligence and policy staff, providing analysis on such key issues as missile programs. The staff's small size and close proximity to policymakers allowed it to calibrate the needs of senior officials in a way that made their information more timely and useful than comparable CIA analyses. Both Kissinger's and Nixon's preferences for working with (and often independently of) small, tightly managed staffs is well known. However, both were genuinely interested in obtaining more and better quality intelligence from the CIA.

For intelligence activities to function smoothly, it was necessary for the DCI to coordinate all the agencies—the CIA, the NSA, the Defense Intelligence Agency, and so on—with a firm hand. In fact, the CIA as a whole had to be the coordinating body. This was evidently understood by President Kennedy when he vested this power in CIA Director John McCone—something that previous DCIs had lacked. "One of the principal influences was the support accorded the DCI by the President and the cooperation of the Secretary of Defense. In a situation where the DCI commanded no resources or outright authority, the position of these two individuals was crucial. While Kennedy and McNamara provided McCone with consistent backing in a variety of areas, Nixon and Laird failed to provide Helms with enough support to give him the necessary bureaucratic leverage," the Senate committee said.

Complicating Helms's plight was the fact that the CIA's internal structures—and those of all the other intelligence agencies—made it extremely difficult to provide the White House with the flow of digested information that it needed. There were two basic problems: one was that the "agreed intelligence estimates" produced under the DCI's aegis were deficient; the other was that there was a self-defeating schism in the CIA itself between the collectors and analysts of intelligence and the covert-operations specialists in the clandestine services (from whose ranks Helms himself had risen).

Raw intelligence—a report on military movements in Eastern Europe, a shift in Soviet missile deployments in Central Asia, or new political alignments in the Middle East or Africa—obviously has value for the United States government. But generally speaking, this is a primitive form of intelligence. To become meaningful to policy-makers, such information—collected through electronic or human means (there is a designation in the CIA for intelligence gathered by agents: HUMINT)—must be analyzed and fitted into a comprehensive estimate. Judgments must be made on how a political move somewhere by somebody may touch on the American national interest, or how a given American policy may affect friend or foe. This is why the CIA employs thousands of first-rate analysts in its Directorate of Intelligence (DDI) and the military agencies do likewise (although on a lesser scale). Ideally, the estimate of a situation should provide decision-makers with sufficient knowledge to be able to respond well.

Lacking authority emanating from the White House (and, apparently, not blessed with the gift of leadership), Helms found it nearly impossible to prod the intelligence agencies to produce good estimates. Each agency on the United States Intelligence Board always, and inevitably, had its policy biases and vested policy interests. Under a strong director of Central Intelligence, the board was able to come up with agreed estimates, with differences among the agencies reasonably composed in a final document (dissenting views were incorporated in it, if needed). Since 1950, this work had been done by the Board of National Estimates (on which all the intelligence agencies were represented) with support from the CIA Office of National Estimates (ONE). The board issued National Intelligence Estimates (NIEs) on a whole variety of questions; when the need arose, it produced Special National Intelligence Estimates (SNIEs). NIEs and SNIEs were valuable instruments.

By the 1970s, however, their quality began to drop alarmingly, and they were often unreadable documents based on the lowest common denominator and riddled with dissents and footnotes. Kissinger was probably right when he remarked to an aide in 1971 that he could no longer cope with "these Talmudic documents," largely devoted to hair-splitting and seldom offering acceptable conclusions.

The board's and ONE's ineffectiveness was further compounded by Nixon's and Kissinger's habits of secrecy. By and large, analysts and estimators can answer only the questions that are asked of them. But because of White House impatience with the intelligence product and the president's insistence on secrecy among officials with the highest security clearances, the intelligence community was asked fewer and fewer important questions. The number of NIEs decreased because nobody wanted to read them. In many situations—the invasions of Cambodia and Laos are good examples—the White House simply did not request SNIEs, a morale-shattering experience for senior intelligence officers. Yet frequently, when left to its own devices, the CIA was able to provide high-quality estimates—such as in the case of NSSM-1, the original Vietnam war study undertaken early in 1969, when each agency was instructed to come up with individual answers. More often than not, the CIA's instincts were correct in Indochina situations and in studies of Soviet strategic developments.

Only in the late 1960s had the CIA begun developing a capability for economic intelligence, something that the British services had perfected decades earlier. And this, in a way, reflected the general attitude of United States administrations toward foreign economic policy. It took the

August 1971 world financial crisis to force the CIA to concentrate on finance, gold movements, trade, world crop forecasts, oil production, and other economic situations of obvious importance to the overall policy-making system. The CIA's other organic weakness was its total compart-mentalization between the covert-operations side and the intelligence-gathering side. They were noncommunicating vessels. The clandestine services (run by the Directorate of Plans [DDP]) quickly turned into the principal CIA activity. All the agency's top managers—from Allen Dulles to Helms—were clandestine operators in the first place. The Senate select committee reported:

> For nearly two decades, American policymakers considered covert action vital in the struggle against international Communism. The generality of the definition of "threat perception" motivated the continual development and justification of covert activities from the senior policymakers' level to the field stations. Apart from the overall anti-Communist motivations, successive Presidential administrations regarded covert action as a quick and convenient means of advancing their particular objectives. . . . Within the Agency, DDP careerists have traditionally been rewarded more quickly for the visible accomplishments of covert action than for the long-term development of agents required for clandestine collection. . . . DDP incentives which emphasize operations over collection and which create an internal demand for projects will continue to foster covert action unless an internal conversion process forces a change. . . . The ethos of secrecy which pervaded the DDP had the effect of setting the Directorate apart within the Agency and allowed the Clandestine Services a measure of autonomy not accorded other Directorates. . . . More importantly, the compartmentation principle allowed units of the DDP freedom in defining operations.

Because the intelligence product was so patently unsatisfactory, Kissinger had a justification for becoming the filter through which intelligence data entered the White House. Now they were interpreted, estimated, and molded into a Kissingerian final product, and the DCI had no independent access to the president. The consequences of such a system presented the obvious danger: Kissinger was both the producer and consumer of intelligence.

A *pro forma* effort was made by Nixon at one point to strengthen the DCI, but it brought no results. In December 1970, he instructed James Schlesinger, then assistant director of the Bureau of the Budget, to undertake an overall study of the intelligence community. Schlesinger spent almost a year on this task, and on November 5, 1971, the president assigned Helms, as DCI, formal responsibility for the review of the budget of the whole intelligence complex—which in theory gave Helms the power of the purse over all the agencies. An Intelligence Resources Advisory Committee was established, but this was as far as matters went. For one thing, Nixon failed to request legislation increasing the DCI's powers; for another, Helms made no effort himself to propose budgetary allocations to the president and presented, instead, the agreed-on views of the community. Nothing changed.

In the area of covert activities, Kissinger also exercised total control in his capacity as chairman of the Forty Committee. Helms was his subordinate in a system in which Kissinger, in effect, was responsible for ultimate policy decisions, since the president was to be protected from responsibility for covert actions. According to the Senate committee:

> The decision-making arrangements at the NSC level created an environment of blurred accountability which allowed consideration of action without the constraints of individual responsibility [the Senate select committee went on]. . . . No one in the Executive—least of all the President—was required to formally sign off on a decision to implement a covert action program. The DCI was responsible for the execution of a project but not for taking the decision to implement it. Within the NSC a group of individuals held joint responsibility for defining policy objectives, but they did not attempt to establish criteria placing moral and constitutional limits on activities undertaken to achieve the objectives. . . . Within the Congress a handful of committee members were informed of most of the CIA's major activities; others preferred not to be informed. The result was twenty-nine years of acquiescence.

Subversion in Chile was of course one of the most important covert activities carried out by the CIA, an activity personally directed by Kissinger with Nixon's blessings. During 1970, the secret effort was centered on preventing Salvador Allende from being elected to office and, then, from being inaugurated as Chile's president. It included Nixon's authorization for Track II—the military coup. In 1971, the Nixon administration set in motion the process to remove Allende from power.

Despite all this activity, the CIA Subcommittee of the Senate Armed Services Committee—the principal congressional watchdog over intelligence—did not hold a single meeting during 1971, and this although public charges abounded about possible CIA involvement in that South American country. (It is interesting to speculate whether the administration would have admitted its plotting in Chile if it had been asked about it, even in the traditional executive closed sessions, at the time. After Allende's overthrow in 1973, Helms and Kissinger at first denied the real extent of American involvement. But when the Senate select committee in 1975 undertook its investigation of intelligence activities, Kissinger changed his mind, as Helms did.)

In January 1971, the Forty Committee approved $1.24 million secretly to support anti-Allende political parties. (The money went for the purchase of newspapers and radio stations that then supported opposition candidates in the April municipal elections.) Simultaneously, the administration began economic warfare against Chile: this was based on National Security Decision Memorandum (NSDM–93) issued the previous November, which recommended suspension of economic assistance to Chile (loans already authorized would be disbursed). The United States surreptitiously marshaled its influence in international financial institutions—the World Bank and the Inter-American Development Bank —to halt the flow of multilateral credits to the Allende regime; and the Export-Import Bank dropped Chile's credit rating to the lowest category, ruling out guarantees to United States investors there. The government made a point of acquainting private banks and businessmen with its new restrictive policies toward Santiago. It was a stunning blow to the Chileans who, with a $1-billion external debt, were vitally dependent on fresh foreign credits. All this was being done without the slightest provocation from Allende, who had just taken office. No expropriations of private American property had yet occurred. Chile's heavy debt had not been a problem before Allende's election, and as a rule the United States was quite lenient with debtors.

Track II having failed in 1970, the administration now turned to pure subversion, in parallel course with the economic acts. The administration also tried to win over the armed forces with military aid. Direct U.S. military assistance and sales to Chile increased during the Allende years, while economic help to the desperately needy and debt-ridden nation was withheld. (In fiscal year 1970, the United States delivered $1.96 million worth of arms under the aid program and $9.14 million under credit sales. In 1971, the figures were $1.03 million and $2.95 million, but they soared again in 1972 and 1973. In 1971, the U.S. Army school in Panama trained 146 Chilean officers; this number rose in ensuing years.)

Nixon and Kissinger anticipated not only the full communization of Chile, but also the creation there of a new continental revolutionary center working in tandem with Cuba, and a major Soviet military presence. After Allende's leftist Popular Unity coalition won 49.7 percent of the votes in the April 4 municipal elections (quite an improvement over Allende's own performance the previous September), the Forty Committee approved over a three-month period a total of $477,000 more for the CIA to support the Christian Democratic Party. Of this, $150,000 was earmarked for Christian Democratic candidates for a congressional by-election in July. But this was no help. The CIA candidates in July lost just as they had in April.

Perhaps the most disturbing aspect of the Nixon-Kissinger policy in Chile—apart from its interventionist immorality—was that it was based on ideological bias rather than on facts. Chilean nationalizations of American property, for example, were just an excuse for these policies.

Chile's constitutional amendment for state control of large copper mines and the expropriation of foreign companies operating them was not approved until July 1971, but Nixon had already acted preventively in January to cut off aid, and the CIA covert activities were going full blast. Nixon had unleashed the subversion even though the intelligence community's own estimates on Chile in 1970 and 1971 took a relatively tranquil view of the Chilean situation. A National Intelligence Estimate (NIE) issued in August 1971 suggested that the consolidation of Marxist leadership in Chile was not inevitable and that Allende had a long, hard way to go to achieve it. Thus far, Allende had taken great care to observe constitutional forms and was enjoying considerable popularity, but, the NIE added, although the Chilean president preferred to adhere to constitutional means, he was likely to use political techniques of increasingly dubious legality to keep power—this was at a time when Allende was talking about a national referendum to create a unicameral parliament, replacing the existing Senate and Chamber of Debuties, to obtain easier passage of his legislation. But he did not have enough Popular Unity votes in the Congress at that point.

The 1971 NIE also said that Allende was trying to avoid a confrontation with the United States over the problems of nationalization. And he was being careful not to subordinate Chilean interests to any Communist or Socialist power or to break existing ties with non-Communist nations on whom he continued to rely for aid. It stressed that Allende was charting an independent, nationalistic course and seemed committed to a policy of nonalignment. (Allende, by the way, never showed any interest in removing Chile from the Inter-American Treaty of Reciprocal Assistance or in leaving the Organization of American States.)

Chilean-Cuban relations were described in the 1971 NIE as those of ideological distance and closer economic ties. Despite Allende's long-standing personal relationship with Castro, he refrained from excessive overtures to the Cuban premier. And although the Russians continued to look for channels of influence into the regime through the Chilean Communist Party, they would probably be unlikely to affect key issues in view of Allende's desire for an independent posture. Neither Allende nor the Chilean armed forces would probably tolerate a permanent Soviet military presence in Chile, the NIE concluded, and in 1971, there was none.

A State Department intelligence note issued in June had said that evidence showed that Allende was sensitive to the concerns of his South American neighbors; his government had warned Argentine and Mexican exiles that they could stay in Chile only if they refrained from political activities, and the most militant Brazilian exiles had been encouraged to leave.

But there was a tragic flaw in these intelligence assessments: the CIA analysts never learned of their colleagues' covert moves against Allende, and could not in fact adequately judge the real situation in Chile. Knowledge that an effort was under way by the United States to undermine the Allende regime would inevitably have altered their estimates.

From the White House, the most urgent matter was believed to be the rebuilding of a network of contacts in the armed forces after the failure of Track II. But, as the Senate committee's report noted, "For their part, Chilean officers who were aware that the United States once had sought a coup to prevent Allende from becoming President must have been sensitive to indications of continuing U.S. support for the coup." Yet by September, "a new network of agents was in place and the [CIA] Station was receiving almost daily reports of new coup plotting." CIA headquarters and the Santiago station busied themselves with fresh intrigue.

One idea proposed by the station was to spread fabricated information showing that the investigation branch of the Carabineros was working with Cuban intelligence services to gather information prejudicial to the army's high command. CIA headquarters decided that this piece of deception would not work and proposed instead that "verifiable" information be given to the leader of the coup group thought to be most likely to succeed. (This "verifiable" information, not identified specifically, also included fabricated CIA letters.) It is not known whether the leader the agency had in mind was in fact General Augusto Pinochet, the army commander who ultimately led the successful coup.

By October, the Santiago station had penetrated this particular coup group. "During late 1971 and early 1972, the CIA adopted a more active stance *vis-à-vis* its military penetration program, including a short-lived effort to subsidize a small anti-government news pamphlet directed at the armed forces, its compilation of arrest lists and other operational data, and its deception operation." These efforts, the Senate committee remarked, "put the United States Government in contact with those Chileans who sought a military alternative to the Allende presidency."

In the meantime, the United States kept applying the economic screws. An example was the unpublicized refusal of the Export-Import Bank in May 1971 to extend a $21 million credit line to LAN, the Chilean airline, for the purchase of three Boeing 707 jet transports. (The Chileans wanted the Boeings because LAN was entirely equipped with United States–built aircraft and it was reluctant to switch to British or Soviet planes.) The reason given to the Chilean government was that the controversy over compensation for expropriated American copper companies had to be settled before the bank could grant LAN the credits. However, the bank acted only one month after the actual expropriation, estimated by the companies at around $500 million, and two months *before* Chile took a stand on compensation. The formal announcement was made in August.

It is not clear what the Americans thought they were gaining; it may have been a desire to force LAN to turn to Soviet sources—which would fulfill the prophecy that Allende's regime was relying on the Russians. Curiously, the negative decision on the airliners coincided with a $5-million Pentagon credit sale of a C-130 transport and "paratrooper equipment" to the Chilean Air Force. Orlando Letelier, then Chile's ambassador to Washington, wondered aloud to friends, "Why is the U.S. willing to sell us war planes, but not peace planes?"

By September, however, Allende began moving quite forcefully in the matter of expropriations. In a decision that enraged Washington, he announced that "excess profits" would be deducted from compensation paid to nationalized copper companies—which the companies interpreted to mean that they would receive no compensation whatsoever. Then the Chilean government took over the operations of Chitelco, the Chilean telephone company, in which ITT held a 70 percent interest. The ITT calculated its loss at about $100 million.

Now the United States and Chile *were* edging toward confrontation. In October, ITT's president, Harold Geneen, wrote the White House proposing an eighteen-point plan of economic warfare designed to assure that Allende "does not get through the crucial next six months."

Kissinger read the proposal and turned it down. The administration preferred to wage its own warfare against Chile; ITT's involvement could cause worse embarrassment than even the disclosure of CIA actions.

On November 5, Kissinger convoked the Forty Committee to authorize further covert action in Chile. This time it was the appropriation of $815,000 to support opposition parties and to try to split the Popular Unity alliance through a harebrained operation devised by the CIA's Santiago station.

With food shortages growing in Chile—Allende's farm policies were increasingly chaotic and the country had no foreign exchange to pay for imports—the Christian Democratic and National parties organized a "March of the Empty Pots" by middle-class housewives in Santiago on December 1. It was the most effective public demonstration against the government since Allende had taken office, and it gave heart to the opposition. There are reasons to suspect that the CIA was behind this effort: a similar march had been undertaken in Brazilian cities in 1964 shortly before the military ousted the left-leaning president, João Goulart, and the CIA was involved in *that* operation; housewives' demonstrations were a classic example of CIA covert political action. Besides, there were known links between Brazilian corporations, some of them part of multinational complexes, and the Chilean opposition.

The second year of American subversion in Chile ended with a Forty Committee meeting on December 15 that approved $160,000 in funds to support two anti-Allende candidates in congressional by-elections scheduled for January 1972.

Meanwhile, Nixon's political predilections in Latin America were demonstrated on December 7, when, with a great show of cordiality, he received General Emílio Garrastazú Médici, the dictatorial president of Brazil. This was at a time that saw extraordinary political repression in Brazil, and the worst tortures and killings in that country's modern history. This reality was evidently absent from Nixon's mind as he greeted Médici at the White House, for he said, "I look forward to our talks because of the enormous success that you have had during your term of office in building the economy of Brazil, in the progress that has occurred during that period. Those who have written about it have called it 'the Brazilian miracle.' " And in a toast to Médici at the White House dinner that evening, he went on:

> The greatest tribute that I can pay to our distinguished guest tonight is that in the brief time that he has been president of Brazil there has

been more progress than in any comparable time in the whole history of that country. This is a great record. . . . Working with you as the leader of that country—because we know that as Brazil goes, so will go the rest of that Latin American continent—the United States and Brazil, friends and allies in the past . . . we shall work together for a greater future for your people, for our people, and for all the people of the American family.

Chapter 18

Since July, when the Viet Cong delegation in Paris urged the United States to "stop all maneuvers" designed to keep President Thieu in power, the question of the approaching South Vietnamese elections had become completely intertwined with the peace negotiations. The Communist side took the view that the Nixon administration could prove its goodwill by withdrawing its political support for Thieu before the October 3 presidential elections.

This, to be sure, would probably have led to Thieu's defeat at the hands of one of his non-Communist opponents in Saigon—if any had been allowed to run—and one of the principal political objectives of Hanoi and the PRG would have thus been met. To Richard Nixon, however, abandoning Thieu was a sinister and unthinkable idea, although Vice President Nguyen Cao Ky and General Duong Van Minh ("Big Minh"), the two opposition candidates, felt just as strongly that the United States should adopt a stance of true neutrality if the elections were to have any serious meaning. The American embassy in Saigon was developing serious doubts about Thieu's plans to eliminate all the other candidates from the October race, and it feared that instability and divisiveness would result. Secretary Rogers was equally uneasy, and he conveyed his feelings to Nixon. But nothing could convince the president and Kissinger that there could be a viable alternative to Thieu in South Vietnam. They feared that the election of Minh or even Ky would open the way for direct peace negotiations between Hanoi and Saigon, cutting the United States out of the diplomatic picture altogether.

Having repeatedly stated in public that the United States would abide by the wishes of the South Vietnamese, Nixon now refused to live up to his word. Having said that he would take "risks for peace," he would now take none. To justify his stand, he portrayed the whole controversy over the 1971 election as a North Vietnamese plot.

At a news conference on August 4, the president said, "Let me emphasize our position. Our position is one of complete neutrality in these elections. We have, under Ambassador Bunker's skillful direction, made it clear to all parties concerned that we are not supporting any candidate, that we will accept the verdict of the people of South Vietnam. . . . We want a fair election." But the next day, the South Vietnamese Supreme Court handed down a decision banning Ky's presidential candidacy on technical grounds. There is every reason to believe that Nixon knew about this the day before. The court was controlled by Thieu and it undoubtedly acted on his instructions; also, Thieu made few major decisions without consulting or, at least, informing Ambassador Bunker, and, moreover, the CIA had been successfully bugging Thieu's office since 1967. Most, if not all, of Thieu's private conversations in the presidential palace were monitored by the CIA at a special listening station at the American embassy three blocks away. Transcripts were shown to Bunker and sent to the White House, marked For Eyes Only.

On the Paris negotiating front, the decision was made to resume secret contacts with the North Vietnamese sometime in August. Kissinger had received private assurance from Hanoi that its June proposals—he had found them mildly encouraging—still stood; now he and Nixon concluded that a counterproposal was in order.

Still, there were inevitable diplomatic delays. For health reasons, David Bruce had resigned from his post as chief American delegate late in July, and his replacement, William Porter, could not make it to Paris before mid-August. (Porter's presence was not actually required in the context of the secret talks, but Nixon thought Hanoi would be happier if the new "open" negotiator were in place just the same. It was a question of atmospherics.) The formulation of the American counterproposal was also slowed down by the president's deepening involvement in the international financial crisis.

On the afternoon of August 15, as Nixon prepared to unveil his new economic measures, Kissinger slipped out of Washington for another clandestine session with Xuan Thuy in Paris. (Le Duc Tho was in North Vietnam; he had evidently judged that it was not worth his while to make the long trip from Asia for a meeting from which he was not expecting too much.) Kissinger used extraordinary precautions to disguise his presence in Paris. After landing at a military airfield, as he usually did, he was driven to a suburban Métro station, where he took the subway to another point in Paris to be picked up by a car that drove him to the North Vietnamese villa in another suburb. After his secret trip to Peking the month before, Kissinger suspected, newsmen would be on the *qui vive* about him.

This was the first time in nearly two months that Kissinger was meeting with the North Vietnamese. But his counterproposal was rather limited in scope: an eight-point plan that differed only slightly from his proposal of May 31. Its full text was never made available, but Nixon subsequently disclosed that its principal new feature was to have all U.S. and allied troops withdrawn from South Vietnam within nine months of the date of an agreement. Kissinger suggested November 1, 1971, as a target, so that the American withdrawal could be completed by August 1, 1972 (which would be shortly before the United States presidential election). And he threw in another sweetener: a personal commitment by Nixon to request from Congress, immediately after the signing of an agreement in principle, a five-year reconstruction program for Indochina.

This was the first time the Americans were willing to talk actual dates, but it is difficult to see how Nixon could have expected Hanoi to go along with the new plan, inasmuch as the United States was proposing to maintain its military presence in South Vietnam during the period of political settlement in Saigon, thus retaining a *de facto* veto over political events in the South. And there was another catch: as the administration already knew that Vice President Ky had been knocked out of the race and that "Big Minh" probably would not make it either, Kissinger was, in effect, offering nothing but U.S. acceptance of Thieu's reelection when he assured Xuan Thuy of "total U.S. neutrality" in the October elections and acceptance of the outcome.

Xuan Thuy was noncommittal, but he hinted at what the final reply would be when he remarked that if Thieu pulled out of the election, it would offer a "favorable opportunity" for a peace settlement.

In South Vietnam, meanwhile, the military and security situation was far from favorable. A secret survey by the American embassy in Saigon, covering events up to the fourth week of June and sent to Washington in mid-July, was, for a change, "the unvarnished truth." Its conclusion was that "the enemy continues to affect adversely internal security in selected areas" although "the national picture reflects gradual internal security improvement." The trouble was that those "selected areas" were Military Regions I and II in northern and central South Vietnam, whence most of the American combat troops had been withdrawn. Region I adjoined the demilitarized zone, the easiest invasion route into the South, and west of the central provinces in Region II were the Ho Chi Minh infiltration trails. If the ARVN could not maintain internal security in Regions I and II, the whole Vietnamization policy was unworkable.

Things were just as bad in three provinces of the Mekong Delta in

Region IV, southwest of Saigon, which had long been considered "pacified" and where there were no American units either. In Kienphong Province, near the Cambodian border, the embassy survey found that there were "sharp enemy reactions against pacification . . . by the North Vietnamese Army and the Viet Cong." What worried the embassy most, however, was the situation in Binhdinh Province, in the coastal area of Region II. There, the survey said, a "serious control problem" existed and "the upper four districts are under enemy military pressure and he is working hard at slowly eroding Government of Vietnam control of the terrain and population." It added, prophetically, that "the crux of the problem appears to be a leadership failure on the part of the Government of Vietnam."

This, indeed, *was* the crux of the problem all along, but now it was being compounded by Thieu's concern with his reelection. His commanders were instructed to concentrate their efforts on electoral politics, with the result that the ARVN was becoming increasingly less effective in the field. On August 12, General Minh, the non-Communist "peace candidate," showed the American embassy a document Thieu had purportedly sent to all the province chiefs explaining how best they could use the government's administrative and military machine to see to it that the Thieu ticket won in the late August National Assembly elections and the October 3 presidential race.

But the United States, bent on observing "neutrality" in the South Vietnamese electoral process, never interfered with Thieu's brazen politicking. After all, he was "our boy," as an embittered official in the Saigon embassy confided to a friend. This was too much for "Big Minh," and he announced on August 20 that he was withdrawing as a candidate. This was exactly what Thieu had wanted: now he was unopposed in his reelection bid. The embarrassing implausibility of this situation was immediately clear to the State Department and even to the American embassy in Saigon. But it was not seen by the White House. A quiet bureaucratic struggle ensued as the opponents of one-man election races—and they included Ambassador Bunker at this point—tried to reverse the situation.

On August 22, Bunker decided to engage his personal prestige in an effort to force a change in Saigon politics, sending a cable to Washington urging a new attitude. An unflappable and highly professional diplomat then close to his seventy-seventh birthday, Bunker was reaching the point where he could no longer stomach Thieu, with whom he had been dealing for four and a half years. An aide recalled: "Bunker was very bitterly disappointed by Thieu's behavior. He took the view that Thieu had screwed up things. Of course, the ambassador would never let this be known publicly. But then, on August 22, he sent that protesting dispatch to Washington."

Bunker's top-secret telegram explained that it would be politically damaging to South Vietnam as well as the United States if Thieu ran alone in the October elections. Then Bunker proposed that the embassy issue a press guidance to American correspondents expressing the United States' regret that the Vietnamese elections were moving in the wrong direction. The idea was that newsmen would write about this "regret," attributing it to high American officials, which would be a strong signal to Thieu to reconsider his position. The second proposal was to tell American newsmen that under Article 56 of the South Vietnamese constitution the vice president—in this case Marshal Ky—could call new elections if the incumbent president, meaning Thieu, resigned from office before the balloting. What Bunker had in mind was an immediate resignation by Thieu to be followed by a new election at a subsequent date in which Thieu as well as Ky and Minh could run. As acting president, Ky would no longer be subject to the Supreme Court ban on his candidacy, and Minh presumably could be convinced to reenter the race. In short, Bunker was proposing something of a *coup d'état.*

Nixon and Kissinger were in San Clemente when Bunker's telegram reached Washington. It was instantly forwarded to the Western White House for a decision, but meanwhile, Kissinger's NSC staff in Washington began drafting a reply based on the correct assumption that the administration wanted no part of the ambassador's proposals. The word was that nothing should be done to undermine Thieu, both because of his position in Saigon and because of the Paris peace negotiations. This was stated in the draft, along with instructions to Bunker to refrain from issuing the press guidance he had suggested. But the next problem was to obtain clearance from Nixon and Kissinger before the reply was sent.

Kissinger could not be found when his Washington staff, after working all day, called San Clemente at 8:00 p.m., West Coast time, to obtain clearance for the cable to Bunker. General Haig told the callers that he thought Kissinger was at a Hollywood swimming pool belonging to an unnamed starlet (this was the period when Kissinger basked in his self-invented reputation as a "secret swinger") and he would try to locate him. Haig finally reached his boss at the Hollywood pool at midnight (3:00 a.m. in Washington); Kissinger called his office, consulted with Nixon in San Clemente, and cleared the telegram. An NSC aide recalled that "in general, it was almost impossible to do business with Kissinger when he was in San Clemente. . . . He could not find time to sit and work with his people. Life came to a standstill at San Clemente at 1:00 p.m.; then Henry would take his children and the nurse to the beach. He simply had no time to see his own people, except for the briefing he received from Haig. . . . The attitude was that a crisis is never what you think it is. The tendency was to minimize crises, to ride out the storm. This was the attitude, for example, in the summer and fall of 1971, at the time of the election charade. The idea was that we should do the best we could by Thieu although we realized that such a decision would have a very profound impact on the Paris negotiations. . . . Nixon was fully involved in the decision on the Bunker proposal although he probably didn't spend more than ten minutes on it."

On August 24, the United States command in Saigon placed all American troops in Vietnam on an alert. The official explanation was that the Communists were planning demonstrations and attacks to disrupt the assembly elections later that week. But the State Department sharply disagreed with this claim: it went to great pains to point out that Viet Cong propaganda urged its followers to vote for "peace" candidates in the elections and that there were no indications that the Communists were preparing any trouble. Rumors of a possible military coup against Thieu were also floated in Saigon, and the State Department spokesman, Robert McCloskey, told newsmen on August 24 that "political dissatisfaction" had been manifested in Saigon over the past week in connection with the electoral developments.

In California, Nixon seemed to have no sense of the crisis. He spent two days—August 28 and 29—cruising in the Pacific aboard the *MoJo,* an eighty-five-foot cruiser owned by a Los Angeles businessman. He was in San Clemente, staying away from the press and any comment on Vietnamese politics, when Thieu formally announced on September 2 that he would run alone for the next presidential term. (This announcement had been preceded by a series of secret meetings between Thieu and his top military commanders in which he had sought new assurances of support, for he had been disturbed over the gains by "peace" candidates supported by the An Quang Buddhist faction in the August 29 elections for the National Assembly.) The die was cast. The unenviable task of explaining the position of the United States toward Thieu was left to Secretary Rogers.

Asked at a news conference on September 3 what the United States had done to push for "contested" elections, Rogers was almost apologetic: "I am not sure in this case whether there was something we should have done that we didn't do. . . . We hoped that there would be a presidential election that would be contested and that would be a fair election. . . . I'm sure that all of you will figure out all the mistakes we have made. I don't know. We certainly tried. And President Thieu said he was disappointed. I think it is a little difficult from this distance to judge."

A few days later, word came from Hanoi through the usual secret channel in Paris that Le Duc Tho would be on hand in the French capital to deliver a reply to the American proposals of August 16.

Kissinger left Washington with his accustomed secrecy late on September 12. From Avord, a French air force base outside Orléans, he and his party transferred on the morning of September 13 to a small French executive jet for the short trip to Ville Coubley, a French airfield near Paris. From Ville Coubley, they were driven directly to the North Vietnamese "safe house" at 11 rue Darthe, in the suburb of Choisy-le-Roi, a few blocks away from the walled-in headquarters of the North Vietnamese delegation.

Le Duc Tho was waiting inside the door of the house to offer Kissinger a polite greeting. But he had nothing else to offer. Speaking in Vietnamese (translated into French by an aide and then into English by General Walters, the defense attaché at the Paris embassy), Le Duc Tho informed Kissinger that the American proposals were unacceptable. Thieu had to go before a peace settlement could be reached, and the South Vietnamese president's decision to reelect himself closed all avenues to an agreement in the foreseeable future. There was some desultory conversation across the table, and Le Duc Tho and Kissinger agreed that they would meet again only when there was something concrete that one side wished to tell the other.

The September 13 session marked the end of the first phase of the secret talks that Kissinger and Xuan Thuy had initiated two years earlier, in August 1969. During that period, Kissinger had made twelve secret trips to Paris, but the cause of peace had not advanced an inch. Neither side, each for its own reasons, was prepared for an agreement. That a temporary break had occurred was, of course, unknown to the public, since no one knew of these talks in the first place.

Nixon and Kissinger had locked themselves into the decision to "ride out the storm" with Thieu on the theory that once the election was out of the way, Hanoi would accept it as a *fait accompli* and, before too long, return to the secret negotiations. This view fitted into the overall assessment, basically unchanged since early 1969, that North Vietnam could withstand American military power only so long, and sooner or later would come to terms with the United States in an acceptable way.

So the strategy was to keep the secret talks going, to maintain the rhythm of American troop withdrawals, and to increase the military pressure on North Vietnam. Aerial activities against Communist forces in South Vietnam reached a new peak: commanders were again assigned monthly bombing and strafing quotas far in excess of existing targets (and again they were forced to "bank" air strikes for the future or engage in pointless and dangerous missions). Over North Vietnam, a new wave of "reinforced protective strikes" occurred as aircraft supposedly on reconnaissance flights hit antiaircraft emplacements and other military objectives. In the Pentagon and in Saigon, air force commanders evolved secret plans for what would later become known as "unauthorized" strikes against major North Vietnamese targets.

Speaking to a group of editors and publishers in Portland, Oregon, on September 26, President Nixon mentioned in passing that in November he would make another announcement about troop withdrawals from Vietnam. And as Thieu was garnering 82 percent of the vote in his uncontested presidential election on October 3, Kissinger and his staff were busily drafting a new peace proposal to be submitted to Hanoi, one they assumed the North Vietnamese would be receptive to, notwithstanding Thieu's "reelection." Kissinger had told Nixon that the North Vietnamese were too pragmatic and practical to keep fighting for lost causes. After all, he said, he had come to know and understand the North Vietnamese in his twelve expeditions to Paris. They were tough bargainers, but they were no fools.

The latest American proposal, an eight-point plan with several new features, was given to the North Vietnamese in Paris on October 11 by General Walters. With it went a suggestion for a meeting on November 1 between Kissinger and Le Duc Tho or "any other appropriate North Vietnamese political leader, together with Minister Xuan Thuy." The most important of the new ideas was that new elections would be held in South Vietnam within sixty days of an agreement in principle and that Thieu would step down one month before the voting. An "independent body representing all political forces in South Vietnam"—the "electoral commission" that was first discussed in 1969 and then discarded—would organize and run the elections. The chairman of the South Vietnamese Senate would run the country between Thieu's resignation and the election of a new president. Within *seven* months of the signing of the preliminary agreement, the United States would withdraw all its forces from

Vietnam, "except for a small number of personnel needed for technical advice, logistics and observance of the ceasefire." At the same time, American POWs and "innocent civilians" in South Vietnam would be released.

This was the third United States peace plan presented during 1971, and from Hanoi's viewpoint it was by far the best. But Hanoi was apparently caught unprepared by it. The North Vietnamese sent back a message through Walters proposing that Kissinger and Le Duc Tho meet on November 20 instead of November 1. Washington agreed at once, not realizing that a struggle had erupted in the Hanoi Politburo, one wing of which (including Le Duc Tho) favored resuming negotiations and the other opposed it.

Encouraged by what he considered a promising North Vietnamese response, Nixon went ahead with his planned announcement of an additional withdrawal of American troops from the South. During a brief news conference on November 12, he disclosed that 45,000 Americans would be pulled out over the next two months and that a further withdrawal would be announced before February 1, 1972. Under the current schedule, American forces in Vietnam were to be reduced to 184,000 men by December 1, and be down to 139,000 men by the end of January. The February decision, however, would be determined, Nixon said, "by the level of enemy activity; . . . the progress of our training program, our Vietnamization program in South Vietnam; and third, any progress that may have been made with regard to two major objectives that we have —obtaining the release of all of our POWs wherever they are in Southeast Asia, and obtaining a ceasefire for all of Southeast Asia."

While Nixon volunteered the information that his announcement on the new troop withdrawal was "somewhat of an indication that we have not given up on the negotiating front," he made it clear that the United States would continue to use its air power in Indochina until a peace settlement was reached. This was part of the administration's basic strategy. He went on to say that if no settlement were obtained, the United States would maintain a "residual force" in Vietnam in order to retain leverage in negotiations for the release of the POWs and "to continue our role of leaving South Vietnam in a position where it will be able to defend itself from a Communist takeover." If there is no settlement, he added, "then we will have to go the other route, and we are prepared to do so."

Nixon's calculations were wrong. Hanoi decided it had no interest in pursuing the October 11 American peace plan. It never explained its reasons. On November 17, General Walters was handed a message that

Le Duc Tho was too ill to meet with Kissinger on the twentieth; when Washington proposed a meeting with another leader or even Xuan Thuy alone, there was no answer.

The best speculation as to the reasons for the North Vietnamese dismissal of the American overtures is that the Politburo had concluded that the stalemate had to be broken militarily in the field rather than diplomatically in Paris. Also, Hanoi evidently suspected the sincerity of the American proposal about the elections. Another consideration was that under the American proposal, an Indochina cease-fire and political settlement would be consigned to subsequent negotiations—*after* the agreement in principle. This was unacceptable to Hanoi because in the interim the United States would not only keep a residual force in Vietnam, but also retain its air power capability. And Hanoi saw no reason to deprive itself prematurely of *its* most important negotiating leverage: the American POWs. Furthermore, Hanoi's military commanders may well have decided that the battlefield situation favored them—as it had not since the 1968 Tet offensive.

Finally, it cannot be excluded that the parallel Politburo decision to mount a do-or-die offensive early in 1972 was motivated to an important degree by fear that Hanoi might be sold down the river by its Chinese and Russian fellow Communists in the name of détente. A successful blow against the ARVN would preempt whatever accommodation the Chinese or the Russians might have otherwise wished to work out with the United States over Vietnam.

In any event, the Nixon administration did not see what was coming. At his November 12 news conference, the president told his audience that "we want to see what the situation is in December and January, which . . . are the key months when infiltration comes along, because that will determine what the activity will be in April, May, June, and July on the battlefield." It was another intelligence failure: Hanoi was planning its "decisive military blow" for *late March.*

North Vietnam had been hit by severe floods at the end of the monsoon season, and Nixon went along with the assessment that Hanoi was at its weakest point since the war began. The president offered the opinion that "the major reason . . . is because of Cambodia and Laos, and the floods, of course, have hurt them, too."

The White House evidently listened to intelligence estimates prepared in Washington rather than to the reports from the field. This may have been due in part to Henry Kissinger's control of the flow of intelligence to the White House, but in any case the administration's relaxed posture was not for lack of information from the field. An NSC official with access to top-secret cable traffic from Saigon has said that "In December 1971, Bunker was sending warning cables to Washington on the Communist buildup, claiming that it was a lot bigger than it was thought at home. Yet the White House and the Defense Department continued to soft-pedal the situation, arguing that the South Vietnamese army . . . could handle the situation itself. Bunker and others were reporting colossal truck movements into truck parks in North Vietnam near the border of the demilitarized zone. . . . The NSC staff at the White House —not Henry but his staff—were advocating preemptive air strikes against these trucks, but the White House was not yet ready to do it."

With the Vietnam peace negotiations hopelessly deadlocked, the United Nations battle over Chinese representation became the last great diplomatic spectacular of 1971. And true to form, Nixon and Kissinger acted on parallel levels of open and private diplomacy—with a considerable infusion of cynicism. The People's Republic of China had made it abundantly clear to the United States and everybody else that it would not accept *any* U.N. seat unless the Nationalist regime on Taiwan was expelled from the organization.

If the General Assembly chose to admit it to membership—even to give it the Security Council seat—and allowed the Nationalists to remain in the assembly as another Chinese entity, Peking would stay away altogether. Huang Hua, then Chinese ambassador in Canada, told me in August, "We can wait outside for another year, for two years, or whatever it takes."

Nixon and Kissinger knew from the outset that the concept of two Chinas—the seating of both Chinese delegations in the General Assembly while conceding the Security Council to Peking—was an unworkable policy, but other political realities dictated the necessity of sticking to it as long as possible.

On the surface, it seemed that the Nixon administration was caught in an insoluble dilemma. But the truth was that no real dilemma existed. Almost as soon as Kissinger returned from Peking in July, he and the president decided to play the problem of Chinese representation as a diplomatic charade.

Still, there was a risk. Inasmuch as the State Department would be instructed to lobby heavily for the Nationalists, Kissinger could not rule out the possibility that the assembly might upset his secret diplomatic strategy and hand the United States a victory it did not really want. It would be rather difficult for Nixon to go to China as the successful architect of a policy that resulted in Peking's exclusion from the world organization for at least another year.

That there was a real link between the U.N. vote and Nixon's journey to China was demonstrated by the fact that Chou and Kissinger tacitly agreed that the announcement of the date for the trip would be held back until after the General Assembly's action. Finally, it was decided that Kissinger would return to Peking sometime in October to "prepare" the presidential visit. The unspoken assumption was that this would be the time of the U.N. vote; Kissinger along with Chou felt that it would be a good idea if he were in Peking during what could be a crisis in relations.

It is not clear whether the two State Department principals instructed to fight the diplomatic battle for Taiwan—Secretary Rogers and George Bush, who had become the United States Permanent Representative to the U.N. in February—were ever told by the president and Kissinger what the real policy was. But there are certainly valid reasons to suspect that they were kept totally in the dark. (Ray Cline, then the State Department's director of intelligence and research, later testified at a congressional hearing that Nixon and Kissinger actually "undermined" the department's efforts in 1971 to save Taiwan.)

It was not only the United Nations seat that was the subject of tacit understandings between Kissinger and Chou. The same applied to the even more complex question of future diplomatic ties. Chou had explained that, as a matter of principle, China could not establish full-fledged diplomatic relations with the United States so long as Washington went on recognizing the Nationalist regime. And when Kissinger told Chou that it was politically impossible for the Nixon administration to ditch Taiwan in the foreseeable future, the premier said he understood Nixon's problem. The two men concluded that Taiwan need not be an obstacle to the evolution of a Chinese-American relationship. A formula could be devised to skirt the issue for the time.

Huang Hua made this same basic point when I visited him on August 6. He told me that Peking would refrain from establishing normal diplomatic relations with Washington or engaging in significant trade until basic political and security problems between them were solved—but his government was ready to receive Nixon regardless of such problems. The solutions could be worked out later. He went so far as to hint that Nixon would be welcome in Peking even if China were unable to enter the United Nations in 1971.

Secretary Rogers had been expected to make a formal statement on the subject of Chinese representation around July 20, but he was delaying it in part because the Taiwan regime would not answer State Department inquiries as to how it would react to a "dual policy." On July 22, he conferred with Nixon at the White House, presumably to be instructed to move with full force in the campaign to save the Taiwan seat. Other officials were forbidden to discuss China policy with foreign diplomats and newsmen.

Finally, at a news conference on August 2, Rogers announced that the United States would support the seating of Peking in the U.N. but would continue to oppose Taiwan's expulsion. This marked the end of twenty years of the old U.S. China policy and the beginning of the Nixon-Kissinger diplomatic charade.

Rogers busied himself with the implementation of what he was led to believe constituted the "real" American policy. He told the news conference that the United States would insist that any expulsion move against Taiwan be considered "an important question," requiring a two-thirds majority in the General Assembly for a decision. A *simple* majority was required to establish that it *was* an "important question." This was the method the United States had used for years to keep out Peking; but in 1971 the first American objective was to win the preliminary vote. If it did, in the next vote Taiwan's foes would have to obtain 85 votes out of 127 —the two-thirds—to oust the Nationalists.

Uneasiness was spreading in Washington, New York, and foreign capitals about what the Americans were trying to do. Many governments simply could not believe that the United States was serious about having two Chinese delegations in the assembly: Peking had made it amply clear that it had to be an all-or-nothing decision, and Taiwan was hinting strongly that it would walk out of the assembly before it could be actually expelled. Senior American officials, not privy to Nixon's secret strategy but able to count potential votes, began telling friendly newsmen that it was entirely possible that the United States would be defeated in the U.N. "This is a real cliff-hanger," a State Department official said in mid-August. "Nobody will know until the moment the votes are cast which way it will go."

On August 20, the United States made its first formal move by submitting as an agenda item for the General Assembly its proposal to seat both Chinese delegations. Albania and seventeen other countries had already submitted a resolution calling for Peking's seating and Taiwan's expulsion. The question was which of these two agenda items the General Assembly would take up first. If it chose to act first on the Albanian resolution, the United States would automatically be defeated because it would no longer be able to invoke the "important question" provision. Otherwise, the State Department would still have a fighting chance. But it was strange that the United States had waited until the last moment to submit its agenda item; the deadline was thirty days before the opening of the General Assembly session.

Having submitted their agenda item so late, the Americans were just as inexplicably dragging their heels about drafting the actual "dual policy" resolution on which they wanted the assembly to vote. There was still no text by September 1, and the United States was having trouble finding cosponsors for it. George Bush, the chief delegate, had conferred in quest of support with ninety-four delegations in less than a month. As a fellow diplomat put it, "It was a quantitative track record," but the results were unpromising. In dozens of foreign capitals, American ambassadors were calling on host governments to obtain backing for the "dual policy." The United States was "calling in all its IOUs," as an official put it, but even its closest friends remained confused.

On September 9, Japan's Foreign Minister Takeo Fukuda arrived in Washington for general talks with Nixon and Rogers. Extraordinary confusion developed over whether Japan would, as had been expected, join the United States in cosponsoring the resolution. Rogers and Fukuda literally had difficulty understanding each other because of deficient English-Japanese interpretation in their talks. But Fukuda did get across the idea that the Japanese government was reluctant to join the United States. Nixon had a long private talk with him on the evening of September 10, but it remained unclear what Tokyo would do in the end.

On September 16, five days before the General Assembly was to convene in New York, Nixon announced at a hastily convoked news conference that the United States would vote to seat Peking in the Security Council as well as in the assembly because "it reflects the realities of the situation." But, he added, the United States opposed Taiwan's expulsion from the assembly. Washington had been noncommittal about the Security Council seat, but now it had to act in order to get "respectable" cosponsorship: Japan, Australia, New Zealand, and others had refused to go along with the "dual representation" in the General Assembly unless Peking got the place in the Security Council. It appeared that Nixon was paying a price to keep Taiwan in the assembly—perhaps this helped to convince the world that he was pulling out all the stops for the Nationalists—but, in truth, he had weakened the State Department's official position. With the Security Council seat already promised to Peking, "dual representation" in the assembly was senseless. And the president and Kissinger knew it.

The General Assembly opened on September 21. From morning until evening, visiting foreign ministers shuttled through Rogers's suite on the thirty-fifth floor of the Waldorf Towers, and twice a day State Department spokesmen issued something akin to war communiqués on the progress of the campaign. ("Yes, Burundi is with us. . . . About Argentina we're not sure. . . .") George Bush and his aides were working just as hard on scores of U.N. delegations.

On September 23, Nixon told the Economic Club in Detroit that he did not think the sudden political upheaval in China would affect his travel plans to the mainland. He was referring to the mysterious fact that, starting September 12, without any explanation, all military flights and most commercial flights in China had been suspended. Intelligence and diplomatic reports filtering out of Peking spoke of Chinese troop movements and strange political activities. This was the beginning of a series of events that resulted in the downfall of Defense Minister Lin Piao, Mao Tse-tung's designated successor. A few weeks later, the world was told that Lin Piao had died in Soviet Mongolia in the crash of a jet airliner aboard which he was fleeing China after the failure of a coup he had attempted against Mao. Many China experts thought that Lin Piao was trying to force Mao to drop his (and Chou's) policies of rapprochement with the United States; unable to change the policy, it now appeared, Lin Piao had tried to stage a coup. The Soviet Union was perhaps involved in the Lin Piao conspiracy—this would explain his aborted escape to Soviet territory.

At the General Assembly, meanwhile, the United States was fighting its losing battle to preserve Taiwan's seat. Whatever support Rogers and Bush had been able to marshal in past weeks was eroding quickly. Argentina, Ecuador, and Mexico were lost at the beginning of October, joining the pro-Peking Latin American bloc that was headed by Peru, Cuba, and Chile. Most of the West European countries, many of which had diplomatic relations with Peking, had opposed the American resolution all along. So had most Asians, the majority of Arabs, and quite a few Africans. The Americans could now count only on a hard core of supporters in Latin America, the Pacific (including Japan), and Africa.

The sense of alarm among American delegates was demonstrated when State Department officials called in reporters to complain that their articles about impending defections from the United States position were undermining the whole strategy. "When an uncommitted delegate reads in *The New York Times* that we've lost this or that vote, he may well be influenced by it and advise his government to hop on the bandwagon," a senior State Department official told me one day. By October 6, Panama was lost and it appeared that Spain and Venezuela would follow. The Algerians, Romanians, and Yugoslavs—the most active campaigners on Peking's behalf—seemed to be picking up new votes every day. The long-awaited debate on Chinese representation was to open on October 18; Nixon, holding a news conference in Washington on the twelfth, completely ignored the subject, and made no appeal for support for Taiwan. As far as the White House was concerned, the United Nations issue concerning China was as good as settled.

On October 16, Kissinger left Washington for Peking to work out the date for the president's visit. He arrived in Peking on the morning of October 20 as the General Assembly debate in New York was in its third day.

At 9:47 p.m. on Monday, October 25, the General Assembly defeated the United States resolution to keep the Nationalists in—exactly as Nixon and Kissinger had known all along it would. Fifty-nine countries had voted against the United States and only 54 for it. (There were 15 abstentions.)

The next vote, 90 minutes later, was taken on the Albanian resolution to seat Peking and to expel Taiwan from the United Nations. It was approved by 76 votes to 35. Now the United States was free to vote for Peking's admission and Bush did so. Nationalist China's delegate, Liu Chieh, and his three advisers, ashen-faced, gathered their papers, got up from their seats, and quietly left the huge hall. Their departure was hardly noticed, as Peking's supporters joined in a victory jig below the rostrum.

On October 26, Peking time, Henry Kissinger left for home after a final meeting with Premier Chou. It was only hours after the United Nations vote. The last potential obstacle to Nixon's journey to China had been removed. On November 12, the Peking delegation to the U.N. arrived in New York. It came almost as an anticlimax when Washington and Peking issued a joint announcement on November 29 that the president's visit to China would begin on February 21, 1972. Nixon did not even bother to announce it personally, leaving the thirty-one-word statement to his press secretary. The diplomatic process of rapprochement with China had been completed in four and a half months.

Small wonder that the president felt a keen sense of pride as he met with the West's top leaders—Pompidou, Heath, Trudeau, and Brandt—

during December to discuss policies for the coming year. He had won worldwide recognition as a masterful conductor of foreign policy, and he basked in this glory. Vietnam was the only dark cloud on the horizon, but the president was confident that he could bring the war to an end—on his terms—in the course of 1972. He saw the new year as the crowning one in what he was pleased to call "the emerging structure of peace"— and 1972 would be an election year, too.

BOOK FOUR

1972

The Year of Détente

Chapter 19

Throughout 1972, Richard Nixon conducted United States foreign policy with an extraordinary blend of military and diplomatic contradictions. Responding to a North Vietnamese offensive, he ordered an awesome escalation of the air war lasting most of the year, climaxing in bombings of Hanoi and Haiphong, and the mining of North Vietnamese waters. But, at the same time, he kept withdrawing American ground troops from South Vietnam. And, the war notwithstanding, the détente with Peking and Moscow was proceeding apace, culminating in Nixon's historic trips to the two Communist capitals.

From the outset of the year, the spotlight was on Vietnam. Acting on Nixon's personal orders, the United States had resumed heavy bombings of North Vietnam just before Christmas 1971. This was in retaliation for the growing North Vietnamese buildup, which the president had been ignoring for months. Another reason for the renewed bombings was the North Vietnamese shelling of Saigon and other South Vietnamese cities during December, an action that, the Americans believed, violated the 1968 Paris "understanding." Then, in mid-January, Nixon suddenly announced ahead of his own schedule, a new withdrawal of American troops from Vietnam, cutting United States forces there down to the bone. In a television interview with Dan Rather of CBS on January 2, he had discussed the reasons for the resumption of the bombings of North Vietnam. Recalling his remarks in November when he had announced the 45,000-man withdrawal from the South, he said:

> At that time, I said that in the event that the enemy stepped up its infiltration, or engaged in other activities which imperiled, in my opinion, our remaining forces as our forces become less, that I would take action to deal with the situation. . . . The enemy did step up its infiltration. They violated the understanding of 1968, when the bombing halt was agreed to, with regard to firing on our unarmed recon-

naissance planes. They shelled Saigon on December 19. Under those circumstances, I had no other choice but to bomb, in this case, selected military targets and supply buildup areas. Those were the only areas that were hit. The results have been very, very effective, and I think that their effectiveness will be demonstrated by the statement I am now going to make. Before the first of February . . . I will make another withdrawal announcement. . . .

Whether or not Nixon was being candid with the interviewer, or even with himself, the bombings, heavy as they were, could not have done away with the massive North Vietnamese buildup. The history of the war showed that air strikes against the infiltration routes and Communist staging areas had only limited impact on North Vietnamese activities and preparations. For Nixon to claim that these latest bombings had been "very, very effective" suggested either that he was being fed deficient intelligence or that he had a political objective in mind.

The political objective might have been the need to justify the new withdrawals he was planning to announce in February. In the first place, Nixon had to maintain the rate of withdrawals for domestic reasons: it was an election year. Second, he and Kissinger believed that withdrawals might make Hanoi more amenable to an acceptable diplomatic settlement. The president evidently reasoned that the December bombings were sufficient warning to the North Vietnamese to refrain from major mischief in 1972. And he did not want to travel to China in the midst of significant military operations in Vietnam.

But Nixon was trapping himself further in the Vietnam situation. He had to bomb as a short-term signal to Hanoi, but he had to keep withdrawing because of the political pressures. Hence his claim of the effectiveness of the air strikes. What the president did not realize was the extent to which Hanoi was building up for a major thrust against the South. He knew from intelligence reports that, as 1972 opened, there was not a single full-fledged North Vietnamese division *operating* in South Vietnam. Hanoi had pulled back its big regular units to reorganize them, but the United States did not guess the intentions of the North Vietnamese. The resumed infiltration, as far as Washington was concerned, did not necessarily foreshadow a big-scale offensive; the North Vietnamese infiltrated every year during the dry season.

Nixon also told Rather that the POW issue was becoming central in American policy in Vietnam: "If the POWs are still retained by North Vietnam, in order to have any bargaining position at all with the North Vietnamese, we will have to continue to retain a residual force in Vietnam, and we will have to continue the possibility of air strikes on the North Vietnamese." The president informed Rather that he had raised the POW question with Soviet Foreign Minister Gromyko, and Kissinger had raised it with Chou En-lai on both his visits to Peking. He added he would raise it himself with Soviet and Chinese leaders during his visits to the Communist capitals. But Nixon was underestimating the degree to which Hanoi had come to depend on the POWs as its ultimate negotiating card.

On January 13, without any elaboration, Nixon announced that 70,-000 more American troops would be repatriated from Vietnam over the next three months. This, he said in a three-paragraph statement, "means that our troop ceiling by May 1 will be down to 69,000." Another announcement on withdrawals, he added, would be made before May 1. There were no new warnings to Hanoi about what the United States might do if the North Vietnamese took advantage of it. The president must have been supremely confident that Hanoi would not challenge him despite all the reports about its military buildup.

A week later, on January 20, Nixon went to Congress to deliver his annual State of the Union address. On Vietnam, he confined himself to generalities though he used the speech to warn the country of the danger of isolationism as a reaction to the Indochina involvement:

> It is my hope that we can end this tragic conflict through negotiation. If we cannot, then we will end it through Vietnamization. But end it we shall—in a way which fulfills our commitment to the people of South Vietnam. . . . The American people have learned many lessons in the wake of Vietnam—some helpful and some dangerous. One important lesson is that we can best serve our own interests in the world by setting realistic limits on what we try to accomplish unilaterally. . . . At the same time, to conclude that the United States should now withdraw from all or most of its international responsibilities would be to make a dangerous error. There has been a tendency among some to swing from one extreme to the other in the wake of Vietnam, from wanting to do too much in the world to wanting to do too little. We must resist this temptation to over-react. We must stop the swinging pendulum before it moves to an opposite position, and forge instead an attitude toward the world which is balanced and sensible and realistic.

Unaware of Hanoi's military plans, the president and Kissinger remained perplexed by the North Vietnamese refusal to keep up the secret peace talks. This was damaging to Nixon not only diplomatically—he had

announced two troop withdrawals since presenting the October proposals and Hanoi was simply not responding—but politically as well. Public
opinion, ignorant of the secret May, August, and October proposals, was
attacking him for his failure to respond to the peace plan put forth
publicly by the Viet Cong the previous July.

In an election year, this was an untenable situation, and Nixon finally
decided to "go public." The idea of revealing the secret negotiations had
been under consideration in the White House from late in November,
when Hanoi invoked Le Duc Tho's illness to avoid a new meeting with
Kissinger. An NSC aide recalled, "Henry had talked about it on many
occasions for months. The notion was that Nixon would have to go public
with this news for the sake of the American public, for American reasons.
This was what we called 'theater' at the White House. The president was
being criticized for not doing enough to achieve peace in Vietnam. Now
it was January, it was an election year, and a policy decision was finally
made."

It was evidently not sufficient to disclose the history of the secret
negotiations. To make his statement more positive, Nixon decided simultaneously to make public the highlights of his October 11 plan, though
with some minor modifications. But he did not identify it as such—
making it appear, instead, that he was presenting a brand-new proposal
on behalf of the United States and South Vietnam. On television on the
evening of January 25, the president said he was presenting "a plan for
peace that can end the war in Vietnam," a plan, he said, that was "both
generous and far-reaching. It is a plan to end the war now; it includes an
offer to withdraw all American forces within *six* months of an agreement
[the October plan had referred to seven months]; its acceptance would
mean the speedy return of all the prisoners of war to their homes" (italics
added). Giving the impression that he was unveiling a fresh set of proposals, he proceeded to tick off all the other ingredients of the October
document: new elections in Vietnam, Thieu's resignation beforehand,
the creation of "an independent body to organize and run the election,
representing all political forces in South Vietnam, including the National
Liberation Front," and international supervision of the cease-fire and the
elections. He added that in a separate offer made the previous July, the
United States had indicated its willingness to "undertake a major reconstruction program throughout Indochina, including North Vietnam, to
help all these people recover from the ravages of a generation of war."

But the president's *coup de théâtre* was the disclosure that his secret
negotiations with Hanoi had been going on for two and a half years. This

was his bombshell answer to the criticism that he was remiss in his efforts to end the war. And he added that his decision to end the long secrecy was also based on his desire to "try to break the deadlock in the negotiations. . . . It is my judgment that the purposes of peace will best be served by bringing out publicly the proposals we have been making in private."

This was the president's account of the secret talks:

> Early in this administration, after ten months of no progress in the public Paris talks, I became convinced that it was necessary to explore the possibility of negotiating in private channels, to see whether it would be possible to end the public deadlock. . . . With the full knowledge and approval of President Thieu, I sent Dr. Kissinger to Paris as my personal representative on August 4, 1969, thirty months ago, to begin these secret negotiations. Since that time, Dr. Kissinger has traveled to Paris twelve times on these secret missions. He has met seven times with Le Duc Tho, one of Hanoi's top political leaders, and Minister Xuan Thuy, head of the North Vietnamese delegation to the Paris talks, and he has met with Minister Xuan Thuy five times alone. . . . This is why I initiated these private negotiations: Privately, both sides can be more flexible in offering new approaches and also private discussions allow both sides to talk frankly, to take positions free from the pressure of public debate. . . . For thirty months, whenever Secretary Rogers, Dr. Kissinger, or I were asked about secret negotiations we would only say we were pursuing every possible channel in our search for peace. There was never a leak, because we were determined not to jeopardize the secret negotiations. Until recently, this course showed signs of yielding some progress.

"Going public," however, did not do away with secret diplomacy. Within twenty-four hours of Nixon's speech, the White House sent a private message to Hanoi indicating readiness to resume secret talks.

Politically, Nixon's announcement of the "new" peace plan and his disclosure of Kissinger's secret travels was a masterful coup. He was able to silence, at least for a time, an important segment of his domestic opposition and to put Hanoi on the spot in terms of the peace negotiations. It *was* a fact that the administration had made more diplomatic efforts toward a settlement than was generally suspected—although the plausibility of the 1971 proposals, except for the October 11 package, was debatable—and it *was* a fact that, in effect, North Vietnam had stonewalled the United States at least since October.

But if the president's move had a measurable impact at home, it had none in Hanoi. The North Vietnamese had already made other plans. It was three weeks before they bothered to reply to the January 26 message proposing the resumption of secret Paris talks.

Even as Nixon spoke in Washington, fresh North Vietnamese divisions and at least six Viet Cong divisions were being massed just north of the demilitarized zone in preparation for a major offensive. This, however, seemingly went unnoticed by American intelligence, which assumed that the Communists would strike from the west, from the Ho Chi Minh Trail staging areas, as they usually did. And to be sure, infiltrations along the trail complex were mounting considerably: between October and late January, some 120,000 troops had moved down from the North, about 30,000 more than in the comparable period the previous year.

That a major offensive would occur in early 1972 was now, belatedly, being taken for granted in Washington. Administration officials, privately briefing newsmen, were saying that this was one reason Nixon had "gone public" on January 25 with the new peace plan and the story of the secret negotiations. Partly because intelligence reports said that Communist political officers were telling their troops that "decisive blows" must be dealt against the Americans and the South Vietnamese during Nixon's China visit, preparations were made for a counteroffensive during February. These included unpublicized strikes against North Vietnamese military targets by planes of the Saigon-based Seventh Air Force. (The Seventh was commanded by Lieutenant General John D. Lavelle, who was later accused of flying "unauthorized" missions against the North; subsequently, a great deal of evidence was developed to show that Lavelle was acting with the knowledge of the Pentagon. But having made his peace pronouncement and getting ready to go to Peking, Nixon did not wish to have American air strikes in North Vietnam known at that point.) On January 30, Defense Secretary Laird predicted that the North Vietnamese "will try to have several spectaculars this year, probably sometime in February, and undoubtedly again this summer and sometime before the presidential elections here in the United States." John Paul Vann, the senior American military adviser in Military Region II and probably the best-informed American in Vietnam, said on the same day that "It is absolutely certain that an offensive will take place. There isn't any question as to what the enemy's intentions are." Vann (later killed in a helicopter crash) added that the North Vietnamese might be prepared to accept 100,000 killed to achieve their political objectives.

But the North Vietnamese were not yet militarily ready to launch their offensive in February. Politically, the judgment in Hanoi was that it might unnecessarily embarrass Peking if an assault started while Nixon was in China. The North Vietnamese, their basic plans made, were in no hurry.

They were waiting for the optimum moment.

On the diplomatic front, Hanoi was also showing its toughness, evidently unimpressed by the Nixon speech. On February 5, Xuan Thuy made a point of questioning the accuracy of Nixon's account of the secret negotiations. And he declared that American POWs would be released *only* when the United States had withdrawn its support from the Thieu government and the war was brought to an end. Even if the United States set a deadline for the total withdrawal of its forces, this would no longer be sufficient to obtain the prisoners' release. The only negotiable issue, it was clear, was President Thieu's removal. Earlier Communist proposals no longer stood, Xuan Thuy said; "You should realize the difference of the conditions in 1971 and the present conditions in 1972. . . . After the October elections in South Vietnam, the Vietnamese people understood still more clearly that Mr. Nixon's words and deeds do not match."

With a total diplomatic deadlock in Paris and the threat of an imminent North Vietnamese offensive, the president prepared to undertake his journey to China.

To Nixon, the Chinese trip fitted into the concept of the double détente—with the ancillary hope that this travel would also help in a quick settlement of the Vietnam war. And he did not want the Russians to misunderstand his intentions in Peking. In his annual report to Congress on foreign policy on February 9—this year it was titled "The Emerging Structure of Peace"—the president insisted that the new China policy was "not aimed against Moscow" and that "there is no reason" for America's progress in normalizing relations with Peking "to jeopardize our relations with its Communist rival." He noted that the United States had "consistently explained to all parties" that to use the new opening to China to exploit Sino-Soviet tensions "would be self-defeating and dangerous."

The next day, February 10, Nixon held a news conference to discuss in detail his forthcoming China trip—and the Vietnam situation. As part of his preparations for the journey, he said, he had invited André Malraux, the former French minister of culture and an old acquaintance of Mao Tse-tung, to come to the White House later in the week to advise him on the Chinese. Nixon recalled that while visiting de Gaulle in Paris in 1969, he had discussed China with Malraux, and "I was particularly impressed with his analysis of the leaders." Now, he added, he had read Malraux's *Anti-Memoirs* (which contains a long section on Malraux's conversations with Mao and Chou in 1965), and he commended it to the newsmen "not only for what it tells about China and its leaders, but also about France, its problems, and the whole World War II and post–World War II era."

It was a very Nixonian touch to invite Malraux to Washington, and to have read the *Anti-Memoirs*. (The last time Malraux had come to Washington was on Kennedy's invitation to show the Mona Lisa.) But it was also very Nixonian to spoil the effect of it all by relating it immediately to self-praise of his homework:

> I give you this only to indicate the breadth of the kind of briefings that all of us who are going to participate in the talks are trying to undertake. . . . Here it is essential to do an enormous amount of homework just to come up to the starting line. I don't want to say that after having read as much as I have, and as much as I will be reading between now and the time we arrive, that I will be an expert, but at least I will be familiar with the men that we will be meeting and the problems that may be discussed.

(Malraux's advice to Nixon was not exactly practical. The writer proposed a "Marshall Plan for China," which to set in motion, he remarked with high emotion, was "an element of the United States destiny." But this was not what Nixon had in mind, and the Chinese surely were not expecting, if indeed they wanted, billions of American dollars.)

A newsman asked Nixon whether he regarded the meetings with the Chinese "as dialogue or negotiation." The president used this opportunity to deliver a capsule lecture on diplomacy:

> They will be primarily dialogue. Here a very subtle but definite distinction is made between the talks that will take place in Peking and the talks that will take place in Moscow. In the talks in Moscow there are certain subjects that we have been negotiating about and those subjects, therefore, will be negotiated, although, of course, there will be dialogue as well. Dialogue is an essential part of negotiation. In the case of Peking, there will necessarily have to be a substantial amount of dialogue before we can come to the point of negotiating on substantive matters.

But Vietnam remained very much on Nixon's mind. And he showed anger with the critics of the latest peace proposals—particularly the candidates for the Democratic nomination. Grimly, he said, "There is, in my view, a very great difference between criticizing policies that got us into war and . . . criticisms by a presidential candidate of a policy to end the war and to bring peace."

Even as he spoke, the Saigon command was announcing more than one thousand sorties by B-52s and air force and navy fighter-bombers against Communist troop concentrations at the confluence of the South Vietnamese, Cambodian, and Laotian borders; also one hundred twenty-five sorties against North Vietnamese artillery north of the demilitarized zone.

Yet there were *some* indications either that Hanoi had not yet fully made up its mind about launching its offensive or at least that it was trying to keep the United States off balance during the final preparations.

On February 14, General Walters in Paris relayed to the White House a secret message from the North Vietnamese that they would be agreeable to resuming secret talks with Kissinger anytime after March 15. Nixon and Kissinger assumed that this was an answer to their communication of January 26, and mulled it over for three days. In the end, they decided that nothing would be lost by continuing the diplomacy. On the morning of the day the president left for China, General Walters was instructed to inform the North Vietnamese that March 20 would be a suitable date for a new meeting in Paris. This exchange was never made public.

On the morning of February 17, Richard Nixon left for China. Never before had a presidential trip been prepared so meticulously. Nixon and his staff overlooked nothing. The departure from the White House was a full-fledged state occasion, complete with an honor guard, the vice president and the cabinet, congressional leaders, some eight thousand "well-wishers" drawn from the federal work force and from public schools in the capital and the Virginia and Maryland suburbs. A red carpet led to the helicopter that the Nixons took to Andrews Air Force Base to board *Air Force One*. Usually, presidential departures were less spectacular: just the cabinet and diplomats saying quiet good-byes at Andrews. But this time was different. The Chinese had agreed to install satellite ground stations near Peking so that the president's activities could be carried live on color television back to the United States. Though Nixon disclaimed any relation between his foreign policy and the reelection campaign, the panoply of his "journey for peace" and the planned saturation coverage of his China "first" in the media could not be lost on the voters. The final touch was a last-minute decision to take along Mrs. Nixon's personal hairdresser on *Air Force One*.

Diplomatically also, the president took precautions. Nixon instructed two senior officials with his party to fly to Tokyo and other Asian capitals as soon as the mainland visit was completed to brief allied governments on his talks with the Chinese. The State Department disclosed these instructions the day before the president left Washington.

The twenty-thousand-mile flight to China was leisurely, as Nixon wanted to be fully rested on his arrival in Peking. The first stop was Hawaii, where the Nixons, the Rogerses, and Kissinger spent forty-six hours at the residence of the commander of the First Marine Brigade. Then there was an overnight rest in Guam. At 10:00 a.m., local time, Monday, February 21, *Air Force One* landed in Shanghai to refuel and take on Chinese navigators. Nixon stayed aboard the plane, not alighting on Chinese soil.

It was 11:40 a.m. in Peking when the president arrived; his landing was carried live to the United States by television satellite (at 10:40 p.m. in the Eastern time zone, an excellent viewing time). An honor guard of the People's Liberation Army was on hand, and Premier Chou En-lai was on the tarmac to greet Nixon and the ranking members of his entourage. There were no crowds at the airport, none along the route to the city, and none in the downtown streets as the motorcade sped to the government guest house where the Nixons would be staying. Television watchers at home may have found this a bit disappointing.

Within the hour, Nixon and Kissinger were invited for an immediate session with Chairman Mao. (Rogers was specifically excluded, despite his rank. The Chinese wanted to deal only with the real principals.) The president had expected to be received by Mao, but the Chinese had never hinted that this would be done instantly on his arrival. It was the highest seal of approval for the nascent relationship: all China would understand it the next day, when news of the Mao-Nixon meeting appeared prominently on the front page of *People's Daily*. (Nixon rated three page-one pictures.)

Mao, accompanied by Chou En-lai, received Nixon and Kissinger in the library of his small house in the Forbidden City; since the president had read Malraux's detailed description of his conversation with Mao, studied other reports, seen innumerable photographs of the seventy-eight-year-old chairman, there was a certain familiarity about the occasion. Mao could be warm, human, witty, and wistful—yet totally in political command of the situation without making his guests aware of it. He had a much clearer, more instinctive vision of what could and should be China's relationship with the United States than what Nixon carried in his briefing book. The president was superbly prepared for the encounter, but during the ninety-minute talk (half of which was consumed in translation), the president found himself deferring to the chairman. Nixon emerged with a feeling that it had been for the most part a formal and ceremonial occasion, a *tour d'horizon* rather than a negotiation. Mao reminisced about his own past, made allusions to history, and just perceptibly, touched on topics ranging from the Indochina war to Taiwan, Japan, and Russia's "hegemony" policies. As Ziegler said later, Nixon spent the time doing what he always did when he first met a foreign leader: measuring Mao's human strength and intellect. But in so doing, he missed much of the substantive subtlety that the chairman was conveying.

Many years later, in a television interview, Nixon talked about his meeting: "As far as the Chinese Communists are concerned, once you put your case on the basis of just peace or friendship, first they consider you to be a fool and second they consider you to be wrong. Because they constantly talk about struggle. They're still Communists . . . and they will continue to be Communists. . . . [Mao] considered himself to be a Communist who was true to the doctrines of the original gospel, Marx and Lenin. He was like an early Christian basically. . . . He considered the Russians, on the other hand, to be deviationists."

Kissinger, who after his two earlier meetings with Chou En-lai had more insight into Chinese thinking and a better intellectual rapport with them, was also taken in by Mao. As he subsequently told the Kalbs, only when he studied the transcript of the Mao-Nixon discussion a few weeks later, did he realize that the chairman had outlined the Shanghai communiqué (the document that capped the presidential visit) in the course of that *first* conversation. Another senior American diplomat who accompanied Nixon to Peking found that Mao's position was both consistent and flexible. "They long considered that the Vietnam war was the most urgent major problem between us," he said, "but they understood that it had to run its course. They wanted assurances that the United States was keen on winding down the war, and Nixon gave these assurances. It was more important than what was said in the communiqué about Taiwan. There is no question that Taiwan remained a fundamental problem, but the Chinese found a way of moving ahead with our bilateral relations without worrying about the immediate legal aspects. . . . Chairman Mao and Chou think big, and in general, they don't allow legal complications to stand in the way of political realities. The Chinese weren't floggers. They would discuss [Vietnam] very thoroughly and meticulously, they would state their position unequivocally, but they didn't flog. They are not hagglers, and they do think more in the context of principles."

The five days the president spent in Peking were devoted to intense private negotiations, public events, and sightseeing. After his meeting

with Mao, Nixon held a brief initial conference with Chou En-lai at the
Great Hall of the People. The president was accompanied by Kissinger,
two NSC senior advisers (John Holdridge and Winston Lord), and a State
Department interpreter; Chou sat with an aide and an interpreter. Following a short rest, the Nixons and the entire American party, including
newsmen went back to the Great Hall of the People for a banquet.

Televised live to the United States, the banquet was the first great
public event marking Nixon's visit. It was Chinese cuisine at its' most
splendiferous. A Chinese Army band played American tunes for the
visitors: "America the Beautiful" and "Home on the Range" were among
the selections. Then, shortly after 8:30 p.m., Premier Chou rose to offer
a toast to

> Mr. President and Mrs. Nixon, ladies and gentlemen, comrades and
> friends. The American people are a great people. The Chinese people
> are a great people. The peoples of our two countries have always been
> friendly to each other. But owing to reasons known to all, contacts
> between the two peoples were suspended for over twenty years. Now,
> through the common efforts of China and the United States, the gate
> to friendly contacts has finally been opened. At the present time it has
> become a strong desire of the Chinese and American peoples to
> promote the normalization of relations between the two countries and
> work for the relaxation of tension. The people, and the people alone,
> are the motive force in the making of world history. We are confident
> that the day will surely come when this common desire of our two
> peoples will be realized. The social systems of China and the United
> States are fundamentally different, and there exist great differences
> between the Chinese Government and the United States Government.
> However, these differences should not hinder China and the United
> States from establishing normal state relations on the basis of the Five
> Principles of mutual respect for sovereignty and territorial integrity,
> mutual nonaggression, noninterference in each other's internal
> affairs, equality and mutual benefit, and peaceful coexistence; still less
> should they lead to war. As early as 1955, the Chinese Government
> publicly stated that the Chinese people do not want to have a war with
> the United States and that the Chinese Government is willing to sit
> down and enter into negotiations with the United States Government.
> This is a policy which we have pursued consistently.

Chou could not resist the gentle reminder that China had been willing
to negotiate with the Americans from the very outset. Nixon rose to reply
to the premier's toast:

> At this very moment, through the wonder of telecommunications, *more
> people are seeing and hearing what we say than on any other such occasion in*

the whole history of the world. Yet, what we say here will not be long remembered. What we can do here can change the world. . . . If our two peoples are enemies, the future of this world we share together is dark indeed. But if we can find common ground to work together, the chance for world peace is immeasurably increased. . . . We have at times in the past been enemies. We have great differences today. What brings us together is that we have common interests which transcend those differences. As we discuss our differences, neither of us will compromise our principles. But while we cannot close the gulf between us, we can try to bridge it so that we may be able to talk across it [italics added].

Nixon became exhilarated as he went on reading the text of his toast, which had been drafted with the most extraordinary care. It was decided that the president would oratorically identify the United States with Mao's early struggles: hence the summons to start "a long march" together though along different roads leading to peace. And Nixon picked up the rhythm of Mao's abrupt phrases: "The world watches. The world listens. The world waits to see what we will do." Then the president quoted Mao directly: "So many deeds cry out to be done, and always urgently. The world rolls on. Time passes. Ten thousand years are too long. Seize the day, seize the hour." And on his own, Nixon added: "This is the hour, this is the day for our two peoples to rise to the heights of greatness which can build a new and a better world."

The president raised a tumbler of *mao tai*, the Chinese firewater, and touched Chou En-lai's glass in salute. Then he moved through the vast hall toasting his Chinese hosts individually in *mao tai*.

The next four days in Peking were spent in point-by-point negotiations over the communiqué to be issued at the end of Nixon's visit. The communiqué was crucial because it created the framework for the new Chinese-American relationship, and all future diplomacy would be based on the understandings—not necessarily agreements—in it. Instead of negotiating specific agreements, they concentrated on defining areas of understanding and clarifying positions. The two sides were dealing with political realities that are more elusive than precise legalisms. Neither the Americans nor the Chinese wanted to be bound by legalisms—on Taiwan, Vietnam, or any other topic—and this made their task more complex. It was one of the great contemporary exercises in flexible diplomacy.

The diplomatic technique, too, was intricate. Nixon and Chou were the principal interlocutors on the main issues. Then, working separately, Kissinger and Deputy Foreign Minister Chiao Kuan-hua, one of China's best professional diplomats, strove to reduce these understandings to communiqué language. Chiao, who had studied in Germany in his youth, spoke fluent German, which helped. Rogers and Foreign Minister Chi Peng-fei worked at a secondary level concerning specific bilateral arrangements.

On Tuesday and Wednesday, February 22 and 23, Nixon and Chou were able to outline their understandings on such issues as Vietnam, Korea, Japan, and the Indian subcontinent. But Kissinger and Chiao had increasing difficulties in putting it all down on paper. While the two drafters struggled with this problem, Nixon and Chou reached on Thursday, February 24, a deadlock over Taiwan. It was not a matter of legalisms: here principles were involved and neither side could yield. Nixon began wondering if there would be any communiqué at all. Then, after another big banquet on Friday evening, Chou and Chiao drove with Kissinger to a nearby suite of conference rooms for a final negotiation. (Earlier in the day, Nixon and Chou had hit upon the idea of producing a two-part communiqué: one section reflecting American views, and the other, Chinese views. This was one of many inventive solutions that emerged in Peking—but it was still necessary to draft the two segments in a mutually acceptable fashion.) They spent an hour discussing a fresh Chinese proposal on how the Taiwan parts of the communiqué should be drafted. Kissinger thought he liked Chou's idea, but he needed Nixon's clearance. While the Chinese waited, Kissinger returned to the president's quarters to consult with him. Rogers, who together with Marshall Green had been unhappy over proposed texts of the Taiwan paragraphs, was chatting with Nixon. It was now well past midnight. Rogers, in his only major involvement in the main negotiations, pressed Nixon to adopt wording about Taiwan that would make clear that the United States was not "dropping" the Nationalists. Nixon mulled it over and agreed. Kissinger went back to the conference table.

Chou was not unreasonable about the changes proposed by the Americans. An hour or so later, the premier retired, leaving Kissinger and Chiao to produce the final draft. Several times during the night, Kissinger excused himself to telephone Nixon for instructions. At 5:00 a.m., with the night's wintry darkness still over Peking, the draft was completed.

In midmorning—it now was Saturday, February 26—the Americans and the Chinese gathered at the Peking airport for a flight to Hangchow, the famously beautiful city where Chairman Mao had a villa. Before boarding the Chinese Airlines Soviet-built jet, Nixon and Chou spent nearly an hour going over the product of Kissinger's and Chiao's nocturnal work. They continued conferring during much of the two-and-a-half-hour flight, with Kissinger, Rogers, and Chiao in attendance. The president added some thoughts of his own. Before the plane landed, Nixon and Chou reached final agreement on the communiqué. It had been a heroic diplomatic enterprise; now Nixon and Chou relaxed.

The day in Hangchow was pure rest. The Nixons were taken on a tour of the West Lake, and in the evening, a banquet at the Hangchow Hotel was given by Nan P'ing, chairman of the Chekiang Province Revolutionary Committee. There was an air of informality, and Nan's and Nixon's toasts were brief and apolitical. But the president was not invited to take leave of Mao, as he had hoped. The next morning, the presidential party and the Chinese flew to Shanghai, Nixon's last stop on the mainland.

(The housing arrangements in the Shanghai Mansions, where the Americans were staying, symbolized the status of different members of the delegation. The Nixons were on the fifteenth floor, Kissinger on the fourteenth, and Rogers, Green, and other State Department officials on the thirteenth. In the afternoon, Premier Chou visited Rogers for forty minutes—as if to make amends for the secretary's exclusion from the meeting with Mao.)

The only serious piece of business in Shanghai was the publication of the Nixon-Chou communiqué, and a press briefing for American reporters by Kissinger and Green to explain what it all meant. The president spent his time visiting an industrial exhibition, then met alone with Green to give him his "marching orders" on how Asian leaders were to be briefed on the China talks. These briefings were Green's mission for the next ten days.

One of the important points Nixon wanted conveyed to the Japanese was that China appeared to have, as a senior official put it, "a tolerant view of the Japanese-American mutual-security treaty, that the nuclear umbrella we provided to Japan was perhaps the best assurance that Japan would not have to go its own nuclear route. . . . The Chinese hadn't said any of these things, but it was sort of implicit in their position, and we felt that there was enough we'd gotten from the talks in Peking so that we could say it to the Asian leaders. We could tell them that China didn't want the United States to pull rapidly out of Asia, that China doesn't want to destroy the United States–Japanese relationship, but that she wants the Vietnam war to come to an end. . . . The Chinese didn't want the destruction of our relationship with Japan because, for one thing, this would probably mean the development of a Japanese nuclear capability. The second reason was that the United States might be all the more constrained to pull rapidly out of the Western Pacific and East Asia. . . . And China is trying to contain the Soviet Union, and wants to have a strong United States and Japan on one flank as well as a strong Western Europe on the other flank in order to do that."

The communiqué separated all other issues from the question of Taiwan, which was addressed alone in the second section of the document. And in the first section, the American position was set forth separately from the Chinese position.

Nixon declared that "peace in Asia and peace in the world requires efforts both to reduce immediate tensions and to eliminate the basic causes of conflict." The American statement went on: "The United States supports individual freedom and social progress for all the peoples of the world, free of outside pressure or intervention." More specifically, it stressed that the Indochinese people "should be allowed to determine their destiny without outside intervention," adding that America's "constant primary objective has been a negotiated solution [to the war]." The January peace proposal "represents the basis for the attainment" of a settlement, but "in the absence of a negotiated settlement the United States envisages the ultimate withdrawal of all U.S. forces from the region consistent with the aim of self-determination for each country of Indochina." This broke no new ground, but it was significant that the Chinese were willing to accept it in a joint communiqué.

On South Korea, the "U.S. side" declared that it would "maintain its close ties with and support for" the Seoul government, and promised to support South Korean efforts "to seek a relaxation of tension and increased communication in the Korean peninsula."

American-Japanese relations were a highly sensitive point, but one sentence sufficed to express the policy: "The United States places the highest value on its friendly relations with Japan; it will continue to develop the existing close bonds." And on the Indo-Pakistani dispute, a subject of intense interest to China, the statement said the United States favored "the continuation of the ceasefire" of December 1971, and "the withdrawal of all military forces to within their own territories and to their own sides of the ceasefire line in Jammu and Kashmir." In a sentence that pleased the Chinese enormously, Nixon said that "the United States supports the right of the peoples of South Asia to shape their own future in peace, free of military threat, and without having the area become the subject of great power rivalry."

The "Chinese side" was much more outspoken and ideological in its opening comments but rather moderate on the substantive points. The preamble used classic Mao rhetoric:

Wherever there is oppression, there is resistance. Countries want independence, nations want liberation and the people want revolution—this has become the irresistible trend of history. All nations, big or small, should be equal: big nations should not bully the weak. China will never be a superpower and it opposes hegemony and power politics of any kind. . . . It firmly supports the struggles of all the oppressed people and nations for freedom and liberation. . . . The people of all countries have the right to choose their own social systems according to their own wishes and the right to safeguard the independence, sovereignty and territorial integrity of their own countries and oppose foreign aggression, interference, control and subversion. All foreign troops should be withdrawn to their own countries.

This opposition to "hegemony" and "foreign aggression, interference, control and subversion" was clearly addressed to the Soviet Union ("hegemony" is the word Peking routinely applies to Soviet policies), and this was fine with the Americans.

On Indochina, the Chinese statement expressed "firm support to the peoples of Vietnam, Laos, and Cambodia in their efforts for the attainment of their goal." It said nothing about the American presence in Indochina, confining itself to the "firm support" of the seven-point peace proposal made by the Provisional Revolutionary Government (Viet Cong) in Paris in July 1971, and the "Joint Declaration of the Summit Conference of the Indochinese Peoples" (a document emanating from a 1970 meeting on Chinese territory of revolutionary Indochinese leaders, right after the Cambodian invasion). Concerning Korea, the Chinese expressed their backing for a 1971 North Korean program for "the peaceful unification" of the peninsula and for the abolition of the moribund United Nations commission on Korea.

On Japan, China "firmly opposes the revival and outward expansion of Japanese militarism and firmly supports the Japanese people's desire to build an independent, democratic, peaceful and neutral Japan."

There was a certain irony, of which the Chinese were probably unaware, about this passage. Just about the time when Kissinger made his first secret trip to Peking, Defense Secretary Laird was in Tokyo guardedly discussing with Japanese leaders the possibility of developing a Japanese nuclear-defense capability for the 1980s. Japan had not yet signed the nuclear-nonproliferation treaty, and the Pentagon was trying to persuade Tokyo to moderate its inflexible stand on atomic weapons. The Pentagon's reasoning was based on the Chinese nuclear threat and the possibility that a Soviet-American SALT agreement might reduce United States nuclear capabilities in the Pacific, thus creating a strategic vacuum. Laird's idea was that Japan should work on a ship-borne nuclear ABM defensive system and develop nuclear depth charges against enemy submarines under a "two-key" arrangement with the United States. Several American correspondents in Tokyo, notably Selig Harrison in *The Washington Post,* reported the general thrust of Laird's suggestions, and despite the correctness of these reports (or because of it), the Nixon administration indignantly denied them. But it was the president's trip to Peking and his tacit understanding with the Chinese about the Japanese-American security pact and the American "nuclear umbrella" that probably helped to put these Pentagon notions to rest. Japan eventually both signed and ratified the nonproliferation treaty.

The "Chinese side" agreed with the Americans that India and Pakistan should pull back to their own territories, but it said nothing about the need to continue the cease-fire, and added that China "firmly supports" Pakistan in the "struggle to preserve . . . independence and sovereignty" and the "people of Jammu and Kashmir in their struggle for the right of self-determination." (The latter point was aimed at India, which had been occupying most of disputed Kashmir since the 1947 partition.)

The communiqué next took up the question of Sino-American relations. It declared that the two sides had agreed to conduct their relations on the basis of the "principles of respect for the sovereignty and territorial integrity of all states, non-interference in the internal affairs of other states, equality and mutual benefit, and peaceful coexistence." It was rather extraordinary that these were almost literally the "Five Principles" that Chou En-lai had proposed at the Bandung Conference in 1955, and that the United States would not even consider then.

Last, the communiqué took up the thorny Taiwan issue. This time the Peking view was set forth ahead of the American one:

> The Taiwan question is the crucial question obstructing the normalization of relations between China and the United States; the Government of the People's Republic of China is the sole legal government of China; Taiwan is a province of China which has long been returned to the motherland; the liberation of Taiwan is China's internal affair in which no other country has the right to interfere; and all U.S. forces and military installations must be withdrawn from Taiwan. The Chinese Government firmly opposes any activities which aim at the creation of "one China, one Taiwan," "one China, two governments," "two Chinas," an "independent Taiwan" or advocate that "the status of Taiwan remains to be determined."

This wholly unequivocal statement offered no compromise, left no legal or political loopholes, and made it absolutely clear that Peking would not enter into formal diplomatic relations with the United States so long as Washington continued to recognize the existence of the Nationalist regime. Of course, Nixon and Kissinger expected this. The point was that this gulf between the two governments *could* be bridged diplomatically; it was a matter of flexible diplomacy and goodwill.

In his formal statement, Nixon went as far as he could. He accepted, in effect, the concept of one China, with Taiwan as part of it—quite a step from the American stance at the United Nations four months earlier—but he refused to abandon Taiwan altogether. He promised, without a due date, a gradual withdrawal of American forces from Taiwan.

> The United States acknowledges that all Chinese on either side of the Taiwan Strait maintain there is but one China and that Taiwan is a part of China. The United States Government does not challenge that position. It reaffirms its interest in a peaceful settlement of the Taiwan question by the Chinese themselves. With this prospect in mind, it affirms the ultimate objective of the withdrawal of all U.S. forces and military installations from Taiwan. In the meantime, it will progressively reduce its forces and military installations on Taiwan as the tension in the area diminishes.

As diplomatists (Sir Harold Nicolson's word for scholars of diplomacy) will readily recognize, this was a masterpiece of drafting, an oeuvre of which Henry Kissinger could be rightly proud. It did not contradict Peking's claim on Taiwan, but did not affirm it. Most important, it removed the United States from a partisan position over the legitimacy of opposing Communist and Nationalist claims as to Taiwan's status. It left it up to the two Chinese sides to make the best of the existing situation: to coexist across the Taiwan Strait or to find a "peaceful" solution. And mindful that Peking did not wish Taiwan's status to be left to future determination by others, Kissinger simply sidestepped this particular point. Last, he tied the rate of American withdrawals from Taiwan to the ending of the Vietnam war. The Chinese were being told subtly that the sooner the Vietnam war ended, the sooner United States military installations on Taiwan would be closed down.

The final section of the communiqué—and it seemed as if both sides breathed a sigh of relief after disposing of the Taiwan question—was highly positive. It described agreement on broadening contacts in "people-to-people" exchanges and improving relationships in bilateral trade, science, technology, sports, and journalism. It disclosed that Nixon and Chou had made arrangements for the two governments to "stay in contact" through "various channels, including the sending of a senior U.S. representative to Peking from time to time for concrete consultations to further the normalization of relations." This meant more Kissinger visits to Peking.

Henceforth there would be no need for third-country channels. (Not announced in Shanghai, but decided by Nixon and Chou, was that the new permanent channel would be the American and Chinese embassies in Paris.) Time had not quite yet come for the exchange of formal diplomatic missions in Peking and Washington, but the Chinese liked Kissinger's idea of establishing "liaison missions."

The farewells were said in Shanghai at a banquet on the evening of February 27, marking the end of President Nixon's stay in China. The host was Chang Ch'un-ch'iao, chairman of the Shanghai Municipal Revolutionary Committee, but Premier Chou En-lai was prominently in attendance, as befitted the coarchitect of the new entente with the United States.

> We people of Shanghai [said Chang], like the people throughout our country, welcome this positive action which conforms to the common desires of the peoples of China and the United States. And we are glad that it is in Shanghai today that we have reached agreement on the joint communiqué after the discussions which took place over the past few days.

Nixon spoke at greater length. Exuberantly, he opened with the classic Nixon touch: "We have been here a week. This was the week that changed the world." Nobody seemed to mind the presidential overstatement, and Nixon (who later said that Chou had told him, "Our meeting will shake the world") continued in a somewhat more realistic vein:

> The joint communiqué . . . will make headlines around the world tomorrow. But what we have said in that communiqué is not nearly as important as what we will do in the years ahead to build a bridge across 16,000 miles and twenty-two years of hostility which have divided us in the past. What we have said today is that we shall build that bridge. And because the Chinese people and the American people, as the Prime Minister has said, are a great people, we can build that bridge. To do so requires more than the letters, the words of the communiqué. The letters and the words are a beginning, but the actions that follow must be in the spirit which characterized our talks. . . . Our communiqué indicates, as it should, some areas of differences.

It also indicates some areas of agreement. . . . Our two peoples tonight hold the future of the world in our hands. . . . If we succeed in working together where we can find common ground, if we can find the common ground on which we can both stand, where we can build the bridge between us and build a new world, generations in the years ahead will look back and thank us for this meeting that we have held in the past week.

The next morning, the Nixons and the large American party boarded their jetliners for the long flight home. The president was joyful: he had carried off one of the greatest postwar diplomatic coups. The week in China had not exactly "changed the world," but it unquestionably created major changes in the world power configuration. And Nixon left China with another very special Chinese gift: the promise of a pair of pandas—Ling Ling and Hsing Hsing—for the National Zoo in Washington.

Air Force One touched down at Andrews Air Force Base outside Washington at 9:00 p.m. on February 28, twenty-five hours after it left Shanghai. (This time there was only one refueling stop en route—in Alaska.) Nixon received a conquering hero's welcome, every second of it nationally televised, with Agnew, the cabinet, congressional leaders, and the diplomatic corps on hand to greet him. The president said:

In the last thirty years, Americans have in three different wars gone off by the hundreds of thousands to fight, and some to die, in Asia and the Pacific. One of the central motives behind my journey to China was to prevent that from happening a fourth time to another generation of Americans. . . . Peace means more than the mere absence of war. In a technical sense, we were at peace with the People's Republic of China before this trip, but a gulf of almost 12,000 miles [the distance had shrunk by 4,000 miles since the Shanghai speech the day before] and twenty-two years of noncommunication and hostility separated the United States of America from the 750 million people who live in the People's Republic of China, and that is one-fourth of all the people in the world. As a result of this trip, we have started the long process of building a bridge across that gulf, and even now we have something better than the mere absence of war. . . . We have set up a procedure whereby we can continue to have discussions in the future. We have demonstrated that nations with very deep and fundamental differences can learn to discuss those differences calmly, rationally, and frankly, without compromising their principles.

Inevitably, the China journey produced an immense diplomatic fallout. As Kissinger remarked to a group of newsmen two days after his return, all nations now had a new "option on the future." And it meant different things to different governments.

To Japan, this "option" was a serious problem. The administration was conscious of the fact that since the announcement of Nixon's China trip the previous July, the Japanese were forced to look for a variety of new policies in terms of their Asian relationships. It took for granted that before long Tokyo would establish its own relationships with Peking, as would other Asian nations. But in the meantime, Japan's actions were highly irritating to Washington. First, ignoring confidential American diplomatic demarches, the Japanese Foreign Office dispatched two of its department chiefs to Hanoi on February 8, two weeks before Nixon's arrival in Peking. Originally, the plan was for the two officials to visit North Vietnam *during* the president's China trip, but the State Department succeeded in persuading Japan to change the timing. A Japanese gesture to Hanoi, the first one of this kind, would be highly embarrassing to the United States just as the president was going to Peking and the North Vietnamese were preparing a major offensive in the South.

On February 24, Japan unexpectedly established diplomatic relations with Outer Mongolia, a country that, for all practical purposes, is a Soviet province in Asia abutting China. This was done without consulting with the United States, a rather unsubtle response to the "Nixon shocks." A month earlier, Soviet Foreign Minister Gromyko had visited Tokyo although the Russians and the Japanese still had not signed a peace treaty after World War II. The consensus in Washington was that Japan, in the wake of the Nixon expedition to China, had decided to embark on annoyingly independent foreign policies. The recognition of Outer Mongolia came four days before Marshall Green and John Holdridge, the presidential emissaries, were due in Tokyo to brief Japanese leaders on the Peking talks.

(That Taiwan would be furious over the Nixon trip and the Shanghai communiqué had been fully anticipated. Not surprisingly, Taipei took exception to Nixon's commitment in the communiqué to withdraw American forces from the island gradually. Rogers had to hold a special briefing on March 2 for Ambassador Shen to assure him that the United States remained committed to the 1954 defense treaty with Taiwan. And the State Department said in a special statement that the American commitment to the Nationalists "is not in question and never has been in question." But the department made a point of noting that 6000 of the 8200 men on the island "relate directly and uniquely" to Southeast Asia, supporting the Vietnam war logistics.)

But Peking, too, had to mend its fences in Asia. On March 3, Premier Chou went to Hanoi for two days of discussions with the North Vietnamese leadership. (His visit was not officially announced: Washington learned of it from intelligence and diplomatic sources.) The assumption was that Chou was reassuring the North Vietnamese that no deal had been struck with the Americans behind their back. It was too much to hope that he would try to dissuade them from launching their offensive.

Cambodia's exiled Prince Sihanouk sat out the Nixon visit to China in Hanoi. Returning to Peking on March 9, he issued a statement that the president had "unsuccessfully" sought to have China act as an intermediary in Indochina. On this point as on all others concerning Nixon-Chou discussions about Indochina, the White House refused all comment.

On March 10, the White House announced that the United States and China had designated their ambassadors in Paris to serve as a direct diplomatic channel. The personalities of the new Chinese-American interlocutors could not have been more different. Arthur K. Watson was a millionaire and former chairman of the board of the International Business Machines' World Trade Corporation. His opposite number, Huang Chen, an ideological playwright, had accompanied Mao on the Long March to Yenan, and was the only Chinese ambassador to hold a seat on the Central Committee of the Chinese Communist Party.

Eager to translate the Peking agreements into deeds, the administration acted on March 13 to issue the first export licenses for mainland China in twenty-one years. They covered $2.2 million for the sale of a satellite-communications–transmitting station (the one brought to Peking in February to help in the television coverage of the Nixon visit) and additional television equipment.

In terms of domestic politics, the president was satisfied that the China journey had been a clear plus. The television and press coverage made him appear a man of peace—a very relevant consideration at a time when the Vietnam war remained stalemated and he could not be certain of a settlement before the elections. And on the conservative side, no noticeable damage was done, although some right-wing commentators and congressmen denounced the China journey and criticized Nixon for clinking glasses with Chou En-lai. The old China Lobby had been defunct for a long time; politically, the conservatives had to stick with the Republican Party. (In fact, when Nixon briefed the cabinet the morning after his return from Shanghai, Transportation Secretary John Volpe volunteered the information that the China journey had helped the president in the New Hampshire primary earlier in the month.) Even before Nixon went to China, right-wing reaction was discounted by the White House. William Safire quoted Kissinger as saying, "Any argument we hear from Taiwan, they'll get from North Vietnam. Any argument we get from Japan, they'll get infinitely more from the Soviet Union. When we think of our right-wing reaction, think of their left-wing reaction."

Still, the president found it necessary to keep justifying his China journey. He, Kissinger, and Rogers did it quite forcefully at the cabinet briefing even though the president concentrated on describing his talks with Mao and Chou and on philosophical remarks about the meaning of the new relationship. Safire, who took notes during this briefing, quoted Nixon as relating that "there was plenty of tough and straight talk. Tough, but elegant and courteous in terms of tone on both sides. But in our private conversations we can discuss these great differences in a civilized tone—there is a chance you can find that glimmer of a hope of common ground."

The China journey had been an extraordinary triumph for Nixon—just as he had planned. As he told his cabinet, "This was an experience which perhaps will not be exceeded in my lifetime."

Chapter 20

No sooner did the president step back into the Oval Office than the problems of Vietnam—contradictory and disconcerting—claimed his attention. On the one hand, Hanoi was continuing its military buildup north of the demilitarized zone and infiltration down the Ho Chi Minh Trail; on the other, it was inviting a renewal of diplomacy.

On February 29, the day after Nixon's return, a message from North Vietnam accepted March 20 as the date for the resumption of the Kissinger–Le Duc Tho negotiations. The president and Kissinger were cautiously optimistic. But even though Nixon had "gone public" in January with the story of the secret negotiations, he decided to say nothing now —not even to his cabinet.

Then something went awry in Hanoi. On March 6, the North Vietnamese, without giving any reason, asked that the March 20 meeting be postponed until April 15. This, however, did not alarm the White House, for the North Vietnamese had lulled the administration into a false sense of security, and intelligence reports from the field were increasingly confusing. False optimism was compounded when Sir Robert Thompson assured Kissinger on March 7, after completing his latest secret mission to Vietnam, that the ARVN would be able to handle internal security after United States troops were reduced to 69,000 men on May 1.

On March 8, therefore, the White House calmly informed Hanoi through the Walters channel in Paris that April 24 would be a better date because Kissinger was expected in Tokyo on April 15. There was no immediate reply, but the White House remained unconcerned. The North Vietnamese always took their time.

Meanwhile, the administration turned to other concerns. The SALT negotiations in Helsinki were entering a crucial period with the approach of Nixon's trip to the Soviet Union; the president was keen on signing a strategic-arms agreement during his Moscow visit. Kissinger's time was consumed in drafting instructions to the SALT delegation and having discussions with Soviet Ambassador Dobrynin. On March 14, Nixon sent a special message to Congress requesting authorization for foreign security assistance programs for fiscal year 1973 totaling $2.15 billion. And on March 21, he received Turkey's Prime Minister Nihat Erim at the White House for conferences and a state dinner, an occasion Nixon used to stress that the United States was not forgetting its NATO allies; he also assured Erim that the United States would support Turkey's program for modernizing her armed forces.

But Nixon and Kissinger were beginning to worry again about Vietnam. On Kissinger's advice, Nixon on March 23 instructed Ambassador Porter, the chief American delegate in Paris, to suspend the weekly semipublic peace talks with the North Vietnamese and the PRG delegations. The judgment was that Hanoi *did* want to resume negotiations but wanted a more favorable psychological environment—hence the foot-dragging—and suspending the semipublic talks would force it to the secret negotiating table.

On March 31, Good Friday, a message from General Walters reached Kissinger at his White House office. It contained the long-awaited North Vietnamese reply: Hanoi would accept April 24 as the date for the next secret negotiating session so long as the United States was willing to resume the semipublic meetings beforehand. Kissinger informed the president, and they decided to advise Hanoi that the weekly meetings would resume on April 13 and that Kissinger would be in Paris on the twenty-fourth. It was late afternoon in Washington—and early dawn of Saturday, April 1, in Vietnam—when Kissinger finished drafting his message.

Just then, word was flashed from Saigon through military communications that Communist forces had launched, at first light, a series of attacks across the demilitarized zone and over Vietnam's western borders from Laotian and Cambodian sanctuaries. Reading the first reports, Nixon and Kissinger were not sure that this was a full-fledged offensive. They could not understand why the North Vietnamese had sent an acceptance of an April date for resumed secret talks almost simultaneously with an offensive, if that was what it was. The White House did nothing further that Friday afternoon, pending developments.

In Vietnam, those developments were swift and lethal. The ARVN was being mauled.

A number of elements formed the overall North Vietnamese strategy. Unlike in the 1968 Tet offensive, or even in 1970 or 1971, the ARVN could no longer count on American ground support: there were only

95,000 United States troops left in Vietnam, and only 6000 of them qualified as combat units. The North Vietnamese generals had concluded that a sustained offensive, massively engaging tank-led main force units, would break the ARVN's back even if the United States provided heavy tactical air support. Articles published in April and May 1972 in *Tap Chi Quan Doi Nhan Dan* (People's Army Review) further explained that the strategy was to capture as much territory as possible, so as to demoralize Thieu's army and tie down the best ARVN divisions along three or four major battlefronts; guerrilla warfare could then erupt again behind the lines and pacification be disrupted, which in turn, would increase Viet Cong influence in villages heretofore controlled by Saigon. As Gareth Porter has written, the offensive "was planned both in order to have the greatest impact on American policy by heavily damaging ARVN's main force divisions and to contribute to a substantive change in the military-political balance of forces in South Vietnam."

If this happened, Hanoi planners reasoned, the United States would be impelled to negotiate on North Vietnamese terms to avoid a total catastrophe. Besides, Hanoi was convinced that Nixon absolutely needed a peace settlement before the November elections. (Contrary to what American analysts believed, the North Vietnamese never contemplated occupying district or provincial capitals for the sole purpose of setting up the PRG's headquarters on South Vietnamese territory. They were playing for bigger stakes.)

Theoretically—and even militarily—the Hanoi plan was sound. But it suffered from these three fundamental political flaws: first, it was a wrong assumption that Nixon would refrain from applying maximal air power to North Vietnam; second, Hanoi misjudged Peking's and Moscow's interest in détente, and their probable reactions to a violent American response; and third, it was a mistake to think that Nixon was determined to have a peace settlement *at any cost* before the elections.

General Vo Nguyen Giap, the North Vietnamese defense minister and the 1954 victor at Dienbienphu, again engineered a textbook offensive operation, one that professors at St. Cyr would have applauded. It consisted of simultaneous thrusts in the north, the west, and the southwest —and an additional diversionary action in the south, in the Mekong Delta. Giap committed 12 fresh divisions (6 well-trained and combat-wise regular North Vietnamese divisions and 6 Viet Cong divisions, the latter less experienced but reinforced with North Vietnamese fillers) to his offensive, in addition to the veteran North Vietnamese division that had been in the South all along. This gave him roughly 200,000 men, plus tens of thousands of Viet Cong irregulars who were infiltrated in areas ostensibly controlled by the Saigon government. This force was formed into a conventional army spearheaded by columns of Soviet-built tanks and disposing of considerable artillery, mortar, and recoilless-rifle firepower besides the normal complement of infantry automatic weapons. As he did at Dienbienphu eighteen years earlier, Giap applied the classic Soviet doctrine of overpowering tank and artillery firepower to open the way for waves of foot soldiers. He used no tactical air cover because North Vietnam had no meaningful air force; Giap did not believe that aircraft were really necessary in the Vietnamese terrain. The Americans had lost more than 3000 aircraft over Vietnam in less than ten years with little to show for it, and the North Vietnamese were unimpressed by the use of tactical air cover. Giap had no helicopters either, but his units were much more mobile on the ground than the Americans or the ARVN. He did have, however, antiaircraft artillery battalions, including SAM batteries, to protect his forces from air strikes.

What Giap was taking on was a South Vietnamese army that, according to its organization table, had 1 million men plus tens of thousands of half-trained regional and local defense forces. The ARVN was also supported by United States and South Vietnamese tactical air forces, and Giap knew that the Americans would quickly engage their heavy bombers for strategic strikes against his forces and, most likely, against key targets in North Vietnam. The American textbook view, as General Abrams had told Nixon a week earlier, was that the Communists simply could not break the South Vietnamese lines. This was a terrible error.

General Abrams's other error was that he had assumed that an offensive by the North Vietnamese, if it came, would aim only at the narrow waist of central Vietnam east from their sanctuaries in order to cut the country in two and then swing upward to isolate the northern part of South Vietnam. Despite intelligence reports about the massing of troops north of the demilitarized zone, Abrams never really thought the brunt of the attack would come from there. As for the ARVN, it was totally dependent on Abrams's judgments. In the spring of 1972, the blind was leading the lame.

The North Vietnamese struck first in the north across the DMZ. After the ARVN defense lines had been softened with a heavy artillery barrage —Giap was faithful to the Soviet doctrine that had worked so well at Dienbienphu—a crack North Vietnamese division penetrated into South Vietnam and quickly destroyed the ARVN's 3d Division, on which Thieu depended to defend the frontier. The division's 56th Regiment defected to the North Vietnamese, who also captured 110 heavy artillery pieces at the firebases along the defensive line. Simultaneously, other North Vietnamese forces began moving out of the Cambodian sanctuaries in the west.

The U.S. government was taken completely aback by the offensive, especially by the fact that the initial thrust came over the DMZ. During Saturday, April 1, there was a sense of uncertainty in Washington as to what was really happening. Abrams's dispatches were less than helpful; he, too, seemed to have trouble understanding the situation. By evening (the morning of April 2 in Vietnam), however, enough bad news had come through to cause considerable concern.

Led by tanks, North Vietnamese regiments attacked the Central Highlands from the west in Military Region II, South Vietnam's narrow waist, aiming at the Pleiku and Kontum population centers. This—but this alone—had been expected by Abrams. Still, the ARVN's 22d Division was unable to hold off the assault and began retreating. Then Giap pulled another surprise. From the Parrot's Beak area in Cambodia, his troops fanned out against Saigon's outer defensive perimeter. One of their objectives was An Loc, 60 miles north of Saigon; the other was Phuoc Long Province, southwest of Saigon and just above the Mekong Delta. The North Vietnamese onslaught was generalized.

Only on Easter Sunday, April 2, did Kissinger (as he admitted later) and the president realize that Saigon was facing a full-scale offensive and that the North Vietnamese were "going for broke" to smash the ARVN before a peace settlement. After several meetings with the president, Kissinger sent a message to General Walters in Paris for urgent delivery to the North Vietnamese there. He said rather plaintively, "The United States side has been showing great restraint in its response in order to give the negotiations every chance to succeed." Confused by the events of the past forty-eight hours, the Americans had not yet decided how and where to retaliate. Kissinger, hoping against hope, had sent the message to signal to the North Vietnamese that the diplomatic track remained open if they suspended military operations.

On Monday, April 3, however, the White House had to face reality. Kissinger, as his aides recalled, became panicky, fearing that the ARVN would collapse. Tactical support by American aircraft for the South Vietnamese forces seemed to make little difference. Nixon received a special daily intelligence report, full of operational details, to keep him abreast of the situation. Also on Monday, Kissinger called the first of what would be almost daily meetings of WASAG. The Pentagon was represented by

Admiral Moorer, the chairman of the Joint Chiefs of Staff, and Deputy Defense Secretary David Packard. The State Department sent Under Secretary for Political Affairs U. Alexis Johnson and Deputy Assistant Secretary for Far Eastern Affairs William Sullivan, the department's principal Indochina expert, who also headed an interdepartmental task force on Vietnam. The CIA was represented by Helms. Top officers from the staff of the Joint Chiefs and NSC staffers were also in attendance. But nothing was decided at the first meeting.

On April 4, WASAG resolved that American air power had to be engaged fully against North Vietnam if the increasingly worrisome offensive was to be halted, or at least discouraged. Nixon readily ratified this decision. There was no other way to act: the unthinkable thought that Vietnamization had failed was beginning to dawn on Kissinger. Nixon, still disposed to listen to Abrams's insistent optimism, had not yet given up on Vietnamization, but he was all in favor of new bombings of North Vietnam. The ARVN had to be assisted, and the president took his usual view that he had to protect the safety of Americans still in Vietnam. And the battlefield situation was becoming grim: the North Vietnamese had penetrated northernmost Quang Tri Province and were advancing on the city of Quang Tri. In the southwest, the North Vietnamese had taken most of Binh Long Province, badly pummeling the ARVN 5th Division, and reaching the outskirts of Loc Ninh, the province's capital.

The Pentagon began to activate a huge air armada. B-52 jet bombers based on Guam and at Utapao in Thailand were ordered to stand by for strike missions. Additional B-52s were flown from the United States to Thailand to beef up the bomber strength. In all, the United States had on hand about 170 of the eight-engine B-52s for the planned missions, 340 air force fighter-bombers (most of them based at Utapao and at Da Nang in northern South Vietnam), and close to 450 navy attack planes from the 6 aircraft carriers on "Yankee Station" in the Tonkin Gulf. This added up to nearly 1000 warplanes in addition to some 500 fighters and fighter-bombers flown by the South Vietnamese. On the morning of April 4, after the WASAG meeting, a Pentagon spokesman, using standard Nixon phraseology, announced that the United States would take "whatever steps are necessary to protect remaining U.S. forces in South Vietnam."

But a major diplomatic problem loomed. The problem was the Soviet Union, and it had two aspects. Nixon was to go to Moscow on May 22, and the eruption of full-fledged hostilities in Vietnam was throwing a monkey wrench into these plans.

How would Moscow react to American retaliation, particularly if it became necessary to go into carpet bombing in the North, hitting targets such as Hanoi and Haiphong? The point had not yet been reached where such raids were required, and the WASAG consensus was that the Russians would not make a major issue of limited aerial action. But Nixon made it clear to his advisers that if he concluded that North Vietnam should be subjected to massive bombing, he would do it no matter what the Soviet reaction—even if the May summit had to be postponed. The second aspect was that the United States could not simply ignore the extent of Soviet support for Hanoi. The Communist offensive could not have been launched without ample supplies of Soviet armor, artillery, and other advanced equipment. This made the Soviet Union an accomplice in the assault that was beginning to threaten the survival of the Thieu regime. How did one publicly register American displeasure with Soviet collusion in the North Vietnamese offensive without, at the same time, creating such tensions with Moscow as to render the May summit impossible? The compromise decision was to issue low-key complaints through State Department spokesmen—the White House wanted to be left out of the picture—so that Moscow would get the point but would not be placed in an impossible diplomatic position. Accordingly, the State Department confined itself on April 4 to a simple statement that the Russians were delivering arms to Hanoi in the context of the offensive. But onrushing events made it impossible for the administration to keep a low profile for long.

On April 5, the North Vietnamese captured Loc Ninh, the capital of Binh Long Province. The ARVN 5th Division, defending Tay Ninh Province and the key town of An Loc, began to come apart. Fleeing South Vietnamese soldiers left behind a number of tanks and artillery pieces in Loc Ninh. In the north, the invaders were moving deep into Quang Tri Province. Saigon commanders were beginning to worry about the safety of Hue, the ancient capital city south of Quang Tri. On April 6, Admiral Moorer pointedly told a press lunch that Soviet tanks and artillery in Vietnam were a "new factor" in the war.

Also on April 6, American fighter-bombers raided military targets 60 miles north of the demilitarized zone. The strikes were announced publicly, and Moorer told his audience that United States aircraft would "inch northward" farther and farther if the Communists kept up the offensive. On April 7, Defense Secretary Laird remarked that Soviet military assistance was "critical" inasmuch as it accounted for more than 80 percent of the modern weapons in the hands of the attacking North Vietnamese.

On April 8, a Saturday, there was more bad news. General Abrams and Ambassador Bunker had finally concluded that Hanoi was embarked on an all-out effort to destroy the Saigon regime. They jointly signed a telegram to the White House predicting that the offensive could go on for months. They recommended heavy American air and naval involvement in the fighting if the Communist attacks were to be blunted.

Nixon was spending the weekend at Key Biscayne when the Abrams-Bunker telegram reached Kissinger in Washington. (Despite the gravity of the Vietnam situation, the president had chosen to maintain his normal schedule. On the day American warplanes first struck north of the DMZ, he had been in Philadelphia to deliver a speech before the annual convention of the National Catholic Education Association; he had spent Friday, April 7, relaxing with his friends, though keeping in constant touch with developments; and on Saturday, he had started the working day with a short speech praising two Miami Customs Patrol officers for seizing twenty-two pounds of heroin worth $5 million on the retail market.)

Now he instantly ordered B-52 raids against military targets in North Vietnam. It was the first time since November 1968 that the heavy bombers went to work over the North. (All previous raids under the Nixon administration had been flown by fighter-bombers.) The war was escalating. And the president wanted political action as well. During lunch, he decided that he should deliver a major speech within the next forty-eight hours to warn Hanoi of the consequences of its offensive.

Though the president had in mind a clear warning to Hanoi that American air power would be used in the South and the North until the offensive stopped, he did not want to burn all diplomatic bridges to North Vietnam. He told Kissinger: "The private thing—we must think about our real interest in having private negotiations and we should not say anything that would really have an effect of torpedoing it—hint at it maybe—we are prepared to negotiate publicly or privately *but not at the point of a gun.*"

William Safire and Winston Lord drafted the speech during Sunday, April 9, as Nixon was returning from Key Biscayne. The president read it in the evening and, without giving any reason, changed his mind about delivering it. He must have decided that the initial bombings had already made the point and that big-power diplomacy must be given another chance. On Monday, as B-52 bombers struck at the North Vietnamese port of Vinh, 150 miles north of the DMZ, in the deepest penetration yet, the president chose to address himself to the Soviet Union. The occasion was a ceremony at the State Department for the signing of the biological-weapons convention, with Soviet Ambassador Dobrynin in attendance along with other foreign diplomats. In a brief speech, Nixon remarked that "each nation in the world must renounce the use of force, the use of aggression against other nations." Then, in a passage meant for Dobrynin's benefit, he said: "We must also recognize another proposition, and that is that a great responsibility particularly rests upon the great powers, that every great power must follow the principle that it should not encourage directly or indirectly any other nation to use force or armed aggression against one of its neighbors."

Yet it is most unlikely that Nixon really expected the North Vietnamese to halt their offensive or the Soviet Union to suspend deliveries of military hardware to Hanoi.

The obvious next step was to expand the air war to Hanoi and Haiphong. Still, it took WASAG three days to agree on a recommendation to Nixon to do so. Actually, the internal administration debate took place on a higher level than Kissinger's crisis-management panel: it involved key members of the cabinet and the military establishment. Kissinger, Moorer, and the Joint Chiefs of Staff favored B-52 strikes against Hanoi and Haiphong, principally for military reasons. They believed that sustained bombings of the North had a good chance of forcing the Communists to reconsider the wisdom of their actions in the South. For Kissinger, it was his old belief that a "fourth-rate industrial power" like North Vietnam could not take such punishment. (He later claimed that his reason for advocating the bombings was his desire to send a "signal" to the Russians that the May meeting might be endangered if they kept assisting the North Vietnamese, but this is not wholly credible. Moscow was not so unsubtle as to require heavy bombings of North Vietnam to understand the objectives of American diplomacy. But, then, Kissinger was also concerned with his personal historical record, with the result that he often seemed to be on both sides of an issue.)

Rogers and Laird, on the other hand, were consistent. They had opposed the 1970 Cambodian invasion on common-sensical and political grounds; now they objected to the proposed bombings for the same reasons. This was not the first time the Pentagon was split between the views espoused by Laird and those held by the uniformed chiefs. Helms was noncommittal, largely confining himself to intelligence presentations, although the CIA, faithful to its traditional estimates, was not convinced that B-52 raids would turn the tide of war.

This left Nixon the final arbiter. He heard all the arguments on Wednesday, April 12, then withdrew in the evening to the hideaway in the Executive Office Building. Presently, he advised Kissinger that he was authorizing bomber strikes on Hanoi and Haiphong for Saturday, April 15, and Sunday, April 16, to see whether that would bring the desired results. He left open the possibility that the raids would be limited to that weekend alone. The Joint Chiefs were told to proceed with "Freedom Porch Bravo," the code designation for the air operation.

With this decision, the president flew to Ottawa on the afternoon of Thursday, April 13, for a scheduled two-day Canadian visit, returning Prime Minister Trudeau's trip to Washington the previous December. Although Nixon and Trudeau discussed the Vietnam situation in private, there was not a single reference to it in the president's public statements. It was as if the war had suddenly vanished. Actually, one reason the raids against Hanoi and Haiphong were held off until April 15—they could have started within hours of Nixon's decision on the twelfth—was that he did not want to be visiting Canada, where antiwar sentiment was strong, during the bombings.

The president was back in Washington on April 15, even as the B-52s prepared to hit North Vietnam in force, in time to preside over a state dinner at the White House for the ambassadors to the Organization of American States. He delivered a speech about the special relationship between the United States and Latin America, but again he refrained from any mention of Vietnam.

Hanoi and Haiphong were severely bombed over the weekend of April 15–16, and again on the seventeenth. In the port of Haiphong, four Soviet merchantmen were slightly damaged, leading to a *pro forma* protest from Moscow. There also was a mild protest from China. The greatest indignation was expressed by liberal opinion in the United States—in Congress and the press—but the administration emphasized through a variety of spokesmen that the air attacks on North Vietnam would be halted only when the Communist offensive was called off.

Those in the administration who had argued that the American retaliatory measures would not hamper relations with Moscow and Peking were vindicated within days of the weekend raids. First, Ambassador Dobrynin reconfirmed that Brezhnev was still expecting Kissinger for a secret visit on April 20. The visit had been planned for weeks as a preparation for the May summit. Brezhnev and Kissinger were to go over the latest American SALT proposal, which Kissinger had given to Dobrynin in March (bypassing the American delegation in Helsinki), and the Russians showed interest in pursuing it. The Vietnam crisis had no effect on these back-channel negotiations, and in fact, both sides felt that the new

Vietnamese situation made Kissinger's visit to Moscow even more desirable. This was of particular interest to the White House, which still thought that Moscow could play a constructive role in Vietnam.

The second vindication came on April 18, when the Chinese Ping-Pong team, which had been touring the United States since the previous week, called on Nixon at the White House. This was the first group from the P.R.C. to come to the United States after the president's journey to China; the Chinese players were returning the April 1971 visit of the American team. Had Peking concluded that Vietnamese events were affecting the nascent relationship, the Ping-Pong team would unquestionably have been called home on a moment's notice.

But nothing of the sort happened, and after playing in Detroit and touring Colonial Williamsburg in Virginia, the Chinese players appeared at the White House Rose Garden at noon on the eighteenth. It was a most cordial get-together.

In Vietnam, the military situation was rapidly deteriorating. The intricate Giap strategy was paying off: his multiple thrusts on three fronts were forcing Thieu to commit nearly his entire strategic reserve—his *masse de manoeuvre*—to battle, opening the rear areas to greatly stepped-up guerrilla activity. This was particularly true in Quang Ngai Province in central Vietnam and in the once-pacified Mekong Delta.

In the north, the North Vietnamese were pressing hard around Quang Tri, obliging Thieu to move up his 2d Division from Quang Ngai after the virtual annihilation of the 3d Division. This was exactly what Giap wanted to achieve. He had successfully deceived ARVN and American commanders who initially assumed that the North Vietnamese simply wanted to gobble up as much territory as possible. Taking advantage of the security vacuum created in Quang Ngai, Viet Cong guerrillas promptly established their control over villages containing some 90,000 inhabitants and seriously undermined pacification programs in villages with 275,000 more. Guerrilla control of these areas would in turn facilitate advances by Giap's regular forces.

In the Central Highlands, main-force Hanoi units, moving at night from the west and spearheaded by tanks, succeeded by mid-April in capturing most of strategic Highway 14. They mauled the ARVN 22d Division and seized its headquarters. Two towns in Binh Dinh Province were also taken and there were big ARVN defections. To prevent the North Vietnamese from taking Kontum and Pleiku (and the guerrillas near the coast were already softening up the government defenses), Thieu had to airlift some of his best Marine and Ranger reserve units from the Saigon area and the Mekong Delta to central Vietnam.

Sixty miles north of Saigon, the North Vietnamese grabbed the town of An Loc on April 16 and held it for three days in furious battle with the 5th Division's best regiment. But with close air support from American planes, the South Vietnamese were able to retake An Loc; the town kept changing hands throughout April, and was reduced to ruin, but at least the road to Saigon was blocked; Thieu was deploying his whole 21st Division and elements of the 9th to prevent a North Vietnamese breakthrough.

Five regiments from the ARVN 9th Division were positioned along the southern sector of the Cambodian border to prevent infiltration from the southwest. Next, however, Giap increased the pressure around Quang Tri and started probes toward Hue. Thieu's response was to dispatch more Marines and Rangers as well as crack paratroop units to the north, thus denuding the Mekong Delta. The North Vietnamese were waiting for precisely such a move; now their regular units began moving into the delta in support of the guerrillas, who had opened a fourth front there. The only way Saigon could cope with the new danger in the delta was to request B-52 strikes there, especially in Dinh Tuong Province. "The heaviest use of B-52s in the heavily populated Delta of the entire war," Gareth Porter wrote.

In less than a month of fighting, the North Vietnamese had succeeded in thoroughly dislocating and disorganizing Thieu's military establishment and causing vast damage to the pacification program. At least two ARVN divisions—the 3d and the 22d—ceased to exist as effective fighting forces; others took heavy losses through casualties and desertions. Some of Thieu's elite units were pinned down where Giap wanted them. United States air power, even with the B-52s ranging from the Mekong Delta to the Red River valley around Hanoi, could not reverse what was turning into a major military catastrophe.

Henry Kissinger's secret mission to Moscow was his first official trip to the Soviet Union; it was kept so secret that neither the American ambassador, Jacob D. Beam, nor General Brent Scowcroft, a senior NSC official then in Moscow preparing the advance logistics of the Nixon visit, was informed. Considering that Kissinger's companion on the nonstop flight from Andrews Air Force Base near Washington to Moscow on the night of April 19 was none other than Ambassador Dobrynin, the secrecy verged on the absurd. It was also insulting to Beam to have him in the dark when his opposite number in Washington not only knew everything but was offered the courtesy of traveling on the VIP jet. Small wonder that morale in the State Department under Rogers had sunk to an all-time low when the White House treated its ambassadors with such contempt.

It was, in any case, a self-defeating policy because American ambassadors, not knowing what their government was doing, were becoming embarrassingly ineffectual. Host governments and fellow diplomats could not but know of this humiliation, and obviously the ambassadors' usefulness was gravely affected.

The first major victim of this approach had been Ambassador Meyer, in Tokyo. But in Moscow, Beam, a diplomat with considerable experience in Communist affairs, was also constantly bypassed by the White House, which evidently believed that it could trust senior Communist officials more than its own envoys. He had found his Western colleagues immensely helpful—the French, for example, kept him informed about talks between Brezhnev and Pompidou, and the West Germans briefed him on Willy Brandt's meetings with Brezhnev—but there was no way he could reciprocate in even minimal fashion. (Nor did the White House inform America's NATO allies directly about its dealings with the Russians, although it demanded full knowledge about European activities.) When it came to China, Beam was unequipped to answer the questions that Foreign Minister Gromyko and other Soviet officials kept asking him, and he had to improvise most of the time, telling the Russians, for example, that trade bans on China were being gradually removed because they were obsolete. (Mercifully, Beam happened to be in Washington when Nixon disclosed the China story.)

Kissinger and Dobrynin landed in the early afternoon of April 20 at a Soviet domestic airfield near Moscow (rather than at Vnukovo, the capital's main airport, where the white-and-blue air force plane could easily have been spotted; Scowcroft's Boeing 707 was parked at Vnukovo because *his* visit was not a secret). Soviet Deputy Foreign Minister Vassily Kuznetsov was on hand to welcome Kissinger and his four advisers— Helmut Sonnenfeldt (the NSC's specialist on the Soviet Union), John Negroponte (who had joined Kissinger's staff the previous September as an expert on Vietnam), Winston Lord, and Peter Rodman. Soviet Foreign Ministry limousines drove the group straight to the Lenin Hills, a complex of official residences and conference rooms some forty minutes from Moscow. Kissinger and his party were put up at Dom Pryomov, a luxurious dacha. They were to spend four days there in absolute secrecy, with top Soviet leaders coming to the Lenin Hills to confer with them. General I. Antonov, chief of Soviet police forces, was in charge of arrangements.

Foreign Minister Gromyko was the first visitor, the evening of April 20. Brezhnev was coming down the next day, and what Kissinger and Gromyko did that evening at Dom Pryomov was to review the agenda: strategic-arms limitations, political aspects of Nixon's visit, now just a month away, and most important, Vietnam.

The next day Brezhnev and Kissinger met for five hours at a secluded nearby government conference villa. This was the first time Kissinger had met Brezhnev; he found him very direct, businesslike, friendly—and totally different from Chou En-lai. With Brezhnev, there was no need for historical analysis, philosophy, and the subtleties of thought and language that characterized the Peking talks. Assisting Brezhnev in the conversations were Gromyko, Dobrynin, Andrei Aleksandrov, Brezhnev's personal foreign-policy adviser who was sometimes described as the "Russian Kissinger," and an interpreter. Lord, Negroponte, and Rodman were there essentially to take notes, since Kissinger wanted a verbatim record of his conversations with Brezhnev. At each day's end, Kissinger sent a summary of the talks to Nixon over the secure communication system installed in his air force plane at the airfield near Moscow.

Kissinger was worried that sooner or later Vietnam might torpedo the May summit even though Brezhnev refrained from making an issue of the escalating war. But Kissinger knew that Washington had contingency plans to increase tenfold the scope of retaliation. Meanwhile Brezhnev indicated to Kissinger that the Soviet Union would under no circumstances halt arms deliveries to the North Vietnamese. Kissinger decided at that point to resort to his diplomatic secret weapon.

What Kissinger has never made public is that his sessions with Brezhnev produced what probably was the first major turning point in the Vietnam negotiations. He told an astonished Brezhnev that the United States would be willing to accept a cease-fire in place in exchange for the departure of the North Vietnamese forces that had entered South Vietnam since the start of the offensive on March 31. This was a veritable diplomatic bomb; Washington had never before *explicitly* agreed to let any North Vietnamese forces stay in the South. An offhand calculation at that point was that between 30,000 and 40,000 fresh North Vietnamese troops had entered South Vietnam since the offensive. Kissinger was telling Brezhnev that Washington would not demand the evacuation of the estimated 100,000 North Vietnamese who had been in the South *prior* to the offensive.

This offer has to be carefully analyzed to understand Kissinger's secret diplomacy. A concession of enormous magnitude was being made to

Hanoi via the Russians. The secret American peace proposals had *hinted* that the United States was not inflexible on the question of North Vietnamese forces, central as this was to the long-range survival of the Saigon regime. The October 1971 proposal had left the matter deliberately ambiguous with the use of the phrase that all armed forces of "the countries of Indochina must remain within their national frontiers." Since Hanoi always took the view that Vietnam was "one country" with "two armies," the North Vietnamese were given the latitude to interpret this phrase as they wished. But they had never been told clearly that their forces could remain in the South.

In the past when Nixon used the expression "cease-fire in place," it was taken to mean that a settlement including "mutual withdrawals" would then be negotiated. Speaking with Brezhnev, however, Kissinger was linking his secret offer with the insistence that Hanoi stop demanding Thieu's removal *before* any agreement. He indicated to Brezhnev that the United States would not allow a Communist government to be imposed on Saigon and wanted, instead, a "genuine political solution." Kissinger also reminded Brezhnev that the American proposal of May 1971 implicitly carried the same notion. Now the idea was for Brezhnev to transmit the new feature of the American position to Hanoi, so that a basis could be established for resuming secret negotiations leading to the cessation of fighting and a final settlement. Brezhnev agreed to do so, and Kissinger thus could report publicly, two weeks later, that the Russians "felt that every effort should be made to resume negotiations."

Kissinger also felt that he had made important progress with Brezhnev on SALT. He was pleased that the Soviet leader had accepted the American proposal made in March that submarine-launched ballistic missiles (SLBMs) be included in the ceilings for offensive weapons contemplated for each side. This point was immensely important to the Pentagon because of the huge Soviet nuclear-submarine–construction program. The American proposal called, however, for the Russians to phase out diesel-powered H-class submarines and some first-generation land-based intercontinental missiles.

Another discussion concerned details of Nixon's visit; Kissinger and Gromyko devoted nearly six hours of April 23 to the preparation of lesser agreements to be signed by American and Soviet leaders, and to an array of housekeeping problems.

Then, and only then, did Kissinger decide to let Ambassador Beam know of his presence in the Soviet Union. In the afternoon of April 23, the telephone rang in Beam's embassy office, and the ambassador was startled to hear Kissinger's voice. He was told that Kissinger wished to see him in the countryside, and that a Soviet Foreign Ministry limousine was on its way to pick him up; the ambassador was not to tell anyone on his staff where he was going.

Within minutes, the Soviet limousine was in the embassy courtyard, and Beam stepped inside. A half hour later, the ambassador was greeted by a smiling Kissinger at Dom Pryomov. Kissinger told Beam that he wanted to brief him about his visit, but, he suggested, it would be safer to talk in the garden to avoid Soviet electronic listening devices. Darkness was falling when Kissinger and Beam strolled into the garden. Kissinger explained the bewildering procedures vis-à-vis the ambassador by confiding to Beam that while he trusted *him,* he did not trust Secretary Rogers, and this was why the State Department was kept out of the important negotiations. He instructed Beam *not* to send a report to the department about the conversations with Brezhnev. This put the ambassador in an extremely difficult position, but, Kissinger said, it was the way the president wanted it. Suddenly, the two men heard a click of safety catches from the bushes, and they were surrounded by Soviet security guards who had mistaken them for interlopers. The incident delighted Kissinger.

Afterward, Kissinger and his party were driven secretly to see the Kremlin, and the quarters Nixon would occupy there. On the afternoon of April 24, Kissinger left Russia as surreptitiously as he had come; only when he was back in Washington did the White House announce that the secret visit had taken place.

On the plane en route from Moscow to Washington, Kissinger undertook to clarify his views on Vietnam for the benefit of his staff. His offer to Brezhnev to let North Vietnamese forces remain in the South (except for the units brought in since March 31) was based, he said, on the assumption that the United States could not stay forever in Indochina. Therefore, the best the United States could do would be to leave the South Vietnamese as strong as possible and to make North Vietnam as weak as possible. Since the United States was unable to weaken North Vietnam by diplomacy, "we would do it by swamping them." Kissinger's idea was that North Vietnam had to be debilitated enough to increase the time span before it could mount still another offensive.

Back in Washington, Kissinger and Nixon reviewed the overall Vietnam situation. They were encouraged by Brezhnev's willingness to communicate Kissinger's peace proposals to Hanoi along with his threats of what the United States would do if the offensive continued. And in fact, Konstantin F. Katushev, a secretary of the Central Committee of the Soviet Communist Party and the man in charge of relations with ruling

Communist parties, went immediately to Hanoi. The president now decided that the time really *had* come to address the nation on Vietnam. In the light of Brezhnev's assurances that Hanoi was ready for "serious talks," the president felt he should be conciliatory, but the battlefield situation was extremely serious, and Nixon believed he had to sound tough as well. Before making his speech, he sent a "signal" to Hanoi: on April 25, the White House announced that the United States and South Vietnam were ready to resume within forty-eight hours the semipublic peace talks in Paris that had been suspended on March 23. This was Hanoi's precondition for the resumption of the secret negotiations, and the White House felt it was worth accepting it.

Speaking to the nation on April 26, the president repeated that the Paris meetings would resume the next day and that, as a goodwill gesture, he was withdrawing 20,000 more Americans from Vietnam by July 1, bringing down the total to 49,000 men. According to Nixon, the new withdrawal was being ordered because "Vietnamization had proved itself sufficiently" and additional Americans could depart "without detriment to our overall goal of ensuring South Vietnam's survival as an independent country."

This was a strange conclusion, given that the ARVN was being savagely mauled, that the North Vietnamese offensive was not abating, and that Nixon had repeatedly promised *not* to make new withdrawals if the safety of the remaining American troops was threatened. But the president preferred to rely almost totally on unleashed American air power, and the new withdrawal had no real military meaning. It did have, however, political and diplomatic value. And he wanted Hanoi to understand that his willingness to resume the semipublic Paris talks and to withdraw additional U.S. troops did not mean the end of American bombings of the North. He insisted that the spring offensive

> is a clear case of naked and unprovoked aggression across an international border. . . . There is only one word for it—invasion. . . . I have ordered that our air and naval attacks on military installations in North Vietnam be continued until the North Vietnamese stop their offensive in South Vietnam. I have flatly rejected the proposal that we stop the bombing of North Vietnam as a condition for returning to the negotiating table. They sold that package to the United States once before, in 1968, and we are not going to buy it again in 1972.

Turning to the political aspects of the war, Nixon proclaimed that "the Communists have failed in their efforts to win over the people of South Vietnam politically." Addressing himself to Congress, where several "end-the-war" bills were under debate, the president charged that the North Vietnamese's "one remaining hope is to win in the Congress of the United States and among the people of the United States the victory they cannot win among the people of South Vietnam or on the battlefield in South Vietnam." It was the kind of political infighting Nixon insisted on mixing with statesmanship.

Meanwhile, Hanoi's attitudes to Nixon's speech were ambiguous: on the one hand, the White House was informed that Le Duc Tho was on his way to Paris and ready to meet with Kissinger on May 2; on the other hand, the Communist offensive was acquiring new momentum. After a few weeks' pause, North Vietnamese units in the north resumed violent attacks. Dong Ha, a town in Quang Tri Province, was captured on April 28. Now North Vietnamese artillery could directly shell the historic city of Quang Tri. The next day, the Communists surrounded Quang Tri. Troops of the battered ARVN 3d Division and units of Thieu's crack Ranger division, freshly flown from the Saigon area, broke ranks and fled toward Hue. Presently, advance North Vietnamese detachments took South Vietnamese firebases defending Hue from the west. Looting broke out in Hue, and government officials and their families abandoned the city, seeking safety in Danang, the principal urban center in central Vietnam.

On April 30, Nixon was attending a barbecue dinner at Treasury Secretary Connally's Picosa Ranch, in Floresville, Texas. Answering after-dinner questions, the president explained again at great length why the United States was bombing North Vietnam, and Connally's guests toasted him in champagne. The critical question one guest asked was whether Nixon had contemplated bombing dams and dikes in the Hanoi-Haiphong area to cause floods and further disrupt the North Vietnamese economy.

The president remarked that while the dikes were a "strategic target, and indirectly a military target," bombing them "would result in an enormous number of civilian casualties. . . . That is something that we want to avoid. It is also something we believe is not needed. . . . The North Vietnamese are taking a very great risk if they continue their offensive in the South. I will just leave it there, and they can make their own choice." Whatever Nixon had in mind, the White House did nothing to deny newspaper stories that the United States would not rule out destroying Red River dikes.

Quang Tri fell to the North Vietnamese on May 1, just as Kissinger prepared to leave for Paris. The loss of Quang Tri was a tremendous blow to Saigon and Washington: it was the first important South Vietnamese city to be taken by the Communists. At that point, Nixon and Kissinger had virtually decided that the next step would be the mining of Haiphong, but they wanted first to "touch all bases," as an NSC official remarked at the time.

Kissinger and his staff left Washington during the night of May 1, arrived at the usual French military airport in midmorning, and switched planes for the short hop to Paris and the limousine ride to the suburban North Vietnamese villa. This was the first time that Kissinger and Le Duc Tho had met since the previous September, and there was a certain coolness between them. Still, Kissinger was somewhat optimistic. The new offer he was bringing from Nixon was that the United States would withdraw all its forces from all of Indochina within four months if Hanoi agreed to an immediate cease-fire and the freeing of the American POWs.

In the course of a four-hour meeting, Le Duc Tho rejected this new proposal—it was, he claimed, little more than the American offer of the previous October. The North Vietnamese, encouraged by the success of their offensive, saw no reason to engage in what a Hanoi diplomat described as "a premature cease-fire." The price the United States would have to pay for a truce, Le Duc Tho indicated, would be Thieu's removal and the establishment of a coalition regime in Saigon. There was no point in Kissinger's discussing American willingness to let North Vietnamese troops remain in the South after a cease-fire (the offer he made in his conversation with Brezhnev). It was a total stalemate.

Kissinger went straight back to the airport to fly home. It was the first secret trip on which he had not spent the night in Paris. He reached Washington in the evening, in time for one of his aides to attend a friend's birthday party. It seemed like the only thing left to do.

But Kissinger did not get the evening off. Nixon and General Haig were awaiting him aboard the presidential yacht, *Sequoia,* to hear the Paris story. The three men debated far into the night what should be done to save South Vietnam. Secretary Rogers, on a European tour that week, was not around when the president made his decision, in principle, to subject North Vietnam to massive bombing and to mine Haiphong harbor so that no new military supplies could reach the North Vietnamese.

Wednesday, May 3, and Thursday, May 4, were spent in continuing top-secret White House meetings involving the president, Kissinger, Haig, and Treasury Secretary Connally. Connally was brought into the strategic debates because Nixon wanted from him a sense of how the nation might respond politically to an all-out air war against North Vietnam. The president remembered Laird's and Rogers's opposition to the 1970 Cambodia invasion, and now he wanted to be reassured by Connally, a professional politician, that he was right about North Vietnam. And Connally did not disappoint him. Simultaneously, Kissinger ordered the NSC staff to prepare option papers for the projected operation (the staff could draw on the 1969 "savage blow" studies and the 1970 Cambodia options); the Joint Chiefs of Staff went to work on the operational aspects.

The mining of Haiphong had first been discussed during the Johnson years, but rejected mainly on political grounds. It was considered again in 1969, but likewise dropped as too dangerous. Now, however, the president was convinced that it was an absolutely necessary move along with sustained B-52 raids against the Hanoi area. Hanoi had not been bombed since the April 15 raids, and Nixon felt the strikes must be resumed. He was now prepared to risk cancellation of the Moscow summit; as he put it to Kissinger, it would make no sense for the president of the United States to arrive in Moscow while "our ally"—the Saigon regime—was on its knees.

General Abrams's daily operational report for May 2, received at the White House on the third, confirmed in Nixon's mind the need for drastic action. Abrams reported that a most critical military situation was developing in the central region, where, he said, three North Vietnamese divisions were attempting to cut South Vietnam in two. If Kontum, a key city in the highlands, could hold out for a "few days," it might not fall to the enemy, but enormous air pressure on North Vietnam plus local air strikes were required to save it. Only the disorganized 22d Division was left to defend central Vietnam. General Abrams was fairly optimistic that the ARVN 1st Division, another crack outfit, could defend Hue, but he was worried that in the southwest the North Vietnamese could break out of An Loc and take Route 1, opening a "corridor" to Saigon. And three mixed North Vietnamese and Viet Cong divisions were now operating in Tay Ninh Province, also directly north of Saigon. Air reconnaissance showed that the North Vietnamese were establishing new weapon and food stockpiles in conquered territories; intelligence specialists concluded that Hanoi was preparing to keep the offensive going well into June and beyond. Laird rushed a six-man top-level team—all generals and admirals, with Assistant Secretary of Defense for Installations and Logistics Barry Shillito at its head—to South Vietnam to determine the ARVN's immediate needs.

By May 4, White House officials were privately telling newsmen that the government no longer felt restrained about bombing the North. A pause had been ordered after the April 15–16 bombings to give diplomacy another chance, but inasmuch as Kissinger's latest Paris effort had collapsed, "we are no longer bound by any restraints." The State Department helped to prepare public opinion for what was to come: a department spokesman announced that Nixon was keeping all the options open except for the recommitment of American combat troops and the use of nuclear weapons (a possibility that was briefly considered aboard the *Sequoia* two days earlier).

A semipublic session of the peace talks was held on May 4, but the North Vietnamese simply restated in public what Le Duc Tho had told Kissinger in private. "We are exceptionally frustrated this week," the State Department spokesman said later in the day. "When it came time to examine the negotiating baggage the other side brought to Paris, they had nothing but empty suitcases." In the midst of these war preparations, Nixon went late on the morning of May 4 to attend funeral services at the National Presbyterian Church for J. Edgar Hoover, who had died at seventy-seven on May 2, and to deliver a eulogy for the man who had run the bureau for forty-eight years. "The good J. Edgar Hoover has done," he said, "will not die."

On Friday, May 5, final planning went into high gear. The President and Kissinger devoted most of the day to conferences with Laird, Connally, Helms, and Moorer. (Secretary Rogers was still in Europe, and Nixon was not yet ready to recall him.) Connally and Moorer favored the mining of North Vietnamese waters. Helms was, as usual, noncommittal. Laird argued against it on operational and political grounds—and Kissinger, oddly, chose that moment to play devil's advocate *against* the mining too. He cautioned the group that mining Haiphong might destroy the Moscow summit and, with it, détente and the SALT agreement on which he had worked so hard.

Nonetheless, by the end of the day the president made up his mind to mine Haiphong. Accompanied only by his daughter Julie, he flew to Camp David for the weekend; that same evening, he dictated the first draft of the speech for the following week announcing the new war measures. As he left, General Haig summoned the NSC staffers to the White House Situation Room at 6:00 p.m. to inform them that it was "98 percent certain" that the president would order bombings of North Vietnam and the mining of Haiphong. A full meeting of the NSC was scheduled for 9:00 a.m. on Monday, May 8, and the staff had the weekend to "game out" the plans.

On Saturday and Sunday, May 6 and 7, Kissinger conducted a WASAG meeting. John Negroponte, his principal staff Vietnam expert, prepared a brief for the Saturday meeting explaining how the operation would work and how effective it was likely to be. At noon, Kissinger had another meeting—with Haig, George Carver of the CIA, Sonnenfeldt as the Soviet expert, John Holdridge as the China expert, and several NSC staffers. He went around the table asking for opinions. Carver said the CIA supported the bombing and mining plan because it could result in great pressure on the Hanoi leadership; this was a departure from the standing CIA position against violent retaliatory acts. Sonnenfeldt said Moscow would not be likely to increase its involvement in the Vietnam conflict unless a Soviet ship in Haiphong were hit, but he gave even odds that the forthcoming summit might be canceled. Holdridge said he doubted China would respond violently. Haig supported the plan so long as it called for a sustained effort over an adequate time period.

Kissinger agonized—pacing back and forth, wondering aloud whether, after all, it would be wise. He knew that Nixon favored action, but he doubted whether it was worth the risk; the ARVN might collapse anyway and the United States had already done enough for Saigon. In the end, however, he was able to rationalize the need for the bombing and mining.

The NSC staff spent all Sunday coordinating operations with the Pentagon, preparing to notify the Russians, Chinese, and others of the U.S. actions, and drafting Nixon's speech. A draft was written by Winston Lord, but Nixon had already dictated his own text on Friday night and refined it on Saturday with Raymond Price, who went to Camp David to work with him. Safire recollected that Nixon told Price to draft "a very businesslike, very factual, short, hard-hitting speech cut down to the bare essentials," and the president instructed Price not to show this draft to either Kissinger or Rogers. Price had the speech ready Saturday night.

On Sunday, May 7, the White House went into high gear—publicly. It announced that Nixon had just telephoned Rogers in Bonn, requesting him to return at once for the National Security Council meeting the next morning. Kissinger, the White House said, also canceled a trip to Tokyo (already postponed once) planned for May 11. He spent Sunday with Nixon at Camp David, and the two men returned to Washington in the evening. The sense of crisis that spring Sunday was further underlined by the announcement that navy jets had shot down three North Vietnamese MiGs near Hanoi. The navy planes were running photoreconnaissance missions, and the MiGs scrambled to intercept them. It was one of the few dogfights of the Vietnam war.

On Monday, May 8, the full NSC met at 9:00 a.m. with the president. Helms, the first to speak, still appeared to have little enthusiasm for the bombing and mining on the theory that even with Haiphong harbor gone, matériel could be easily moved to North Vietnam by rail from China. Rogers spoke out strongly against both measures, and told the president that America had already done enough for South Vietnam.

Secretary Laird was also outspoken against both actions. Vietnamization was working well, he thought: Hue had not yet been taken, and the ARVN was proving itself. Besides, the Pentagon already had a $4-billion deficit in 1972 and the navy had expended all the ammunition allocated for the current fiscal year.

Nixon's approach was different. He told the group they faced a tough situation, in view of the approaching Moscow summit: in reality a Soviet ally had invaded an ally of the United States. He did not wish to hear the argument that retaliation against North Vietnam would kill the Moscow meeting because the president of the United States was not prepared to go to the Soviet Union in the first place if Russia had done nothing to discourage an attack on America's ally.

Connally was the strongest advocate of retaliation. As one of the participants described it, he practically jumped out of his chair, pointed his finger at Nixon and said that, in effect, he would not be a real president if he failed to act. He made disparaging comments about Laird's reservations. Vice President Agnew, too, strongly favored the decision to "go."

The only comment Kissinger made during the whole meeting was that there was a 50-50 chance that the Soviets would cancel the summit if the United States engaged in the bombing and mining. A participant said later that if a secret ballot had been taken at the meeting, the decision might have gone against the bombing of the North. Yet few of the NSC members seemed disturbed when the decision was made. The president ended the meeting at noon; then he went off with Kissinger and Connally to his Executive Office Building hideaway. This was where he formalized his decision at 2:00 p.m.

Before delivering his speech, Nixon met in the Roosevelt Room at 8:00 p.m. with congressional leaders. Safire wrote later that it was "as tense a session as I attended in four years." Several senators, notably Majority Leader Mansfield (just back from a trip to China) and Senate Foreign Relations Committee Chairman Fulbright were openly critical of the president's decision. After the briefing, Nixon left Moorer (who was for it), Laird (who opposed it), and Rogers to mollify the congressmen. Mansfield's comment was: "The war is enlarged. . . . We are embarking on a dangerous course. . . . We are courting danger here that could extend the war, increase the number of war prisoners, and make peace more difficult to achieve." And Fulbright noted that since the Senate had declared that the Tonkin Gulf Resolution used by Lyndon Johnson was void, Nixon was acting illegally in blockading North Vietnam.

But it was too late: the decision had been made and now—at 9:00 p.m. on May 8—the president was facing the television cameras to make his announcement. And unknown to anyone except Nixon, Kissinger was meeting in his West Wing office with Ambassador Dobrynin, giving him an advance copy of the presidential text, assuring him that American actions in North Vietnam were not directed against the Soviet Union, and expressing the hope that the Brezhnev-Nixon meeting would start on schedule on May 22. Still, the president was in no mood to exculpate the Soviets. In fact, he opened his speech with a critical reference to Moscow:

> Five weeks ago, on Easter weekend, the Communist armies of North Vietnam launched a massive invasion of South Vietnam, an invasion that was made possible by tanks, artillery, and other advanced offensive weapons supplied to Hanoi by the Soviet Union and other Communist nations. The South Vietnamese have fought bravely to repel this brutal assault. Most tragically, there have been over 20,000 civilian casualties, including women and children, in the cities which the North Vietnamese have shelled in wanton disregard of human life.

Describing American peace proposals in detail, Nixon said that in the two weeks since the United States offered to resume negotiations, "Hanoi has launched three new military offensives. . . . In those two weeks, the risk that a Communist government may be imposed on the 17 million people of South Vietnam has increased, and the Communist offensive has now reached the point that it gravely threatens the lives of 60,000 American troops who are still in Vietnam."

The United States, he said, now has

> a clear, hard choice among three courses of action: immediate withdrawal of all American forces, continued attempts at negotiation, or decisive military action to end the war. . . . It is plain . . . that what appears to be a choice among three courses of action for the United States is really no choice at all. The killing in this tragic war must stop. . . . There is only one way to stop the killing. That is to keep the weapons of war out of the hands of the international outlaws of North

Vietnam. . . . I therefore concluded that Hanoi must be denied the weapons and supplies it needs to continue the aggression. . . . I have ordered the following measures which are being implemented as I am speaking to you:

All entrances to North Vietnamese ports will be mined to prevent access to these ports and North Vietnamese naval operations from these ports. United States forces have been directed to take appropriate measures within the internal and claimed territorial waters of North Vietnam to interdict the delivery of any supplies. Rail and all other communications will be cut off to the maximum extent possible. Air and naval strikes against military targets in North Vietnam will continue.

Now on May 8, there were thirty-five foreign-registry ships (most of them flying the Soviet flag) in Haiphong and four more in other North Vietnamese ports. Nixon said that the countries with ships in these North Vietnamese ports "have already been notified that their ships will have three daylight periods to leave in safety" and that "after that time, the mines will become active and any ships attempting to leave or enter these ports will do so at their own risk."

As a condition for lifting the blockade, Nixon listed his terms:

First, all American prisoners of war must be returned. Second, there must be an internationally supervised cease-fire throughout Indochina. Once prisoners of war are released, once the internationally supervised cease-fire has begun, we will stop all acts of force throughout Indochina, and at that time we will proceed with a complete withdrawal of all American forces from Vietnam within four months. Now, these terms are generous terms. They are terms which would not require surrender and humiliation on the part of anybody.

This was essentially what Kissinger had offered to Le Duc Tho on May 2, and this time, no political conditions were attached. In fact, Nixon said, his terms "would allow negotiations on a political settlement between the Vietnamese themselves." This was a crucial point, but the president also had a message for the Soviet Union:

We respect the Soviet Union as a great power. We recognize the right of the Soviet Union to defend its interests when they are threatened. The Soviet Union in turn must recognize our right to defend our interests. No Soviet soldiers are threatened in Vietnam. Sixty thousand Americans are threatened. We expect you to help your allies, and you cannot expect us to do other than to continue to help our allies, but let us, and let all great powers, help our allies only for the purpose of their defense, not for the purpose of launching invasions against their neighbors. Otherwise the cause of peace, the cause in which we both have so great a stake, will be seriously jeopardized. Our two nations have made significant progress in our negotiations in recent months. We are near major agreements on nuclear arms limitation, on trade, on a host of other issues. Let us not slide back toward the dark shadows of a previous age. We do not ask you to sacrifice your principles, or your friends, but neither should you permit Hanoi's intransigence to blot out the prospects we together have so patiently prepared. We, the United States and the Soviet Union, are on the threshold of a new relationship that can serve not only the interests of our two countries, but the cause of world peace. We are prepared to continue to build this relationship. The responsibility is yours if we fail to do so.

One of the most notable features of Nixon's speech was that nowhere in it was there any suggestion that a North Vietnamese withdrawal from the South must occur as a condition for the bombing and mining to cease. This omission, which was consistent with the offer Kissinger made to Brezhnev two weeks earlier, was deliberate. As early as 1970, an NSC staff review of Indochina cease-fire consequences had convinced Kissinger that there was no way to win the removal of the North Vietnamese from the South, though the United States had been paying lip service to this notion. But now the official U.S. position had become that a *permanent* cease-fire in place was to follow the end of the fighting. Inevitably the conclusion was reached that in the end South Vietnam would be marked with military "leopard spots."

Nixon's decision to blockade and bomb North Vietnam was the most drastic move in the war since Lyndon Johnson had begun the vast buildup of American forces in Indochina in 1965. The majority view in Washington was that Moscow would call off, or at least delay, the summit meeting. However, the State Department, largely on the basis of dispatches from Ambassador Beam, was inclined to think that it would be held as scheduled. Preparations in Moscow to receive the president proceeded normally.

Beam's analysis was that the Russians expected the Vietnam war to end sooner or later—with their help—and decided to "grin and bear it." But, Beam warned, he had the impression that the Kremlin was "praying" that there would be no serious incidents involving their shipping in Haiphong. Still, opposition to the summit meeting, led by Pyotr Shelest, the Politburo member from the Ukraine, erupted at a Kremlin meeting on May 9. It is unknown how Brezhnev handled this, but the restrained official statement concerning the blockade issued on May 11 seemed to put an end to the argument. A few days later, a small announcement in *Pravda* said without elaboration that Shelest had resigned from the Politburo.

In Washington, Soviet officials were acting as if nothing had happened. Soviet Foreign Trade Minister Nikolai S. Patolichev happened to be having dinner with Commerce Secretary Peterson (who had taken over Commerce the previous January) at his home overlooking Rock Creek Park the night of the speech. Peterson and Patolichev watched Nixon together, but the Soviet official offered no reaction afterward; the two men simply resumed their discussion of the trade agreement Nixon and Brezhnev were planning to sign in Moscow. Across town, at the home of Navy Secretary John Warner, the guest of honor—Deputy Commander of the Soviet Navy Admiral Vladimir Kasatonov—was likewise sphinxlike. The next day the Peterson-Patolichev and Warner-Kasatonov negotiations proceeded normally. And on the eleventh, Patolichev visited Nixon at the White House. (The visit was Kissinger's idea—it was his way of testing the waters.) Patolichev told newsmen: "We never had any doubts" that the summit would be held as planned. "I don't know why you asked this question. Have *you* any doubts?"

Now Nixon felt vindicated in his brinkmanship—and his correct reading of the Russians. Still, he could not let well enough alone. Daily, the White House announced that telegrams by the thousand were pouring in, the vast majority in favor of the blockade decision. Only years later was it discovered that most of the 22,000 telegrams had been sent by Nixon's own reelection campaign committee. The bitterness of the Nixon White House toward public opinion was reflected in a confidential memorandum sent by Haldeman to Charles Colson:

> We have the ironic situation that, after initially reacting to the Monday announcement with almost hysterical predictions that we had blown the Russian summit and our whole "Generation of Peace" foreign policy, the columnists and commentators—with a considerable amount of egg on their faces—now have the gall to say that the Monday decision was wrong and reckless but that the Soviet Union is showing great restraint in continuing the summit nevertheless. It is again the most devastating proof of the fact that whatever we do and however it comes out, we are going to be torn to pieces by our liberal critics in the press and on television.

Yet Nixon did have bona fide support in many quarters—even in the Democratic Party. This included Jimmy Carter, the little-known governor of Georgia, who, after commenting that "we are headed for a major defeat in South Vietnam," urged the nation to "give President Nixon our backing and support—whether or not we agree with specific decisions."

As Nixon readied himself to fly to the Soviet Union, he also had the satisfaction of noting that the battlefield situation in Vietnam had begun to stabilize. There were no new Communist breakthroughs around Hue or along Saigon's outer defense perimeter. It was a welcome breathing spell, perhaps a good augury.

Chapter 21

Curiously, Nixon chose a day shortly before his departure for Moscow to send a message to Congress requesting funds for the operations of Radio Free Europe and Radio Liberty. It was a Nixonian quirk because RFE, broadcasting to Eastern Europe, and Radio Liberty, broadcasting to the Soviet Union, had long been an irritant in relations with the Communist countries. They had been funded for years by the CIA as a part of covert political action programs, but Congress moved to end this arrangement and to replace it, at least temporarily, with financing through the State Department. In the message he sent on May 10, the president declared that they "are not spokesmen for American official policy—that role belongs in broadcasting to the Voice of America." Rather, he said, "they are expressions of our profound conviction that a responsible, independent, and free press plays an indispensable part in the social and political processes that look to better understanding and more effective cooperation, not only within a nation, but also among nations."

This, of course, was a fiction, because RFE and Radio Liberty were essentially propaganda outlets. As it happened, Radio Free Europe was a very competent operation with an enormous listenership in Eastern Europe, but it could hardly be considered part of an "independent and free press."

President and Mrs. Nixon, Kissinger, Rogers, and a large group of NSC and State Department officials left Andrews Air Force base shortly after 9:00 a.m. on Saturday, May 20. (Always keen for a "first," Nixon characteristically noted that he was off on "the first state visit a president has ever made to [Russia]"; Roosevelt's Yalta did not count because it was a mere working session. The president wanted to spend Sunday in Salzburg, Austria, his last chance to complete his preparations, which had preoccupied him for the last three days before his departure. SALT and Vietnam were the political centerpieces, and Nixon became almost totally absorbed by these subjects. He worked aboard the plane and, again, after his Sunday meeting and lunch with Austrian Chancellor Bruno Kreisky. Running into a group of newsmen in the gardens of Klessheim Palace, where he was staying, the president told them that "there are so many substantive conversations involved here that it requires a great deal of concentration. . . . Now I have to go over all the final papers to be prepared for a number of very intensive discussions on a number of pretty knotty issues." He could not resist stating the obvious: "Where conferences of this type fail is where one side or the other is not prepared, does not know what the real heart of the problem is. In this case, that will not be the problem. We will be able to go very directly to the points of difference and the points of agreement, and then we can talk about the points of difference. I look forward to perhaps the most intensive negotiations that I have participated in on substantive matters, and that is why I will not be doing any sight-seeing."

Richard Nixon was no stranger to Moscow. He had first gone there in 1959 as vice president to open the American National Exposition (this was part of the on-and-off predétente efforts between the Russians and the Eisenhower administration that included Nikita Khrushchev's visit to the United States and the elusive "spirit of Camp David") and, later, as a globe-trotting private citizen. In 1959 he had engaged in a verbal brawl with Khrushchev over how the United States and the Soviet Union could destroy each other; his later visits had been more discreet, and Soviet leaders, looking ahead to the future, had gone out of their way to receive him—just in case.

Now it was a triumphal return. And for Americans back home it was another White House television spectacular: his visit was covered by correspondents permanently stationed in Moscow, others who gradually drifted in ahead of him, and two planeloads of White House press arriving just before *Air Force One*. Moscow was not so exotic as Peking, but it was still a big event, to be reported in every detail.

Greeting the Nixons at the airport at 4:00 p.m., May 22, were President Nikolai V. Podgorny of the Supreme Soviet of the U.S.S.R., the nominal chief of state (and still active at that time in the Kremlin leadership), Premier Aleksei Kosygin, Foreign Minister Gromyko, Ambassador Dobrynin, and innumerable other dignitaries. Protocol did not require Brezhnev to be present inasmuch as he held no formal *government* post: he was the general secretary of the Soviet Communist Party. There were warm handshakes, the anthems, the honor guard, and then Nixon climbed with Podgorny and Kosygin into a big black Soviet Ziv limousine for the drive to the Kremlin. There were inevitable comparisons between

Nixon's receptions in Peking and in Moscow: in the Chinese capital on the first day, the population seemed unaware of the president's presence; in Moscow, however, the government brought out tens of thousands of citizens to watch the motorcade.

The Nixons, Kissinger, Haldeman, and Ehrlichman were installed in newly decorated Kremlin apartments. Secretary Rogers, the White House speech-writers, and the rest of the American contingent were put up at the nearby Rossiya Hotel, the most modern in Moscow. As soon as the president could refresh himself, he was led to Brezhnev's office in another section of the Kremlin for their first meeting, a two-hour late-afternoon session, during which they conferred alone except for interpreters. This was one occasion at which Kissinger had not been asked to be present. The president had met Brezhnev, then a little-known Politburo member, during his 1959 visit, but it was a fleeting encounter that left no particular impression on him. This was a get-acquainted meeting—and the two men had ample opportunity to take each other's measure. They exchanged pleasantries, talked about Nixon's schedule—he was to visit Leningrad and Kiev in addition to Moscow—and engaged in a general *tour d'horizon* of world affairs. They did, however, discuss in general terms some of the problems involved in the SALT negotiations, such as the question of land-based mobile ICBM launchers and how submarine-launched missiles would be counted in the proposed interim pact on offensive arms.

The truth was that the SALT agreement was rather far from completion, much further than was generally realized. Neither the Helsinki negotiations nor the secret talks between Kissinger and Dobrynin in Washington (of which the American team in Helsinki was unaware) had produced a breakthrough. Kissinger's optimism after his secret trip to see Brezhnev in April had been premature.

Even with Nixon in Moscow, the situation remained studded with enormous difficulties. Privately, some American advisers were beginning to doubt the wisdom of pushing for an accord that week, though the president and Kissinger felt that the political dynamics of the situation required Herculean efforts to do so. This was the background for the extraordinary decision not to have Gerard Smith, chief American SALT negotiator, join Nixon in Moscow for the final phase of the talks. Smith and his delegation were permitted to come only at the last moment, when Nixon and Brezhnev had struck their deal on the excruciatingly complex problem of nuclear-missile–firing submarines, a problem that came within inches of killing the agreement.

In the meantime, the president was finding himself very much at ease with the ebullient but very businesslike Brezhnev. Both men were practicing, rough-and-tumble politicians, and they understood each other even when the negotiations reached the toughest stage. A touch of ribaldry even developed between them, something that would have been unthinkable with Mao or the exquisitely nuanced Chou.

The dinner in the huge Granovit Hall at the Grand Kremlin Palace the first night of Nixon's Moscow stay set the political tone for the visit. Speeches were sober and to the point. President Podgorny stayed away from specifics as he set forth the principles of the Soviet negotiating position, but he left no doubt that hard bargaining lay ahead. He did Nixon the courtesy of refraining from even the most indirect mention of the Vietnam war and the difficult circumstances in which the Soviet leadership was receiving him. In his reply to Podgorny's toast, the president struck a softer note than his host, and singled out SALT for special mention as the principal summit topic.

Official protocol called for President and Mrs. Nixon to depart Granovit Hall at 10:00 p.m. and walk to their Kremlin apartments. This they did, but Nixon had little sleep that night. Tension kept him awake, as it often did, and despite the long and hard day—the flight from Salzburg, the meeting with Brezhnev and the Kremlin dinner, followed by an hour's talk with Kissinger—Nixon had a white Moscow night. First he read. Then, on impulse, he decided to break out of the confinement of his rooms and seek serenity in the Kremlin's open courtyards. He got dressed shortly after 4:00 a.m., and walked downstairs, tailed by stunned Secret Service agents, their walkie-talkies abuzz, and Soviet security men. In Washington, Nixon's nocturnal wanderings had taken him to the Lincoln Memorial. At the Kremlin, he broke his stride to stare at Lenin's statue. He chatted briefly with a Soviet military guard, and went back upstairs after about a half hour. He spent another half hour working at his desk, then went to bed at 5:30 a.m. as the sun was rising.

Tuesday, May 23, was a day of hard negotiations for Nixon, who managed to show no signs of his lack of sleep. He led the American delegation at a plenary session with the Russians in Catherine Hall in the morning, then conferred with Brezhnev for five hours in the afternoon and evening, in a meeting broken only for ceremonies of signing the first agreements on environmental protection and medical science and public health. (Because both sides realized that the major agreements to be negotiated would not be ready until the end of the week, the decision had been taken to have daily signings of lesser accords. These had been completed ahead of time. In this fashion, there would be a steady flow of positive news from Moscow—including television and photo coverage of the signing ceremonies showing Nixon and Soviet leaders—while the real negotiations proceeded behind closed doors. Nixon did no sight-seeing in Moscow and his public appearances were limited, but both governments—and especially the Americans—wanted to avoid a news void that could lead idle U.S. newsmen to damaging speculations.)

The Tuesday plenary session—involving Nixon, Kissinger, Rogers, Beam, and several other senior delegation members on the American side, and Brezhnev, Kosygin, Gromyko, Dobrynin, Andrei Aleksandrov, and other assorted high officials on the Russian side—was essentially a general discussion, of SALT, Vietnam, and trade, punctuated with good-humored asides and playful (albeit heavy-handed) repartee.

It was determined from the outset that the "big items"—SALT and Vietnam—would be handled in separate sessions by Nixon, Kissinger, Brezhnev, Kosygin, and when required, Podgorny. For the Russians, Gromyko served chiefly as liaison between the "first" American team and his principals, although he also participated in the trade negotiations alongside Kosygin and Foreign Trade Minister Patolichev, and at one stage joined the SALT bargaining. For the Americans, Rogers and Peter Flanigan, the White House coordinator of foreign economic policy, were the principal trade negotiators, although Nixon remained in close touch with this topic. Other specialists conferred separately on lesser issues.

The first major skirmish between Nixon and Brezhnev was over SALT: it was the topic of the five-hour conference they held Tuesday afternoon and evening. And it was only then that the president fully understood the depth of Soviet-American differences in the realm of strategic arms.

In terms of the ABM treaty, negotiations in Helsinki and Vienna, as well as the Kissinger-Dobrynin back-channel talks, had resulted in a basic agreement that each side would limit defensive deployments to one single ABM site, each with no more than 100 ABM launchers and 100 interceptor missiles. The Soviets, who had already developed an ABM system around Moscow, chose the option of retaining it there instead of constructing antiballistic defenses around their ICBM launching sites. They had agreed not to install offensive ICBM launchers within the radius covered by the Moscow ABM system.

The United States, which had been building the Safeguard defensive system to protect the Minuteman launcher silos in North Dakota, opted for maintaining it, leaving Washington unprotected. The differing Soviet and American decisions on ABM sites were largely based on the economic and operational convenience of not having to dismantle existing deployments and establish new ones. Besides, American nuclear doctrine attached more importance to the protection of ICBM launchers than to the protection of cities, so that the United States could retain a second-strike capability in the event of Soviet attack. This, in addition to the largely invulnerable nuclear-submarine force, was considered by the Pentagon the best deterrent against nuclear aggression. To conform to the one-site concept, the United States agreed to halt ABM construction around launcher sites in Montana.

The problem of radar installations supporting the ABM systems, however, was unresolved. The United States took the view that so-called phased-array radars (also known as "heavy" radars), ideally suited for tracking incoming missiles because of their electronic-scanning capability, should be restricted to the 150-kilometer radius in which ABMs were deployed around Moscow, and it was willing to accept similar qualitative limitations on its "heavy" radars in North Dakota. But the Russians balked at these restrictions. Less sophisticated mechanical-scan radars (known as "light"), the Americans also believed, should be kept at the numerical level existing at the time of the signing of an agreement.

The controversy was important because the deployment of phased-array radars outside the agreed ABM locations would enable one side secretly to expand antimissile-launcher deployments (it is easier to spot and identify launchers than radars, particularly if the latter are not operational at a given time, through satellite-surveillance techniques), and offered early-warning advantages on a nationwide basis; the fundamental concept of the proposed ABM treaty was that neither the United States nor the Soviet Union would deploy antiballistic systems capable of defending its entire territory. The American position was that all things considered neither side should take the other's commitments on faith: they should be spelled out in the treaty. And there was also the question of how many "light" radars could be located elsewhere—as well as the precise definition in watt potential of "heavy" and "light" radars.

Nixon and Brezhnev tackled this ABM problem first, and quite successfully, considering its technical complexities. Possibly because the Russians were eager to obtain an ABM treaty—this is what they had wanted all along, being much less interested in an offensive-weapons pact —Brezhnev largely accepted Nixon's position, though he persuaded him to include some technical aspects of radar-potential measurements in the "agreed interpretations" appended to the treaty rather than in the treaty itself. This precedent of "interpretations" was a dangerous one, particularly when Nixon was subsequently maneuvered into "unilateral statements" in the pact on offensive arms. Agreed interpretations, in lieu of formal treaty language, are bad law since either party can change its mind concerning an interpretation and thus open up an area of potential violation. Unilateral statements are even worse inasmuch as they do not bind the other side even morally or politically.

The problems with offensive weapons were much more complicated than the ABM question, although the United States had abandoned many of its original positions in the course of the thirty months of negotiations preceding the summit. It gave up its 1970 proposal (known as option "E") for "equal aggregates" in offensive weapons between the two countries. The idea was that the United States and the Soviet Union would each limit the number of nuclear launchers—land-based ICBMs, submarine-deployed launchers, and manned bombers—to 1900 (Washington also hoped for a sublimit of 250 on Russia's huge SS-9 missiles, the biggest in the world, with frightful megatonnage). This would have been exact parity. But the Russians were not disposed to accept numerical limitations, given their inferiority in MIRV technology, and they insisted that American Forward Based Systems (FBS) stationed in NATO countries and attached to the Sixth Fleet in the Mediterranean be counted under the equal-aggregates ceiling. The United States flatly refused, but, as a *quid pro quo,* it had to drop the equal-aggregates notion.

In the end, Washington agreed to swap a freeze on land-based ICBMs deployed at the time of an agreement for Moscow's willingness to forget FBS. Numerically, this favored the Russians, who already had more ICBMs than the United States (and more powerful ones) and were feverishly building additional ones—including the monster SS-9s—as well as engaging in a breathless submarine-construction program, clearly trying to beat whatever SALT deadline might be imposed. The Americans retained the MIRV edge, however, and Kissinger was able to persuade the Pentagon and the White House Verification Panel that a freeze on ICBMs was an acceptable deal—provided that the Soviet Union compromised on related problems.

When Nixon arrived in Moscow, therefore, there were basic agreements on an ICBM freeze—at 1054 ICBMs for the United States and 1618 for the Soviet Union (including those under active construction at the time of the SALT signing)—and on the fact that only an interim agreement on offensive weapons could be aimed for. The United States, because of the MIRV advantage, which meant more *warheads* than the Russians could deploy, had not been building ICBMs since 1968, but both sides would be free to pursue development and testing of MIRVs and even more advanced systems.

But there were still four major problems that Nixon and Brezhnev had to resolve. One was the question of mobile land-based ICBMs. Because these weapons can easily escape detection by satellite observation—they can be moved or concealed—mobile missile systems can destabilize the whole strategic balance. The United States, which had built none, had insisted throughout the SALT negotiations on banning them. The Russians had resisted having a treaty obligation on this point.

The second problem involved the size of missiles. The United States was concerned that the Soviet Union might convert launchers for such "light" missiles as the SS-11 and SS-13 into launchers for the "heavy" SS-9 or even more potent rockets. This, in time, could eat away the American MIRV advantage and equip the Soviet Union with a formidable array of superweapons. Besides, American negotiators assumed that the Russians would achieve a MIRV breakthrough before long. Here, again, the Russians were holding back: they were reluctant to accept the American definition that all their missiles except the SS-9 were "light."

The third problem, a related one, had to do with the dimensions of silos. Still fearing Soviet conversions into "heavy" missiles, the United States stipulated in Helsinki that in the process of modernizing or replacing ICBM silos, their dimensions could not be increased by more than 10–15 percent. The two governments were able to define an ICBM as "any land-based strategic ballistic missile capable of ranges in excess of the shortest distance between the northeastern border of the continental United States and the northwestern border of the continental Soviet Union." But they left it to Nixon and Brezhnev to define missile size and silo dimension.

The fourth and the most intractable problem was the number of nuclear submarines and launcher tubes permitted. The Soviet Union wanted to be allowed more nuclear-powered submarines with more launchers—a maximum of 62 boats and 950 launchers (the United States had at the time 44 modern nuclear submarines with 710 launchers)—and the United States agreed to this *in principle:* the Pentagon wanted to wait to increase the American underwater fleet until the new Trident submarine was fully developed, sometime in the late 1970s, instead of building additional obsolescent Poseidon-class boats. Nixon's commitment to go ahead with the Trident was a major condition exacted by the Pentagon from the White House in exchange for its support for the overall SALT agreement.

There was, however, a catch: the Americans demanded that for each new nuclear submarine and each new launcher, the Russians must phase out older boats, such as their diesel-powered submarines, or old land-based ICBM launchers. In other words, the overall Soviet nuclear force should not grow in absolute terms as it was modernized and transferred to the sea under a complex replacement formula. Moscow went along with this but rejected categorically the American estimates as to *how many* older submarines or ICBMs would have to be dismantled to earn it the right to a new nuclear boat or to *x* additional tubes. Whereas American calculations were that the Soviets had in 1972 between 41 and 43 Yankee-class nuclear submarines, operational or under construction, the Russians insisted they had 48. In this instance, it was advantageous for Moscow to claim as many as possible because fewer "sacrifices" would be required to allow the Soviet Union to reach the permissible limit of the 62 boats and 950 launchers.

At his first meeting with Brezhnev, President Nixon quickly realized that this last issue was the most critical in the whole SALT negotiation. Brezhnev simply would not concede an inch on it. Problems of ABM radars and other related details were settled fairly quickly; the two SALT delegations in Helsinki were accordingly instructed to draft a final version of an ABM treaty. Under "agreed interpretations," rather than in the treaty itself, the two governments set forth commitments such as that phased-array radars outside ABM defense sites might be used only for tracking objects in outer space or for "national technical means of verification." (The latter phrase, incorporated in both the ABM treaty and the interim pact on offensive weapons, refers to satellites, telemetry, and over-the-horizon radar that the United States and the Soviet Union would legally employ to monitor the SALT agreements—although, of course, they were used all along for strategic-intelligence gathering.) Independent electronic and photographic verification had to be the *sine qua non* of SALT inasmuch as neither side accepted on-site inspection.

On the question of mobile land-based ICBMs, Nixon and Brezhnev worked out something of a compromise, and it did not fully meet American intentions. Realizing that the Russians would under no circumstances accept a formal ban on deploying mobile missiles, the administration had begun compromising even before Nixon left Washington for Moscow. On May 20, Ambassador Smith had officially informed the Soviet delegation in Helsinki that "in the interest of concluding the Interim Agreement the U.S. delegation now withdraws its proposal that [the Agreement] . . . explicitly prohibit the deployment of mobile land-based ICBM launchers," although, he warned, the United States would consider such deployment "during the period of the Interim Agreement as inconsistent with the objectives of that Agreement." When Nixon and Brezhnev held their evening session on May 23, the president put it in even stronger terms. Any Soviet deployment of mobile missiles would be considered as cause for abrogating the interim agreement as well as the ABM treaty, Nixon warned. Brezhnev indicated that he understood the American position, but the actual text of the interim agreement took no cognizance of this. Smith's declaration on the subject in Helsinki was simply included as a "unilateral statement" by the United States in "Enclosure 3" attached to the SALT agreements.

The Russians had their way on this point because Nixon and Kissinger believed it was not worth jeopardizing the whole SALT deal over this issue; there were no indications that the Soviet Union had built any mobile ICBMs. It was probably imprudent to relegate the ambiguous language of Smith's declaration to a "unilateral statement," but Kissinger, thinking of the technique applied to the Shanghai communiqué with China, was convinced that "unilateral statements" were, in the absence of an agreement, a brilliant and highly civilized diplomatic device.

Nixon had just as little success with Brezhnev on the question of "heavy" ICBMs. He could not persuade him to accept the notion that any missile in the class of the Soviet SS-9 should be considered "heavy" and that neither side should convert "light" into "heavy" rockets. Brezhnev was not about to tie his hands when it came to building huge missiles— the Soviet answer to the Americans' MIRV advantage. Consequently, Nixon caved in. The American position was thus confined to another "unilateral statement" appended to the interim agreement: "The United States would consider any ICBM having a volume significantly greater than that of the largest light ICBM now operational on either side to be a heavy ICBM. The U.S. proceeds on the premise that the Soviet side will give due account to this consideration." (As it turned out, two years later, the Soviet side did *not* "give due account to this consideration." The secret negotiating record shows that the United States delegation had stipulated that inasmuch as the Soviet SS-11, the largest "light" missile operational in 1972, had a volume of 69 cubic meters, anything over 70 cubic meters would be considered as being "significantly greater." In 1974, however, the Soviet Union fielded a brand-new SS-19 with a volume close to 100 cubic meters as a replacement for the SS-11.) Because their position on "heavy" missiles was no more than a pious expression of hope, the Americans could not even subsequently claim that the Russians were guilty of violating the SALT agreement.

Nixon and Kissinger were similarly outmaneuvered on the related point of silo dimension. What they did not know was that the Russians had developed a so-called cold-launch technique, in which compressed air is used to "pop up" (elevate) the missile in the silo before its engines are ignited; in this fashion, a SS-19 can be fitted into a SS-11 silo enlarged by no more than 15 percent.

(It is important to note that Kissinger misled Congress as to his own errors here and the meaning of clauses in the SALT interim agreement. At a special White House briefing on June 15, 1972, he told congressional leaders:

> The agreement specifically permits the modernization of weapons. There are, however, a number of safeguards. First there is the safeguard that no missile larger than the heaviest light missile that now exists can be substituted. Secondly, there is the provision that the silo configuration cannot be changed in a significant way and then the agreed interpretative statement or the interpretative statement which we made, which the other side stated reflected its views also, that this meant that it could not be increased by more than 10 or 15 percent. We believe that these two statements, taken in conjunction, give us an adequate safeguard against a substantial substitution of heavy missiles for light missiles. So, we think we have adequate safeguards with respect to that issue. . . . As far as the break between the light and the heavy missiles is concerned, we believe that we have assurances through the two safeguards.

But this was not true. No safeguards existed concerning the conversion of light into heavy missiles; the Soviets had never indicated acceptance of American "unilateral statements." The administration also never disclosed the full SALT negotiating record, including its precise stipulation of what the United States regarded as a "significantly greater" volume of missiles.)

Nixon and Kissinger may have been outflanked that evening in Moscow because they lacked the technical competence to comprehend the issues fully. Having kept Smith and his experts in Helsinki, the president was advised by Kissinger, a nuclear strategist but not a weapons expert, and Helmut Sonnenfeldt and William Hyland—who specialized in Soviet political affairs and not in missilery. The NSC's own SALT experts were left behind in Washington. Brezhnev, on the other hand, had the vast professional knowledge of Deputy Premier Leonid V. Smirnov, the man in charge of Soviet missile production, whom the Americans had never met before.

In the end, the May 23 negotiating session was a net minus for the

American side on the vital ICBM issue; Nixon and Kissinger were beaten diplomatically and technically. Brezhnev granted them some points on the ABM radars, a consolation prize for that day's negotiations. Now three out of the four outstanding SALT problems had been resolved, and the two teams turned their attention to the controversy over submarines. Here, however, neither side would budge. Late in the evening, Nixon and Brezhnev broke off, instructing Kissinger and Gromyko to take over the negotiations on submarines while they turned to other matters.

On Wednesday, May 24, Nixon started his day at the Aleksandrov Gardens, laying a wreath at the tomb of the Unknown Soldier; this was one of two public appearances in the Soviet capital. Then, he returned to the Grand Kremlin Palace for a session with Brezhnev and the Soviet team on trade and other bilateral questions.

In the afternoon, it was back to St. Vladimir Hall for the daily ritual of signing agreements. The president and Kosygin signed an agreement on space cooperation (it subsequently resulted in a joint flight by American astronauts and Soviet cosmonauts and other joint space projects); Rogers and V. A. Kirillin, chairman of the Soviet Committee for Science and Technology, signed one on scientific and technological exchanges and cooperation.

Then it was time for Vietnam. In all, there were four separate Soviet-American conferences on this topic during the summit. The first, with Nixon and Brezhnev, took place Wednesday night at a government dacha in the Lenin Hills.

The report from Saigon that morning, routed via Washington, had been rather encouraging to Nixon: the North Vietnamese offensive, now approaching the end of its second month, had slowed down, and the North Vietnamese forces around Hue were making no effort to capture it. The ARVN was able to stabilize its lines in the Central Highlands and north of Saigon. Nixon and Kissinger thought that the bombing and the mining of the North—which had gone on unabated during the previous days—was a major reason for the improvement. Perhaps, they reasoned, Hanoi no longer believed the spring offensive could destroy the Thieu regime, and it was developing second thoughts about the whole enterprise.

Brezhnev left with Nixon and Kissinger for the country so suddenly after the signing ceremonies at the Kremlin that the two NSC aides who were to attend the meeting—Winston Lord and John Negroponte—were left behind at their hotel, and with them were all the position papers on Vietnam, including Nixon's "talking points." Making their way to the

Kremlin, Lord and Negroponte found General Antonov, head of Soviet police forces, who presently procured what he described as the best car in Moscow. Careening to the dacha at eighty-five miles an hour, Lord and Negroponte reached the estate while Brezhnev was demonstrating his hydrofoil boat on the river to Nixon and Kissinger.

The Vietnam session opened at 8:00 p.m. in a simply furnished room and lasted until 11:30, when Brezhnev finally called a dinner recess. The men sat around an oval table, a grandfather clock stood in a corner, and through the window one could see white birches and the garden sloping down to the river. Brezhnev, Kosygin, Podgorny, and Aleksandrov sat on one side of the table; Nixon, Kissinger, Lord, and Negroponte on the other. (The president faced Aleksandrov, who doubled as the inter-preter.)

Nixon took the floor first, speaking quietly for about twenty minutes, without notes. He made the point that if the Soviet Union's allies attacked America's allies with Soviet equipment, the United States had no choice but to react. Nixon went on to say that the United States had laid out its negotiating terms and that if Hanoi did not find them acceptable, it would pursue the bombing and the mining.

Kosygin, Podgorny, and Brezhnev each spoke for about one hour, in that order. They were critical of American policies in Vietnam but said, in effect, that there was nothing the Soviet Union could do about them. Kosygin was the most bitter: "I was in Hanoi [in 1965] when the Ameri-cans started bombing and I shall never forget it." But as Sonnenfeldt had predicted, even Kosygin confined his protest to the danger of a Soviet ship being hit by American bombs. The general line of Brezhnev's re-marks was that détente was moving ahead, so why should the United States spoil it all by destroying North Vietnam and being condemned for it by the rest of the world? None of the three Russians suggested that the continuing war in Vietnam was an obstacle to détente. At one point, Kosygin turned to Nixon and said: "You have Henry Kissinger, he's a smart man, why don't you get him to find the right solution for the war?" The Russians talked and talked and talked—for so long that Nixon turned to Kissinger to whisper, "God, this cannot go on like this." Then, in a rather unusual gesture, he lit a small cigar. The sumptuous dinner was all cordiality, Kosygin leading the toasts with Georgian brandy. Nixon had two or three brandies, bottoms up.

The second meeting on Vietnam was held between Kissinger and Foreign Minister Gromyko at the Kremlin during the afternoon of Thurs-day, May 25. There Kissinger dropped two diplomatic bombs. After

Gromyko made it clear that the Soviet Union could live with the existing situation in Vietnam, Kissinger told him that the American air action over North Vietnam did not *necessarily* have to continue until all the POWs were returned. This was an abrupt departure from the position stated by Nixon only two weeks earlier that the return of the prisoners was the *first* condition for the end of bombing in the North. Thus, again, Kissinger was producing a secret diplomatic line at variance with the public U.S. position. Clearly, he was using the bombing as a bargaining chip.

Kissinger's second surprise was the sudden introduction of the theme of the Vietnamese political situation. This had not been discussed previously and was also a departure from Nixon's speech of May 8, in which no mention at all was made of Vietnamese politics. Kissinger announced that the United States was prepared to back a tripartite electoral commission in South Vietnam, including elements from the Saigon regime, the Viet Cong, and the neutralists. This was a real shift: the United States had opposed such a tripartite commission out of fear that it could evolve into a coalition government, which Saigon and Washington had always rejected. The secret American proposal of October 1971 had spoken only of an "independent body," representing all political forces in South Vietnam, to organize and run the elections—a far cry from a tripartite commission. Gromyko was so taken aback that he said to Kissinger, "Let me make quite sure I got right what you said." Kissinger replied: "Yes, I'm talking about a tripartite commission."

Kissinger and Gromyko discussed Vietnam again on Friday, May 26, covering roughly the same ground. The net effect of these discussions was that the United States made it clear to the Russians that its private negotiating position was infinitely more flexible than the public posture. This covered the North Vietnamese presence in the South, the willingness to suspend bombing even before the release of the POWs, and the support for a tripartite electoral commission. Kissinger was edging closer and closer to Hanoi's views—except for the immediate removal of Thieu—and was laying the foundations for what would become the ultimate settlement.

The last discussion on Vietnam was conducted by Nixon and Brezhnev on May 29 at their farewell meeting. They agreed that Podgorny would go to Hanoi as soon as possible to convey to the North Vietnamese the views Kissinger had expressed in Moscow. The precise nature of Podgorny's mission has thus far been kept secret, although his presence in Hanoi between June 15 and June 18 was publicly announced at the time. Kissinger was delighted that Podgorny would serve as an intermediary, and he expressed pride to his associates that the Russians "are going to help us."

On Wednesday afternoon, May 24, while Nixon was busy at signing ceremonies, Kissinger tried to break the SALT deadlock in a meeting with Gromyko and Smirnov. Then he raced with Nixon to the Brezhnev dacha for the first Vietnam session and the midnight dinner—complete with Georgian brandy toasts. The president returned to Moscow to retire for the night, but Kissinger, with Winston Lord, rushed back to the Foreign Ministry and SALT negotiations with Gromyko, Smirnov, Dobrynin, and Georgy Kornienko, a member of the collegium of the ministry and an expert on American affairs. (Sonnenfeldt and Hyland awaited Kissinger at the ministry.) The group worked until 4:00 a.m. Thursday, finally recessing out of sheer exhaustion. Some progress was made during the night, but the two sides could not agree on defining at what precise point a submarine was "under construction"—a key point in determining the schedule of substitutions.

Negotiations were proceeding simultaneously on all fronts. Nixon had a midmorning conference with a sleepy Kissinger, reviewing the Vietnam discussion of the previous evening and the status of SALT following the predawn negotiations at the Foreign Ministry. Then he met for two hours with Brezhnev and his advisers for another general look at the world situation. Rogers and Flanigan were completing trade talks with Kosygin and his team. In the afternoon, Kissinger was back at the Foreign Ministry, this time to drop his Vietnam bombs. Navy Secretary John Warner and Admiral S. G. Gorshkov, commander in chief of the Soviet navy, signed an agreement on the prevention of accidents at sea.

In the evening, the Nixons, Brezhnev, and all the American and Soviet dignitaries involved congregated at the Bolshoi Theater to attend a performance of the ballet *Swan Lake*. This was Nixon's second public appearance in Moscow. But not even *Swan Lake* could entirely interrupt the SALT negotiating process. The deadline was quickly approaching, and the Russians wanted the SALT agreements to be signed the following day. In the course of the performance, Hyland kept vanishing to take telephone calls from the NSC staff in Washington. (Nixon and Kissinger needed constant contact with the Pentagon—they did not want to risk problems with Secretary Laird and the Joint Chiefs during the bargaining with the Russians—and the NSC experts in Washington served as the link.)

From the Bolshoi, the president went back to the Kremlin, but Kissinger—again—headed for the Foreign Ministry to pick up the negotiations. He presented a new proposal on submarine replacements approved by Nixon. But the meeting broke up at 3:00 a.m. without a solution. The Russians said they needed instructions from Brezhnev before proceeding further. Now both sides knew they had only the daytime hours of Friday to reach an agreement—or to see SALT disintegrate and the summit collapse. Nixon was becoming increasingly uncomfortable. Conferring with Kissinger in the Kremlin apartments in midmorning on Friday, May 26, he made it clear that he was prepared to go home without an agreement if the Soviets rejected the final American offer on the submarines, submitted during the night.

Curiously, the issue separating the two sides was minor in comparison with the other SALT problems resolved earlier in the week, chiefly by dint of Nixon's concessions. The United States had agreed in Helsinki that the Soviets could build up to a limit of 62 nuclear submarines and 950 launching tubes from what they already had in 1972 *provided* they retired older submarines and obsolescent land-based ICBMs to make up the difference, and the concept of replacements was acceptable to the Russians. The week-long argument in Moscow was over the precise quantitative and qualitative formula for replacements; for example, was an extra tube on a Soviet nuclear submarine worth 1, 2, or 3 old land-based SS-7 launchers? And, above all, what was the exact numerical difference between the existing Soviet nuclear-submarine fleet and the proposed SALT ceiling?

The numbers involved were ridiculously small compared to the overall Soviet and American nuclear arsenals. In Yankee-class submarines, the difference was 5 or 6 Soviet boats; in launcher tubes, the difference was 128 (the Russians said they had only 640, while the American count was 768). At the Foreign Ministry meeting in the early hours of Friday, the Soviet team tacitly agreed to go along with the American estimate of 41–43 nuclear submarines already deployed by the Soviet fleet or "in construction." This meant that the Soviet Union would have to retire 19–21 (not 14) of its conventional boats to be allowed to reach the permitted total of 62. The Russians and the Americans also found a definition for submarines "in construction"—this was necessary to determine *when* old boats had to be phased out—but they were completely stymied by the problem of the 128 tubes and how older Soviet submarines would be replaced. The most important political negotiation since World War II was on the verge of failing over what essentially were minor military details.

For Nixon, however, this was a matter of principle. He had already compromised—in the Helsinki negotiations and in his meetings with Brezhnev in Moscow—over several important issues. He knew that the Pentagon (and, for that matter, the State Department, which had taken a dim view of the Helsinki concessions) firmly opposed any capitulation on the submarines, as telegrams and telephone calls from Washington were reminding him every day. A SALT agreement would require Senate approval, and the president could not risk being undermined by the bureaucrats, who would inevitably take their case to the senators.

The proposal made by Kissinger at dawn on Friday was something of a compromise, but one Nixon thought could be sold to the Pentagon. It provided for establishing a "baseline" of 740 tubes from which the Russians could build up to the 950 limit. It was not exactly splitting the difference (which would have resulted in a 708-tube baseline), but the Americans insisted that the 30 tubes on H-class submarines, which the Soviets were expected to keep, be included in the 740 baseline. They also demanded that tubes on the old, noisy diesel-powered G-class boats be counted in the 950 total if the Russians chose to upgrade them.

The submarine controversy was one of the most confusing (and esoteric) in the history of contemporary diplomacy—and Nixon and Kissinger were at the self-inflicted disadvantage of lacking technical experts to advise them. John Newhouse, a disarmament specialist, has noted that "after the White House party returned to Washington, several meetings of the Verification Panel were devoted largely to trying to establish exactly what had been agreed on SLBMs [submarine-launched ballistic missiles] and what, precisely, it all meant." In short, the larger question is whether the president and Kissinger knew precisely what they were doing. Many members of the American delegation in Helsinki, all professional experts in strategic weaponry, had serious doubts on that score. The agreements were so ambiguous that later it was impossible to say with authority whether the Soviets were actually violating them. In fact, Kissinger was forced to renegotiate secretly with Dobrynin in July 1972 one of the clauses in the submarine agreement (the Senate was not informed of this until *two years* later, after it had voted to ratify the SALT package).

The morning of May 26 was one of nearly unbearable tension for Nixon and Kissinger as they awaited the Soviet reply to their final compromise offer. The signing of the SALT agreement had been officially scheduled for 5:00 p.m., and the news media, naturally, were unaware that it might never take place. The president simply had no idea what would happen next; for one thing, he was to host a dinner for Brezhnev and other Soviet leaders at the American embassy that evening. What kind of a dinner would it be, he wondered, if SALT collapsed?

Meanwhile, Brezhnev was presiding over an emergency meeting of the Politburo to decide whether to accept the American proposal. He, too, was eager for a SALT agreement, but like Nixon, he had to have the support of *his* political and military establishment. Shortly after 11:00 a.m., as the Politburo session ended, Gromyko telephoned Kissinger to say that the negotiators could reconvene immediately in Catherine Hall. Brezhnev had evidently carried the day, for the Russians immediately informed Kissinger that they were accepting the American position on all points, including the tube baseline and the handling of the G- and H-class submarines. This was the breakthrough and the salvaging of SALT.

But the immediate problem was that the SALT documents were not ready for signature. Under the bizarre procedure devised by Nixon and Kissinger—and accepted by the Russians—to keep the American SALT delegation, and therefore the Russian one also, away from Moscow during the negotiations, both the ABM treaty and the interim agreement on offensive weapons were being drafted physically not in Moscow, which would have made sense, but in Helsinki.

As each point of the agreement was hammered out in Moscow, Americans and Russians had to telephone and cable instructions to their Helsinki people, who, in turn, drafted the documents. By Friday morning, they had everything ready except the special protocol on the submarines as they awaited word from Moscow. Now the problem was to bring the two delegations and completed drafts to Moscow so that the signing could take place after dinner (the time was delayed from the original 5:00 p.m.). Kissinger at least had the foresight to have a U.S. Air Force plane standing by in Helsinki, but it was already 2:30 p.m. when the delegation received its cabled instructions.

Working furiously throughout the afternoon, the delegations drafted the submarines protocol and amended the text of the interim agreement to conform with it. Then they rushed to the plane, putting the finishing touches on the documents while flying to Moscow. They arrived at Vnukovo just as the dinner at the American embassy was getting under way; parts of the documents still had to be retyped at the Foreign Ministry because of errors made by the breathlessly working secretaries. It was a most unconventional diplomatic exercise.

While this scenario was unfolding, the attention of the press was taken with the communiqué on the establishment of a Joint United States–Soviet Union Commercial Commission, the result of the week's trade talks. The communiqué said the commission was instructed to negotiate "an overall trade agreement" between the two countries and a series of related accords. For the Soviet Union, the most important provision in this planned trade pact was Nixon's commitment to grant it most-favored-nation treatment in terms of tariffs on Soviet goods entering the United States. Actually, in the past, among America's trading partners only Communist countries (except Poland and Yugoslavia) had been deprived of the MFN benefit, and this was why the new commission was mandated to negotiate "reciprocal MFN treatment." However, only Congress has the right to grant most-favored-nation status, and the president had overcommitted his government. For a variety of reasons, he would not be able to deliver on his pledge. The trade commission was also to negotiate reciprocal availability of government credits, reciprocal establishment of business facilities to promote trade, and an agreement for an arbitration mechanism for settling commercial disputes. Further in the future, the joint commission was to study possible American-Soviet "participation in the development of resources and the manufacture and sale of raw materials and other products." In general, the idea was that détente would increase trade and economic cooperation between the United States and Russia in many fields. Quite a few American policymakers believed that economic motives were paramount in the Soviet interest in détente. And Nixon and Kissinger, for their part, had the idea that the United States would "reward" the Russians for correct political behavior—however that was defined in their minds—with economic advantages.

But as with all else concerning détente in its early euphoric days, expectations in the economic field considerably exceeded the real possibilities. To be sure, the Russians were hungry for American technology to modernize their industry and American food imports to make up for their chronic farm-production deficiencies. There was very little, however, that the United States was interested in buying in the Soviet Union. And the wild hopes for Soviet-American cooperative projects to produce petroleum and natural gas in Siberia, for example, proved unfeasible. In any event, the trade communiqué provided copy for the hundreds of newsmen in Moscow.

The president's dinner at Spaso House—the American embassy—had to be delayed until 8:30 because of the last-minute SALT-drafting problems, and the signing itself was held at 11:00 p.m. in St. Vladimir Hall, carried live on television to the world (it was reasonably good watching time in the eastern United States—5:00 p.m.).

With Nixon signing first, followed by Brezhnev, the two leaders affixed their signatures to three documents: a treaty of indefinite duration limiting antiballistic defense systems to one in each country; a five-year interim agreement on offensive strategic arms providing for a freeze, effective July 1, on the construction of new land-based ICBM launchers (it left the United States with 1054 launchers and the Soviet Union with 1618); and a protocol to the interim agreement stipulating that the United States might have no more than 44 modern nuclear ballistic-missile submarines and 710 missile launchers, and the Soviet Union no more than 62 such submarines and 950 launchers. A Standing Consultative Commission was established to assure compliance "with the obligations assumed and related situations which may be considered ambiguous." Both governments committed themselves to "continue active negotiations for limitations on strategic offensive arms."

Nixon and Brezhnev rose from the table and shook hands. They stood at attention as the anthems of the United States and the Soviet Union were played. Then Nixon turned to Brezhnev and said quietly: "This was one of the greatest days in our lives." Brezhnev replied softly, "Yes, it was." But they had to sign the documents again the following morning: the papers they had signed at the Kremlin were inaccurate because of typing errors that had not been caught in time.

It was almost inevitable that a confusing negotiation would be completed in confusion. Not only had Nixon and Brezhnev signed flawed documents Friday night, but no copies of the texts of the SALT agreements were available to newsmen, who had to depend on a chaotic briefing by Kissinger in a hotel rooftop nightclub to learn what had been agreed to. Kissinger did his best, but the reporters, unfamiliar with the background of the week's excruciating debates, had difficulty understanding why the United States had accepted this or that. It was impossible to give adequate explanations of "unilateral statements" and "agreed interpretations."

It took a long time not only for reporters, but for Congress and the bureaucracy to understand fully, assuming that they *did* understand, what had been accomplished in the SALT negotiations. Only Nixon and Kissinger know everything that was *said* by both sides in the negotiations— as distinct from what appears in the official texts. There is no certainty that even the actual negotiating record, still maintained in absolute secrecy, is complete.

There was an agreement made by Nixon and Kissinger in Moscow that does not appear in the text of the interim agreement. This was the

American commitment *not* to dismantle the heavy but quite obsolescent Titan ICBMs in exchange for modern ballistic submarines—the Tridents —that the United States hoped to start building in the late 1970s to reach its allowable ceiling. The Russians had pressed this point, preferring to have the Americans give up, for example, some of the relatively advanced Polaris submarines under the replacement-and-modernization *quid pro quo* formula.

Strictly speaking, this was not a "secret agreement," inasmuch as Kissinger mentioned it in passing at a Washington news briefing in June —which he decided to do at the last moment after some of his aides warned him he was certain to be asked about secret agreements in SALT (as indeed he was) and should not be untruthful. Why Kissinger chose, in the first place, to keep the Titan provision out of the official text is one of those White House mysteries.

The House Select Committee on Intelligence had this to say about SALT in its report in 1976:

> It is clear that, in the final stages of the SALT talks, U.S. negotiators did not fully consult or inform intelligence experts, who had been key figures in previous treaty sessions. Only Russian technical experts were on hand. Dr. Kissinger's private talks with Soviet leaders in this period were not disseminated. Some officials assert that "ambiguities" which plague the accords may have been the result of U.S. policy-makers' self-imposed intelligence blackout at the critical moment. The record indicates that Dr. Kissinger, U.S. architect of the accords, has attempted to control the dissemination and analysis of data on apparent Soviet violations of the SALT pact. . . . The spectre of important information, suggesting Soviet violation of strategic arms limitations, purposefully withheld for extended periods from analysts, decision-makers and members of Congress, has caused great controversy within the Intelligence Community.

More and more, serious commentators have concluded that the Nixon-Kissinger SALT diplomacy was deficient. Lord Chalfont, a former British cabinet minister and specialist in strategic problems, wrote in mid-1976 that "while the strategic arms limitation talks have been going on, and partly as a result of American concessions during those negotiations, the Soviet Union has achieved a position of strategic nuclear superiority over the United States."

Still, the agreements Nixon and Brezhnev signed in 1972 were a milestone in the nuclear age. Obviously, if they so desire, the superpowers can go to war regardless of agreements; this was always clear. But as

John Newhouse noted, "the two sides have engaged in a frank, open, nonpolemical dialogue on the weapons most vital to their security. . . . That is itself a watershed."

After the signing of the SALT agreements, the balance of Nixon's stay in the Soviet Union—three and a half more days—was largely ceremonial although he and Brezhnev had more conversations, and Kissinger kept up his diplomatic missionary work, mainly on Vietnam, with Gromyko and his colleagues.

On Saturday, May 27, the president, accompanied by Podgorny, flew to Leningrad for the day. First, he visited the Piskaryev Cemetery, where thousands of Russians killed during the wartime siege of the city are buried. There he was shown the memorial to a twelve-year-old girl named Tanya, her picture, and her diary, which described the siege until the moment of her death. Nixon was touched so deeply that the memory of Tanya would stay with him for years and keep recurring in his speeches. Addressing the Executive Committee of the Leningrad Council of Workers Deputies, his lunch hosts at Mariinsky Palace, the president spoke of Tanya: "She was a beautiful child—brown eyes, a pretty face. The pages of her diary were there for all to see. She recorded how first her mother died, her father died, her brothers and her sister, and then only she was left. . . ." But then, however, Nixon had to use Tanya to make a political point. He went on to say: "As I think of Tanya, that twelve-year-old girl in Leningrad, I think of all the Tanyas in the world—in the Soviet Union, in the United States, in Asia, in Africa and Latin America, wherever they may be. I only hope that the visit that we have had at the highest level with the Soviet leaders will have contributed to that kind of world in which the little Tanyas and their brothers and sisters will be able to grow up in a world of peace and friendship among people—all people in the world." The self-conscious statesman once again could not leave well enough alone. In the afternoon, the Nixons dutifully visited the Pavlovsk Museum, then flew back to Moscow.

On Sunday, the Nixons attended services at Moscow's Baptist Church, and the president spent the afternoon in his Kremlin apartment polishing the television speech he was to deliver in the evening (it was not really another "first": he had addressed Soviet audiences in 1959 during his vice-presidential visit) and catching up on paper work. At 8:30 p.m. Nixon went to the Green Room in the Grand Kremlin Palace to face the cameras of the Soviet State Television and the American networks. It was an explanation of his presence in the country and a pitch for détente. Because White House speech-writers have the notion that American presidents abroad must use a few words in the language of the country they are visiting (this patronizing aberration was not invented by Nixon's men), Nixon opened with a "Dobryy vecher" ("Good evening") and closed with "Spasibo y do svidaniye" ("Thank you and good-bye"). He told an old Russian peasant story to illustrate a point (White House speech-writers have every kind of research material at their fingertips) and mentioned the diary of Tanya he had seen in Leningrad the day before: "Let us think of . . . the other Tanyas and their brothers and sisters everywhere."

On Nixon's last day in Moscow, he and Brezhnev had a brief private conversation—this was when Nixon learned that Podgorny would go to Hanoi within two weeks—and then they signed a twelve-point declaration on the "Basic Principles of Relations Between the United States of America and the Union of Soviet Socialist Republics." The key points were that "in the nuclear age there is no alternative to conducting their mutual relations on the basis of peaceful coexistence"; that they "attach major importance to preventing the development of situations capable of causing a dangerous exacerbation of their relations"; that they "have a special responsibility . . . to do everything in their power so that conflicts or situations will not arise which would serve to increase international tensions"; that they "will continue their efforts to limit armaments on a bilateral as well as on a multilateral basis"; and that they "make no claim for themselves and would not recognize the claims of anyone else to any special rights or advantages in world affairs."

The last point was of special interest to the Soviet leaders: it was an explicit recognition of the Soviet Union's global *political* parity with the United States—something the Russians had sought since the end of World War II but which the Americans granted only when they accepted the concept of nuclear *equivalence* between the two superpowers. For the first time, the United States recognized the equal role of the Soviet Union in international problems ranging from Asia to the Middle East.

This recognition was further spelled out in the joint communiqué on the Nixon-Brezhnev talks, the final document of the Moscow summit, issued simultaneously with the "Principles." In the section on "International Issues," the communiqué said that the United States and the Soviet Union "intend to make further efforts to ensure a peaceful future for Europe, free of tensions, crises and conflicts." Specifically, foundations were laid for the European security conference, a long-cherished Soviet objective, with the statement that "the conference should be carefully prepared" but held "without undue delay." The communiqué mentioned the need for "a reciprocal reduction of armed forces and armaments" in Central Europe, but it made no commitment for a special conference on this subject although the United States and NATO had been advocating it since 1968.

Concerning the Middle East, the two governments confirmed "their desire . . . to play their part in bringing about a peaceful settlement" that "would open prospects for the normalization of the Middle East situation and would permit in particular, consideration of further steps to bring about a military relaxation in that area." On Indochina, each side stated its public position (the same device used in the Shanghai communiqué with China) without any mention of the private views exchanged in the Nixon-Brezhnev talks.

Nixon's Moscow visit ended with a noontime Kremlin reception, where Brezhnev bade him farewell. Podgorny and Kosygin went to the airport to see the Nixon party in the rain board a Soviet airliner for the flight to Kiev, in the Ukraine, the president's last stop in the Soviet Union. However, the plane was unable to start its engines, and, after an hour's delay, the Americans were transferred to another jetliner. *Air Force One* followed.

In Kiev, the president attended a dinner offered by the Ukrainian authorities, delivered a brief speech extolling the wartime courage of the city's inhabitants and praising them for their reconstruction efforts, and retired at midnight for his last night on Soviet soil. The next day, he laid a wreath at the Tomb of the Unknown Soldier in the Park of Eternal Glory to the Soldiers of the Great Patriotic War and, accompanied by his wife, visited the famous St. Sophia Cathedral and Museum. Then, it was back to the airport and a long flight to Tehran, the next point on the presidential itinerary.

Nixon had spent eight days in the Soviet Union, but for him and the rest of the American group it was more like eighty. It had been very hard work.

Mohammed Riza Shah Pahlevi of Iran was a close ally of the United States. Following Britain's departure from the Persian Gulf in 1971, his country had become the center of pro-Western military power in the Middle East. Aside from Israel, Iran was the only Middle Eastern nation openly friendly to the United States at this juncture. The shah was being armed to the teeth by the United States and Great Britain, and expanding his influence in the whole gulf region. Finally, Iran was a leading oil producer and a major source of supply for the West.

For all these reasons, Nixon found it desirable to pay a call on the shah on his way home. It was an overnight visit, and as the president said in a toast to the shah, "We will always be grateful for that little respite after our eight days in the Kremlin. And while the Kremlin is a great palace, to be there for eight days is a long time." So ostensibly the twenty-four hours was a time to relax while making a friendly goodwill gesture. But Nixon and the shah held two private conferences—one on the evening of the president's arrival and the other on the morning of Wednesday, May 31, before his departure for Warsaw. Their joint communiqué reflected no more than had been expected—curiously, nothing was said about oil, but as one American official remarked, Nixon had not come to Tehran to bargain over petroleum prices. What Nixon and Kissinger *did* negotiate with the shah—in the most absolute secrecy—was the covert involvement of the United States in the insurgency conducted for decades against the Iraqi government by Kurdish tribal rebels led by General Mustafa al-Barzani. This was one of the most shameful actions undertaken secretly by the White House, in terms both of the original support for the Kurds and of their subsequent abandonment—in each case for reasons of political expediency.

The shah had been quietly backing the Kurdish rebellion for some time, chiefly because Iran disputed its common boundary line with Iraq at the head of the Persian Gulf. Tankers carrying oil from Iran's huge Abadan refinery and terminal had to navigate Iraqi waters before reaching the gulf itself. The shah was concerned that if the dispute worsened, the Iraqis might block the movement of the tankers. Armed incidents had occurred between Iranian and Iraqi forces in border areas, and the shah had concluded that he could best keep the Baghdad regime in check by encouraging the Kurdish rebellion. It was a useful diversion. Actually, Iran had no desire to see the Kurds achieve autonomy: there were about one million Kurds living in Iranian territory, and the shah did not want them to develop separatist sentiments if Barzani succeeded in setting up a Kurdish state next door in Iraq. Iran thus simply used the Kurds to harass the Iraqis.

To do so effectively, the Iranians felt they needed American assistance in arms and money, preferably through the CIA. Their first request was made in January 1970, when the shah was still short on weapons and the big oil money had not begun to flow into his treasury. But both the State Department and the CIA opposed American involvement with the Kurds. On January 20, Joseph Sisco, assistant secretary of state for Near Eastern affairs, said in a secret memorandum to the CIA's acting deputy director for plans (clandestine services), "The U.S. does not support the concept of an autonomous entity. . . . We thus do not wish to become involved, even indirectly, in operations which would have the effect of prolonging the insurgency, thereby encouraging separatist aspirations and possibly providing to the Soviet Union an opportunity to create difficulties for Iran and Pakistan."

As frictions between Iran and Iraq increased in 1971, the shah renewed his request in August of that year and again in March 1972. Again he was turned down. Kissinger discussed the matter with Sisco in March and agreed with him that the United States should stay out of the Kurdish rebellion.

When Nixon arrived in Tehran at the end of May, the shah raised the Kurdish question once more. He told the president and Kissinger that the situation had changed radically with the signing of a Soviet-Iraqi friendship treaty on April 6, 1972. The shah had been alarmed by the visit of a Soviet naval squadron to the Iraqi ports of Umm Qasr and Basra immediately after that, and by the prospect that Iraq would be receiving even greater Soviet military assistance. As it was, the Iraqi Air Force was made up almost entirely of MiG-19 and MiG-21 jet fighter-bombers; now the shah feared a major military threat from Iraq.

What is unclear to this day is why at that juncture Iran thought it needed American arms and money to help the Kurdish insurgency; by then it had adequate supplies of both. There is no known record of the conversation between the shah and Nixon, but the Iranian ruler was evidently convincing in his argument; Nixon and Kissinger agreed to give the request favorable consideration, and the president promised a prompt decision.

One possibility is that Nixon agreed with the Iranian view that Iraq should be weakened as much as possible. The radical regime in Baghdad was a formal ally of the Soviet Union and outspokenly anti-American. Nixon may have also feared that Iraq's growing military power might be used against Israel. In any case, he committed himself to a policy directed against a Soviet ally within twenty-four hours of leaving the Soviet Union. If nothing else, it was a good illustration of the underlying weakness of détente—despite all the rhetoric of the preceding days—and of the quintessential fact that nothing had really changed in American and Soviet national interests.

Another secret agreement made by Nixon and the shah provided for unrestricted sales of *all* conventional weapons systems by the United

States to Iran. A major program of military supplies to the Iranians had been started in 1971, with minimal publicity, but now the shah wanted an open-ended arrangement. He argued that the Soviet Union and Iraq posed a danger to Iran, indeed to the entire Persian Gulf area, and that he had to build the most powerful arms establishment in the region. A parallel problem, he told Nixon, was that Iran needed a modern army and air force to cope with radical rebel movements on the Arabian peninsula —in Oman, for example. The president agreed that the Iranians should receive everything they needed; this view was reflected in the joint communiqué's statement on the "vital importance" of the Persian Gulf's "security and stability" and Iran's "determination to bear its share of this responsibility."

The president, however, never informed Congress of this commitment. It became known only four years later when a Senate committee came across relevant documents that told the story, including a secret NSC memorandum signed by Kissinger. A staff study by the Senate Foreign Relations Committee noted that Nixon's decision to sell Iran the most modern aircraft and "in general to let Iran buy anything it wanted" prevented any review of this program either by the Pentagon or by the State Department. The program, indeed, may have made little sense the way Nixon set it in motion, but the figures tell the tale: Iran's overall military expenditures rose from $1.94 billion in 1972 (when Nixon visited the shah) to $5.28 billion in 1974. Iran's *purchases* of arms rose from $415 million in 1972 to $870 million in 1974. Between 1971 and 1976, Iran spent a total of *$10.4 billion* on military purchases (1975 and 1976 being the highest years in this buying binge). According to the U.S. Arms Control and Disarmament Agency, in 1974 Iran was the world's leading arms importer, ahead of Israel, West Germany, Syria, North Vietnam, and Saudi Arabia.

The Kurdish question, meanwhile, must have been much on Nixon's mind because he acted on it as soon as he returned to Washington—still in total secrecy. In late June, John Connally, who had resigned as treasury secretary two weeks earlier to work on Nixon's reelection campaign, visited Tehran to deliver a personal message from the president to the shah that the CIA had been ordered to assist the Kurds. (He stopped in Iran in the course of a world tour on Nixon's behalf.) Kurdish emissaries came to Washington early in July to discuss operations with Helms and Kissinger's aide Colonel Louis Kennedy.

Nixon's decision was taken without approval of the Forty Committee, the executive panel coordinating covert intelligence operations, and without the knowledge of Secretary of State Rogers. On August 7, Helms sent a telegram to the Tehran CIA station chief informing him that the State Department was unaware of the Washington visit by the Kurdish envoys, adding, "Thus do not discuss with the ambassador." Later that day, however, Helms discovered that the ambassador in Tehran, Joseph Farland, knew about Connally's mission and its purpose. So he sent a telegram directly to Farland: "Nixon has, since his talks with the shah, taken a personal interest in the matter. He has felt that we should do all we can to prevent the Soviets from exploiting the Iraqis to their advantage and to the jeopardy of Iran. . . . I must say in all frankness, however, that not everyone in State sees it in this light. The project has been held tightly here in Washington and I know you will help us hold it tightly over there."

A few days later, Kissinger decided to acquaint the Forty Committee with the Kurdish operation in a one-paragraph memorandum. The members, including Under Secretary of State for Political Affairs U. Alexis Johnson, were simply asked to initial it. There was no discussion.

Actually, American aid to Barzani's guerrillas was exceedingly small. Between August 1972, when it was initiated, and March 1975, when it was ended at the request of the shah, who settled his border problem with Iraq, it totaled only $16 million. Perhaps its value lay in the fact that Barzani trusted the United States more than he did Iran, not realizing that the two governments were in cahoots to use him as a pawn. Poor Barzani was so grateful for the support he was getting that he sent Kissinger a gift of three rugs and later, when Kissinger was married, a gold-and-pearl necklace. Within the White House, however, this was a deep secret. A CIA memorandum to General Brent Scowcroft, deputy head of the NSC staff, said, "The relationship between the United States Government and the Kurds remains extremely sensitive. Knowledge of its existence has been severely restricted; therefore, the fact that Dr. Kissinger has received this gift should be similarly restricted."

What Barzani did not know was that as early as October 1972 the CIA was apprised of secret negotiations between Iran and Iraq through Algeria. The Iranians had sent word that if Iraq was willing to sign a new treaty over the disputed waters, they would "be willing to allow peace to prevail in the Kurdish area." Although Baghdad was not yet ready to do business with the shah, the CIA went on considering Barzani an expendable asset. A CIA internal memorandum remarked, "Iran, like ourselves, has seen benefit in a stalemate situation . . . in which Iraq is intrinsically weakened by the Kurds' refusal to relinquish its semi-autonomy. Neither Iran nor ourselves wish to see the matter resolved one way or the other.

... [The Kurds] are a uniquely useful tool for weakening Iraq's potential for international adventurism."

During the 1973 Arab-Israeli war, Barzani offered to undertake an offensive against Iraq. But neither the White House nor the CIA wanted this to happen, because it might have upset the shah's strategy. On October 16, 1973, Kissinger sent a memorandum to William Colby, the new director of Central Intelligence, advising him that Nixon concurred in the judgment that no such offensive was desirable and that Barzani should be so informed. He added that Iran took the same view.

In March 1975, when the shah made peace with Iraq, he withdrew his support from the Kurds, and the United States did likewise. Deprived of outside aid, Barzani's insurgency collapsed and thousands of Kurds were killed. The House Select Committee on Intelligence, which studied this episode, concluded that "even in the context of covert action, ours was a cynical enterprise."

This, then, was the principal result of Nixon's visit to Tehran in May 1972. As the president said, he enjoyed every minute of it—the sumptuous dinner at the shah's Niavaran Palace, the sight-seeing, and the relaxation. Kissinger, too, had a fine time. After the shah's dinner, the Iranian prime minister took him to a nightclub to admire belly dancers over caviar and champagne.

On May 31, the president flew to Warsaw—his last stop before returning home. The United States had good political relations with Poland going back to 1959, when Vice President Nixon had received an enthusiastic reception there. Besides, a special relationship had always existed between Poles and Americans, what with millions of citizens of Polish descent living in the United States. This time Nixon was keen on making it clear that Poland, too, should be part of détente and benefit from it. He met twice with Edward Gierek, first secretary of the Polish Communist Party (who came to power after the Christmas 1970 food riots), and chief of state Henryk Jabłonski, attended a dinner at the Palace of the Council of Ministers, and hosted a lunch for Polish leaders at the suburban Wilanów Palace. A Moscow-length joint communiqué was issued, and Secretary Rogers and Foreign Minister Stefan Olszowski signed a convention providing for the opening of an American consulate in Kraków, Poland's old royal city, and of a Polish consulate in New York. In midafternoon of June 1, Nixon went to Okęcie Airport to board *Air Force One* for the nonstop flight to Washington.

He had been gone from the United States for thirteen days, and it was the toughest diplomatic journey he had ever undertaken. But the president was bringing home the fragile gift of détente.

Chapter 22

The late spring and summer of 1972 were Richard Nixon's time of apotheosis. He was riding high. In foreign affairs, he had scored what were believed to be extraordinary achievements. The Moscow summit and the signing of the SALT agreements had ushered in the era of détente and, together with the China journey, were the greatest turning point in America's international relations since World War II. Even the president's severest critics had to grant him his achievements in statesmanship.

Returning from his summit journey on the evening of June 1, the president dramatically flew by helicopter from Andrews Air Force Base to Capitol Hill to deliver a nocturnal address to a joint session of Congress on his sixteen-thousand-mile trip. The president, greeted with a standing ovation and continually interrupted by applause, reported that "everywhere we went . . . we could feel the quickening pace of change in old international relationships and the people's genuine desire for friendship for the American people." This was Nixon at his statesmanlike best:

> Everywhere new hopes are rising for a world no longer shadowed by fear and want and war, and as Americans we can be proud that we now have an historic opportunity to play a great role in helping to achieve man's oldest dream—a world in which all nations can enjoy the blessings of peace. . . .
>
> To millions of Americans for the past quarter century the Kremlin has stood for implacable hostility toward all that we cherish, and to millions of Russians the American flag has long been held up as a symbol of evil. No one would have believed, even a short time ago, that these two apparently irreconcilable symbols would be seen together. . . . This summit has already made its news. It has barely begun, however, to make its mark on our world, and I ask you to join me tonight—while events are fresh, while the iron is hot—in starting to consider how we can help to make that mark what we want it to be.

The president asked Congress to approve the agreements he had reached in Moscow—the SALT treaty, for one, required Senate ratification—so that the United States could "join with other nations in building a new house upon that foundation, one that can be home for the hopes of mankind and a shelter against the storms of conflict."

And he was determined to keep striking while "the iron is hot." The next day, he invited congressional leaders of both parties to a special private briefing. On June 13, he sent up to the Senate for ratification the ABM treaty and the Interim Agreement on Strategic Offensive Weapons. Separately, he sent them to the House of Representatives as well, to obtain "an expression of support"; he wanted the full Congress to stand behind SALT. He began also to prepare Congress for future requests for funds to develop the Trident submarine and the B-1 bomber. On June 15, he brought to the State Dining Room of the White House 122 members of five congressional committees to brief them personally on the ABM treaty and the interim agreement. The administration, he told them, would make Rogers, Laird, Helms, and Gerard Smith available for congressional appearances to explain the agreements—but *not* Kissinger, because in this instance "executive privilege" had to prevail. This was the first major instance when Nixon invoked executive privilege in a foreign-policy situation, and he was not challenged.

Kissinger *was* made available to brief the congressional group *on the record,* and not under oath, at the White House right after Nixon completed his own briefing. This was when he misleadingly assured the congressmen that the "unilateral statements" appended to the ABM treaty and the interim agreement provided all the necessary "safeguards." Largely on the strength of these assurances, the Senate subsequently ratified the SALT package. The only serious skeptic was Henry Jackson, the Democratic senator from the state of Washington and one of the few people in Congress who understood the strategic equation.

Despite the ovations Nixon received from Congress, he was still facing serious opposition, particularly in the Senate, to his Vietnam policies. A number of "end-the-war" amendments, curtailing funds for the conduct of the conflict, had been attached to the foreign-assistance authorization bill for fiscal year 1973, and the president was determined to kill them.

On June 10, he wrote a letter to Senate Majority Leader Mike Mansfield and Minority Leader Hugh Scott declaring that "I share with you the desire to withdraw our remaining forces from Indochina in a timely and honorable manner." But, he wrote, "Congressional amendments which can be misconstrued by our adversaries to be hostile to my peace proposals of May 8 do not serve this objective. . . . I have made clear to the North Vietnamese that we are fully prepared to participate in meaningful negotiations to achieve a settlement and I am hopeful that they will be convinced that such negotiations are in the best interests of all parties." The president was preparing the resumption of secret diplomacy with Hanoi, and he considered it absolutely vital that there should be no collapse in his political position at home. For, as he saw it, his policies in Vietnam appeared to be vindicated. His violent military reaction against North Vietnam had succeeded in saving Thieu's regime; by late June, the offensive was grinding to a halt and the revived ARVN was counterattacking, retaking Quang Tri and blocking North Vietnamese moves above Saigon. The continuing bombings and the quarantining of Haiphong and other Northern ports were having a powerful impact on the war without interfering with the double détente. Moreover, his seeming inflexibility toward Hanoi was gradually leading back to the conference table in Paris, just as he and Kissinger had predicted. The Russians and the Chinese were keeping up their military and economic assistance to North Vietnam, but they were also beginning to engage in discreet diplomacy of their own to push Hanoi toward a negotiated settlement.

The day after the SALT briefing for the congressmen, Kissinger went to Peking to reassure the Chinese leaders about the Soviet-American negotiations. It was June 16, and Podgorny was already in Hanoi on a mission that included relaying to the North Vietnamese the secret American proposals Kissinger had made three weeks earlier. The timing was perfect. In Peking, there was a complete *tour d'horizon* in meetings between Kissinger and Chou En-lai, their first personal contact since Nixon's visit in February. They discussed Vietnam for four hours, and Kissinger seemed keen on enlisting Chinese support for a negotiated settlement. For one thing, he was eager to resume secret meetings with the North Vietnamese before the Democratic National Convention—"for theater," as the White House saying went. Whereas in Moscow Kissinger was a negotiator, in Peking he was the candid philosopher. He told Chou that if the Americans could be friends with China, they must also be friends with Hanoi.

The secret record shows that Kissinger told the Chinese premier that the trouble with the North Vietnamese was that they were too greedy, that they wanted everything at once, that they were afraid of the process of history. Why was Hanoi so afraid of history, and why couldn't it see the whole process as two separate stages? The first step, he said, would be American disengagement. History would then run its own course in Vietnam. Kissinger went on to complain that Hanoi kept asking the United States to overthrow a friend, the South Vietnamese, with whom Washington had already been fighting diplomatically so that the war could be ended. Kissinger, having propelled the Russians into a form of mediation, was now trying to obtain the same from the Chinese.

But Chou En-lai was less responsive. He took the position that China had done all it could to help the North Vietnamese while the Russians were a "treacherous bunch" who had done nothing for Hanoi since May 8. He made it clear that the Chinese would not repeat the mistake they made in 1954, together with the Russians, of advising the North Vietnamese; this had forced Hanoi to accept the 17th parallel as the dividing line between the two Vietnams. Though Chou was not completely ruling out a discussion with North Vietnam, he told Kissinger that China would not press Hanoi one way or another, even though it did not necessarily approve of the North Vietnamese strategy of invading the South with conventional forces. He also volunteered the opinion that history was against the United States, Communism would prevail in Vietnam and Cambodia, but Laos would continue to be ruled by its king.

The two men enjoyed talking with each other, sometimes philosophizing, sometimes exchanging specific views, sometimes joking. During a conversation about Germany and European problems, Chou smilingly said, "I studied in Germany and my deputy foreign minister did too, so we all are pro-German." One of Kissinger's aides felt that "Henry was much more candid with the Chinese than with the Russians, as if he were saying that, in a sense, we and the Chinese were allies. And Chou was equally candid." So Kissinger left Peking with a sense of cautious optimism; at the right moment perhaps the Chinese might quietly apply their diplomacy to help persuade Hanoi that the time had come to modify its stance.

Meanwhile, China was acting toward North Vietnam in a manner that Hanoi found disturbing. Soviet ships with war matériel for North Vietnam were not permitted to enter Chinese ports, although vessels of East European registry were. Arms, ammunition, and fuel transported aboard Polish, East German, and Yugoslav ships were then moved by the Chinese overland to North Vietnam, but this was not an adequate substitute for the use of Haiphong. Besides, the rail line from China was under constant air attack on the North Vietnamese side, as were the roads leading south.

It is unclear to what extent the message Podgorny brought to Hanoi in June—that the United States was now willing to accept a tripartite electoral commission in Saigon as part of the settlement—affected the evolution of North Vietnam's diplomatic stance. Hanoi in any case had to face the reality that the war could not go on much longer: the B-52 strikes in the Hanoi-Haiphong area (some of them damaging the Red River dikes and raising the long-feared threat of massive floods) were taking their toll; the sea blockade was increasingly painful; and the spring offensive had failed to produce the expected results. The Soviet Union and China, moving toward détente with Washington, could no longer be regarded as unconditional allies.

Even before Podgorny turned up in Hanoi, therefore, the North Vietnamese began rethinking the politics of the war. They were beginning to consider a settlement based on a "ceasefire which would permit President Thieu to remain in power while explicitly recognizing the PRG as a legally coequal administration," as Gareth Porter has written. Under these circumstances, Podgorny's intervention must have had an important if not decisive influence on Hanoi's thinking.

From Richard Nixon's point of view, this was of course splendid. In July, Kissinger would be going back to Paris to start the final phase of the peace negotiations. Diplomatic progress was glacially slow, but the situation was promising. Nixon had every reason for satisfaction. Even in the Middle East, he was collecting unexpected dividends: in July, President Sadat suddenly expelled all Soviet military personnel from Egypt, including most of the advisers—apparently because Moscow was unwilling to supply him with modern weapons for a new war against Israel.

Helped by his foreign-policy triumphs and the relative improvement in the economic situation at home, Nixon was certain to be renominated by his party to run for a second term. There was little question that he would beat McGovern in November. He had fielded a new cabinet team for the balance of the first term, picking George Shultz, a first-rate choice as treasury secretary to replace Connally, and Richard Kleindienst as attorney general. Peter Peterson had been at the Commerce Department since early in the year, busying himself with the implementation of the economic aspects of the summit agreements with the Soviet Union.

There was only one small cloud on this brilliant summer sky. On June 17, there was a mysterious break-in at the offices of the Democratic National Committee in the Watergate office building in Washington.

On June 15, Nixon had received Mexico's President Luis Echeverría at the White House for two days of talks and a state dinner. Meetings between American and Mexican presidents were now routine both for reasons of goodwill and for dealing with bilateral problems ranging from salinity of waters in the border area to illegal migrants. Then Nixon had flown to Florida for a weekend vacation at Key Biscayne, and retired on Friday night, June 16, after eleven o'clock.

Several hours later, a White House Plumbers team broke into the offices of the DNC at Watergate. The team was directed by Howard Hunt, the former CIA officer who had worked for a year as a White House consultant. Hunt monitored the operation by walkie-talkie from a room in the Watergate Hotel next door, but the men who actually went into the Democratic offices were James McCord, another retired CIA man, and three Cubans, two of whom had participated in Hunt's burglary in the Los Angeles offices of Daniel Ellsberg's psychiatrist the previous September.

A Watergate building guard, suspecting a break-in, called the police, and presently the four burglars were arrested by plainclothesmen. Hunt fled. It was dawn of Saturday, June 17. It developed quite quickly that the four men had CIA ties, and this discovery instantly placed a special political stamp on the whole operation. To compound matters, Hunt's cover name—"Eduardo"—with a "WH" (White House) notation and a White House telephone number were found in the address book carried by one of the Cubans. Hunt, in hiding, was quickly identified as Eduardo. Some kind of White House connection with the aborted burglary had been established.

Despite all these potentially damaging discoveries, Nixon seemed undisturbed. He remained in Key Biscayne and returned to Washington on Monday, June 19. Because of the burglars' links with the CIA, the president discussed the matter with General Vernon Walters, the agency's deputy director, while Ron Ziegler, the White House press secretary, dismissed the Watergate affair as a "third-rate burglary."

On Thursday, June 22, Nixon held an afternoon news conference in the Oval Office. The first question concerned charges by Democrats that the Watergate burglars had a "direct link" to the White House. Perfectly relaxed, the president replied:

> Mr. Ziegler and also Mr. Mitchell, speaking for the campaign committee, have responded to questions on this in great detail. They have stated my position and have also stated the facts accurately. This kind of activity, as Mr. Ziegler has indicated, has no place whatever in our electoral process, or in our government process. And, as Mr. Ziegler has stated, the White House has had no involvement whatever in this particular incident. As far as the matter now is concerned, it is under investigation, as it should be, by the proper legal authorities, by the District of Columbia police, and by the FBI. I will not comment on

those matters, particularly since possible criminal charges are in-volved.

This answer seemed to satisfy the reporters; they did not follow up on it. At a second news conference a week later, Watergate was not even brought up. The president seemed chiefly concerned at that moment with foreign affairs and with his reelection in November: his role as a world statesman and peacemaker was his strong suit, and after Peking and Moscow, he was determined to take maximum advantage of it. Although the June 22 news conference was supposed to be devoted exclusively to domestic matters, he delivered an exhaustingly extended reply to a ques-tion as to whether the SALT agreements would affect the new defense budget. He noted that a debate had developed in Congress and the press over the ratification of the SALT package—Defense Secretary Laird had taken the public position that if the Senate approved the ABM treaty but rejected the interim agreement on offensive arms, the security of the United States would be in "serious jeopardy"—and proceeded to make a sales pitch for the strategic accords. He was aware that many senators had reservations about the interim agreement, believing that the United States had conceded too much to the Russians in Moscow, but he went on to "strongly urge" congressional approval of both agreements.

In line with his commitment to the Joint Chiefs that the Trident submarine and B-1 bomber would be authorized in compensation for SALT, Nixon added pointedly that Congress "should then vote for those programs that will provide adequate offensive weapons." He continued his explanation:

> If we have a SALT agreement and then do not go forward with these programs, the Soviet Union will, within . . . a very limited time, be substantially ahead of the United States overall, particularly in the latter part of the seventies. If the United States falls into what is a definitely . . . inferior position to the Soviet Union overall in its defense programs, this will be an open invitation for more instability in the world and . . . for more potential aggression in the world, particularly in such potentially explosive areas as the Mideast.

The argument was inconsistent to say the very least: after signing an agreement that he had described only three weeks earlier in the most glowing terms and defending it against critics who saw holes in it, Nixon was now playing up potential strategic weaknesses in order to get Con-gress to approve new defense programs. Brezhnev, he said, "made it absolutely clear to me that in those areas that were not controlled by our offensive agreement that they were going ahead with their programs." The president further argued that unless the United States moved to develop new strategic weapons, "there will be no chance that the Soviet Union will negotiate Phase Two of an arms-limitation agreement. . . . Now in the event that we do not therefore have any new offensive systems under way or planned, the Soviet Union has no incentive to limit theirs."

Nixon, speaking the logic of the nuclear age, was urging continuation of an arms race in order to deter strategic escalation. Both sides seemed to perceive this apparent contradiction as a reality, perhaps as something more real than SALT. At the June 29 news conference, the president pushed his argument further. The reason for the need to build the B-1 bomber, he said, was to "offset" the advantage the United States had given the Soviet Union in land-based ICBMs—but then he bogged down in another contradiction. The United States had accepted these ceilings, Nixon said, because it already *had* a strategic advantage over the Soviet Union in its B-52 bombers. This was positively Alice-in-Wonderlandish. But, at the same time, his argument reflected the reality that neither government wished to acknowledge publicly: a continued arms race was all but inevitable. Nixon was right that SALT had frozen the construction of new Soviet ICBMs and ABM launchers and limited the Soviet submarine-building program, yet none of it—as he knew—made much of a dent in the nuclear balance of terror.

With the Moscow summit hardly out of the way, the American and Soviet governments moved to begin a new economic relationship. This relationship was launched with an economic "shock" of sorts: a massive purchase of American grain by the Soviet Union in which the Marxist businessmen of the Kremlin taught Yankee traders a bitter lesson and, in the process, forced a painful increase in domestic food prices in the United States.

This 400-million-bushel (17-million-ton) transaction, the largest on record, also demonstrated the U.S. government's virtual inability to conduct foreign economic affairs on a rational and coordinated basis. The decision to sell the Russians this volume of grain was made essentially by Agriculture Secretary Earl Butz, a former member of the board of directors of the Ralston Purina Company. Butz did it without consulting anyone in the administration—although some White House officials said later that the freewheeling secretary did "touch base" with Nixon, to the extent of telling him that big wheat sales to the Russians would mean bigger farm incomes—an important factor in an election year.

The president, who understood election-year politics better than agricultural economics, apparently gave Butz the nod, but there is nothing to indicate that the wheat sale was subjected to a government policy review, normally a necessary precaution in an operation of this magnitude. As a *fait accompli,* the Western White House in San Clemente announced an initial sale on July 8.

The only knowledgeable parties at the outset of this murky affair were Butz and one or two of his assistant secretaries, the Soviet government, and two or three American grain-exporting corporations—which reaped enormous profits from it at the expense of American consumers, farmers, and taxpayers. Among those high in the administration who were not given adequate advance notice of the dimensions of the wheat transaction was Commerce Secretary Peterson, supposedly the government's principal economic negotiator with the Russians. Peterson went to Moscow in July for ten days of talks with Soviet leaders (including a three-and-a-half-hour session with Brezhnev), heading the American delegation to the first meeting of the Joint United States–Soviet Union Commercial Commission established during the May summit. He learned how huge the grain deal was from a Washington-dateline story he happened to read on a news-agency ticker at the American embassy in Moscow. The Russians, of course, said nothing to Peterson about the new wheat purchases, then in negotiation, because, from their viewpoint, their success depended on maximal secrecy. Peterson sent a protest to Washington—he thought a serious error was being committed—but it was too late.

The wheat sale to the Russians resulted from two converging situations: a dramatic crop failure in the Soviet Union in 1972, requiring huge grain imports to stave off severe belt tightening, and vast surpluses accumulated in the United States under the long-standing subsidy program to farmers operated by the Agriculture Department. But this was not simply a supply-and-demand situation: it was a much trickier enterprise.

For one thing, when the Soviet government first proposed a wheat purchase in July, it did not tell American exporting companies just how much it ultimately planned to buy, nor did it disclose the real scope of the Russian crop failure. The Russians, of course, wanted to buy cheap on what was basically a depressed market. Compounding this Soviet trading strategy was the Agriculture Department's ignorance—even though the American embassy in Moscow was sending accurate reports and the department had an intelligence unit dealing with world crop estimates. Also, the Agriculture Department grossly overestimated

United States grain surpluses in storage.

However, Butz wanted to sell—and sell no matter what. His philosophy was that American farmers should produce as much as possible so that the United States could export food in massive quantities (even before Butz's plant-and-sell campaign, American farmers were producing much more food than the nation could consume). He believed that it was wrong to pay farmers subsidies for *not* planting, as had been done for many years, so long as there was an ever-increasing world export market. But he was prepared to go on paying subsidies during the transition period, which included 1972, to compensate the farmers for low prices. He wanted to help the United States balance of payments through food exports and to raise farmers' incomes—the latter objective was, of course, principally political in motivation.

When the Soviets first informed American exporters of their interest in purchasing grain, word of it was relayed to Butz, who, in effect, cleared the sales. Both Butz and the exporters went along with the Soviet secrecy ploy for their own reasons. In this instance, the name of the game was to buy up vast amounts of wheat from farmers at commodity exchanges around the country at the lowest possible prices. To achieve this goal, farmers could not be told about the Soviet inquiries; Butz, friend of the farmer, saw to it. Given the low prices paid by the Russians for the wheat, which left only a small profit margin for the exporters, the Agriculture Department paid the corporations hundreds of millions of dollars in sales subsidies. The final sales price to the Russians, as congressional experts remarked later, was "unrealistically low"—courtesy of the American taxpayers.

But this was not the end of the operation. After each transaction was completed, the Russians came for more wheat, and the exporting corporations strove mightily to find it. By August, there was little grain left on the open market—and farmers, beginning to realize that they had been had, raised their prices. The corporations, having committed themselves to low selling prices to the Russians on new orders, now needed more cheap wheat. And again, Butz came to the rescue: the Agriculture Department promptly sold them millions of bushels from government stocks while maintaining the sales subsidy. Once more the taxpayers were making wheat cheap for the Russians and helping to enrich the exporters. On August 31, for example, the Agriculture Department sold the Continental Grain Company 60 million bushels of cheap wheat—nearly 30 percent of all the grain sold to the Soviet Union in 1972—in what was described as the biggest single government sale in history to a private company. Furthermore, the Soviets received $750 million in credits from the United States to pay for the grain. And one of the assistant secretaries of agriculture involved in the Soviet wheat deal soon became a vice president of one of the big grain-exporting companies.

The results of this astounding undertaking were quick to come. Butz could have removed farm subsidies when the world wheat price began approaching the United States support price—and thereby have saved the taxpayers $200 million—but, as he told a senior official, it was impossible in an election year. There was the outcry from American farmers that despite the subsidies they had been cheated out of higher profits because of Butz's manipulation of the market. Loading terminals, rail lines, and embarkation ports became hopelessly clogged with the Soviet wheat shipments; the infrastructure was not prepared to handle such a volume of grain so suddenly. Probably most important, the domestic price of wheat rose at once from $1.50 to $2.50 a bushel because of sudden shortages. Butz had miscalculated what the United States had on hand. This was the beginning of a major food-price spiral. The final touch in the Butz wheat saga was that the ungrateful Russians haggled with the United States well into November to obtain ship-charter rates to ship their wheat that were lower than the prevailing American freighter costs.

While the Soviet wheat deal was being secretly put together in the United States, Secretary Peterson was busy in Moscow discussing a wide range of cooperative economic projects. He saw Gromyko, Foreign Trade Minister Patolichev, and Brezhnev. Brezhnev talked about "big" projects for the United States and the Soviet Union: possible joint oil and natural-gas projects in Siberia, the huge Kama River truck plant then under construction, timber operations. He wanted twenty-year credits (his idea was that the Americans should finance all these projects), and argued that undertakings of this magnitude would in time help the U.S. balance of payments and reduce unemployment because most of the industrial plant would come from American factories.

Peterson took a less enthusiastic view of Brezhnev's proposals. The financial risk alone would render the projects difficult, inasmuch as the Export-Import Bank would be guaranteeing the credits extended by American companies. He preferred to see multinational companies— including Japanese, West Germans, and others—involved in these ventures. In the case of energy projects, Peterson feared the Russians would have "too much leverage if only American money was in the ground." (They could, for example, shut off production for political reasons.)

The immediate aim was negotiation of a formal trade agreement—

including most-favored-nation treatment for the Russians—under the provisions of the May summit decisions, and on his return from Moscow, Peterson wrote that "there has been some encouraging progress."

The main points involved were repayment by the Soviet Union of the wartime Lend-Lease debt—it stood at $11 billion but Washington was willing to settle for $500 million—and new long-term credits to the Russians. The American position was that until the Lend-Lease debt was settled, something the Soviet Union had refused to do, the Export-Import Bank would not make fresh credits available. There were also questions of tariff treatment, a maritime agreement, controls of strategic exports, and antidumping pledges.

Brezhnev eventually agreed to the debt settlement when Kissinger flew to Moscow on September 10 for a broad policy discussion. A joint statement was issued by the two governments in Moscow on September 14, and the White House said that a comprehensive trade agreement with the Soviets would be signed before the end of the year.

Within days of Kissinger's visit to the Kremlin, three Soviet delegations arrived in Washington to start formal negotiations on various aspects of this proposed agreement. Rapid progress was made, but on September 27 the negotiations ran into what ultimately would become an insuperable obstacle. This was an amendment to the pending East-West trade-relations bill (required, among other reasons, to grant the preferential tariff treatment to Communist countries) forbidding any economic concessions to the Soviet Union so long as there were any restrictions on the emigration of Soviet Jews.

This amendment, which had been sponsored in the Senate by Henry Jackson and in the House by Ohio Representative Charles Vanik, had broad bipartisan support. In Jackson's words, it would "establish a direct legislative link" between trade with Communist nations and "the freedom [of Jews] to emigrate without the payment of prohibitive taxes amounting to ransom." Thirty-four nationwide Jewish organizations stood foursquare behind the amendment.

The Jewish issue posed an immensely serious problem for the U.S. government—even though, ironically, a State Department compilation of data from refugee organizations showed that Jewish emigration from the Soviet Union in the first half of 1972 had already exceeded the total of 14,000 departures during all of the previous year. The administration took the view that this question, involving both human rights in general and Soviet sovereignty over its internal affairs, should be the object of "quiet diplomacy" by the United States rather than an open confrontation involving Congress. In fact, both Nixon and Rogers had raised the matter of Jewish emigration during the summit meeting, and some American officials suggested that this may have been why departures during June had reached a record level. But the day after the amendment was introduced, the State Department formally announced its opposition to it; passage of the amendment would be likely to force the Russians into a corner, possibly induce them to restrict Jewish emigration again, and damage détente as such. But the lawmakers were adamant and a deadlock developed.

Meanwhile, détente was making headway in other areas. One of the additional agreements hammered out between Brezhnev and Kissinger in September was that a conference on the reduction of NATO and Warsaw Pact military forces in Central Europe would open in 1973, about the same time as the Soviet-advocated European security conference. At the May summit, Nixon and Brezhnev had reached a specific accord on the security conference, but the question of mutual balanced force reductions (MBFR, in diplomatic jargon), advocated by the West for over four years, had remained vague in the final Moscow communiqué.

The administration thought that Brezhnev's specific acceptance of MBFR was a significant political breakthrough, although the Russians still preferred direct talks among nations with troops stationed in Central Europe. In 1972, NATO maintained about 1 million men in Europe, including United States units, and the Warsaw Pact around 1.2 million, of whom 275,000 were Soviet troops in East European countries. The idea, as worked out in Moscow in September, was that preparatory sessions for the security conference, strictly a political exercise, would begin about the same time in 1973 as the MBFR parley. The United States and its NATO partners agreed at the same time to send delegates to a preliminary ambassadorial-level meeting to be held late in November in Helsinki, the proposed site of the security conference.

On September 30, Nixon ceremoniously signed the congressional resolution approving the five-year SALT interim agreement on offensive weapons. This accord, being an executive agreement and not a treaty, did not require Senate ratification (unlike the ABM treaty, which the senators approved in August), but the president had insisted on concurrent House and Senate resolutions endorsing the nuclear freeze so that the record would show that he had Congress behind him on SALT.

Signing the resolution and the ABM treaty (he delayed final action on ABM, pending the vote on the interim agreement), Nixon declared that "this is not an agreement which guarantees that there will be no war, but what this is, is the beginning of a process that is enormously important, that will limit now and, we hope, later reduce the burden of arms and thereby reduce the danger of war." Three days later (after a White House ceremony marking the entry into force of the SALT accords attended by Soviet Foreign Minister Gromyko) the president entertained Gromyko at a Camp David dinner. With Kissinger in Moscow in mid-September and Gromyko in Washington early in October, the détente contacts between the two superpowers were becoming quite intimate. And now a Brezhnev visit to Washington was being planned for mid-1973 to establish the tradition of annual summit meetings.

Getting along with the Russians did not preclude Nixon from enjoying a sense of *Schadenfreude* over their sudden reverses in the Middle East. This came on July 23 when President Sadat suddenly expelled all Soviet military personnel—except for some 200 advisers at SAM sites—from Egypt and closed Egyptian air and naval bases to Soviet planes and ships. Sadat's move, never clearly explained, caught the Soviet Union as well as the United States completely by surprise. It was one of the most significant developments in the Middle East in three years—since the Russians first established their military presence in Egypt.

Nixon was careful to hide his delight, particularly because many Middle East specialists suspected that Sadat acted out of anger and disappointment that the Russians had virtually ignored the Arab-Israeli dispute at the May summit meeting. Sadat had expected Brezhnev to press Nixon to use American influence with Israel to force it into concessions. Already annoyed by Russia's refusal to supply Egypt with modern arms and by what he saw as Soviet attempts to meddle in internal Egyptian affairs, Sadat appeared to feel that Brezhnev's attitude at the summit was the last straw. If this was Sadat's motivation in expelling the Russians, Nixon did not want to gloat publicly and rock the boat of détente.

At a news conference in the Oval Office, he said that "The situation there is still one that is not clear and any comment upon it, first, might possibly be erroneous, and second, could very well be harmful to our goal of a just settlement. . . . It might exacerbate the problem by trying to evaluate what happened between Sadat and the Soviet leaders."

By the end of July, American intelligence reported that the Russians had started repatriating their 10,000 combat troops from Egypt. Likewise, the 18 Tu-16 twin-jet reconnaissance bombers, whose primary mission was to track Sixth Fleet warships in the Mediterranean from Egyptian bases, were being removed with their crews. Some 70 MiG-21 jet fighter-bombers and 6 advanced MiG-23s, all flown by Soviet pilots, were also being taken out. Soviet naval facilities at Alexandria, Port Said, Mersa Matruh, and Sollum were being closed down.

Simultaneously, Sadat proceeded to send diplomatic signals to Washington. Their essence, as a State Department official put it, was: "You said you wanted us to expel the Russians and now we did it. . . . So what are you going to do to help us?" A message also came from King Faisal suggesting, in effect, that the United States take advantage of the new situation to resume the peacemaking diplomacy in the Middle East that had been virtually suspended for a year.

"It *was* a good opportunity," a senior State Department official recounted later, "but it was an election year and we were marking time. It was clear that Sadat was taking the first step to engage the United States in active diplomacy, yet the timing was terrible. If the United States and the Soviet Union resumed joint peace efforts, we'd have a crisis with Israel. And the word from the White House was, 'Don't rock the boat.' They were glad that the Russians were out, but Nixon and Kissinger didn't want to resurrect the Rogers Plan at that point. They said it was like a 'red flag' to Jews."

If there was any chance for Middle Eastern diplomacy during 1972, it vanished completely when 11 Israeli athletes were killed by Arab terrorists at the Olympic Games in Munich early in September. Grieved and angry, Israel advised friendly governments that it would engage in no further diplomatic negotiations until all Arab terrorism was eradicated. Moreover, the Israelis served notice that they would soon engage in "a major military effort" in the Middle East, including the resumption of raids into Syria and Lebanon, to put an end to terrorism. When Foreign Minister Abba Eban visited Washington on September 22, he told Rogers that his government would not have anything to do with the standing American proposal to enter into peace talks with Egypt on the basis of reopening the Suez Canal. He made it plain that Israel blamed Egypt as well as the other Arab countries for tolerating terrorist activities. Negotiations, Eban told newsmen, could not proceed until the "obstacle" of terrorism "is out of the way." The United States was in no position to disagree, and the official comment by the State Department was that priority must be given to combating international terrorism although "options must be kept open" for peace talks.

The only American diplomatic initiative in 1972 occurred early in July when Rogers visited Sana, the capital of the Yemen Arab Republic, to restore diplomatic relations broken during the 1967 Arab-Israeli war.

Yemen was the first of seven Arab states that had severed ties with the United States to resume them.

Even in the absence of war in the Middle East, an assured supply of petroleum constituted an important aspect of U.S. security, to say nothing of economic health, yet the Nixon administration continued to exclude oil problems from its serious consideration of the Middle East crisis. The 1971 agreements with Persian Gulf and Libyan producers seemed to have had a tranquilizing effect on the administration as well as on the industry. Everyone assumed that the Middle Eastern governments simply would not defy the United States by raising prices again, after having been warned in 1971 that any further increases would be regarded as a threat to American interests. Besides, Nixon took it for granted that his friendship with the shah of Iran was a guarantee that the Iranians would create no problems for the United States. Blindly, both the administration and the industry went on ignoring mounting signs that OPEC member governments in the Middle East were considering nationalizing foreign-owned companies. (The shah, for example, had said that Iran would take over the companies if oil revenues were not satisfactory.) And when the State Department suggested to the "big seven" oil companies in mid-1972 that they make immediate "participation" offers to the host governments to escape nationalization—the idea was for joint ownership of production facilities—all but two "reacted with horror," as one official put it.

In the last week of June, Colonel Georges R. Guay, the defense attaché of the American embassy in Paris, was instructed to deliver a secret message to the North Vietnamese suggesting that semipublic peace negotiations be resumed in mid-July to be followed by a private meeting between Kissinger and a Hanoi representative. (Guay, who spoke French, had become the go-between with the North Vietnamese delegation when General Walters left Paris for his new post as CIA deputy director.) The White House was mainly interested in the secret talks, but it was willing to meet Hanoi's standing demand that semipublic meetings be conducted at the same time.

The American message was delivered in Paris just as the North Vietnamese Politburo was conducting an unpublicized review of its war policies. Xuan Thuy and Le Duc Tho were both in Hanoi, but a positive reply came at once. Semipublic meetings would resume on July 13 and Kissinger and Le Duc Tho would confer on July 19.

Nixon then made a quick goodwill gesture. On June 28, without any elaboration, the White House announced that 10,000 more ground troops would be withdrawn from Vietnam within two months. At that point, there were 49,000 men left in the country, and now the target was for 39,000 troops by September 1. To be sure, the air force had been reinforced in bases in Thailand and the navy in the Gulf of Tonkin to conduct the bombings and the blockade, but in terms of the negotiations the important thing was the number of Americans on the ground in Vietnam.

On June 29, at a White House news conference, responding to a question as to whether he could keep his original pledge to wind up the war during his first term, Nixon said: "We have returned to the negotiating table, or will return to it, on the assumption that the North Vietnamese are prepared to negotiate in a constructive and serious way. We will be prepared to negotiate in that way. If those negotiations go forward in a constructive and serious way, this war can be ended, and it can be ended well before January 20."

He refused to say what specifically had led to resuming the Paris meetings—the Moscow and Peking talks had to remain secret—but again, he let his optimism shine through: "It would not be useful to indicate the discussions that took place in various places with regard to returning to the Paris peace table. Let it suffice to say that both sides considered it in their interest to return to the Paris peace table. We would not have returned unless we thought there was a chance for more serious discussions and more constructive discussions than we have had in the past." The president flatly ruled out American acceptance of a coalition government in Saigon and made no reference to the fact that the United States now accepted a tripartite electoral commission in Saigon after the cease-fire as a compromise formula.

Nixon denied press and diplomatic reports from Hanoi that American bombs were hitting Red River dikes, threatening North Vietnam with floods. This was becoming an acute issue with American and international public opinion, but the president said he had had the reports checked and "they have proved to be inaccurate." Before long, photographs would become available showing dikes that were damaged purposely or accidentally—but he insisted that the United States "has used great restraint in its bombing policy . . . we have tried to hit only military targets and we have been hitting military targets. We have had orders out not to hit dikes because the result in terms of civilian casualties would be extraordinary."

At this point, the president evidently felt that the United States was approaching the new negotiations from a position of strength, and he went out of his way to insist that his decision to bomb and mine the North had been the correct one: "It has always been my theory that in dealing with these very pragmatic men . . . who lead the Communist nations, that they respect strength, not belligerence but strength, and at least that is the way I am always going to approach it, and I think it is going to be successful in the end."

In the meantime, the president moved camp to San Clemente for a two-week vacation starting on the eve of July 4. Kissinger came along, and the two men met at least once a day to study military dispatches from Vietnam and relevant diplomatic reports in preparation for the resumption of the Paris talks. Only slight attention was given to the semipublic session held on July 13, involving William Porter, the chief American delegate, and his North Vietnamese counterpart, Xuan Thuy. It happened to be the one hundred fiftieth plenary session in fifty months of talks. The assumption in San Clemente was that Xuan Thuy would simply repeat the standing Hanoi line on the cessation of bombings and a coalition regime in Saigon, which he did. Porter was instructed to do no more than restate the United States position as set forth by Nixon on May 8. For that matter, Kissinger planned to go no further in his meeting with Le Duc Tho on July 19.

Bizarre as it may appear, Kissinger (with or without Nixon's knowledge) brought the International Brotherhood of Teamsters into the Vietnam negotiating picture at this point. Harold Gibbons, a Teamsters vice president from New York, had made a visit to Hanoi during the spring with two other labor leaders invited by the North Vietnamese; he had been included in the invitation because he was said to have a liberal reputation and Hanoi was looking for American friends wherever it could find them. Before and after his Hanoi trip, Gibbons visited Kissinger at the White House for conferences. According to an NSC aide, Kissinger showed Gibbons classified reports from Saigon as well as negotiating memoranda "which normally were not shown to anybody at the State Department." Trying to explain the strange relationship between the Teamsters vice president and the White House adviser on foreign policy, another aide said, "Henry wished to be seen by Hanoi as a man to be trusted, and when somebody went to North Vietnam, Henry was anxious that this impression be conveyed to the North Vietnamese."

On July 17, Gibbons turned up at San Clemente in the company of Irving Taub, lawyer for James Hoffa, imprisoned president of the Teamsters Union. They came with the union's Executive Committee, which had an appointment with Nixon, and they brought a most extraordinary proposition. Kissinger received the two men on the terrace of his bungalow. This was their proposal: if Nixon granted Hoffa a pardon, the Teamsters chief would go to Hanoi to negotiate a Vietnam peace settlement. Taub showed Kissinger telegrams that purported to be invitations to Hoffa to visit Hanoi. In brief, Gibbons's and Taub's mission in San Clemente— which was also the mission of the Executive Committee—was to obtain a presidential pardon for Hoffa. An NSC official familiar with this conversation said later, "It was an improbable plot inasmuch as no one could believe that the North Vietnamese would wish to receive Hoffa of all people in Hanoi, but Henry seemed to take it seriously and he kept listening to Gibbons." It is possible that Kissinger received Gibbons three times because he was aware of the closeness between the Teamsters and some of Nixon's friends.

Another visitor to San Clemente was France's defense minister, Michel Debré, who called on Nixon on July 7 with a message from President Pompidou to the effect that the North Vietnamese were interested in serious negotiations and that, in the opinion of the French government, the outlook for peace was improving. The French were always in close touch with the North Vietnamese, but Kissinger's inclination was not to take their judgments too seriously. Wrongly, he thought the French diplomats were simply transmitting Hanoi's views. On July 12, another diplomat, Ambassador Dobrynin, arrived at San Clemente for a long conference with the president and Kissinger. The discussion centered on Vietnam, and the Soviet diplomat, too, was making optimistic sounds.

The preparations for Kissinger's approaching Paris trip included a meeting, chaired by Nixon, with General Haig and Sir Robert Thompson. Haig and Thompson had just come back from South Vietnam, and they gave the president and Kissinger a fairly optimistic report on the military and security situation there.

Nixon and Kissinger were simultaneously considering drastic military actions against Hanoi if no peace came. One of these secret options was a South Vietnamese invasion of North Vietnam after the American elections, presumably supported by United States air and naval power. It is hard to imagine the ARVN invading the North even with American logistical and tactical support, but the idea was intriguing to the White House. General Haig had asked the commander of the ARVN I Corps whether he thought an invasion would be feasible. The South Vietnamese shrugged and said it was really up to the Americans; he was still licking his wounds from the spring offensive. Kissinger remarked that the United States "would not be bashful" after the elections in terms of military action against Hanoi. The B-52 bombings and the mining of the ports were, in Kissinger's opinion, only a prelude to *real* operations, if they became necessary.

Late on July 17, shortly after meeting with the Teamsters delegates, Kissinger quietly left San Clemente for Washington. The next evening, he boarded an air force jet for Paris for his unannounced meeting with Le Duc Tho and Xuan Thuy. The attention of White House reporters on July 18 was centered on the president's return from San Clemente to Washington, and somehow Kissinger's absence was not noticed. His flight to Paris opened an entirely new phase in the Vietnam peace negotiations even though the initial results were less than promising.

Kissinger, Le Duc Tho, and Xuan Thuy met for more than six hours on July 19, and as the American side had expected, little happened. The North Vietnamese continued to insist on the formation of a coalition government in Saigon, although they knew perfectly well that the United States was immovable on this point. Occasionally, Tho would use other phrases to describe a coalition arrangement, but, as Kissinger noted, he was still talking about the same thing. The Hanoi diplomats also complained about the continuing bombing in the North and expressed fears that their dikes might be hit, causing terrible floods.

For his part, Kissinger repeated the offer contained in Nixon's May 8 speech, but also reverted to some of the aspects of the January proposal: Thieu's resignation after a cease-fire, to be followed by general elections in the South and a rapid withdrawal of American forces. In fact, he hinted that the United States might shorten the deadline for the total withdrawal of its troops from the four months offered by Nixon. Kissinger chose not to raise the matter of a tripartite electoral commission—he did not think Hanoi was yet ready to discuss it—but his mention of new elections (which Nixon had ignored in the May speech) was a way of getting the North Vietnamese to focus again on this point. He assumed the Russians had referred to the idea in Hanoi; now it would be up to Tho to bring it up if he wished.

As to Tho's protests about the bombings of the North, Kissinger told him, in effect, what Nixon had said at his news conference on June 29: that the United States would keep up the raids until the North Vietnamese accepted its peace terms. This was the first time in the war that the United States had taken such an extreme position; even on May 8,

Nixon had tied the bombings to the ending of the Communist offensive. Now it was indefinite heavy bombings until North Vietnam compromised on peace terms.

Yet Tho chose not to break off the talks—something he might have done in the past. Instead, Kissinger and Tho parted with an agreement to keep in touch and, if possible, to meet again in a matter of weeks. This was encouraging to Kissinger, as was the willingness of the North Vietnamese to have the two governments simultaneously announce that private negotiations were being held. The old secrecy could be abandoned —although neither government went beyond a barebones announcement.

As soon as his meeting with Tho and Xuan Thuy was over, Kissinger drove back to Orly Airport for the flight home (it was no longer necessary for him to conceal his comings and goings by traveling through out-of-the-way military airports), and that same evening he reported to Nixon on his day's diplomatic activities in Paris. Kissinger told Nixon that he felt, despite the inconclusive character of his meeting with Tho, that the United States and North Vietnam were now seriously engaged, and they agreed it would be useful if another session could be held within two weeks or so.

There were valid diplomatic reasons for doing this, of course, but Nixon also saw considerable political advantage in keeping up the diplomatic momentum. The Democrats had just nominated George McGovern as their presidential candidate—he was one of the principal spokesmen of the antiwar movement—and Nixon's plan was to wrest away from him the *cachet* of the peace candidate, while retaining at the same time a statesmanlike posture toward the negotiations. The president revealed this new strategy at an Oval Office news conference on the afternoon of July 27. Rather roughly, he remarked that "We would hope . . . that Congress, in its actions, will not in effect give a message to the enemy, 'Don't negotiate with the present administration; wait for us; we will give you what you want—South Vietnam.' " But he chose to be noncommittal about the resumed peace talks.

When a reporter asked him whether a settlement could be obtained through a political agreement between the two Vietnamese factions without first holding elections, Nixon hedged because the question veered very close to the concept of the tripartite electoral commission, which he still wanted to keep under wraps. For one thing, President Thieu had not yet been told that this was what Nixon had in mind. "That is a very perceptive question, but it is one . . . that I should not comment upon for the reason that negotiations are now under way. . . . At a time that matters are being discussed, it is not well for me to state anything with regard to what is happening in the negotiations."

This was a neat clue the president had thrown to the newsmen, but as so often happened, nobody picked it up. The main interest at that point was whether the United States was bombing the 2700-mile system of dikes and dams in North Vietnam—the State Department had acknowledged the day before that there had been inadvertent damage to the dikes from nearby bombings—and a number of questions were directed to that issue. Nixon did not mind these questions; they gave him an opportunity to deliver a long statement about American bombing policy and the situation in Vietnam in the wake of the Communist offensive.

At this point, in fact, it was the president who went on the offensive. He said that had the United States really wanted to destroy the dikes, it could have done so in a week; instead, it was trying to avoid civilian casualties. Quite primly, Nixon remarked that "Our restraint, it seems to me, rather than being subject to criticisms, should be subject to objective analysis and . . . a considerable amount of support."

Warming to his subject, the president accused all his critics—including United Nations Secretary General Kurt Waldheim—of "a hypocritical double standard" in denigrating the United States. They were the victim of "enemy-inspired propaganda" concerning American attacks on civilian targets, he said, not raising their voices against the Communist bombings of civilian centers in South Vietnam. He cited a report from Ambassador Bunker in Saigon that 45,000 civilian casualties, including 15,000 killed, had been caused by the Communist spring offensive.

Nixon's anger went beyond what he considered misrepresentation of what was happening in Vietnam. He was seriously concerned that the charges of dike bombing could damage him politically at home on the eve of the elections; at the same time he was worried that Hanoi might actually believe that the United States was planning to destroy North Vietnam's flood-control system and might retaliate by again halting the renewed Paris negotiations. And the diplomatic situation was in a highly sensitive stage.

Meanwhile, unknown to the outside world, around July 20, Chairman Mao Tse-tung received the Viet Cong foreign minister, Mme. Nguyen Thi Binh, as she stopped in Peking en route from Paris to Hanoi. The Chinese believed, along with the Americans, that the main stumbling block in the peace negotiations was the Communists' insistence on President Thieu's ouster as a condition for a settlement. Unlike the Americans, however, the Chinese had their own reasons to think that it was the Viet Cong rather than the North Vietnamese who made a fundamental issue of it. In Peking's view, the Viet Cong enjoyed much greater autonomy within the Vietnamese Communist camp than the United States realized or was willing to believe. The Chinese thought that once the Viet Cong was persuaded to drop its demand for Thieu's removal, Hanoi would be prepared to separate the political and military problems and an agreement with the United States would then be possible.

Mao, consequently, took it upon himself to change the PRG's mind. The chairman told Mme. Binh that the PRG had to know how to act tactically when required by the circumstances. He said to Mme. Binh: "Do as I did—I once made an accord with Chiang Kai-shek when it was necessary." This was in the 1940s. He added that the Viet Cong had to negotiate with Thieu in the context of the larger talks with the United States in order to end the war.

About a week later, French Foreign Minister Maurice Schumann came to Peking and was received by Mao for a three-hour audience. Mao apprised him of the conversation with Mme. Binh, adding that she had accepted his advice. In Schumann's view, this was a great breakthrough in the peace negotiations. On his return to Paris, he quietly met with Mme. Binh and North Vietnamese diplomats. As he recounted it later, he received confirmation that Mao had, indeed, intervened and that the Viet Cong had taken his counsel. Of Mme. Binh, Schumann said, "She was a changed woman."

Schumann's next step was to inform the United States of his conversations with Mao and then with Mme. Binh and the North Vietnamese in Paris. He did so through diplomatic channels; word reached Nixon and Kissinger immediately. They were skeptical about this information, however. Kissinger, for one thing, was not inclined to take Schumann very seriously, for he considered him a lightweight. His underestimation of most other diplomats was one of Kissinger's frequent errors. Two months later, when they met in Washington, Schumann was finally able to convince Kissinger that differences *had* existed between the PRG and North Vietnam, and that Mao *had* played a key role in resolving them. When Kissinger, Le Duc Tho, and Xuan Thuy met again on August 1, the conversation revolved almost entirely around a formula for a mutually acceptable political settlement linked to a cease-fire. Kissinger sought to narrow down the discussion to the question of what would happen in Saigon *after* a cease-fire. While Le Duc Tho maintained his insistence on a coalition government—he would not budge from this position—Kissinger began to sketch, instead, a tripartite electoral commission, including the Viet Cong, that would supervise new elections after a cease-fire, the total withdrawal of American troops, and Thieu's resignation. Le Duc Tho indicated noncommittal interest, and he said he needed more clarifications from Kissinger as well as instructions from home. They agreed to reconvene on August 14, although this was not mentioned in the official announcements of the latest private session.

Kissinger and Nixon decided that at the next meeting Kissinger could be more explicit about the tripartite commission formula if Le Duc Tho was still interested in it. The question of North Vietnamese withdrawals from South Vietnam had ceased to be an issue—it had not even been mentioned in the new series of discussions—and everything was turning on the political formula.

The difficulty was that President Thieu had not yet been told about the tripartite commission plan. Kissinger obviously could not pursue it with the North Vietnamese so long as he lacked Thieu's assent—and he sensed it would not be easy to obtain, since it was so perilously close to the creation of a coalition government. The United States therefore found itself in the extraordinary position of having to negotiate secretly with *both* Vietnamese factions—its ally and its enemy—to sell the tripartite commission idea.

Kissinger dispatched General Haig and John Negroponte to Saigon to convince Thieu. Not unexpectedly, Thieu turned down Kissinger's emissaries. He told them that he controlled 90 percent of South Vietnam (an exaggerated claim) and that the Communists would be unlikely to garner more than 10–20 percent of the vote in an election. Why, then, he asked, was a tripartite electoral commission necessary? Was it not clear that such a commission could easily be turned into a coalition regime? Instead of such a commission, Thieu said, there should be a referendum in South Vietnam, preferably under the supervision of the Saigon government.

On August 14, Kissinger presented the commission idea to the North Vietnamese in the form of an actual proposal. Le Duc Tho was still noncommittal, but still interested. Although the North Vietnamese kept advocating a coalition government, Kissinger felt he was making progress. The meeting was adjourned without setting a new date, but the two men agreed to resume the negotiations as soon as practicable.

After leaving Tho, Kissinger raced to a Swiss resort to help his parents celebrate their fiftieth wedding anniversary. Then his air force plane picked him up in Zurich for the flight to Saigon. The aircraft landed in

Tehran to refuei at 5:00 a.m., but Kissinger slept through it. American embassy officials and a United States Army general, the ranking United States military officer in Iran, came out to the airport at dawn to greet him, but Kissinger, asleep, of course did not appear. The refueling stop-over was so quick that David Engle, an NSC aide, almost missed the plane when he went out to the terminal to buy caviar.

Kissinger spent two days negotiating with Thieu in Saigon, and his tack was entirely different from the ones he took with the Russians, the Chinese, or the North Vietnamese.

His problem in Saigon was to *prepare* Thieu for a settlement. The idea was to remind Thieu that a presidential election was approaching in the United States, the administration must be forthcoming in its peace diplomacy, and it must not let Senator McGovern suggest that Saigon was blocking peace. Consequently, he said, the administration must, as a matter of political realities, come forth with seemingly attractive proposals, knowing full well that Hanoi would reject them. Political risks had to be reduced.

Then Kissinger proceeded to make some extravagant promises. After the elections, he told Thieu, it would be a "different story": the United States would not hesitate to apply all its power to bring North Vietnam to its knees; Thieu should start planning an invasion of North Vietnam after the elections—he suggested specifically ARVN landings in Vinh or Dong Hoi. Thieu appeared nonplussed by this idea, but finally replied that if an invasion were mounted, Thanh Hoa should be the prime objective. Actually, Thieu had been urging an invasion of North Vietnam as early as March 1971, during the Laos incursion, but could muster no American encouragement and eventually dropped the idea. It was first revived by General Haig in June 1972.

It is of course hard to judge whether Kissinger was playing a complicated double game with the two Vietnamese factions, or whether he really believed that a final blow at Hanoi late in the year would leave the South Vietnamese in a strong enough military position to go along with the peace proposals he had in the works. There was, to be sure, a certain logic in Kissinger's approach. The spring offensive, if nothing else, had convinced him that the Vietnam war must be ended as soon as possible and the United States finally extricated from it. During the flight from Saigon, following his talks with Thieu, Kissinger mused in front of his staff, "We just can't let the Vietnam issue plague us for four more years." The problem, he said, had to be resolved between the November elections and the president's anticipated second inaugural the next January. He was optimistic that with quiet Soviet and Chinese support, and the stalling of the North Vietnamese offensive, Hanoi would meet him halfway before long—meaning a decision to wind up the conflict on the basis of the secret concessions he had spelled out in Moscow and Peking. Kissinger's problem was to convince the president to accept this course of action and, simultaneously, to force Thieu to face reality and endorse the American diplomatic stance. As for Nixon, Kissinger wanted to "lock him irrevocably into a decision" before the elections. And Thieu was to be given maximum military advantage before a cease-fire. Kissinger told his aides on the plane over the Pacific, "One thing is for sure: we cannot stand another four years of this. . . . So let's finish it brutally once and for all."

Kissinger stopped for one day in Tokyo for general conversations with the Japanese government. There was no need to inform it of the status of the peace negotiations, but he was now more careful about relations with Japan; besides, the new prime minister, Kakuei Tanaka, was to meet with Nixon in Honolulu at the end of the month, and Kissinger wanted to prepare the ground politically. Earlier that week, William D. Eberle, the White House's special representative for trade negotiations, had met with Tanaka to review economic differences between the two governments.

Kissinger returned to Washington on August 19, and immediately took a helicopter to Camp David, where Nixon was resting before the Republican nominating convention, to bring him up to date. When Kissinger was away for more than one or two days on a negotiating journey, he cabled daily reports to the president, but it had now become routine for him to meet with Nixon the moment he returned from abroad. Secretary Rogers was rarely present at these debriefing sessions.

The North Vietnamese, Kissinger reported, had not yet accepted the tripartite electoral commission package, and Thieu was intractable. It was a double deadlock, and would take time before it could be broken. He spoke of the need to provide Thieu with maximum military support—new aircraft, helicopters, and heavy weapons, and even a promise of aiding a South Vietnamese invasion of the North after the American elections if necessary—to win his assent for the U.S. negotiating position with Hanoi. And Kissinger also told Nixon that the United States should be prepared for an escalation of the air war against the North if peace could not be negotiated before the elections.

The president took notes on his yellow pad, asked some questions, but no decision was taken on what should be the next step in the Vietnam political quagmire. Nixon said that, for the time being, the bombings in the North should continue while Kissinger kept working the diplomatic track. At that point, Nixon's mind was on the approaching Republican convention and his acceptance speech.

Virtually unopposed, Richard Nixon was renominated as the presidential candidate of the Republican Party at the Miami Beach convention on August 22. Facing Senator McGovern, an unimpressive candidate leading a divided party, Nixon seemed to have little to worry about. The only subject on which he might be vulnerable was Vietnam. But Nixon could rightfully claim that he had brought half a million American troops home without losing the war, and although the United States was still savagely bombing North Vietnam, he could point to serious negotiations with Hanoi and better prospects for peace than at any time since he took office.

Logically, then, Nixon emphasized his foreign-policy achievements and his "statesmanship" when he stood before the Republican convention on the night of August 23 to deliver his acceptance speech. Toughness was Nixon's policy, and he displayed this, too, lashing out against proposals to grant an amnesty "for those few hundred Americans who chose to desert their country rather than to serve it in Vietnam." Inasmuch as the amnesty proposals covered deserters as well as draft evaders (many of whom were serving prison terms), it was unclear where and whether he was drawing a line. The president seemed to be lumping them all together when he said, "The real heroes are two and a half million young Americans who chose to serve their country rather than desert it."

After enumerating his global foreign-policy successes, and appealing to the voters "to give us the chance to continue these great initiatives that can contribute so much to the future of peace in the world," after invoking the "need" to continue an arms buildup so that the "incentive" to reduce arms would be preserved, Nixon once more told the story of Tanya, the Russian girl whose diary he said he had read at the Leningrad cemetery. He urged his listeners

> to think of Tanya and the other Tanyas and their brothers and sisters everywhere [as] we proudly meet our responsibilities for leadership in the world in a way worthy of a great people. . . .
> I ask you, my fellow Americans, to join our new majority not just in the cause of winning an election, but in achieving a hope that mankind has had since the beginning of civilization. Let us build a peace that our children and all the children in the world can enjoy for generations to come.

Chapter 23

The president's reelection campaign was launched within twelve hours of his acceptance speech. At noon on August 24, Nixon was in Chicago addressing the annual national convention of the American Legion, and he repeated his theme of statesmanship and global responsibilities not quite three hours later in an unusually long speech at the dedication of the Dwight David Eisenhower High School in Utica, Michigan. He went into foreign policy again in the course of lengthy remarks made on his arrival in San Diego (here not surprisingly he put the accent on the need for a strong navy). Shortly after 7:00 p.m., he was at San Clemente, again speaking at length and again emphasizing foreign affairs.

Nixon took a five-day vacation in San Clemente before flying to Honolulu to meet Prime Minister Tanaka and to confer with Ambassador Bunker about political problems in Saigon. On August 27, the Nixons entertained Hollywood celebrities at a San Clemente reception. The president chatted easily about movies—he noted, for example, that no X-rated films had ever been shown at the White House although on one occasion he allowed an R film—yet he managed even here to inject remarks linking foreign policy with his reelection.

On August 29, he held an open-air news conference at the Western White House. Vietnam was a major topic. Nixon broke no new ground because negotiations were then in a state of suspended animation. There was no new date fixed for the resumption of the private talks in Paris, and there were serious problems with Thieu. But the president did announce that he was withdrawing 12,000 more American troops from Vietnam. By December 1, he said, there would be only 27,000 ground forces left in the country. But he declined to speculate about further withdrawals. "We are going to look at the situation again before the first of December, after the election, incidentally, because we are not going to play election politics with this next withdrawal—or this next announcement, I should say, because I am not suggesting that there will be another withdrawal."

The truth was that Nixon had decided to keep the 27,000 troops in

Vietnam indefinitely—as a bargaining chip in the negotiations. And the United States needed this bargaining chip, in addition to the continuing bombings of the North, to obtain the release of the POWs. "As long as there is one POW in North Vietnam . . . there will be an American volunteer force in South Vietnam."

North Vietnam had now been under intense American air assault for nearly four months and the president told the newsmen, "I am not going to put any limitation on when the U.S. activities in the air would stop." With the negotiations temporarily stalled, this was, of course, a signal to Hanoi to accept the American peace terms—the terms Kissinger had already privately modified earlier in the month in Paris—or keep suffering the bombings.

In the course of the news conference, Nixon made two interesting statements that would come back to haunt him. Asked about the status of the Watergate investigation and illegal political contributions to his campaign, he said that "we are doing everything we can to take this incident and investigate it and not to cover it up. . . . What really hurts in matters of this sort . . . is if you try to cover it up. . . . We want all the facts brought out and that as far as any people who are guilty are concerned, they should be prosecuted."

Turning again to foreign policy, Nixon declared that "abroad this country does not follow Hitlerite policies" and "the president of the United States is not the number-one warmaker of the world." He was offering an aura of respectability at home and the image of Richard Nixon as the great peacemaker abroad. Public-opinion polls suggest that at that point he was largely believed.

Nixon's next item of business was a quick trip to Honolulu on August 30. There, he and Kissinger held a long meeting with Ambassador Bunker, summoned from Saigon, to determine how best President Thieu should be handled in the context of the peace negotiations. Though Bunker was not apprised of all the fine points in Kissinger's bargaining with the North Vietnamese, he was instructed, in effect, to bring Thieu in line. It was a very tall order.

Then the president turned to the official part of the program in Honolulu: a two-day conference with Japan's Prime Minister Tanaka. It was another effort by the administration to improve the fragile relationship with the Japanese both in terms of overall Asian strategy and the seemingly intractable question of trade between the two countries.

Nixon and Tanaka promptly agreed to maintain indefinitely the Japanese-American Treaty of Mutual Cooperation and Security. This was the linchpin of America's strategic posture in the Far East, a fact that China —thinking of the Soviet Union—tacitly welcomed in the Asian balance of power. At that point, the United States supported an improvement in Chinese-Japanese relations, and the Nixon-Tanaka communiqué on September 1 expressed the hope that the prime minister's forthcoming trip to Peking would advance "the trend for the relaxation of tensions in Asia."

Nixon and Tanaka also agreed that the United States would try to expand exports to Japan and the Japanese would seek to promote imports from the United States. The point was that the United States was running a $3.4-billion annual trade deficit with Japan, a major factor in continued international monetary instability.

But the discussions on trade also covered a subject that eventually led to a major international scandal. This was the desire of the Lockheed Aircraft Company to sell its Tristar jet airliners to Japanese airlines and its P-3C Orion antisubmarine patrol aircraft to the Japanese Self-Defense Forces. With the Tristar, Lockheed was competing with the McDonnell-Douglas DC-10; with the Orion, the Japanese had to decide whether to buy it from Lockheed or to develop an aircraft of this type on their own. There are reasons to believe that Nixon used the Honolulu meeting to try to convince Tanaka to favor Lockheed in both instances.

Lockheed was in dire financial straits, having been saved from bankruptcy two years earlier by congressional approval of a Nixon administration proposal for federal guarantees of loans from a syndicate of private banks. Sale of the Tristars and Orions to the Japanese would immeasurably improve Lockheed's position: the Orion sale alone was worth more than $1 billion. Nixon may have acted legitimately in pushing Lockheed sales, inasmuch as they would increase U.S. exports to Japan—although McDonnell-Douglas might have taken a dim view of the president's favoring its competitor. Concerning the Orion, it was U.S. policy (though never stated publicly) that Japan should continue to rely on American sources for sophisticated military supplies rather than create its own capabilities, and Nixon was perhaps simply conveying this policy to Tanaka.

As it turned out, All-Nippon Airlines did buy the Tristar; and Tanaka, in his capacity as chairman of the Japanese Defense Council, concluded that Japan should *not* build its own patrol aircraft—which meant that it would purchase the Orions. Exactly how or why these decisions were made is not known. But subsequent disclosures by the Senate Subcommittee on Multinational Corporations showed that Lockheed had paid more than $12 million in illegal fees and commissions to its Tokyo sales agents, who, in turn, paid off members of Tanaka's government. Lockheed's principal agent was Yoshio Kodama, a shadowy figure in Japanese politics, a convicted war criminal, a man with close ties to the CIA—and Tanaka's friend and active supporter. The prime minister was forced to resign from office in 1974 because of his involvement in an unrelated financial scandal, and in mid-1976, he was arrested in connection with the Lockheed payoffs. It is unknown whether Nixon was aware that Tanaka and his associates were on the receiving end of the Lockheed bribery chain. But Senate investigators discovered that the White House kept senior Lockheed officials posted about the Nixon-Tanaka conversations both before and after they took place.

The United States, Nixon said in San Clemente in late August, was prepared to bomb North Vietnam indefinitely in search of peace. But intelligence reaching the White House early in September suggested that even after close to four months the heavy bombing raids were not having the desired effect. Separate but concurring studies prepared for the National Security Council by the CIA and the Defense Intelligence Agency found that despite the bombings North Vietnam could go on fighting "at the present rate" for two years. North Vietnamese "ant tactics" kept troops and supplies moving despite the air attacks; they were preparing new "high-point" offensives throughout South Vietnam; some 20,000 fresh North Vietnamese had infiltrated into the South since mid-July, making a total of approximately 100,000, with only one training brigade remaining in North Vietnam; they now had the largest number of regular troops in the Mekong Delta, southwest of Saigon, with the total estimated at 20,000–30,000 men, compared with 3000 a year before; and the delta had become the "biggest problem" in pacification.

Neither the bombing nor the mining of the ports seemed to have deprived North Vietnam of the supplies it needed to pursue the war. Fuel could no longer come in tankers, but a third underground petroleum pipeline had been completed between the Chinese frontier railroad terminal of Pingsiang and Hanoi. (The first two pipelines were laid in 1970 and 1971; work on the third one had begun in May, after Haiphong was mined, and it was opened within three and one-half months, *despite* the bombings.) Simultaneously, the North Vietnamese had built additional pipelines southward from Hanoi to supply forces in South Vietnam; one reached down to the Ashau Valley, opposite the Laotian border. It was virtually impossible for air strikes to cut the four-inch pipelines, but whenever a pipeline was hit, technicians turned it off at pumping stations and rapid repairs were made. The railways from China continued to function because Hanoi had marshaled all available rolling stock and manpower. (The "ant tactics" involved moving supplies by rail up to a bombed-out bridge or a severed highway; supplies were then moved by barges, trucks, bicycles, or back packs to railroad cars waiting beyond the damaged section and reloaded. At the same time, tracks and bridges were repaired.) Pilots kept reporting "secondary explosions" along the infiltration trails—these were munitions caches exploding—which suggested that matériel continued moving southward.

As a consolation, the intelligence agencies told the NSC that if it had not been for the bombings, the North Vietnamese could have doubled their operations and would have been spared losses estimated at 100,000 killed on the battlefield and in bombing attacks—compared with 30,000 ARVN fatalities—since the start of the spring offensive.

The overall conclusion was that while North Vietnam had failed to win the offensive, it had not been put out of commission and was capable of further aggressive action. This was not what Nixon had expected.

Hanoi's refusal to abandon the idea of a coalition government in Saigon as the price for peace was no doubt bolstered by this sense of military strength. But presumably because of Chairman Mao's intervention, Hanoi and the Viet Cong were making less of an issue of Thieu's immediate fate. Le Duc Tho had remarked several times on August 14 that what existed in South Vietnam were "two armies," "two administrations," and three "political groupings." Subtly, he was shifting his position from a total rejection of Thieu and his regime to the recognition that there *was* a Saigon army and a Saigon administration in the South. (The three political groupings were the Thieu government, the Viet Cong, and the neutralist faction between them.) This was the real turning point in the peace negotiations.

While Le Duc Tho had shown interest in Kissinger's tripartite electoral commission formula, the North Vietnamese were still quite suspicious. An article published early in September in *Hoc Tap,* the monthly theoretical journal of the North Vietnamese Communist Party, charged that the United States was attempting to "liquidate" the Viet Cong administration in the South through new stratagems. The article made no mention of the tripartite commission, but suggested that whatever Kissinger had in mind was still unacceptable.

On September 11, the Viet Cong delegation in Paris issued a new proposal calling for what it termed a tripartite "government of national concord." In it, the three "political groupings" would be "in equal strength and on equal footing." The Saigon faction—without Thieu— could "appoint its people to participate in the government of national concord." Close study of the statement showed a certain give in the Communist position: it was the first time the Communist side said publicly that a settlement had to reflect the "reality" of "two administrations, two armies and other political forces." It was one thing for Le Duc Tho to say it privately to Kissinger and another for the Viet Cong and Hanoi to state it in public. And the phrase "government of national concord" was, at least, a semantic breakthrough.

The Americans publicly dismissed the new proposal as "an undisguised attempt to put the Viet Cong in power in South Vietnam without an election." But Nixon and Kissinger thought an attempt should be made to hold another meeting with the North Vietnamese, and messages were exchanged through the usual channels; the date was set for September 15. First, however, Kissinger was to go to Moscow to discuss various matters with Brezhnev—including Vietnam.

During Kissinger's four-day stay in the Soviet capital—September 10–14—Vietnam came up only once, on September 13, at a session between Kissinger and his advisers and Brezhnev, Gromyko, Dobrynin, and Aleksandrov. Kissinger was not certain that the Viet Cong's new proposal was the breakthrough for which he had been waiting for three years; the Russians told him they thought it was.

Meanwhile, a stark and intense drama was developing behind the scenes. The plan was for Ambassador Bunker to obtain Thieu's agreement to the tripartite commission while Kissinger carried out his Moscow talks and prepared to meet Tho in Paris. Kissinger was determined to present the North Vietnamese with a proposal *agreed to by both Washington and Saigon* at their forthcoming session. But late at night on September 13, Kissinger, who was at Brezhnev's guest house, received a cable from Bunker advising that despite all the efforts in recent days, Thieu had rejected the tripartite commission proposal. "Henry blew a gasket," an associate recounted later. Pacing around the dacha at midnight, Kissinger briefly toyed with the idea of rushing to Saigon to try to change Thieu's mind, but concluded that the time had come for the United States to act unilaterally. Shortly after midnight, he telegraphed President Nixon requesting permission to meet with Tho as planned and to inform him that Washington would stand firm on the question of the electoral commission regardless of Thieu's views. Kissinger reasoned that with the American elections only seven weeks away, Nixon could not risk a collapse in the Paris peace negotiations.

Nixon's reply reached the American party the next morning, September 14, as it prepared to leave for London. It said, in effect, that Kissinger could go ahead and tell Tho that the United States accepted the tripartite commission. But this decision was not wholly popular in the White House: Haig, for example, complained privately to friends that Kissinger was giving away too much.

The Nixon-Kissinger decision was another major turning point in the tortured history of Vietnam negotiations. For the first time, Nixon was ready to make a major offer to Hanoi without Thieu's concurrence—indeed, in the face of his outright opposition.

Kissinger flew to Paris from London on September 15, reverting to complex secrecy procedures. (Kissinger had spent the previous night at Claridges—after a meeting with British officials—and a State Department Vietnamese-language interpreter, urgently summoned from Washington, was put up at another hotel to maintain the cover. The interpreter met Kissinger at 6:30 a.m. in Claridges lobby, and then the whole group was driven in a British military vehicle to the Royal Air Force's Bryce-Norton Base near London. There, they boarded a U.S. Air Force prop-driven twin-engined Convair plane for a choppy flight to the Villa Coubley field outside Paris.)

Kissinger's meeting with Tho and Thuy was relatively brief: he orally communicated the new American position and asked questions about the Viet Cong proposal of September 11. Tho, in turn, questioned Kissinger about modalities of presidential elections in South Vietnam after a cease-fire. This was, in a way, a preliminary step before the negotiations were to enter their final stage.

Kissinger noted that Le Duc Tho was no longer talking about the need to remove Thieu as a precondition for peace. The fact was, as Gareth Porter has written, that Hanoi was ready "to accept the continuation of the Thieu regime under conditions which would deprive [the South Vietnamese government] of its claim to exclusive sovereignty over South Vietnam and obligate Thieu to loosen his grip over the political life of the Saigon-controlled zone." Hanoi and the PRG had evidently accepted Mao's pragmatic advice. A peace agreement had finally become possible.

Back in Washington, Kissinger conferred in the small hours of September 16 with Nixon and then, separately, with Secretary Rogers. Rogers, however, received only a partial version of what had been going on: Kissinger remained obsessively distrustful of him, although he now took William Sullivan, deputy assistant secretary of state for Far Eastern affairs and head of the Interdepartmental Vietnam Task Force, into his confidence. But Sullivan and his personal aides were instructed to write out in longhand all papers pertaining to the negotiations so that no typing would be done by secretaries and there would be no danger that Rogers saw any copies.

Nixon and Kissinger decided that matters had progressed sufficiently in Paris for Kissinger to take the unusual step of holding a news conference later in the day. They felt that now the public should be informed about where the negotiations stood, although they had no intention of revealing everything. But the news conference produced nothing but confusion. Kissinger was optimistic when he said that the "fact that these talks are going on would indicate a certain seriousness." But then, without elaboration, he remarked that the September 11 Viet Cong proposals left "something to be desired," warned against setting "arbitrary deadlines" for ending the war, and said that he would "not be surprised" if the Communists soon launched new offensives and "other high points" in Vietnam (though of lesser scope and duration than the spring offensive).

He seemed to attach little importance to the Viet Cong suggestion that Thieu should go—he knew that Hanoi had tacitly dropped this demand—but he went out of his way to say that the "basic principle" of United States policy continued to be the refusal "as a result of the negotiations to impose a particular form of government that guaranteed predominance to one side" in Saigon. This formulation carried an important nuance that was undoubtedly lost on his audience: Kissinger was no longer opposing a "government of national concord" in Saigon but arguing against the possibility that the Communists would win the upper hand in a tripartite government.

On September 26, Kissinger was back in Paris. (This time the White House announced the meeting ahead of time.) For this crucial session, Tho had received new instructions from Hanoi, and now he formally advised Kissinger that North Vietnam no longer demanded Thieu's removal—this made official what Kissinger already knew—and no longer insisted on a coalition government, in so many words. Instead, Tho proposed a National Council of Reconciliation and Concord. Kissinger still thought that this might become a "*de facto* coalition government," but the negotiating gap was being bridged. He told Tho they should continue discussing the proposal.

After returning to the suite he was occupying at the American embassy residence on the rue du Faubourg St. Honoré, Kissinger cabled Nixon that he was remaining in Paris for another day of talks. The message reached the president aboard *Air Force One* as he was flying from Washington to New York for a "Victory '72" dinner at the Americana Hotel. Ziegler gravely told newsmen, "Dr. Kissinger is staying in close touch with the president concerning the current talks."

The pulse of diplomatic activity was quickening elsewhere too. In Moscow, Premier Kosygin and President Podgorny had received the North Vietnamese ambassador, Vo Thuc Dong, on September 25. In Hanoi, *Nhan Dan,* the official newspaper, published a long article bearing the authoritative "Commentator" signature, urging the United States to join with North Vietnam in guarantees that "neither side dominate political life in South Vietnam" under a peace settlement. This was taken to be a reply to Kissinger's comment that the United States would not "impose a particular form of government that guaranteed predominance to one side." Even more important was a statement that "the correct way is to proceed from the reality of the situation in South Vietnam and to form during the transition from the restoration of peace to the holding of free and democratic elections a provisional government of national concord without domination by any side." To American officials, this indicated that Hanoi might be edging toward acceptance of the American view that a cease-fire must precede a political settlement in South Vietnam.

Also on the same day, French Foreign Minister Schumann told a small group of newsmen in an off-the-record conversation in Washington that a Vietnam peace settlement was "within reach" if both parties were prepared to "reach out" for it.

In Paris, Kissinger had his second meeting with Le Duc Tho on September 27. He heard more North Vietnamese explanations about the transition government and, for his part, submitted again the formal American position for the tripartite electoral commission. They parted with an agreement to meet again within two weeks; Tho was returning to Hanoi for additional instructions from the Politburo, and Kissinger needed to review the situation with Nixon. Flying home, Kissinger seemed encouraged. There was a good chance, he told his associates on the plane, that the "Vietnam cancer" could be removed before the November elections.

He was back in Washington on the evening of September 27, but Nixon was away in Los Angeles at another "Victory '72" dinner. When he returned to Washington the next day, Kissinger and Haig joined him for the evening aboard the *Sequoia* for a long review of the negotiations. The situation looked extremely promising, but, as Kissinger pointed out, they did not yet have a peace agreement sewed up. That morning, in fact,

Hanoi radio had broadcast the text of an article in *Hoc Tap,* the theoretical journal, charging that the "American propaganda machine is trying to give the impression that the United States and North Vietnam are getting closer" in the peace talks. Nixon and Kissinger were not sure what to make of this.

The continuing difficulty was President Thieu's refusal to go along with the American position. On instructions from Nixon, Ambassador Bunker had told Thieu that Hanoi appeared to be moving toward a settlement. But Thieu was not impressed. So Nixon dispatched Haig and Negroponte to Saigon to try once again to persuade the South Vietnamese president to relent. They left the next day; the White House did not disclose their real mission, and the announcement simply said that Haig was going to Saigon to confer with Thieu and make a "general assessment of the situation there."

Later on September 29, Nixon received Foreign Minister Schumann for two hours. The conversation was entirely devoted to Vietnam, and at one point, Kissinger, still uncertain about Hanoi, asked Schumann, "Are you sure North Vietnam won't insist on Thieu's departure?" Schumann replied that, yes, he was sure, and he knew that both the Russians and the Chinese were for leaving Thieu in place. Nixon raised the question of whether Hanoi believed that he sincerely wanted a peace settlement. Schumann said he thought so, but volunteered to convey the president's sentiments to the North Vietnamese on his return to Paris. (He did so at a secret meeting with Le Duc Tho on October 7 at La Celle château, in St. Cloud, near Paris.) As Schumann recalled it later, Nixon "asked me to intervene with the North Vietnamese so that they would understand how far the United States could go and how far it couldn't go. They couldn't go as far as to forcing President Thieu to resign."

The stage was set for the breakthrough.

The presidential election was now a month away; Nixon felt he could take no chances in terms of peace predictions, and he remained extremely cautious. He was under mounting attack for maintaining the bombings over North Vietnam—they had now been going on for five months and more than 800,000 tons of "air ammunition" had been dropped on Indochina in the first nine months of 1972, more than the total tonnage for 1971—and the criticism was getting to him. Watergate, too, would not go away.

All of this came out at the president's news conference on October 5. The first question was about corruption in his administration, and Nixon's response was bitter, sarcastic, and self-righteous:

I have noted that this administration has been charged with being
the most corrupt in history, and I have been charged with being
the most deceitful president in history. The president of the
United States has been compared in his policies with Adolf Hitler.
The policies of the U.S. Government to prevent a Communist
take-over by force in South Vietnam have been called the worst
crime since the Nazi extermination of the Jews in Germany. And
the president who went to China and to Moscow, and who
brought 500,000 home from Vietnam, has been called the number-
one warmaker in the world.

Nixon kept insisting that there was no link between the elections
and a Vietnam peace settlement:

Under no circumstances will the timing of a settlement, for example,
the possible negotiation of a cease-fire, the possible negotiation of, or
unilateral action with regard to, a bombing halt—under no circumstances will such action be affected by the fact that there is going to
be an election November 7. If we can make the right kind of a settlement before the election, we will make it. If we cannot, we are not
going to make the wrong kind of a settlement before the election. We
were around that track in 1968 when well-intentioned men made a
very, very great mistake in stopping the bombing without adequate
agreements from the other side. . . . The election, I repeat, will not
in any way influence what we do at the negotiating table.

He acknowledged that Hanoi might be delaying an agreement in the
hope that he would be defeated next month; however, Nixon added, "We
are talking," and "if we have the opportunity, we will continue to talk
before this election and we will try to convince them that waiting until
after the election is not good strategy."

The very next day, October 6, the diplomatic pieces began falling into
place. Hanoi confirmed that Le Duc Tho would be in Paris on the eighth
to meet with Kissinger. The president and Kissinger heard from General
Haig that Thieu still stubbornly resisted the settlement being worked out
by Kissinger and Le Duc Tho. Nixon thought it over and told Kissinger
that it was now too late for the United States to change course. If a deal
could be made with Hanoi on terms that Nixon could accept, then it must
be done regardless of Thieu's attitude. With this, Kissinger, Haig, and a
large staff of advisers flew to Paris on the morning of October 7.

The breakthrough in the Vietnam peace talks came on October 8. Tho
opened the conversation by saying that inasmuch as Kissinger was eager
to settle the war before the American elections, the North Vietnamese
had brought a document to serve as a draft peace agreement—it was the

first time Hanoi had presented a genuine negotiating document rather than just a series of demands.

The highlights of the Hanoi plan were an immediate cease-fire in place in Vietnam, a total U.S. withdrawal from Vietnam, and the return of all American POWs within sixty days. Politically, it proclaimed Vietnam —North and South—to be one country, temporarily divided. To bring about eventual unity, the North Vietnamese blueprint offered a vague political process in the South where an "administrative structure" would be in some way established prior to the elections. The document appeared to separate military from political issues—certainly not making a cease-fire contingent upon a political solution—and in this sense it met Kissinger's conceptual approach. He remarked that this was a "very interesting document" for that reason.

Kissinger indicated to Tho that he was willing to accept his document as the basis for subsequent negotiations, and another meeting was scheduled for the next day, October 9, at 3:00 p.m. Back at the American embassy residence, Kissinger instructed Winston Lord, John Negroponte, and David Engle to draft a counterproposal. As it stood, he said, the Hanoi draft placed almost all the operational obligations on the United States and South Vietnam and virtually none on North Vietnam, except to cease firing and return the POWs. Hanoi's troops were not expected to go home. One of Kissinger's ideas was that there should be a National Council of Reconciliation and Concord in Saigon, as Tho had originally proposed, in lieu of the vague "administrative structure." The council, not a coalition government, would operate alongside the Thieu regime and the electoral commission during the preelection period.

Having instructed his staff to write the counterproposal, Kissinger went out to a restaurant with a date. The three men finished their work at 3:00 a.m. and went to sleep, leaving the document for Kissinger. But they were awakened by him at eight o'clock. He was furious; the draft was too hard. "You don't understand," he said. "I want to meet their position." He also wished to keep a number of issues open for further discussion. He gave his staff until 1:00 p.m. to revise the counterproposal along the lines he had indicated. (An American official, familiar with the events of that week, said later, "Henry was rushing things too much; it was getting too sloppy.")

Before going into the second meeting with Tho, Kissinger sent a two-paragraph telegram to Ambassador Bunker informing him very briefly of the situation and instructing him to tell Thieu. Trying to preserve his negotiating freedom on all fronts, Kissinger sent only scant reports on the situation to Saigon and even to Nixon.

Kissinger and Tho met daily on October 9, 10, and 11. On the eleventh, they reached an agreement in principle, although two issues were left unresolved: the question of releasing civilian prisoners in South Vietnam (Kissinger did not want to press Thieu on this point); and the cessation of all military aid by the United States to South Vietnam and by North Vietnam to the Viet Cong (and North Vietnamese regulars in the South) except on a one-to-one replacement basis. Kissinger told Tho that he now had to return to Washington to seek Nixon's approval before there could be another meeting on October 17 to make the agreement final. But Tho insisted on an understanding that a peace accord would be signed on October 31. The North Vietnamese conveyed their concern that after the election the president's position might harden and the agreement, evidently favorable to them, might become unhinged. Kissinger, who told Tho on six different occasions that Saigon's concurrence had to be obtained for the signing, related later that the North Vietnamese fought for the October 31 date "almost as maniacally as they fought the war." Kissinger promised Tho to make a "major effort" to meet the deadline. Then he flew home on October 12, leaving Lord and Engle behind to keep liaison with the North Vietnamese.

Kissinger went straight from Andrews Air Force Base to the White House to present the 58-page draft agreement to Nixon. They spent two hours together. On October 13 the draft was shown to Rogers and several State Department experts, including Sullivan and Deputy Legal Adviser George H. Aldrich. The CIA's George Carver was also brought in. The consensus was that the Hanoi draft was basically acceptable, although a number of provisions had to be tightened. Carver warned Kissinger that he might have great difficulty bringing Thieu around to agree to the settlement as it was now shaping up, but the warning did not fully register.

On the morning of October 14, the president had breakfast at the White House with Kissinger, Rogers, and Haig. They reviewed the draft and concluded that final agreement should be possible after a few more negotiating sessions in Paris. The American public was unaware of how advanced the negotiations were. Neither the White House nor Hanoi was eager to publicize the substance of the negotiations although Kissinger found the time privately to guide several Washington newsmen as to how their stories should be written. The official position of the United States and North Vietnam was that a lot of work was still required before an agreement could be completed. In Paris, Le Duc Tho told newsmen as he was leaving for Hanoi that "there are still many difficult things to settle." At the White House, Ron Ziegler said, "you can assume that we would not challenge" Tho's comment. The fact that Kissinger and the North Vietnamese planned to meet again on October 17 was kept secret, and Ziegler refused to say when—or even whether—the private talks would be resumed. Likewise, the White House would not say whether further consultations with Thieu were required.

As for Kissinger, he was privately bubbling with optimism. His plans were to return to Paris on October 17 for a final meeting with Xuan Thuy (Tho was no longer expected back in Paris in time for the next negotiating session because of his stops in Moscow and Peking en route to Hanoi) and then to go on to Saigon for what he hoped would be wrap-up conferences with Thieu between October 19 and 23.

Next, he would fly secretly to Hanoi to initial the agreement on October 24—his presence in the North Vietnamese capital would be revealed publicly only after the ceremony—and the peace accord would be signed by the four foreign ministers in Paris on October 31. The Hanoi trip would be Kissinger's greatest coup, and he was visibly excited about it. It was a beautiful scenario.

(The day before Kissinger left for Paris, Richard Nixon allowed himself an emotional outburst, attacking "the so-called public-opinion leaders of this country" for not supporting him after he had ordered the bombings and mining of North Vietnam. In a slashing and totally unexpected indictment of his critics at a Washington conference of the National League of Families of American Prisoners and Missing in Southeast Asia, Nixon included the news media, the universities, and even the business community. What triggered Nixon's furious performance? Observers recognized that this was part of the Nixon behavior pattern: a man of immense public self-control, he would sometimes explode almost irrationally when he felt himself attacked or misunderstood.)

Kissinger arrived in Paris on the morning of October 17 with Sullivan and Aldrich. They went immediately into session with Thuy, but it quickly developed that important textual differences remained between the two sides. The afternoon turned into evening, Kissinger, growing nervous and impatient, announced that he simply had to leave for Saigon before Orly Airport closed at 11:00 p.m. He was anxious to stay on schedule. Thuy told him that the final details could presumably be worked out in Hanoi after Kissinger arrived there on October 24. (The North Vietnamese liked the idea of having Kissinger in Hanoi to wind up the talks and initial the accord in their capital.)

Kissinger and Sullivan arrived in Saigon on the morning of October 19. Nobody there had a clear idea of what was happening: Kissinger had of course kept everyone in the dark. Ambassador Bunker had not seen the text of the agreement and was only vaguely aware of its provisions. Thieu knew next to nothing.

Kissinger and Bunker met for three and a half hours with Thieu at the presidential palace. And for the first time Thieu saw the draft peace agreement (and only in the English version, which was all Kissinger had with him). He reacted with undisguised fury. His attitude was described by a participant as that of a "trapped tiger." His first objection was that he had not been consulted. The text was still incomplete (the provisions for the release of civilian prisoners in the South and the question of military-equipment replacements remained subject to further negotiation), but he opposed most of the clauses. He said he was not ready for a cease-fire and he could not understand why the Americans had given up their demand for an Indochina-wide cease-fire in favor of a truce confined to Vietnam alone. For the next three days Thieu claimed that the worst flaw in the proposed agreement was that the North Vietnamese were not required to leave the South. He protested that the document recognized post-truce areas of control in the South for both his forces and the Communists. This, he said bitterly, had the effect of granting the Communists sovereignty over some areas.

Sessions at the palace grew increasingly tense—a participant said Thieu was acting almost paranoid—and the Saigon leader accused Kissinger of negotiating an agreement behind his back and then demanding his endorsement of it in three days. He took exception to the concept of the tripartite commission and to the expression "administrative structure," which was still in the text despite Kissinger's preference for the "Council of Reconciliation and Concord." Either way, he said, this presaged a coalition government.

Kissinger, who by now had developed a deep resentment toward Thieu, argued that the proposed agreement, combined with American guarantees, gave the regime a "fighting chance" and "decent interval" after the cease-fire and now inevitable U.S. withdrawal. "We were successful in Peking, we were successful in Moscow, we were even successful in Paris. There is no reason why we cannot be successful here."

Thieu's young foreign-policy adviser Hoang Duc Nha replied, "So far history has shown that the United States has been successful in many fields. But history does not predict that in the future the United States will be successful here."

Still, Kissinger thought that Thieu would in the end be persuaded, and he so advised Nixon from Saigon. Late on October 21, Nixon dispatched an extraordinary message to Hanoi, saying that despite a few remaining problems "the text of the agreement could be considered complete" and that peace could be signed on October 31. The plan still was for Kissinger to go to Hanoi on the twenty-fourth.

While Kissinger kept negotiating with Thieu, he sent Sullivan to brief Laotian Premier Souvanna Phouma in Vientiane and the Thai leaders in Bangkok. Sullivan told the Thais that as part of the peace agreement the North Vietnamese would withdraw from Laos and Cambodia. If Hanoi violated this commitment, he said, the United States would "obliterate" North Vietnam. This, however, was not entirely accurate. The United States never had a firm commitment from Hanoi on quitting Cambodia —although it had secret assurances that a truce in Laos could be arranged (as, indeed, it was, a month after the Vietnam accord). Kissinger made a quick trip to Phnom Penh to confer with President Lon Nol, but he did not show him the peace plan or tell him that Hanoi resisted a commitment on ending the Cambodian fighting. Instead, he pressed Lon Nol to seek a unilateral cease-fire. Lon Nol thanked him and asked when the North Vietnamese were leaving.

Kissinger and Bunker held their last meeting with Thieu on the morning of October 23. Despite Kissinger's entreaties, Thieu remained totally opposed to the peace plan. Kissinger reported this to Nixon who, in turn, informed Hanoi that the Saigon talks had hit a snag and that, after all, the signing of the peace agreement could no longer be done on October 31. Heavyhearted, Kissinger canceled his Hanoi trip and, dejected and exhausted, returned to Washington.

On his arrival in the capital late on October 23, after flying for twenty hours, Kissinger went directly to the White House. The question was what to do next. Kissinger, with Nixon's approval, had made a commitment to the North Vietnamese that the peace agreement could be signed, and now the whole diplomatic edifice was collapsing because of Thieu's iron opposition. Nixon and Kissinger knew that the United States would be accused of bad faith when in truth the problem was that it could not control its ally. The two men talked far into the night. Next morning, Kissinger was back at the White House for another conference with Nixon —and Rogers.

No decision on how to proceed was taken on October 24. The president signed two veterans' benefit bills dealing primarily with Vietnam veterans, and delivered a short speech, noting that "this has been a long war. It is a difficult one. It is very controversial. People in the United States have disagreed about it, whether we should have gotten in, how it is being conducted, and what we should now do."

On October 26, a new crisis developed. The North Vietnamese had evidently concluded that the Americans had used them for domestic political purposes and were reneging.

Their response was to "go public" with a broadcast disclosing the highlights of the once-hoped-for agreement. The broadcast was monitored during the night by the Foreign Broadcast Information Service (a CIA operation) and Kissinger was awakened at 2:00 a.m. to be told about it. He instantly telephoned the president at the White House. The decision was later made that Kissinger would hold a news conference at noon to explain the situation. Kissinger's overwhelming concern was that Hanoi not think that it was being deceived by the United States.

With Nixon's specific approval, he confirmed Hanoi's disclosures and used the expression that "peace is at hand," saying that only a few more meetings with the North Vietnamese were required to iron out final details. The point was to reassure Hanoi, on the one hand, and to warn Saigon, on the other, that the United States was determined to conclude a Vietnam peace agreement. Just as important, the statement served to undercut McGovern two weeks before the election.

Nixon and Kissinger were deeply concerned that the negotiations with the North Vietnamese would now collapse. While still in Saigon, Kissinger had urged Nixon by cable to suspend American bombings north of the 20th parallel as a gesture of goodwill. He even suggested the end of U.S. tactical air support to the ARVN to show his annoyance with Thieu. Nixon agreed to the former but refused the latter. (The pressure on everyone involved was intense: before his return from Saigon to Washington, Kissinger had a series of bitter cable exchanges with Haig, who thought that the American negotiating position was eroding.)

At his televised and immensely "virtuoso" performance on October 26, Kissinger was, in effect, telling Hanoi to cool it, that the United States would deliver despite the unexpected delay. Some of Kissinger's colleagues say that he did not believe at that point that peace was really "at hand," but that he was both anxious to commit Nixon to a quick peace and to keep McGovern on the defensive. He seemed worried that after the elections Nixon might reopen the whole diplomatic situation; he feared that given Nixon's natural inclinations, the president might revert to "toughness" after being reelected.

There is a school of thought that Nixon and Kissinger—especially

Nixon—had secretly welcomed Thieu's rejection of the peace agreement at that juncture. Some students of the history of the negotiations believe that the White House never intended to sign the agreement before the elections. They cite the fact that in two cables to North Vietnamese Premier Pham Van Dong between October 21 and 23 Nixon sought to reopen some of the provisions in the agreed-upon text. Another evidence of White House duplicity is that the United States was preparing to turn over vast amounts of new weapons to South Vietnam before the signing of the agreement so that Thieu could fend for himself.

These arguments cannot be rejected out of hand because there is circumstantial evidence to support them. The military resupply program —known as Operation Enhance—was far from complete late in October when the agreement was to be signed. Under peace provisions, no new military equipment could be introduced into South Vietnam except for one-to-one replacements. And without this equipment, desperately needed by the ARVN after the Communist spring offensive, Thieu might not have been able to survive for long after the cease-fire. Nixon and Kissinger had to assume that the Communists would not simply give up their decades-long dream of the reunification of Vietnam only because the United States was getting out of the war. If South Vietnam was to remain non-Communist, Thieu had to be left in the strongest possible position.

Kissinger's press conference of October 26 also raises disturbing questions. At no point did he blame Thieu for blocking the signing of the agreement, suggesting instead that it was a question of working out additional "technical" matters with Hanoi—even though four days earlier he appeared to be ready to go to the North Vietnamese capital to initial the text. Kissinger was also implying that the United States had never accepted finally the text of the agreement.

Whatever the truth, the fact remains that the turn of events late in October did help Nixon politically. As far as the voters were concerned, the Nixon administration was presenting them with "peace at hand," and they were willing to accept Kissinger's explanation about last-minute "technical problems." Nobody had seen the text of the agreement, and it was impossible to question the accuracy of what Kissinger was saying. Likewise, the president had suspended the bombings of North Vietnam, thus removing one of the most damaging aspects of his Vietnam policies. Hanoi's angry denunciations of American manipulations, whatever they were, made no real difference.

But of course, it was now too late to resolve the "technical problems" in time for a signing before the election. The widespread belief was that it could be done right after November 7, and that the worst was over. Nixon, who left on a campaign tour a few hours after Kissinger's news conference, reinforced this impression. In fact, the president was presenting the situation that had developed in the past twenty-four hours as a triumph for the cause of peace. Speaking in the evening in Huntington, West Virginia, he said that "as all of you have read or heard on your television tonight, there has been a significant breakthrough in the negotiations with regard to Vietnam. . . . I can say to you with confidence that because of the progress that has been made, I am confident that we shall succeed in achieving our objective, which is peace with honor, and not peace with surrender, in Vietnam. There are still differences to be worked out. I believe that they can and will be worked out." He repeated the same theme in Ashland, Kentucky, several hours later.

In a radio address on "One America" on October 28, the president said that "in the difficult job of seeking an honorable negotiated settlement in Vietnam, I have been able to count on the support of a majority of Americans. . . . That is why America has been able to preserve its pledge that we shall not betray our allies, or abandon our men held prisoner or missing in action, as we work for a full generation of peace." In Saginaw, Michigan, also on October 28, Nixon declared that "as you know, we can now look forward with confidence to winning the kind of peace in Vietnam that all Americans want."

In a televised address on November 2—his "Look to the Future" speech—Nixon said that "we have reached substantial agreement on most of the terms of a settlement." But he added pointedly: "There are still some provisions of the agreement which must be clarified so that all ambiguities will be removed. I have insisted that these be settled before we sign the final agreement. That is why we refused to be stampeded into meeting the arbitrary deadline of October 31."

Now there was a perceptible hardening in Nixon's line on the peace agreement. There were no more references to "technical problems," and the deadline to which he had agreed a week earlier had suddenly become "arbitrary." On November 2, he spoke of "central points." Yet in the euphoria of the "breakthrough"—and in the absence of public knowledge concerning the secret Vietnam diplomacy from Paris to Saigon—the president's words went unquestioned. From West Virginia to Kentucky, Michigan, Illinois, Oklahoma, Rhode Island, North Carolina, New Mexico, and California—his final campaign swing—Nixon was getting all the mileage he could from the "breakthrough" and his prudent handling of a still "ambiguous" situation. But he was also laying the foundation for a wholly new phase of war and diplomacy—after the elections.

On November 7, Richard Nixon was reelected by a landslide for a second four-year term. Only Massachusetts and the District of Columbia went against him. Among other things, this victory handed the president the mandate to deal with the Vietnam situation as he saw fit. Nixon himself viewed the vote as an expression of national confidence in his conduct of foreign policy.

His winning margin was established so quickly that the president was able to deliver a short televised address to the nation from the Oval Office at 11:54 p.m. on election night.

> We are united Americans—North, East, West, and South, both parties —in our desire for peace, peace with honor, the kind of peace that will last, and we are moving swiftly toward that great goal, not just in Vietnam, but a new era of peace in which the old relationships between the two superpowers, the Soviet Union and the United States, and between the world's most populous nation, the People's Republic of China, and the United States, are changed so that we are on the eve of what could be the greatest generation of peace, true peace for the whole world, that man has ever known.

But to bring the war finally to an end, Nixon had to resolve two principal issues. One was to get the Paris negotiations back on the track; there had not been any meaningful communication between Washington and Hanoi since "peace at hand" broke down with the events of October 26, except for a decision worked out through Colonel Guay's Paris channel on November 4 that Kissinger and Le Duc Tho would meet again on November 20. This, however, was not made public. The president and Kissinger, no longer under electoral-deadline pressures, thought that in the two weeks before the return to Paris they could work out a negotiating position that would take care of what Nixon regarded as "central points" and "ambiguities." Kissinger, however, continued to talk about "technical problems" only.

The other issue was President Thieu. In October, Nixon had allowed him to exercise, in effect, a veto over the peace settlement. The president may even have found it desirable to have a delay in the signing to obtain more concessions from Hanoi—the negotiations during October had moved at an astounding tempo—and in this Thieu had been useful. The anti-Kissinger faction at the White House—notably Ehrlichman and

Haldeman—had been pressing the president late in October to hold off on the signing, and he may have taken their advice. All three, after all, were instinctive cold war ideologues no matter what Nixon had been saying in his public speeches. Kissinger was nonideological in big-power dealings, and he wanted the agreement he had negotiated to be signed as soon as possible. He resented having been left out on the limb with his "peace at hand" proclamation.

Now Thieu could not be permitted to block peace much longer. As Nixon and Kissinger held their conferences after the elections at the White House, the hideaway in the Executive Office Building, and during a short November vacation in Key Biscayne, the president agreed that the United States would sign an acceptable document regardless of Thieu's objections.

There were two ways of handling Thieu, the White House thought. The first was simply renewed diplomatic pressure. Then there were arms. Under Operation Enhance, covering the period between May and October, the South Vietnamese had been receiving weapons primarily to offset the losses they suffered during the spring offensive. Since May, they had been given 153 aircraft, 106 helicopters, 240 tanks, 141 TOW antitank weapons (in short supply in the United States), 750 heavy mortars, 175-mm. artillery guns, and vast amounts of lighter weapons, ammunition, and fuel.

But Thieu argued—and Nixon agreed—that South Vietnam would need much more to face the Communists after the cease-fire. The truce contemplated under the agreement would be a cease-fire in place, meaning that the ARVN and the Communists would remain exactly where they were the moment hostilities ceased: a "leopard-spot" situation. Even as the October negotiations were moving ahead, both sides in Vietnam were increasingly engaged in land-grabbing operations, each wanting to be in the best possible military position when the fighting stopped officially. And Nixon understood that land grabbing would go on, perhaps less blatantly, after the cease-fire. This was a Vietnamese reality. Just as Operation Enhance was filling South Vietnam with new equipment during October, the North Vietnamese were infiltrating fresh troops and supplies into the South in preparation for the truce and taking advantage of the start of the dry season.

By late October, the Pentagon—acting with Nixon's personal approval—launched Operation Enhance Plus designed to give Thieu still greater military muscle. These deliveries would have to stop, of course, once the agreement was signed. But Enhance Plus also increased Nixon's leverage over Thieu. If he remained totally intractable, shipments under Enhance Plus, which had started in the first days of November, would be halted. Although this was the strategy that Nixon decided to apply in his bargaining with Thieu, the president at the same time was willing to give Saigon enough time to allow the completion of Enhance Plus.

For this reason, Nixon appeared to be perfectly happy to let the postelection negotiations with North Vietnam drag on much longer than may have been necessary. As it was, Thieu had three months of grace after October 31. Between November 1 and January 27, 1973, when the peace agreement was signed, South Vietnam received an additional 266 warplanes and 277 helicopters. Saigon thus faced "peace" with its air force increased by roughly 75 percent and strongly equipped ground forces. The two Enhance operations cost the United States $1.23 billion, according to Pentagon figures, but the real figure had to be much higher: the Defense Department was writing off equipment for South Vietnam at way below real replacement cost. In some cases, weapons were disposed of at 8.9 percent of acquisition cost as "excess defense equipment."

Nixon moved quickly to have the Saigon situation resolved before Kissinger returned to Paris. On November 8, the day after the elections, General Haig was dispatched to South Vietnam to discuss the "minimum changes" to be negotiated with Hanoi and to explain the military *quid pro quo* to Thieu.

Haig, who unlike Kissinger was still on speaking terms with Thieu, told him on November 9 that he should not take too much comfort from the American elections. He warned him that although Washington would do its best to improve the terms, it would not give up its commitment to the tripartite electoral commission.

Thieu reopened his objections to the draft language defining the areas of military control by the two sides in South Vietnam and resisted anything that would bind him militarily. The North Vietnamese were overextended in the South at that stage—many of their units had not been advised to prepare for a cease-fire—and now Thieu was stalling while the ARVN tried to improve its position. Haig still could not break the impasse.

Kissinger returned to Paris on November 20—to settle what he had said the previous month would be the final details. But again, he miscalculated the situation. On Nixon's instructions, he convinced the North Vietnamese to include in the text a definition of the demilitarized zone as a provisional political division line. This was designed to pacify Thieu. He also read "for the record" a South Vietnamese document demanding sixty-nine changes in the text.

The next day, he retracted about one-half of these proposed changes, and he said later that it was inconceivable that the North Vietnamese would have taken the demands seriously. However, it was probably a mistake for him to have ever raised them so late in the game.

The talks dragged on for four more days and the Americans began detecting hesitations on Tho's part. Old questions were being asked again. Then, on November 25, the North Vietnamese asked for an eight-day recess. Tho raced back to Hanoi.

Kissinger paid a courtesy call on Foreign Minister Schumann—he wanted the Frenchman's reading of the situation—and then flew to New York to brief the president, who was spending the night at the Waldorf Towers.

As for Thieu, he now sent his own emissary—his foreign policy adviser Nguyen Phu Doc—to present his case at the White House. Doc conferred with Nixon on November 29 and 30, arguing that the acceptance of the peace agreement as it now stood would be suicidal for South Vietnam. Nixon insisted that there was no basic alternative, even if some of the provisions could be improved, and he tried to persuade Doc that his regime could survive with the new arms being provided under Enhance Plus. Besides, he said, South Vietnam could count on American help if Hanoi engaged in massive violations of the cease-fire. This was the first secret commitment to Thieu that Nixon is known to have made.

Nixon was not speaking lightly. The Pentagon had been working since October on contingency plans for support of the ARVN after the cease-fire and for action in the event of massive North Vietnamese violations. This included the reintroduction of American tactical air forces in Vietnam and the planning of air strikes. Plans were being developed jointly by the American command in Saigon and the Joint Chiefs of Staff in Washington. These were completed on November 27 when MAC/V cabled to the National Military Command Center a top-secret operational blueprint carrying the title "Organizational Changes in Southeast Asia."

This immensely detailed document provided that upon the signing of the peace agreement MAC/V would be "disestablished" and replaced by the Defense Attaché Office (DAO) in the American embassy in Saigon, functioning as a permanent minicommand. To vest operational and coordinating responsibilities for continuing military activities in Vietnam in the Defense Attaché Office, normally small, was one of the deceits the United States was preparing to carry out: DAO was to be staffed with 50 military personnel and 1345 Defense Department civilians (military personnel become Defense Department civilians in such cases when they exchange uniforms for civilian garb), of whom 219 would be "intelligence personnel." The document noted that 6 military personnel out of the total of 1345 in DAO "will perform traditional DAO missions and/or functions."

DAO's real mission would be to coordinate and support "in-country military operational requirements for CINCPAC [Commander in Chief, Pacific] within the purview of CINCPAC." The plan placed major emphasis on continued intelligence operations in South Vietnam. The DAO's Operations and Intelligence Division would "be responsible for continuing essential aspects of operations, intelligence, contingency planning, force development. . . ." The "Readiness Operations Section" was to "monitor, evaluate and report RVNAF [Republic of Vietnam Armed Forces] operational activities and employment of forces, monitor . . . reconnaissance operations over RVN [Republic of Vietnam] and contiguous waters and monitor ceasefire violations." Monitoring cease-fire violations was supposed to be the responsibility of the international supervisory force set up under the peace agreement, but the MAC/V document said the "Readiness" section "will establish and operate a command center to function on a 24-hour-a-day basis and will provide a direct link with the USSAG in Thailand" (United States Support and Assistance Group, the American military command with authority over B-52 and fighter-bomber squadrons stationed in Thailand).

That the United States contemplated the possibility of again conducting air operations in Vietnam was shown in the mission description for DAO's Plans and Liaison Branch. This branch was to "participate in the planning for resurgence and reintroduction and employment of Tac Air [tactical air operations] . . . to include strike planning." The Liaison Section was charged with providing "U.S. military representation to RVNAF JGS [Joint General Staff] for all matters pertaining to training, operations and intelligence. . . . [It] will also monitor and program off-shore training [schools] requirements."

Under the plan, the Intelligence Branch was to act "as primary U.S. element for collection, evaluation and dissemination of intelligence information pertaining to NVA/VC [North Vietnam Army/Viet Cong] activities in the RVN." And a Surveillance Section was to "coordinate U.S. air reconnaissance and surveillance operations" over South Vietnam—even though the agreement negotiated by Kissinger stipulated that "the United States will not continue its military involvement or intervene in the internal affairs of South Vietnam."

For that matter, the peace agreement also provided that within sixty days of the signing the United States would withdraw from Vietnam *all* "troops, military advisers and military personnel, including technical personnel and military personnel associated with the pacification program, armaments, munitions and war material." This was why the administration, preparing to violate the agreement even before it was signed, devised the ruse of the Defense Attaché Office and Defense Department "civilians."

The DAO's Surveillance Section was also in charge of coordinating "humint" (human intelligence) activities. This indicated that the Pentagon planned to maintain its wide network of intelligence agents in Vietnam. Furthermore, since the section was to serve as "in-country contact point for coordinating unilateral humint operations by Department of Defense collection units from out-country," military-intelligence agents would also be brought from the outside.

This was not all. The DAO was also to provide daily intelligence summaries on South Vietnam and "adjacent territories," indicating that military-intelligence operations in Cambodia and Laos (and, presumably, North Vietnam) would be run out of Saigon by Americans. A Counter Intelligence Section was to "formulate security policies to prevent, detect, neutralize hostile espionage and subversion attempts, conduct discreet liaison with ARVN counterintelligence and police agencies." So much for noninterference in South Vietnamese internal affairs after the cease-fire. Likewise, the Pentagon planned to maintain electronic intelligence operations in South Vietnam—clearly aimed at North Vietnam—through the assignment of 161 "civilian" personnel from the National Security Agency. One of their tasks would be cryptology—the breaking of codes.

The plan took into account the possibility that American military-intelligence operations would "not be authorized" in South Vietnam under the cover of the Defense Attaché Office. In that event a small group within the DAO "would be required to obtain the total intelligence output" of South Vietnamese military intelligence and "forward it in some meaningful format to an agency capable of collating, analyzing, and disseminating this intelligence." To accomplish this objective, the top-secret Fast Pass operation—a standing arrangement for exchange of intelligence with South Vietnam—"would be appreciably expanded," apparently through covert techniques.

What appeared to concern the Pentagon was that there were "shortfalls" in South Vietnamese "human intelligence," particularly in Cambodia and Laos and along the borders. The plan provided for stationing American military-intelligence personnel not only in Saigon but in Danang, Pleiku, Bien Hoa, Can Tho, "and other areas as required." This, of course, would be another violation of the peace agreement.

Finally, the document discussed at vast length the support, logistical, training, and advisory responsibilities of the DAO in connection with the South Vietnamese armed forces, still another violation.

The document as a whole constituted an added guarantee to Thieu —and a highly secret one—as well as an assurance that American military interests in Indochina would not be excessively damaged by a cease-fire in Vietnam. After all, wars would be still fought in Cambodia and Laos. On November 30, the Joint Chiefs of Staff met with Nixon at the White House to discuss this and other contingency plans for the postwar period.

But diplomacy was being kept alive, and Kissinger was again getting ready to fly to Paris. First, however, he wanted to shut off all speculation about American military activities in Vietnam in the event peace could *not* be secured. The White House announced on November 30 that there would be no further statements regarding U.S. troop levels in Vietnam (another withdrawal announcement had been scheduled for the end of November) because this subject was under current negotiation. On December 2, Kissinger went to Key Biscayne to consult with the president, and they discussed diplomatic strategy for two days.

On December 4, Kissinger, Haig, and Sullivan flew to Paris. There, they found a new attitude on Tho's part. Kissinger's impression was that Hanoi had suddenly developed "cold feet." Battlefield conditions were turning against the Communists while, at the same time, the United States was rushing new military equipment to South Vietnam under Operation Enhance to beat the cease-fire deadline. F-5A jet fighter-bombers were being borrowed from South Korea, Nationalist China, and Iran to beef up the South Vietnamese Air Force because it would take too long to get them from the United States. Hanoi's strategic doctrine called for a cease-fire only under optimal conditions; the North Vietnamese might be rethinking the entire agreement. Still, Kissinger kept negotiating with Tho despite the North Vietnamese on-and-off attitude toward parts of the agreement.

On December 14, Tho told Kissinger that he had to go home for a few weeks to study the situation. Before leaving, he handed Kissinger the text of a protocol for implementing the cease-fire, including international supervision, which the Americans found totally unsatisfactory. Kissinger returned to Washington, but he was still hopeful that an agreement was within reach. He saw Nixon at the White House that night.

Sullivan and William Porter were left behind in Paris to continue technical talks with the North Vietnamese. On December 15, when the two delegations met at the Neuilly-sur-Seine home of an American jeweler, the North Vietnamese proposed sixteen changes in the text. Among other things, they now demanded that the release of the American POWs be conditional on the freeing of thousands of civilian prisoners held by Saigon. (Until then, the matter of the Saigon prisoners had been left for negotiations to come after the truce between the two Vietnamese factions.) Sullivan and Porter passed this on to Kissinger, who immediately ordered his staff to prepare a paper on Hanoi's "perfidy," to form the basis of his Washington press conference the next day.

A close study of the documents suggests, however, that the "perfidy" was somewhat exaggerated. Aside from the reopened question of the POWs, the differences between Hanoi and Washington were not all that great at that point.

The question, therefore, arises: why did the president feel impelled on December 18 to order Operation Linebacker II—the "Christmas" bombing of Hanoi, Haiphong, and the rest of North Vietnam? Unlike his past practice, Nixon remained totally silent about this move. He did, however, send a secret cable to Hanoi on December 15 warning that bombings would resume if negotiations were not reconvened within seventy-two hours.

A theory held privately among many key officials is that he and Kissinger had decided that drastic action was necessary to discourage the prowar faction in North Vietnam from forcing a reconsideration of the peace agreement. The Americans had heard from intelligence sources that the October decision to go for a settlement had carried by only a small margin in the Hanoi Politburo. As Kissinger put it, the United States was applying leverage against Hanoi to assist it in its decision-making process. These officials believe that Nixon in effect launched the Christmas bombings to force Hanoi to make "marginal decisions" about changes in the text of the agreement. One participant remarked at the time, "We are bombing them to force them to accept our concessions."

The administration realized that the bombings could not be continued indefinitely. On the day the bombings were resumed, Haig went to Saigon with a secret letter from Nixon urging Thieu to accept the settlement. Haig also told Thieu that, while the United States was "brutalizing" North Vietnam, it would sign a peace agreement if Hanoi would make a few changes in the text; if Thieu remained adamant, he could no longer count on American assistance. On December 21, Thieu handed

Haig a letter for Nixon saying that he felt that he had been given an ultimatum and that he could not believe the president of the United States would deal in such a manner with an ally. When Kissinger read the letter, he commented bitterly: "All the Vietnamese parties are against us."

Nixon was vacationing in Key Biscayne while American B-52s were systematically smashing Hanoi and Haiphong in around-the-clock raids. Despite worldwide outrage over the carpet bombings, the president remained absolutely silent in public about Vietnam. On December 22, Nixon said to Kissinger and Haig that he was determined to maintain the aerial offensive until Hanoi gave signs that it was interested once more in "serious negotiations," one of his favorite phrases.

Nobody knew what decisions the North Vietnamese were trying to reach, but they did not interrupt the technical-level discussions with Sullivan in Paris until December 27. Two days later, Hanoi evidently concluded that it could not accept the bombings any longer: in the evening of December 29, a message was received in Paris that North Vietnam was prepared to resume negotiations on the "highest level"—with Kissinger—on January 8, and talks on the technical level on January 2.

The message was flashed through White House communications to Key Biscayne in the early morning of Saturday, December 30. The president was awakened and immediately telephoned Kissinger, who was spending the holidays with friends in Palm Springs, California. They decided that the bombings could now be halted.

But Nixon did not choose to announce personally that he was stopping the raids. When they were ordered on December 18, he had let the announcement be made by the Pentagon, not wishing to be personally associated with this brutality, although it had been his decision. (For that matter, Kissinger, too, recoiled from being identified with Linebacker II even though there is no doubt he supported it strongly. He had gone to the extreme of telling some of his newspaper friends that it was not his handiwork: when Nixon heard about this, he hit the roof. Next to a question about his relations with Kissinger, in a briefing book containing anticipated press questions, the president wrote in scratchy longhand: "He has advised and supported every action I have taken.") So it was left to Deputy Press Secretary Gerald L. Warren to announce at the White House at 9:00 a.m. on December 30, "The president has ordered that all bombing will be discontinued above the 20th parallel as long as serious negotiations are under way."

. . . .

In Vietnam, the United States had been fighting a savage, but open and visible war. Across the world—in Chile—the Nixon administration was engaged in 1972 in the third year of its silent, secret, and deceitful war against the elected government of President Salvador Allende.

The Vietnamese war was waged with planes and tanks to prevent— in the words of three successive presidents of the United States—the Communist take-over of South Vietnam. The war against Allende was conducted with economic and subversive weapons to bring about the fall of the Marxist regime which Richard Nixon and Henry Kissinger saw as the forerunner of Communism in South America. In Vietnam, the terrible war was designed, as Kennedy, Johnson, and Nixon said, to guarantee the political self-determination of a nation. In Chile, it was meant to *deprive* a nation of political self-determination. But Nixon, the president who launched the war against Allende, never admitted its existence.

After two years of subversion against Allende and the expenditure of millions of dollars on covert CIA actions in Chile, Nixon had this to say on February 9 in his foreign-policy report to Congress:

> In our view, the hemisphere community is big enough, mature enough and tolerant enough to accept a diversity of national approaches to human goals. We therefore deal realistically with governments as they are—right and left. We have strong preferences and hopes to see free democratic process prevail, but we cannot impose our political structure on other nations. We respect the hemispheric principle of non-intervention. We shape our relations with governments according to their policies and actions as they affect our interests and the interests of the inter-American system, not according to their domestic structures.

This was sheer hypocrisy given the United States track record of interventions in internal affairs of Latin American countries in the past decade or so—first Cuba, then the Dominican Republic, and now Chile —but Nixon went on:

> Our relations with Chile are an example. Chile's leaders will not be charmed out of their deeply held convictions by gestures on our part. We recognize that they are serious men whose ideological principles are, to some extent, frankly in conflict with ours. Nevertheless, our relations will hinge not on their ideology, but on their conduct toward the outside world. As I have said many times, we are prepared to have the kind of relationship with the Chilean Government that it is pre-

pared to have with us. In this context, its actions thus far on compensation for expropriated U.S.–owned copper companies are not encouraging. The application *ex post facto* of unprecedented legal rules which effectively nullify compensation is, in our view, inconsistent with international law. We and other public and private sources of development investment will take account of whether or not the Chilean Government meets its international obligations.

To the uninitiated, which included the Congress of the United States, what Nixon was saying did *sound* reasonable. Indeed, there was a dispute between the two governments concerning the payment of compensation for nationalized copper mines in Chile. The previous September, Allende had announced that "excess profits," covering an indeterminate number of years, would be deducted from compensation payments—and this was an unusual procedure. But there had been contentious nationalizations elsewhere in the past, and in modern days, they were not made into a *casus belli* by the United States.

That Nixon and Kissinger had launched their secret war against Allende a full year before his September 1971 nationalization decree was, of course, unknown to Congress. It was unaware of White House–directed efforts to prevent Allende's inauguration in 1970 at all costs, including a plan to trigger a military *coup d'état* to achieve that goal, and subsequent CIA activities to produce chaos in the country in order to bring down the regime.

The prevailing impression was that the president was doing no more than taking perfectly proper measures to protect American corporate interests in Chile; this was, in effect, what he had said in his February report to Congress. Three weeks earlier, on January 19, Nixon had issued a public warning that unless there was "prompt, adequate, and effective" compensation for American property seized in foreign countries, the United States might terminate new bilateral economic aid to them and withhold its support from loans under consideration in multilateral development banks. Chile was not singled out by name, but the message was clear.

What Nixon was doing in his January proclamation was publicly justifying, *ex post facto,* the economic warfare that had been applied against Chile for two years. The principal instrument in this warfare was the secret National Security Decision Memorandum (NSDM-93), issued in November 1970, providing for a policy of economic pressure through all possible means, including denial of United States and international credits to Chile. This policy was born from a basic decision taken by the White

House on September 15, 1970, which CIA Director Helms summarized in his private notes on that meeting with the words, "Make the [Chilean] economy scream."

In 1972, therefore, Nixon was making official what his administration had been doing all along behind the scenes. Bank figures told what the United States was doing to Chile: Export-Import Bank credits dropped from $29 million in 1969, when Allende began his campaign (they stood at $234 million in 1967), to zero in 1971. Loans from the Inter-American Development Bank, in which the United States holds an effective veto, went from $46 million in 1970 to $2 million in 1972. The World Bank, where the United States also wields a powerful influence, made no loans to Chile at all after 1970. Private American bankers, watching the actions of the administration, followed suit, severing Chilean credit lines. They were cut from $300 million in 1969 to $30 million in 1972.

In February and March 1972, Chilean negotiators met in Paris with representatives of foreign countries to reschedule payments on Chile's outstanding $800-million external debt. The United States was the only government to refuse the rollover of its part of the debt, tying it to copper compensation payments. Allende may have not realized it at the time, but his 1971 move on "excess profits" deductions from compensations handed Nixon the perfect excuse to legitimize the economic warfare against Chile. And in the long run, the United States had the power to destroy the Chilean economy, which, unlike that of Cuba, was not being subsidized by the Soviet Union. The Russians and some East European governments did grant Chile $600 million in credits and loans late in 1972, but according to the Inter-American Committee on the Alliance for Progress (a U.S.–dominated institution in Washington), they were "tied to specific development projects and could be used only gradually."

The Soviet Union was not eager to assume total responsibility for faraway Chile, where Moscow, for its own reasons, sought no confrontation with the United States.

In the course of the year, the Kissinger-chaired Forty Committee at the White House approved $2.5 million in secret funds for CIA subversive operations in Chile. Of this total, $965,000 went to *El Mercurio,* the chief organ of the opposition, even though the intelligence community's 1972 NIE had found that opposition news media "had been able to resist government intimidation and persisted in denouncing the government." That there was official pressure on *El Mercurio* is undeniable—the newspaper *was* the regime's chief public enemy—but it did not need close to $1 million to keep freedom of the press alive in Chile.

Other CIA funds went to subsidize opposition candidates in three congressional by-elections during 1972—with no success. On October 26, the Forty Committee authorized $1,427,666 (one of its largest single appropriations) to help the opposition prepare for the congressional elections in March 1973. This was the first down payment; more money for these mid-term elections would be approved early in the new year. October 26 was the day Kissinger held his Vietnam "peace is at hand" news conference, but Chile was important enough to engage his attention.

There are no indications that the CIA was directly involved in the October 1972 antiregime strike by Chilean truckers. But it kept as busy as ever establishing links with disaffected military groups and leaders who might be thinking of a coup against Allende. In January 1972, the agency's Santiago station had identified the group with the greatest antiregime potential. As the Senate Select Committee on Intelligence Activities noted in its report, the CIA "had successfully penetrated it and was in contact through an intermediary with its leader."

The State Department was aware of the CIA's secret operations in Chile, but its public posture was that the United States was keeping its hands off Allende. On March 23, for example, the department spokesman, Charles W. Bray III, said in a formal statement that "any ideas of thwarting the Chilean constitutional process following the election of 1970 were firmly rejected by this administration."

Throughout the year, official policy was to keep Allende at arm's length although the State Department engaged in mid-December in desultory talks with the Chileans about the debt rescheduling. But $10 million in aircraft and tanks went to the Chilean armed forces in 1972. This was part of the larger strategy. When the administration learned that Allende was coming to New York early in December to address the United Nations General Assembly, it successfully discouraged him from visiting Washington, though the Chilean president had hoped against hope that a meeting with Nixon might help to improve relations.

On December 4, Allende, disabused of his hopes, bitterly told the General Assembly that Chile has been the "victim of serious aggression. . . . We have felt the effects of a large-scale external pressure against us." Later that afternoon, he spoke at length in private of his expectations of doing well in the congressional elections, though he did not think that his Popular Unity coalition would win majorities in the two houses. Foremost on his mind was the state of the Chilean economy and his vanishing foreign-currency reserves. "I don't know how I'll be able to import food next year to feed my people," he told me. In the evening, he left for Moscow.

Substantial covert operations conducted by the United States in 1972 were not limited to Chile. Another major target was Italy, where the Nixon administration was concerned over the growing strength of the Communist Party. The same philosophy applied to both situations: in Chile, the White House attempted to get rid of a regime it suspected of moving toward Communism (after having failed to prevent it from taking power); in Italy, the effort was to preclude Communist gains although there was no imminent danger of Communist control of the government.

Italian parliamentary elections were not scheduled until 1974, but both Graham Martin, the United States ambassador to Italy, and Kissinger felt that "investments for the future" should be made as early as 1972. Acting on Martin's advice, Kissinger obtained an authorization from the Forty Committee for a secret expenditure of $11.8 million in Italy that year, even though only $9.9 million was actually spent. The beneficiaries of this largess were the ruling Christian Democratic Party, a highly corrupt organization that had been steadily losing support among Italian voters, which received $3.4 million; a political organization created and supported by the CIA, which got another $3.4 million; other pro-Western political parties and organizations, given $1.3 million; and 21 individual candidates for parliamentary seats who received $1.8 million. According to standard procedure, this money would be channeled to recipients by the CIA. Ambassador Martin, however, after a furious battle with the CIA's station chief in Rome, persuaded Kissinger that, in a departure from precedent, *he* should be in charge of deciding where the secret funds went.

One of the recipients Martin selected was General Vito Miceli, head of the Italian Defense Information Service, who received $800,-000 to undertake propaganda operations. In this case, the CIA had the wit to warn the ambassador, albeit to no effect, that Miceli was linked to neo-Fascist groups. CIA cables quoted Martin as saying, "I do [care], but not a helluva lot" whether Miceli would be successful. "Important thing is to demonstrate solidarity for the long pull," Martin allegedly told the station chief. The argument over the Miceli payment led Martin, according to a cable from the station chief, to tell him that if he kept dragging his feet about contacting the Italian general, the ambassador would "instruct Marine Guards not to let you in this building and put you on the airplane." However, Kissinger approved payments to Miceli. Two years later, he was arrested for plotting to overthrow the government.

Kissinger appears to have supported Martin on all points during this whole enterprise. The nearly $10 million spent in Italy in 1972 raised to *$75 million* the total given pro-Western political parties by the United States over a twenty-year period in that country. Like their predecessors, Nixon and Kissinger believed that foreign elections could be bought with money.

The president's and Kissinger's dislike and contempt for "small-fry" Communists did not prevent the United States from concluding an anti-hijacking agreement with Cuba in December 1972. This was the first important accord worked out by the two countries (negotiations were conducted through the Swiss government) since they broke diplomatic relations in 1961.

Providing for prosecution and eventual extradition of hijackers bringing captured aircraft or sea vessels to either the United States or Cuba, the agreement was the result of necessity rather than a move toward an improvement in political relations. There had been two hijackings of American airliners to Cuba in the latter part of 1972—coming on top of a long series of earlier incidents of this type—and the administration concluded that only Cuban cooperation could discourage further attempts. For Havana, the hijackings had turned into a major embarrassment; both governments swallowed their pride and negotiated the agreement.

But there was no follow-up. Cuba insisted that the United States lift the ten-year-old economic blockade of the island as a condition for entering into any talks leading to a resumption of relations. Nixon, who, among other motivations, felt politically committed to the Cuban exile community in Florida, refused to consider any concessions to Castro (although Kissinger was intrigued by the notion of extending the détente to Cuba).

Meanwhile, American and Soviet delegations met in Geneva on November 21 to open the second main phase in the SALT talks, now known as SALT II. This was the follow-up on the interim agreement negotiated in Moscow during the May summit, and the objective was to expand the area of controls over offensive weapons with a reduction in strategic arms as the ultimate goal. Nixon wrote Gerard Smith, the chief American delegate, that "now you face a task which in many respects is even more complex and more difficult, for both sides will now be obligated to make long term commitments, in a permanent agreement, to a stable strategic relationship for this decade and beyond."

BOOK FIVE

1973

The Year of "Peace"

Chapter 24

From a reviewing stand in front of the White House, Richard Nixon once more watched an inaugural parade in his honor. It was January 20, 1973, and the president felt on top of the world. His landslide victory, he believed, gave him a fresh mandate to run the country—and its foreign policy—as he saw fit. His second term, he told his associates, would consolidate all the great foreign-policy achievements of the first quadrennium. He would streamline his administration and turn the nation back to peace for the first time in more than a decade. After all, the settlement in Vietnam was worked out for all practical purposes.

But again, Nixon was misjudging America—and the future. The awesome bombings of North Vietnam, terminated just three weeks earlier, had left a deep impression on public opinion; the president had already lost much of the support he had had in his race against a weak Democrat in November. Anti-Nixon sentiment inspired a "counterinauguration" ceremony held after dark at the National Cathedral, where Eugene McCarthy, the poet and former senator, warned starkly against further American involvements in Indochina. In Congress, there were hostile stirrings against Nixon's war policies.

Yet Nixon, buoyed by his electoral victory, still believed that Indochina could be "saved" through military action. If necessary, he would do it surreptitiously—as he had in December. Top-ranking officers at the Pentagon had been taken by surprise by the decision then to unleash B-52s over Hanoi and Haiphong. For one thing, Nixon did not want arguments over the military validity of Linebacker II; the air force, knowing that North Vietnam had built up its SAM defenses to the highest point in the war, would have been loath to jeopardize its B-52s. So total secrecy prevailed. On the highest level, only Defense Secretary Laird and the Joint Chiefs knew about the plans beforehand, the latter only because they had to come up with target lists. In the Office of the Secretary of Defense, three officers had advance knowledge on a need-to-know basis, and Laird recorded their names in case of news leaks. The director of the Pentagon's Vietnam Task Force, in charge of coordinating all war operations, learned about the bombings only after they started. CINCPAC in Hawaii was informed just barely in time to activate the B-52s on Guam and in Thailand.

But were the Christmas bombings truly necessary to extract a "better" peace agreement? Both Nixon and Kissinger claim that they were. Yet a close study of United States and Vietnamese negotiating positions between October 1972 and January 1973, as well as a comparison between the October and January texts, demonstrates the opposite.

What the United States (and Saigon) won from the bombings in exchange for the deaths of 2200 civilians in Hanoi alone (the North Vietnamese figure), the destruction of large swaths of Hanoi and Haiphong (and in Hanoi, of the 1000-bed Bach Mai Hospital), and the loss of many B-52s (North Vietnam claimed 34, probably a more accurate figure than the 15 officially admitted by the Pentagon) were minor changes in the wording of the agreement. By any standards of diplomacy, more or less the same result might have been achieved through negotiation, even if things had dragged on a bit longer. Instead of negotiation, U.S. aircraft dropped 36,452 tons of explosives over the North in twelve days—ten times the total tonnage dropped between 1969 and 1971.

Although the B-52 raids against Hanoi and Haiphong ended on December 31 (Vietnamese time), American bombings of military targets in North Vietnam and the mining of its waters continued for two more weeks. Thus the president kept up the air war well into January, even though negotiations in Paris had already been resumed. One must conclude, therefore, that the real reason for all the bombings was Nixon's determination to leave North Vietnam weak and battered before the signing of the agreement. Simultaneously, Operation Enhance Plus to resupply the South Vietnamese armed forces could be completed. President Thieu, who now had the world's fourth largest air force, consequently became more amenable to the settlement.

Knowledgeable American diplomats believe that after the United States refused to sign the proposed peace agreement in October, and after Kissinger in November reopened a number of already settled points, Hanoi decided to take a new look at the situation. Le Duc Tho's first reaction was himself to reopen areas in the text to which he had previously agreed—for example, the North Vietnamese consent that the demilitarized zone would be maintained after the settlement—so as to give Kissinger a taste of his own medicine. But American experts also think that the Hanoi Politburo developed second thoughts about the entire agreement in the light of American behavior.

The president and Kissinger, however, were unable to understand that North Vietnam would not negotiate under the threat of bombing. They concluded, rather, that the bombings were necessary to restore a winning margin to the Politburo's propeace faction. This was Kissinger's explanation to his staff. In other words, the ostensible point of the bombings was to restore the diplomatic status quo that the United States had upset in the first place in October and November. The Americans discovered subsequently through NSA intercepts of classified North Vietnamese communications that North Vietnam had only a two-day supply of SAM missiles on hand when the bombings ended. For the United States and Saigon, the new situation had obvious military advantages. But considering how minor the differences were between the October draft and the postbombing text, it is just as obvious that the president and Kissinger behaved with extraordinary cynicism.

Kissinger and Le Duc Tho held their first and stormy meeting of 1973 on January 8. Tho, who barely greeted Kissinger, started out by telling him, "I am a personal victim of yours," referring to the breakdown in the talks. He bitterly condemned the Christmas bombings, made proud claims of the number of B-52s the North Vietnamese had shot down. Kissinger let it pass.

They reconvened the next day, and now Tho was entirely businesslike. By January 13, they had worked out the final text of the agreement and the complex accompanying protocols. Suddenly, everything was going easily with neither side required to make serious concessions. On January 13, Kissinger and Tho shook hands: they had completed their work in Gif-sur-Yvette. They agreed that the documents would be initialed on January 25, and formally signed by the four foreign ministers —of the United States, North Vietnam, South Vietnam, and the PRG— on January 27.

A cease-fire in Vietnam was to start at 2400 hours GMT, January 27. The United States had abandoned its insistence on an Indochina-wide cease-fire, but Kissinger won an oral commitment for a quick truce in Laos. No such promises, however, were made regarding Cambodia. The United States' formal commitment was to end all its military activities against North Vietnam the moment the cease-fire went into effect, and to remove and deactivate all mines it had sown in North Vietnamese waters.

The United States pledged not to continue "its military involvement or intervene in the internal affairs of South Vietnam," and to withdraw within sixty days all remaining troops and advisory and technical personnel, and to dismantle all its bases in the country. There was no concurrent commitment by North Vietnam to withdraw its forces from South Vietnam; their existence was not even acknowledged. The agreement took care of this matter by proclaiming that at the time of the cease-fire "the armed forces of the two South Vietnamese parties [Saigon troops and Communist troops] shall remain in place." This was the galling point for President Thieu, who had been protesting that the agreement sanctioned the North Vietnamese presence in the South, which it did. Kissinger had tried without success to have Hanoi repatriate its forces at least from the northernmost Quang Tri Province.

Prisoners of war were to be released by both sides within the sixty-day period during which the United States completed withdrawal of its forces. This met Nixon's demand for the freeing of the American POWs in exchange for total United States military withdrawal from Vietnam. Although Le Duc Tho had tried to link the release of the American POWs to that of the thousands of political prisoners held by Saigon—it was the only major new demand he had made when the negotiations resumed in January—he dropped it quickly. Instead, the agreement left it up to the South and North Vietnamese governments to work out directly the liberation of the captives.

To guarantee the cease-fire, the agreement provided that pending a new permanent South Vietnamese government, "the two South Vietnamese sides shall not accept the introduction of troops, military advisers, and military personnel . . . armaments, munitions, and war material into South Vietnam." This meant theoretically that no fresh North Vietnamese forces might enter the South and no more American equipment might be given Thieu. However, both Vietnamese sides in the South were permitted "periodic replacements" of destroyed, damaged, or worn-out equipment "on the basis of piece-for-piece" of identical items.

The agreement created a Four-Party Joint Military Commission to enforce the execution of the general cease-fire, the withdrawal of American forces, the dismantling of American military bases, and the release of war prisoners. This commission was to be disbanded after sixty days and replaced by a Two-Party Joint Military Commission of unlimited duration—made up of Saigon and PRG representatives (the PRG was not mentioned by name; the agreement spoke only of the "two South Vietnamese parties")—to enforce the cease-fire between Vietnamese factions, the prohibition of the introduction of troops into South Vietnam, and the release of civilian prisoners held by Saigon. Each side was to have 825 men on this commission.

The agreement also set up an International Commission of Control and Supervision to police the cease-fire and all the other provisions in the peace settlement. The ICCS (with Canada and Indonesia representing the pro-Western orientation and Hungary and Poland representing the pro-Communist side) was set at 1160 personnel. This was a compromise between a 5000-man force, desired by the United States, and the 250-man force Hanoi wanted. It is hard to believe that Kissinger really expected the ICCS to keep the South Vietnamese and the Communists apart if they wanted to fight. But like everything else in the agreement, it was a question of getting the United States out of direct participation in the war, obtaining freedom for the POWs, and hoping for the best.

The military provisions of the agreement offered little chance for a real peace in Vietnam after the departure of the Americans. But the political arrangements were even more of an abstraction. Nixon, to be sure, lived up to his pledge not to turn South Vietnam over to the Communists; in the short run, the agreement was a triumph for Thieu inasmuch as he was allowed to remain in power. In the long run, however, he was left on his own and, sooner or later, would have to face the Communists alone. Both Saigon and Hanoi understood this fact of life —Thieu with special and justified trepidation.

The way Thieu read the agreement, American recognition of Vietnam's "unity" as spelled out in the 1954 Geneva agreements was an invitation to Hanoi to unify the country in its own way. He was not reassured by another article stating that "the reunification of Vietnam shall be carried out step by step through peaceful means on the basis of discussions and agreements between North and South Vietnam, without coercion or annexation by either party, and without foreign interference."

Thieu scored a point when Hanoi agreed to preserve the demilitarized zone (Hanoi had wanted to do away with it), but he lost a point when Kissinger and Le Duc Tho drafted a paragraph declaring that, "pending reunification," the military demarcation line at the 17th parallel "is only provisional and not a political or territorial boundary." Thieu had opposed free civilian movement across the demarcation line—he assumed that this would offer Hanoi a chance of infiltrating fresh troops while claiming that they were civilians—and Kissinger supported him. In the end, a compromise absolved the United States of any responsibility: the agreement said that "modalities of civilian movement" across the DMZ was one of the questions Saigon and Hanoi would "promptly" start negotiating "with a view to reestablishing normal relations in various fields."

For the United States, the Vietnam war had been fought to prevent a Communist take-over in the South. For four years, the Nixon administration had tried to negotiate a political formula that would guarantee South Vietnam's political survival when the cease-fire finally came. For four years, Hanoi had opposed such political guarantees. Finally, they produced a compromise that recognized Thieu's continuance in power until other arrangements were made but also, in effect, granted the Communists representation in a new power structure. Both Vietnamese sides understood that they were being left with a situation in which each would do its best to prevail regardless of what the agreement specified. This is where the military and political contradictions of the accord became emphatic. In a strict sense, Hanoi had scaled down its political demands, but the North Vietnamese knew that time would be working for them. So, indubitably, did Kissinger, but the objective in the negotiations was to extricate the United States from the war without turning Saigon over to the Communists overnight. Richard Nixon could thus claim he had kept his word.

Hundreds of thousands had died and been maimed so that the 1973 peace agreement could proclaim these unenforceable platitudes:

> The South Vietnamese people's right to self-determination is sacred, inalienable, and shall be respected by all countries. The South Vietnamese people shall decide themselves the political future of South Vietnam through genuinely free and democratic general elections under international supervision. Foreign countries shall not impose any political tendency or personality on the South Vietnamese people. . . . The two South Vietnamese parties will: achieve national reconciliation and concord, end hatred and enmity, prohibit all acts of reprisal and discrimination against individuals or organizations that have collaborated with one side or the other; ensure the democratic liberties of the people: personal freedom, freedom of speech, freedom of the press, freedom of meeting, freedom of organization, freedom of political activities, freedom of belief, freedom of movement, freedom of residence, freedom of work, right to property ownership, and right to free enterprise.

What the agreement did, then, was to create a *de facto* situation of new confrontation in Vietnam—with the United States no longer there.

The agreement called for "democratic general elections," but it failed to say when they would be held. This, for different reasons, suited both Vietnamese parties. Thieu did not want to be trapped by an election deadline because he needed time to reorganize his political forces. (This is why Kissinger had dropped earlier American proposals specifying an electoral period and did not revive the idea for Thieu to resign ahead of time.) Hanoi had no interest in elections at all; it had other ideas on how to deal with Saigon.

Specific political arrangements provided that "immediately after the cease-fire, the two South Vietnamese parties shall hold consultations in a spirit of national reconciliation and concord, mutual respect, and mutual non-elimination to set up a National Council of Reconciliation and Concord of three equal segments." This was a compromise between the coalition government, the tripartite electoral commission, and the opposition to both expressed by Thieu. But it was a neuter. It was not a government designed to supersede the Thieu regime, but a body meant to function alongside it until after the elections and the establishment of a permanent government. To make sure that Hanoi did not regard the council as a government, Kissinger had prevailed on Le Duc Tho to drop the phrase describing it as an "administrative structure." The three segments in the council were to be the Thieu faction, the Communists, and a neutral groupment that nobody had defined. It took uncounted hours of negotiations to refine the council formula even though it was unlikely that it would ever come into being.

Quite optimistically, the agreement stated that after the council had assumed its functions, the two Vietnamese parties would negotiate and sign an agreement "on the internal matters of South Vietnam"—this, it was hoped, within ninety days of the cease-fire. Then the council would busy itself with "national reconciliation" and organize the elections. In this sense, the council resembled Kissinger's electoral commission. Another council function would be to settle in an unspecified manner the question "of Vietnamese armed forces in South Vietnam," something that obviously would be impossible until a permanent government was formed. The reduction of the "military effectives" of the two South Vietnamese parties would be a matter for negotiations.

In other words, the agreement left South Vietnam's political future— a subject of four years of intense negotiations in Paris while the war raged on the battlefield—up in the air.

A separate section of the agreement dealt with the postwar relationship between the United States and North Vietnam. The pertinent articles said:

> The United States anticipates that this Agreement will usher in an era
> of reconciliation with the Democratic Republic of Vietnam as with all
> the peoples of Indochina. In pursuance of its traditional policy, the
> United States will contribute to healing the wounds of war and to
> postwar reconstruction of the Democratic Republic of Vietnam and
> throughout Indochina. The ending of the war, the restoration of
> peace in Vietnam, and the strict implementation of this Agreement
> will create conditions for establishing a new, equal, and mutually
> beneficial relationship between the United States and the Democratic
> Republic of Vietnam. . . . At the same time this will ensure stable peace
> in Vietnam and contribute to the preservation of lasting peace in
> Indochina and Southeast Asia.

Here Kissinger was on slippery ground. While the agreement stressed
"strict implementation" as a condition for economic reconstruction assistance, Kissinger erred in committing the United States to this without
consulting Congress, for he underestimated congressional sentiment
against this (particularly in the light of Hanoi's treatment of American
POWs, a highly emotional issue).

The agreement declared that the signatories would respect the "neutrality" of Laos and Cambodia, but this "respect" was not formally linked
to any cease-fires there; the United States was determined to keep bombing Cambodia in support of the Lon Nol regime, and Hanoi had equally
little intention of respecting Cambodian neutrality. Another article declared that the Paris signers "refrain from using the territory of Cambodia and the territory of Laos to encroach on the sovereignty and security of one another and of other countries." Hanoi was willing to accept
this provision because, as in the case of South Vietnam, it never admitted
that its troops were operating there in the first place. The provision that
"foreign countries shall put an end to all military activities in Cambodia
and Laos" applied equally to the United States and North Vietnam, but
neither was about to respect it.

Still, this was the best agreement the United States could obtain under
the circumstances, Kissinger believed. As a matter of reality, the agreement was weighted in North Vietnam's favor, but the alternative was
continued war—and besides, Nixon had some extra cards up his sleeve.

After his handshake with Le Duc Tho on January 13, Kissinger flew
to Key Biscayne to present his oeuvre to Nixon, and on January 14, they
took two decisions. Both of these were based on the plan to keep the
agreement secret: the White House had had enough of peace "at hand"

and was holding out for peace *in hand.* First the president ordered all military actions against North Vietnam ended. The next day, the White House announced that because of the "progress" in the Kissinger-Tho negotiations, "President Nixon directed that the bombing, shelling, and any further mining of North Vietnam be suspended." (Still hedging, Nixon preferred the word "suspended" to the word "ended.") The second was to send General Haig and John Negroponte to Saigon to persuade President Thieu to accept the agreement that the United States was now unequivocally determined to sign. Carrying a personal letter from Nixon to Thieu, the American emissaries arrived in Saigon on January 15 and met immediately with the South Vietnamese leader.

Nixon's letter was described as "very blunt," a "final ultimatum." It informed Thieu that the peace agreement would be initialed on January 23 and formally signed on January 27. It told him that if he did not go along, the United States would sign alone and cease supporting the Saigon regime. Nixon added that his decision was "final and irrevocable." Haig handed Thieu the president's letter, offering him no further explanations. But he met with Thieu once more to clarify some points. Then he departed for Laos, Cambodia, and Thailand, giving Thieu four days to make up his mind.

While Haig was away, Thieu and his advisers met around the clock in an effort to save what was already beyond saving. On January 19, Foreign Minister Tran Van Lam told newsmen in Saigon that a peace settlement was "very close" although his government was "still seeking clarification of terms." He said: "We want to make it clear there is no objection [to the agreement]; we have used the word 'clarification.'" What Thieu wanted was a definition of South Vietnamese war prisoners to be released by Hanoi; a ban on stationing the joint military commissions in strongly pro-Communist areas; the freedom for his national police to move everywhere fully armed; permission for his air force to fly over areas controlled by Saigon; and the handing over of the southern portion of the DMZ to South Vietnamese forces. But Haig had already told him it was too late to introduce changes.

Haig was back in Saigon on January 20. He went straight to the presidential palace, where Thieu told him, "I have two choices: to be a short-term hero, like Diem, who was done in by friendly Americans, or to think of the long-term fate of my country." With this, he handed Haig a letter to Nixon. "It was very Asian," said one American diplomat; "it didn't really say yes, but it did not reject the agreement either." Because there still were last-minute problems, Thieu said, he was sending Foreign

Minister Lam to Paris to be available to Kissinger, whose experts, working with the North Vietnamese, were putting the finishing touches on the texts of the protocols that accompanied the main agreement. The Americans interpreted Thieu's letter as meaning that he had "caved in," but the South Vietnamese president did not give the United States a specific oral or written acceptance of the Paris agreement. (On his way home, Haig stopped in Seoul, having received an urgent message from Kissinger to brief President Park Chung Hee on the situation; there still were South Korean units in Vietnam. This detour made Haig miss a Redskins game in Washington for which he had tickets, and he blamed Kissinger for deliberately making him miss it.)

In his address following his inauguration for his second term as president of the United States, Nixon spoke principally of his foreign policy:

> When we met here four years ago, America was bleak in spirit, depressed by the prospect of seemingly endless war abroad and of destructive conflicts at home. As we meet here today, we stand on the threshold of a new era of peace in the world. . . . Let us resolve that this era we are about to enter will not be what other postwar periods have so often been: a time of retreat and isolation that leads to stagnation at home and invites new dangers abroad.

He avoided direct references to the Vietnam peace agreement, but emphasizing his "missions" to Peking and Moscow, he said that "because of America's bold initiatives, 1972 will be long remembered as the year of the greatest progress since the end of World War II toward a lasting peace in the world." Then, Nixon proceeded to define a new American role:

> We shall respect our treaty commitments. We shall support vigorously the principle that no country has the right to impose its will or rule on another by force. We shall continue, in this era of negotiation, to work for the limitation of nuclear arms and to reduce the danger of confrontation between the great powers. We shall do our share in defending peace and freedom in the world. But we shall expect others to do their share. The time has passed when America will make every other nation's conflict our own, or make every other nation's future our responsibility, or presume to tell the people of other nations how to manage their own affairs.

The rhetoric was admirable.

Earlier in the day, Nixon attended the swearing-in of five new cabinet officers and other key officials, having reshuffled his government for the second term. Among them, Elliot Richardson came from HEW to replace Melvin Laird as defense secretary (Laird had had enough). Peter Peterson was let go, at the Commerce Department, partly because of pressure from Kissinger, and Frederick Dent took his place. James R. Schlesinger was the new CIA director, in place of Richard Helms, whom neither Nixon nor Kissinger liked and who was perceived as a potential embarrassment. He was exiled to be ambassador to Iran. John Scali was named permanent representative to the United Nations. Donald Rumsfeld, a rising star, was appointed ambassador to NATO. Henry Kissinger, who had been vaguely talking about quitting after completing the Vietnam negotiations, stayed on at the White House. He had plenty more to worry about.

The next day, January 21, the president again turned his attention to Vietnam. Meeting with Kissinger and Haig (who was reporting on his talks with Thieu and other Asian leaders), he formally authorized initialing of the Vietnam peace agreement. The White House was proceeding on the assumption that Thieu had been convinced and would no longer block the conclusion of peace.

At 12:30 p.m., Paris time (7:30 a.m. in Washington), January 23, Kissinger and Le Duc Tho initialed the Vietnam peace agreement at an unpublicized ceremony in the conference room of the Communist villa in a Paris suburb. Then the two men rose and, reaching over the table separating them, exchanged the pens they had used for the initialing. There were broad smiles and handshakes. This was the culmination of three and a half years of secret war-and-peace diplomacy that had begun in a Paris apartment in August 1969. Kissinger, the State Department's William Sullivan, and other members of the American delegation left the villa wreathed in smiles, but they were uncommunicative with the horde of newsmen waiting outside. The world had to wait a half day more to learn that the Vietnam war had come to an end.

This announcement was made simultaneously in Washington and Hanoi at 10:00 p.m., Washington time. In Hanoi, it was in the form of a terse radio bulletin. In Washington, it was handled by the president in a brief televised address to the nation from the Oval Office:

> The agreement will be formally signed by the parties participating in the Paris Conference on Vietnam on January 27, 1973, at the International Conference Center in Paris. The cease-fire will take effect at 2400 Greenwich Mean Time, January 27, 1973. The United States and the Democratic Republic of Vietnam express the hope that this agree-

ment will insure stable peace in Vietnam and contribute to the preservation of lasting peace in Indochina and Southeast Asia.

Throughout the years of negotiations, we have insisted on peace with honor. . . . In the settlement that has now been agreed to, all the conditions that I laid down . . . have been met.

Nixon listed them: the cease-fire to take effect four days hence, the release of the POWs within sixty days, the withdrawal of all American troops during the same period, and the fact that "the people of South Vietnam have been guaranteed the right to determine their own future, without outside interference." But this was overselling the agreement: the South Vietnamese had not, in reality, been "guaranteed" anything except that Thieu would not be ousted instantly. Nixon was also misleading the nation in stating that throughout the negotiations the United States had been "in the closest consultation" with Thieu and that "this settlement meets the goals and has the full support of President Thieu and the Government of the Republic of Vietnam." Declaring piously that the terms of the agreement must be "scrupulously adhered to," the president again parted company with the truth when he said that "we shall do everything the agreement requires of us, and we shall expect the other parties to do everything it requires of them." Even as Nixon spoke, the Defense and State departments were quietly refining ways of getting around the accords; so were Saigon and Hanoi. Nixon went on to claim that "our insistence on peace with honor has made peace with honor possible." He failed to explain, however, that if this was "peace with honor," it could have been achieved much earlier—certainly the past October—as a peace with less bloodshed and destruction.

This is how an American diplomat put it later: "We could have insisted [in October] on a cease-fire throughout Indochina, and we had reasons to believe that Hanoi was thinking of meeting us halfway. We had a secret agreement with them that a cease-fire in Laos would be signed thirty days after the Vietnam cease-fire, and subsequently, we got this down to twenty days. If we had held out in October, we could have gotten the Cambodia cease-fire. We had a hell of a lot of leverage. But in January, Kissinger could not change the October draft, which was written under the pressure of the American elections, without opening himself to major charges of deception by the North Vietnamese. Anyway by January he felt that Cambodia was too much trouble. He was psychologically exhausted, and willing to believe that Hanoi didn't control the situation in Cambodia. Hanoi had told us in October that foreign troops should leave Laos and Cambodia—and this, of course, was put in the final agreement—but we did not negotiate a cease-fire there on that basis although we could have. By January, there was too much haste and uninterest on our part. We never had a clear-cut perception of what we wanted politically."

The last thing Kissinger said to Tho about Cambodia, just before they initialed the agreement on January 23, was that the United States would continue to bomb there until at least a *de facto* cease-fire developed.

On January 26, the president issued a proclamation designating 7:00 p.m., eastern standard time, of January 27—the moment the cease-fire was going into effect—as a National Moment of Prayer and Thanksgiving and the twenty-four–hour period beginning then as a National Day of Prayer and Thanksgiving to mark the end of the Vietnam war. The Agreement on Ending the War and Restoring Peace in Viet-Nam was signed in Paris, but even this ceremony demonstrated how far apart Saigon and Hanoi remained in terms of real peace. Thus one set of the nine-article agreement, refraining from any specific reference to the South Vietnamese Provisional Revolutionary Government (the Viet Cong), was signed by the four foreign ministers: William Rogers for the United States, Tran Van Lam for the Republic of Vietnam (Saigon), Nguyen Duy Trinh for the Democratic Republic of Vietnam (Hanoi), and Mme. Nguyen Thi Binh for the PRG (Viet Cong). But even so, Rogers's and Lam's signatures were affixed on one numbered page and those of Trinh and Mme. Binh on a separate numbered page. The South Vietnamese had refused to sign on the same *page* as the Communists. Then Rogers and Hanoi's Trinh signed a separate agreement, containing the same text but incorporating a different preamble that stated that Hanoi was signing "with the concurrence of the Provisional Revolutionary Government of the Republic of South Vietnam." This was because Saigon declined to sign any document that appeared to legitimize the Viet Cong.

The same method was used for the signing of a fourteen-article Protocol on Prisoners and Detainees, an eighteen-article Protocol on the International Commission of Control and Supervision (the most difficult and confusing of all the Paris documents), and a nineteen-article Protocol on the Cease-Fire in South Vietnam and the Joint Military Commissions. Finally, Rogers and Trinh signed a bilateral Protocol on Mine Clearing in North Vietnam.

The truce in Vietnam was preceded by a violent period of land grabbing, chiefly by the Communists, who were determined to control as much territory as possible when hostilities ceased—not only for strategic advantage, but to legitimize their presence in these areas for political reasons. Seizing a village, the Communists would hoist the PRG flag and await the arrival of inspectors from the International Commission of Control and Supervision to confirm Communist control. This would give the PRG greater influence in political negotiations with Saigon—if they were ever undertaken. Thus land grabbing went hand in hand with flag planting. The freshly rearmed South Vietnamese were doing the same thing for similar reasons. Between Friday and Sunday morning, the Communists captured several hundred South Vietnamese hamlets. On Saturday, they took the provincial capital of Tay Ninh and held it for a few hours before being pushed out by the ARVN. The South Vietnamese, of course, were counterattacking everywhere with artillery, air strikes, and helicopter gunships. When the truce came, the Communists held some three hundred and fifty hamlets they had taken in the preceding forty-eight hours.

What the Communists had launched was, according to their own statements, a "general uprising" designed to maximize their territorial gains before the cease-fire deadline. Gareth Porter has written that

> planned in meticulous detail for months, it was to be the Communists' final offensive effort: a combination of military attacks, overthrow of local RVN governments, destruction of Saigon's control over refugees, and stepped up efforts to induce Saigon soldiers to revolt against their commanders. . . . Directives from higher Party echelons emphasized that the military operations in support of the uprising would continue until the cease-fire became effective, after which "we continue motivating the people to rise up and to launch military proselytizing attacks [propaganda within enemy armed forces] . . . in order to shatter the enemy force and achieve our basic objective of liberating the rural areas."

But if Hanoi had no intention of observing the armistice, neither did Saigon. On January 24, Thieu had told the population, "If Communists come into your village, you should immediately shoot them in the head," and anyone who began "talking in a Communist tone" should "be killed immediately." According to *Tin Song*, the Saigon newspaper that spoke for the regime, policemen and soldiers were to kill those who "urge the people to demonstrate, and those who cause disorders or incite other persons to follow Communism." Deserters and inciters to desertion were to be shot. The orders were to arrest and detain "neutralists" and those who "incite the people to create disorder and confusion, or to leave those areas controlled by the government in order to go into Communist-controlled areas or vice versa."

For Thieu, the question was one of survival. For the Communists, it was achieving the goal of assuming power in South Vietnam—without American interference. No sooner was the peace agreement signed than a new war had begun. It simply had to be that way, and the small International Commission of Control and Supervision force was in no position to stop it. By mid-February, it was crystal clear that the Vietnam war was continuing in earnest and that neither side (particularly Saigon) had the slightest desire to implement the political aspects of the peace agreement Kissinger and Tho had so laboriously drafted.

Under the circumstances, Thieu had every interest in keeping the conflict going. He did not even mind—politically—the Communist offensives. If Hanoi's and the PRG's actions became too menacing, he was counting on the reintroduction of American air power. He knew the American contingency plans, including the covert organization of a command in Saigon (the huge Defense Attaché Office), one of whose missions was to coordinate the return, if necessary, of United States tactical air support. He had in his desk two private letters from Nixon—one sent on November 14, 1972, and the second on January 5, 1973—assuring him that the United States would "react very strongly and rapidly" and "respond with full force" if Hanoi seriously violated the truce.

United States policy, meanwhile, was proceeding—as usual—on two more or less parallel tracks. One was to provide Saigon with all possible support, covertly as well as openly, in resisting Communist pressures. The other track was to seek accommodation with North Vietnam, at least until all American POWs were safely out—by March 27, the sixty days after the cease-fire. And the two tracks occasionally intersected: there were secret understandings with the North Vietnamese, and there were secret understandings with the South Vietnamese about how best the Paris agreement could be interpreted in their favor.

The public policy was stated by Nixon at a White House news conference on January 31. He confirmed that he would confer with Thieu in San Clemente early in the spring, and he announced that Kissinger would be leaving for Hanoi on February 10 to discuss the postwar relationship with the North Vietnamese. Nixon said he had raised with congressional leaders the question of American aid in rebuilding Indochina, including North Vietnam (though he did it *after* Kissinger had committed the United States to it in Paris), and noted that resistance was developing against this idea. But, he said, "I look upon this as a potential investment in peace. . . . To the extent that the North Vietnamese, for example, participate with us and with other interested countries in reconstruction of North Vietnam, they will have a tendency to turn inward to the works of peace rather than turning outward to the works of war." Nixon's concept was sound. But North Vietnam and the United States Congress had different priorities.

The president's thin skin—and his meanness—also showed at the January 31 news conference. Having read sarcastic press comments about "peace with honor," he felt compelled to answer them in bitter Nixonian style: "I know it gags some of you to write that phrase, but it is true, and most Americans realize it is true, because it would be peace with dishonor had we . . . 'bugged out' and allowed what the North Vietnamese wanted: the imposition of a Communist or a coalition Communist government on the South Vietnamese." In similarly angry tones, Nixon rejected the notion of amnesty for American war deserters and draft evaders: "It is a rule of life: we all have to pay for our mistakes. . . . Many Americans paid a very high price to serve their country . . . in a war that they realize had very little support among the so-called better people, in the media and the intellectual circles and the rest, which had very little support, certainly, among some elements of the Congress—particularly the United States Senate. . . . Amnesty means forgiveness. We cannot provide forgiveness for [deserters]. Those who served paid their price. Those who deserted must pay their price . . . a criminal penalty for disobeying the laws of the United States."

During February, the United States concentrated on its double-track policy toward Vietnam. Kissinger and a group of aides spent February 11 to 13 in Hanoi. Visiting Hanoi had long been one of Kissinger's fondest desires—it would cap his Vietnam diplomacy beautifully—and on his brief trip there in mid-February he enjoyed himself hugely. He was greeted by Le Duc Tho and conferred with Premier Pham Van Dong and Foreign Minister Nguyen Duy Trinh (who was also the vice premier). But he was not invited to meet Le Duan, first secretary of the Communist Party and *primus inter pares* in the Hanoi leadership. A lengthy communiqué was issued on February 14, covering most of the areas of present and future relationships between the United States and North Vietnam. (There was no reference to Cambodia in it: Kissinger's January optimism about Cambodia had been greatly exaggerated.) A major subject of discussion had been American cooperation in North Vietnam's postwar reconstruction, and the communiqué announced formation of a United States–North Vietnamese Joint Economic Commission. As it happened, Nixon had sent a secret letter to Premier Pham Van Dong on February 1, promising $4.75 billion in postwar reconstruction aid "without any political conditions." This was raising the ante: Nixon had said in 1972 that Hanoi would be given $2.5 billion after a final cease-fire.

Kissinger could not have failed to see the vast damage inflicted on Hanoi by American bombers less than two months earlier, but his hosts were delicate enough not to point this out. The visit, after all, was meant to mark the beginning of a new era. Yet Kissinger did not abandon his habitual cynicism. After his return, he told a senior State Department official, "You know, they were never so congenial as they were to me on this trip. Never. This time they were all buddy-buddy, even though we'd been bombing Hanoi and Haiphong." This proved, in Kissinger's mind, his theory that the only thing Asians respect is brutal power.

The North Vietnamese had timed the release of the first batch of American POWs to coincide with Kissinger's stay in Hanoi. He saw them leave aboard an American medical-evacuation plane on the morning of Monday, February 12. A few hours later, millions of Americans—including Richard Nixon—could see on television the arrival of the prisoners at Clark Air Force Base in the Philippines. Some of them had been in prisons for more than eight years. (In all, 566 POWs were ultimately released. At least 72 had died in brutal captivity.) It was an emotional moment, as the 116 men first released came down the ramps at Clark, some of them on crutches, smartly saluting the officers awaiting them at planeside and walking over to the buses for the trip to the base hospital.

Nixon had issued orders that there should be no ranking government officials awaiting the POWs. As he told reporters at San Clemente, "I think that after what they have been through they deserve some time to themselves. I don't think VIPs should go in and try to exploit them. . . . Let's let them get back home. Let's let them see their families again, and then if they want to see anybody, the secretary of defense or the president, we will be available." He did, however, take a telephone call from Clark from air force Colonel Robinson Risner, the senior officer aboard the first evacuation plane. The White House said that "on behalf of the former prisoners, Colonel Risner expressed their desire to thank the president in person for ending the war and obtaining their release."

But the United States still had to make President Thieu feel secure. Kissinger, who had developed an intense dislike of Thieu during their October negotiations, preferred to stay away from Saigon. Instead, he sent William Sullivan, the State Department's Southeast Asia expert, who had accompanied him to Hanoi.

Sullivan reached Saigon on February 14, hours before the Hanoi communiqué was issued, and immediately went to see Thieu in Ambassador Bunker's company. His principal mission was to reassure the South Vietnamese president that Kissinger had not sold him down the river in Hanoi—again—and to advise him how to act in order to retain continued United States support. The first thing Sullivan did was to hand Thieu an advance copy of the Hanoi communiqué. Their seventy-five-minute discussion was fully described in a telegram, marked Secret, from Bunker to Rogers.

Thieu was unhappy over proposed American economic aid to North Vietnam, and according to Bunker's telegram, Sullivan "impressed on Thieu the fact that we had made it clear to the North Vietnamese that no economic assistance would be forthcoming unless they carried out the agreement faithfully." This was not quite the way Kissinger had put it in Hanoi, but it *was* American policy. The Bunker telegram went on to describe the reassurances to Thieu: Sullivan "told Thieu that he felt that there were two important factors in GVN favor. One was that the DRV needed a period of rest and the other was that they appeared to be disappointed with the Soviets and the Chinese, and wanted some ties with the United States which they could use to balance against them." If Sullivan indeed believed this, he (and Kissinger) either misunderstood Hanoi's thinking or engaged in wishful thinking.

Cambodia was very much on Thieu's mind, and he asked Sullivan what seemed to lie ahead. As Bunker reported, Sullivan said that "while we saw signs of the situation in Laos moving toward a cease-fire, the situation in Cambodia was much more complicated, with the various factions involved refusing to talk to each other." Sullivan added that "prospects for a formal settlement were not immediately foreseeable." Thieu commented that North Vietnam could sustain its troops in Cambodia, even if they had to withdraw from Laos, because they could "do this through Vietnam or the Ho Chi Minh Trail if this was not sealed off." The United States, of course, was still bombing the Laotian trails.

Thieu then told Sullivan, according to Bunker's dispatch, that in Vietnam "he saw only two guarantees for a peace." One, he said, was "U.S. willingness to react to violations of the agreement and giving South Vietnam the means to resist new aggression, the other was to keep the Russians and the Chinese from continuing to build up the DRV's war potential. Therefore, it was not only a question of the U.S. using economic assistance as a lever on North Vietnam but also a question of persuading the Chinese and the Russians to cooperate."

Sullivan sidestepped Thieu's request for these peace "guarantees," but he told him frankly that, in effect, he had to behave to make continued American support possible. As Bunker put it in the secret telegram, Sullivan informed Thieu "that the GVN had many opponents in the U.S. —people who had a vested interest in the agreement failing and who would be anxious to leap on the GVN at any opportunity . . . it was highly important for the GVN to assume such a position that none of these critics had any opportunity to blame him. . . . Thieu's speeches on early political settlement and elections were excellent from the point of view of the U.S. public opinion . . . he was now in the position of trying to consolidate peace and the obstacles were coming from the Communist side . . . he should continue in this vein, pushing for early contact with the NLF [National Liberation Front] on reconciliation, the setting up of the National Council, etc."

The Americans must have known that Thieu had no intention of doing any of these things, but Sullivan advised him that it "would help his position with Congress if he came [to the United States] with a spirit of confidence in the future and made it clear that the Communists were responsible for all obstacles to the implementation of the agreement."

Thieu still pushed for more American guarantees. He told Sullivan that North Vietnam would use the tanks it was currently infiltrating toward South Vietnam "to test the U.S. reaction" in about six months "by launching massive attacks at perhaps one or two locations in the country." He emphasized again that "the best guarantee to prevent this kind of attack was the U.S. threat of intervention, and the means which [the United States] gave the GVN to resist on their own." Sullivan's comment, according to the Bunker telegram, was that "the real guarantees for the peace were the presence in the area of U.S. air power, economic assistance to North Vietnam, and Chinese/Russian differences over Indochina."

American policy, then, was to manipulate both sides in Vietnam in order to preserve the precarious peace. On the one hand, the United States was militarily ready to move at once: warplanes were standing by in Thailand and on Guam as well as aboard navy carriers in the Gulf of Tonkin. The minicommand in Saigon was equipped to coordinate whatever air operations were required. On the other hand, the United States kept dangling the carrot of economic aid before Hanoi.

Supposedly an agreement means what it says. But in the case of the Vietnam accords, there were so many ambiguities—some deliberate and some inadvertently accepted by both sides—that both Washington and

Hanoi found it desirable as well as necessary to develop their own interpretations. In certain instances, American legal experts discovered *ex post facto* that they did not know the real meaning of certain crucial provisions of the basic agreement and the accompanying protocols.

All of this made it necessary for the State Department to come up late in February with a thirteen-page, single-spaced document, classified Secret, setting forth its interpretation of what Kissinger had negotiated and initialed and Secretary Rogers had signed. The work of George H. Aldrich, then the department's acting legal adviser, this document, entitled "Interpretations of the Agreement on Ending the War and Restoring Peace in Viet-Nam," was couched so as to bend the pact as much as possible in favor of the United States and South Vietnam. It also provided new insights into the secret negotiating history of the Paris agreement, and showed how much the negotiators had depended on "understandings" not incorporated in the text of the agreement.

Concerning aerial reconnaissance over North Vietnam by American or South Vietnamese aircraft, for example, a subject that had created a host of problems after the 1968 bombing halt, the document said, "we have assured the DRV that such activity 'will cease completely and definitely.' " But in discussions about Saigon's reconnaissance by unarmed aircraft over *South* Vietnam, "the DRV has told us that the PRG [Viet Cong] will not tolerate reconnaissance over areas controlled by [it] and will fire at any GVN aircraft overflying such areas. . . . We have responded that we would consider such firing a violation of the cease-fire." This set of private understandings had to lead to trouble: the South Vietnamese obviously would be overflying Communist-held areas in the South—it was one of the few ways they could be sure of what was going on—and PRG gunners would just as obviously fire at these planes. If the United States chalked this up as a violation against Hanoi, it, presumably, considered some way of responding. Aldrich chose to determine that only "armed combat aircraft" were prevented from flying reconnaissance over South Vietnam, but how were Communist gunners to know whether a plane was armed?

This conflict was aggravated by the fact that the Paris negotiators had been unable to define the respective "areas of control" in South Vietnam's "leopard-spot" situation. Yet, as the State Department's paper observed, "the concept of separate areas of control by the two South Vietnamese parties is critical to the definition of the cease-fire and is one of the basic assumptions of the Agreement." The document then told the inside story of the negotiations on this point, winding up with a most unhappy conclusion:

We tried unsuccessfully to include in the Cease-Fire Protocol an article making it clear that the Two-Party Joint Military Commission
(Saigon and PRG) should base its determination on a census of military forces, including their location, strength, and deployment. The
DRV refused to accept this concept and clearly preferred a political
exercise of drawing lines on a map. In view of this unresolved disagreement, the Two-Party Joint Military Commission is left with no
guidance on how to determine the areas of control in South Viet-Nam.

This was a clear admission that the cease-fire was unenforceable inasmuch as nobody could define who controlled which piece of South Vietnamese real estate. It may have been "critical to," and a "basic assumption of," the Paris agreement, but the concept of the control areas was
unresolved, and this seemed to undermine the whole peace settlement
from the very outset. It is mystifying why Kissinger, who haggled over so
many lesser matters, allowed this gaping hole in the agreement. But it
certainly explains why the North Vietnamese went on their flag-planting
rampage just before the truce went into effect.

The State Department "Interpretations" tried to enable the South
Vietnamese to keep supplying Phnom Penh by river transport. Although
the Paris agreement prohibited the movement of warships into areas of
South Vietnam controlled by the other side, the Aldrich document provided a loophole: "We have informed the GVN that military escorts of
convoys proceeding up the Mekong to Phnom Penh are, in our view,
permissible if the GVN agrees that the ship channel remains an area
under government control. This would be true even if areas of shore line
are clearly under PRG control, but it is far from clear that the PRG would
accept that interpretation." The Mekong ship channel could be declared
under the Saigon government's control for the simple reason that the
South Vietnamese had warships on the river and the Communists did not.

The State Department also attempted to weaken the provision requiring departing United States forces to take home military equipment belonging to them. The idea was that, in addition to equipment delivered
from the United States and elsewhere under the pretruce Enhance programs, the South Vietnamese should be able to retain weapons held by
American units. While the agreement specified that actual "transfers" of
material would not be permitted after the cease-fire, the State Department decided that it was unclear "whether transfer of title or transfer of
possession is the critical act." In other words, the department was suggesting that transfers of "title" might be permissible *after* the cease-fire
and, if so, transfers of actual equipment during the sixty-day period for
the completion of American troop withdrawals. American negotiators,

the document said, chose not to explain their interpretation to the North Vietnamese, but "the North Vietnamese said nothing to us inconsistent with our interpretation. . . . We can make a reasonable case, but we must recognize that it is far from compelling and that the International Commission may or may not agree with our view."

In the case of U.S. military bases in South Vietnam, the "Interpretations" said they would not be dismantled (the agreement called for the dismantling of all bases "of the United States") because "we transferred title to all U.S. bases prior to the conclusion of the agreement." Aldrich noted that "we avoided making this intention clear to the DRV during the negotiations. . . . Nevertheless we can expect a dispute on this issue."

Then there was the question of continued military assistance to Laos and Cambodia. The Paris agreement on Vietnam did not restrict foreign assistance, but it urged that it be halted at the "earliest possible time." The administration hoped to be able indefinitely to shore up friendly forces in both countries (although Congress was reluctant) and the State Department paper noted that a halt "could not occur until cease-fire agreements were concluded in Laos and Cambodia and, perhaps, until subsequent political settlement agreements were concluded in these countries." This reference was designed to make sure that weapons could flow, especially to Cambodia, for a very long time.

The next maneuver was invented by the State Department to help Thieu further in replacements of combat aircraft. Under the agreement, military equipment could be replaced on a one-to-one basis when it was "destroyed, damaged, worn out, or used up." During the Enhance programs, the United States had arranged to provide South Vietnam with "a large number" of F-5A jet fighter-bombers borrowed from South Korea, Iran, and Taiwan because they were not available in the United States. (F-5s, also known as "Freedom Fighters," and less sophisticated than the jet aircraft flown by U.S. armed forces, are built only for export and no significant stocks are kept on hand.) However, as the State Department now said, "We may wish at some future time to replace these F-5A aircraft with F-5E aircraft so that the F-5As can be returned to the three countries from which they came." The problem was that the F-5E (the Freedom Fighter's "Tiger" version) is a more advanced and better armed plane than the older "A" type. To justify the switch, Aldrich offered this argument: "If [the F-5As] are at some point returned to the countries of origin, I believe they can be reasonably argued to be 'used up.' . . . In general, that term was understood to mean all types of consumption which would make the item unavailable for further use by the GVN. An aircraft which has been transferred to another country is certainly no longer available to the GVN and should be considered 'used up' and therefore subject to replacement."

Aldrich went on with these legal acrobatics: "A second and more difficult question is whether an F-5E can be a legitimate replacement for an F-5A. . . . [The agreement] requires that the replacement be 'on the basis of piece-for-piece of the same characteristics and properties. . . .' It seems obvious, however, that the GVN will have to be prepared to justify this replacement on the grounds of substantial similarity between the aircraft; if a decent argument cannot be made, the replacement cannot be justified." As it happened, Saigon did not even bother to make "a decent argument." By the time the F-5Es were ready for delivery, most of the truce control systems had broken down and the South Vietnamese simply started flying the Tigers.

Under the agreement, all American "armaments, munitions and war material" had to be withdrawn from Vietnam within sixty days of the truce. But the State Department now said that cars and trucks for the South Vietnamese civilian police "need not be considered 'war material,' " and, consequently, could be left behind. The document failed to say that the South Vietnamese national police were an important element of Saigon's counterinsurgency effort.

One of the gravest problems facing South Vietnam was posed by the obligation of the United States to repatriate all its military personnel. Saigon's armed forces still desperately needed American advice, and American training and operational coordination. But ways were found to get around this provision of the pact. First, the South Vietnamese military establishment was secretly backed up by the huge Defense Attaché Office in the American embassy. Then, the State Department satisfied itself that the agreement was sufficiently ambiguous to suggest that American civilians employed by South Vietnamese or United States "contractors," rather than by Saigon's armed forces, were not necessarily covered by the Paris provisions and could probably stay. This was a very fine line indeed. Aldrich's document also revealed that the United States was violating a secret understanding with the North Vietnamese about American civilians working directly for the South Vietnamese armed forces. These were in their majority "instant civilians" paid by the Defense Department.

The United States has assured the DRV that we shall withdraw from South Viet-Nam within twelve months from the signature of the Agreement all our civilian personnel "working in the armed forces of the Republic of Viet-Nam." We have also assured the DRV that the majority of them will be withdrawn within ten months. These assurances clearly cover all U.S. Government employees whose principal duties are with GVN armed forces. It is unclear whether it applies to U.S. nationals employed by contractors of either the United States or the GVN.

These assurances had been made in Paris because the North Vietnamese raised the question of American civilians in South Vietnam, and, as an American diplomat put it, "we were a bit caught by the language." Nevertheless, he said, "we have taken advantage of certain ambiguities."

As soon as the agreement was signed, an American diplomat with ambassadorial rank was rushed back to Washington to recruit top-level civilians to replace the military men who were leaving South Vietnam. These efforts to make up for the departure of United States military were quite successful. So much so that in May 1974—fifteen months after the signing of the agreement—there were still 9000 American civilians in South Vietnam, most engaged directly or indirectly in supporting Saigon's armed forces, especially in aviation. This violated the secret commitment with Hanoi.

The Vietnam cease-fire was violated by all sides—with or without excuses—from the day it went into effect. After the brief and artificial euphoria of the signing of the peace settlement—most of it engendered by Nixon and Kissinger (and the rather naïve American press, which had not done its homework)—bleakness again descended on the Indochina scene.

In the first three weeks after the truce, 213,000 South Vietnamese civilians were made homeless as a result of stepped-up fighting between opposing factions. This was the highest refugee rate since the spring 1972 Communist offensive. The Agency for International Development reported that during the first month, civilian casualties—dead and wounded—were running at a monthly rate of 5000, compared with 3500 in the first eight months of 1971. The new war seemed even more ferocious without the Americans. In Cambodia, North Vietnamese and Khmer Rouge troops were gradually eroding the resistance of the Lon Nol regime.

The only bright spot in Indochina was Laos, where a cease-fire, favored by Hanoi, was signed between the Pathet Lao rebels and Premier Souvanna Phouma's government on February 22. The two sides were to engage in political negotiations aiming to form a coalition regime, but it promised to be a long and complex process. The cease-fire forced the United States to end country-wide bombings in Laos, but the administration persuaded Souvanna Phouma, still its client, to let American aircraft fly reconnaissance missions and to look the other way as B-52s kept pounding the Ho Chi Minh Trail.

In Saigon, President Thieu was calmly disregarding the provisions of the peace agreement on freedoms of the press, speech, and political association. Instead, he was concentrating on rebuilding his political power base. It was dictatorship as usual. And nobody had expected North Vietnam and the PRG in its areas in South Vietnam to blossom forth with democratic freedoms. Nevertheless, the outside world acted as if the peace settlement were a serious enterprise. A twelve-nation International Conference on Vietnam met in Paris on February 26 to place its seal of approval on the settlement. It brought together the foreign ministers of the United States, North Vietnam, South Vietnam, and the PRG, who were signatories to the January agreement; also, of Canada, Indonesia, Poland, and Hungary, whose countries were represented on the International Commission of Control and Supervision; of the Soviet Union and Britain, who were permanent cochairmen of the Geneva conference on Indochina (convened in 1954 and in recess since 1962); and of China, a signatory of the 1954 and 1962 Geneva agreements who could not be ignored at this juncture. On March 2, the Paris conference produced a high-sounding declaration, approving and supporting the Vietnam peace agreement. But it was easily the most useless major international conference in many a year.

In Washington, President Nixon was trying to be positive about the Indochina situation. At a news conference on March 2, he announced that he would confer with President Thieu in San Clemente early in April, that the Laos cease-fire would work because it carried "an unequivocal provision" for the withdrawal of all foreign forces, and that the situation in Cambodia was "much more complex because you don't have the governmental forces there that can negotiate with each other." Nixon noted that the Lon Nol regime had tried a unilateral cease-fire in February, but it was not reciprocated. He added that until there was an agreement, "we, of course, will provide support for the Cambodian government." He omitted the fact that the United States was continuing to bomb in Cambodia.

The president then delivered an extraordinarily impassioned appeal in favor of economic reconstruction aid to North Vietnam. He launched into it after denying, in reply to a question, that such aid was a condition for the Vietnam cease-fire. Nixon recalled the "very substantial" opposition after World War II to help for "most militaristic" Germany and Japan. He said that as a congressman he had voted for it "even though it was submitted by a Democratic president, because I was convinced that the chances for having peace in Asia and the chance for having peace in Europe would be considerably increased if the Germans and the Japanese . . . were turned toward peaceful pursuits, rather than being left in a position of either hopelessness, which would lead to frustration and another war, or confrontation." He added:

> If the North Vietnamese, after twenty-five years of war, continue to think that their future will only be meaningful if they engage in continuing war, then we are going to have war in that part of the world, and it would not only threaten South Vietnam, but Cambodia and Laos and Thailand, the Philippines, the whole area. If, on the other hand, the people of North Vietnam have a stake in peace, then it can be altogether different. And so we believe that once the Congress, both Democrats and Republicans, considers this matter . . . they will decide, as they did twenty-five years ago, based on that precedent and what happened then, that the interests of peace will be served by providing the aid. The costs of peace are great, but the costs of war are much greater.

A week later, however, the administration began to reveal its concern over what was happening in Vietnam. First, the Pentagon announced that 300 tanks and 30,000 North Vietnamese troops had moved down the Ho Chi Minh Trail since the beginning of the year. This was not particularly new since Hanoi made a heroic effort to insert as much equipment as possible into South Vietnam before the truce deadline. Sometimes it took as long as two months between the time North Vietnamese troops and equipment entered the funnel at the top and the time they came out at the bottom in South Vietnam or Cambodia. But there was a purpose in these North Vietnamese movements.

On March 13, the State Department said that the United States was watching the North Vietnamese activities "very closely and with some concern." The problem of infiltration was further complicated by the fact that Saigon and the Communists had been unable to agree on the official points of entry into South Vietnam from the North and Cambodia for the purpose of resupply as provided in the agreement. This was to have been settled fifteen days after the cease-fire, but it remained unresolved a month after that target date. Hanoi and the PRG refused to designate their chosen points of entry until South Vietnam gave assurances that the agreement's wording on one-for-one replacements of equipment would be interpreted literally in the context of the same "characteristics and properties." In the light of the negotiating history, they were worried that the United States would be giving Saigon superior war matériel under the replacement clause; given the Aldrich "Interpretations," the Communists had reason to be suspicious.

All these arguments may sound esoteric and technical, but they were vital to both sides. The very enforcement of the cease-fire hung in the balance. It was bad enough that from the outset nobody could define the respective areas of control; now everything was paralyzed by disagreements and deadlocks on other points. Under the circumstances, the Communists felt free to infiltrate the South from locations of their choosing, and Saigon had no inhibitions about accepting equipment the United States was willing to supply, regardless of the truce requirements. North Vietnam utterly disregarded the one-for-one provision for replacements. Neither the International Commission nor the Saigon-PRG Military Commission (which was not functioning) could control the situation. The cease-fire was a fiction.

Nixon's reaction to the breakdown in the six-week-old cease-fire came on March 15 at a news conference. He volunteered the information that "we have informed the North Vietnamese of our concern about [the] infiltration and of what we believe it to be, a violation of the cease-fire . . . and the peace agreement." This was the first time the United States had accused Hanoi of violating the peace agreement, *as distinct from the cease-fire,* and Nixon stressed that he was "primarily concerned about the equipment, because as far as the personnel are concerned, they could be simply replacement personnel." Then, like an echo from the past, the president said, "And I would only suggest that based on my actions over the past four years, that the North Vietnamese should not lightly disregard such expressions of concern when they are made with regard to a violation."

This not-so-veiled hint of military retaliation, presumably a warning that American air power could be recalled to Vietnam, had also been made in a private message Nixon had sent to Premier Pham Van Dong in Hanoi a few days earlier. But newsmen in the White House briefing room did not follow up on it. Watergate was the dominant topic, and most of the questions were addressed to the hearings North Carolina's Senator Sam Ervin was planning to hold on Nixon's election campaign irregularities, to the emerging battle between the president and Congress over executive privilege, and to the role of the FBI in investigating the various misdeeds.

Then the president ever so softly dropped the other shoe on North Vietnam. Following the creation of the United States–North Vietnamese Joint Economic Commission during Kissinger's visit in Hanoi, the two sides had begun meeting in Paris to explore how the United States could provide postwar reconstruction aid to North Vietnam. By late March, the two delegations had reached virtually complete agreement on operating procedures, and on March 27, Maurice J. Williams, the chief American negotiator, dispatched a top-secret telegram to Washington reporting this progress. He noted that the only unresolved point involved how the North Vietnamese were to report on the modalities of using the aid. First, there was silence. Then Williams was instructed to break off the talks. The signing of the agreement with Hanoi, planned for July 23, 1973, never took place.

Nixon, counseled by Kissinger, had decided that North Vietnam would be denied promised reconstruction aid in retaliation for what the White House regarded as a violation of the peace agreement: the infiltration of new military equipment into South Vietnam as well as Hanoi's failure to remove its troops from Cambodia. But there are reasons to believe that the president may have used the cease-fire problems as a handy justification for halting the economic negotiations in the knowledge that Congress would never approve help to the Communists. The decision to back away from aid to North Vietnam left unborn for years what might have been a postwar relationship with Hanoi. Perhaps the North Vietnamese did not want it either—except wholly on their terms. In any event, the administration never acknowledged publicly that the United States had been one step away from an economic pact with Hanoi *or* that it retreated from it.

Relations between the two South Vietnamese parties over a political settlement—supposedly the heart of the Paris agreement—never went well, although the actors went through the required motions. A Two-Party Political Conference convened on March 19 at La Celle château in St. Cloud, with appropriate ceremonies. But the PRG's chief delegate, Minister of State Nguyen Van Hieu, was poker-faced, and Saigon's envoy, Deputy Premier Nguyen Luu Vien, though all smiles, had come without the slightest authority to negotiate. After three sessions, Hieu and Vien could not even agree on an agenda, although the agreement specified that the establishment of a National Council of Reconciliation and Concord was to be the first point of business. Hieu spent his time denouncing the United States and charging that the Saigon regime was guilty of 46,000 violations of the cease-fire during the first two months. Vien kept insisting that the conference should deal with the removal of North Vietnamese troops from the South, even though the "nonexistence" of such forces had in effect been decided by Kiss'nger and Le Duc Tho.

If any proof was needed that Thieu had absolutely no intention of negotiating *anything* political with the PRG, he provided it on March 29, two days before leaving for California to meet Nixon, by formally inaugurating a new political party. It was called the Democracy Party, and it was one of three parties allowed to exist under a new law. Seventeen parties, including all leftist, Buddhist, and traditional nationalist parties, were abolished. Thieu said his party's mission would be to compete with Communists in the elections to be held under the provisions of the Paris agreement. Not many people in Saigon took this seriously.

Having consolidated his political power, Thieu could afford high-visibility goodwill gestures. Thus he released Truong Dinh Dzu, the "peace candidate" in the 1967 presidential elections who had spent five years in prison. (Dzu, a lawyer, was Thieu's best-known political prisoner; his crime had been advocating peace negotiations with the Viet Cong for the establishment of a coalition government; he had further annoyed Thieu by polling 18 percent of the vote.)

Communist members of the Four-Party Joint Military Commission and, later, the PRG delegation to the Two-Party Joint Military Commission were allowed to come to the capital, although they were kept isolated and nearly incommunicado at Tan Son Nhut air base. They spent a good deal of their time giving interviews to foreign newsmen and hardly ever went out of town. Inasmuch as there was a deadlock on the implementation of key points in the cease-fire protocol, the military commissions had very little to do. There were no Saigon military delegates in the PRG-held areas because the Communists never designated the control and entry centers.

The twelve long years of American military presence in South Vietnam ended on March 29, 1973, when the last soldier of the last United States unit boarded an air force jet transport in Danang, in the north, for the flight home. During those years, 2.5 million young Americans had served and fought in Vietnam to implement policies of three American presidents. At the height of the war, 540,000 American soldiers were there. More than 50,000 died, more than 300,000 were wounded, and more than 1000 became war prisoners or vanished in Indochinese jungles. American society had been torn asunder by the Vietnam war.

Now it was all over. The provisions of the peace agreement for the departure of all American forces from Vietnam were met. The last prisoner for whom the North Vietnamese could account was released at the same time.

President Nixon marked this occasion with an evening speech to the nation from the Oval Office at the White House. It should have been a solemn moment, a historic moment. The president succeeded in making it bitter. His address was shot through with Churchillian travesties: "Never have men served with greater devotion abroad with less apparent support at home." And he had to end it with this phrase: "If we meet the great challenges of peace that lie ahead . . . then one day it will be written: This was America's finest hour."

The president asked that

on this day, let us honor those who made this achievement possible . . . every one of the 2 ½ million Americans who served honorably in our nation's longest war. . . . Let us honor them with the respect they deserve. And I say again tonight, let us not dishonor those who served their country by granting amnesty to those who deserted America. Tonight I want to express the appreciation of the nation to others who helped to make this day possible. I refer to you, the great majority of Americans listening to me tonight, who, despite an unprecedented barrage of criticism from a small but vocal minority, stood firm for peace with honor. I know it was not easy for you to do so.

Nixon ended with a threat: "The leaders of North Vietnam should have no doubt as to the consequences if they fail to comply with the agreement."

Having issued this warning to Hanoi, the president welcomed President Thieu at San Clemente for two days of conferences. (The choice of the locale was deliberate: the White House realized that Thieu's popularity in the United States was limited and that to bring him to Washington on an official visit might have resulted in demonstrations and unpleasantness. But everything was done in San Clemente to please Thieu. He was given a formal welcome with full military honors.)

Behind closed doors in the Casa Pacifica, Thieu argued for increased American military aid—his point was that Hanoi's violations of the peace agreement relieved the United States of any obligation to observe the prohibition on supplying him with new equipment—and for substantial economic aid. The departure of American troops had deprived South Vietnam of hundreds of millions of dollars annually in local expenditures by the United States, and Thieu was facing an economic catastrophe. Nixon was reassuring, but cautious. The United States was not prepared to abrogate the Paris agreement, he told Thieu, but ways would be found to shore up the South Vietnamese military establishment. Nixon also promised Thieu direct military support, if needed. On economic aid, the president explained that, to a large degree, the decisions were in the hands of Congress, which was reluctant to keep pouring money into South Vietnam. Their joint communiqué made it plain that the "allies" would not tolerate continued North Vietnamese violations of the truce. This was Nixon's strongest warning to Hanoi since the Paris settlement and his strongest public assurance of military backing for Saigon.

Thieu went home with practically everything he wanted: strong personal support from Nixon that would further consolidate his political base at home; the virtual commitment of U.S. military action if Hanoi's pressures and truce violations persisted; promise of as much military equipment as the United States could supply without openly violating the Paris agreement; and a formal assurance that the Nixon administration would go to Congress to get the funds Thieu needed to survive for the next two years. When he returned to Saigon after a two-week absence— he had also visited Italy, West Germany, France, South Korea, and Taiwan—Thieu received a hero's welcome.

Nixon also gave him a new American ambassador: Graham A. Martin, one of the toughest United States career diplomats, the man who, as ambassador to Italy, had arranged the secret payments of $10 million to pro-Western political parties in 1972, to stem Communist advances. Martin was the perfect envoy to replace the gentler Ellsworth Bunker in the new twilight period of South Vietnamese history, a time calling for public toughness and a talent for coordinating covert American activities in Thieu's support.

No sooner had he reached Washington after his conferences with Thieu than the president found himself facing a new Cambodian crisis. Khmer Rouge guerrillas—now fighting in the name of Sihanouk's National United Front of Kampuchea—had launched an offensive that threatened to destroy the American-supported regime of President Lon Nol.

Communist forces in Cambodia had been under steady bombardment by American B-52s, but the strikes were not having sufficient effect. On April 7, as the huge bombers struck Cambodia for the thirty-first consecutive day in the current phase (they were interrupted at the time the Paris agreement was signed), Nixon and Kissinger dispatched General Haig to Phnom Penh and Saigon to "assess the situation." A White House statement said that the president was concerned over the refusal of Hanoi to withdraw its troops from Cambodia, the level of violence there, and the continuing cease-fire violations in South Vietnam. But actually, the Cambodian situation was ambiguous. Unable to obtain a commitment in Paris in January for the withdrawal of North Vietnamese troops from Cambodia or for pressure on the Khmer Rouge to sign a truce with Lon Nol, Kissinger presented Le Duc Tho with a unilateral "understanding." He said that the United States "understood" that it was free to bomb in Cambodia without violating the Paris agreement so long as the North Vietnamese forces remained in the country. Inasmuch as Hanoi had never accepted this "understanding," the United States found itself trapped in Cambodia.

The combination of this "understanding" with Haig's April recommendations for maximal military support for Lon Nol served to push the Nixon administration not only into a frustrating deadlock in Cambodia, but also into a bitter struggle with Congress over the bombings.

Chapter 25

The shadow of Watergate was lengthening over Richard Nixon and the White House. The Watergate burglars had been convicted in January, but new revelations in March and April showed that the White House had been deeply involved in illegal activities in connection with the 1972 reelection campaign; it was no longer just the question of the break-in in the offices of the Democratic National Committee.

Nixon's response was to invoke his preoccupation with foreign policy as his reason for not having paid enough attention to the political activities of his associates in what he called "this whole sordid affair." In effect, he urged the nation to let him go on concentrating on international problems now that, according to him, adequate steps had been taken to resolve the Watergate situation. In other words, the president's strategy was to hide behind foreign policy, his strongest point, and to ride out the storm.

This was made clear in a speech he delivered on television on April 30 announcing the resignations of his chief of staff, H. R. Haldeman; the head of the White House Domestic Council, John Ehrlichman; counsel to the president, John Dean; and Attorney General Richard Kleindienst.

Political commentators have correctly observed that during my twenty-seven years in politics I have always previously insisted on running my own campaigns for office.

But 1972 presented a very different situation. In both domestic and foreign policy, 1972 was a year of crucially important decisions, of intense negotiations, of vital new directions, particularly in working toward the goal which has been my overriding concern throughout my political career—the goal of bringing peace to America, peace to the world. That is why I decided, as the 1972 campaign approached, that the presidency should come first and politics second. To the maximum extent possible, therefore, I sought to delegate campaign operations, to remove the day-to-day campaign decisions from the president's office and the White House.

He then informed the nation that since March 21, he had "personally assumed the responsibility for coordinating intensive new inquiries into the matter," and that he was now shifting Elliot Richardson from the Defense Department to be the new attorney general with "absolute authority to make all decisions bearing upon the prosecution of the Watergate case and related matters." The Watergate speech then became also a foreign-policy speech:

> It is . . . essential that we not be so distracted by events such as this that we neglect the vital work before us, before this nation, before America, at a time of critical importance to America and the world. . . . There is vital work to be done toward our goal of a lasting structure of peace in the world—work that cannot wait, work that I must do.

For example, the president said, he would be meeting the next day with West Germany's Chancellor Willy Brandt "for talks that are a vital element of the 'Year of Europe,' " the new policy toward the Western allies that Nixon and Kissinger were seeking to develop in 1973, following the Vietnam settlement. The president had launched the "Year of Europe," a policy that never got off the ground despite the accompanying fanfare, in comments at the White House on February 15, and Kissinger followed it up with a major speech on March 23.

Then, Nixon said, the administration was busy preparing for the Brezhnev summit visit in June, for negotiations for a second round of SALT agreements, and for mutual reduction of military forces in Central Europe; and it was facing "the difficult tasks of maintaining peace in Southeast Asia and in the potentially explosive Middle East."

All this, of course, was true, and in a curious way Watergate did not yet seem to be seriously interfering with Nixon's conduct of foreign policy. If anything, the president was again immersing himself in it after turning the Watergate scandals over to Richardson. And aside from Indochina and foreign economics, his policies were prospering in a variety of fields. Late in December 1972, a confident Nixon had told Kissinger that 1973 would be "a great year."

And this confidence was reflected in Nixon's annual report to Congress on foreign policy, sent up on May 3. The 1973 message was about three months late, in part because Kissinger, its actual author, had been busy with Indochina problems, his China trip, and other international matters, and in part, of course, because with Watergate a great many things were running way behind schedule.

The double détente seemed to be functioning especially well. The second phase of SALT negotiations had started on March 12 in Geneva, and Nixon was optimistic that he and Brezhnev could sign new accords on controlling offensive nuclear arms during the approaching June summit. Relations with China, too, were developing satisfactorily. In mid-February, Kissinger and eight advisers spent five days in Peking in conferences with Premier Chou En-lai (who hosted another banquet for Kissinger at the Great Hall of the People), Foreign Minister Chi Peng-fei, and other senior Chinese officials. Chairman Mao unexpectedly invited him for a long chat. On February 22, the first anniversary of Nixon's breakthrough visit to China, an upbeat joint communiqué reported that the talks "were conducted in an unconstrained atmosphere and were earnest, frank and constructive," and that the two governments had found that the progress in their relations during the past year was "beneficial to the people of their two countries."

(Kissinger, however, committed one major error in Peking. He rejected Prince Sihanouk's overtures, made through intermediaries, for a meeting to discuss the Cambodian situation. Still euphoric after the signing of the Paris agreement, Kissinger saw no reason to sit down with the titular head of the Cambodian rebel movement. He was assuming that the "understanding" on Cambodia he had placed before the North Vietnamese would, sooner or later, take care of the whole matter. Before long, Kissinger would regret having snubbed Sihanouk.)

Aside from a general review of world and bilateral problems, the principal practical result of Kissinger's visit to China was the decision for the United States and China to exchange ambassadorial-level liaison missions. This was the formula Kissinger and Chou devised to set up permanent diplomatic representation, getting around the fact that full-fledged diplomatic relations were still impossible. That both governments regarded the liaison offices as extremely important was proved by Nixon's appointment of seventy-five-year-old David Bruce, the most distinguished living American diplomat, to head the Peking mission, and Chou En-lai's selection of Huang Chen, the Chinese ambassador to Paris and the only diplomat to serve on the Central Committee of the Chinese Communist Party, to run the Washington office. The Chinese went even further: they sent another diplomat of ambassadorial rank, Han Shu, to serve as Huang's deputy.

When Huang Chen reached Washington on May 29, the administration went to unusual lengths to honor him. A diplomatic dinner was held at the State Department for him and members of his mission the evening of their arrival. The next morning, as a special gesture of friendship, Nixon received him at the White House (just before leaving for Iceland to confer with President Pompidou). New ambassadors usually waited days or weeks to be received by the president. Nixon and Huang spent twenty-five minutes together, after exchanging public remarks. To Huang, the resumption of official relations with the United States was being achieved after "a detour of more than twenty years." To Nixon, the meeting was an occasion to tell Huang that he would like to revisit China soon. He thanked the Chinese for the welcome they had given Ambassador Bruce in Peking two weeks earlier, saying he hoped "that we can see that your accommodations are handled as well here." Smiling, he added: "If there are any slip-ups, we will fire Dr. Kissinger." The Chinese diplomat did not seem amused. Actually, the Chinese needed no help: after several weeks at Washington's famous Mayflower Hotel, they acquired a 400-room hotel next to the Portuguese and French embassies' residences, and remodeled it as an office-and-residence compound.

The exchange of liaison missions capped a series of other Chinese-American goodwill gestures. On March 2, Secretary Rogers and Foreign Minister Chi Peng-fei, meeting in Paris during the Indochina peace conference, agreed in principle on settling outstanding financial issues: the disposition of $196 million of private American claims for assets frozen or blocked in China.

On March 9, the White House announced that the last three Americans held prisoner in China would be set free the following week. One of them, John T. Downey, a CIA official, had been serving a life sentence since 1952, when he was captured on the mainland. The Chinese agreed to commute Downey's sentence after an appeal from Nixon to Chou En-lai; the president had sent word to Peking that Downey's mother was critically ill. The other prisoners were an air force pilot and a navy pilot shot down over China in 1965 and 1967 respectively after straying into Chinese air space during raids against North Vietnam.

Trade with China was rising spectacularly. In 1970, total exchanges stood at $5 million. In the first eleven months of 1972, following Nixon's trip to Peking, they had risen to $220 million and included the Chinese purchase of ten Boeing 707 jets. In 1973, China started buying American wheat, cotton, and tobacco. It even bought two American motion pictures: *Tora! Tora! Tora!* (the story of the events leading to the Japanese attack on Pearl Harbor) and *The Sound of Music.* The Chinese post office and Western Union set up telegraph and Telex links between New York and Peking. A group of top American business executives established a

National Council for United States–China trade. By the end of 1973, total trade rose to $900 million, of which $840 million was American exports.

Not only in trade, however, was the pattern predominantly one-way from the United States to China. It was Peking's policy to restrict trips by its citizens to the United States to a minimum while allowing considerable numbers of visits by Americans. In 1972, some 3000 Americans received visas—congressmen, journalists, scholars, scientists, and businessmen—and in 1973 this number grew to 5000. The Chinese did send a troupe of acrobats in January (they were received by Nixon) and a delegation of eighteen journalists in May; a few other delegations came later. But this pattern did not concern the White House: it saw Chinese-American relations improving steadily, and that was all that mattered.

The Nixon administration's hope to make 1973 the "Year of Europe" resulted from a long series of considerations. The obvious one was that the years of preoccupation with Vietnam had obscured relationships with Western Europe, and that the time had come to strengthen them again. The related consideration was that the establishment of Soviet and Chinese détentes had caused concern and misunderstandings that required careful handling. Besides, the agreement with the Soviet Union on the European security conference and the force-reduction negotiations directly affected Continental interests—and joint preparations had to be made for these diplomatic enterprises.

But perhaps the most important consideration was economic. The emergency measures taken in 1971—the temporary suspension of dollar convertibility, the import surcharge, the freeing of the price of gold, the devaluation of the dollar, and the Smithsonian Agreement on currency rates—had not resolved the basic imbalances in trade between the United States, Western Europe, and Japan, or the accompanying financial distortions. The United States was still buying too much abroad and selling too little. Nixon had hoped that a basic international monetary reform—including trade negotiations—could be set in motion during 1972. Nothing meaningful, however, had happened. As 1973 began, the situation was deteriorating. The United States was stymied in its exports by foreign restrictions, and speculators were mounting a new assault on the dollar.

In his economic message to Congress on January 30, the president said that if Americans were to import goods and to invest funds abroad,

> we must be able to pay by selling abroad the things that we produce best, and selling them on the best terms that we can freely obtain.

. . . We must be able to pay in a way that is sustainable so that we are not confronted with the need for sudden and possibly painful adjustments. . . . Existing arrangements are not favorable to us in either respect. We have been buying from abroad in rapidly increasing amounts. . . . But our exports, with which we seek to pay for these imports, have been subject to high barriers, particularly in the case of our agricultural products. We have not been able to sell enough to pay for our overseas expenditures, and so we have had to pay by incurring more and more short-term debts abroad. This is not a situation that can go on indefinitely; its sudden ending could be disruptive.

At a news conference the next day, Nixon said that the problems of Europe "will be put on the front burner," emphasizing again the question of trade. He noted that the character of the European Economic Community (the Common Market) was changing with the entry in 1973 of Britain and other countries, and that the United States must determine its position toward it: "We can either become competitors in a constructive way or . . . engage in economic confrontation that could lead to bitterness and which would hurt us both."

On February 1 and 2, Nixon discussed these problems with Prime Minister Edward Heath. But neither the Nixon-Heath discussions nor other diplomatic efforts could arrest the deterioration in America's financial posture. On February 12, Treasury Secretary George Shultz announced a 10-percent devaluation of the dollar. The principal purpose of the second devaluation was to make American goods abroad cheaper and thereby more competitive while making foreign imports dearer and more prohibitive. In fourteen months, the United States had decreased the value of the dollar by nearly 20 percent in terms of other currencies —and the line had to be held there. The devaluation did not come as a particular shock—it had been expected by experts—but Nixon wanted to convey a warning to the Europeans and Japan that things simply could not go on in the same old way. At a joint news conference with Shultz on February 13, the president served notice that the United States would get tough on trade.

The monetary shocks of the previous two years had finally convinced Nixon of the importance of international economics. The administration still had not evolved a fully comprehensive foreign economic policy (Kissinger's mind was always on something else, Butz had his own ideas on how to maneuver with food surpluses, and the State Department was kept at bay by the White House), but the president was increasingly aware of trade and monetary problems. On March 22 he sent up to Congress an

Annual International Economic Report, the first one ever prepared by a president, again insisting on world trade reform. In an accompanying message, Nixon wrote that "our major difficulties stem from relying too long upon outdated economic arrangements and institutions despite the rapid changes which have taken place in the world. . . . I have concluded that we must face up to more intense long-term competition in the world's markets rather than shrink from it."

Economics, in this case, had to be related to international politics, and Nixon and Kissinger decided that the time had come for a grand gesture, after all the public carping about how the Europeans and the Japanese were shortchanging the United States in trade. The grand gesture they devised was a "new Atlantic Charter"—three decades had elapsed since Roosevelt and Churchill had signed the original Atlantic Charter in the midst of World War II—that would tie Western Europe and Japan close to the United States in everything from economic policy to military affairs. Usually, such a proposal would be made publicly by the president or his secretary of state, but Nixon decided to assign it to Kissinger although nominally he was only an assistant to the president. The White House notion was that Kissinger, now internationally famous, would have more effect than Secretary Rogers, who was falling more and more into oblivion.

Kissinger chose the annual meeting of The Associated Press editors in New York on March 23 to deliver the "new Atlantic Charter" statement. It was one of his and Nixon's greatest foreign-policy duds—although James Reston, in a front-page article in *The New York Times*, compared it to the launching of the Marshall Plan in 1947. Aside from the *Times*, virtually nobody in a position of influence in the United States paid much attention to it. As for the West Europeans, they were aghast. In full prosperity, they saw no reason to attach themselves organically to the United States through new charters or declarations. They correctly suspected that the principal American motivation was to use such a new link to enforce economic pressures—and they wanted no part of it. The overriding European interest was to preserve the economic status quo, which was favorable to them, while remaining assured of United States military protection through the nuclear umbrella and the continued stationing of 300,000 United States troops on the Continent.

That the Europeans may have been selfish and ungrateful was beside the point. What mattered was that this was the way they felt about the American initiative; it was strange that Kissinger, a European by birth and cultural heritage, seemed to understand European politics so little. In any event, all that the Atlantic Charter idea produced was a year of pointless wrangling with the Europeans over what kind of declaration, if any, should emerge. Nixon tried to keep the "Year of Europe" concept alive (he was even planning to visit Europe in another grand gesture toward the end of 1973) in meetings with Premier Giulio Andreotti of Italy in mid-April and Chancellor Brandt at the beginning of May, and in talks with Pompidou in Iceland at the end of that month. But it was in vain.

The Nixon administration was learning international economics the hard way. First, there had been the trade and monetary crises of 1971 and 1973 that might perhaps have been avoided had the White House (even under Lyndon Johnson) been paying more attention to these problems. Then, there was energy.

Early in 1970, Nixon had refused to abolish oil import quotas in favor of a tariff system, responding largely to a huge lobbying campaign mounted by the big oil companies. By 1973, however, it finally dawned on the administration that domestic consumption was so greatly outstripping production that the freeing of imports had become necessary—even if it further damaged the trade balance—and that steps had to be taken to augment the output of energy at home. OPEC was increasingly aggressive, and all signs were that prices would keep rising. In a special message to Congress on energy policy on April 18, Nixon announced that he was ending "quantitative controls on oil imports" and establishing a National Energy Office. Heretofore there had been no centralized agency in the government dealing with energy. The president told Congress that as a result of the gap between energy consumption and production, "we face the possibility of temporary fuel shortages and some increases in fuel prices in America."

But the president again found it necessary to lead the nation astray in his judgment about the future. "If our energy resources are properly developed, they can fulfill our energy requirement for centuries to come," he said. Either he knew not what he was talking about, always a possibility in the increasingly isolated White House, or he felt that his statements must be "positive" regardless of circumstances.

In addition to ending the oil import quotas, Nixon ordered an acceleration in the leasing of undersea oil lands on the Outer Continental Shelf. He called for the revitalization of the depressed coal industry, even at the risk of setting aside certain environmental standards under the Clean Air Act; his comment was that "our concern for the 'general welfare' . . . should take into account considerations of national security and economic prosperity, as well as our environment." Finally, he proposed deregulation of natural gas prices to encourage the search for new production sources. The gas and oil industry had been demanding deregulation for years, and it was a hot political issue.

By late spring, Watergate had invaded every province of Nixon's conduct of foreign policy. His appeal on April 30 to be left in peace to be able to concentrate on world affairs went unheeded. And Nixon's grasp on the management of foreign affairs was perceptibly weakening. In the preceding weeks, the existence of the 1969–71 secret wiretapping program had been revealed, and Nixon had to acknowledge that he had approved it on "national security" grounds and that Kissinger, as head of the National Security Council apparatus, had been actively engaged in selecting wiretap targets. This was the first time that Kissinger had been tarred with the Watergate brush; his credibility, too, was coming under a cloud.

The president's new vulnerability was quickly reflected in congressional attitudes toward his Indochina policies. Throughout the four years of war under his presidency, Congress had repeatedly failed to approve any form of antiwar legislation, and the signing of the Vietnam peace settlement in January had defused criticism on the Hill. But the realization that the conflict in Laos and Cambodia was continuing—and that American bombers were continuing their destructive work in those two countries—revived congressional efforts to impose limits on the president's war powers.

On May 15, the Senate Appropriations Committee approved an amendment to the supplemental-appropriations bill, prohibiting the use of any funds provided in that bill, or subsequently appropriated, to support American combat activities in Cambodia and Laos. Nixon was sufficiently worried—and angry—to issue a special statement the next day condemning the action. He was very concerned, he said, that "having persevered to success these long years, the Congress has, on the very eve of negotiations to achieve compliance with [the peace] settlement, taken action that could severely undermine prospects for success." Then, he was applying the same peace-through-war policy in Cambodia that he had used against North Vietnam. But the vote in the Senate committee was only the first shot in the congressional battle with Nixon. He was once more invoking "national security" considerations to justify the misdeeds of Watergate. In his mind, there was a clear linkage between what had been done by the White House Plumbers and the protection of his conduct of foreign policy. He also feared that the unfolding Watergate investigation would further damage the secrecy that was fundamental to his method of diplomacy.

But the graver problem was of course Watergate. On May 22, the same day he was defending his Vietnam policies in a speech in Norfolk, Virginia, Nixon issued a statement in which he made the point that "it is not my intention to place a national security 'cover' on Watergate, but to separate national security issues from Watergate." His argument was that the Plumbers operation, organized in the first place to do away with news leaks that interfered with his secret diplomacy, had gotten out of hand, and now he was worried that investigations would reveal more national-security information, that "other sensitive documents are now threatened with disclosure." Providing his own extraordinary version of White House intelligence operations (the 1969 wiretaps, which he pronounced "legal," the 1970 Huston Plan, and the 1971 creation of the Plumbers Unit), the president argued that they were absolutely necessary for the conduct of foreign policy:

> By mid-1969, my administration had begun a number of highly sensitive foreign policy initiatives. They were aimed at ending the war in Vietnam, achieving a settlement in the Middle East, limiting nuclear arms, and establishing new relationships among the great powers. These involved highly secret diplomacy. They were closely interrelated. Leaks of secret information about any one could endanger all. Exactly that happened. News accounts appeared in 1969, which were obviously based on leaks—some of them extensive and detailed—by people having access to the most highly classified security materials. There was no way to carry forward these diplomatic initiatives unless further leaks could be prevented. This required finding the source of the leaks.

What did he mean when he said that his initiatives could not be carried forward unless new leaks were prevented and their sources discovered? There is no evidence to suggest that even a single diplomatic effort had been derailed by leaks (Kissinger's subsequent testimony made the same charges, but offered no proof) or that the White House investigations had "produced important leads that made it possible to tighten the security of highly sensitive materials." The truth is that the administration was unable to track down a single leak.

As to the events of 1971, the president singled out the publication of the Pentagon Papers by *The New York Times* as the event that triggered the operations by the Plumbers (although the Plumbers had been organized in April and the *Times* publication occurred in June). He said that this disclosure had raised

> serious questions about what and how much else might have been taken. . . . Other governments no longer knew whether they could deal with the United States in confidence. Against the background of the delicate negotiations the United States was then involved in on a number of fronts—with regard to Vietnam, China, the Middle East, nuclear arms limitations, U.S.–Soviet relations, and others—in which the utmost degree of confidentiality was vital, it posed a threat so grave as to require extraordinary actions.

But again, the argument did not hold water. American diplomacy had not been affected in the slightest by the publication of the Pentagon Papers—the best proof of this being that Kissinger was able to visit Peking secretly four weeks later. No foreign government was disturbed by the Ellsberg leak. A classified State Department study in 1971 showed that not a single friendly or neutral government had raised the question of confidence; the only place inquiries were made at all was in Canada, with which the United States was not engaged in any secret negotiations.

Nixon's basic assumption was that the impressive record he had built in international affairs—and his image as a world statesman—would protect him from domestic onslaughts. But it was at that point that he ceased to be an effective manager of foreign policy. Foreign governments were now, in 1973, beginning to question whether Nixon could still be an *interlocuteur valable;* from now on his conduct of foreign policy depended on the momentum that he had developed earlier—and on the performance of Henry Kissinger.

Leonid Brezhnev's visit to the United States in June for the second Soviet-American summit was just such an effect: the result of momentum. At the 1972 Moscow summit, Nixon and Brezhnev had agreed to meet annually; whatever Brezhnev might think of Nixon and Watergate (and there were indications that he, for one, was convinced that the American president would survive his crisis), he was in no position to cancel the trip. As for Nixon, the summit would be the perfect opportunity to shine again as a great peace statesman, turning public attention away from Watergate. Even the Senate seemed willing to help Nixon: Senator Ervin, the chairman of the Senate Watergate committee, agreed to suspend the sessions—America's greatest television attraction in years—during Brezhnev's stay in order not to embarrass the White House.

To prepare the summit, Kissinger had gone to Moscow on May 4 for five days of conferences with Brezhnev and his advisers. He was invited to stay at a Soviet government hunting lodge near the village of Zavidovo, ninety miles from Moscow, close to Brezhnev's own dacha. As usual, the American ambassador was not included. But actually, Brezhnev and Kissinger had little to negotiate. The American and Soviet delegations that had been meeting in Geneva since March to prepare a SALT II agreement had made little progress, and it was obvious that neither side was ready to take another major step in controlling strategic offensive weapons. For one thing, the Soviet Union was on the very verge of MIRVing its missiles; she certainly was not interested in any new limiting accords before achieving this breakthrough.

But a summit meeting requires new agreements—failure to produce any might cast new doubts on détente—and Brezhnev and Kissinger worked out a number of accords to be unveiled in Washington: one entitled On the Prevention of Nuclear War, another, Basic Principles of Negotiations on the Further Limitation of Strategic Offensive Arms. (The latter provided that SALT II should conclude by the end of 1974, an acknowledgment of how hard it was to move ahead in the control of nuclear weapons, much harder than Nixon had thought when the first SALT pact was signed a year earlier.)

When Kissinger returned to Washington on May 11 to brief Nixon, he found the president weary and depressed. Secretary Rogers called on him, too, before leaving on a tour of eight Latin American countries, and Kissinger of course stayed on for this meeting; he would not take the chance of letting Rogers confer alone with Nixon, even about Latin America, which was furthest from Kissinger's thoughts (except for Chile). And it was in keeping with the White House way of running foreign policy that the secretary of state was away from Washington while the summit was being prepared and new negotiations with North Vietnam were in the offing.

Coincidentally, it was also on May 11 that the White House announced that Kissinger and Le Duc Tho would meet in Paris to review the status of the peace settlement and "to find measures to bring about the strict implementation of that agreement." Both Nixon and Kissinger knew that unless a quick deal could be worked out with Hanoi over Cambodia, Congress might deprive the administration of military leverage there. On May 4, the House Democratic Policy Committee had overwhelmingly voted in favor of cutting off funds for further bombings in Cambodia, and on May 10 the full House had passed a resolution to that effect. On May 15, two days before Kissinger was to meet Tho, the Senate

Appropriations Committee approved its similar amendment.

Meeting Le Duc Tho on May 17, Kissinger was obviously negotiating from a weak position. The North Vietnamese knew what had been happening in Congress; they figured that the best policy was to wait. Likewise Tho gave not at all on the question of cease-fire enforcement: he knew that Nixon would be unable to reintroduce American air power in Vietnam.

On May 24, Kissinger was at the White House reporting to Nixon on his unproductive Paris effort. The president was annoyed. He desperately needed a foreign policy success to offset Watergate; not even the Soviet summit would be enough. He kept asking Kissinger whether some agreement with the North Vietnamese might be possible the following month, but Kissinger said he was not certain. Later that day, at the State Department for an afternoon reception for returned Vietnam POWs, Nixon delivered a long, rambling speech during which he repeated once more that when he took office three hundred Americans a week were being killed in Vietnam, there was no plan to end the war, no hope for the POWs, no communication with China, and "we were in constant confrontation with the Soviet Union." Then he went on the offensive:

I think it is time in this country to quit making national heroes out of those who steal secrets and publish them in the newspapers. . . . In order to continue these great initiatives for peace, we must have confidentiality, we must have secret communications. It isn't that we are trying to keep anything from the American people that the American people should know. It isn't that we are trying to keep something from the press that the press should print. But it is that what we are trying to do is to accomplish our goal, make a deal. And when we are dealing with potential adversaries, those negotiations must have the highest degree of confidentiality. And I can assure you that . . . I am going to meet my responsibility to protect the national security of the United States insofar as our secrets are concerned. . . . What I am concerned about is the highest classified documents in our National Security Council files, in the State Department, in the Defense Department, which if they get out, for example, in our arms control negotiations with the Soviets, would let them know our position before we ever got to the table. They don't tell us theirs. They have no problem keeping their secrets. I don't want, and you don't want, their system and that kind of control, but I say it is time for a new sense of responsibility in this country and a new sense of dedication of everybody in the bureaucracy that if a document is classified, keep it classified.

When Kissinger returned to Paris on June 6, the negotiations centered on preserving the Vietnam cease-fire. It took five days to hammer together a communiqué reaffirming the original agreement and clearing up a few of its ambiguities. But Kissinger and Le Duc Tho were able to agree only on minor points: New cease-fire orders were to be issued by Communist and Saigon commands, and local commanders at "places of direct contact" were to meet within twenty-four hours to work out their own cease-fires. The South Vietnamese were to allow Communist representatives on the Two-Party Joint Military Commission to move with greater freedom. The commission was to define the South Vietnamese "areas of control"—the point on which the original Paris agreement failed to give it any guidance—"as soon as possible." But none of this worked. After August, the two Vietnamese factions stopped holding meetings altogether. For all practical purposes, the Vietnam cease-fire became a fiction.

It was in these circumstances that Leonid Brezhnev and his delegation —Gromyko, Dobrynin, Foreign Trade Minister Patolichev, Civil Aviation Minister Boris Bugayev, Kremlin foreign-policy adviser Aleksandrov, and a number of others—arrived at Andrews Air Force Base from Moscow on May 16. They eschewed protocolary greetings and were taken by helicopter to Camp David to rest over the weekend. But, in advance of the official welcome, Nixon telephoned Brezhnev at the Maryland retreat from his vacation home in Key Biscayne to offer him private greetings. He also sent Kissinger to Camp David for more preparatory talks.

The second Soviet-American summit opened formally at 11:00 a.m. on Monday, June 18, when Brezhnev and his party flew by helicopter to the south lawn of the White House where Nixon awaited them with the cabinet.

(This was Brezhnev's first visit to the United States, and he was visibly delighted. He was all smiles as he debarked from the Marine helicopter and got into a black limousine to be driven the several hundred yards to the south portico of the White House.)

The first meeting lasted nearly four hours; it was a *tour d'horizon* that the White House described as being on "a more general, philosophical level." But Brezhnev and Nixon had an evident camaraderie, continuously joking and poking each other when in public. At the White House lawn reception, the Soviet leader waved to the VIP crowd and clenched his hands above his head in a boxer's gesture of triumph. Nixon, the introvert, tried to keep up as best he could.

The formal White House dinner that evening was another cordial occasion, full of jokes and laughter. But earlier in the day Leonid Zamyatin, director general of the Soviet news agency, Tass, had put the situation into sharper focus at a press briefing. In the knowledge that no major agreements on SALT were possible, the Russians had decided to concentrate on economic matters, specifically on the trade agreement that both governments had agreed to negotiate a year earlier. This, however, had been stymied by congressional refusal to grant Moscow most-favored-nation tariff treatment so long as obstacles were posed to the emigration of Soviet Jews. Addressing himself to this point, Zamyatin said the Soviets hoped that "common sense and political farsightedness will prevail in Congress," and when asked about Jewish emigration, Zamyatin heatedly answered that "those who ask such a question create the impression of proceeding from a position which is tantamount to interference in the internal policies of another sovereign state."

The next day, Brezhnev personally—and openly—took up the controversy surrounding Jewish emigration. He did so at a lunch he gave at Blair House, the official residence for visiting dignitaries, across the street from the White House, for seventeen members of the Senate Foreign Relations Committee and eight other congressmen. First, he cited statistics showing that Jewish emigration had been increasing despite the imposition of a departure tax. He said that 95 percent of Soviet Jews were free to leave. Then he told his guests: "We came to consolidate good things, not to quarrel. We can stay at home and quarrel. Any of you who wants to spoil good relations can make up bad questions, spread the rumor that sometime in the future we will impose a new tax. I can't understand why these things should impair good relations between us."

During the three-and-a-half-hour lunch, of which an hour and a half were taken up by an informal, wide-ranging speech by Brezhnev, the Russians stressed the need for equality and nondiscrimination in the economic relationship. Brezhnev left no doubt that the Soviet Union was eager to expand all these relationships—suggesting that he believed American businessmen shared this interest—but he warned, in effect, that there could be no trade agreement unless Congress extended the most-favored-nation clause to Moscow.

Economic matters dominated the summit for the rest of the day, but on Wednesday, June 20, Brezhnev and the president spent most of their time at Nixon's Aspen Lodge discussing formulas for a new SALT agreement. With nuclear forces of both superpowers quantitatively frozen under the 1972 pact, the new problem was *qualitative* control—which meant limiting MIRV technology, if possible. But this was the thorniest aspect of arms limitation; neither side was prepared to give up its MIRV freedom, and both were working furiously to develop new qualitative advantages. Nixon and Brezhnev's decision was to issue fresh instructions to their SALT delegations in Geneva to continue the negotiations. Then they turned to the proposed conference on reducing military forces in Central Europe.

Still, economics and trade remained foremost on the Russians' minds. In fact, they began to link them with SALT and the East-West talks on European force reductions. Arms control could be achieved more quickly, they suggested, if Soviet-American trade could be expanded. This was the opposite of the American philosophy that political and military agreements should pave the way for stepped-up economic cooperation.

Friday morning, June 22, his last day in Washington, Brezhnev was still pushing Soviet-American trade, this time playing the role of super-salesman at a Blair House meeting with fifty-one leading American business executives—ranging from Armand Hammer, the oil millionaire interested in joint ventures with the Russians for petroleum and natural-gas exploration, to Fred M. Seed, president of Cargill, a major wheat exporter, and Donald M. Kendall, whose company was swapping Pepsi-Cola for Russian vodka. Brezhnev, paying no attention to the fact that the session was running way beyond the allotted time, treated the businessmen to a ninety-minute discourse on trade between the two countries now, as he said, that the cold war was over. And Foreign Trade Minister Patolichev, at a luncheon given by the National Association of Manufacturers, promised that "we . . . will do anything and everything to help you develop your trade with us, and we hope you will do the same." The business executives gave him a round of enthusiastic applause.

The curious thing about the Soviet performance was that it won over America's most powerful corporate executives—proof, perhaps, that capitalists hold sales and profits above ideology. But Brezhnev left the politicians unconverted. Congress still held out for Soviet capitulation on Jewish emigration—it was couched in terms of defending "human rights" in the Soviet Union—as the price for a trade agreement that would include tariff preferences.

Whatever else may have been achieved in the Nixon-Brezhnev talks, the public was treated to the spectacle of a whole slew of agreements being signed. It started out at a State Department ceremony on June 19, with the summit barely under way, when Rogers and Gromyko signed agreements on transportation, oceanography, and culture, and Secretary Butz and Gromyko signed an agricultural agreement.

The most interesting of the four—all of them drafted ahead of time

—was this last. Its preamble recognized "the desirability of expanding relationships in agricultural trade and the exchange of information necessary for such trade," and its most important provision was for a "regular exchange of relevant information, including forward estimates, on production, consumption, demand and trade of major agricultural commodities" and "methods of forecasting the production, demand and consumption of major agricultural products, including econometric methods." This was quite crucial, because the catastrophic American wheat sale to Moscow had resulted to a large degree from Washington's total ignorance of Soviet production, consumption, and demand. The administration, presumably with Butz's concurrence, was obviously right in signing this five-year agreement, but as it developed later, it did not work. The Soviets went on regarding farm data, particularly crop forecasts and production estimates, as highly classified intelligence information; the United States went on selling wheat to the Russians without much of an idea of what it was doing.

As for the cultural agreement, it brought instant criticism from the liberal establishment. An editorial in *The Washington Post* expressed the general dismay well:

> The agreement on what is called "cultural exchange" is something very different, involving not technological and economic interests which Americans and Soviets share but fundamental values which they do not share at all. That Mr. Nixon, in his eagerness to carry off a successful summit with Mr. Brezhnev, should act in a way to sweep aside those differences is a matter for deep regret. . . . Many experts feel that the more the Soviet Union loosens up its political and economic relations with the West, the more it tightens the cultural screws at home. . . . Given these harsh facts, what was called for at this summit was, at the least, continuation of the modest but valuable exchange programs of the last 15 years or, at best, a candid statement by Mr. Nixon on his intention to make American participation in the exchanges more reflective of American values than of Soviet control. . . . By extending the agreement from 2 to 6 ½ years, he relinquished some of the all-too-small bargaining leverage with which Americans had protected the substance of the exchanges. . . . It has the effect of adding legitimacy to Soviet cultural controls and of letting the Kremlin pass off its regimented culture as the genuine Western article. . . . If that is what Mr. Nixon means to extoll in the nature of "détente" and a "generation of peace," he risks giving a bad name to what is an otherwise welcome accommodation between two great powers with a common interest in coming to terms in certain hard-headed and mutually beneficial ways.

The *Post* editorial was an illustration of the uneasy and ambivalent manner in which many Americans looked at détente. This uneasiness deepened with the passage of time, but meanwhile, Nixon was extracting every drop of success from the "summit." The spectacle went on unabated. At Camp David, Nixon gave Brezhnev a Lincoln Continental: television faithfully recorded pictures of the Soviet leader driving the president around in his new car. Then more agreements: on June 20 a convention on taxation, designed to avoid the payment of double income taxes by American and Soviet citizens (the first tax convention the United States had negotiated with a Communist country); and the declaration on Basic Principles of Negotiations on the Further Limitation of Strategic Offensive Arms, a set of seven ambiguous and vague guidelines for the SALT delegations in Geneva. Briefing newsmen on the significance of this accord—and straining to give it special importance—Kissinger underlined the fact, already widely known, that Nixon and Brezhnev had decided to set a 1974 target for the new SALT pact rather than wait until the interim agreement expired in 1977. Both the Basic Principles and Kissinger's briefing reflected a certain sense of unreality. There was little reason to think that all the monumental SALT problems could be resolved in eighteen months—but the White House was engaging in "theater," and Brezhnev seemed willing to help out a partner in trouble.

Also on June 21, the two leaders signed a new agreement on the peaceful uses of atomic energy aimed at developing new types of plants to satisfy worldwide energy needs. The following day, Treasury Secretary Shultz and Patolichev signed two protocols on Soviet-American business relations: one providing for discussions on the establishment of a Soviet-American chamber of commerce; the other dealing with office space in Moscow for American companies. (The Soviet government listed ten companies and banks to which it had issued accreditations to do business in Moscow; they included Occidental Petroleum, General Electric, International Harvester, the Chase Manhattan Bank, the Bank of America, and the First National City Bank.) But the big coup of the summit, if this is what it was, came on June 22. It was an eight-article agreement On the Prevention of Nuclear War, and it had been saved as a big secret for Brezhnev's last day in Washington. Actually, it added little to the safeguards worked out in the past, most notably the 1972 accord on preventing nuclear war by accident or "unauthorized act."

The new agreement provided for "urgent consultations" between Moscow and Washington if relations between them—or relations between one of them and another country—would "appear to involve the risk of nuclear conflict." But Article I, covering the first eventuality, was a piece of redundancy, and the second eventuality appeared to apply to the danger of a nuclear war between the Soviet Union and China. The idea seemed to be—and Kissinger confirmed it, in effect, in a press briefing on the new agreement—that if Washington perceived that the Soviets and Chinese were on the brink of war, it would intervene diplomatically with Moscow to talk it out of it. Again, it was a provision of dubious practicality if the Soviets had already reached the decision to pulverize China's cities.

The agreement was promptly forgotten, but its signing provided another opportunity for a display of summit cordiality, champagne toasts, and Nixon-Brezhnev clowning.

After all this, Nixon and Brezhnev flew aboard *Air Force One* to El Toro Marine Air Naval Station in California (circling en route for 20 minutes at 1000 feet above the top of the Grand Canyon so that the Soviet leader could admire the landscape). From El Toro, they went by helicopter to San Clemente, where Nixon had invited Brezhnev to stay at his house— Casa Pacifica. They had a quiet family dinner that evening, chatting easily about world affairs.

Most of Saturday, June 23, was spent in further conferences, chiefly on the Middle East and Europe. Brezhnev taped the television speech to the American people that was scheduled to be aired on Sunday night, and while American and Soviet teams were drafting the final communiqué, still another agreement was signed back in Washington: it provided for a limited expansion in airline service between the two countries. In San Clemente, Brezhnev was Nixon's guest of honor at a Mexican-style poolside reception attended by Hollywood celebrities. Bob Hope was there and so was Frank Sinatra.

Because of Brezhnev's fondness for American Westerns, Nixon had invited "several Western movie stars that you will recognize." But, the president added, "because this is a house of peace, every one of them has checked his holster belt with the pistols at the door before he came in." It was a lively party. At one point, Chuck Connors, in cowboy garb, lifted Brezhnev off the ground and carried him around.

The summit ended formally Sunday morning, June 24, when Nixon bade farewell to Brezhnev in San Clemente. He accepted Brezhnev's invitation to visit Moscow in 1974 for the third summit.

The joint communiqué restated what had been said and signed during the past eight days, but it also disclosed a major new decision: that the East-West conference on the reduction of military forces in Central

Europe would open in Vienna on October 30. Nixon had insisted on this *quid pro quo*—he would not have the political European security conference (already slated to begin in July) without an agreement on the military parley. The communiqué also reported that Nixon and Brezhnev believed that Soviet-American trade should aim at reaching a total of $2–3 billion over the next three years, an overoptimistic estimate.

But the greatest Soviet deceit—and Nixon's greatest failing—in the 1973 summit related to the Middle East. The joint communiqué devoted three carefully drafted paragraphs to this theme, but they concealed not only deep disagreements but the danger building up in that area. They said:

> The parties expressed their deep concern with the situation in the Middle East and exchanged opinions regarding ways of reaching a Middle East settlement.
> Each of the parties set forth its position on this problem.
> Both parties agreed to continue to exert their efforts to promote the quickest possible settlement in the Middle East. This settlement should be in accord with the interests of all states in the area, be consistent with their independence and sovereignty and should take into due account the legitimate interests of the Palestinian people.

But there was much more to this story. Kissinger himself acknowledged in his briefing on the communiqué that the Middle East had been one of "the most complex areas" of American-Soviet discussion and that there was no agreement on how the crisis should be resolved. What Kissinger failed to say—then or afterward—was that the United States had, for well over two months, advance intelligence that Egypt was preparing to attack Israel, that Nixon never raised this question with Brezhnev, and that Brezhnev throughout that cordial summit never warned the president of the impending war.

Diplomacy is made up of subtleties. But the diplomatic art is not only the conveying of subtlety; it is also the ability to detect it and understand it. Secret intelligence is an essential adjunct of diplomacy, and it cannot be discarded if it happens to run contrary to one's intellectual prejudices or vested interests. There are cardinal rules of good diplomacy and statesmanship. In the context of the Middle East situation before and during the 1973 summit, Nixon and Kissinger succeeded in violating all these rules—with disastrous consequences for the cause of peace they were supposedly serving.

First, considerable complacency over the Middle East had reigned in

the Nixon administration during the early part of the year; it was shared
to a certain extent by Israel. The principal reason for this was President
Sadat's expulsion of Soviet military personnel and most advisers from
Egypt the year before, together with the assumption that the Soviet
Union would not embark on new Middle Eastern adventures with the
ever-present danger of big-power confrontation. When Prime Minister
Golda Meir visited Nixon on March 2, there was no special sense of crisis
in the region; still the president agreed to grant Israel's request for
deliveries of forty-eight Phantoms and thirty-six Skyhawks over a four-
year period.

By April, however, the situation had begun to change. Intelligence
reports told of the resumption of Soviet arms shipments to Egypt and
Syria. Experts at the State Department became convinced that before
very long Sadat would create a new crisis and, quite possibly, break the
three-year-old cease-fire on the Suez Canal. He was impatient with the
stalemate, and his domestic political situation in Egypt was deteriorating.

Late in April, American defense attachés in Cairo were able to obtain
a detailed three-phase Egyptian attack plan against Israel. The first phase
called for crossing the Suez Canal into the Sinai Peninsula under cover
of Soviet-supplied SAM-6 and SAM-7 antiaircraft missiles. The second
phase provided for a follow-up advance, after breaching the Bar-Lev
Line, and the capture of the Mitla Pass, opening all of the Sinai to swift
advances by Egyptian armor. The third phase would be the conquest of
the entire peninsula up to the 1967 armistice lines. There were no plans
to invade Israel proper, as Sadat apparently expected to engage in diplomatic negotiations from a position of overwhelming strength. What the
American military attachés did not know was when the attack would be
launched.

The Defense Intelligence Agency, to which the attachés reported,
immediately disseminated the Egyptian plan to other members of the
Washington intelligence community as well as to the White House and
the State Department. It is certain that Kissinger was made aware of this
information. Nixon should have received it in his daily intelligence summaries. But there is no indication that either the president or his principal
foreign policy adviser reacted in any fashion to these reports. At the State
Department, the Egyptian attack plan was taken with utmost seriousness
by the Intelligence and Research Bureau and several officials in the office
of the assistant secretary for Near Eastern affairs. Officials also noted with
interest Syrian President Assad's trip to Moscow on May 3. Reconnais-
sance-satellite photography and agents' reports provided data on the

arrivals and deployment of new Soviet equipment, movements of the
Egyptian Army and its accelerated training in river-crossing operations,
presumably in preparation for a Suez thrust. Collating this data with the
Egyptian offensive plan, the Intelligence and Research Bureau drafted a
detailed study, specifically predicting an Egyptian attack coordinated with
a Syrian assault on the Golan Heights to occur between late June and
midautumn. The prediction of Syrian involvement was essentially a logical inference from what was known about Soviet military deliveries to
Damascus. (U.S. intelligence was not able to obtain the Syrian attack plan
until the first weeks of September.)

On May 31, Ray Cline, then director of the Intelligence and Research
Bureau, presented the secret study to Secretary Rogers, who had just
returned from Latin America. A copy went to Kissinger at the White
House. Still, there was no high-level reaction. This seems incomprehensible. One explanation is that Nixon, caught between his Watergate worries
and his briefings for the summit, could not spare the time to consider
developing dangers in the Middle East. The other explanation is that
Nixon and Kissinger simply refused to believe that on the eve of his
American visit Brezhnev would thus betray détente in the Middle East.
That Syria's president received a visit from Sadat on June 12 likewise
seemed to have no impact on the White House.

As a senior State Department official put it, "There was a complete
estrangement between the department and the White House at that time.
Rogers had absolutely no clout, and he could not convince Kissinger to
consider our studies seriously even if he believed them himself. All
Rogers worried about was how long he would stay on as secretary of state.
But we were also getting the word from the White House that they didn't
think the Egyptians could absorb and use all that new Soviet equipment
so well and so quickly. The fellows over at the NSC didn't think either
that the Russians knew what Sadat was planning. But we had no sound
information on that point. The CIA station in Cairo was plain lousy."

The Israelis were informed of the State Department study, but they,
too, remained complacent. They knew about the Egyptian river-crossing–
training program, but refused to believe that Sadat's army had acquired
the capability to storm across the canal. They were confident of their
strength, convinced that Egypt would be defeated again if it went to war.
The Israeli view was that Sadat had to negotiate on Jerusalem's terms—
in face-to-face talks—if he wanted diplomatic progress.

Meanwhile, however, a new and subtle dimension began to emerge.
Early in May, the Russians had started urging the United States through

all possible channels to "do something" in the Middle East to avoid a war. "Something," of course, meant to pressure Israel to become more flexible. This was what Dobrynin told Kissinger in their back-channel conversations, other Soviet embassy officials told the State Department, and the Soviet Foreign Ministry told the American embassy in Moscow. But the White House evidently failed to relate these messages to the warnings from American intelligence, though it began to dawn on Nixon and Kissinger that the Middle East situation was more explosive than they had realized. When Brezhnev, in Washington, kept pressing Nixon to adopt a strong stance toward Israel, he spoke in generalities, but there is no question that he was familiar with the Egyptian timetable. Soviet military involvement in Egypt had become too great, and the Egyptians had even told the Romanian government as early as April that they were planning an attack against Israel in the autumn.

Nixon, for his part, is not known to have told Brezhnev that the United States government knew of the Egyptian offensive plan, let alone to have protested Soviet military deliveries to Cairo. To have done so might have ruined the possibility of a festive summit, the political triumph Nixon so desperately needed. Thus a chance—however slight—to reverse the quickening drift toward war may have been lost out of concern for Nixon's personal political survival.

What Nixon did choose to do in the aftermath of the summit was to cover his diplomatic flanks. On June 30, in San Clemente, he received the permanent representatives of the fifteen member nations of the NATO Council, so as to reassure them that the United States and the Soviet Union had not formed a "condominium" to run the world at the expense of others. On July 6, he received the head of the Chinese liaison office in Washington, Ambassador Huang Chen, to assure him that none of the agreements reached with Brezhnev was a danger to China.

The summit meeting with the Russians had been a political reprieve for Richard Nixon. For eight days, he had been able to forget Watergate and perform as president of the United States—not as defendant in a deepening political scandal. But this illusory period did not last long: the pressures were building daily.

After Brezhnev's departure, the president remained behind in San Clemente for a week-long working vacation, but even there he could not escape Watergate.

On May 10, the House of Representatives had approved the second supplemental appropriations bill of 1973, including the provision prohibiting any newly appropriated funds, or any funds previously appropriated by Congress, from being used to support U.S. combat activities in or over Cambodia or Laos. In plain language, this meant that the administration would have to cease the bombings in Cambodia at once. By June 26, the Senate accepted (in conference) the House version and stood ready to vote.

Nixon, his aides recalled later, was livid with rage. He felt that Congress was betraying him, ignoring his appeal for a free hand in Indochina, where his diplomacy could be supported by the weight of bombs. He instantly vetoed the bill, explaining that he had done so "because of my grave concern that the enactment into law of the 'Cambodia rider' to this bill would cripple or destroy the chances for an effective negotiated settlement in Cambodia and the withdrawal of all North Vietnamese troops." Reminding Congress that an equitable "framework for peace" in Indochina had "finally" been put together in Paris in January, he said, "we are now involved in concluding the last element of that settlement, a Cambodian settlement. It would be nothing short of tragic if this great accomplishment, bought with the blood of so many Asians and Americans, were to be undone now by congressional action."

This was political blackmail, but Nixon was also misleading Congress. The last effort to persuade Hanoi to withdraw its forces from Cambodia had failed when Kissinger met with Le Duc Tho in Paris in May and early June. There were *no* negotiations on Cambodia in progress. Besides, relatively few North Vietnamese troops were in Cambodia in the summer of 1973; most of the fighting against the Lon Nol regime was being done by Khmer Rouge rebels. But Nixon went on to expostulate that a "total halt to U.S. air operations in Cambodia" would "virtually remove Communist incentive to negotiate and would thus seriously undercut ongoing diplomatic efforts to achieve a cease-fire in Cambodia" and would "effectively reverse the momentum towards lasting peace in Indochina set in motion last January and renewed in the four-party communiqué signed in Paris on June 13."

The president's rhetoric evidently worked, because the same day, June 27, his veto was sustained by the House by a surprising 241–173 majority. But the triumph was very shortlived. Two days later, the Senate approved, 64–26, Senator Fulbright's amendment to the supplemental appropriations bill barring the use of funds for American combat activities in Southeast Asia *after* August 15. This was a compromise of sorts, giving the administration forty-six days to prove that, indeed, bombings would help negotiations. The House passed the compromise version a few hours later, 236–169.

The administration lost the battle and Nixon had no choice but to sign the bill into law. He still wanted to have the last word, however. On August 3, he wrote identical letters to the Speaker of the House and the Senate Majority Leader informing them that the administration would obey the law, but noting that he would be "remiss in my constitutional responsibilities if I did not warn of the hazards that lie in the path chosen by Congress." With nothing to justify this assertion, Nixon again insisted that "we have had every confidence" that a Cambodian settlement could be achieved, but "the incentive to negotiate a settlement . . . has been undermined, and August 15 will accelerate this process." Despite the end of the bombings, "we will continue to provide all possible support permitted under the law"—a reference to continued shipments of military material and to covert operations that the United States conducted in Cambodia until the bitter end.

On August 14, Washington time, B-52s flew their last bombing mission over Cambodia. For the first time in four years and five months, Cambodia was free of the threat of American bombing that Richard Nixon had initiated clandestinely in March 1969.

Nixon's congressional defeat over Cambodia was the first major public display of the loss of confidence in him as president and commander in chief. Now the spirit of Watergate was affecting all his foreign policy-making. For five years, Nixon's opponents had sought the passage of a war powers act to limit presidential authority to involve the United States in wars through executive acts. On July 18, the House approved legislation requiring the president to report to Congress within forty-eight hours commitment of American troops to hostilities anywhere in the world. (Then, the president would have sixty days to seek congressional approval for such an act, although Congress retained the prerogative to act on its own before that deadline.) A somewhat different version passed the Senate on July 20. A conference compromise between the two houses was necessary, and as it developed, three months went by before further action was taken. This gave Nixon extra time to lobby against the bill, but to no avail. On October 12, both houses approved the conference report. On October 24, the president vetoed the legislation. But on November 7, the House overrode the veto 284–135 (a bare two-thirds majority), and the Senate did it by an easy 75–18, with large numbers of Republicans deserting the White House. This was the first time the Ninety-third Congress had overridden a presidential veto. From that day the president of the United States no longer enjoyed the freedom to commit American forces to wars of his choosing, ending a tradition that had begun when Truman went into Korea in 1950.

Nixon's problems with Congress were multiplying. On July 12, the Senate Foreign Relations Committee had rejected the nomination of G. McMurtrie Godley to be assistant secretary of state for East Asian and Pacific affairs to replace Marshall Green, too outspoken a man, who had been sent away as ambassador to Australia. The committee's rejection of Godley—a highly unusual act—was based on the fact that he had directed activities of the CIA's Clandestine Army in Laos as well as air strikes in that country in his capacity as ambassador during the past four years. The committee concluded that, under the circumstances, Godley was not suitable for a sensitive policy-making post. It was obviously a slap at Nixon, who reacted with a public statement expressing his deep regret that a "distinguished Foreign Service officer should be penalized for faithfully carrying out the policies of his government, which were not set by him."

Congress's attitude toward administration policies in Indochina was motivated to an important degree by President Thieu's behavior in Saigon, which many on the Hill found simply appalling. Amnesty International, a London-based organization concerned with the treatment of political prisoners throughout the world, charged in a report in July that Thieu was holding 100,000 civilians in his prisons despite the Vietnam peace agreement. Simultaneously, a Saigon organization of dissident priests and students claimed that there were 202,000 political prisoners in South Vietnam, subjected to "unbearable" physical conditions and torture. In April, Thieu had imprisoned the presidents of four South Vietnamese labor unions—they were still imprisoned in July—for opposing his Democracy Party. He was planning a Thieu-type parliamentary election for August, also in disregard of the political machinery set up by the Paris agreement.

The mounting pressures were beginning to take their toll on Nixon. On July 12, he entered Bethesda Naval Hospital in Washington with viral pneumonia. On his return to the White House eight days later, he spoke at length to his staff in the Rose Garden. It was the first time in thirteen years that he had been hospitalized, he told them; in fighting spirit, he went on: "Any suggestion that this president is ever going to slow down while he is president or is ever going to leave his office until he continues to do the job and finishes the job he was elected to do, anyone who suggests that, that is just plain poppycock." Again, he invoked foreign policy as his most important mandate: "Here in this office is where the great decisions are going to be made that are going to determine whether we have peace in this world for years to come. We have made such great strides toward that goal. . . . And what we were elected to do, we are going to do, and let others wallow in Watergate, we are going to do our job."

After spending a weekend of rest at Camp David, Nixon devoted much of the balance of July and the beginning of August to foreign affairs. On July 24 and 25, he conferred with the shah of Iran, entertained him at a White House dinner, and attended the shah's dinner at the Iranian embassy.

In a welcoming speech, he noted that the shah was the first foreign statesman he was seeing after the Brezhnev summit (in 1972, Nixon had stopped in Tehran to see the shah after the Moscow summit) and that Iran was in a "very key, central area" in a region that posed "a potential threat to peace." There is no record of whether Nixon raised the question of oil or OPEC, but he and the shah talked at length about Persian Gulf defenses; American arms were flowing to Iran at a more and more rapid rate.

On July 26, Nixon was busy coping with requests from the Senate Watergate committee and Judge John J. Sirica for presidential tape recordings and documents (the committee had just learned from Alexander Butterfield that the president had been secretly recording all the conversations in the Oval Office and his living quarters); he decided to hold them back on the grounds of executive privilege. But on July 30, he was once again the host, receiving Australia's Prime Minister Gough Whitlam. He spent most of his time on July 31 and August 1 with Prime Minister Tanaka—trade and monetary reform continued to be the outstanding issues vis-à-vis Japan—but Watergate was now continuously on his mind. Toasting Tanaka at the White House dinner, Nixon said: "Let others spend their time dealing with the murky, small, unimportant vicious little things. We have spent our time and will spend our time in building a better world." (Both he and Tanaka would be out of office within a year under remarkably similar circumstances.)

The next day, the president continued the international offensive, welcoming Albert-Bernard Bongo, president of Gabon, to the White House. Then it was back to Watergate. On August 15, he argued that his invocation of executive privilege on testimony by John Ehrlichman and others about White House activities was justified because "disclosure would unquestionably damage the national security." He would not make his tapes available to investigators because, he said, in the future "no one would want to risk being known as the person who recommended a policy that ultimately did not work. . . . No one would want to speak bluntly about public figures here and abroad."

And a few days later, at the national convention of the Veterans of
Foreign Wars in New Orleans, he offered a bitter and defensive account
of his diplomatic policies. In particular, he addressed himself to the now
growing public criticism of the bombing in Cambodia:

> The president of the United States has been accused of a secret
> bombing campaign against the defenseless and neutral country of
> Cambodia in 1969. That was two months after I became president.
> . . . I remember the meeting in which that decision was made. Mr.
> Laird, who was then secretary of defense, remembers; he was there.
> Henry Kissinger, to whom you will give an award tonight, remembers
> it; he was there. The chairman of the CIA was there. The secretary of
> state, Secretary Rogers, was there. And we looked over what was, to
> us, a totally indefensible position. . . . So we decided to do something
> about it. . . . We found that there was a strip of land ten to fifteen miles
> wide in which there were no Cambodians whatever. It was totally
> occupied by the enemy, the North Vietnamese. . . . The suggestion
> that these staging areas . . . a few thousand yards from American
> troops were what we call neutral territory, exempt from counterattack
> or bombing, is simply ludicrous. . . . The Communists had made a
> mockery of the neutrality of these border regions. . . . The United
> States was under no moral obligation to respect the sham.

The president also went on defending his 1972 decisions to mine
Haiphong harbor and order the massive Christmas bombings of Hanoi.
He recited in detail the history of the double détente, argued against cuts
in the defense budget, and ended on the usual note intended to enhance
his stature as the statesman of peace. The VFW convention then presented Nixon and Kissinger with its Peace Award.

But his fighting words notwithstanding, it was in military policy that
Nixon found himself most persistently attacked. In mid-July, the Senate
Armed Services Subcommittee on Research and Development had eliminated more than $500 million from the administration's request for funds
for the development of new strategic weapons during fiscal 1974. On
August 1, the full Senate Armed Services Committee, which normally
gave the Pentagon almost everything it wanted, removed $885 million
requested for accelerated development of the Trident missile-launching
submarine. These were major blows. Nixon's commitment to develop the
Trident had been part of the *quid pro quo* with the Joint Chiefs of Staff by
which they agreed to support the 1972 SALT agreements. Moreover, the
interim agreement on offensive weapons was, from the American viewpoint, based on the concept that the first Tridents—a submarine vastly

superior to the Polaris in range and nuclear firepower—would be deployed by 1978, two years ahead of the original schedule. This was why the Pentagon temporarily accepted a lower number of ballistic submarines than was granted the Soviet Union under the SALT freeze. The navy saw no sense in building additional obsolescent Polaris submarines with Poseidon missiles to stay within the allowable 41-submarine ceiling; it preferred to await the availability of the Trident to phase out its 41 Polaris boats. New Trident I missiles to be placed aboard the new boats could hit Moscow from a distance of 4000 miles. The Trident II missile, still in development, would have a 6000-mile range. The Poseidon missile had a 2500-mile range.

The administration, and especially the Pentagon, believed that the committee's action placed the United States at a grave strategic disadvantage. The Russians were moving apace in their modern submarine-building program; in 1973, they had around 33 and, under the SALT agreement, they were permitted to build up to 62 if they retired older boats and equivalent numbers of land-based ICBMs. The navy's idea, therefore, was to be able to deploy 10 Trident submarines by 1978, each with 24 Trident missiles.

The committee, however (including such pro-Pentagon members as Barry Goldwater, Peter Dominick, and Harry Byrd), argued that the Tridents, costing $1.3 billion each, were too expensive and not really necessary. It took the view that the Polaris was adequate and, in effect, invulnerable to Soviet attack. It authorized funds for the continuing development of the Trident, but on a slow schedule, making it unlikely that the new boat would be operational before the early 1980s. The overriding consideration was that U.S. missiles were mostly MIRVed: there would be 7000 MIRVed warheads in the American arsenal in 1975—5000 of them on submarine-based Poseidons and most of the rest on Minuteman III land-based missiles. (MIRVed Minutemen were flight tested in late 1973.) The committee concluded that the MIRV advantage left the United States with a considerable edge, even without the Trident, though the MIRV monopoly would end very soon. The senators also cut from the Pentagon's request $15.4 million to start the development of the cruise missile, a winged missile with its own guidance system. The Pentagon likewise lost funds for a new mobile ICBM missile.

There was more bad news in the strategic field. Despite worldwide protests, the French (who never signed the test-ban treaty and who, under de Gaulle, had removed their armed forces from the NATO military framework) exploded nuclear devices July 21 and 29 on a test range

in the South Pacific. At the same time, they began building new inter-
mediate-range ballistic missiles with hydrogen-bomb warheads at launch
sites in southeastern France. The Pacific testing was related to the expansion of the French nuclear strike force—an expansion deemed necessary
because of serious reservations about the wisdom of relying on the
American nuclear umbrella over Europe.

But the worst news, long anticipated as it may have been, came on
August 17, when James Schlesinger, the new secretary of defense, announced that the Soviet Union had successfully flight tested MIRV-
equipped missiles. American intelligence, using over-the-horizon radars
and telemetry monitors, had established the day before that the Russians
had finally been able to test MIRVed SS-17 and SS-18 missiles (the SS-18
was the largest Soviet rocket, with immense throw-weight) on a test range
on the Kamchatka Peninsula in northeastern Siberia. The SS-18 carried
at least six hydrogen warheads in the MIRV cluster, each warhead pack-
ing one-megaton (the equivalent of one million tons of TNT) power.
(The American Minuteman II carried three smaller warheads.) Schlesinger added that the Russians might also have tested MIRVed SS-16 and
SS-19 missiles, the latter being the newest addition to the Soviet arsenal.
They had begun a series of "very adventuresome" tests in May, he said,
achieving their MIRV breakthrough in mid-August.

Actually, it had taken the Soviet Union a year longer to flight test
MIRV missiles than the CIA had predicted in 1969 (the Defense Department had argued at the time that the Russians were already on the verge
of MIRVing), but the shock was no less for that. Politically, it was the kind
of news Nixon did not need, less than two months after having enthusias-
tically hailed détente and the success of his summit meeting with Brezhnev. The Soviet MIRVing changed the whole strategic power picture.
Now, the Soviet Union had a combination of huge missiles, with throw-
weights vastly exceeding the American Minuteman's, and with MIRV
technology. Schlesinger, an expert in strategic weapons (much more
accomplished in this area than Kissinger), observed, "One may have been
surprised that they have all these missiles [but] it is the breadth of the
development, not the race, that is surprising." In his view, which turned
out to be accurate, the Soviets intended to arm all their ICBMs with MIRV
clusters, and they would be ready to deploy them operationally by 1975.
By the end of the decade, the Russians were likely to have as many
MIRVed missiles as the United States.

As for the SALT negotiations, he said, the Soviet MIRVing had great
significance because "our ability to monitor is rapidly, very rapidly deteri-

orating. . . . Once they come through the flight test, [our] ability to verify will be substantially undermined." MIRV flight testing was detectable through American intelligence means—long-range radars and telemetry —but the actual deployment could be determined only with the greatest difficulty, and probably not very reliably. Therefore, he said, the new phase of SALT talks must aim to prevent strategic "imbalance" in the Soviets' favor, though he admitted that Moscow was not "particularly interested" in MIRV limitations. "The minimal point one can make is that the Soviets are unwilling not to demonstrate technology that the United States has demonstrated. . . . Imagery is important."

The new defense secretary chose not to be alarmist, though. He said, quite correctly, that "a first-strike capability, if properly understood in terms of a disarming capability, is obtainable by neither side; neither the Soviets nor ourselves." Nevertheless, the entire development served to change defense politics in Washington. Above all, it set Schlesinger against Kissinger, who seemed to have more faith in a reasonable SALT II agreement with Moscow. Schlesinger took the view that no matter what Nixon and Brezhnev had decided at the summit, there simply was no chance for a new SALT treaty by the end of 1974, or even beyond it. An agreement would be possible only if the Russians agreed to broader verification procedures, which he did not expect them to do, and to a MIRV-limitation accord, which he did not think Moscow would ever accept.

Kissinger was more optimistic. The problem was that Kissinger, as the coauthor of détente, was intellectually tied to this policy and could not envisage its defeat; to him "imagery" mattered, too. The MIRV issue and its effect on SALT was the beginning of an increasingly strained relationship between the two top intellectuals in the Nixon administration.

On August 20, at the State Department, Rogers, holding his first news conference since February 15 (and his last as secretary of state), seemed closer to Schlesinger's position. He said that the Soviet MIRV success "has somewhat reduced," but not ruled out, the chances for a SALT agreement on qualitative limits, but it was now "a matter of greater urgency than before" that a SALT agreement be negotiated by the end of 1974. This was the official White House line. On September 20, the Pentagon announced that it had detected successful Soviet MIRV flight tests on a third missile, the SS-19.

Rogers's news conference also served to remind Americans how badly the Vietnam cease-fire was deteriorating. In disgust, Canada had withdrawn its contingent from the international truce-supervisory commission at the end of July, and Rogers now announced that Iran was taking its place. Everything was coming apart in Nixon's foreign-policy structure.

Not only that, but it had become clear that Richard Nixon had neither the time nor the attention span required to be an effective manager of American policy. And indeed, it was the president's own conclusion that the foreign-policy apparatus had to be newly strengthened from within, that he had to give up a part of the decision-making burden. What Nixon needed was a man with a commanding personality to assume the direction of American international affairs; he himself could no longer spend long hours with Kissinger going over the concepts and details of new policies.

The logical answer was to transfer maximum authority to the long-neglected State Department, where power would be vested in the secretary of state. But in Nixon's judgment, this could not be done so long as William Rogers remained at the post. Rogers was fine for ceremonial and advisory purposes when Kissinger and Nixon ran the show from the White House, but he could not be left on his own. Then there was the Kissinger-Rogers problem. Nixon knew that Kissinger would not stay for a moment in the White House if Rogers's hand were strengthened. After four and a half years Kissinger was still insecure about Rogers, seeing him as his great rival (which Rogers was not and could not be) and suspecting Rogers of plots against him. But the president could not let Kissinger go.

Under the circumstances, the only solution was to elevate Kissinger to be secretary of state while letting him retain his White House post as the president's assistant for national security affairs.

The president met privately with Rogers at the White House on August 19, explained the situation, and in effect, asked for his resignation for the good of the country. Again, he drew heavily on their old personal friendship. Rogers, increasingly uncomfortable in the administration, had really no choice. When he held his news conference on the twentieth, he had already submitted his resignation.

Nixon arrived in San Clemente late on August 20 for a long weekend after addressing the VFW in New Orleans. Kissinger was with him, and the next day Nixon invited Kissinger and his two children to swim in his pool. According to the Kalb brothers, Kissinger's biographers, it was there, at the shallow end of the pool, that Nixon informed Kissinger that he proposed to nominate him the next day as the new secretary of state. Actually, this was no great surprise. Kissinger had known for several days from General Haig that there would soon be a new secretary of state, and

Nixon himself had told Kissinger that Rogers planned to resign.

Now, in the San Clemente pool, Kissinger promptly agreed to wear two Washington hats: he would have total and undisputed control of foreign policy—except for whatever supervision Nixon cared to exercise. But of course Kissinger knew that by now the president was largely out of commission. With a new man at the State Department, the détente policies he and Nixon had so laboriously evolved might be eroded. In his own mind, he had decided to leave if someone else received the State Department.

On August 22, Nixon held a news conference in San Clemente, his first in five months. He told reporters that Rogers had wanted to leave at the end of the first term—which was news to Rogers—but had agreed to stay on for another eight months "because we had some enormously important problems coming up, including the negotiations which resulted in the end of the war in Vietnam, the Soviet summit, the European security conference, as well as in other areas." Now he was out, as of September 3. And the Kissinger appointment was of course easy to explain. The man's qualifications, he said, were "well known," and holding both foreign-policy posts, he would effect "a closer coordination between the White House, the national security affairs, the NSC, and the State Department."

It was a measure of what interested public opinion at that moment that not a single question was asked about Kissinger's nomination. The only question on foreign policy—and this, too, related to the growing cluster of charges against Nixon—had to do with the secret bombings of Cambodia, and whether the president owed "an apology to the American people." Nixon considered that the public not only did not need an apology, it did not *want* one. Then he moved on to questions about still another scandal erupting in his administration: the charges that Vice President Agenew had been involved in bribe taking. "The vice president has not been indicted," he replied angrily. "Charges have been thrown out by innuendo, and otherwise, which he has denied to me personally and which he has denied publicly."

Whether the public was interested or not, the fact was that the Kissinger appointment was an event of considerable significance. For a start, the new secretary of state was in a difficult position. He was the first foreign-born secretary of state and the first Jew in the United States to be designated to the senior post in the cabinet. His being Jewish, some observers thought, might interfere with American policies in the Middle East. He was the most important spokesman for an administration that was wallowing deeper and deeper in scandal, and soon he would become, by default, the nearest thing the United States ever had to a prime minister. Yet Kissinger was confident that he was politically unassailable in his new job. "I will conduct the foreign policy of the United States regardless of religious and national heritage," he proclaimed. "There is no other country in the world in which a man of my background could be considered for an office such as the one for which I have been nominated, and that imposes on me a very grave responsibility which I will pursue in the national interest."

Still, the Senate Foreign Relations Committee would not confirm Kissinger until September 18, for it was concerned with his part in the 1969 wiretaps (it even set up a special subcommittee to meet with Attorney General Richardson to assure itself that the proposed secretary of state was personally above reproach), the Cambodia bombings, and the American role in Chile, where a military group had just overthrown the government of President Allende. Eventually Kissinger satisfied the senators—he denied that he did more than supply the FBI with the names of aides who had access to classified information, and he denied that the administration had anything to do with Chile—for on September 21 the full Senate voted overwhelmingly to consent to his nomination. On September 22, Kissinger was sworn in at the White House as secretary of state.

At the swearing-in ceremony, Nixon made a rather bizarre speech, devoting several minutes to the fact that, according to the White House barber, Kissinger was the first secretary of state since World War II who did not part his hair. Acheson, Dulles, and Rogers had parted their hair, he informed the audience, and the balding Dean Rusk parted whatever hair he had. But "the parting of the hair has no relevance to the functions of the secretary of state," he went on, and then uttered the usual platitudes: "Dr. Kissinger assumes this office at a watershed time in American foreign policy, at a time when America is at peace for the first time in twelve years, at a time when we recognize that the only thing more difficult than getting peace is keeping it, at a time, therefore, when building the structures of peace is so important."

Kissinger replied, in an obvious allusion to the Watergate tensions, that if his European origins "can contribute anything to the formulation of our policy, it is that at an early age I have seen what can happen to a society that is based on hatred and strength and distrust, and that I experienced then what America means to other people, its hope and its idealism. . . ."

By late September, Nixon had in place a wholly new national-security team: Kissinger at State, Schlesinger at Defense, and William Colby, since September 4, as the new CIA director. And Richardson was the back-up at the Justice Department with his past experience in foreign policy. Ironically, Nixon now had the intellectually best equipped cabinet he ever assembled.

But the problems and crises were too much even for such a group to keep under control. In a real sense, the United States government was headless: the president had ceased to function as such, and improvisation was the best that was left to the new men. Yet MIRVing by the Soviet Union, growing oil shortages, and the winds of war in the Middle East were not matters for haphazard invention. Nor was the immediate threat of crisis that was, tragically, of Washington's own making.

Chapter 26

On September 11, the Chilean armed forces staged a revolution to oust the government of President Allende, who had been in office for three years and one week. Allende died in the Moneda Palace as he defended himself in his office. The last photograph the world has of Allende shows him wearing a helmet and holding a submachine gun. It remains unclear whether he was killed or committed suicide; his widow claims he was murdered.

The military revolution interrupted democratic rule in Chile that had lasted for forty-one years—the last successful military coup in that country had occurred in 1932—a record of democratic continuity unmatched in Latin American history. But the 1973 revolution also produced a staggering bloodbath: thousands of Allende's supporters were killed in pitched battles with the troops; many hundreds were executed without trial; tens of thousands were imprisoned; brutal and vicious torture became commonplace. Chile became the most repressive dictatorship in the West.

In making a balance sheet of the Nixonian "structure of peace," it is beyond question that the president and Kissinger must share in the blame for these terrible events. The Nixon administration did not directly organize the anit-Allende revolution, of course. This was done by the Chilean armed forces themselves. But through the CIA's covert operations in Chile, the application of vast economic pressures, and military assistance to the Chilean armed forces, the United States government did without any question help to create a situation in which the anti-Allende coup became possible. In the famous phrase of a United States congressman, Washington did everything it could to "destabilize" Chile and make it ripe for the coup.

To finance covert CIA operations in Chile, the White House Forty Committee had approved $8,809,166 in secret funds between 1970 and 1973. Much of this went to support anti-Allende political parties and press. Propaganda was a principal means by which the CIA made for the "destabilization" and a revolutionary climate. As the Senate Select Committee on Intelligence Activities pointed out in its report, "A CIA project renewal memorandum concluded that *El Mercurio* [Chile's principal newspaper, the bastion of antiregime opposition, and a major recipient of CIA funds] and other media outlets supported by the Agency had played an important role in setting the stage for the September 11, 1973 military coup which overthrew Allende."

Even before that, the U.S. government had, of course, also involved American companies in its plot, personally directed by Nixon, to encourage a military coup to keep the Chilean president-elect from being inaugurated (Nixon later denied he had given such orders, but it was his word against sworn testimony by former CIA Director Helms).

When 1973 began, the United States had been deeply engaged in anti-Allende policies for nearly two and a half years. Its aim at the outset of the new year was to help antiregime parties win a two-thirds majority in both legislative houses in the March elections in order to block Allende's legislation. In October 1972, the Forty Committee had approved $1,427,666 to assist opposition candidates. On February 12, 1973, the committee authorized an additional $200,000 for that purpose; in all, the Forty Committee approved a total of $1.2 million for subversive operations in Chile in 1973.

Money, however, did not buy votes in Chile. The vote tally for the March 4 congressional elections showed that Popular Unity, the Allende coalition, had won 43.4 percent of the vote, considerably more than it had received in 1970, when Allende was first elected with a plurality, but no majority, in a three-way race. The 1973 results were better than Allende had expected. If nothing else, they showed that close to half the voters supported the government. And the very fact that elections were held at all (not even the opposition had claimed that they were rigged) made a mockery of Kissinger's prediction in 1970 that "I have yet to meet somebody who firmly believes that if Allende wins, there is likely to be another free election in Chile." Certainly the elections did not provide any basis for a foreign country to intervene in Chile to "save democracy."

The Nixon administration was thus forced to reassess its Chilean strategy. Now only direct action could oust Allende. Two alternatives were open: one was continued economic pressure to "destabilize" Chile, and the other was stepped-up CIA activity in conjunction with groups in the Chilean armed forces.

Coincidentally or not, Chilean-American negotiations on the rollover of Chile's huge external debt (held mainly by the United States) were suspended because of a complete impasse on March 22, less than three weeks after the congressional elections. The deadlock was partly due to American insistence that the question of compensation payments for expropriated property, mainly copper mines and ITT's telephone company, be made part of the debt renegotiation. Rightly or wrongly, the Chileans refused to accept this requirement.

In his annual foreign-policy report to Congress on May 3, Nixon made no mention of Chile—for the first time in three years. Evidently, this was a subject the administration no longer cared to discuss publicly.

In the late spring and early summer, the Allende regime came under mounting internal and external pressures. Copper miners, the mainstay of the Chilean economy, struck because of the government's refusal to raise their wages (there is no indication that the CIA was behind this strike) when Chile acted on June 5 to suspend foreign shipments of copper. This damaged Chile's disastrous foreign-exchange position even more, further limiting food and other imports. And because of American pressures, the Chileans no longer had access to credit lines elsewhere in most of the West.

On June 20, thousands of teachers, physicians, and students went on strike to protest the government's handling of the copper miners' stoppage, by now in its third month. The next day, Allende's supporters and opponents fought a bloody battle in Santiago, using guns and bombs. The government obtained a court order closing down *El Mercurio* for six days because of its open advocacy of insurrection, but within twenty-four hours a higher court had voided the order. Chile under Allende had not yet become the dictatorship Washington believed it to be.

The situation grew increasingly serious for Allende. On June 29, a Santiago garrison rebel unit took over the capital's downtown area, attacking the Moneda Palace and the Defense Ministry building across the street. The president still had the loyalty of the armed forces, however, and the uprising was quickly suppressed. On July 17, another military conspiracy was foiled; Allende's naval aide-de-camp was killed by unidentified gunners.

On July 26, truck owners throughout the country went on strike, and a week later, owners of 110,000 buses and taxis joined them. On August 27, Chilean shop owners also proclaimed a strike, and on September 4, the Confederation of Professional Employees launched a strike of indefinite duration. This was the war of the middle class against Allende, and it paralyzed the country. Now it seemed to be only a question of time before the army moved against Allende. All along, the strategy of Allende's opponents, strongly encouraged by the United States, was to create such a state of chaos in Chile as to compel the armed forces to intervene. It was succeeding.

While there is no evidence that the CIA directly supported the strikes, agency funds were passed to private Chilean groups that were linked to the strikers. And on August 20, the Forty Committee, chaired by Kissinger, approved $1 million to back opposition political parties and private organizations in Chile.

Now the anti-Allende army men began to move into key posts. General Carlos Prats González, an Allende supporter, resigned on August 23 as defense minister and army commander. To replace him as army chief, Allende named General Augusto Pinochet Ugarte—a fatal mistake. Pinochet, however, was thought to be loyal, and he insisted on his loyalty in several conversations with Allende and Orlando Letelier, the new civilian defense minister. Yet there are reasons to believe that the CIA's Santiago station was aware of Pinochet's inclinations.

If there was any single event that triggered the coup, it was Allende's decision to call a national referendum on the question of replacing the two-house parliament with a unicameral congress. His timing could not have been worse, but Allende was evidently now desperate. His idea was that a unicameral congress could assure the passage of social and economic legislation he considered necessary. To his enemies, this was the sign that the president was going down the road to a Marxist dictatorship.

In Washington, the administration watched the Chilean events with intense interest. A joint antisubmarine-warfare exercise with the Chileans, code-named Operation Unitas, had been scheduled for mid-September, but the State Department ordered the U.S. Navy to cancel it. The administration did not want U.S. warships in or near Chilean ports if a revolution erupted. This did show a certain foresight on Washington's part, but the naval task force was kept in the general vicinity of Chile as a precaution that the administration never explained.

When the coup came early on September 11, Kissinger immediately convoked WASAG, the crisis-management group at the White House. As he testified that week at the Senate hearings on his confirmation, his principal concern was that the naval task force should be free of any involvement with the Chilean upheaval, and he strongly denied that the United States had participated in any way in plotting Allende's downfall. The Senate committee took his word for it, but his testimony appears to border on perjury.

Colby, who took over as CIA director four days before the Chilean revolution, was more candid. Much of his knowledge about the Chilean operations derived from his earlier experience as the agency's deputy director for operations (as clandestine services were now called). In secret testimony before the Senate Subcommittee on Multinational Corporations on March 12, 1974, Colby said of the CIA's activities in Chile that "our object was to help create conditions which would make it impossible for Allende, or Popular Unity, to succeed himself" in 1976. He added that "we did have interest in groups opposed to Allende to help insure that his government wasn't successful."

Ironically, the intelligence analysts maintained until the end that Allende presented no "Marxist danger." A National Intelligence Estimate on Chile issued a week before the coup said that "a political standoff" was the most likely course of events there. As summarized by the Senate intelligence committee, this NIE said that "Allende had not consolidated the power of his Marxist regime," that "the bulk of low-income Chileans believed that he had improved their conditions and represented their interests," and that "the growth in support for his coalition reflected his political ability as well as the popularity of his measures." The NIE warned, however, that the "growing polarization of the Chilean society was wearing away the Chilean predilection for political compromise." The intelligence analysts did make one mistake: unaware of the covert activities by their colleagues on the clandestine side and their connections with the Chilean Army, they predicted that "there was only an outside chance that the military would move to force Allende from office."

Whatever the actual degree of American participation in preparing the September 11 revolution in Chile, the Nixon administration embraced the new military junta, headed by General Pinochet, with boundless enthusiasm. It took upon itself the task of helping Pinochet look good in the eyes of the world. CIA agents in Santiago assisted Chilean military intelligence in drafting bogus "Z-Plan" documents alleging that Allende and his supporters were planning to behead Chilean military commanders. These were issued by the junta to justify the coup. And on October 15, when the junta's repression was reaching its bloody climax, the Forty Committee approved $34,000 in covert CIA funds to finance an anti-Allende radio station and to pay for foreign travel by junta spokesmen on public-relations assignments. It was never explained why the United States had acquired responsibility for building up Pinochet as an admirable statesman.

The Senate Select Committee on Intelligence Activities described the CIA's postcoup operations in Chile as follows:

The goal . . . was to assist the Junta in gaining a more positive image, both at home and abroad, and to maintain access to the command levels of the Chilean government. Another goal, achieved in part through work done at the opposition research organization before the coup, was to help the new government organize and implement new policies. Project files record that CIA collaborators were involved in preparing an initial overall economic plan which has served as the basis for the Junta's most important economic decisions. . . . Access to certain Chilean media outlets was retained in order to enable the CIA Station in Santiago to help build Chilean support for the new government as well as to influence the direction of the government, through pressures exercised by the mass media. These media outlets attempted to present the Junta in the most positive light for the Chilean public and to assist foreign journalists in Chile to obtain facts about the local situation. Further, two CIA collaborators assisted the Junta in preparing a *White Book of the Change of Government in Chile.* The *White Book* . . . was written to justify the overthrow of Allende.

Chile was one of the shadowy sides of Richard Nixon's "structure of peace." He and Kissinger, through secrecy, deceit, and manipulation, helped to bring internecine war and awesome terror to a small, peaceful country. But their secretive manipulations were applied as well to another crisis that was erupting simultaneously: the fourth Arab-Israeli war.

The principal conclusion to draw from the Arab-Israeli war fought between October 6 and 25, 1973, is that it should not have happened in the first place. The second main conclusion is that once war did erupt, the Nixon administration, having recovered from its initial confusion, proceeded to manipulate the situation to serve what it perceived as long-term U.S. interests at the cost of a great many Arab and Israeli lives—and almost brought about a big-power confrontation. American policy also became intertwined with efforts to persuade the Arabs to lift the oil embargo imposed against the United States, Western Europe, and Japan on October 16, halfway through the war, and not lifted until the following March. Later, Henry Kissinger was hailed as a diplomatic wizard for having negotiated the cease-fire and subsequent disengagements of Arab and Israeli forces; what was overlooked was that what he did was to stabilize a situation that should not have developed in the first place, a situation that in a very special way he had welcomed.

It must be remembered that American diplomacy was operating in the most adverse possible domestic political conditions. Four days after the war broke out, Vice President Agnew resigned after pleading *nolo contendere* in a tax-evasion case, the Justice Department having agreed to drop more serious bribery charges against him. With the war still in progress, the Watergate affair reached one of its worst crises, when Nixon fired the special prosecutor, Archibald Cox, and Attorney General Richardson resigned in protest.

It is unlikely that Nixon could have played a serious managerial role in the Middle Eastern affray, although he went through all the required motions. Often, he was not consulted at all on developing policies or even at supreme moments of tension, and he was misled by his closest collaborators; top figures in his administration were fighting over policies when he might have arbitrated them. Nevertheless, the basic decisions were made—or confirmed—by him, and Nixon must in the end be held accountable.

It has never been adequately explained why Nixon's administration—and, most notably, Henry Kissinger—so completely ignored the signs of an approaching Arab offensive against Israel. That Israeli intelligence, one of the most respected in the world, and the Israeli cabinet also minimized the significance of these signs does not entirely exculpate the United States government. Washington, after all, had its own intelligence sources, its own ability to make political assessments, and its open channel to Moscow. Israeli complacency should not have been so readily duplicated in Washington, especially in light of what the Russians had been telling the Americans for months.

September, in any event, brought additional signs that should have alerted the Nixon administration as well as the Israelis. On the tenth, King Hussein of Jordan flew to Cairo for a two-day meeting with Sadat and Assad. Hussein was not asked to participate in the war, but was asked simply to deploy his forces along the Jordan River to tie down as many Israeli troops as possible. This tripartite Arab meeting was known publicly, but the White House seemed to attach no significance to it.

On September 13, Israeli and Syrian jet fighters fought the first major air battle since 1967, with Syria losing thirteen MiGs and Israel one Phantom. Again, the administration refused to see this as a danger sign. In Damascus, however, Assad resolved that the time had come to set a date for attacking Israel. He conferred with Sadat by telephone. In the next two days, the Egyptian General Staff completed its preparations, setting October 6 as the date to launch the war. On September 22, Sadat sent a secret message to Brezhnev telling him so. There is nothing to indicate that the Soviets tried to dissuade the Egyptians; they were careful not to pass this information on to the United States, spirit of détente or not.

In the last week of September, new and disturbing data reached Washington. Through satellite observation and electronic tracking, American intelligence learned that Egyptian forces were moving toward the Suez Canal in division strength, that they were deploying new communications facilities and engaging in a major logistic buildup. In the north, Syrian armor was involved in unusual movements; CIA analysts thought that Assad's tanks were abandoning their normal defensive emplacements. On September 25, intelligence services reported that three Soviet freighters, possibly loaded with surface-to-surface missiles, had sailed through the Bosphorus into the Mediterranean and appeared to have set course for Alexandria. All this information reached Kissinger and, presumably, Nixon (it was contained in the president's daily CIA intelligence summary).

Kissinger had become secretary of state on September 22, moving his key advisers from the White House NSC staff to Foggy Bottom. With a few exceptions, senior State Department officials were not brought into Kissinger's personal orbit and given easy access. Among those virtually frozen out was Ray Cline, director of the Intelligence and Research Bureau, who at the end of May had prepared the study warning that the Arabs might launch a war before the autumn.

Kissinger's first formal appearance as secretary of state was at the U.N. General Assembly in New York, which had opened its annual session on September 18. On September 25, he hosted a lunch at his Waldorf Towers suite for thirteen Arab foreign ministers and permanent delegates. After running through a series of self-deprecating Kissingerian jokes, he told his guests that the United States wanted to "promote progress toward peace" in the Middle East, and arranged to have private meetings in the next few days with Egyptian and Jordanian diplomats to start evolving a negotiating formula. Complications developed on September 28, when Palestinian commandos captured five Soviet Jews traveling by train through Austria and demanded that the Austrian government stop using Schönau Castle as a transit point for emigrants en route to Israel. Austria's chancellor, Bruno Kreisky, himself a Jew, agreed promptly. But such was the shock in Israel that Golda Meir flew to Vienna to try to change his mind. She was unsuccessful. The Austrian incident suggested to some American officials, including Kissinger, that the Israelis might respond, as they had to past terrorist acts, with retaliatory strikes against Palestinian camps in Lebanon and Syria. Kissinger developed the wholly erroneous notion that Israel was planning to strike at Egypt and Syria in a preemptive action—which in fact the Israelis did not contemplate until October 5. He sent messages to Jerusalem, pleading with the Israelis "not to preempt."

On Wednesday, October 3, American intelligence learned that the Russians had begun to evacuate dependents of their official personnel from Cairo and Damascus. Aeroflot Ilyushin-18 transports were diverted from their normal routes (sometimes in mid-flight) to pick up Soviet families in the two Arab capitals. American intelligence analysts concluded that this meant Moscow was anticipating an immediate outbreak of hostilities. But despite all the accumulation of fresh data about Arab military movements along Israel's borders and the Soviet military sealift to Alexandria, the consensus was that the Russians feared an Israeli strike. Whether anyone had planned it that way, the Schönau incident became a superb piece of "disinformation" for the Arabs.

On Friday, October 5, U.S. intelligence reported that Syrian armor beyond the Golan Heights was at combat readiness. Intercepts from Egyptian military communications west of Suez indicated that main units were poised to move out. The CIA's new study of the situation concluded that everything suggested that war was possible, but refused to predict, flat out, that the outbreak was imminent. As far as is known, the only senior official in the United States government who believed on October 5 that an Arab-Israeli war might erupt within the next twenty-four hours was Ray Cline. His forecast reached neither Nixon nor Kissinger.

By now the Israelis were suddenly taking the situation with seriousness. An Israeli Army spokesman issued this statement: "Israeli forces are following with attention events on the Egyptian side of the Suez Canal and all steps have been taken to prevent the possibility of a surprise on the part of the Egyptians." But everything was closing down early in Israel that Friday: the observance of Yom Kippur, the Day of Atonement, was beginning at sundown. No newspapers appeared the next morning to publish the army's cautionary statement.

At noon on October 5, Defense Minister Moshe Dayan, Chief of Staff Lieutenant General David Elazar, and Army Chief of Intelligence Major General Eliahu Zeira met at Dayan's office. Large Soviet military transports were reported to be landing in Cairo and Damascus, most likely with war equipment, and Dayan, who the week before had deployed an armored brigade on the Golan Heights, now put Israel's regular forces on alert. He ordered all holiday leaves canceled; officers in charge of the general mobilization plan were told to stand by. Yet the official Israeli estimate still was that there was "little likelihood" of war, and this was dutifully passed on to United States intelligence. The military group then

moved to Mrs. Meir's office for further conferences with several other
cabinet ministers. General Elazar repeated for Mrs. Meir's benefit the
conclusions in the intelligence estimate, adding that the Americans were
taking a similar view. The prime minister decided not to visit her daughter at a Negev kibbutz, and stayed in town for the high holy days. She had
a premonition.

At 4:00 a.m., General Elazar telephoned Mrs. Meir at home to say that
"irrefutable" intelligence had come during the night to indicate that the
Arabs would attack on both fronts at 6:00 p.m. Mrs. Meir called a cabinet
meeting for 7:00 a.m. Dayan conferred with Elazar, Zeira, and the air
force commander, Major General Binyamin Peled, who reported that his
aircraft would be ready to launch preemptive strikes against Egypt and
Syria by 1:00 p.m. Elazar was in favor of them, also demanding a general
call-up of reserves.

All this was discussed with Mrs. Meir at the early-morning meeting at
her home. She and Dayan rejected the preemptive strikes on the grounds
that they would turn the United States against Israel—and America was
the only ally the Israelis had. But the prime minister agreed to a limited
call-up of reserves. They worried that either Egypt or Syria, or both,
feared an Israeli attack, possibly as a retaliation for the Austrian episode.
The day before, Mrs. Meir had sent a message to the Israeli embassy in
Washington, with instructions that it be delivered to Kissinger, suggesting that the Americans advise the Egyptians and the Syrians that Israel
had no plans to preempt, but that, if attacked, Israel would respond "with
great strength." Kissinger received the message in New York at 8:00 p.m.
Friday (which was 2:00 a.m. Saturday in Tel Aviv), but did nothing about
it.

Mrs. Meir now called in the American ambassador, Kenneth Keating,
from his residence in suburban Tel Aviv. It was 8:00 a.m. She told Keating that war was imminent and that the United States should appeal to
the Soviet Union, Egypt, and Syria to head it off. She repeated that Israel
would not preempt. It took Keating four hours to get to his office, draft
and send the coded telegram to Kissinger, and for this message to reach
the secretary at the Waldorf Towers. By now it was noon in Israel and
6:00 a.m. in New York. Kissinger, who should have done it the previous
evening, called Nixon in Key Biscayne, awakening him. The president
instructed him to telephone Egyptian, Syrian, and Israeli diplomats in
New York as well as Dobrynin in Washington. Kissinger did so, appealing
to the Arabs to act with restraint. Then the secretary telephoned United
Nations Secretary General Kurt Waldheim, and dispatched cables to King

Faisal and King Hussein—something that might have been done days earlier.

The last hour before the Arab attack was total confusion. First, Dobrynin called Kissinger back to say that the Kremlin would inform Cairo and Damascus that their fears of Israel were groundless; if war broke out, he said, the Soviet Union would stay out of it under terms of her détente understanding with the United States. The Egyptian foreign minister, Mohammed el-Zayyat, telephoned Kissinger too, to say that Israeli naval units had attacked the Syrian port of Latakia. Kissinger, in turn, called Eban at the Plaza Hotel to inquire about this report. Eban put in a call to the Foreign Ministry in Jerusalem, but instead of a reply to the Egyptian charge, he was told that "the war has broken out." It was 1:55 p.m. Israeli time, and Mrs. Meir was in a cabinet meeting in Tel Aviv; it was 7:55 a.m. in New York. Kissinger got the word five minutes later, and relayed it to Nixon in Florida.

Egyptian troops, moving under the cover of SAM-missile batteries firing in diagonal trajectory against Israeli aircraft, were throwing their pontoons over the Suez Canal and beginning to cross the waterway just before 2:00 p.m. Simultaneously, Syrian armor and infantry were striking at Israeli positions on the Golan Heights. The war the United States and Israeli governments never believed would happen had started.

When the postmortems came, weeks later, Kissinger chose to blame the American intelligence community for failing to alert the government. And to be sure, the CIA was not blameless. But political conclusions are primarily the business of policy-makers, and this was the case with Kissinger, who had always insisted on molding his own intelligence estimates. Yet at a news conference on October 12, Kissinger washed his hands of all responsibility. Three times in the week preceding the war, he said, American and Israeli intelligence agencies were asked for their assessment and had come back with the answer that "hostilities were unlikely to the point of there being no chance of it." This was an oversimplification at best; among other things, Kissinger seemed to have forgotten the studies that Cline had been providing.

Kissinger flew back to Washington on Saturday afternoon and called a meeting of WASAG. The conclusion was reached that Israel would defeat the Arabs in less than a week. The administration did not seem all that alarmed on the first day of the Yom Kippur war. Kissinger realized he would not be able to go to Peking as scheduled, but Nixon decided there was no reason to cut short his Key Biscayne weekend.

When the president returned to the White House on Sunday night, October 7, he had what he described as a "rather long talk" with Kissinger about the Middle East situation. Thereupon he dispatched a personal message to Brezhnev urging the Russians to exert their influence to bring the war to an end and expressing his belief that both superpowers would exercise maximum restraint in the crisis. Brezhnev's reply, received during the night, was called "constructive" by White House officials.

On Monday, the eighth, Nixon and Kissinger appeared together before newsmen in the Oval Office. The president told the reporters about his late-night meeting with the secretary; "This morning, I was here around 7:30 or so and studied all of the reports," he went on, "both with regard to the military situation and the reaction to our diplomatic initiative." He and Kissinger, he said, "have been meeting for a good part of the morning here on particularly that diplomatic initiative, and having in mind the importance of getting strong support for the position that the United States will take."

This diplomatic initiative was consultations with the permanent members of the United Nations Security Council and the parties to the hostilities. The fighting had been going on for forty-eight hours, but the Security Council did not meet until late on Monday to attempt to secure a cease-fire. This diplomatic confusion only mirrored the military and intelligence confusion.

In any case the Russians were showing no interest in a cease-fire mandated by the Security Council, for the simple reason that their clients appeared to be winning. They wanted to wait a while longer. The Israelis, facing Egyptians on the Sinai side of Suez, were likewise unenthusiastic about a cease-fire in place that would confirm whatever conquests Egypt had achieved in the first two days. They had hopes of recouping. Kissinger spent the balance of Monday in meetings and telephone conversations with Dobrynin and Simcha Dinitz, who had just returned from Jerusalem. There was another private Nixon-Brezhnev exchange; in the evening a Kremlin message said that the Russians would "consider" going along with a cease-fire. But Nixon's diplomatic initiative collapsed before it could get off the ground. The council did not act. Kissinger, feeling betrayed by the Russians, declared that "détente cannot survive irresponsibility in any area, including the Middle East."

On Tuesday, October 9, while the situation in the Middle East kept deteriorating, the president found himself caught up in ceremonial activities as well as in meetings not directly related to the Arab-Israeli war. It was also the eve of Agnew's resignation—a day when Nixon did not know where to turn first.

He spent the morning greeting President Félix Houphouët-Boigny of the Ivory Coast, then conferring with him. But both before and after Nixon spoke with Kissinger. In the afternoon, he met with his top advisers on energy and environment, including the secretaries of interior and commerce, then issued a statement warning the nation that "we may face fuel shortages for the next few years," adding that the shortage of heating oil in the coming winter could reach 400,000 barrels a day. He suggested that Americans lower their thermostats by four degrees to make up for it. He made no reference to the war; the Arab oil embargo was only eight days away.

Later in the afternoon, the president and Kissinger discussed at length the major issue of whether to send military supplies to Israel, which, suffering unexpectedly high losses, was now urgently requesting them—replacements for the aircraft (mostly Phantoms) they were losing to the Egyptian SAM missiles near Suez, electronic countermeasure devices to neutralize the SAMs, and just about everything else needed to pursue what could be a lengthy war. Then Nixon spent the evening entertaining Houphouët-Boigny at a White House dinner.

The next day continued this hectic pace—with its peculiar mixture of trivia and urgent seriousness. Early in the morning, the president learned from the daily CIA summary that the Soviet Union had initiated an airlift of military equipment to Cairo and Damascus. The Arabs, too, were now evidently expecting a long and difficult war, and the Kremlin—Brezhnev's promises earlier that week notwithstanding—was fully involved. This, as Nixon and Kissinger recognized, was a major escalation. The United States had to react in some fashion, but they were not sure at the moment just how it should be done.

In midmorning, the president was informed that Agnew had decided to resign. Facing proceedings before a federal court in Baltimore, the vice president had struck a bargain with Attorney General Richardson that he would not be prosecuted on more serious charges if he agreed to plead no-contest on a single income-tax–evasion charge. The other part of the bargain was that he would step down from office. This secret bargaining had Nixon's approval; in the midst of his own Watergate troubles he could not be burdened with a vice president under federal indictment.

Next, Zaire's President Mobuto Sese Seko called at the White House to discuss his country's economic problems. Late in the morning, the president spent a half hour conferring National Medal of Science Awards for 1973 on eleven recipients. It was a major occasion with the cabinet and members of Congress in attendance, and Nixon used it to deliver a speech urging a strong national defense.

During lunch, Nixon received more intelligence reports on the Soviet airlift to the Arabs; he discussed them over the phone with Kissinger. Other reports told him that it was beyond the Israelis' capability to win the war during that week. They were counterattacking on the Golan Heights, but they were on the defensive in the Sinai, losing more and more aircraft.

Early in the afternoon, Nixon received Agnew's letter apprising him of his resignation, and attaching a copy of the one-sentence letter to Henry Kissinger: "I hereby resign the Office of Vice President of the United States, effective immediately." (The formal resignation was addressed to Kissinger in his capacity of secretary of state and principal member of the cabinet, as prescribed in the Constitution.) Nixon chose to reply warmly with a "Dear Ted" letter:

> Your departure from the Administration leaves me with a great sense of personal loss. You have been a valued associate throughout these nearly five years that we have served together. However, I respect your decision, and I also respect the concern for the national interest that led you to conclude that a resolution of the matter in this way, rather than through an extended battle in the Courts and the Congress, was advisable in order to prevent a protracted period of national division and uncertainty. As Vice President, you have addressed the great issues of our times with courage and candor. Your strong patriotism, and your profound dedication to the welfare of the Nation, have been an inspiration to all who have served with you as well as to millions of others throughout the country.

Afterward, the president held two Oval Office meetings—one with Senate Minority Leader Hugh Scott, Senator Robert Griffin, House Minority Leader Gerald Ford, and Representative Leslie Arends; the other with Senate Majority Leader Mike Mansfield and Speaker of the House Carl Albert—to discuss the selection of a new vice president. Then it was back to the Middle East and a ninety-minute briefing with ten senators (including Mansfield and Scott) and nine congressmen (including Ford) on the crisis.

By Friday evening, October 12, Nixon had decided to nominate House Minority Leader Gerald Ford of Michigan to be vice president, subject to congressional approval. He had made up his mind during a night and a day at Camp David.

"We have to recognize," Nixon said, "that the peace that we have worked so hard to build, not only for ourselves but for all the world, is now threatened because of a new outbreak of war in the Mideast. This is a time, therefore, that we need a strong and effective leadership. . . . Never in our history has the world more needed a strong America, a United America." He described Ford as "a man . . . who has been unwavering in support of the policies that brought peace with honor for America in Vietnam and in support of a policy for the strong national defense for this country, which is so essential if we are to have peace in the world." By the next day, Nixon announced that Ford would start getting daily intelligence briefings and participating in National Security Council meetings—even before being confirmed and sworn in.

In reconstructing American policy during October 1973, it becomes evident that Kissinger persuaded Nixon that, once having broken out, the Arab-Israeli war should be manipulated so as to create the conditions he considered necessary for successful long-range peace diplomacy by the United States. The rewards of such a policy, Kissinger reasoned, would be the disappearance of the threat of an Arab oil embargo, the establishment of a new relationship between the United States and the Arab world, and ultimately, the elimination of Soviet influence in the Middle East. But for this policy to work, it was necessary that neither the Arabs nor Israel win the war militarily. What Kissinger needed was a stalemate among the three bloodied and exhausted combatants so that, at the proper time, they would turn to the United States in search of peace. To Kissinger, therefore, the war itself was but a cruel sideshow, serving the larger interests of American policy as he perceived them. In a sense, Kissinger was applying his Vietnam-war strategy to the Middle East. He believed, now as then, that peace can only follow a terrible and debilitating spasm of war.

Edward R. F. Sheehan, a sympathetic but perceptive student of Kissinger's Middle East diplomacy, has written that Kissinger "once told a friend, 'I never treat crises when they're cold, only when they're hot. This enables me to weigh the protagonists one against the other, not in terms of ten or two thousand years ago but in terms of what each of them merits at this moment.' " Sheehan, who has had access to Kissinger's written records, has described as follows the secretary's responses in the middle of the first week of the October war, when he realized that the strategic balance was shifting away from Israel:

He had no mind to restore it straightaway, because he recognized instinctively that the new balance tendered him an exquisite chance to use the war as an extension of diplomacy. If he allowed neither side to win decisively, then he might manipulate the result to launch negotiations, and—ultimately—to compose the Arab-Israeli quarrel. . . . In keeping with his early perception that the war must be used to promote a settlement, Kissinger decided to withhold major deliveries to Israel so long as the Russians exercised restraint and so long as he hoped that Sadat would accept a ceasefire.

Kissinger's policy, however, was enormously dangerous, precisely because it assumed that the Russians would act with restraint and that Sadat would go for a truce at the right moment. Both these assumptions were wrong. In the end, it was Israel's military brilliance that saved the day— and with it America's policies and Kissinger's prestige.

Kissinger's view on the war changed almost daily. For the first four days, he like most American officials believed that Israel would beat back the Egyptians and Syrians fairly easily. According to Sheehan, Kissinger "complained constantly to his aides of 'irrational Arabs,' 'demented Arabs.' . . . Certain that Israel would crush Egypt, he feared that the Soviet Union would intervene, forcing the United States to intervene on the side of Israel and risking a war of the great powers." But he was underestimating the lethal combination of Soviet-supplied SAMs and massive thrusts by Egyptian armor, artillery, and motorized infantry.

By October 10, Kissinger changed his assessment. The Egyptians had not been thrown back; instead, having broken through the Bar-Lev Line, they were advancing in Sinai and pouring more troops across the Suez Canal. The Israelis were reeling back in the south, taking heavy losses in aircraft and tanks, although they had succeeded in stopping the Syrians on the Golan Heights. This suggested to Kissinger the possibility of a stalemate that his diplomacy could then exploit. It also legitimized the cruel charade the administration had been playing from the outset with Israel, at Kissinger's instigation, over the question of military supplies.

Aside from Israel itself, the principal victim of this charade was Simcha Dinitz, the ever-trusting Israeli ambassador in Washington. On instructions, Dinitz began requesting shipments of American arms on Monday, dealing directly with Kissinger. Kissinger took the view that Israel did not need new supplies because it would win the war by Thursday anyway, but this was not what he told Dinitz. His explanation was that Defense Secretary Schlesinger and the Pentagon were dragging their feet, even to the point of defying presidential orders. Now Schlesinger had lent himself to this game only most reluctantly, since he harbored profound doubts about the wisdom of holding back arms for Israel strictly on Kissinger's say, and his personal view was that the Israelis should be helped most expeditiously. But on Tuesday, October 9, Kissinger again invoked Schlesinger's alleged insubordination. It did not seem to have occurred to Dinitz that, if Kissinger was telling him the truth, it was a most extraordinary state of affairs in an administration in which the secretary of state had the president's ear and was the dominant personage in town.

It would be pointless to chronicle in detail the story of Kissinger's manipulations and Dinitz's frustrations during that first week of the war, and of their innumerable conversations. It has been recorded elsewhere, based largely on Kissinger's own version of these events and Dinitz's supportive testimony at the time. Suffice it to say that on October 10, Nixon and Kissinger secretly shifted their strategy while keeping alive the official charade. Now the real reason for denying help to Israel was Kissinger's hope for a military deadlock that would open the way for mediation on his part. The discovery of the Soviet airlift to Syria and Egypt did not alter this policy: Kissinger still wanted to keep the Israelis on a short leash.

Commercial Boeing 707s of El Al, the Israeli airline, were now allowed to land at Oceana Naval Air Station in Virginia and at JFK International Airport in New York (on a remote runway) at night to pick up sophisticated weapons, but they had to have their tail insignia painted over. This silly piece of deception was ordered by Kissinger, but the first El Al jet taking off from Oceana was filmed by a television network and correctly identified. In any event, the arrangement was wholly unsatisfactory. El Al had too few large planes—no more than eight or ten were available for this makeshift airlift—and the Israelis needed the pilots anyway for combat duty.

A senior Pentagon officer who helped to run procurement for the Israelis offered this description: "El Al planes did not want to make pickups beyond the Eastern seaboard because it was wasting too much precious time, but once they flew to an air force base in Utah. . . . We had to have airlift priorities, but the Israelis kept changing them constantly. . . . The Pentagon had the ETA [estimated time of arrival] of the El Al planes as soon as they left Tel Aviv, and it had projected loads for them. But the Israelis often rejected these loads; they wanted to fly the most important items first. Then, there was the problem that the Israeli 707s had no cargo doors, unlike United States Air Force cargo planes, and ammunition had to be hand loaded. Lift forks were useless. . . . This was not known publicly at the time, but we were then short of fuel at air force bases, and we had a hell of a time refueling the El Al Boeings."

The only possible answer was an airlift by U.S. military aircraft, and in midweek this was what Schlesinger proposed. But Kissinger would not hear of it. It was a major concession that he allowed U.S. Air Force pilots to fly to Israel the two or three Phantoms he agreed to release during the first week. To keep back major deliveries, he invented the charter ploy. First, the Israelis were told to try to find private charter cargo planes. If these were available, he told Dinitz, they could take all they could carry. No charter operator, however, was willing to risk planes in a war zone or to incur Arab hostility afterward. Besides, nobody would insure the charters. When Dinitz reported this to Kissinger, the secretary said that Nixon would instruct Schlesinger and the Department of Transportation to find charters. This did not work either, of course, and Kissinger again blamed the Pentagon.

By Thursday it evidently began to dawn on Kissinger that his strategy was backfiring. Israel was in dire military straits, but the Arabs were being resupplied around the clock by huge Soviet Antonov-22 transports flying tail-to-nose airlifts into Cairo and Damascus. (To shorten flying time, the Russians were brazenly going over Yugoslavia, which did not mind it, and Turkey, which dared not protest.) Israel needed massive aid. Kissinger's attempt at obtaining a cease-fire in place, reluctantly accepted by Israel on October 12, was rejected by Sadat the next day. Kissinger was now willing to authorize an open American airlift, but he still had an absurd and time-wasting condition: American planes would fly only as far as the Lajes Air Force Base on Terceira Island in the Azores; the cargo would then be transferred to the commercial airport on Santa Maria Island to be picked up by El Al 707s. Dinitz, at his wits' end, told Kissinger that he would appeal to friendly senators and the American Jewish community to "go public" in favor of aid to Israel if the airlift were not launched by the next day. Kissinger again blamed the Pentagon, but he and Schlesinger met with Nixon that evening and the clearance was finally given. (The air force wanted Portuguese permission to refuel at Lajes—the huge C-5 Galaxies could fly nonstop to Israel, but with reduced loads, and C-130s needed refueling either in the Azores or in mid-air—and this forced a delay until noon on Saturday, October 13, when the Lisbon government finally provided clearance.)

The Pentagon had been ready and willing to start supplying Israel from the first day of the war, but Kissinger was not entirely incorrect in claiming that some high officials there were reluctant to launch the operation. Schlesinger, of course, was simply (and reluctantly) obeying the rules of the game laid down by the White House, but Deputy Secretary William Clements may have been doing more than that. A Texas millionaire whose oil-drilling–equipment company had extensive interests in the Middle East, Clements was pro-Arab and opposed to aid to Israel. Even when the White House began to release arms for the Israelis, Clements tried to slow down the shipments. Kissinger, who did not mind reinforcing his playacting with an occasional bit of righteous indignation, upbraided Clements in a telephone conversation in Dinitz's presence. "If *you* had *your* way," Kissinger told Clements, "you'd be sending planes in the opposite direction." (The playacting, incidentally, went on until the end. When Mrs. Meir visited Nixon on October 31, the president pointed to Kissinger, saying, "This is the man who got you the airlift.")

In any case, once the full-fledged airlift was authorized, there was no foot-dragging at the Defense Department. It was coordinated by a special Mideast Task Force in the office of the assistant secretary of defense for international security affairs (ISA), working twenty-four hours a day. As a member of the task force recalled, "It seemed as if the Pentagon was run by Golda Meir and Mota [Mordechai] Gur [then Israeli defense attaché in Washington]. The Israelis sent their requests to the task force in ISA, and we routed them to the Joint Chiefs of Staff. Sometimes Gur or the chief of the Israeli supply mission in New York would call, saying he had Golda at the other end of the line, and that she was pressing for all kinds of things. . . . They wanted tanks, 155-mm. shells, blankets, snowsuits, tents—and everything had to be airlifted. The Defense Department ordered different military depots to send the equipment to air force bases at Dover, Delaware, or McGuire, in New Jersey, or to be sealifted. . . . The task force met once or twice a day with representatives of the Joint Chiefs, the Office of the Secretary of Defense, and the services to review the Israeli requests. Depots were ordered searched, then action came at the next meeting. Israel would ask for, say, a hundred and twenty tanks, and we had to determine the stocks, approve maybe thirty of them, get them moving, then approve more. A lot had to come from army units because there wasn't enough equipment in supply. . . . The Israelis would ask for pilotless drones to get photography behind Arab lines, to spot the SAMs, and we'd try to get them going. The air force had to strip their own units, check production lines, and often, divert to Israel aircraft programmed for elsewhere."

But by the end of the first week of the war, Nixon and Kissinger had to change their strategy once again. Since military stalemate could no longer be induced through the denial of arms to Israel, the new plan anticipated a stalemate through a reassertion of Israeli strength. Kissinger thought this kind of manipulation was still possible, but now he had to reckon seriously with the Russians, whose long-range intentions were unknown. Meanwhile, as strategic gears shifted in Washington, the world was treated to one of the great ironies of the year: the Nobel Committee voted on October 16 to award the Peace Prize for 1973 to Kissinger and Le Duc Tho for negotiating the Vietnam peace agreement. The Vietnamese cease-fire was in tatters, which may have been one reason for Le Duc Tho's refusing his half of the prize, but Kissinger accepted his. Nixon, who apparently had expected the prize himself, congratulated Kissinger by telephone.

Nobel Peace Prize or no, October 16 marked a turning point in the Arab-Israeli war and, with it, in diplomacy. But it was not what Nixon and Kissinger had anticipated, and once more, they had to refashion their strategy to avert what they perceived as another kind of potential disaster: a crushing defeat of the Egyptian armies by the revived Israeli forces. Now, for the second time in ten days, the objective of American policy was again to prevent an exaggerated Israeli victory. In this endeavor, the White House suddenly found an ally in the Soviet Union, which overnight had rediscovered détente.

The turning point was the crossing of the Suez Canal to the *Egyptian* side by a tank force led by General Ariel Sharon, a daring and imaginative Israeli commander. This thrust to the west, while tens of thousands of Egyptian troops were fighting on the eastern side of the canal, in the Sinai, had been conceived during the first week of the war as one of those classically unconventional but brilliant Israeli military moves. Having first been the victim of Arab surprise attacks on the Day of Atonement, the Israeli Defense Force (the Zahal, as it is called in Hebrew) produced a stunning surprise of its own with Sharon's crossing at the southern end of the canal, starting with a successful commando probe on the night of October 15.

Dayan, Elazar, and Sharon, who planned the operation, had waited until Dinitz flashed the word from Washington on October 13 that the big airlift was under way before they gave the final green light. Without the fresh deliveries of arms and munitions, the crossing could not have been risked. The Americans, naturally, were not told what the Zahal had in mind; they might have been less generous had they known that the Israelis had more ambitious plans than just to defend themselves on the Sinai front. The invasion of "African" Egypt reversed the course of the war.

Even before the magnitude of the Israeli feat was fully understood, the Russians were worrying about the war they had helped to set in motion. Ten days of fighting had elapsed, much too long for a desert offensive war, and the Israelis were still lodged in the passes controlling most of Sinai; the Egyptians held only a fifteen-mile strip east of the canal. In the Golan Heights, Israel was on the counteroffensive. And now the Zahal was assured of unlimited American supplies.

On October 16, as Sharon's tanks were racing, Patton-like, across Egypt, Premier Kosygin arrived in Cairo for secret conferences with Sadat. Sadat's first reaction to Kosygin's notion of negotiating a cease-fire was completely negative: Sadat still thought he was winning the war and he had not yet comprehended what Sharon's armor was achieving behind Egyptian lines.

But in Washington, the Arabs were attempting a peacemaking end run of their own at a meeting with Nixon on October 17. As a result of a cabled appeal from King Faisal, Saudi Foreign Minister Omar Saqqaf led a delegation composed of his Algerian, Moroccan, and Kuwaiti colleagues (and supposedly representing eighteen other Arab states, including Egypt and Syria) to a lengthy morning White House conference. Saqqaf's proposal, contained in a four-page document in Arabic script, was for a settlement based on a formula "somewhere between" demands for an Israeli pullback to the pre-1967 lines and American proposals for a cease-fire in place. Nixon, not surprisingly, was uncommunicative about the results of this meeting, and he refused to say whether the question of oil had been discussed. It was an immensely touchy point at that particular moment: only the day before, American oil companies had started receiving telegrams from the Middle East informing them that oil-producing countries had suddenly stopped all shipments to the United States, Western Europe, and Japan. There had been no formal declaration, but all signs were that an embargo had, indeed, been applied. On the morning his foreign minister was visiting Nixon, King Faisal announced that Saudi Arabia was "symbolically" reducing oil production by 25 percent.

What the administration had feared most—an oil embargo—had finally happened. Most likely, it had been triggered by the decision to mount the big airlift for Israel: the Arabs had warned that they would stop the oil if the United States became significantly engaged on the side of Israel, and they kept their word. That afternoon for the first time, Nixon made a point of attending the daily WASAG meeting on the Middle East. For a moment, at least, he set aside his Watergate concerns.

Along the Suez Canal, meanwhile, the Israelis were on the offensive everywhere. General Elazar announced that 100 Egyptian tanks had been knocked out in an all-day battle—one of the largest armor encounters in history—on the east side of the canal. Counterattacking Israeli tank formations were pushing the Egyptians back to the waterway. On the western side, Sharon had the Egyptian Third Army on the run. His tank spearheads were advancing north toward the Ismailia-Cairo highway and south toward the town of Suez, and the Israelis were destroying SAM sites as they went.

In Cairo, the realization that the Egyptians might be facing a catastrophic defeat began to sink in. Sadat, reading hourly reports from the front, became more amenable to Kosygin's pressures for a cease-fire, but he wanted assurances of Soviet intervention if the Israelis violated the truce. Kosygin told Sadat that he could count on the Russians.

Late on October 18, Kosygin returned to Moscow. That same night (the time difference between Moscow and Washington is seven hours), Dobrynin came to see Kissinger with a cease-fire proposal. Given what had happened in the last forty-eight hours, it seemed to make little sense: the Russians suggested that there be a cease-fire in place, which would keep the Israelis indefinitely on the Egyptian side of the canal; that Israel commit itself to withdraw to the pre-1967 lines, which would mean abandoning East Jerusalem; that there be an international peace conference (obviously with the Russians) to seek a final settlement; and that the United States and the Soviet Union become the guarantors of the cease-fire.

Kissinger told Dobrynin that his proposal would never be accepted by Israel, but he passed it on to Eban, who was still in New York, and Dinitz. Eban telephoned Mrs. Meir. The prime minister replied that Israel was in no hurry for any kind of cease-fire and instructed Eban to come home and attend a Sunday cabinet meeting that would review the whole diplomatic situation. Israel wanted time to conclude its military operations.

On Friday morning, October 19, Dobrynin came to Kissinger with another message: Brezhnev wanted Kissinger to come to Moscow for "urgent consultations on the Middle East"—or, if that were impossible, Gromyko would come to Washington. Kissinger checked with Nixon— and informed Dobrynin that he would leave that evening for Moscow. He preferred to negotiate with Brezhnev, who could make decisions virtually on the spot, rather than with Gromyko, who would have to keep asking for instructions. Yet Nixon and Kissinger also had an interest in delaying a decision on a cease-fire. They knew Israel could use the extra time. So

Kissinger kept delaying his departure. He made a point of attending a dinner at the Chinese liaison office and staying late—and did not depart from Andrews Air Force Base until shortly after 1:00 a.m., Saturday, October 20.

Earlier on Friday, Nixon had sent a message to Congress requesting $2.2 billion in emergency military aid for Israel along with $200 million for Cambodia. This would be an outright grant to Israel, the first one in many years, and not a credit line. The president told Congress that in the first twelve days of the war, the United States had authorized $825 million in military equipment for Israel—conventional munitions, air-to-air and air-to-ground missiles, artillery, crew-served and individual weapons, fighter-aircraft ordnance, as well as "replacements for tanks, aircraft, radios and other military equipment which have been lost in action."

Israel was making good use of it. Sharon's tank army penetrated forty miles west of the Suez Canal, and his advance units stood fifty-five miles east of Cairo on the Ismailia highway. A separate column was fanning out toward the south to take the town of Suez and complete the encirclement of the Egyptian Third Army. On the east side of the canal, the Egyptian Second Army was being eviscerated by Israeli air and armor attacks. On the Syrian front, the Israelis had pushed the enemy back from the Golan Heights area, were approaching Quneitra, and had Damascus within the range of their long guns. As an Israeli officer remarked, "This is better than 1967." But now Israel had to contend with Soviet-American diplomacy, and in the end, this would cost it all its 1973 gains as well as some territory in the Sinai.

Much has been made of the allegation that Nixon granted Kissinger a diplomatic "power of attorney" on his October mission to Moscow. And it is true that Kissinger did receive (in flight) a message granting him "plenipotentiary" powers in negotiating with Brezhnev over the *Middle East* crisis, i.e., permitting him to speak and sign in a binding manner in the name of the president in matters pertaining to that crisis. But legal and constitutional experts point out that the president could not have delegated to Kissinger, or to anybody, his powers as commander in chief without the concurrence of Congress. If Nixon had become incapacitated during Kissinger's Moscow visit, presidential authority would have been vested constitutionally in the vice president. (To be sure, Ford had not yet been confirmed by Congress—he was not sworn in until December 6—but in such an instance congressional action would have been instantaneous.) Nixon never explained his plenipotentiary grant to Kissinger, but his aides thought at the time that it was, in fact, a Watergate precaution—inasmuch as he was in the midst of his confrontation with Special Prosecutor Cox and Attorney General Richardson over his tapes, the most critical point in the whole Watergate investigation. As it happened, Kissinger remained in cable contact with Nixon during his two-and-a-half days in Moscow, and often conferred by telephone with White House aides.

Certainly the timing of these various crises could not have been more dramatic—or more confusing. But it is clear that the president tried to use the Middle East crisis as a lever to exact what he wanted from his attorney general in the Watergate situation. On October 15, when Richardson had met with General Haig, now the White House chief of staff, to be briefed on the Middle East and the state of Soviet-American relations, Haig had gone out of his way to impress on him the gravity of the international situation. Cox, he went on, would have to be fired because, as Richardson described it later, "The problems generated by Cox's investigation were causing an intolerable diversion of the president's time and energy from far more important matters." Richardson's reply is well known: that he himself would quit if Cox were dismissed, for he had accepted the post of attorney general on the understanding that he would guarantee the special prosecutor's independence.

Involved negotiations among Cox, Richardson, and the White House followed, concerning the form in which Nixon's tapes might be made available to the special prosecutor and Judge Sirica. By Friday night, Richardson was advised that Nixon had just written him a letter "instructing you to direct . . . Cox" to make no further attempts "by judicial process" to obtain presidential materials. Late on Saturday, he met with the president.

This is Richardson's own recollection of this meeting: "For me, by far the hardest part was having to refuse his urgent appeal to delay my resignation until the Middle Eastern crisis had abated. 'I'm sorry,' the president said, 'that you insist on putting your personal commitments ahead of the public interest.' I said in as even a voice as I could muster, 'I can only say that I believe my resignation *is* in the public interest.' " The president's final comment was, "Brezhnev would never understand it if I let Cox defy my instructions."

Nixon accepted Richardson's resignation, but he would not accept that of Deputy Attorney General William D. Ruckelshaus; he had Haig dismiss him. Solicitor General Robert H. Bork became acting attorney general, and it was he who fired Cox. This extraordinary Saturday Night Massacre shook the Nixon administration to its very foundations.

Kissinger, meanwhile, was off on his plenipotentiary mission. He and Brezhnev had quickly agreed that a Middle East cease-fire was necessary, but they adjourned their first meeting without a decision.

The American and Soviet teams reconvened in Brezhnev's private office on Sunday afternoon, conferring for four hours around a long conference table next to Brezhnev's desk. Kissinger and Brezhnev each produced a draft of a cease-fire resolution to be presented to the U.N. Security Council. The Russians now seemed agreeable to including references to the 1967 Security Council resolution (the famous 242) providing for Israeli withdrawal from occupied territory in linkage with "secure" borders, plus a call for immediate negotiations to establish "a just and durable peace in the Middle East"—a victory for Kissinger—and Brezhnev obtained Sadat's concurrence; Kissinger, after consulting with Nixon, sent a message to Mrs. Meir in the president's name urging her to accept the cease-fire. On Monday Kissinger cabled instructions to U.N. Ambassador John Scali to request an immediate Security Council session, and by the end of the day, the council had approved Resolution 338, ordering the cease-fire and the negotiations. (China abstained from voting.)

His mission in Moscow completed, Kissinger could go home—but he stopped in Israel for five hours (the Israelis had asked him to do so) to explain what he had accomplished in Moscow to Mrs. Meir, the cabinet, and the military chiefs. The real problem was to make the Israelis stop fighting. They were closing a circle around the Egyptian Third Army on the western side of the canal, and they needed several more days to complete the operation. Kissinger told Mrs. Meir that the cease-fire should take effect immediately, but as an American official put it, "We knew the Israelis wouldn't do it." Mrs. Meir and her colleagues kept questioning Kissinger about future U.S. intentions, whether Israel would be asked to make concessions, whether American military aid would continue, and how Israeli war prisoners could be freed. Kissinger offered more assurances, but insisted that the time had come for negotiations. As he told an aide, "It took the war to unfreeze the positions" on both sides. He was right, but the cost to Israel had been enormous: when all the figures were in, 1854 soldiers had been killed—0.06 percent of the population and more than twice the number killed in the 1967 war—and at least 1800 more hospitalized wounded.

In any event, the cease-fire did not hold. In Washington, Dobrynin protested, and in New York, the Security Council passed a second cease-fire resolution on Tuesday, October 23. The cease-fire was broken again on Wednesday, in part because several Egyptian units had tried to escape the encirclement, and renewed fighting allowed the Israelis to reach the town of Suez. That Wednesday, Nixon received a cable from Sadat suggesting that a joint Soviet-American peace-keeping force police the truce. (A similar message went to Brezhnev.) The Americans vigorously opposed this idea, for the last thing they wanted was Soviet combat troops in the Middle East; nor did they want to commit American forces there, either. But the Russians fastened on this notion, and late in the day Dobrynin so informed Kissinger.

New intelligence reports signaled that seven Soviet airborne divisions were on the alert in southern Russia and Hungary. Vague reports also suggested that one or more Soviet ships had entered the Mediterranean, possibly carrying nuclear warheads that could be fitted on SCUD surface-to-surface missiles the Russians had earlier supplied to the Egyptians. Neither Nixon nor Kissinger could adequately interpret these reports. What were the Soviet intentions? Bluff? Plans to impose a cease-fire?

Key members of U.S. intelligence agencies have acknowledged that they could not be sure of the accuracy of the reports about the Soviet airborne troops. For example, there was no actual knowledge of troops being staged at airports, let alone embarking on aircraft. Perhaps the Soviet airborne units had simply been on a low-level alert ever since the outbreak of the war—the same kind of precaution that had led the Nixon administration to order the Sixth Fleet to stream toward Israel's coast.

Around 10:00 p.m., Dobrynin called Kissinger to read him the text of a message from Brezhnev to Nixon. The White House never released the message, but this is what it said in part: "Let us together . . . urgently dispatch Soviet and American contingents to Egypt" so that the cease-fire could be implemented "without delay. . . . I will say it straight, that if you find it impossible to act together with us in this matter, we should be faced with the necessity urgently to consider the question of taking appropriate steps unilaterally. Israel cannot be allowed to get away with the violations."

Kissinger telephoned Nixon at the White House living quarters to pass on Brezhnev's warning, and then he assembled his experts to study the situation. The combination of the Brezhnev message with the reports of Soviet airborne forces being placed on the alert seemed to suggest that the Russians were ready to move unilaterally. But nobody could be sure. A letter was drafted and sent over Nixon's signature telling Brezhnev that the United States could not accept unilateral Soviet action. The message reaffirmed the summit agreement to work for Middle Eastern peace, but noted that this did not provide for the dispatch of forces to the area. The president proposed, instead, a peace-keeping force with troops from nonnuclear powers.

What happened next, and how and why it happened, remains a mystery. During the night, the White House issued a worldwide military alert —Defcon 3 (Defense Condition 3, on the scale of 5 possible Defcons; Defcon 1 is war). Among other forces placed on alert were nuclear-bomb–bearing B-52s. The alert was a signal to Brezhnev that, as Nixon had written, the United States would not tolerate unilateral moves by the Soviets. The alert was not announced publicly (Americans learned about it the next morning, by accident, when several airmen were stopped by the police for speeding to their bases, and explained why they were doing it), but it was assumed that the Russians would discover it immediately through their electronic intercepts of American military communications.

Among the questions one might ask about this development were: Who actually ordered the alert? Was the United States overreacting? Was it really intended for the benefit of the Russians? Or was it a form of pressure on Israel to obey the U.N. cease-fire order before the international situation really got out of hand?

There is some support for the last interpretation. At 2:30 a.m., Thursday, October 25, Ambassador Dinitz was urgently summoned to the White House by Kissinger. There, he was told of the alert and given a copy of Brezhnev's message and asked to pass it on to Jerusalem. Dinitz immediately called Mrs. Meir on a secure line and read her the Soviet communication; her first reaction was, "When the Russians are threatening, this is no time to make concessions," but she told Dinitz that efforts would be made to ensure the end of the fighting. Moreover, the Russians evidently did not really want a confrontation with the United States. For Moscow made no further moves that week, although the fighting went on throughout Thursday and Friday, when the Egyptians tried again to break out of the encirclement. Brezhnev advised Nixon on the twenty-fifth that he accepted the small-power peace force, and the truce became operative late on October 26. The next day the first contingent of the emergency peace-keeping force, commanded by a Finnish general, reached the besieged town of Suez.

At a news conference on October 25, Kissinger said that President Nixon had called "a special meeting of the National Security Council" at 3:00 a.m. to order the alert, and that "all the members of the National Security Council were unanimous in their recommendations as the result of a deliberation in which the president did not participate, and in which he joined only after they had formed their judgment." Kissinger refused to say at the time *why* the NSC had recommended an alert, promising to explain everything "upon the conclusion of the present diplomatic efforts." He never did. But most curiously, there is no record of a National Security Council meeting that night. The only meetings of the NSC in 1973 were on March 8 and April 12. "All the members" were "unanimous in their recommendations," Kissinger said, but the only people who "met" when the recommendation order was given for Defcon 3 were he and Schlesinger. (William Colby, not a statutory NSC member, joined them *after* the decision was taken.)

Nixon said two days later that he ordered the alert shortly after midnight, after "we obtained information which led us to believe that the Soviet Union was planning to send a very substantial force into the Mideast, a military force." But Schlesinger's own recollection was that the "abbreviated National Security Council" meeting was held at 11:00 p.m., and that it was he who initiated the idea; he made a point of saying that "the president was in complete command at all times during the course of the evening." But this hardly explains why, in a grave international situation that was considered liable to lead to war, the president was resting upstairs when he might have been with his aides. The only point on which there is agreement is that, after the alert order was issued, Haig went upstairs to tell Nixon what had been done.

The suspicion that the alert is linked not only to the Middle East crisis but to Watergate has never been wholly dispelled. Coming as it did only two days after the Saturday Night Massacre, it led immediately to public questioning on this point. And the president allowed himself considerable exaggeration about the crisis: the White House "theater" was still in operation. At a news conference on October 26, Nixon, answering a question about suggestions that he resign or be impeached, said that a confrontation had been avoided because of his relationship with Brezhnev, and "as long as I can carry out that kind of responsibility, I am going to continue to do this job." The events of the week had brought about "a real crisis," he added, "the most difficult crisis we have had since the Cuban confrontation of 1962."

But this simply was not so. In 1962, Soviet ships had been on the verge of breaching the American blockade of Cuba, imposed after Khrushchev had placed nuclear weapons on the island. American forces were on a *full* alert. An American reconnaissance plane had been shot down. No comparable situation had arisen now: indeed it could be argued that the 1970 crisis over Jordan and the alleged preparations for basing Soviet submarines in Cuba had been vastly more dangerous. But the telling thing was that Nixon brought up his foreign-policy record in the context of Watergate. His somewhat rambling reply went like this:

> Well, I have noted speculation to the effect that the Watergate prob-
> lems may have led the Soviet Union to miscalculate. I tend to disagree
> with that, however. I think Mr. Brezhnev probably can't quite under-
> stand how the president of the United States wouldn't be able to
> handle the Watergate problems. He would be able to handle it all
> right, if he had them. But I think what happens is that what Mr.
> Brezhnev does understand is the power of the United States. What he
> does know is the president of the United States. What he also knows
> is that the president of the United States, when he was under unmerci-
> ful assault at the time of Cambodia, at the time of May 8, when I
> ordered the bombing and the mining of North Vietnam, at the time
> of December 18, still went ahead and did what he thought was right;
> the fact that Mr. Brezhnev knew that regardless of the pressures at
> home, regardless of what people see and hear on television night after
> night, he would do what was right. This is what made Mr. Brezhnev
> act as he did.

Between the October crisis and the end of the year, diplomacy in the Middle East functioned better than might have been expected when the furious fighting finally died down. Under the auspices of the U.N. com-mand, Israeli and Egyptian officers met at Kilometer 101 on the Cairo-Suez road and negotiated relief for the surrounded Egyptian Third Army —the first time Israelis and Egyptians had negotiated face to face since 1948.

By November, the U.S. government was undertaking a policy of rap-prochement with the Arabs even though the oil embargo was still in force. Kissinger's view was that Egypt was the key to a new relationship with the so-called confrontation states. On November 7, Kissinger held his first meeting with Sadat in Cairo. As Edward Sheehan wrote, this encounter, "simply because it happened, was the food of history." For Kissinger, it was the beginning of America's political return to the Arab world: now, he believed, the United States could· successfully mediate in the Middle East. The meetings with Sadat during November and December led to the reestablishment of full-fledged American-Egyptian diplomatic rela-tions for the first time since 1967. Kissinger also made a Syrian "break-through," in conferences with President Assad that produced the list of Israeli prisoners held by Syria (Israel and Egypt had exchanged their prisoners earlier) and smoothed the way for Israel's attendance at the long-term negotiations in Geneva. The secretary also held long meetings with King Faisal, and went to Israel several times.

The two-day Geneva conference opened on December 21, with Israeli, Egyptian, and Jordanian foreign ministers in attendance, but the
Syrians absent. (Kissinger and Gromyko were there to make sure it went
reasonably well.) It was the first time Arab and Israeli diplomats had been
present in the same room to exchange their views on a possible peace in
the Middle East. But the only result was that Egypt and Israel were urged
to begin discussing the disengagement of their forces on both sides of the
Suez Canal. And on December 26, Egyptian and Israeli officers conferred
in Geneva about outstanding military problems in the areas where their
troops were in place, separated only by small U.N. contingents.

For Nixon, the aftermath of the October war was quite positive politically. He could claim, however extravagantly, that the Middle East was on
the road to peace as a result of American efforts—ignoring the fact that
the cost of the Yom Kippur war had been so enormous as to make it
debatable whether, in reality, much that was worthwhile had been
achieved to move beyond the *status quo ante bellum.* The Israelis certainly
did not think so.

But in other respects the outcome was not so positive. Relations with
Western Europe were strained, largely because most of America's allies
(except for the Netherlands) had quickly assumed a pro-Arab position.
West Germany had protested the Americans' use of its ports to move war
matériel to Israel from American depots in Europe. But, worse, the
American people themselves were suffering from the oil embargo. The
shortages that had been anticipated earlier in the year were now drastically compounded.

On November 7, the president delivered an address to the nation
about energy shortages. He warned that because of the embargo more
than 2 million barrels of crude oil a day that should have reached the
United States from the Middle East during November would not be
available. (In 1973, crude-oil imports from the Middle East represented
roughly 13 percent of total U.S. oil consumption.) Therefore, he said,
"We must . . . face up to a very stark fact: we are heading toward the most
acute shortages of energy since World War II. . . . Our supply of petroleum this winter . . . could fall short by as much as 17 percent." He
announced various measures being taken to conserve energy: a ban on
further conversion from coal to oil by industry and utilities (this had been
a trend for nearly twenty years); reduction in allocating fuel for aircraft
aimed at cutting back around 10 percent in airline flights; a 15-percent
reduction in the supply of heating oil for homes, offices, and other estab-

lishments; additional reduction in energy consumption by the federal government; and a speedup in the licensing and building of nuclear-power plants. Temperature in government offices would be kept to 65–68 degrees, and Nixon appealed to citizens to set home thermostats down to 68 degrees, too, which, he noted, is "really more healthy . . . if that is any comfort."

This was the first time since World War II that Americans had been asked to accept personal sacrifices so that the national economy would be spared major dislocations, and they responded with little enthusiasm to the idea; the attitude only worsened throughout the 1973–74 winter. (For example, there was widespread annoyance that Nixon had requested a 50-mile-per-hour highway speed limit, even though this alone would save 200,000 barrels of oil a day—10 percent of what normally came from the Middle East each day.)

The president said that he would request emergency energy legislation from Congress to develop domestic energy resources, so that the United States would be able to meet its own energy needs by 1980. But this was an impossible target date, as energy experts in and out of government hastened to point out. Still, Nixon had made it into a political goal, basically to enhance the idea of leadership being provided by his administration. Again he listed his achievements in 1973—he mentioned the ending of the Vietnam war and the record low unemployment rate, and proclaimed, "I have no intention whatever of walking away from the job I was elected to do. . . . In the months ahead, I shall do everything that I can to see that any doubts as to the integrity of the man who occupies the highest office in this land—to remove those doubts where they exist." Now, foreign policy *and* the energy crisis became reasons for the public to accept his continuation in the presidency. These were Nixon's last weapons.

On November 8, Nixon sent over to Congress the long list of proposals for emergency laws on energy. They ranged from mandatory conservation measures (such as exemption of energy-development projects from the National Environmental Protection Act and the establishment of year-round daylight saving time) to the grant of authority to the president "to allocate and ration energy supplies." Authorization for construction of the pipeline to bring oil from newly discovered fields in the Alaskan North Slope to warm-water ports in the south was deemed a "first order of business" (construction of the pipeline had been held up for years by court suits brought by environmental-protection groups). And Nixon also called for the creation of a Department of Energy and

Natural Resources in the cabinet. The latter was indeed an urgent matter, for no agency existed in the government to coordinate energy problems: the Federal Power Commission, the Interior Department's Bureau of Mines, the Commerce Department, and the State Department each had a piece of the pie, but nobody was in charge and there was no coherent energy policy. Nixon asked as well for a separate Energy Research and Development Administration to administer the $10-billion "Project Independence" he had devised. "This new effort to achieve self-sufficiency in energy," he said, "is absolutely critical to the maintenance of our ability to play our independent role in international affairs."

Nixon was absolutely right that energy independence was related to an independent foreign policy. But the trouble was that while the administration pushed hard for the lifting of the oil embargo, it was also, in effect, telling OPEC producers that America would not need their petroleum after 1980. This, inevitably, convinced the producers that they should raise their prices as much as possible to earn all they could before the United States became independent of them. The shah of Iran was among the first to react in this fashion to Project Independence. Iran was not a party to the embargo, but it more than doubled its crude-oil prices as soon as the Arabs imposed the ban. Other non-Arab OPEC producers —such as Venezuela and Nigeria, which provided much of the oil imported by the United States—quickly followed suit. OPEC understood instantly that it was a seller's market, and it moved to extract the maximum advantage from it.

The northeastern United States was running short on heating fuel by the onset of winter, and long queues were forming at gasoline stations. New measures were announced: refineries were ordered to reduce gasoline production in favor of heating oil throughout the winter (this, Nixon said, meant that the national gasoline supply was being cut by 15 percent); gasoline stations were asked to shut down on Sundays to discourage long weekend driving; fuel for airlines was cut again; and ornamental outdoor lighting for homes and businesses was forbidden.

On December 4, Nixon established a Federal Energy Office to "provide the centralized authority we must have for dealing with the energy crisis," and named William Simon, a New York bond specialist and deputy secretary of the treasury, to be its executive director. But energy was becoming a political football, and the creation of the FEO was only the beginning in a long series of reshuffles and reorganizations in the management of energy problems. This was the first time that Washington was becoming directly involved in operational energy matters as well as in policy-making, a step the big oil companies had successfully prevented since World War II.

The Arab oil embargo, meanwhile, weakened the much-vaunted détente with the Soviet Union. Negotiations for a new SALT agreement were completely stalled. The deadlock was of such magnitude that on November 30, Defense Secretary Schlesinger announced that the administration would propose the development of new strategic weapons as insurance against a failure to obtain a SALT II agreement: a larger ICBM (now that the Russians had MIRV warheads for their huge missiles, American strategic superiority had, in effect, vanished), mobile land-based missiles (which in 1972 Nixon and Kissinger had fought to put in the forbidden category), more MIRV warheads for existing missiles, new armaments for bombers, and accelerated production of ballistic-missile submarines.

This statement reflected the Pentagon's belief that the United States had to insist on "essential equivalence" with the Soviet Union in strategic weapons to avoid allowing the Russians to establish superiority in specific types of arms. But the judgment in the civilian agencies, including the NSC staff, was that what really mattered was overall equality. The argument sounded highly abstract to the uninitiated, but it deeply affected major issues—from defense budgets to the negotiating posture in SALT—and deeply divided the administration.

There were also emerging doubts about the Soviet Union's compliance with the 1972 SALT agreement. The administration refused publicly to discuss possible Soviet violations, but critics such as Senator Jackson brought it into the open. Joseph Alsop wrote in a column in mid-December that the administration's failure to deal adequately with Soviet SALT violations was "proof that the government is being increasingly paralyzed [by Watergate] in its most vital functions." The question of violations, he wrote, is in "total abeyance . . . because the President gained much political credit from SALT, and he is now too beleaguered to endanger that credit." Even Kissinger acknowledged the SALT problems, but he was still optimistic that SALT II would be signed before the end of 1974. By coincidence or not, at the end of the year the Pentagon announced that Minuteman III missiles—without nuclear warheads—would be tested for the first time in flight over the continental United States: from the North Dakota launching sites to the splash-down range in the Pacific. This, the Pentagon said, was necessary to "demonstrate the effectiveness and reliability of the Minuteman strategic deterrent force."

Things were going equally badly at the East-West negotiations in Vienna on the mutual balanced reduction of military forces in Central

Europe. The nineteen-nation conference had opened on October 30 and adjourned on December 13 without making the slightest progress. An American spokesman said that NATO and the Warsaw Pact countries were "significantly apart" on many issues. Moscow made it sound even worse: an editorial in *Pravda* on December 17 charged that NATO had advanced proposals intended to alter the regional balance of power.

Détente clearly was functioning better with China and Romania, the two Communist countries that, in varying degrees, opposed Soviet foreign policy. Chairman Mao and Premier Chou En-lai had received Kissinger in Peking on November 10; while there was no effort to reach specific new agreements—Washington's continued recognition of Taiwan still made normal diplomatic relations with Peking impossible—the atmosphere was quite warm. The United States had withdrawn a Phantom squadron from Taiwan in September, and the Chinese chalked it up as a goodwill gesture. One thing Kissinger did learn in Peking was that the Chinese were concerned about Watergate, reasoning that the weakening of the administration, to say nothing of the president's possible fall, would play into the hands of the Soviet Union; they believed that Brezhnev would not have risked the Middle East adventure in October if it had not been for the erosion of Nixon's authority. Yet the Chinese loyalty to Nixon, even beyond matters of policy, never flagged.

Although Romanian President Ceauşescu during a December visit to Washington warmly congratulated Nixon for his role in the reestablishment of peace in Vietnam, the peace itself was not being implemented at all. The Vietnamese cease-fire was being violated by both sides to such an extent that it was possible to say that full-fledged war was still raging in Indochina.

The only relatively positive development had been the formation on September 14 of a coalition government in Laos, incorporating representatives of the American-supported regime of Prince Souvanna Phouma and those of the Communist Pathet Lao movement led by Souvanna's half-brother, Prince Souphanouvong. Souvanna remained the premier, and Souphanouvong became a deputy premier; the Pathet Lao received five out of twelve cabinet posts. But when Kissinger went to Paris on December 20 for what was to be his last meeting with Le Duc Tho, the encounter produced nothing but mutual recriminations over Vietnam, and over Hanoi's continued refusal to disengage from Cambodia. The following day, the State Department sent a classified four-page cable to the heads of all U.S. diplomatic posts summarizing Washington's views on the implementation of the Vietnam cease-fire:

Communist violations of the Paris Accords . . . have reached a danger-ously high level. The build-up in men and arms of North Vietnamese forces in South Vietnam gives the Communists a capability for offen-sive action greater than that deployed before their spring 1972 offen-sive. The United States Government intends by every possible means to deter Hanoi from continuing on its present course. One of our efforts must be to bring to bear on Hanoi the pressure of external public opinion and to encourage other governments to exert a re-straining influence on North Vietnam.

The fighting continues. Ceasefire violations are numerous, and in the past two months they have become more serious and blatant. . . . None of the bodies established to implement the ceasefire has functioned effectively because the Communists have failed to facilitate the work of these peace-keeping mechanisms. . . . Further the ICCS has been largely crippled in its supervisory role because of persistent obstructionism on the part of its Communist members, Poland and Hungary.

There has been no progress toward a political settlement. North Vietnam remains determined to gain power in the South, by military means if necessary; and the South Vietnamese remain determined to prevent this. Communist efforts to win greater support from the South Vietnamese people have failed dismally. The current level of hostilities initiated by the Communists may reflect their conclusion that they have no chance to win a political contest in South Vietnam and that the military route represents their only hope of gaining control of the South. . . . Since January 27, over 70,000 fighting men have moved illegally into the South, bringing total Communist com-bat strength to between 180,000 and 190,000. This infiltration has recently been increased back up to wartime levels. . . .

While committing major violations of the Agreement, the Commu-nists have unleashed a massive propaganda barrage claiming alleged US and GVN ceasefire violations. Hanoi has sought to pin the blame for the deteriorating military situation on US encouragement of and assistance to GVN. . . .

The State Department's conclusion was that "while we cannot predict their decision, the Communists clearly have a viable option to launch another major offensive." This, it added, could take the form of "massive, coordinated assaults on all fronts, as in 1972," or "a creeping offensive, with gradually increased pressure on weak spots in South Vietnamese defenses, culminating in large-scale assaults against major targets." It added, in a phrase that best summed up the whole situation, that "be-cause of inevitable GVN counter-blows, such a strategy would tend to obscure the question of who is to blame for the renewed warfare."

It was hardly a happy note on which to end this negative, troubled year.

BOOK SIX

1974

The Year of the End

Chapter 27

For Richard Nixon, 1974 was a year of eight months and nine days. And during this short time, the foreign policy of the United States suffered further deterioration under a president subordinating it to his own survival—and a secretary of state whose own star was declining. And 1974 was marked by wars: the old ones in Indochina and a new one in Cyprus. There was in addition a major revolution—the military overthrow of the ancient dictatorship in Portugal—whose meaning and implications the Nixon administration wholly misunderstood. True, American diplomacy brought about the disengagement of military forces in the Middle East, new relationships were established with the Arabs in a dramatic personal performance by Nixon, and the oil embargo was lifted. And Richard Nixon had his last hurrah in the Kremlin, where he strove to salvage détente, and his own standing in the eyes of the American Congress and people, five weeks before the end. It was an unhappy and perplexing period.

The Middle East, in all its multifarious aspects, almost entirely dominated America's foreign policy during the first three months of 1974. On January 9, the president sent identical letters to the heads of the Canadian, West German, French, Italian, Japanese, Dutch, Norwegian, and British governments inviting their foreign ministers to attend a conference in Washington on February 11 to work out a "consumer action program" on energy in general and oil in particular. Nixon's idea was that oil-consuming industrialized nations should form a united front, then meet with the producers to seek a "concerted" program that "would satisfy the legitimate interests of both the consuming and producing countries." This was, of course, a sound approach. The industrialized countries, immensely vulnerable to OPEC pressures, needed a coordinated policy and, by the same token, a basic understanding with the producers on supplies and prices. But it was an enormously complicated proposition. The industrialized nations were far apart on their policies, while the producers took the view that any long-term arrangements must include concessions in trade patterns, allowances for inflationary distortions, and what they considered economic "justice" from those who had once "colonized" them politically and economically.

In a broad sense, this marked the opening of a new era in international relations, but this was not yet fully understood in Washington or elsewhere in the West.

Within a week, Nixon had good news to announce: the agreement between Egypt and Israel on the disengagement of their military forces that Kissinger had been able to hammer out in five days of furious shuttling between Jerusalem and Aswan (where President Sadat was spending a part of the winter). Actually, it was a surprisingly easy negotiation, as Kissinger himself remarked at the time, and the formula came from Israeli Defense Minister Dayan. Kissinger's original notion was that the disengagement should be discussed by Israeli and Egyptian teams in Geneva, but Dayan urged Kissinger to come back to the Middle East as soon as possible in January; after consulting with Sadat, he agreed to do so.

Dayan had proposed five zones in the canal area for the purposes of disengagement: an Egyptian zone of some ten miles east of Suez in the Sinai, a United Nations buffer zone, an Israeli zone in the Sinai, and two zones on either side of the canal in which no SAM batteries would be allowed. The Israelis would withdraw their forces from the west bank of the canal, where General Sharon's tanks had nearly destroyed the Egyptian Third Army in October.

Sadat was basically in agreement with this concept, but he did not want the disengagement maps to show the SAM-free zones. He was willing to have the five zones, but with only three of them showing on the maps. Somewhat reluctantly (Edward Sheehan quoted Sadat as saying, "It's difficult for me to sign a document which limits the forces in my own territory"), Egypt agreed to trim its forces on the east bank from 60,000 to 7000 men. The Israelis likewise accepted a limitation of forces in their zone adjoining the U.N. buffer area.

But some fast diplomatic footwork was required. Sadat was unwilling to specify the forces' limitations in the agreement because it might look as if Israel had imposed them. So Kissinger came up with the idea that the official agreement would simply mention the limitations, while letters from the U.S. government to Israel and Egypt would spell out precisely what they were. Israel, for its part, needed a series of assurances from the

United States, now that it had to give up a slice of Sinai after having, in effect, won the Yom Kippur war. (Kissinger, perhaps unwittingly, compounded Israeli worries by gratuitously telling Foreign Minister Eban that Nixon was anti-Semitic. Later that year, the president, just as gratuitously, told Syria's President Assad, "You can depend on Kissinger; he's an American, not a Jew.")

There were secret agreements, too. Kissinger gave the Israelis a secret memorandum of understanding, which conveyed an Egyptian commitment to clear the Suez Canal (with American technical assistance), rebuild cities along the waterway, and resume peacetime activities. This was crucial for Israel: if Sadat rebuilt the shattered cities, he would, presumably, be unlikely to start a new war in the area. The memorandum also assured Israel that "the United States will make every effort to be fully responsive on a continuing and long-term basis to Israel's military equipment requirements." And Sadat secretly promised Kissinger that nonmilitary Israeli cargoes would be allowed to go through the Suez Canal. Both governments agreed to let the United States maintain aerial surveillance over the disengagement area.

The only tangible result of the October war was that Israel lost its Bar-Lev defenses on the canal and surrendered a fifteen-mile strip of territory in the Sinai. But for Sadat this was something of a political triumph: high as the military cost had been, the Egyptians were back in the Sinai for the first time since 1967.

On January 18, Israeli and Egyptian chiefs of staff signed the disengagement agreement at Kilometer 101 on the Cairo-Suez road. What was achieved was a little less—the strip on the eastern bank of the Suez Canal given the Egyptians—than the *status quo ante bellum*. In a war that was avoidable, this was an extraordinarily costly restoration of the situation that had existed prior to October 6, 1973.

Though Nixon viewed the disengagement as an American foreign-policy victory, it did not bring the end of the paralyzing oil embargo. Sadat had promised Kissinger to intervene with producing governments once the disengagement was achieved, yet the Saudis and the others were unresponsive. They wanted to extract more Israeli concessions and broader Western commitments on economic relationships. And in any case, the Americans were choosing peculiar ways to seek an end to the embargo. First, Kissinger had told the producers that the embargo, combined with Watergate, might quicken Nixon's impeachment. Then, during the Christmas holidays, he hinted in a magazine interview that the United States might, conceivably, have recourse to armed force to reopen oil supply lines. Other published articles, generally believed to have been inspired by the administration, suggested blueprints for an invasion of the Persian Gulf area. The nervous apprehension about American interventionism did little to speed the lifting of the embargo. Fortunately for Nixon—who on January 19 expressed his satisfaction that after seven "gasless Sundays" and other conservation measures, gasoline consumption had gone down 9 percent and heating-oil consumption 16 percent —the 1973–74 winter was unusually mild.

But the great problem was the rising cost of fuel. OPEC producers were hiking their prices while big oil companies were showing record profits. Nixon noted that prices of imported oil from nonembargo countries had risen from $4 a barrel in September to $12 in January. Congress, he said, would be asked to act immediately on a windfall-profit tax, and the oil companies would be required to provide a "full and constant accounting" of their inventories—something they had zealously kept to themselves in the past.

On January 23, the president asked for additional legislation to meet "the short-term emergency" and laws "to help us achieve self-sufficiency in energy." Sounding like a populist, Nixon told Congress, "We must not permit private profiteering at the expense of public sacrifice. . . . In equal measure, we must not permit the big oil companies or any other major domestic energy producers to manipulate the public by withholding information on their energy supplies." Then, in an unusual confession of past error, the president remarked, "The Arab oil embargo will temporarily close some gasoline stations, but it has opened our eyes to the short-sighted policy we had been pursuing."

On February 11, the conference of foreign ministers of oil-consuming industrialized nations met in Washington, and Nixon told the participants that "we are here at . . . a watershed in world history." Then he proceeded to warn them that despite his administration's best efforts, there was "a growing sense of isolationism" in the United States.

The warning was intended to impress, particularly on the West Europeans, that the United States was increasingly concerned about the inability of the allies to act together. Washington resented the Europeans' dealing with the Arabs during the October war to assure oil supplies in total disregard of what it considered to be the need for a concerted policy.

But Nixon's exhortations fell on deaf ears. The conference produced no tangible results but, rather, a bitterness, which the participants tried only half-successfully to hide from public view. Kissinger had tense exchanges with France's sardonic foreign minister, Michel Jobert, and in the end, the West remained divided. A few weeks later, the president put it bluntly in a speech in Chicago: "We are not going to be faced with a situation where the nine countries of Europe gang up against the United States—the United States which is their guarantee for their security. That we cannot have."

At his first news conference of the year, on February 25, in reply to a question about the embargo, Nixon noted that Kissinger's attempt to obtain a Syrian-Israeli disengagement might have "a positive effect, although it is not linked to the problem of the embargo directly." But, he warned, "If the embargo is not lifted, it will naturally slow down the efforts that we are making on the peace front."

On March 1, a Federal grand jury in Washington indicted seven administration officials, most of them men who had worked in the White House and were close to Nixon, on charges of conspiracy to obstruct the administration of justice and other offenses. Among the seven were Haldeman, Ehrlichman, Colson, and former Attorney General Mitchell.

Nixon was now fighting a rearguard battle, increasingly falling back on his residual statesmanship in foreign policy and on his campaign to extricate the United States from the energy crisis. On March 6, he vetoed the energy-emergency bill, charging that Congress had "succeeded only in producing legislation which solves none of the problems, threatens to undo the progress we have already made, and creates a host of new problems." His earlier populist pronouncements notwithstanding, he faulted the bill that set domestic crude oil prices at a level so low that "the oil industry would be unable to sustain its present production of petroleum products, including gasoline." He seemed unaware of the contradiction between his earlier protests against excess profits and his determination to let the companies bring the prices of so-called new oil—the production developed after 1972—up to the level charged by foreign sellers. The Senate sustained the veto.

On the same day, Nixon held another news conference, trying vainly to focus attention on the energy crisis. The House Judiciary Committee was now moving toward formal impeachment proceedings against him, and the reporters could talk of little else. But again Nixon linked the embargo with Kissinger's efforts to obtain a Syrian-Israeli military disengagement: "We believe that the progress . . . that is taking place on the diplomatic front will inevitably have a constructive effect on the oil-producing countries. . . ."

On March 8, the president conducted a cabinet meeting, a rare occasion, to discuss Kissinger's peacemaking efforts in the Middle East and the energy situation. The next day, Nixon flew to Key Biscayne for a brief rest. He returned to Washington late on March 11. On the twelfth, he conferred with King Hussein, promising Jordan additional military aid and urging him to use whatever influence he had to help Kissinger to work out the Israeli-Syrian accord. Whereas the negotiations in January for an Egyptian-Israeli disengagement had been relatively easy, the talks with the Syrians were turning into a diplomatic nightmare, and it would take Kissinger nearly four more months to win an agreement.

On the evening of March 12, Nixon addressed the Veterans of Foreign Wars—one of the few friendly forums left to him—in still another defense of his foreign policy.

The Western world could not achieve even a semblance of unity in the difficult days of 1974, but Richard Nixon's stubborn policies in the Middle East paid off when the Arab oil producers finally lifted their embargo, on March 18. Nixon wasted no time in making sure that it was understood as a victory for him and that the credit should accrue to him. Speaking in Houston on March 19, he announced that "It will not be necessary for us to have compulsory [oil] rationing," that the order closing gasoline stations on Sundays was being rescinded, and that the administration was increasing oil allocations to industry and agriculture "so that they can have the necessary energy to operate at full capacity." He promised, too, that "the problem of peace in the Middle East will be high on the agenda" on his trip to Moscow late in June for the third summit with Brezhnev.

Nixon's assessment of the political situation, as the proceedings against him gained momentum, was that his last defense lay in his image as the great peacemaker. As early as March, his administration began planning his Moscow trip. On the twenty-fourth, Kissinger broke away from his Middle Eastern negotiations to fly to Moscow for four days of conferences to prepare the summit with Brezhnev and his advisers. If the Russians had any reservations about receiving Nixon at a time when he might be facing impeachment proceedings, they gave no sign of it. They were deeply annoyed with American activities in the Middle East, but interestingly, they chose to blame the secretary of state, long their favorite interlocutor, rather than Nixon for working out direct settlements between Israel and its Arab antagonists instead of working with the Soviet Union in the context of Geneva. When Senator Edward Kennedy was received by Brezhnev at the Kremlin on April 22, just a month after Kissinger's visit, Brezhnev said to him, "Just between us—it is official, but no publicity—I berated Kissinger here in Moscow for the United States' behavior in the Middle East. We had agreed, at the United Nations and elsewhere, that the United States and the Soviet Union would work together to secure peace. Then Kissinger began a series of ruses and attempted to go it alone in the Middle East. So I agree, we must act together, or there will be no tranquillity in the Middle East. Israel, too, wants peace and tranquillity, and guarantees of independence. Israel, too, knows our strength, and would want us to guarantee. It was even agreed, even to better relations with Israel. Then, there was the Kissinger trickery—which is not the way to deal with this. At San Clemente, I kept Nixon up almost all night on the Middle East, trying to convince him of the need to act together. Otherwise, there would be an explosion in the Middle East. Nixon did not heed my words. Then Nixon wrote a letter to me, saying that he underestimated the gravity of the problem. Kissinger now agrees that we must act together. . . . The Soviet Union has shown some restraint in the Middle East."

Brezhnev's self-serving comments suggest that the Russians were developing uncertainties about their dealings with Nixon and Kissinger.

The president spoke proudly about American peacemaking in the Middle East, but there were fewer and fewer references to the 1973 Vietnam agreements and virtually none to "peace with honor." In the fourteen months since the signing of the Paris settlement, not the slightest progress had been made toward the creation of a National Council or toward general elections. To be sure, this had been an impossible proposition from the start, Thieu was not about to negotiate any joint political venture with the Communists, and the PRG, not unexpectedly, wanted to do business only on its own terms.

Besides, the Communists were steadily building up their military strength (there was nobody to monitor them or stop them) for what inevitably had to be a denouement on the battlefield. After March, the two South Vietnamese factions gave up even the pretense of negotiating.

Likewise, Saigon was incapable of defending itself in the field. Its most powerful weapon—the huge air force the Americans had given Thieu— could only function against the North Vietnamese and the Viet Cong if the United States supplied enough fuel and ammunition. And it was precisely in that area that Thieu and Nixon were running into trouble.

In April, the administration asked Congress to raise the existing $1.12-billion ceiling on military assistance to South Vietnam during the balance of fiscal 1974, but in May a Senate-House conference refused. Congress had no more stomach for financing the war between the Vietnamese. When it came to authorizing military funds for Saigon for fiscal 1975, the White House asked for $1.6 billion; the House held it down to the previous year's $1.12-billion ceiling, while the Senate, infuriating Nixon, lowered it to $900 million. The Pentagon then tried an end run: having discovered that it still had $266 million in unexpended moneys for Vietnam from previous years, it tried to spend it—but again, Congress blocked the move. A House-Senate conference report declared, "No accounting change would be permitted by the [Defense] Department involving the $266 million in question," and, "It cannot be emphasized too strongly that the statutory ceiling of $1.12 billion enacted in Fiscal Year 1974 remains unaltered and shall not be circumvented by accounting adjustments."

On April 25, a virtually bloodless military revolution led by young officers overthrew the dictatorial regime of Premier Marcello Caetano in Portugal, an extension of the iron rule that had been established nearly a half century earlier by Antônio do Oliveira Salazar, the West's most durable dictator. What brought down Caetano was Portugal's fourteen-year war against the nationalist movements in its African territories: Angola, Mozambique, and Guinea-Bissau. The nation was exhausted by the war that could not be won, and young Portuguese officers had gradually espoused the independence cause. Many of them, indeed, were also captivated by the Marxist or generally leftist views of the African leaders with whom they had come in contact. But the April revolution had repercussions far beyond Portugal and its African lands.

For the Nixon administration, Caetano's fall was unmitigated bad news. A dictatorship with which the United States had useful, if not cordial, relations was being replaced by leftist officers who muttered about American imperialism while trying to make radical reforms; mindful of the previous year's events in Chile, they developed, not unnaturally, an obsessive fear of the United States. And indeed, as seen from Washington, Portugal could become a focus of Marxist contagion in southern Europe at a time when Generalissimo Francisco Franco, the Spanish dictator, was nearing death, and the power of the Communist Party was growing in Italy.

But the Portuguese revolution had still another meaning. The new government instantly suspended hostilities in Africa and promised independence to the three colonies (or, rather, "overseas territories") by the end of 1975. In one stroke, the entire geopolitical map of Africa was affected. If black rulers were to replace the Portuguese in Angola and

Mozambique, the white regimes of Rhodesia and South Africa would lose the protective belt that for so many years had protected them from nationalist black guerrillas to the north of them. Besides, the victorious movements in Angola and Mozambique were of a Marxist persuasion (the CIA, playing both ends against the middle, had secretly supported the weakest of the Angolan rebel factions, while the Soviets backed the much more popular leftist movements), and this gave the shivers to Kissinger and his fellow policy-makers. Nonetheless, even Kissinger began to recognize that the basic balance of power in Africa was shifting dramatically —and permanently. Kissinger's assessment in the NSC study of 1970 that white regimes in Africa were there to stay forever had been demolished by forces of history that he had failed to perceive. And the Lisbon revolution had turned the Horn of southern Africa into one of the world's most strategic and contested areas.

Richard Nixon did not fully appreciate the Portuguese events and their implications or even pay much attention to them. He apparently could concentrate only on the Middle East and détente with the Soviet Union. Nevertheless, he preserved the façade of total involvement in world affairs, and spent the month of April in frantic activity.

On April 2, President Pompidou died in Paris, and Nixon immediately decided to attend the funeral. It was expected of the American president to represent the United States personally at the burial of the leader of a major Western ally; besides, it would be an opportunity for noncontroversial international exposure. On the same day, Nixon found time to receive Secretary of Commerce Frederick Dent, to discuss Dent's forthcoming trip to the Soviet Union, Bulgaria, and Romania. This was détente business.

But the next day Nixon was engulfed again by personal problems. The Joint Congressional Committee on Internal Revenue Taxation released a staff analysis of his tax situation, suggesting that he had taken an illegal deduction of $432,787.13 on his 1969 return for donating his vice-presidential papers to the National Archives. The law permitting such deductions had been set aside by Congress effective July 1969, but Nixon had had the papers delivered to the archives after that date and, ignoring the legislation, claimed the whopping deduction. His response to the Joint Committee's staff analysis was to insist that while the actual delivery had been made *before* the July deadline, he was ordering the payment of the full amount plus interest to the Internal Revenue Service. But he was misleading the nation: the dates on the documents transmitting his "gift" to the archives had been falsified by one of his lawyers.

Publicly, he was keeping up a brave front. On April 6, he went to memorial services for Pompidou at Notre Dame Cathedral, visited Acting President Alain Poher, appeared at a reception for foreign leaders, and spent the rest of the day receiving heads of state and government at the American embassy residence.

State funerals are excellent occasions for quick top-level diplomacy, and Nixon covered all the bases during his stay in Paris. Speaking to reporters, he remarked incongruously, given the circumstances of this visit, "We always like to come to Paris. I look forward to coming back someday when I have many hours as a tourist to try the restaurants again. Forty years ago, I majored in French, had four years of French. After four years, I could speak it, I could write it. I read all the classics. And today, I just understand a little."

The president preferred to be away from the White House as much as possible. The Paris trip was a welcome change of scene, and two days after returning to Washington, he was off again, this time to inspect tornado damage in Xenia, Ohio. On April 10, he visited four towns in Michigan's Eighth Congressional District in his first tour of the year in anticipation of the 1974 congressional elections. At each stop, Nixon delivered an unusually long speech—he seemed to have the need to talk about himself and his programs—emphasizing his foreign-policy achievements. He reminded his audiences that "for the first time in twelve years, America is at peace with all nations in the world," that the Vietnam POWs had returned home, and that in Paris "I met with the heads of thirty-five governments"—which was a wild exaggeration. Inevitably, Nixon kept overselling himself. In one of his speeches, he said that he had gone to Europe the previous week as part of his effort to "build a permanent peace" (there was no mention of Pompidou's death), and "that is why we are working for peace in the Mideast, that is why I will be going to the Soviet Union to talk to our adversaries to reduce the burden of arms that rests on the shoulders of the men and women who work wherever they are throughout the world and also reduce the danger of war."

On April 11, the president was back in Washington to confer with Algeria's President Houari Boumedienne and to preside over a White House working dinner for his visitor. But on April 13, he fled Washington again, this time for a three-day rest at Key Biscayne.

Returning on April 17, Nixon received West Berlin's Mayor Klaus Schütz. In the evening, he entertained Latin American foreign ministers (they were en route to Atlanta for the annual meeting of the Organization of American States). "You can expect that the United States will not seek to impose its political preferences on your countries," he told them. "We will not interfere in the domestic affairs of others in this hemisphere." This was just seven months after the overthrow and death of Salvador Allende, but Nixon seemed oblivious to the implications these events might have in the minds of Latin Americans.

Kissinger was preparing to return to the Middle East, and Egyptian Foreign Minister Ismail Fahmy came to the White House on April 18 to discuss the disengagement of Israeli and Syrian troops. Earlier in the day, the president had gone to Constitution Hall for the annual congress of the Daughters of the American Revolution to deliver a speech that heavily emphasized foreign policy. Now Nixon was not only *justifying* the long war in Vietnam, but assiduously creating the illusion that all was well in Indochina. He addressed himself to these matters in his Foreign Assistance Program message to Congress on April 24, requesting a $940-million appropriation "to assist South Vietnam, Cambodia and Laos in their efforts to shift their economies from war to peace and to accelerate the reconstitution of their societies." The president also asked for $330 million for Israel, $250 million for Egypt, and $207 million for Jordan. For Israel and Jordan, most of these funds were to be earmarked for military use; the money for Egypt was for clearing the Suez Canal, repairing the damage in adjacent areas, and restoring trade. Planning a trip to the Middle East the following month, Nixon was keen on presenting Israel and the Arabs with the kind of aid that, in his judgment, would encourage both sides to go along with the American peace initiatives.

A casual look at Nixon's official schedule during April and his speeches, pronouncements, and messages would indeed suggest that the president was fully concentrating on foreign affairs and that he was fully in command of America's international policies. This was the impression he strove to create, always emphasizing his global statesmanship. On April 25, for example, he flew to Jackson, Mississippi, to give a long speech before the state's economic council. Once again he recounted his Paris trip, telling his audience that he had conferred with thirty-five heads of government and heads of state *in addition to* the leaders of Britain, France, Italy, West Germany, and the Soviet Union. The number of foreign leaders with whom he had met during the three days in Paris kept growing. But Nixon was never free of Watergate, no matter how much he traveled, where he went, or how deeply he tried to hide behind foreign policy.

On April 11, the House Judiciary Committee had issued a subpoena for additional presidential tape recordings. On April 29, the president went on television to announce that he would deliver to the committee the next day 1200 pages of transcripts of his private conversations about Watergate with his principal aides and associates between September 1972 and April 1973. It was the product of forty-two tapes covering that period, and the publication of this material became the turning point in the impeachment hearings being held by the House Judiciary Committee. He evidently now realized that he was in mortal danger of impeachment, and his speech was an impassioned plea to let him remain at the White House.

But the president's appeal went unheeded. During May the noose of Watergate was drawn tighter and tighter around his neck. On May 7, the president advised the House Judiciary Committee that he would supply no more of his tapes. Two days later, the committee began examining in closed session such documentary evidence as was available to it. But it needed additional White House materials. Consequently, on May 15, the committee issued a subpoena for the tapes and his diaries. On May 22, Nixon advised the committee that he would not produce any of these materials.

In an increasingly unreal way, Nixon went on vaunting his foreign-policy achievements—as if everything were perfectly normal in Washington. He was determined to carry out his scheduled trips to the Middle East in June and to the Soviet Union during late June and early July, and evidently could not believe that it was already too late for this strategy to work, that no matter what he achieved in Cairo, Jerusalem, or Moscow, Congress would move inexorably to impeachment.

He kept up the façade—relentlessly. At a Republican rally in Phoenix, Arizona, on May 3, he repeated his recital of foreign-policy achievements, then said: "The time has come to get Watergate behind us and get on with the business of America." The next day, he was in Spokane, Washington, to inaugurate Expo '74, and this, too, became a forum for plugging world statesmanship.

Back in Washington on May 7, the president turned his attention to the energy crisis. For once Congress had gone along with him, approving legislation to proceed with the Alaska pipeline and to create the Federal Energy Administration. He was highly pleased but, as usual, overdid it in his public reaction. On May 8, he swore in William Simon as the new treasury secretary (George Shultz, one of the best minds in the cabinet, had had enough of the government and quit); Simon had served as the head of the energy program, and Nixon liked his toughness.

On May 11, he was back on the stump. At the commencement exercises at Oklahoma State University at Stillwater, Nixon talked football, energy crisis, foreign policy—and Watergate. "Having presented all of the evidence to the Congress of the United States, I trust that the House of Representatives will act promptly so that we can reach a decision, so that the president, the Congress can get on with the people's business, as we should."

At the White House, his attention seemed to remain riveted to security and diplomatic affairs. On May 14, he received General George Brown, whom he had nominated to be chairman of the Joint Chiefs of Staff, and General David Jones, picked to be the new chief of staff of the air force. On May 19, he sent a message to Valéry Giscard d'Estaing congratulating him on becoming the president of France. Within three days he conferred with Japanese Foreign Minister Masayoshi Ohira; NATO's Secretary General Joseph Luns; the foreign ministers of Britain, Iran, Turkey, and Pakistan, in Washington for the annual meeting of the Central Treaty Organization's Council; Aziz Ahmed, Pakistan's minister of state for foreign affairs and defense; and eight members of the Presidium of the Supreme Soviet of the Soviet Union. All the visitors to the Oval Office reported that Nixon was alert, interested, and fully informed.

Chapter 28

All this frantic activity did not obviate the need for some convincing demonstration that President Nixon could keep delivering. White House hopes were pinned on Kissinger's shuttle negotiations for the disengagement of Syrian and Israeli troops. But this was an excruciatingly tough problem. Neither side was willing to give up an inch of territory: Syria's President Assad insisted that the Israelis pull away from Quneitra and the surrounding area beyond the Golan Heights they had taken in their counteroffensive; Mrs. Meir and the Israeli cabinet kept arguing that this kind of withdrawal was unacceptable for military-security reasons (the prime minister told Kissinger that too much Israeli blood had been shed around Quneitra as a result of hostilities initiated by the Syrians to justify any concessions). And while Kissinger kept flying between Damascus and Jerusalem, the Israelis and Syrians were fighting an escalating war of attrition on the ground and in the air.

Oddly, it was Nixon who may have salvaged the negotiations. Twice in late May, Kissinger was prepared to give up, convinced that the deadlock was unbreakable. But the president instructed him to keep shuttling and keep talking, and simultaneously urged Mrs. Meir several times to be more flexible. This may have been diplomacy of desperation, but it worked in the sense that Kissinger remained long enough to go on persuading Syria and Israel to compromise. The negotiations broke down once more—on May 27 when Kissinger was in Damascus—and again he was on the verge of returning to Washington; this time, Assad encouraged him to go to Jerusalem for one more try. And on May 29 the breakthrough was finally achieved.

Nixon made a point of personally announcing the disengagement agreement that day (simultaneous announcements were being made in Damascus and Jerusalem) in a statement he read to White House reporters. He saw it as a triumph for *his* administration—and, therefore, for him —but Kissinger emerged as the principal hero. The Judiciary Committee went on with its impeachment proceedings, while Kissinger stood proud

and alone in the limelight. One cannot but feel that Nixon must have
hated him at that moment, even more than when he had won the Nobel
Peace Prize the year before.

For his part, Kissinger was increasingly hostile to the president—in
private, of course. He had expressed intellectual contempt for Nixon
from the very outset, but dependent as he was on the president's goodwill
for his continuing advancement and stardom, he treated him with extraordinary deference. Still, he had convinced himself that the president
could have never evolved his foreign policy without him—a judgment
that is arguable, since Nixon was not a neophyte in world affairs—and he
seemed to resent the president's personal reputation as an international
statesman. It was an amazing partnership: both men insecure to the point
of paranoia, but each needing the other for foreign-policy glory.

With the onset of Watergate, it became clear to Kissinger's closest
aides that the secretary of state was hoping for the impeachment of the
president. He seemed to have forgotten his own involvement in the 1969
wiretapping program, one of the articles of impeachment. The fear was
simply that Nixon's incapacitation in office would destroy *his,* Kissinger's,
foreign policy. During the May shuttle in the Middle East, he was angry
that Nixon had twice ordered him to keep negotiating when he judged
that he should break off the talks and fly home. And when Nixon's instincts proved to be right and the breakthrough was achieved, he was
even angrier.

In his White House announcement, the president sounded most
statesmanlike:

> It is obviously a major diplomatic achievement, and Secretary Kis-
> singer deserves enormous credit for the work that he has done . . . in
> keeping this negotiation going and finally reaching an agreement
> when, at many times over the past few weeks, it seemed that the
> negotiations would break down. . . . This particular agreement, to-
> gether with the agreement that was reached earlier on disengagement
> of Egyptian and Israeli forces, now paves the way for progress in
> Geneva and, of course, with the various governments involved, to-
> ward our objective and, we trust, their objective as well, of achieving
> a permanent peace settlement for the entire Mideast area. . . . The
> prospects . . . are better than they have been at any time over the past
> twenty-five years.

Undeniably, the May disengagement (largely patterned after the Egyptian accord, and enforced by a United Nations Disengagement Observer
Force) was an important step toward peace, but to say that prospects for

a permanent peace were now better than at any time in a quarter century was a gross exaggeration; as the president should have known, the basic positions in the Middle East remained unchanged, and no new solutions had been invented for such fundamental problems as that of the Palestinians.

Nixon tried to create the impression that new significant developments were in the offing. This served, among other things, to set the tone for his forthcoming journey to the area. On the evening of the announcement, Nixon had entertained eleven congressmen at dinner aboard the presidential yacht, *Sequoia,* talking about the bright prospects in the Middle East. Watergate was politely ignored. Still, even as he prepared to travel, he had to keep fighting the Watergate battle. For the release of his taped conversations had marked the beginning of the end. Now the Judiciary Committee and the special prosecutor demanded that additional tapes and documents be turned over to them, and the president was facing the possibility that the case would go to the Supreme Court.

On the eve of the Middle Eastern trip, therefore, Nixon again turned to his foreign-policy record to defend his presidential credentials. On June 5 the forum was the Naval Academy in Annapolis, Maryland, where he went to deliver an address at the commencement ceremonies. Then on June 9, the day before the trip, he attended a luncheon where he was honored by the National Citizens' Committee for Fairness to the Presidency, a hard-core organization of his supporters headed by Rabbi Baruch Korff. There he was among friends, including William Simon, Earl Butz, and Nebraska's Senator Carl Curtis. Characteristically, Nixon opened his remarks with the comment, "Tomorrow . . . Mrs. Nixon and I will start a very long journey of fifteen thousand miles in which we will visit five nations, four of which have never been visited by a president of the United States." He was still claiming firsts. The audience was reminded that "I have visited over eighty countries over the past twenty-seven years" and that "I have visited many countries that no president has ever visited before." Then came the appeal for national support, the smooth phrase in which Watergate and Nixon's personal fate became intertwined with the institution of the presidency and the future of the world: "We are grateful to each and every one of you and to the hundreds of thousands and millions throughout the country who recognize that what is involved, not only in what has happened over the past few months and years but what is involved in the future, is the American presidency and what it can do for this nation, what it can do not only for Americans but for all the people who inhabit this globe." There was a standing ovation for Nixon as he left the hotel ballroom, walking to his car in the bright spring afternoon sunshine. Only a few of the bystanders noticed that the president had a slight limp.

The next morning, June 10, came the departure for the Middle East. Nixon, still limping, left the White House and strolled to the south lawn for the farewell ceremonies. His last act before leaving was to sign a letter to Representative Peter W. Rodino, Jr., chairman of the House Judiciary Committee, reiterating his refusal to comply with subpoenas for presidential tape recordings and documents. He had already refused to comply with the subpoena that was issued on May 15, and on May 30, as Nixon was hailing the Middle East disengagement agreement, Rodino had written him that this refusal was a "grave matter." Now the president responded: "The question of the respective rights and responsibilities of the Executive and Legislative branches is one of the cardinal questions raised by a proceeding such as the one the Committee is now conducting," and "the question at issue is . . . where the line is to be drawn on an apparently endlessly escalating spiral of demands for confidential Presidential tapes and documents." He could not accept the "doctrine" that the Judiciary Committee "should be the sole judge of Presidential confidentiality."

Through a bizarre quirk in legal research, Nixon's letter cited as precedents for his refusal two cases that, from the viewpoint of popularity, could not have been worse choices.

One was a 1962 Senate resolution declaring that a federal court needed its permission to obtain evidence in its power for the trial of the Teamsters Union president, James Hoffa. The other one was a House subcommittee's refusal to turn over to the courts for trial testimony obtained in executive session concerning Lieutenant Calley of My Lai massacre fame. One would have thought that common sense would have counseled Nixon not to associate himself in the public mind with Hoffa or Calley—however remotely.

Now the idea was to deflect attention from the Watergate investigations with the trips to the Middle East and Russia. From a foreign-policy standpoint, a visit to Moscow fitted into the rhythm of annual meetings to which Nixon and Brezhnev, perhaps mistakenly, had agreed in 1972. But the excuse for the Middle East trip was less convincing. Although presidential goodwill visits may be a good idea under certain circumstances, the situation in the Middle East in June 1974 was not propitious, and there was little Nixon could in fact accomplish there, except to shore up relations with the Arabs and Israelis. The trip might conceivably have been justified as being designed to bolster Nixon's position vis-à-vis Brezhnev, but this, too, seemed marginal. In the end, all rhetoric to the contrary notwithstanding, the president embarked on this 15,000-mile trip for personal reasons that were essentially related to Watergate. And he did so despite a developing illness that he kept secret from his family and staff. He knew that there was something wrong with his left leg—the mounting pain was responsible for the limp of the past days—but he was going to clench his teeth and brave it.

Air Force One brought Nixon to Salzburg, Austria, on the evening of June 10. The plan was for him to spend a day there before going on to Cairo. But June 11 turned out to be a day of crises in Salzburg, for Watergate had followed the presidential party to Austria, and Nixon's health was at stake.

Secretary of State Kissinger, who was in the presidential party, precipitated the first crisis by calling a special news conference at which he discussed the accusations that he had played an active role in the 1969–70 wiretapping program, and that he had knowledge that David Young, one of his assistants, was involved in the White House Plumbers operation. He announced that he had written a letter to Chairman Fulbright of the Senate Foreign Relations Committee formally requesting that his earlier testimony on the subject be reviewed by that body in order to clear his name once and for all. To the completely stunned group of correspondents, he charged that documents he had submitted to the Fulbright committee were being leaked to the House Judiciary Committee and then to the press in a way that undermined his credibility. Alternately choking with anger and shaken by emotion, Kissinger declared, "In these circumstances, it is not appropriate for me, as secretary of state, to go with the president to the Middle East without having a full discussion of the facts as I know them. . . . I do not believe it is possible to conduct the foreign policy of the United States under these circumstances when the character and credibility of the secretary of state is at issue. And if it is not cleared up, I will resign."

Kissinger's extraordinary performance produced a major shock in Salzburg and in Washington. For one thing, it totally overshadowed Nixon and the Middle East. As John Herbers, White House correspondent of *The New York Times,* wrote, the Kissinger "ultimatum" seemed "to threaten what is widely believed to be one of the purposes of the journey —to divert public attention from Administration scandals."

Why did the secretary choose to hold his Watergate-related news conference at that moment, and why did he do it in Salzburg, on foreign soil, in utter violation of all rules of diplomatic behavior? Inasmuch as Kissinger had all along been expressing fears that Watergate might, indeed, ruin the administration's foreign policy, he was engaging in a self-serving exercise without any regard as to how it might affect the embattled president for whom he worked.

Kissinger's explanation is not convincing. The reason, he said, had to do with articles written about a news conference he had held at the State Department five days earlier, on June 6, when several questions were asked about his role in the wiretapping and about David Young. The questions that had irritated him the most were whether he had been contacted by Watergate prosecutors regarding a possible perjury investigation of his sworn testimony on the subject before Senate committees, and whether he had retained counsel "in preparation for a defense against a possible perjury indictment." Kissinger's reply on June 6 had been, "I have not retained counsel, and I am not conducting my office as if it were a conspiracy. I stand on the statements that I have made and I will answer no further questions on this topic." But now Kissinger, stung by adverse press comments in the interval, was not only willing to answer questions but eager to go on the offensive. He said that he had contacted Fulbright on Sunday, the day before the trip, to deliver the letter requesting a review of his case by the Senate Foreign Relations Committee. But he omitted to say that he had also talked with Senate Majority Leader Mike Mansfield, who had counseled him against raising the topic with the press on the eve of a presidential journey. Kissinger had considered holding a news conference on Sunday, but evidently took Mansfield's advice. On arriving in Salzburg, however, he abruptly decided to "go public." Nixon, he knew, could not jettison him at that point, and Fulbright's committee, still awed by "miracle-maker" Kissinger, immediately agreed to review his record. Later that day, the secretary shrugged off questions as to whether he really planned to resign.

But Kissinger was treading on dangerous ground. At that point, the only allegations against him were that he had volunteered names of people to be wiretapped and that he had regularly received FBI "logs" of intercepted telephone conversations. In Salzburg he said that his participation had been entirely passive, that he submitted names of potential leakers only when he was asked for suggestions, and that he read no more than brief "summaries" of pertinent FBI reports when national security was thought to be endangered. This, he said, he had already told the Foreign Relations Committee at his confirmation hearings in 1973. In the absence of other evidence, these statements were accepted at face value.

There was no proof that he had not spoken the truth. After all, nobody had accused him of a crime: wiretapping was legal if authorized by the president or the attorney general.

Since then, however, a considerable amount of information—including sworn testimony—has emerged to suggest that Kissinger was not a passive participant in the wiretap affair. Testimony by former Attorney General Mitchell and others, FBI memoranda obtained by the House Judiciary Committee, and depositions taken from a number of former officials (including Nixon) in Morton Halperin's successful wiretap suit (Halperin was the first NSC official to be wiretapped) depict the secretary of state as being quite actively involved. Kissinger had discussed the measures to be taken to stop news leaks with Hoover by telephone and personally. In a deposition taken early in 1976, Nixon said, "My recollection is that they went back and forth, Hoover and Dr. Kissinger, as to who might be the individual or individuals who should be surveilled." Nixon also said under oath that Kissinger had the power to recommend to Hoover that wiretaps be removed if they were no longer necessary. Hoover, he testified, "would give very great weight to Dr. Kissinger's recommendation that a tap be removed, just as he would give very great weight to a recommendation that a surveillance be instituted."

In his own deposition, also given early in January 1976, Kissinger insisted that it was Hoover who had suggested the first four names of wiretap targets, including Halperin, and that he had been simply asked "to supply the names of key individuals having access to sensitive information which had leaked."

Kissinger's truthfulness relates in an even deeper sense to his cavalier conduct of American diplomacy. The fact is that virtually nobody—possibly not even Richard Nixon and Gerald Ford—knows precisely what promises and commitments Kissinger made to foreign leaders during his eight years in power: to Mao Tse-tung and Chou En-lai, Brezhnev and Dobrynin, Le Duc Tho, Sadat and King Faisal, Golda Meir, or any number of other foreign presidents, foreign ministers, and ambassadors.

What the public and Congress know is essentially what Kissinger has chosen to tell them. Periodically, Americans are allowed to look behind the curtains of Kissingerian secrecy, either because enterprising newsmen or scholars have been able to pierce them and discover bits of the hidden truth or because the secretary himself has contrived to leak highly classified information to a select few in a manner designed to present him in a favorable light. Major published accounts on such matters as the SALT and Middle East negotiations have leaned heavily on material surreptitiously made available by Kissinger but doing little for serious history.

In the case of SALT, for example, favored authors were selectively fed NSC study and decision documents. Crucial instruction telegrams to American SALT negotiators, which tell a great deal of the inside story, were withheld. So were the telegrams from the negotiators to Kissinger, which were sometimes even more revealing of internal administration struggles. (Some of the instances in which Kissinger misled Congress and the public about the 1972 SALT agreement [the meaning of "unilateral" interpretations] and the 1973 Vietnam peace settlement [secret State Department "interpretations" of the Paris text and various secret assurances to Hanoi] are already known.)

As a negotiating technique, Kissinger had led many foreign leaders to believe in diplomatic positions which the administration never had any intention of actually adopting. The Vietnam talks were a case in point, as were Kissinger's discussions with Sadat on different Middle East settlement possibilities. Likewise, Kissinger's deliberate imprecisions could result in dangerous policy shifts by foreign governments.

Most disturbing of all, the United States government has no complete *written* record of Kissinger's secret diplomacy. The record is incomplete because it is based on Kissinger's own "memcons" (memoranda of conversation) dictated after negotiating sessions at which often no other American was present. Some of the memcons were produced by NSC note-takers, but edited or censored by Kissinger before being placed in the files. We do not even know whether *all* the memcons are in the files. It is, then, a matter of accepting on faith that Kissinger recorded everything *truthfully* and *completely*—and his diplomatic practice justifies skepticism. Kissinger's total control of the record for eight years may have resulted in a manipulative version of the events in which he participated. Only Kissinger knows how truthful, accurate, and forthcoming he has been in his written record and in his face-to-face reports to Nixon and Ford. Even these two presidents had to take Kissinger's word on faith because they had no alternative. To a degree, of course, this is true of any secretary of state and any president, but no man in American history has been given the diplomatic latitude enjoyed by Kissinger. And neither President Nixon nor President Ford seems to have comprehended the depths of Kissinger's manipulative talents. The stunning Salzburg press conference was a superb demonstration of them.

While Kissinger was imperiling Nixon's trip in one way, Richard Nixon was faced with another terrible problem. The pain in his left leg that had developed in Washington was now worse, and the leg was swollen and inflamed. He called Major General Walter Tkach, his personal physician, to his quarters at Klessheim Palace in Salzburg and asked him to take a look at the leg. Tkach quickly concluded that a blood clot had developed in one of the veins. He diagnosed it as phlebitis, and bluntly told the president that there was an imminent danger that the clot might break free and move instantly to his lungs or his heart. Death could ensue quickly. Tkach's urgent advice was to cancel the rest of the trip, enter a hospital in Salzburg for preliminary treatment, and then return to Washington for prolonged care. Excessive movement—and the Middle East schedule called for plenty of it—could loosen the clot. Lieutenant Commander William Lukash, another White House physician, told the president the same thing: he simply had to cut the trip short.

But Nixon would not hear of it. As quoted in *The Final Days,* Bob Woodward and Carl Bernstein's account of Nixon's fall, he replied, "The purpose of this trip is more important than my life. I know it is a calculated risk." In Nixon's terms, this made sense. But it was absolutely vital that his condition be kept a secret: if word of his illness leaked out, the purpose of his journey would be defeated. The two doctors had to abide by presidential orders.

Air Force One landed at Cairo's International Airport about 3:30 p.m. on June 12. President Sadat was on hand to greet Nixon, and the two men rode to Qubba Palace, on the other side of the capital, in an open limousine, cheered by hundreds of thousands of people lining the streets. Sadat knew how to organize crowds. To the Egyptian president, Nixon's presence was of vast importance. He had made up his mind to play the American card in the intricate politics of the Middle East—this decision implied the exclusion of the Soviet Union from Egyptian affairs—and now, speaking before the crowd in Arabic, he told his visitor this. Sadat's notion was that the United States might be prepared to support Arab demands that Israel withdraw from the territories occupied in the 1967 war. Kissinger had indirectly led Sadat to expect this during their earlier meetings—although, as was his custom, the secretary never made the American position entirely clear.

Nixon, concealing his pain, stood with a frozen smile as Sadat spoke. Then he delivered his noncommittal response. "Certain roadblocks along the long and difficult road toward permanent peace have been removed," he said carefully.

In the evening, there was a state dinner at Qubba Palace and the exchange of long toasts in the palace gardens. It was 11:30 when Nixon finished giving his toast; it was well after midnight when he could finally get to bed, exhausted and in excruciating pain. But the diplomatic charade resumed the next day with a train excursion to Alexandria. This was Sadat's idea; he wanted to show off his guest to additional millions of Egyptians whom he had lined up along the Cairo-Alexandria railroad track. Watergate, of course, was meaningless to the applauding Egyptian masses, and both presidents basked in the preprogrammed adulation of the crowds. Nixon and Sadat were using each other: there was no real diplomacy to occupy them. In fact, they had almost nothing to say to each other during the train ride.

As Tkach and Lukash watched in horror, Nixon spent much of his time standing in the observation car alongside Sadat, waving to the crowds. (They were the only ones in the railroad car who knew of the president's condition.) At one point, Nixon went to a private compartment to get a pain-killer from Lukash; then he rejoined Sadat for more crowd-pleasing exposure. Toward the end of the trip, Nixon and Sadat invited a group of reporters for a chat. The president seemed to be at ease, and none of the newsmen suspected the physical torture he was enduring. His platitudinous conversational style was unchanged: he said that he was impressed with the crowds' "respect and trust" for Sadat, that the Egyptian masses were showing "a very deep feeling of affection and friendship for America," and that this was a foundation for a lasting relationship. He gave the reporters a rundown on Egypt's economic needs and emphasized America's desire to help develop the country. To a reporter's inane question whether the United States should have luxury railroad cars such as Sadat's, the president answered with a rambling comment about the deplorable state of the roadbed between Washington and New York. The situation verged on the absurd.

In Alexandria, there was another mammoth reception for Nixon as he and Sadat rode to Ras el-Teen Palace, a place of exquisite luxury that stands in almost shocking contrast to the Cairo and Alexandria slums and the poverty of the Nile Delta peasants whom Nixon could see from the train.

During a private meeting at Ras el-Teen Palace late that afternoon Nixon indicated to Sadat that the United States favored Israel's withdrawal to the pre-1967 lines. This was what Sadat had been hoping to hear. Details of this conversation of June 13 have never been disclosed publicly, but Edward Sheehan, who had access to Kissinger's materials, offered this version in his book *The Arabs, Israelis and Kissinger:*

In reply to Sadat's questions, Nixon did tell his host that the American objective in the Sinai was to restore the old Egyptian international border. Dr. Kissinger was sitting there when Nixon said it. Moreover, Sadat probed Nixon about American recognition of the Palestine Liberation Organization. Nixon answered to the effect that, at some appropriate future time, the United States would endeavor to bring the P.L.O. into the negotiating process. His response was cautious, but that much was clear.

The president's remarks to Sadat were of overwhelming importance because they constituted a secret change in America's support for the 1967 U.N. Security Council resolution that coupled Israeli withdrawals from occupied territories (but not necessarily all of them) with guarantees of secure borders and the establishment of a lasting peace. The Israelis were never apprised directly of this secret shift in American policy. Nixon, of course, may have been willing to tell Sadat what he wanted to hear in order to make his visit successful. When Sheehan's version was first published in magazine form in early 1976, the State Department claimed that it was based on Sadat's interpretation. But Sheehan stands by his version, insisting that his sources were "participants in the meeting," and there is no reason to disbelieve him.

Nixon's largess to Sadat also included the offer of nuclear-power plants for peaceful purposes to be built by the United States in Egypt and the gift of a helicopter for the Egyptian leader's personal use. The news that the Americans were to build nuclear reactors in Egypt came, not surprisingly, as an enormous shock to the Israelis, who learned of it only when they read the text of the Principles of Relations and Cooperation Between Egypt and the United States issued by Nixon and Sadat on June 14. The document said that after the two governments negotiated an "agreement for cooperation in the field of nuclear energy under agreed safeguards," the United States would "be prepared to sell nuclear reactors and fuel to Egypt, which will make it possible for Egypt by the early 1980s to generate substantial additional quantities of electric power to support its rapidly growing development needs." Pending such an agreement, the document said, Washington and Cairo would conclude later that month "a provisional agreement for the sale of nuclear fuel to Egypt." Israel's anger over this news was compounded by the fact that only two months earlier Kissinger had flatly denied to Ambassador Dinitz reports in the Egyptian press that negotiations were under way on just this point. The Israeli concern was, naturally, that the Egyptians would be able to use wastes from the power-plant fuel to manufacture nuclear weapons. The technology was well known, and, in fact, this was what India had done, a month earlier, on May 18, exploding a nuclear device made from power-plant plutonium provided by Canada.

Promising nuclear reactors to Egypt evidently formed a part of a policy of winning over Sadat at almost any cost. To justify this rash move, Kissinger sent a message to Jerusalem explaining, not very convincingly, that the Soviet Union would give the Egyptians nuclear reactors, without safeguards, if the United States did not do so first. (This, incidentally, was the rationale invariably used by the Nixon administration to explain its vast and reckless sales of military equipment. It was always the race to preempt the Soviet Union—even if the Russians did not have the immediate capability of matching American deliveries.) But in any event, the commitment to Egypt proved self-defeating. The reaction at home was so adverse that it virtually nullified the spectacular aspects of Nixon's presence in Egypt. It is odd that this possibility had not occurred to him beforehand. But his judgment on public opinion was becoming more and more beclouded.

On the afternoon of June 14, the president was back aboard *Air Force One* for a short flight to Jidda and a meeting with King Faisal. This twenty-four-hour visit to Arabia was grueling for the increasingly fatigued Nixon. He had a few free hours in what was left of the afternoon, but then he conferred with the king and had to spend the evening attending Faisal's state dinner at the royal guest palace. It was a long, regal meal with, of course, the ceremonial toasts afterward.

Faisal and Nixon had met several times in the past, and now the king minced no words in conveying his views about the Middle East situation. "The injustice and aggression that were wrought upon the Arabs of Palestine," he said, "are unprecedented in history, for not even in the darkest ages had a whole population of a country been driven out of their homes to be replaced by aliens." The Arabs had launched the 1973 war against Israel because all their appeals "to the conscience of the world . . . were in vain." Turning to his principal personal preoccupation, the king told Nixon that "there will never be a real and lasting peace in the area unless Jerusalem is liberated and returned to Arab sovereignty, unless liberation of all the occupied Arab territories is achieved, and unless Arab people of Palestine regain their rights to return to their homes and be given the right to self-determination."

Nixon, ever conscious that Faisal could again use his oil weapon against the West, chose to be vague and conciliatory. He reminded the king of American-Saudi cooperation in economic and military spheres—

Washington was beefing up and modernizing the Saudi Arabian Army and Air Force—and said that the new element was that the United States "is playing a role, a positive role, working toward the goal of a permanent peace in the Mideast." The next morning, at a second conference reviewing standard problems, Nixon argued that Western economies could not withstand constant increases in the price of oil; Faisal agreed, but pointed out that the pressure for price increases was coming from other OPEC countries, and Saudi Arabia had to maintain a united front with them.

After the meeting, Nixon received an unexpected political bonus. In a short public speech, King Faisal rose to the president's defense in the Watergate battle, ending with the words, "We beseech Almighty God to lend His help to us and to you so that we both can go hand in hand, shoulder to shoulder in pursuance of the noble aims that we both share, justice, and prosperity in the world."

It was the last time Nixon and Faisal met. Within less than a year one would be out of power, the other felled by an assassin's hand.

Nixon's whirlwind tour continued with another day-long descent into yet another country. The Syrian visit was only twenty-four hours, but diplomatically, it was one of the most important on the Middle Eastern tour; President Assad had the reputation of being one of the most difficult and intractable Arab leaders in the "confrontation states." And the special bitterness between Israel and Syria was much deeper than that between the Israelis and their other neighbors, the Egyptians and Jordanians. The Golan Heights were, as far as the Israelis were concerned, the only truly nonnegotiable territorial issue (besides Jerusalem). Yet to Assad, Middle Eastern peace without the return of Golan to Syria was out of the question. And the Syrians, heavily armed by the Soviet Union, remained much closer to Moscow than the Egyptians were; they kept getting new equipment after the Russians turned off the flow to Egypt in the aftermath of the 1973 conflict.

But Assad was also a highly intelligent leader and a first-rate political strategist. He knew when to compromise, and the best example was his last-minute decision to accept the disengagement with Israel only two weeks before Nixon's visit. Just like Sadat, but independently, Assad had made up his mind that Syria's interest would best be served if Damascus enjoyed good relations with the United States as well as with the Soviet Union. Considerable credit for this goes to Kissinger, who had established an excellent personal relationship with him and kept persuading him that all the Arab states had much to gain from encouraging an active and evenhanded United States presence in the Middle East.

One result of these negotiations was that when Nixon came to Damascus, the two presidents could formally announce resumption of diplomatic relations between the United States and Syria. Nixon allowed himself to be lighthearted when he replied to Assad's toast at the state dinner at the Damascus Orient Club the evening of his arrival. "You . . . have told me that there is a Syrian saying to the effect that the guest's respect and admiration for his host is directly measured by the amount of food the guest consumes at the host's dinner. . . . I can now see why Henry Kissinger gained seven pounds in his thirteen trips to Damascus over the past thirty days. And whenever we wear him out on his other travels throughout the world, we will send him back here to build him up."

The subject of occupied territories came up at a private meeting between Nixon and Assad, with Kissinger in attendance. According to Sheehan, "In response to questions, Nixon informed President Assad . . . that the United States favored the substantial restitution of the 1967 frontiers on the Golan Heights . . . within the framework of a general peace." But Sheehan also noted that "it was clear from the context of the conversations" with all Arab leaders that "Nixon expected . . . Arab governments to confer full peace and recognition upon Israel in return for the old frontiers." When Assad said that Syria would never relinquish the Golan Heights, "Nixon replied that the purpose of interim diplomacy . . . was to nudge the Israelis backwards upon the Heights, step by step, 'until they reach the edge, then tumble over.' "

There is nothing in the public record to indicate that Nixon told Assad that the United States continued to insist on "defensible frontiers" for Israel. From the Israeli viewpoint, the frontier would be indefensible if the Syrians returned to the Golan Heights and could again point their guns at the Israeli settlements below. Once more, Nixon and Kissinger were playing double diplomacy in the Middle East in the name of even-handedness.

No surprise, then, that Israel was the most difficult and delicate segment of Nixon's Middle Eastern tour. The Israelis were suspicious of American policies and felt insecure. The new prime minister, Yitzhak Rabin (who had been army chief of staff in 1967, then ambassador to Washington, and briefly, education minister), had taken office only thirteen days before. And indeed, Nixon's twenty-four-hour visit proved once more that the president—and Kissinger—found it easier to deal with confrontation-minded Arab leaders, who were at best very uncertain new friends, than with Israelis, who were old friends and virtually allies.

Israel's obsessive fear was that the Nixon administration would sell it down the river for the sake of an American-dictated peace settlement that, among other things, would establish the primacy of the United States over the Soviet Union in the Middle East. Nixon and Kissinger thought that the Israelis were paranoiac on the subject, but, as a senior Israeli official said, "Paranoia is part of our defensive arsenal." As they saw it, there was a lot of recent history to justify Israeli fears. There was the two-year struggle to obtain new jet aircraft from the United States in 1969 and 1970, the Rogers Plan negotiations conducted with the Russians behind their backs, the denial of desperately needed equipment during the first week of the Yom Kippur war after Washington failed to prevent the conflict, the inexorable American pressures to keep the Israelis from achieving a total victory after they had crossed the Suez Canal and surrounded an Egyptian army, and finally, the friendships Nixon and Kissinger were developing in Cairo and Damascus.

In public, the Israelis were immensely polite. But eventually Nixon laid it on the line: "There are two courses that are open," he said at the inevitable state dinner. "The one is an easy one, an easy one particularly politically, I suppose, and that is the status quo. Don't move, because any movement has risks in it, and therefore resist those initiatives that may be undertaken, that might lead to a negotiation which would perhaps contribute to a permanent, just, and durable peace. . . . The other, I believe, is the right way. It is the way of statesmanship, not the way of the politician alone. It is a way that does not risk your country's security. That must never be done. But it is a way that recognizes that continuous war in this area is not a solution for Israel's survival." In other words, Israel must start negotiating with the Arabs under American auspices.

In private meetings with Rabin and his key cabinet members, Nixon and Kissinger pushed a new specific idea: with the Egyptian and Syrian disengagements out of the way, Israel should now negotiate with Jordan for the ultimate return of most of the West Bank territory taken in 1967. Their point was that the choice facing the Israelis was to negotiate at once with King Hussein or to have to do so later with the Palestine Liberation Organization; the longer negotiations with Jordan were delayed, the stronger the PLO would become, eventually being recognized as the spokesman for the entire Palestinian cause. This, Nixon and Kissinger told Rabin and his associates, was inevitable and Israel might as well understand it.

The Israelis were as aware of this danger as the Americans. But, as Rabin pointed out, the West Bank was a highly emotional issue for Israel. Golda Meir had made a pledge to call a general election if new negotiations involved withdrawal from this territory. She felt she needed a specific mandate from her people to proceed with this kind of negotiation. Rabin said he could do no less. The meeting ended with no commitment from Israel about talks with Hussein.

The joint statement issued by Nixon and Rabin on June 17 made no reference to Jordan. But it was specific about American pledges of military and economic support for Israel. It also disclosed that the United States would let Israel purchase nuclear-power reactors and fuel for them. This would be done exactly in the same way as in the Egyptian agreement. Nixon had evidently decided to be evenhanded in distributing nuclear reactors in the Middle East.

Across the Jordan, matters were no less difficult. King Hussein had long enjoyed a special relationship of his own with the United States, and he had always played an odd-man-out role in Middle Eastern politics. He fought Israel in the 1967 war, losing all of the West Bank, including the Old City of Jerusalem, but he never engaged in serious flirtation with the Soviet Union and his military forces never depended on Soviet equipment, relying instead on Britain and the United States while Saudi Arabia kept him afloat financially. Hussein was the only Arab leader not to break diplomatic relations with the United States during the 1967 war, and in the years that followed, Hussein succeeded in maintaining discreet but valuable contacts with Israeli leaders.

Although Jordan contained one of the largest concentrations of Palestinians—post-1948 refugees and their children, all deeply committed to the hope of someday regaining Palestine—Israel never really regarded Hussein as an enemy. In 1970, when Palestinian commandos rose against the king and Syrian armor entered Jordan to support them, the Israelis, acting in conjunction with the United States, stood ready to engage their forces in Hussein's defense. It was obviously in their interest, because Hussein's fall would signal the rise of a radical Palestinian-led state on Israel's exposed eastern flank. In 1973, Hussein's decision to stay out of the Yom Kippur war may have been a crucial factor in Israel's survival. In every sense, then, Israeli governments felt different about Hussein than about other Arab leaders.

After 1967, such Israeli personalities as Moshe Dayan and Yigal Allon considered various plans to establish some kind of a Palestinian state on the West Bank in collaboration with Hussein. For reasons of Israeli and Jordanian internal politics and different external factors, nothing ever came of these ideas. But there always was a potential interest in Jerusalem to negotiate with Jordan even when the Israelis, quite unwisely, kept creating new Jewish settlements on the West Bank and applying too much repression against the West Bank Arabs. Over the years, the Israelis had allowed trade and the movement of persons between Jordan and the West Bank, keeping at least one bridge over the Jordan River open to this traffic.

Under the circumstances, the Israelis—notably Rabin and Foreign Minister Allon—did not think that Nixon and Kissinger were altogether unreasonable in urging them to enter into negotiations with Hussein before the PLO gained the upper hand. But they wanted to know in greater detail what the Americans had in mind and what, if any, were Hussein's conditions.

Hussein's view was that his neutrality in 1973 merited a reward from both the United States and Israel in finally regaining some, if not all, of the West Bank territory (though he was realistic enough to understand that Israel would never yield East Jerusalem). Meeting with Nixon and Kissinger on June 17 and 18 at Amman's Basman Palace, he conveyed this quite forcefully to his visitors. He also adduced the argument already invoked by the Americans that Israel would be wiser to negotiate with him than wait until the PLO became the accepted official voice of the Palestinians.

As he had said in Cairo and Damascus, Nixon told Hussein that the United States favored Israeli withdrawals from occupied Arab territories as part of a general peace. In the case of Jordan, he said, this meant the return of most of the West Bank. Hussein reminded Nixon that in January he had quietly proposed that negotiations with Israel begin with a seven-mile pullback from the Jordan River and the creation of a United Nations–controlled demilitarized zone. Israel had rejected Jordan's proposal then, but Hussein wanted to know now whether Jerusalem might not wish to rethink it.

Hussein also offered some long-range ideas: "The Palestinian problem has never been a refugee problem, but one of the inherent rights of a people to return to their homeland and to determine their own future. Once the occupied territory has been evacuated by the Israelis, only Palestinians can decide what its future is to be. They can choose continued union with Jordan, a new form of federation, or the creation of a separate state."

In responding, Nixon confined himself to generalities, preferring to stay away from a public discussion of Hussein's specific proposals. And the joint statement on June 18 noted simply that "the President promised the active support of the United States for agreement between Jordan and

Israel on concrete steps toward [a] just and durable peace." It also noted that the administration had submitted proposals to Congress "for a substantial increase in American military and economic assistance for Jordan in the coming twelve months."

In retrospect it seems regrettable that the United States did not seriously follow up the possibilities of step-by-step diplomacy involving Jordan and Israel. But Israeli and American domestic problems foiled this. In Jerusalem, the Rabin government was too weak to risk an opening with Jordan. Instead, in July, Israel publicly proposed a package-deal political settlement with Jordan, ruling out major withdrawals from the West Bank. It was an ill-advised move, but Rabin had concluded that it would be safer politically to deal first with Egypt over the Sinai under a plan that Kissinger had advanced in Cairo and Jerusalem. And after the Middle East tour, the Nixon administration no longer had the capability of acting creatively.

En route home, the president stopped in the Azores for the night and for a meeting with Portugal's new president, General Antônio de Spínola. Lajes Air Force Base on Terceira Island, where Nixon spent eighteen hours, was considered strategically vital by the United States (especially after the 1973 Middle East war when the American airlift to Israel was able to refuel there), and the president wanted to establish a good relationship with the revolutionary Portuguese regime. The long history of American support for the Salazar and Caetano dictatorships made it urgent to present a fresh image, and the visit to the Azores provided a good opportunity for it. Nixon was the first foreign chief of state to step on Portuguese soil since the April revolution, and this heightened the drama of the occasion.

Before going to Moscow, Nixon had six days in Washington to rest from his trip, catch up with routine work that had accumulated in the Oval Office, and size up the state of the impeachment proceedings. Outwardly, he continued to function as president. His public appearances and activities during the short Washington interval between his foreign travels were limited, but he had to do his homework for Moscow—and take care of his leg. The phlebitis seemed to have receded despite the enormous exertions of his Middle East tour, and his doctors no longer feared for his life. He was receiving medication and none of the physicians dared suggest that he postpone the Russian journey.

Whatever hopes the president might have had of restoring his political standing at home on the basis of his latest performance as a world statesman on the Middle Eastern expedition were totally disappointed. The television clips, the sight of millions cheering him from Cairo to Amman, and all the grave rhetoric about peace no longer made any difference. Impeachment now appeared all but certain.

On June 25 Richard Nixon undertook his final foreign journey. If Nixon, now continuously subject to depressions and drinking too much, still had any sense of political reality, he must have understood that short of a miracle in Moscow, the trip could no longer influence the inexorable approach of impeachment. Four days before he left for Europe, the Judiciary Committee opened the second phase of its work: taking direct testimony from witnesses. The end was approaching. But Nixon kept up a brave front in public and acted with aplomb.

Departing from Andrews Air Force base early on the morning of the twenty-fifth, the president thanked the officials gathered for coming out "to see us take off on another journey for peace." He seemed to be saying these words almost automatically, like a tired old missionary repeating his theme before plunging once more among the pagans. And indeed, his agenda was a modest one.

The first item was to confer in Brussels with NATO heads of state. The Belgians treated him with deference and respect—many Europeans never understood why something so bizarre as Watergate should be sufficient grounds to impeach an American president—and it was like the old days all over again.

Nixon's toasts included all the conventional remarks about the Atlantic alliance, world peace, détente. Later, the president and his NATO colleagues signed a Declaration on Atlantic Relations, a cliché-ridden document that fell instantly into oblivion. Finally, Nixon held separate meetings with West Germany's new chancellor, Helmut Schmidt, British Prime Minister Harold Wilson, and Italian Prime Minister Mariano Rumor, and then was the smiling host at an evening reception for NATO luminaries. It was the apparently busy day, full of intentional "statesmanship," that the president enjoyed so much. Now he was ready for Brezhnev.

Brezhnev himself was in a peculiar position. He had to be the cordial host, yet he did not want to become too closely identified with his troubled guest, nor did he want to be pushed into too much negotiating. When Nixon arrived in Moscow on the afternoon of June 27, Brezhnev made a point of greeting him at the airport, a gesture not required by protocol (President Podgorny was the Soviet Union's official head of state) and one he had not made in 1972. But when Nixon, giving his toast at the dinner at the Kremlin's Granovit Hall that evening, said that all the recent Soviet-American agreements "were possible because of a personal relationship that was established between the general secretary and the president of the United States," Brezhnev politely ignored it.

On June 28, Soviet and American officials signed three agreements: on cooperation in energy matters, in housing and other construction, and in artificial-heart research. These agreements were important in expanding the texture of détente, but they made no politically helpful headlines at home.

The next day the summit moved to Brezhnev's Crimean vacation home in Oreanda on the Black Sea, not far from Yalta. The Soviet leader was repaying Nixon's hospitality at San Clemente the year before. At the seaside compound, Nixon and Brezhnev spent two days talking, mainly about SALT and the Middle East.

These talks made it clear to Nixon that no meaningful progress on SALT was possible at that time. In the spring, when Kissinger visited Moscow, the United States had proposed that the planned permanent agreement on offensive weapons impose ceilings on the new MIRVed missiles as well. The Russians, still busy catching up qualitatively and quantitatively with the American MIRV technology, said no. The Crimea discussions now established that a permanent agreement was out of the question, that the two sides should aim for a new interim accord to run from 1975 to 1985, and that some modifications should be introduced in the ABM treaty. By all accounts, the Nixon-Brezhnev talks on SALT were so frank and detailed in terms of the weaponry involved that Kissinger would say later that what the two leaders had done would have violated all the "intelligence codes in previous periods."

The SALT situation was further complicated by the fact that neither side had come to the meeting with a fully agreed negotiating position. Nixon and Kissinger had been unable to work out a consensus with Defense Secretary Schlesinger and the Joint Chiefs of Staff. Brezhnev, according to all indications, had similar problems with his military establishment. The armed forces on both sides were loath to give up any strategic advantage, or potential advantage, for the sake of a political agreement. This confirmed the foolishness of having unprepared summit meetings sheerly on the basis of the political momentum.

From Oreanda, Nixon flew to Minsk, capital of Byelorussia, for an overnight visit, where he visited the Katyn war memorial, then attended a luncheon at the government guest house. He was back in Moscow in the late afternoon.

Most of his final working day in the Soviet Union was taken up in conferences with Brezhnev at the Kremlin. SALT was again the center of their discussions, and they finally agreed to abandon the concept of a *permanent* accord on offensive weapons and go, instead, for a new ten-year pact. At one point, the negotiations became so difficult that Brezhnev asked for a recess in order to meet with his full Politburo in another part of the Kremlin, presumably to obtain its approval. The two men also agreed to a special protocol to the 1972 ABM treaty, which is of unlimited duration, providing that each country would be limited to only one defensive ABM site. The original treaty had called for two sites each in the Soviet Union and the United States, but the administration had opted for a single site, to protect the Minuteman silos at Grand Forks, North Dakota, since the Americans never saw much sense in erecting ABM defenses around cities. In the light of the American decision to maintain only one ABM site, Brezhnev now agreed that the Soviets would do likewise. His choice, however, was to concentrate antiballistic defenses around Moscow. (Subsequently, responding to a congressional decision, the United States dismantled the ABM system at Grand Forks.)

At a news conference given just before the presidential party left Moscow, Kissinger gave vent to disappointment over the SALT failure and his annoyance with the armed forces—American as well as Soviet. "Both sides have to convince their military establishments of the benefit of restraint," he observed, "and that is not a thought that comes naturally to military people on either side." Warning against the idea of maintaining nuclear superiority, whether by the United States or by the Soviet Union, Kissinger sounded almost desperate: "One of the questions we have to ask ourselves as a country is what in the name of God is strategic superiority? What is the significance of it, politically, militarily, operationally, at these levels of numbers? What do you do with it?"

Concluding the summit, Brezhnev and Nixon joined in presenting their meeting to the world as another major diplomatic accomplishment. Toasting Brezhnev at dinner, the president allowed himself a phrase he hoped would be heard in Washington: "The progress that we have made and will make in the future not only was possible because of the support of our people, it is possible and will be possible because of the initiative taken by the leaders of both countries." And Brezhnev, too, wanted to make the summit appear an important step forward. Responding to Nixon's toast, he said, "You and we already have every reason to say that the results of this meeting, like the outcome of the two previous ones, can be described as constructive and weighty."

Richard Nixon left Moscow on the morning of July 3, arriving at

Loring Air Force Base in Maine just as the sun was setting over the eastern seaboard of the United States. It was the end of his last foreign journey as president.

But had the Soviet summit been worth that last effort? The consensus was that, in real terms of American foreign policy, nothing was lost and nothing was gained. In terms of Nixon's own stature, however, it was a pointless enterprise. Indeed, it probably harmed him more than it helped him.

Writing in *The Washington Post,* Murrey Marder, an experienced diplomatic correspondent, correctly observed that the threat of Nixon's impeachment "was inextricably entwined in the negotiating strategy on both sides, although both would deny it. No American president ever has engaged in high-stake international diplomacy under such a cloud." And, as Rowland Evans and Robert Novak said in a column from Moscow, "The President's calculated and self-serving effort to enshrine *détente* as a special Nixon creation—its future coexistent with his own—has both embarrassed and angered his Soviet hosts."

Though he was not responsible for it, Nixon was also made to share blame for Soviet actions in blocking live broadcasts about Russian dissidents by American television networks from Moscow. Soviet technicians at Moscow's television studios pulled the plugs the moment network correspondents began reporting on the hunger strike on which Andrei D. Sakharov, a noted physicist and political dissenter, had embarked to dramatize the plight of Soviet political prisoners. The reaction in the United States, where détente had been criticized all along because of Soviet violations of human rights, was instant. Nixon, whose own record on respect for human rights in foreign countries was less than enviable, became tarred with the brush of Soviet censorship. The conservative columnist George F. Will commented that, in the light of reports that Soviet dissenters were being rounded up on the eve of the summit, "it would have been an act of simple decency, and a useful political and diplomatic stroke, for Mr. Nixon to have made use of his 'personal relationship' with Brezhnev by explaining to him that the arrests must stop or the summit would stop . . . one reason Brezhnev censored the broadcasts to America is that he knew that he could do it without provoking a protest from Mr. Nixon, whose opinion of the press is no secret to Mr. Brezhnev."

But the President seemed oblivious to all these impressions as he stood before the television cameras at Loring Air Force Base on the evening of July 3 to report to the nation on the Moscow summit. (He had chosen this remote base for his return so that his remarks would come early enough to make the evening news.) It was the same old litany:

> It is always good to come home to America. This is particularly so when one comes home from a journey that has advanced the cause of peace in the world. . . . In the past month, Mrs. Nixon and I have traveled over twenty-five thousand miles, visiting nine countries in Western Europe and the Middle East, as well as, of course, the Soviet Union. . . . Among the nations of the Middle East, among those of the Western alliance, and between the United States and the Soviet Union, new patterns are emerging, patterns that hold out to the world the brightest hopes in a generation for a just and lasting peace that all of us can enjoy.

But the words sounded hollow and unreal. And the man facing the cameras seemed to belong to an unreal world. His speech delivered, the president climbed back aboard *Air Force One* and went to Florida to spend the Fourth of July holiday at his Key Biscayne hideaway.

July 8 was a busy day for Richard Nixon. James St. Clair, his chief counsel, and Leon Jaworski, the new Watergate special prosecutor, appeared before the Supreme Court to present their cases. St. Clair's task was to defend Nixon in the suit brought by Jaworski to obtain sixty-four presidential tapes that the White House was refusing to provide; this was *United States of America* v. *Richard Nixon, President of the United States.* But the Boston lawyer was also there to argue Nixon's countersuit, which contested the right of a federal grand jury to name him as an unindicted coconspirator in the Watergate cover-up. This was *Richard Nixon, President of the United States,* v. *United States of America.* Nixon still believed that offense was the best defense.

The Supreme Court was being asked to rule on whether the president must obey subpoenas or whether he has the constitutional prerogative to ignore them. Jaworski's point was simple: can the president interpret the Constitution to suit himself and is there anybody, including the Supreme Court, "to tell him otherwise"? St. Clair's was equally simple, but quite defiant: "The president is not above the law. . . . What he does contend is that as president the law can be applied to him only one way, and that is by impeachment."

Nixon must have known that if the Supreme Court ruled against him, he was finished. He would have to produce everything the Judiciary Committee and Jaworski wanted; impeachment would be inevitable and would be followed by a Senate trial if Nixon chose to go down fighting.

The alternative was resignation either after the court ruled against him or when the House impeached him. But the president spent much of the morning at the Oval Office with Vice President Ford, briefing him on the trip to Belgium and the Soviet Union. As usual, he was more at ease plunging into his favorite subject, when he did not have to think about the Supreme Court, the Judiciary Committee, or Jaworski.

On July 9, he received Treasury Secretary Simon, who was about to leave on a trip to the Middle East and Europe. Another long foreign-policy discussion ensued. Then he saw all his top economic advisers in a long session, and finally conferred with former Labor Secretary James D. Hodgson, who was to assume his new post as ambassador to Japan. For the next few days, it seemed like business as usual in the Oval Office. Then, on July 12, the president and his family flew to San Clemente for a two-week rest. Before leaving, he received in the Rose Garden the Wu Shu Martial Arts and Acrobatic Troupe from the People's Republic of China—the occasion for a typical little speech to the effect that "normalization of relations between our two countries continues to be a major goal of American foreign policy." The Chinese briefly demonstrated their skills, and Nixon, pointing to the three youngest members of the troupe, added, "If I ever need a bodyguard, I will just take these three with me."

At this point Nixon found it necessary to come forward in defense of Henry Kissinger's reputation. Following Kissinger's outburst at Salzburg the month before, Nixon wrote to Senator Fulbright on July 15, accepting full responsibility for the wiretaps and justifying once more the need for deep secrecy in the conduct of foreign affairs. The committee was reviewing Kissinger's earlier testimony at his request. The letter said:

> Without secret negotiations and essential confidentiality, the United States could not have secured a ceasefire in Vietnam, opened relations with the People's Republic of China, or realized progress in our relations on the SALT negotiations with the Soviet Union. . . . I ordered the use of the most effective investigative procedures possible, including wiretaps, to deal with certain critically important national security problems. Where supporting evidence was available, I personally directed the surveillance, including wiretapping, of certain specific individuals. I am familiar with the testimony given by Secretary Kissinger before your Committee to the effect that he performed the function, at my request, of furnishing information about individuals within investigative categories that I established so that an appropriate and effective investigation could be conducted in each case. This testimony is entirely correct; and I wish to affirm categorically that

Secretary Kissinger and others involved in various aspects of this investigation were operating under my specific authority and were carrying out my express orders.

The wiretap program was, of course, a subject the Judiciary Committee was investigating as part of its impeachment proceedings. In fact, it was the subject of one of the twenty-nine proposed articles of impeachment that John Doar, the committee's chief counsel, presented to the committee on July 19.

In the midst of the national trauma surrounding Nixon, a major international crisis erupted on July 15, just as the president was beginning his California vacation. This was the *coup d'état* against President Makarios of Cyprus engineered by the Greek military junta in Athens, Greek army officers commanding the Cypriot National Guard, and their shady allies on the island. Operation Aphrodite was a plan to assassinate Makarios and set up a right-wing pro-Greek regime in Nicosia, possibly leading to *enosis,* or union, between Greece and Cyprus—or, at least, with the ethnic Greek regions of the strategic Mediterranean island. The idea was hatched principally by General Dimitrios Ioannides, the former head of the military police who had recently become chief of the Athens junta. But the coup was a virtual open invitation to Turkey to invade Cyprus to protect the Turkish Cypriot population (the United States had prevented a Turkish invasion in 1964 and again in 1967 by applying forceful diplomacy in Ankara), and it served as a possible prelude to open warfare between Greece and Turkey. That Ioannides and his cohorts had acted as they did was explicable in terms of their desire to divert attention from the awesome political repression that they were applying at home. There are even indications that Ioannides was willing to risk a war with Turkey despite his subsequent claims that the Turks had assured him privately that they would not move if Makarios was, indeed, deposed. The whole affair was, in any case, an act of utter folly.

But what is not understandable is why the Nixon administration failed to do anything to prevent the coup even though it was in a position to do so. Washington had ample advance notice through CIA channels that the coup was in the offing. Besides, Makarios himself had written a letter on June 2 to Greece's figurehead president, Phaedon Ghizikis, charging that a junta was conspiring to murder him and overthrow his government. The United States government had a copy of the letter. And on July 5, a Nicosia newspaper published a report that Makarios's intelligence services had discovered a coup plot.

Actually, Kissinger did instruct the American ambassador to Greece, Henry Tasca, to inform the Greek government that the United States would disapprove of any violence in Cyprus. According to Laurence Stern's authoritative account of the Cyprus crisis published in the quarterly *Foreign Policy* in 1975, "when the Athens junta sought in July 1974 to establish a puppet surrogate in Cyprus, with ample advance notice to Washington, the United States entered the quietest demurrer of all its Atlantic allies." The junta "considered the warnings from Tasca as window-dressing," and there was "no record of any attempt by Kissinger or [Joseph] Sisco to call in the Greek ambassador in Washington . . . to register the U.S. government's severe disapproval of any coup action against Makarios." He quoted a Greek Foreign Ministry official as saying that if Kissinger had warned the ambassador, "it would have been a most valuable weapon in our hands. We could have gone screaming to the generals saying, 'Look what we are being told in Washington.' "

The problem, of course, was that the Greek junta was one of the Nixon administration's most valuable "clients." President Johnson had applied a limited arms embargo to Greece when the junta captured power in April 1967, but Nixon ordered the resumption of full-scale military assistance in 1970. The principal channel of communications between the junta and Washington was the CIA; the State Department was virtually left out of the picture. Likewise, the junta allowed the CIA to establish secret camps in Greece where Cambodian and Ugandan guerrillas were trained. The Pentagon, too, had its own direct line to Athens: Admiral Elmo Zumwalt, then chief of naval operations, obtained home-porting rights for the United States Sixth Fleet in a harbor near Athens. Nixon's personal friends were prospering in business in Greece, and the junta gave them preferential treatment. When Ambassador Tasca, a noted sympathizer of the military regime, concluded that Ioannides had gone too far in domestic repression, he was, according to Stern, "counseled strictly against intervening publicly to influence events in Athens. . . . Kissinger insisted that Tasca make no waves." Stern quoted Tasca as saying later that former Secretary of State Rogers "was more interested in getting people back to democracy. Kissinger thought that was less relevant."

Kissinger also had deep antipathy for Makarios. He regarded him as the Castro of the Mediterranean, even though the archbishop tolerated extensive American intelligence operations based in Cyprus. When the July 15 coup came, Kissinger appeared to be pleased with it. Makarios, who escaped assassination and flew to New York to address the United Nations, was received with ill grace by Kissinger; the secretary of state refused to consider him the president of Cyprus. This was in marked contrast to the attitude of Britain and other European governments.

It eventually occurred to Kissinger, however, that the anti-Makarios coup might lead to a Turkish invasion of Cyprus. On July 17, he presided over a WASAG meeting at the White House. Then he telephoned Nixon in San Clemente to tell him that Joseph Sisco, under secretary of state for political affairs, was being rushed to the area to prevent the invasion.

Sisco first flew to London to confer with British Foreign Secretary James Callaghan and Turkish Prime Minister Bulent Ecevit. (Britain, Greece, and Turkey were coguarantors of the 1960 Zurich agreement which granted independence to the unified Cyprus state.) Then he began commuting between Ankara and Athens, trying to persuade the Turks not to invade and the Greeks to remove their puppet regime in Cyprus. But it was too late. On the morning of July 20, Turkish forces, backed by jet aircraft and warships, began landing on Cyprus. Ioannides prepared to send his army from Thrace into Turkish territory. Kissinger ordered Sisco to remain in Athens and dissuade the Greeks from attacking Turkey. From his State Department office, he kept telephoning top Greek and Turkish officials in Athens and Ankara, trying his hand at transatlantic diplomacy.

As for Nixon, he remained calmly in San Clemente. Clearly, he was no longer making policy, and indeed, he seemed to have abandoned his public role as a world statesman for peace. Other things, some of them incongruous, were on his mind.

On July 17, for example, he issued a statement expressing his sadness over the death of the baseball star and sports broadcaster Dizzy Dean. On July 18, as American diplomats tried desperately to prevent a Turkish invasion of Cyprus, he spoke by telephone to a Washington meeting of the National Citizens' Committee for Fairness to the Presidency. As the crowd at the Washington hotel chanted, "We love Nixon," the president told Korff: "Your efforts to build a grass-roots organization . . . with two million members reminds me of something General de Gaulle once said —it is one of my favorite quotations. He said that France is never her true self unless she is engaged in a great enterprise. Here in America, we have all been guided by that same sense of national purpose. . . . In these difficult times, when world peace depends so fundamentally upon the strength and unity of America, you have joined together, Democrats and Republicans, to support an office which is bigger than any party, the Office of the Presidency of the United States."

On July 21, the day after the invasion of Cyprus, Nixon attended a dinner at the Bel Air home of his friend Roy Ash, director of the Office of Management and Budget. In what was his last speech on foreign policy as president of the United States, he took credit for the Cyprus cease-fire, proclaimed earlier that day. The struggle between Greece and Turkey, he said, "is one that could only be averted by the leadership of the United States of America."

Events in the Mediterranean continued on their tumultuous way. On July 22, Greek armed forces in Athens overthrew the junta and called Constantine Caramanlis, a liberal opposition leader, to return from exile in Paris to form a civilian democratic government. Still in San Clemente, Nixon sent a congratulatory message to Caramanlis—an extraordinary hypocrisy, considering his long and warm support of the junta. But the Cyprus cease-fire and the restoration of democracy in Greece failed to end the crisis in the eastern Mediterranean. In fact, a whole series of new crises still loomed ahead. On August 14, when Nixon was no longer president, the Turks staged a second invasion, breaking out of their perimeter on Cyprus and occupying additional territory with the aid of fresh troops. And the Cyprus affair also marked the first major defeat for Kissinger.

Not only did his mismanagement of the Cyprus situation trigger a wave of anti-American sentiment in Greece and Cyprus (the Greeks on the mainland bitterly resented the American role in the conflict), but Congress moved in August—over Kissinger's strong protests—to suspend military assistance to Turkey, on the grounds that Turkey's use of American weapons to commit aggression against another country violated the U.S. laws under which military aid had been provided. Never before had Kissinger failed so badly in his diplomatic endeavors and never before had Congress acted against him when his personal prestige was on the line. Earlier rejections of the administration's request for appropriations for Indochina had been aimed at Nixon. But this time it was a clear vote against Kissinger. The cut-off of aid, in turn, produced deep anti-American sentiment in Turkey, where the government in reprisal, closed down all U.S. military installations, including the vital and top-secret intelligence operations of the National Security Agency.

Thus did the American performance in the Cyprus crisis result in profound anti-Americanism all over the territories of two important allies —an unprecedented state of affairs. And on this note of failure, the Nixon administration's foreign policy came to an end.

The end came quickly. On July 24, with Nixon still in San Clemente, the Supreme Court handed down the unanimous opinion that the president must turn over to Judge Sirica "forthwith" the sixty-four White House tapes Jaworski had subpoenaed. The judge was to determine whether the tapes were relevant to the Watergate cover-up trial of Nixon's former aides.

The president chose to continue his isolation in San Clemente. Although he briefly considered defying the Supreme Court decision, he issued a statement a few hours later announcing that he would comply with the subpoenas and turn the sixty-four tapes over to Sirica. He surely knew that the so-called June 23 tape—his three conversations with Haldeman six days after the Watergate break-in—would establish beyond the slightest doubt his involvement in the cover-up from the very outset. This was the "smoking gun" for which the investigators had long been looking.

Still, as if awaiting a miracle, he was not ready to quit. On July 25, he went to Los Angeles to deliver a televised speech on the national economy at a conference sponsored by California business organizations. The next day, the president calmly conferred with Kissinger and West German Foreign Minister Hans-Dietrich Genscher. He was again in his element. But on July 27, a Saturday, the Judiciary Committee voted the first article of impeachment against him: complicity in the Watergate cover-up. On Sunday, July 28, Nixon finally returned to the White House. On Monday, the committee voted the second article of impeachment: Nixon's abuse of power and the violation of the constitutional rights of American citizens. This article covered the national-security wiretaps as well as the misuse of the FBI and the CIA, thus formally linking the president's management of foreign policy to his overall guilt as president. On Tuesday, it was the approval of Article III, charging Nixon with unlawful defiance of the committee's subpoenas for the tapes and other materials. But the article charging the president with complicity in ordering the secret bombings of Cambodia in 1969 failed to pass.

Now it was a question of days. Most important of all, Henry Kissinger and General Haig had concluded that Nixon must resign. Both of them felt that further resistance—going through the impeachment process in the full House of Representatives and a trial in the Senate— would only prolong the agony and grievously damage the United States. Kissinger was particularly worried about the whole structure of American foreign policy coming unhinged. Policy had already been paralyzed since late spring—even before Nixon's Middle East trip—and now it was imperative that the United States reassert its power to make decisions and to act. Some decisions could be taken only by the president, no matter how much latitude Kissinger might enjoy.

Consequently, on Thursday, August 1, although the president still resisted any idea of caving in, Haig instructed Ray Price, a White House speech-writer, to start drafting Nixon's resignation address. In fact, Nixon was planning a different kind of statement, one disclosing the contents of the June 23 tape but insisting that it was not grounds for impeachment. He spent the weekend at Camp David working with his assistants on the statement, then returned to the White House on Sunday night.

The statement was released on Monday, August 5; the president did not have the emotional strength to go on television to read it himself. Nixon said that he was turning over the tapes to the Judiciary Committee and Judge Sirica and making them public. He acknowledged that they were "at variance with certain of my previous statements," but he insisted that even though he had discussed "the political aspects of the situation" six days after the Watergate break-in, his foremost concern at that time was with national security. He never abandoned this line of defense. He repeated his earlier claim that he had become concerned "about the possibility that the FBI investigation might lead to the exposure either of unrelated covert activities of the CIA or of sensitive national security matters that the so-called 'plumbers' unit at the White House had been working on, because of the CIA and plumbers connections of some of those involved." And, he added, "I therefore gave instructions that the FBI should be alerted to coordinate with the CIA and to ensure that the investigation not expose these sensitive national security matters." This was his conclusion:

> Whatever mistakes I made in the handling of Watergate, the basic truth remains that when all the facts were brought to my attention, I insisted on a full investigation and prosecution of those guilty. I am firmly convinced that the record, in its entirety, does not justify the extreme step of impeachment and removal of a President. I trust that as the constitutional process goes forward, this perspective will prevail.

On Tuesday, August 6, the president suddenly called a cabinet meeting for midmorning. The cabinet members were sure that Nixon would tell them he had decided to resign, but they were wrong. They found Nixon in fighting spirit, assuring them that he had no intention of resigning and that he would resist all pressures to do so.

After the meeting, Nixon asked Kissinger to stay behind for a private conversation in the Oval Office. The other cabinet members returned to their offices, wondering how the president proposed to carry on the fight. But one of them, Defense Secretary James Schlesinger, resolved that the time had come to take precautions. Back at his Pentagon office, he met with the chairman of the Joint Chiefs of Staff, and the two men agreed that they would refuse to obey any orders from the president that might threaten public order, national institutions, or national security. Schlesinger had doubts about Nixon's mental stability, and he wanted to ensure that, remote as this possibility might be, the president would not suddenly trigger an international crisis to justify a suspension in the impeachment proceedings or engage the armed forces in a political operation designed to keep him in power. As far as Schlesinger and General Brown were concerned, Richard Nixon had ceased to be commander in chief.

By Wednesday, August 7, it was clear even to Nixon's staunchest supporters in Congress that he would be impeached and, most likely, be found guilty by the Senate and removed from the presidency. The effect of the June 23 tape was absolutely devastating. Resignation, they told him, was the only way out. That evening the president asked Kissinger to join him in the Lincoln Sitting Room, the place where for five and a half years they had secretly plotted the course of American foreign policy. He wanted to know how history would regard his statesmanship. Kissinger replied that his place in history was assured. Then, in the scene described by Woodward and Bernstein in *The Final Days,* Nixon, his face covered with tears, asked Kissinger to kneel with him in prayer. That night Richard Nixon made the decision to resign.

On Thursday, August 8, Ray Price was summoned by the president and instructed to draft the resignation speech. Nixon spent much of the day in routine Oval Office occupations as if all were normal. He signed a message to Congress transmitting the annual report on the Trade Agreement Program for 1973, his final act in the field of foreign policy. In the message, he addressed himself to problems of worldwide inflation and trade and monetary reform, and emphasized that "economic issues should be managed and negotiated in parallel with political and security issues, in order to make progress on all three fronts." He urged the Senate to approve the trade-reform bill, already passed by the House, adding, "the rest of the world is waiting for us on the trade negotiating problem." Reading the message, one has the impression that Nixon fully expected to be around for the balance of his term, personally encouraging the trade negotiations and guiding the American negotiators. (Another statement to emerge from the White House press office on August

8 was Nixon's veto of the agricultural-environment and consumer protection appropriation bill on the grounds that it exceeded the budget and was inflationary. The semblance of normality at the White House was eerie.)

At 9:01 p.m., Richard Nixon sat for the last time in front of the television cameras in the Oval Office. It was the thirty-seventh time he was thus addressing the nation. His years in office, he said, "have been a time of achievement in which we can all be proud." True to his deepest interest, the same old themes were singled out:

We have ended America's longest war, but in the work of securing a lasting peace in the world, the goals ahead are even more far-reaching and more difficult. We must complete a structure of peace so that it will be said of this generation, our generation of Americans, by the people of all nations, not only that we ended one war but that we prevented future wars.

We have unlocked the doors that for a quarter of a century stood between the United States and the People's Republic of China.

We must now ensure that the one-quarter of the world's people who live in the People's Republic of China will be and remain not our enemies, but our friends.

In the Middle East, a hundred million people in the Arab countries, many of whom have considered us their enemy for nearly twenty years, now look on us as their friends. We must continue to build on that friendship so that peace can settle at last over the Middle East and so that the cradle of civilization will not become its grave.

Together with the Soviet Union, we have made the crucial breakthroughs that have begun the process of limiting nuclear arms. But we must set as our goal not just limiting but reducing and, finally, destroying these terrible weapons so that they cannot destroy civilization and so that the threat of nuclear war will no longer hang over the world and the people.

We have opened the new relation with the Soviet Union. We must continue to develop and expand that new relationship so that the two strongest nations of the world will live together in cooperation, rather than confrontation.

Around the world—in Asia, in Africa, in Latin America, in the Middle East—there are millions of people who live in terrible poverty, even starvation. We must keep as our goal turning away from production for war and expanding production for peace so that people everywhere on this earth can at last look forward in their children's time, if not in our own time, to having the necessities for a decent life.

At 9:36 a.m. on Friday, August 9, Richard Nixon said his last farewell to his cabinet and White House staff. Then he and Mrs. Nixon boarded the helicopter that, for the last time, took them to Andrews Air Force Base and to the waiting air force jetliner and the flight to San Clemente. At 11:35, Haig delivered a letter to Secretary of State Henry Kissinger at his White House office.

> Dear Mr. Secretary:
>   I hereby resign the Office of President of the United States.
> Sincerely,
Richard Nixon

The resignation became effective at noon, as *The Spirit of '76* flew high over Middle America.

Chapter 29

History alone can judge the foreign policy of Richard Nixon. Time, too, must elapse before Richard Nixon can be judged adequately as a statesman. A great many secrets of his foreign policy remain hidden from us, and may remain so for a long time—if not forever. After all, secrecy had been one of Nixon's principal instruments in the evolution and conduct of America's foreign affairs. And it was this secrecy that, ultimately, precipitated his fall. Nevertheless, it is possible even now to reach certain conclusions about Nixon's international performance.

The broad, conceptual strokes of his policies were undoubtedly correct: détente with the Soviet Union and the opening to mainland China. It is hard to quarrel with Nixon's theme that the world must move from an era of confrontation to an era of negotiation. But reality does not sustain his claim that confrontations are altogether behind us. Détente itself has changed in appearance and character since the first Nixon-Brezhnev summit in Moscow in 1972. The Middle East and Africa, to mention two crucial areas, are still arenas of confrontation between the American and Soviet superpowers. So are the Mediterranean and the Indian Ocean. Nixon seems to have disregarded the fundamental truth that great national interests—American as well as Russian—are not likely to be diluted by détente for a long time to come. SALT was unquestionably a step forward, but not the breakthrough claimed by Nixon and Henry Kissinger. Despite it, both sides were developing new generations of overkill weapons systems. And no progress whatsoever has been made in the efforts to reduce conventional forces in Central Europe.

In establishing the relationship with China—probably the most dramatic and innovative move in America's postwar foreign policy—Nixon brought "one-quarter of the world's people," to use his words, into contact with the United States and the rest of the outside world. This was beneficial to the cause of peace and to all concerned, and to be sure, it was also calculated as a deft policy stroke in America's relations with Communist powers, the triangular policy.

Nixon had, indeed, ended America's longest war with the signing of the Vietnam peace accords in January 1973. But to achieve the "peace," Nixon had brutalized Vietnam. And within a little more than two years, South Vietnam fell and the country was unified under Hanoi's aegis. This was, it is fair to say, an all but inevitable denouement. As it was, America's participation in the war was unnecessarily prolonged by four years at an immense cost in lives; the 1973 accords set the stage for two more years of fratricide, a period that might have lasted even longer had not Congress cut off the funds for Nixon's desired and indefinite support of the corrupt Saigon regime. Cambodia, under American bombardment since 1969 and an open battlefield since 1970, suffered untold destruction after Nixon ordered it invaded in order to "shorten" the Indochina war. And that, too, was in vain. Today, Cambodia is totally isolated from the outside world under the peculiar revolutionary system imposed by its new Communist rulers.

In the eastern Mediterranean and the Middle East, Nixon and Kissinger conducted some of their most dangerous policy experiments. Although Kissinger was later able to negotiate a limited Israeli withdrawal in the Sinai, peace in the Middle East is not yet at hand. Greece and Turkey remained at swords' points over Cyprus, and the danger of war continued in the Aegean.

Despite Nixon's pious words about American leadership for peace in the world, his administration's policies were characterized by extraordinary immorality. Such dictatorships as the Greek junta, Caetano's regime in Portugal, the moribund Franco regime in Spain, Park's government in South Korea, the Brazilian military government, and the shah's repressive government in Iran were among Nixon's and Kissinger's favorites. Respect for human rights in all these countries—and, for that matter, in the Soviet Union—was never a matter of interest or concern. Subversion of governments not to Nixon's and Kissinger's liking—even if they were democratically elected—was an accepted policy.

In one of his last pronouncements as president, Richard Nixon urged the industrialized nations, starting with the United States, to regear their production from war to peace. But it was under Nixon that America had become the world's greatest arms merchant, purveying billions of dollars' worth of weapons to Iran, Saudi Arabia, and other oil-rich nations around the Persian Gulf regardless of the dangers to peace implicit in it. If one of Nixon's motivations in so doing was to curry favor with the OPEC cartel, this, too, was a fiasco. The United States has never been so dependent on OPEC oil—and so much at the mercy of the OPEC price manipulations—as it is now. Nixon's Project Independence, designed to free America of reliance on foreign energy sources, was never more than an impossible and arrogant dream.

Nixon's principal defense in his impeachment drama was that everything he did in the context of Watergate was motivated by his concern for national security. Later, it developed that much of this secrecy was intended to cover up misdeeds, ranging from the bombing of Cambodia to the subversion in Chile, and a police state in America had almost been created in order to build this illusory "structure of peace." Having promised the "structure of peace," Richard Nixon exacted an immense price from Americans—and the world—for giving only the illusion of peace.

Index